THE MUSIC
OF THE
ENGLISH CHURCH

Also by Kenneth R. Long
CHURCH CHOIR MANAGEMENT

THE MUSIC
OF THE
ENGLISH CHURCH

by

KENNETH R. LONG

HODDER AND STOUGHTON
LONDON SYDNEY AUCKLAND TORONTO

In memoriam
ROGER PIERS WHITE
who died in a vain attempt to save a drowning chorister
Sydney, 7 October 1957

TO ELIZABETH

for her indispensable
help and encouragement

Acknowledgment

I want to record here my grateful thanks to the several publishers who have generously allowed me to quote from publications in their copyright. They include:

Ascherberg, Hopwood & Crew Ltd: Ex. 172.

Banks & Son (Music) Ltd.: Exs. 138, 163 and 176b,c.

Blandford Press Ltd. for extracts from *The Treasury of English Church Music, II, III and IV*: Exs. 4, 9c, 9e, 10a, 13a, 13b, 14b, 16b, 25a, 36a, 37f, 87, 92, 118, 119, 120, 121, 141, 142a, 142b, 146, 147c, 147d.

The Carnegie United Kingdom Trust for examples from the ten volume *Tudor Church Music*: Exs. 2, 3, 5, 6, 8, 9b, 9f, 9g, 11a, 11b, 12a, 12b, 14a, 15a, 16a, 17c, 18b, 22, 24b, 26e, 27f, 28e, 28f, 29a, 29c, 29f, 33c, 34, 35a, 35b, 36d, 37a, 37b, 37d, 46, 47, 48, 64, 65, 66a–e, 67, 68, 78, 79, 80, 83, 84, 86a.

Faber Music Ltd. (for J. Curwen & Sons Ltd.): Ex. 178.

Galliard Ltd.: stanzas by Sydney Carter and Jim Stringfellow on p. 436.

Herbert Jenkins Ltd.: Ex. 87.

Music Publishers: for Ex. 88, copyright © 1968 by Hinrichsen Editions Ltd.; and Ex. 89, copyright © 1969 by Hinrichsen Editions Ltd.

Novello & Company Ltd.: Exs. 9h, 28c, 32b, 33b, 36b, 81, 82, 99, 110, 111, 112, 113, 115a, 115b, 116, 117b, 122, 123, 124, 125, 126, 127, 128, 129, 135, 136, 137, 139, 140, 147a, 147b, 147e–g, 148, 150b, 151, 152, 153, 154, 155, 156, 157a, 157b, 158, 159, 164, 165, 166, 167, 168, 169a–c, 171, 180.

Oxford University Press Music Department: Exs. 9a, 9d, 10b, 11c, 18a, 21, 26a–d, 27c, 28a, 28b, 28d, 29b, 29d, 29e, 33a, 33d, 35c, 37c, 50, 58, 73a, 86d, 97, 101, 109, 130, 147h, 149, 150a, 176a, 176d, 176e, 177, 179.

Routledge and Kegan Paul Ltd.: Ex. 98.

Schott & Company Ltd.: Exs. 70, 90, 96.

Stainer & Bell Ltd.: Exs. 1, 10c, 15b, 17a, 17b, 19, 20a, 20b, 24a, 25b, 27a, 27b, 27d, 27e, 33e, 35d, 36c, 37e, 38, 39, 40a–c, 41, 42, 43, 44, 45, 49, 51, 52, 53, 54, 55, 56, 59, 60a–d, 61, 62, 63a–f, 69, 71, 72, 73b, 74a, 74b, 75a, 75b, 76, 77, 85, 86b, 86c, 86e, 86f, 91, 105, 107, 114, 170, 173a, 173b, 174, 175.

I should also like to thank my publishers, the music block-makers and the printers for the enormous trouble they have gone to throughout, and especially in incorporating late additional material and ensuring, as far as possible, the accuracy of the text. Whatever mistakes may remain are entirely my own responsibility. My grateful thanks to them all.

Foreword

A history of English church music is much needed at the present time, for there have probably been few periods in our history when a wider and more intelligent interest in this part of our great heritage prevailed. This interest is not confined to the specialist church musician, but extends to include a large number of men and women, many of them not particularly musical, both in this country and across the world.

There do not appear to have been many attempts to write a comprehensive one-volume history of this branch of music, and this is the more surprising in that it is one in which England has particularly excelled.

Although histories of music have naturally mentioned English church music, few books have been devoted exclusively to this subject. It is therefore fitting that, at this present juncture, this very considerable work should appear to stimulate further the interest in this subject.

The method of writing which has been adopted is very different from the two-volume *A History of English Cathedral Music 1549 to 1889* by John S. Bumpus which appeared in the early years of this century. It is instructive to compare the music there discussed and the method of its discussion with that which appears in this book. Nothing short of a revolution has taken place in the music of our churches since Mr. Bumpus penned his chatty and voluminous account of the subject. Not only has most of the music which he talked about been re-edited and is now performed in an entirely different way, but vast quantities of music, at that time unknown, have come to light, and now find a place in the repertoire of our choirs.

The situation had changed greatly between Bumpus's book and *English Cathedral Music from Edward VI to Edward VII* by Edmund H. Fellowes. This was first published in 1941, and for a long time was the standard work on the subject; recently a new edition has appeared revised by Sir Jack Westrup. Fellowes was nurtured in the English cathedral tradition; he grew up in the days when cathedral music was of the kind described by Bumpus and was performed in the old-fashioned way. It was hearing Tudor music thrashed whilst he was a cathedral Minor Canon that led him to undertake the vast researches which completely transformed our whole outlook on Tudor music. All of us—and those who are now revising the editions of the music which he made are generous enough to admit it—are immeasurably in his debt for his imaginative and far-reaching research. His book was on a smaller scale than this present volume, and made no attempt to deal with many of the subjects which are here reviewed.

The Singing Church by C. Henry Phillips, was first published in 1945 and appeared in a new edition, prepared by Professor Arthur Hutchings, in 1968. This was a very general historical survey smaller in range than that undertaken by the present author. Its brevity made it impossible to discuss matters in detail, and the author's intention was to give a bird's eye view on each subject.

So, with these three works as predecessors, appears this compendious volume. Its author is modest about his achievements, but I write with real knowledge when I say that it represents a quite enormous task which has filled a great many of his normal waking hours and some of those during which he ought to have been asleep. The result seems to me to be a most valuable contribution to this fascinating subject; it can be cordially recommended, in my view, to those who wish to make a full study; those who wish to skim through it will find much to interest and to stimulate.

Had circumstances been otherwise thirteen years ago, when I was honoured by an invitation from the publishers to write a history of English church music, I might at this moment have been writing the Preface to it rather than a Foreword to Mr. Long's book. At that time I had little leisure, for I held two appointments in Canterbury: Organist and Master of the Choristers at the Cathedral, and Warden of the Royal School of Church Music, whose headquarters were there before they were moved to Croydon in 1954. Had I been the author my pride in my achievement would certainly have been considerable—modesty would none the less have prevented me from doing what I can now do: commend it unreservedly to the attention of all students and other lovers of church music in all parts of the world.

Director   Gerald H. Knight
The Royal School of Church Music
Addington Palace
Surrey

8

Preface

This book is primarily a history of the music, rather than of the musicians, of the English Church. It is concerned with the growth and development of the art of liturgical music and of the circumstances under which it was written and performed: individual composers are of interest only in so far as they illustrate, initiate, or contribute to that development. Something else I have tried to do—and this, I think, distinguishes this history from earlier ones—is to show English church music as part of the far wider pattern of western European musical culture and to examine the effect upon it of such great continental movements as the Renaissance and Baroque. In addition, I have sought to project it against its religious, political, economic and social background, all of which profoundly influenced its development and practice. Parallel with the main history of cathedral music, some attempt is also made to trace the outline of music in the parish churches, though evidence is scanty for the earlier centuries. Organ building is much too vast a subject for adequate treatment here but again a thumbnail sketch of its development is integrated into the general history to help make the overall picture as complete as possible. It is my hope that this rather broader treatment of the whole subject will illuminate it more fully than perhaps have some previous books and may also explain much that other histories have left unexplained.

For whom is the book intended? I have tried to make it a handy work of reference not only for organists, choirmasters and students but for *all* who are interested in English church music—including not only the parson, choir members, musical church officers and members of the congregation, but also the increasing number of people with no particular religious affiliations but who yet take great interest in cathedral music and have become familiar with it through the medium of the gramophone. On the other hand I hasten to point out that the book is not intended as a work of profound scholarship for specialists in the field (though I should like to think that perhaps even some of them may wish to keep a copy within reach). Perhaps I was unwise to try to make it so all-embracing because in one place I feel obliged to explain something as rudimentary as the difference between counterpoint and harmony (which all but the veriest beginner ought to know) while elsewhere I go into some detail about such technical matters as rhythmic counterpoint, harmonic rhythm, canon, *musica ficta*, degree inflection, *basso continuo* and the like, as well as discussing the liturgical pattern of Byrd's *Gradualia*, a rather complex subject which will concern very few people. But by and large I hope that my main purpose will have been achieved and that I have written the sort of book all interested in church music will find useful and stimulating.

With such an enormous mass of material to deal with, selection has caused most headaches. To give only one example: should as many composers as possible have been included even if, as a consequence, they would each receive only brief mention? So often this method ends by giving little more than their dates and a list of their more significant works; such information is more the province of a dictionary than a history. Alternatively, should fewer composers be dealt with but these in greater depth? In striking some balance between these two methods I have tried to keep in mind the primary aim — to write a history of the music rather than of the musicians. Fortunately it is generally (though not invariably) true that the greatest composers are also the ones who most aptly illustrate the growth of their art and who are often the most original and enterprising; because of their prestige, their experiments and innovations have considerable influence on their contemporaries and successors. These then are the men whose impact on their art is likely to be the most decisive and I have therefore treated them at some length. That others have been dismissed in a few lines or even not mentioned at all is not necessarily a reflection on their relative abilities and merits as composers; it merely means that in my estimation (itself a subjective and very fallible yardstick) they did not so conspicuously illustrate, initiate, or contribute to, the development of their art. This problem of selection caused the greatest difficulty in all fields.

It will sometimes be found that the same matter has been discussed two or three times in different parts of the book. This may either be because on each appearance it is approached from a different point of view (thus the division of a text into short clauses appears on p. 45 as part of a historical survey and on p. 101 as an aspect of polyphonic technique): or it may be that the reference is very brief and it therefore seemed tidier, for the sake of a sentence or two, to repeat the matter so as to make each section as complete as possible in itself, rather than send the inquirer on the fiddly business of hunting up references in another part of the book and then turning back again.

I must further confess that some inconsistencies will be found in the music-type examples. Instead of taking them all from library editions, which few church musicians will ever see, I have sometimes preferred to use popular or older editions which many folk are likely to have either at home or in their choir libraries, even though such editions may not be so accurate or scholarly. The example is then more easily identified and its relation to the whole more readily seen.

Like most general historians, I have had to lean heavily on the work of other people. Much of what I have written has been compiled from material published by scholars who have specialised in some particular period or subject, and between the covers of this one book I have compressed the essence of several others, many of them detailed studies of a particular period or of individual composers. My only defence is to claim that such men would be poorly rewarded if, after they have done some notable piece of research, their work should be ignored by the general historian. I can only hope that footnote references and the bibliography will encourage readers to go to these source-books and enquire more deeply. I am particularly indebted to Frank Ll. Harrison on the fifteenth and sixteenth centuries and to Christopher Dearnley on the English Baroque, to Paul Doe on Tallis, Joseph Kerman and James Jackman on Byrd, Denis Stevens on the Tudors and on Tomkins, Walter Collins and David Brown on Weelkes, Edward Thompson on Robert Ramsey, Percy Scholes on the Puritans and, of course, to Fellowes on almost everybody. To all these writers, and to the many others listed in the bibliography, I am under an immense obligation. Most of all I am indebted to Peter le Huray: I have unblushingly plundered his splendid book *Music and the Reformation in England 1549–1660* and I can only hope that what I have written will stimulate readers to turn to his authoritative, highly original and utterly absorbing book for a more thorough and detailed treatment of the period. Certainly all future writers on the subject must profit from his work.

This book owes its existence to Mr. Leonard Cutts of Hodder and Stoughton who, in 1957, conceived the idea of it and suggested to Dr. Gerald Knight, Director of the Royal School of Church Music, that he should write it. Dr. Knight was far too heavily committed to undertake this somewhat burdensome assignment and therefore suggested that I should tackle it. This is a great pity as I am sure Dr. Knight would have made a much better job of it. When I first accepted the commission I estimated the book would take four years to write: in the event it has taken fourteen. For this there are several reasons — pressure of other work, inaccessibility of much material and the difficulty of finding time to visit the main music libraries (especially as I live in the north of England). More frustrating still, it has seemed that every time a section has been completed, an important new book or article was sure to be published which completely invalidated what I had written, so making it necessary to begin again. This happened so often that there were times when I thought the job would never be done. Even now I am not satisfied with it — but one must draw a line somewhere. That the task has at last been completed is due largely to Dr. Knight who has ever been ready with warm encouragement and good practical advice. He has given up much precious time to checking the various typescripts after each rewrite and has given further time to the laborious grind of reading the proofs. No author could hope for a more wise and gracious Svengali and I owe him an inestimable debt.

Of others who have given generously of their time and knowledge I should particularly like to thank Mr. Alan Percival and the late Prof. Thurston Dart for help in the early stages, and Prof. Walter Collins for specialist advice on Thomas Weelkes. Mr. John Smith, of Manchester University Extra-Mural Department, though not a musician, brought his splendidly logical mind to bear on some of my more hazy thinking in Chapters 2 and 3, and Mr. James W. Chant read sections of the typescript and made some useful comments. Mrs. Jennifer Porter checked later sections of the revised manuscript and offered suggestions which I have been most happy to incorporate. Miss E. Leach, Librarian of Manchester Arts Library, gave valuable help in compiling the first section of the bibliography. The first to read the whole book through in its complete form was Dom Anselm Hughes and I am anxious to pay a warm tribute to him for his painstaking and detailed comments.

Most of all I must thank my wife who, since the day we were married, has accepted 'the book' as a silent but very demanding member of the family, always lurking in the background and even sharing our holidays with us. She has put up with my fits of preoccupation and depression and, in later stages, has given up an enormous amount of time to such tedious chores as checking, proof-reading, and helping with the indexing.

But although I am profoundly grateful to all these people for their help and ideas, I accept sole responsibility for the final outcome. Though I have tried to check and recheck the accuracy of my statements it is inevitable that some errors, false statements, dangerous generalisations and misprints will slip through. I should be grateful if those with a lynx eye for spotting such things would kindly write and tell me so that if ever the book should go through to a second edition they can be corrected.

Finally, may I emphasize strongly that no amount of reading can ever be a satisfactory substitute for listening: reading can only stimulate and supplement listening. To get the best from this book, therefore, readers are urged to familiarise themselves with as much of the music discussed as possible. Ideally, if you live near a cathedral or choral foundation, attend its services as often as you can so as to hear a wide range of cathedral music performed by the traditional choir of men and boys for which it was originally conceived. Failing this, or in addition to it, make maximum use of broadcasts and recordings. Excellent recordings are available of many of the works mentioned here. Happy is he to whom the great corpus of English church music is not so much a field of academic study as a glorious living reality.

Altrincham
July 1971

Contents

CONTENTS

CONTENTS

CONTENTS

CHAPTER I

The English Reformation

Probably many of us, faced with the question 'What was the Reformation?', would take refuge in the words of the schoolboy who answered, 'When Henry VIII started the Church of England so that he could have six wives'; but of course the Reformation cannot be assigned to any specific date nor ascribed to any one person. Basically it was a long period of dissatisfaction with the many superstitions and abuses which had crept into Western religious practice and of growing unrest at the increasing worldliness and materialism of the Papacy as a temporal power: these feelings, finding expression either in attempts at reform or in acts of open defiance, culminated in the emergence of various 'protest-ant' bodies under the leadership of men like Luther, Zwingli and Calvin.

In England the Reformation is often said to have extended from 1534, the year of Henry's break with the Papacy, to 1662, the last authorized revision of the Book of Common Prayer; but if it be allowed that these dates serve conveniently to define and contain the movement there is still no doubt that the *spirit* of the Reformation can be traced back at least to John Wycliffe (1329–84) and stands clearly revealed in the pages of his contemporaries, Chaucer and Langland. Henry VIII is particularly identified with the movement only because he was quick to recognise its irresistible strength and, bowing to the inevitable, was astute enough to turn it to political and personal advantage, yet it is often forgotten that in spite of his break with Rome, his Dissolution of the Monasteries, the introduction of the 'Great Bible' in English into every church, and his acceptance of Cranmer's Litany, he remained a Catholic, if no longer a Roman Catholic, to the end of his days.

A BRIEF HISTORY OF THE BOOK OF COMMON PRAYER

Long before any attempt was made at liturgical reform there was a strong movement afoot to have a vernacular Bible made accessible. A petition from Convocation to Henry, dated 19 December 1534, for an English version of the Bible was answered by Item 7 in the first set of Royal Injunctions (1536) requiring every parish to possess a copy of the Bible in English (Coverdale's translation). In September 1538 the King's Vicar-General, Thomas Cromwell, issued further Injunctions directing that a Bible 'of the largest volume in English' be set up in some convenient place in every church and that the Creed, Lord's Prayer and Ten Commandments should be taught in English. These 'Great Bibles', in Miles Coverdale's translation, were eventually issued in the early summer of 1539. In 1543 the reading of the Scriptures in English was introduced for the first time into public worship, so paving the way for the further substitution of English for Latin. Nor was there long to wait. On 11 June 1544 the Litany appeared, almost in the very form in which we have it today: it was Cranmer's own work and was drawn from many different sources — the old Western litanies, the liturgies of Constantinople and Sarum, Luther, etc. At this time Cranmer and others were making various experiments in reforming the service-books but the King, far too wily to overplay his hand, firmly restrained too much zeal in making changes and so the revisions remained in draft form.

However, immediately after the death of Henry the tide of reform, impatient at delay, swept on faster than ever. Edward VI came to the throne on 28 January 1547 and ten weeks later Compline was sung in English in the Chapel Royal. Next, the Mass itself was invaded and the Epistle and Gospel were read in English. Innovations and reforms now followed one another hotfoot; more and more English was introduced into public worship whilst various features of the old services were abolished one after another. Then on 8 March 1548 'The Order of Communion' was put out by Royal Proclamation as a sort of supplement to the Roman Mass. It is significant that these changes were all made without reference either to Parliament or Convocation.

This period of experiment and change culminated in 1548 with what was, perhaps, the most important single event of the whole of the English Reformation, the publication of the first 'Booke of the Common Prayer' of Edward VI, which came into use on Whitsunday, 1549. This event, which we shall discuss in more detail presently, was really the birth of the Anglican service as we know it. From this point onwards the progress of the Reformation showed itself in successive revisions of the Prayer Book. The first Prayer Book itself was very short-lived. It fell between two stools; it went much too far to mollify the traditionalists yet not far enough to satisfy the radicals. Probably it was only intended to be an interim measure, a basis for trial and further discussion. Certainly on such matters as Vestments and Prayers for the Dead the book met with considerable opposition and only three years later a much more drastic and Protestant revision was adopted, a revision which clearly showed the influence of Continental reformers. This book of 1552 added the Introductory Sentences, Exhortation, Confession, and Absolution at the beginning of the Daily Offices: in the Communion Office the ninefold Kyrie Eleison, Benedictus qui venit, and Agnus Dei were omitted, the Gloria was transferred to the end, the Ten Commandments were added, and the ancient canon was split into three parts — the Prayer for the Church Militant, the Prayer of Consecration, and the first alternative Prayer after Communion — while commemoration of the Blessed Virgin Mary, thanksgiving for the Patriarchs and Prophets, the sign of the cross and the invocation of the Holy Ghost at the consecration were all swept away. The altar itself was replaced by a table set amongst the people; Vestments and Prayers for the Dead were abolished. This book represents the most Puritan of any Anglican formulary: the extent to which Civil Powers had by this time intruded themselves into Church affairs is shown by the fact that it was authorized by Parliament alone; Convocation was not consulted.

Hardly was the ink dry on this book, however, when came another reversal of fortune. The King died on 6 July 1553 and was succeeded by his half-sister, Mary Tudor. Her uncompromising allegiance to the Roman Church was not tempered by any desire to conciliate the progressives, neither did she possess her father's rare genius for running with the hare and hunting with the hounds. Within a few months of her accession the 1552 book was repealed and Roman forms of worship were restored: then she settled in grim earnest to the task of sending heretics (men, women and boys as well as clerics) to the stake. Fortunately her reign was a short one and great must have been the general relief when, on 17 November 1558, Elizabeth became Queen.

After Mary's excesses there was in many quarters a feeling of revulsion against the Catholics and folk were much more receptive to the ideas of the reformers. The new Queen was cautious and did her best to reconcile Papists and Puritans by constitutional methods. The upshot of all this was the Prayer Book of 1559, basically the book of 1552 with a few small but important changes (such as the reintroduction of Vestments): these changes inclined much more to the spirit of the 1549 book than to that of 1552. However, in spite of all the Queen could do, the Prayer Book remained a battleground for the rest of her days, with the Puritans gradually gaining the ascendancy.

As soon as James came to the throne in 1603 the Puritans presented their 'Millenary Petition' to him setting out their grievances: the King, rather fancying himself as a skilled arbitrator, called both Episcopal and Puritan divines to state their cases to him. This conference, held at Hampton Court in January 1604, made surprisingly few alterations to the Prayer Book but it deserves our gratitude for one thing—it resulted in the Authorized Version of the Bible of 1611. The rest of his reign, and that of his successor, witnessed the growing strength of the Puritans. Bigoted Calvinism coupled with political power and military organisation led ultimately to the overthrow of King, Government and Church, and in 1645 the Prayer Book was proscribed and its place taken by the *Directory for the Plain Worship of God in the Three Kingdoms.*

The Restoration of Charles II to the throne in 1660 at last brought about some extension of religious liberty though it was not until William III's Toleration Act of 1689 that Churches other than Anglican were recognised as legal and even then Roman Catholics continued to suffer various disabilities. But just as people had reacted to Mary's persecutions by swinging over towards reform, so Puritan austerity ultimately strengthened the Established Church. Charles immediately brought the Prayer Book back into use; then, following the Savoy Conference held the next year, a further revision was undertaken the outcome of which was the Prayer Book of 1662, a version destined to remain the only official service-book of the Church of England for over three hundred years. The new book showed a marked reaction against Puritan concepts and it is significant that the word 'Priest' was used again as well as 'Minister'.

In the Georgian era, a literary pride in 'our incomparable liturgy' went hand in hand with much slovenliness in its performance and worship all too often degenerated into a duet between the parson and the clerk. In the first half of the nineteenth century the Oxford Movement resulted in a genuine attempt to carry out the services more worthily and Tractarian reverence for Christian antiquity restored the Eucharist as the central act of worship. A new table of lessons appeared in 1871 and the following year saw the passing of the Shortened Services Act. In 1906 a Royal Commission reported that 'the existing law of worship is too narrow for the present generation' and a new revision of the Prayer Book was accordingly begun.

In 1927 this further revision secured the support of the Convocations and the Church Assembly but was rejected by the House of Commons. It had tried to undo the worst effects of the 1552 Protestant revision of the 1549 book and was markedly Catholic in its emphasis, restoring some of the richness, beauty and symbolism of mediæval worship. In 1928 a slightly modified version of it again failed to get Parliamentary support but in 1965 many of its provisions were given legal authority: (in practice, parts of it had been widely adopted in many parishes during the intervening years, though without legal sanction).

Such then is, in brief, the story of the English Book of Common Prayer.

THE FIRST PRAYER BOOK OF 1549

Let us now see what the compilers of the 1549 Prayer Book set out to do and how far they succeeded in doing it. They were guided by five main principles:

1. All public worship must be 'understanded of the people': everything said and sung must therefore be in the vernacular, English replacing the Latin throughout. (Latin was still permitted in College Chapels where it was considered to be 'understanded of the people'; at that time Latin was still the language of scholarship.)

2. Services must be simple and straightforward so that even the humblest folk could follow and join in. The old services were considered much too elaborate and ornate.

3. There must be uniformity of worship throughout the realm so that a visitor from another part of the country would feel quite at home when worshipping in a different church: there would no longer be 'some following *Salisbury* Use, some *Hereford* Use, and some the Use of *Bangor*, some of *York*, some of *Lincoln*; now from henceforth all the whole Realm shall have but one Use.'[1]

4. The Daily Offices should provide for the continuous serialised reading of the entire Bible. Only Holy Scripture should be read in church; lives of the Saints and the 'planting in of uncertain stories and legends'[2] should no longer be permitted. In giving practical effect to this objective the Calendar was so arranged that the Old Testament would be read through once a year, the New Testament three times a year, and the Psalter once a month.

5. Finally, the object of the compilers was, in very truth, *reform* as opposed to revolution, a purifying and a return to those things 'ordained of a good purpose, and for a great advancement of godliness' but which 'in continuance of time have been corrupted'.[3] In his Preface, Cranmer, after listing various abuses and corruptions which had crept in, went on to say 'These inconveniences therefore considered, here is set forth such an Order, whereby the same shall be redressed.'[4] The reformers wanted the new services to be rooted in the traditions of the past and were anxious to conserve all that was best in the old books: attempts were even made to fit the new English words to the old plainsong melodies.

Of these five guiding principles it was perhaps the striving for simplicity which resulted in the greatest changes; this process of simplification operated in three directions:

(a) a greatly simplified Calendar
(b) simplified services
(c) one book to replace many.

(a) The Calendar. The mediæval Church had introduced into the Calendar a plethora of special days in honour of various Saints (many of purely local repute), six principal and many lesser feasts of the Blessed Virgin Mary, commemorations of the dead, days in honour of Martyrs, Confessors, Virgins and Matrons, and votive Masses and Requiems

---

[1] Cranmer's Preface to the first Book of Common Prayer (1549). It is retained in the Prayer Book of 1662 under the title *Concerning the Service of the Church*.
[2] Ibid.   [3] Ibid.   [4] Ibid.

for local worthies. Octaves of several of these were kept. It is not surprising then that the compilers of the new Prayer Book fell upon the Calendar with a particularly heavy hand. Saints' days, other than the commemorations of Apostles, were all banished while the principal Holy Days, especially those of Holy Week, were shorn of their ancient ceremonies and traditions and were marked merely by a Proper Preface. Inevitably, in purging away the dross much that was richly imaginative and symbolical had to be sacrificed as well — a heavy price to pay.

(b) Simplified services. To see how the services themselves were simplified and curtailed we need look no farther than the Daily Offices. In the pre-Reformation Church, especially in its monastic foundations, it had become customary to keep eight 'Hours of Prayer'; these were:

Mattins (or Vigil)	at midnight
Lauds	in the very early morning
Prime	at dawn (or sometimes at 6.00 a.m.)
Terce	third hour (9.00 a.m.)
Sext	sixth hour (noon)
None	ninth hour (3.00 p.m.)
Evensong (or Vespers)	in the evening
Compline	at bedtime

In practice the first two (sometimes three) were usually aggregated. The content of these services owed much to the ancient traditions of pre-Christian synagogue worship and their main purpose was the systematic reading of the Bible serially and the weekly recitation of the entire psalter. Mattins and Vespers were the longest: Mattins consisted of the Lord's Prayer (said privately), versicles and responses, Venite, a hymn, psalms with their antiphons, three lengthy lessons and, on festivals, Te Deum. Lauds and Vespers each included five psalms whilst Psalm 119 was recited daily, divided between the three lesser hours of Terce, Sext and None.

In the 1549 book the eight ancient 'Hours' of the monastic routine were abolished and their place taken by the two offices of Morning and Evening Prayer. Morning Prayer was derived from a fusion of the three early Hours — Mattins, Lauds and Prime — and Evening Prayer had been distilled from Vespers and Compline. The Canticles are notable survivors from the pre-Reformation services: Te Deum, probably composed by Bishop Niceta in the fourth century, reached us by way of the monastic Mattins; Benedicite, a Greek addition to Daniel 3 found in the Apocrypha (The Song of the Three Holy Children), was taken from Sunday Lauds; Benedictus came from Lauds, Magnificat from Vespers and Nunc dimittis from Compline. Lessons were so appointed that the whole Bible was to be read in course, the Old Testament once a year and the New Testament thrice yearly; and whereas previously the entire psalter had been recited or sung through once a week, from now onwards its recitation was to be spread over a month. The psalms were not printed as they were already available in the Bible.

(c) One book to replace many. In the mediæval Church the multitude of prescribed services together with all the variations and interpolations of an over-busy Calendar involved the use of a large number of books. These included:

1. the Missal or Mass book	for use at the altar, containing the full service of the Mass including the priest's part of the chant (but not the choir's part);

2. the Gradual	originally the book containing the responds sung between the Epistle and Gospel (the *responsoria graduali*). Later the word was used more loosely to describe the book containing the choir music of the Mass;
3. the Breviary	the priest's book for the Daily Offices (roughly corresponding to the Missal for the Mass);
4. the Antiphonary	containing the choir chants for the Offices (i.e. the musical parts of services other than the Mass — Cf. the Gradual);
5. the Processional	containing chants for use in processions, e.g. litanies;
6. the Manual	for occasional Offices (Baptism, Matrimony, Churching, Visitation of the Sick, Burial of the Dead);
7. the Pontifical	containing those services where a bishop or prelate officiates (consecration of a church, ordinations, etc.) and usually his own personal property.

By the time Edward VI had come to the throne several other books had been added to these of which we may mention:

8. the Primer	which followed no set pattern but generally included the Hours of the Blessed Virgin Mary, sometimes the Hours of the Holy Spirit, Hours of the Trinity, etc. for public worship and also various private devotions, usually in the vernacular;
9. the Consuetudinary	which prescribed details of rites and ceremonial, directed the 'actors' and gave orders of ecclesiastical precedence. It also gave the rules and customs of discipline of a particular religious order or monastery;
10. the Ordinal or Directorium (later known as Pie)	which (i) brought together the opening words of all the different participants drawn from the various books listed above, i.e. a book of cues; and (ii) gave a complex series of rules and orders of precedence governing the occurrence and concurrence of movable and immovable feasts.

Some of these books were so bulky that they were often bound in several volumes; thus the Missal often ran into five volumes while the Breviary sometimes extended to seven. To find the way through so many books at any given service was no easy matter and that was why it was necessary to have the Ordinal or Pie which acted as a general index to the others and included a Perpetual Calendar: but then the Ordinal itself was difficult to follow. What a nightmare taking a service must have been! As Cranmer himself so feelingly tells us in his introduction to the Book of Common Prayer: 'The number and hardness of the Rules called the *Pie*, and the manifold changings of the Service, was the cause, that to turn the Book only was so hard and intricate a matter, that many times there was more business to find out what should be read, than to read it when it was found out.'[5] This is probably no exaggeration. The whole system was complicated, bulky and, in days when all books were hand copied, very expensive.

To make matters worse, the Roman rite underwent various local modifications centred round the practice of particular monasteries or cathedrals. Such modifications were known as a 'Use'. In this same introduction Cranmer complains about these various 'Uses' and announces his remedy: 'And whereas heretofore there hath been great diversity in saying and singing in Churches within this Realm; some following *Salisbury* Use, some *Hereford* Use, and some the Use of *Bangor*, some of *York*, some of *Lincoln*; now from henceforth all the Realm shall have but one Use.'[6]

Small wonder then that the reformers were utterly ruthless. From now onwards, apart from the Bible itself, only one book was to be used throughout the land and everything necessary for the conduct of public worship must be found within its covers. To achieve this, Cranmer performed miracles of compression but even so, much of great beauty and significance perished and our services have been left the poorer.

A word must be said about the literary quality of the Prayer Book. A most happy accident of history wrought a miracle for which Anglicans have cause to be grateful. It so happened that the birth of the reformed Church coincided with one of the golden periods of English prose, a period which extended from Malory to Coverdale and which might well be called the swan-song of Middle English, expressed in prose rather than verse. This period culminated in two of the mightiest, and certainly most influential, achievements in the whole history of English letters—the superb Tyndale–Coverdale translation of the Bible (1535, which became the basis of the Authorized Version of 1611) and the Book of Common Prayer (1549).

The actual authorship of the Prayer Book is veiled in some obscurity. A number of bishops and divines were assembled at Chertsey in September 1548 to consider the new book and it seems likely that these men were the so-called 'compilers'. But their contribution was probably very small. Almost certainly they met to discuss a draft which had been prepared beforehand and their discussion would have been concerned more with doctrinal issues, rubrics, and problems of organisation, administration and authorization than with the niceties of literary expression. Probably most, if not all, of the actual drafting was done by Thomas Cranmer himself. His style has much in common with other great writers of his age, like Lord Berners and Sir Thomas More. It smoothly and harmoniously blends three apparently disparate elements—the strength and directness of Saxon (but not its disjointedness), the elegance of French and the rolling sonority of Latin—yet though rooted in the past there is no hint of pastiche. It established a new standard of dignity and grace; it is always clear and concise, elegant but not inflated, scholarly but not abstruse or pedantic, and always marvellously flexible. But it was in liturgical writing that Cranmer found his greatest inspiration: to his other gifts he added an exquisite ear for the language of devotion, a language to which he imparted a music of its own expressed in majestic rhythm and a melodious arrangement of words. Such things as the various exhortations, the General Confession and Absolution, the General Thanksgiving, and the Litany give classic expression to the thoughts and feelings of the worshipping Church and are at the same time incomparable as literature. Whereas magnificent architecture, masterpieces in painting or coloured glass, in stone or wood carving, are adornments and aids to worship, here is a work of art which is itself an actual vehicle of worship.

[5] Ibid.   [6] Ibid.

The Reformation Bible and Cranmer's Book of Common Prayer have remained the two supreme glories of English religious literature. At no other period in our history could they have appeared in so perfect a form; at the same time they provided a splendid model for a language then at the close of a formulative era and seeking new ways forward. There is no doubt that the repetition of their beautiful and smoothly flowing phrases day by day and week by week had a profound and ennobling influence on the development of English language and thought for the next four hundred years.

It is sad to realise that the Act of Uniformity of 1549, intended to unite the whole Church of England in one order of worship universally accepted, in fact split the Church into two—the traditionalists and the reformers, the conservatives and the progressives, the 'High' and the 'Low'—a split which has divided the English Church throughout its history and which unhappily still shows little sign of being healed.

CHURCH MUSICIANS AND THE REFORMATION

The Reformation brought about a great change not only in the work but also in the daily lives of church musicians. Previously, nearly all of them had been employed either in the Chapel Royal or in one or other of the eight hundred or so monasteries and abbeys dotted about the country, some fifty of which maintained choral foundations and choir schools while the wealthier of them employed quite large forces of lay musicians as directors, singers, composers and copyists. With the dissolution of the monasteries (1536–40), most of these musicians were thrown out of work and it is likely that, at a conservative estimate, upwards of two thousand men were dismissed (a much more significant percentage of the population then than it would be now). What happened to them? Some, but not many, would have been lucky enough to secure appointment to one of King Henry's 'Cathedrals of the new foundation'—Canterbury, Winchester, Durham, Oxford, Chester, Gloucester, Worcester, Rochester, Norwich, Ely, Peterborough and Carlisle; others would have found their way into one of the royal or private chapels. Most would have abandoned church music for a livelihood and taken up other occupations, retaining music as a spare-time interest, secularising it, and probably taking private pupils.[7] This great enrichment of secular art no doubt contributed much to the high level of musical skill in all sections of the community in the Elizabethan period a generation later.

The few musicians who did manage to retain or secure appointments in the Henrician Church found themselves faced with almost insuperable difficulties. The Act of Uniformity, which was passed on 21 January 1549, decreed that 'the Book of Common Prayer and none other' was to be used on and after 9 June of that year. This meant that in five months all the plainsong and traditional music built up over centuries would be ruthlessly swept away and masses, motets, and all settings of the Latin would become illegal. But what was to replace them? Little time was left to answer this question.

Of course some settings of sacred texts in English were already available. Probably the earliest of these were the carols, a form which reached the height of its popularity in the fifteenth century. Known manuscript sources of the period yield nearly a hundred 2- and 3-part settings of English and macaronic carols.[8] In the next century (c. 1530) one of the earliest examples of music printing in England was an anthology of sacred and secular

[7] See p. 207 for an interesting parallel.
[8] See John Stevens: *Mediæval Carols*. Musica Britannica Vol. IV. (Stainer and Bell.)

pieces, vocal and instrumental, which included carols by Ashwell, Cowper, Gwynneth and Richard Pygott.

Then there were the metrical psalms. In *c.* 1543[9] appeared what was, in effect, a sort of hymnbook for use in the home or private chapel—Myles Coverdale's *Goostly psalmes and spirituall songs.* Its words and music were largely Lutheran in origin: it included thirteen metrical psalms, metrical versions of Magnificat, Nunc dimittis, the Lord's Prayer, Creed and Ten Commandments, and a number of Latin and German hymns. The music drew largely on Gregorian chant and German chorales and all settings were in unison. It is interesting to note that the usual English genius for compromise saw nothing in the least incongruous in this curious marriage of the ancient plainsong tones of the Roman Church with the metrical psalmody of protestant extremists. Unfortunately King Henry's anti-Lutheranism led to the book's being banned after a brief life and Bishop Bonner's order for its burning is dated 26 September 1546. Only one copy has survived. Two other metrical psalters must be mentioned. Sometime before his death in 1549 a Thomas Sternhold issued a small collection of nineteen metrical psalms without music. This collection, together with further translations of his own and successive additions by John Hopkins, Thomas Norton and others, was destined to become the most famous of all English metrical psalters—Sternhold and Hopkins, later to be known as the 'Old' Version. As subsequent editions appeared more and more psalms were added; in 1556 an edition with tunes was published and in 1562 the book reached completion. From then onwards innumerable editions and reprints appeared with various minor changes and additions: indeed, Sternhold and Hopkins held the field virtually unrivalled till 1696 when a 'New' Version by Nahum Tate and Nicholas Brady was brought out. Another metrical psalter that deserves mention is Robert Crowley's *The Psalter of David newely translated into Englysh metre . . . whereunto is added a note of four parts* (1549): this contained translations of the entire psalter and was the first such book to contain harmonised music, but it met with little success and was short-lived. The important thing is that both Sternhold's first two editions and Crowley's psalter were available to church musicians in the first few months after the Act of Uniformity.

But carols and metrical psalms were essentially simple, suitable for the home, private chapel or (later) parish church; in cathedrals they were a poor substitute for the rich and elaborate music associated with the Latin rite. Something more was needed. Fortunately some composers had been quick to see which way the wind was blowing and had anticipated the new Prayer Book by setting English words to more elaborate music for use by cathedral choirs. For their texts they turned to the metrical psalters and, even more, to the Primers. The Primers had originally been intended for private devotions and were important because they paved the way for the substitution of English for Latin in public worship. Beginning with a publication by Wynkyn de Worde of *c.* 1494 a number of Primers were issued of which Marshall's (*c.* 1535), Hilsey's (1539) and the 'King's' Primer (1545) were particularly important. They contained English translations of the daily 'Hours' of Mattins, Lauds, Prime, Terce, Sext, None, Vespers and Compline, translations of the Apostles' Creed and Lord's Prayer, and various private prayers in English. A unique set of Edwardian partbooks in the Bodleian Library, usually known

[9] Dr. Peter le Huray in his *Music and the Reformation in England 1549–1660* (Herbert Jenkins 1967) suggests 1538–9 and Dr. Gustave Reese in *Music and the Renaissance* (Dent 1954) gives 1539–40, but the Rev. Maurice Frost in *English and Scottish Psalm and Hymn Tunes* (S.P.C.K. and Oxford 1953) prefers 1543.

as the 'Wanley' manuscripts,[10] include some fifty or so canticle settings and motets designed as choir music of cathedral standard (*a 4* and *a 5*) the texts of which have been taken from these Primers. What is interesting is that most of the Wanley pieces would have been composed at least a year or two before the Act of Uniformity.

The new services offered considerable scope to the musician: musical settings could be provided for the Versicles and Responses, Psalms, Canticles, the Litany and the Office of Holy Communion; in addition, there came into being what was later to develop into an important form of sacred music peculiar to the English—the anthem. At first, however, anthems were merely motets with English words. Cranmer himself was far more than just an inspired translator and adapter; he fully deserves to rank with Ambrose and Gregory in the hierarchy of musical bishops. Like them he concerned himself with all aspects of public worship; like them also he had given much thought to the purpose, style and standard of whatever music was to be admitted into church services and he was particularly anxious that if music were to be used at all it should add to the expressiveness of the words, not obscure them or detract from them. He himself composed a number of simple plainsong-like melodies to carry his English translation-of some Latin processions but, alas, neither the translations nor their musical settings have survived. In a covering letter to the King, dated 7 October 1544, which accompanied these translations occurs a famous and oft-quoted passage in which the Archbishop summed up his ideas about how sacred words should be set to music:

> ... if Your Grace command some devout and solemn note to be made thereunto ... I trust it will much excitate and stir the hearts of all men unto devotion and godliness. But in my opinion, the song that should be made thereunto would not be full of notes, but, as near as may be, for every syllable a note, so that it may be sung distinctly and devoutly as be in the matins and evensong Venite, the hymns, Te Deum, Benedictus, Magnificat, Nunc dimittis, and all the psalms and versicles; and in the mass Gloria in excelsis, Gloria Patri, the Creed, the Preface, the Pater Noster, and some of the Sanctus and Agnus. As concerning the 'Salve festa dies', the Latin note, as I think, is sober and distinct enough, wherefore I have travailed to make the verses in English and have put the Latin note unto the same. Nevertheless, they that be cunning in singing can make a much more solemn note thereto. I made them only for a proof, to see how English would do in song. But because mine English verses lack the grace and facility that I wish they had, Your Majesty may cause some other to make them again that can do the same in more pleasant English and phrase ...

Though this letter refers mainly to the translation of 'Salve festa dies' which it was accompanying, the fact that he lists by name the other sung portions of the offices clearly suggests that he favoured the principle of 'for every syllable a note' in all music which the congregation were expected to sing or understand. His intention was to make the services simpler and easier to join in; he recognised that florid music was out of place as a vehicle for popular worship and sought to discourage its use. No doubt the tropes were his main target: tropes were long, decorative, and often highly florid interpolations of words and sometimes music placed between the words of an authentic text (e.g. Surge—*infida gens, dejecta perfidia, quem demonstravit stella regem regum venerare*—et illuminare—*cogita, spera et suspira, coelestia contemplate*—Jerusalem). Yet it must be emphasized that in the passage just quoted Cranmer has in mind only simple unison

[10] Bodleian Library: Mus. MSS. E. 420–2 (Tenor partbook missing).

settings intended for congregational participation; his remarks were not intended to apply to more elaborate choir settings in several voice-parts: failure to appreciate this dictinction was later to lead composers to some misunderstanding and confusion. Furthermore, he is expressing only a personal opinion (though doubtless an influential one!).

Of course the principle of 'for every syllable a note' was well established long before Cranmer's day and is exemplified in the hymns and sequences of the Sarum rite, in various special prayers and hymns set in *conductus* style, and in such works as Pygott's *The mother, full mannerly*, Taverner's *Playn Song* and *Small Devotion* Masses and Tye's *Euge bone* Mass. As a general principle it is fairly sound and it guards against excessive elaboration in music intended for a congregation to sing, but its too rigid application can have a constraining effect; thus, passing notes can often make a melody easier rather than harder to sing. In any case, most composers had the good sense to accept Cranmer's dictum as a useful guide rather than a rule to be slavishly followed. Nevertheless the Archbishop's known views, as expressed in this letter five years before the Act of Uniformity, undoubtedly had considerable influence on contributors to the Wanley manuscripts and on other composers, both then and later.

MERBECKE'S 'BOOKE OF COMMON PRAIER NOTED'

The old Latin services had their prescribed musical counterpart and the chant for any part of the offices for any particular day was set down by authority (as in the modern *Liber Usualis* of the Roman Church). When the new English Prayer Book appeared, choirmasters would have felt the need for some equivalent musical lectionary bearing the stamp of authority. However, such a book has never appeared: the nearest we have ever got to it was John Merbecke's *Booke of Common Praier Noted* (i.e. set to music) of 1550. It is clear that in its production Merbecke must have worked in fairly close collaboration with Cranmer and we find the principle of 'for every syllable a note' strictly applied. Merbecke's setting is typical of the mood of the English Reformation: though ostensibly a new setting for the new English words, we find that in fact it draws heavily on the past. Thus, in the familiar Communion setting, the Introit Psalm was set to a traditional psalm-tone, the ninefold Kyrie was a simplified version of the Kyrie from the ancient Mass for the Dead, the Gloria and Credo retain their ancient and familiar intonations, Sanctus and Benedictus were derived from the Mode II setting of *In Dominicis*, whilst the Agnus Dei was adapted from an old Sarum melody. What he himself composed consists of a kind of quasi-plainsong, not far removed in spirit from the chant of the old Roman services: it does, however, differ from true plainsong in one important particular—it is printed with notes of four different time values (*breue, semy breue, mynymme* and what he calls a 'close') and in his short preface Merbecke makes it plain that he wants these relative note lengths to be carefully observed and the music sung in tempo.

There is no evidence to show that Merbecke's book was ever used. Only two years after its publication the revised Prayer Book of 1552 superseded the 1549 book and the changes made were such that his setting would no longer fit. Neither did he make any attempt to revise it: probably by this time his anti-popery sentiments had reached the stage where he regretted writing his *Common Praier Noted* because its plainsong derivations and similarities would inevitably appear to him to conjure up the shade of the

Scarlet Woman. Perhaps there were musical reasons too why it was so soon forgotten. Merbecke's work was a curious hybrid; in some ways it was like plainsong yet it had to be sung in tempo: furthermore, a rather dull unison setting could hardly have been very popular with folk who were used to the richness of pre-Reformation polyphony.

THE MODERN REVIVAL OF MERBECKE

It was the nineteenth-century Tractarians who rediscovered and popularised Merbecke's Communion setting in a commendable endeavour to revive congregational participation. Unfortunately their musical scholarship was not as good as their intentions and editions appeared which showed a complete misunderstanding of the style and spirit of the original. Typical of these is the barbarous travesty which appeared in Stainer's *Cathedral Prayer Book* (1891), divided into bars and harmonized in four parts! But more enlightened scholarship has brought its own problems: a sincere attempt to realise Merbecke's intentions has led to sharp controversies as to what those intentions were. There are three main schools of thought:

    (a) those who favour strict adherence to Merbecke's own note-values;
    (b) those who feel the music should be printed in notes of equal value and treated in the manner of true plainsong; and
    (c) those who would redistribute the note values and treat the melodic line in a sort of speech-rhythm fashion.

In addition, each of these methods can be employed either strictly or flexibly. In practice these differences are not of great moment; what is important is that the congregation should become familiar with whatever method is adopted and should be able to join in with confidence and spirit.

Many different editions of Merbecke's Communion Service are now available though all have been adapted, in greater or less degree, to accommodate the 1662 version of the words. (More recently Merbecke has undergone still further alteration to accommodate the changes made in the Series II experiment.) Many editors have not contented themselves with making the minimum adjustment necessary but have considerably modified the original; such editions are best avoided. Of the many versions available, the following are the only ones which can be considered true to the original:

    edited by Basil Harwood (Novello)
    edited by Dom Anselm Hughes (Faith Press)
    edited by J. Eric Hunt and Dr. Gerald H. Knight (S.P.C.K.)

Ideally Merbecke's setting should be sung unaccompanied but a discreet organ accompaniment gives most congregations more confidence. When used, the accompaniment causes least offence when treated on plainsong lines.

THE 'PARISH CHURCH' AND 'CATHEDRAL' TRADITIONS

Merbecke's setting is unique at this period in that it was liturgical music written expressly for congregational use. As we have seen, the reformers laid great stress on the importance of the active participation of the congregation in public worship, yet in cathedrals and similar institutions it was clear that ordinary worshippers could never hope to join in the elaborate music performed by professional choirs; it became equally clear that not only would highly skilled singers resent having to restrict their efforts to what a congregation could manage but also that their specialised knowledge and skill would be wasted in so doing. Hence another legacy of the English Reformation was the emergence, or more accurately the retention, of two quite separate, yet complementary, streams of church music—the 'parish church tradition' and the 'cathedral tradition'. These two traditions are perhaps mostly clearly differentiated in the choir offices of Mattins and Evensong. To this day considerable misunderstanding still exists about the role played by these two traditions. How often people attending a cathedral service for the first time come away disappointed because 'no one sang' or because when they did sing they got black looks from their neighbours. In some parish churches congregations resent the intrusion of an anthem ('We don't want to hear the choir—we want to sing ourselves'); in others, an anthem is favoured so long as it isn't in Latin; in some, all anthems are welcomed including those in Latin; in yet others the service is a replica of the cathedral type of service. So much confusion exists about the function and place of music in worship that some further discussion is necessary.

CHAPTER II

The place of Music in Worship

From the early days of Christianity there have always been those who viewed music with misgivings; these misgivings, which many still share, resolve themselves into two questions: 'To what extent, if at all, should music be admitted into public worship?' and 'If admitted, what sort of music is most justifiable and appropriate — plainsong, unison-singing, harmony, polyphony, congregational singing or singing by a trained choir, accompanied or unaccompanied, organ, instruments, orchestra, band or, in these days, "pop" group?' These questions have continued to exercise the minds of all Christians who care about music.

The early Fathers were sharply divided in their attitude to music. They all recognised that because of its direct appeal to the hearts and minds of men it had immense power — but was this power an instrument of good or evil? Did it derive from God or the Devil?

God mingles the sweetness of harmony with the divine Truth so that while we are enjoying the pleasures of hearing the music we may unconsciously gather up the benefits of the words which are being spoken. This is just what a wise doctor will do when, obliged to give bitter medicine to a sick man, he lines the medicine cup with honey.

Basil of Caesarea (*c.* 330–379) Sermon I.3.

Thus does the devil stealthily set fire to the city. It is not a matter of running up ladders and using petroleum or pitch or tow; he uses things far more pernicious — lewd sights, base speech, degraded music, and songs full of all kinds of wickedness.

John Chrysostom (*c.* 347–407) *De poenitentia* VI.

Certainly it was generally thought that even if the Devil had not personally invented music he was quick to subvert its power to his own ends and therefore the only safe music was that used in praising God:

Nothing will delight your sight except what you see to be essentially good and right. Nothing will please your ears but what nourishes your soul and tends to your improvement . . . So, if it is pleasure to hear music, let your best pleasure be to sing and hear the praises of God.[1]

Lactantius (*c.* 240–*c.* 320) *De Vero Cultu* 6.21.

But even here, in the Church itself, dangers still existed. Although most churchmen admitted that music could be a valuable adjunct to public worship they were deeply

[1] These three passages in translation are quoted from Erik Routley: *The Church and Music*, pp. 236, 239–40, 233. (Duckworth, Rev. Ed. 1967.)

suspicious of the pleasurable emotions which it excited. Music, from being an aid to worship, could quickly become an end in itself, tickling the ear and stimulating sensuous thoughts instead of uplifting the spirit: thus it could easily prove more a distraction than a help and even, at times, a barrier between man and his God. This view receives its classic expression in the famous passage in St. Augustine's *Confessions* where he says:

The pleasures of the ear did indeed draw me and hold me more tenaciously, but You have set me free. Yet still when I hear those airs, in which Your words breathe life, sung with sweet and measured voice, I do, I admit, find a certain satisfaction in them, yet not such as to grip me too close, for I can depart when I will. Yet in that they are received into me along with the truths which give them life, such airs seek in my heart a place of no small honour, and I find it hard to know what is their due place. At times indeed it seems to me that I am paying them greater honour than is their due — when, for example, I feel that by those holy words my mind is kindled more religiously and fervently to a flame of piety because I hear them sung than if they were not sung: and I observe that all the varying emotions of my spirit have modes proper to them in voice and song whereby, by some secret affinity, they are made more alive. It is not good that the mind should be enervated by this bodily pleasure. But it often ensnares me in that the bodily sense does not accompany the reason as following after it in proper order, but having been admitted to aid the reason, strives to run before and take the lead. In this matter I sin unawares, and then grow aware.

Yet there are times when through too great a fear of this temptation I err in the direction of over-severity—even to the point sometimes of wishing that the melody of all the lovely airs with which David's Psalter is commonly sung should be banished not only from my own ears but from the Church's as well: and that seems to me a safer course which I remember often to have heard told of Athanasius, bishop of Alexandria, who had the reader of the psalm utter it with so little modulation of the voice that he seemed to be saying it rather than singing it. Yet when I remember the tears I shed, moved by the songs of the Church in the early days of my new faith: and again when I see that I am moved not by the singing but by the things that are sung—when they are sung with a clear voice and proper modulation—I recognise once more the usefulness of this practice. Thus I fluctuate between the peril of indulgence and the profit I have found: and on the whole I am inclined—though I am not propounding any irrevocable opinion—to approve the custom of singing in church, that by the pleasure of the ear the weaker minds may be roused to a feeling of devotion. Yet whenever it happens that I am more moved by the singing than by the thing that is sung, I admit that I have grievously sinned and then I should wish rather not to have heard the singing.

Augustine (354–430) *Confessions* X. 33.[2]

In other words, the problem posed by Augustine is briefly this: up to a point music in worship is a good thing; beyond that point a bad thing. But where does this point occur? How are we to strike the right balance? Obviously it is a highly personal matter; those who are unmusical may find any form of music an unwelcome intrusion whilst many musical folk would consider a fine anthem far more inspiring and uplifting than a sermon. Most people will come somewhere between these two extremes and since we

[2] Ibid.

cannot each have services arranged to meet our special needs, the amount of music to be admitted must be arbitrarily regulated by the appropriate authority.

How then has the first of our two questions been answered in Britain? Except for the Quakers (and even they have come to accept it now) nearly all Christian sects in Britain admitted some sort of music as part of their public worship though of course there have been wide differences in the amount and type of music employed. This leads directly to a consideration of our second question, which has always been a burning issue—what sort of music should be used? Speaking broadly, this question can be put in another way—should church music be simple and straightforward so that everyone can join in, or should it be a sacramental act of worship in itself in which we, or our musical representatives, offer back to God the finest fruits of those musical gifts which he himself has bestowed—polished works of art, noble, beautiful, but necessarily more difficult and elaborate?

On the face of it the answer is obvious: a church service is not a musical appreciation class and God is not a music critic. He is not concerned with the aesthetic values of what we sing, our musical skill or the quality of our voices, be they pleasing or raucous, so long as we give the best we can and sing from our hearts. Hence, church music should be simple enough for every member of the worshipping community to be able to join in—high and low voices, old and young, skilled and unskilled, educated and uneducated, musical and unmusical. This point of view was strongly held by the Puritans and was also the basis of much nineteenth-century missionary endeavour and street-corner evangelism: it still has many adherents, especially amongst certain nonconformist sects. But principles, however good, are not always satisfactory in practice and this particular one has often had an unexpectedly pernicious effect. Why is this?

The reasons themselves and the many arguments to which they give rise are fundamental to any understanding of the function and place of music in worship. They may be summarised as follows:

1. In order to be sung by all conditions of men, melodies must move mainly by step and avoid too many leaps, must be restricted in range, elementary in rhythm (hence the popularity of hymn-tunes in triple time) and easy to memorise. Admittedly there are many splendid tunes that do satisfy these requirements but in the long run such restrictions must eventually become a strait jacket, stifling vitality and imagination and tending towards uniformity and monotony. Some would claim that plainsong is the best answer—that it fulfils the given requirements and is free from these objections: this is certainly true of some simple chants but in more advanced melodies not only is the range too wide but they are by no means easy to memorise.

2. In practice, music which is easy enough for the unmusical to enjoy is often strangely irksome and unsatisfying to more musical people who feel instinctively that it cannot give adequate expression to their inmost thoughts. After all, song is a natural outlet for the expression of our noblest and deepest feelings and when these feelings are of worship, praise and thanksgiving to Almighty God, we are woefully conscious of how inadequate even our utmost skill is to convey all that is in our hearts without having that expression arbitrarily scaled down to what less gifted people can do. Such artificial limitations and restrictions must inevitably give way as we open the flood-gates of pent-up emotions. Hence musical people tend, often unconsciously, to develop, extend, decorate or elaborate simple basic material to a point where less musical folk can no longer participate. Indeed it is a common phenomenon in most of the arts for some new form to begin in a simple

fashion, then to grow increasingly complex and elaborate—almost of its own volition—until it reaches the summit of its finest fulfilment; after this, further elaboration leads to decay and decline until ultimately some process of reform or reaction is instituted to cut away a superstructure of accretions, mannerisms and inessentials which obscure, or are in danger of obscuring, the basic art-form itself. Art tends naturally to proliferate; reforms tend to simplify. It follows that the simpler music is to start with, the stronger will be the natural and inevitable pull towards elaboration. So the development of church music has often been a sinuous line winding its way between the musicians, who were constantly enriching it with new conceptions, advancing techniques and increasing resources (sometimes to the point of extravagance); and the reformers, like Pope John XXII, Cranmer, Calvin, the Council of Trent, and others, who tried to constrain it and prevent excesses.

3. Many people feel that church music at its best is something far more wonderful than just an opportunity to 'give 'em a good sing and let 'em get their emotions off their chests'. Not only is it an aid, an accessory, to worship but it can itself become a positive act of worship, something which can be presented to God as a special offering, a yielding back to him of the talents which he himself has entrusted to our care.

If we accept this view, we must now go on to consider what sort of music makes a truly worthy offering. Is it enough that it should be sincere both in conception and execution; that its intrinsic quality is unimportant so long as it comes from the heart? The answer must surely be 'No'. If a cleaner leaves the chancel in a dirty and untidy condition it is small comfort that she is a devoted Christian: we are not pleased if an electrician, however sincere in his religious beliefs, is so incompetent that he burns the church down: neither is it much consolation when the new spire collapses to reflect that the architect, however useless at his work, is 'a man of God'. Sincerity then, important as it is, must be coupled with professional skill and, in matters of art, with an artist's vision and perception as well. In other words, bad music (and, incidentally, bad poetry) is not excused merely because its composer had pious intentions. Herein lies the fallacy that 'God is not a music critic'. Of course he's not—but he has endowed us with critical faculties and these should surely be used to help us in our task of making certain that only the best should be given back to him. Who would build a church out of corrugated iron if better materials were readily available? Who would lay a piece of coconut matting in front of the altar if he could afford a carpet? Who would send fallen and bruised apples to a harvest thanksgiving? Why then should we sing inferior music when far better is at hand? These same arguments apply not only to the composition but also to the per-formance of sacred music. It is not sufficient that we should sing just because we ourselves happen to enjoy singing: that is merely being self-centred. If we are making a gift of our music to the Almighty we should at least take the trouble to perform it as well as we possibly can; (hence the introduction of 'congregational practices' and other aids in some churches).

4. Let us return to the theme 'God is not a music critic—he is not concerned with the aesthetic values of what we sing'. This may be very true but it can also be a dangerous argument. If we abandon quality as a criterion in selecting music for public worship how else will our choice be guided? Only too often those responsible for selecting the music will put down what they themselves enjoy or what they think the congregation will enjoy. But as we have just seen, personal enjoyment is self-centred, not God-centred, and such music is no longer 'worship' in its best sense. Here we come back to St.

Augustine's 'It is not good that the mind should be enervated by this bodily pleasure. But it often ensnares me, in that the bodily sense does not accompany the reason as following after it in proper order, but having been admitted to aid the reason, strives to run before and take the lead. In this matter I sin unawares, and then grow aware . . . Yet whenever it happens that I am more moved by the singing than by the thing that is sung, I admit that I have grievously sinned, and then I should wish rather not to have heard the singing.'

5. Again, if we accept that church music is an act of worship, does it necessarily have to be a personal act? What about those who are quite unable to sing even the simplest melodies; are they to be excluded? There is a strong body of opinion in the Church which believes that because in our public worship we are no longer individuals but a corporate group, part of the Church Universal, we are therefore justified in calling upon those who are obviously more musically capable than others and can therefore offer a more beautiful musical gift to lead the people in their singing and even, at times, to present worship on behalf of the less musical—much as some town might commission a master-craftsman to create a work of art as a gift from the townsfolk to some royal visitor; though the townsfolk themselves did not actually make it, it is still their gift. When this happens the chosen musicians must always be conscious that, as leaders or delegates, they are responsible for the worship of others, approaching their work with humility and subjugating their own individual personalities to the objective impersonality of public worship. If this viewpoint can be accepted it becomes plain that a choir singing an anthem, an organist playing a voluntary, or even an orchestra or a band performing at a service, does so—or should do so—on behalf of the congregation. As we shall see, this doesn't mean that, having delegated a part of worship, responsibility is ended and the congregation takes no further interest.

6. What of those churches, cathedrals and musical foundations where there is a fully professional choir of highly skilled musicians and the music is so elaborate and rarefied that even the most musical members of the congregation cannot hope to join in in any part of the service, and are in fact discouraged from doing so? How can such a situation be justified? Many, of course, believe that it never can be justified; that it is the negation of corporate worship. Others think that there are two answers to this. First, they believe that many people attach far too much importance to being able to 'join in'. After all, we cannot audibly 'join in' quite a large part of the service—the Epistle, Gospel, lessons, prayers and collects (except for the 'Amens'), and the sermon, to mention only a few— though we recognise all these things as part of our pattern of worship: neither can we 'join in' magnificent architecture, stained glass windows, mosaics, rich tapestries and intricate wood-carving and wrought ironwork, yet these can be a very real aid to devotion, producing an atmosphere which is conducive to worship, lifting us out of the mundane world of everyday things and attuning our hearts to the spiritual. Music has this capacity in very high degree even if it has no words at all (as in an organ voluntary), or if the words cannot be heard (as in a complicated polyphonic motet) or cannot be understood (as in a Latin anthem). This is where Cranmer's 'for every syllable a note' theory cannot be applied too rigorously to choir music because it fails to take into account that a highly melismatic and almost wordless work like Taverner's *Western Wynde* Mass can still be deeply moving and spiritually uplifting. Second, although we may not be able to join in with our lips and voices, this does not prevent us from joining in actively (not passively) with our hearts and minds. We should concentrate our thoughts on the

offering that is being made on our behalf, listening intently, and either following the words in our books (if that is practicable) or at least identifying ourselves with them as closely as possible. Thus we can take part mentally even when we cannot take part vocally. The fact that the best choirs consist of professional musicians who receive payment for their services is a stumbling block to some people, but if it is remembered that a musical training is both lengthy and costly and that the daily round of choir practices and sung services makes it difficult for singers to take up other full-time employment, it becomes clear that they must be paid a living wage as must the clergy, organists, vergers and other full-time officials.

Enough has now been said to indicate that the choice of music for performance in public worship presents problems which admit of no easy solution. To choose simple, easily singable music is not the only answer nor is it necessarily the best. It is therefore a matter for great rejoicing that the Church of England has been particularly liberal in its attitude to music and makes generous provision for almost all shades of opinion. Within its walls can be heard all types of music from Byrd to Barnby and from plainsong to 'pop' song. This wide range is made possible because from its very inception, as we have seen, two different traditions were established, one associated with the parish church, one with the cathedral, and both having their roots in the pre-Reformation Roman Church. These traditions are both still flourishing today: what then, in practical terms, are their characteristics and requirements?

THE PARISH CHURCH TRADITION

In a parish church we should experience the practical realisation of the dreams and ideals of the early reformers—a service 'understanded of the people' in which they can and should take a large and active part. The ideal to aim for is whole-hearted congregational participation and the worshipping community can fairly claim to share in almost everything that is sung. For this reason the music is much more simple and there is less of it than in cathedral services. The congregation should be helped and encouraged to join in:

1. The Ordinary of the Communion Service. To facilitate this a unison treatment is probably best. Merbecke's setting has become very popular though musically it is rather dull. A number of unison settings simple enough for congregations to learn have been published in recent years.
2. The recitation of the General Confession, Lord's Prayer, Creed and (when used) the General Thanksgiving. In the nineteenth century it became customary to sing all these on a monotone (often with the support of a crawling organ accompaniment) but the modern practice of reciting them in the ordinary speaking voice has been found less artificial, less tiring and far more meaningful.
3. Responses. These should be sung in the so-called 'Ferial' version, not the 'Festal' which is too high for untrained voices.
4. The Psalms. Though ideally the congregation ought certainly to join in the singing of the psalms there are practical difficulties to overcome. Prior to the Oxford Movement the psalms had very generally been sung in metrical versions: these were easy to sing and to memorize but usually the verse was of poor quality. It is far more difficult for untrained people to sing the Prayer Book version rhythmically

37

and reasonably well together, either to Gregorians or to Anglican chants. Indeed, the report of the Archbishops' Committee on music in worship goes so far as to say: 'It may be a regrettable fact, but it has to be admitted that the psalms, whether they be sung to plainsong tones or to Anglican chants, do not lend themselves readily to singing by the average congregation.'[3] Many churches solve the problem by restricting themselves to a few popular psalms on which they ring the changes week by week. A better and more helpful way, and one which should certainly become much more general, is to provide the congregation with 'pointed' psalters; these are more effective still if occasional congregational practices are held. In some churches it may be better to accept realities and read the psalms aloud: responsorial reading between the parson and people or between people on the north and south sides of the church can be greatly inspiring if done well. Anglican chants should be chosen carefully; high reciting notes are tiring and discouraging for untrained singers and chants having a reciting note higher than C should be avoided.

Confusion is worse confounded because a wide variety of psalters is in use, each offering a different system of 'pointing'. To avoid perpetuating this problem, the Commission responsible for issuing *The Revised Psalter* has authorized and will continue to authorize the publication of only one method of pointing. By having only this one official version it is hoped to ensure uniformity of practice wherever the book is in use. Even then individual choirmasters will inevitably and justifiably alter the pointing to agree with their own feelings and interpretation — as they have done with other psalters.

5. Canticles. Familiar tones or chants should normally be used so that even without pointed books people will soon memorize the pointing. New tones or chants can be added from time to time once the pointing has become well established. Fully-composed 'settings' as used in cathedrals should not normally find a place in parish church worship though in some churches they may be fittingly used to mark some special occasion.

6. Hymns. People enjoy singing hymns but a critical mind and discriminating taste for both words and music are needed when choosing them. From a practical point of view extreme high notes should be avoided: tunes like *St. Gertrude* ('Onward, Christian soldiers') and *Austria* ('Glorious things of thee are spoken') should be transposed down into a more comfortable key. Descants by the choir, unison verses and varied harmonisations are all useful so long as they do not distract the congregation from their part. New hymns and tunes should be introduced occasionally (one at a time!); they then need fairly frequent repetition for a few weeks to become assimilated.

Anthems. Since 1662 the Prayer Book has permitted the performance of an anthem after the Third Collect and this is the only musical part of the service in which the congregation is not expected to take an active part, though they should of course take a passive part by listening attentively. It must be emphasized that anthems, unlike the motets of the Roman rite, are not an essential part of the service and should not, therefore, be sung unless they are appropriate, of spiritual and musical merit, and can be adequately performed. There is a natural and human tendency for choirs to over-reach themselves

[3] *Music in Church*, p. 34. (Church Information Office: Rev. Ed. 1957.)

and tackle music beyond their capabilities; this must be guarded against. Neither should meretricious music be performed merely because it appeals to an influential parishioner or because 'we've always had it'. The anthem is an art form peculiar to the English Church. It has been greatly developed and enriched over the centuries and now the whole corpus of anthem literature constitutes an important branch of liturgical music, one which is essentially English. Incidentally, the anthem is the common ground on which the parish church and cathedral traditions meet.

The function of the parish church organist is different from that of his colleague at the cathedral. Whereas in the cathedral the organist merely accompanies the choir when an independent accompaniment is called for, in the parish church, especially the smaller church, his main task is to encourage, guide, and often lead the singing of the people. In the past this lead was frequently provided not by an organ (which few country churches could afford) but by the parish clerk, or by a gallery band or a barrel organ.[4] The introduction of a surpliced choir seated in the chancel was a nineteenth-century innovation stemming from the Oxford Movement,[5] but it must be pointed out that in parish churches the choir exists specifically to lead the singing of the congregation and not, as in cathedrals, to offer worship on behalf of the congregation.

THE CATHEDRAL TRADITION

The cathedral tradition is essentially one of delegation: music is offered on behalf of the people by a highly trained all-male choir of which the men are usually professional musicians and the boys have been carefully selected and then given a thorough and lengthy musical training — often in a choir school attached to, or part of, the foundation. Often such schools are boarding establishments. We may note the following characteristics:

1. Fully choral services are sung not only on Sundays but on weekdays as well.
2. Far more music is sung than is customary in a parish church and much of it demands a technically accomplished choir. Most of this music is too difficult for parish choirs to attempt.
3. Those sung parts of the prescribed services which remain unvaried from day to day (the Ordinary of the Mass, Responses, Canticles, etc.) are sung to fully-composed settings, some of them highly elaborate.
4. The set psalms for the day are sung *in toto*. The two sides of a cathedral choir are known as Decani (i.e. the side containing the Dean's stall) on the liturgical south and Cantoris (the side containing the Precentor's stall) on the liturgical north; it has long been the custom for the psalms to be chanted antiphonally from side to side, Decani and Cantoris, either verse by verse or, less commonly, half-verse by half-verse.
5. The Te Deum and Benedictus in Mattins and the Magnificat and Nunc dimittis in Evensong are not sung to tones or Anglican chants; instead they are provided with full settings in the style of anthems. Somewhat confusingly, these canticle settings are called 'Services'. To distinguish them from ordinary statutory church services, the word 'Service' will be dignified with a capital letter throughout this book when it refers to such through-composed canticle settings. Since in such a Service all

[4] See pp. 231-4.   [5] See pp. 326-9.

canticles are normally set in the same key, it is customary to speak of (say) Stanford's Morning Service in C or Wesley's Evening Service in E or, more familiarly, Stanford in C and Wesley in E. These canticle settings, like anthems, are an art form peculiar to the English Church: they too form a considerable and important corpus of religious music.

6. An anthem after the Third Collect, though optional in the Prayer Book ('In Quires and Places where they sing here followeth the Anthem'), is considered almost obligatory in cathedrals. Cathedral-type anthems are usually longer and more elaborate than those used in parish churches—though many of the more popular anthems are regularly sung in both.

7. In modern times cathedral organists are careful to select only music of the highest quality or proved excellence; their music lists include the finest music of all periods.

These, then, are the two traditions but the dividing line between them is extremely fluid. Many of the larger parish churches with sufficient resources model their worship on the cathedral pattern and sing quite elaborate music: if they are geographically situated many miles from the cathedral city they can do valuable work in bringing the riches of cathedral music to the notice of a wider circle of worshippers. Such churches become, in fact 'deputy cathedrals'. At the same time there is a growing tendency for cathedral Chapters to go in for a popular 'nave' type of service on parish church lines. This of course is quite legitimate providing such services are additional to, and not in place of, those daily choral services which must always be the first care and responsibility of cathedral bodies.

It is hardly surprising to find that it is the cathedral, with its daily choral services, its skilled professional choir, its fine organ and capable organist, its echoing acoustics, and its opportunities for extended anthems and Services, which has always appealed to composers much more strongly than the humbler parish church: furthermore, most church composers were themselves cathedral organists and wrote for their own needs. As, therefore, we trace the main stream of Anglican church music in the following pages it is almost inevitably cathedral music with which we shall be mainly concerned. It is a thousand pities that most Anglicans, unless they are fortunate enough to live near a cathedral or choral foundation, never have the opportunity of hearing the great music which is one of the chief glories of our public worship.

CHAPTER III

Music at the Time of the Reformation

ORIGINS AND DEVELOPMENT OF RENAISSANCE STYLE

From the twelfth to the fourteenth centuries France had been the centre of musical art in Western Europe. In this period the influence of the polyphonic School of St. Martial (*c.* 1100–50) was succeeded by that of Leonin (second half of twelfth century) and Perotin (*c.* 1183–*c.* 1220). Then the *Ars antiqua*, as represented by such composers as Franco (fl. *c.* 1250–after 1280) and his contemporary Pierre de la Croix, gave place to the *Ars nova* which culminated in the work of Philippe de Vitri (1291–1361) and Guillaume de Machaut (*c.* 1300–*c.* 1377), a poet-composer who set his own poems to music. But though France dominated the scene, music in other countries flourished and developed until, in the fourteenth century, distinctive national schools emerged in Italy, Spain and England.

With the coming of the Early Renaissance in the fifteenth century the centre of gravity moved round from one geographical region to another. During the first half of the century England became for a time the leading country in European music and our national school of composers included such distinguished musicians as Leonel (Lyonel) Power, Henry IV and Thomas Damett. Among those listed in the Old Hall MS. and other sources we may mention Cooke, Aleyn, Sturgeon, Burell, Byttering, Tyes, Excetre, Pycard, Rowlard, Queldryk, Jervays, Fonteyns, Olyver, Chyrbury, Typp, Swynford, Pennard, Lambe, Mayshuet, Trowell, Robert of Brunham, Bedingham, Benet, Bloym, Bodoil, Driffelde, Forest, Gervasius, Hothby, Markham, Sorbi and Standley. Little is known about these men but they undoubtedly constituted an important school of composers, probably the first such school in England. The greatest of them all, John Dunstable (*c.* 1370–1453), spent much of his life abroad and was acclaimed on the continent as one of the supreme musicians of his day. Several other Englishmen, like Walter Frye and Robert Morton emigrated to France, the Netherlands or Italy and were in great demand in foreign courts.

But England's glory was short-lived and by the middle of the century her fame was surpassed by that of the Northern French School of composers at the Burgundian court of Philip the Good, centred on Dijon. Of the brilliant constellation of musicians there gathered, two shone with a lustre which seems all the brighter from this distance of time—Gilles Binchois (*c.* 1400–60), specially famed for his chansons, and Guillaume Dufay (*c.* 1400–74), primarily a church composer.

The Italians, who had been very active in the first quarter of the quattrocento, experienced a resurgence during the last quarter in the work of the frottolists and the composers of *laude* and *canti carnascialeschi* (carnival songs).

But by far the most important composer of this period was Johannes Ockeghem (*c.* 1420–95) who, though Flemish by birth, spent much of his life at Tours in the service of successive kings of France. Ockeghem was the first of a long line of composers, often known as the Franco-Netherlandish or Flemish School, which extended on through Obrecht (*c.* 1450–1503) and the illustrious Josquin des Prés (1450–1521), through Willaert, Gombert and Arcadelt, to Philippe de Monte (1521–1603), composer of over 1,100 madrigals, and Orlando di Lasso (1532–94), perhaps the most famous of them all. Though these composers were born in the Flanders region most of them emigrated to other countries, especially Italy.

Many writers on musical history have dismissed the earlier members of the Franco-Netherlandish school as little more than contrivers of highly ingenious puzzle canons, intricate rhythmic labyrinths and complex notational conundrums. This charge is unjust. It is true that the fifteenth century was a period of experiment and immense technical development; inevitable too that at such a time there should be a delight in technical virtuosity for its own sake (we have experienced much the same thing in our own day and for the same reason). But this relish for musical brain-teasers was not solely the prerogative of the Franco-Netherlandish school; musicians of most west European countries indulged their technical prowess in this way and indeed some of the most complex of such puzzles were those devised by English composers of the Dunstable era. Although many of the Franco-Netherlandish musicians certainly subscribed to the prevailing fashion of their time by writing intricate technical exercises, such pieces represent only a minor and comparatively unimportant aspect of their work. These composers are now honoured not for their puzzle canons but for the profound beauty and expressive power of their finest achievements.

If the fourteenth century saw the rise of a number of separate 'national' schools, the fifteenth century, often called the Early Renaissance, was one of cross-fertilisation. As we have seen, musicians began to emigrate and settle in foreign courts—Englishmen to the continent, continentals to England, and Frenchmen to the Court of Burgundy, while Flemish musicians were in great demand everywhere. Later there was a general exodus of the best north European musicians to Italy when they accepted pressing and highly lucrative offers to join the sumptuously endowed papal choir of the Sistine Chapel which, after the return of the papacy from Avignon to Rome in 1377, rapidly grew in fame and prestige until it was universally recognised as the most important and influential centre of sacred music in all Western Europe. At times the Sistine Choir seems to have consisted almost entirely of singers imported from abroad, mainly from the Netherlands: (it must be remembered that in those days the best singers were also, generally speaking, the best composers).

As a result of all this coming and going the various centres became not only disseminators of their own styles and techniques but also recipients of those of others. Indeed the various musical schools influenced each other to such an extent that styles and techniques began to merge together and differences between them grew ever smaller until by the middle of the sixteenth century one common style had evolved, a sort of *lingua franca* shared by nearly all west European countries. Though within this common language a discriminating ear can still distinguish certain national characteristics (such as, in England, a bolder use of discord) and some stylistic traits peculiar to particular composers, it is nevertheless true that even for most musicians a work by Palestrina (Italy) sounds much like one by Victoria (Spain), Orlando di Lasso (modern Belgium), Handl (modern Czechoslovakia) and Byrd (England), all composers of the late sixteenth century. Once this *lingua franca* had become established it remained virtually unchanged for the next sixty to seventy years; composers were, in the main, content to share their common heritage and there was no great striving after that 'originality' so much prized by today's composers.

During the period in which this common language was being formulated there also came about a gradual shift of emphasis from a preoccupation with technical considerations to increasing artistic awareness and imaginative expressiveness. In the fourteenth and earlier fifteenth centuries composers were of necessity cramped by the limited technical resources available to them: many accepted these limitations unquestioningly and worked within them; the more adventurous wrestled with constraints and reached out to explore new ways of giving expression to their conceptions. They experimented with new procedures and a bolder harmonic vocabulary based on the tonal system, so enriching the language of music. At times, as we have seen, they took an innocent delight in technical dexterity for its own sake, yet this period of preoccupation with technique was an essential phase in the slow evolution of polyphonic music.

The outcome of this long period of progress and consolidation was that by the beginning of the sixteenth century practically all the basic features of Renaissance style had become firmly established and composers found themselves possessed of a technical apparatus of the utmost precision, refinement and flexibility, capable of expressing in musical terms a wide range of feelings and emotions, both religious and non-religious, with sensitivity and subtlety. The stage was now set for the triumphal entry of the great composers of the Late Renaissance in whom four centuries of development were to reach their apotheosis. By a happy accident of time it was halfway through this century, when much of the world's greatest sacred music was being composed, that the Reformed Church of England was born.[1]

THE SIXTEENTH CENTURY

Just as Beethoven bestrode the Classical and Romantic periods, so another colossus, the great Flemish composer Josquin des Prés (1450–1521), formed a similar link between the Early and Late Renaissance: he closed one era and was himself the beginning of the next. His earlier works betray a typically Early Renaissance fascination with recondite technical devices, especially the complexities of proportional notation and elaborate canonic construction, though with an artist of his calibre even the solution to some intricate technical problem is made a valid and genuine form of musical communication (as in Bach's use of fugue). Josquin's astounding technical brilliance quickly won him wide acclaim but as he grew older his interest shifted from 'How?' to 'Why?'; from technique *per se* to the larger problem of 'What is it I am trying to express?'; he became increasingly concerned with expressing in musical terms the mood and even the meaning of his text. In search of this objective his technical apparatus became much simpler, more free, and used with much greater artistry. Unlike his predecessors Ockeghem and Obrecht, Josquin had a natural feeling for melody; indeed, he was one of the first to write melodies with an implied harmonic basis rooted in major and

[1] It is worth pointing out that until the Second World War the music of the twelfth to fifteenth centuries was virtually unknown except to scholars and a handful of cognoscenti. Now, thanks to the enterprise of the B.B.C., gramophone recording companies, and the more adventurous choirmasters and choral directors, there are increasing opportunities to grow familiar with it. Whereas it used to be looked upon merely as primitive and inarticulate, or at best a preparation, a foreshadowing of greater glories to come, it is now more and more appreciated and enjoyed for its own sake.

minor tonalities, i.e. the type of melody which was to govern all music in the Baroque, Classical and Romantic eras. These melodies were so contrived as to constitute a projection in musical terms, as near as may be, of the natural rhythm and often the natural speech inflections of the words set. This intimate relationship between words and music was to become one of the most striking characteristics of Late Renaissance style.

Josquin, like many of his musically gifted compatriots, spent several years in Italy and was for a time in the Sistine Choir: in fact throughout the sixteenth century, and for most of the seventeenth, Italy retained her pre-eminence as the musical centre of Europe and continued to attract foreign musicians. In addition to the magnificent choral foundations in Rome itself, Italian ducal courts vied with one another in the splendour of their music—like those at Ferrara, Florence, Mantua, Milan, Modena, Parma and Verona, to name only a few—while the music at St. Mark's, Venice, became a serious challenger to the supremacy of Rome itself. At first most of the finest musicians in Italy were immigrants, mainly from the Netherlands, including Josquin, Willaert (*c.* 1485–1562), Arcadelt (*c.* 1504–68) and de Rore (1516–65). A later and even better known immigrant was the great Spanish composer Victoria (1548–1611).

By the second half of the sixteenth century, however, Italian musicians had once again come into their own and there followed that remarkable flowering of native genius which made the Late Renaissance one of the greatest periods of musical history and one which in particular is often referred to as the 'Golden Age' of purely choral writing. Amongst the better known stars in this galaxy we may mention Andrea Gabrieli (*c.* 1520–1586), Merulo (1533–1604), Nanini (*c.* 1543–1607), Ingegneri (*c.* 1545–92), Vecchi (1550–1605), Marenzio (1553–99), Giovanni Gabrieli (1557–1612), Gesualdo (*c.* 1560–1613) and Felice Anerio (*c.* 1560–1614) whilst above them all shines the towering genius of the man who is almost universally acknowledged to be the living embodiment and supreme practitioner of all that was best in this great period—Giovanni Pierluigi da Palestrina (*c.* 1525–94).

THE SIXTEENTH CENTURY IN ENGLAND

After the great burst of creative activity in the earlier part of the fifteenth century, English music seems to have burnt itself out and for the next thirty or forty years became increasingly conservative and more isolated from the exciting developments taking place on the continent. From being, for a brief time, in the vanguard of progress, England lost her lead and dropped far behind. It is almost true to say that from then onwards, in most branches and aspects of musical development, England has been not a pioneer but a reluctant follower of continental trends. (Of the few exceptions, perhaps the most important was the rapid development of keyboard writing by Byrd, Bull and others in the late sixteenth century.)

This conservatism has become a tradition. English musicians like to sit on the fence while carefully watching continental movements and experiments from a safe distance. Then, when the tumult and the shouting dies, they make a careful assessment to see if the experiment has yielded some useful result or a measure of genuine artistic gain. If so, then in some mild manifestation or suitably Anglicised it will slowly be absorbed and integrated into English music. This applies just as much to serial composition in the twentieth century as to madrigal writing in the sixteenth and opera in the seventeenth.

This practice of subjecting new techniques to the test of time and assessing them by their artistic merit rather than their novelty value has the advantage of avoiding extremes and excesses, but in playing for safety the excitement and challenge of the true pioneer is missing; originality and experimentation is discouraged and all too often the end product is a dull and shoddy imitation. This was the curse laid upon so much music written in the eighteenth and nineteenth centuries.

The time-lag between the first appearance of some new development abroad and its ultimate adoption in England has varied from a few years to half a century or more (as with madrigals and opera). To cite an extreme case, it took well over two centuries, perhaps nearer five, for the pedal organ to cross the Channel and become generally established.[2] Thus our musical progress has been evolutionary rather than revolutionary, safe rather than adventurous.

So it was that composers active in England at the beginning of the sixteenth century — including those whose music appeared in the Eton Choirbook (c. 1490–1502) and their contemporaries and successors, like William Pasche, Hugh Aston, John Lloyd, Nicholas Ludford, John Redford and William Whytbroke — still exhibited characteristics of the Early Renaissance School of Dufay and Ockeghem and had little in common with their illustrious contemporary Josquin des Prés. To the style of writing adopted by these composers Dr. Frank Ll. Harrison has given the name 'differentiated' because in it ritual plainsong (usually in the tenor and often decorated and rhythmically varied) was adorned by additional voice-parts differentiated from each other by melody, relative speed of movement, rhythm or phrasing. The development of the melodic lines themselves involved a good deal of thematic repetition, often rhythmically varied; the interplay of different phrase lengths and rhythmic groupings impelled the music forward and at the same time bound it together. Imitation, though often present, was more decorative than formal and so had not the structural importance it was to assume in the latter part of the sixteenth century. Sections for full chorus were contrasted with passages for two, three, or even four, solo voices.

As the century advanced, however, imitation became a method of construction. The text was divided into short clauses:

Patrem omnipotentem – – factorem coeli et terrae – – visibilium omnium et invisi-bilium – – Et in unum Dominum Iesum Christum – – filium Dei unigenitum – – et ex patre natum ante omnia sæcula – – Deum de Deo, lumen de lumine – – Deum verum de Deo vero – – genitum no factum – – consubstantialem patri – – per quem omnia facta sunt:

Each clause was set to a short musical phrase which rhythmically, and often melodically, was a musical projection of the natural rhythm and inflection of a good reader. The musical phrase, technically known as a 'point', was announced first by one voice-part then subsequently taken up by a second while the first continued to sing a counter-melody. Then a third, fourth, and often more voices entered with the 'point' rather in the manner of a fugue but with much greater freedom. These vocal lines were related to an underlying harmonic framework. When one point had been exhausted another was introduced, often in a different voice part from that which introduced the previous point. Sometimes for the sake of variety or to give verbal emphasis a clause would be

[2] See pp. 62, 231, and 334–5.

set in block harmony; later composers became adept at achieving a smooth transition from polyphony to block harmony and back again. At first there was a tendency for the music to grind to a close at the end of each point only to start up again with the introduction of the next, a series of stops and starts like a ride on the London Underground: even Tallis, great composer that he was, occasionally fell into this trap—as in *Absterge Domine* and *Derelinquat impius*.[3] However, composers soon became highly skilled at overlapping points, so concealing the joins and building continuous movements of much greater length. Inevitably, the more closely the voice-parts imitated each other the more they lost their individual identities, their 'differentiation'. Thus the differentiated style of the Early Renaissance and the imitative polyphony of the Late Renaissance are fundamentally opposed though, superficially, they often sound similar.

To return to the composers active in the early part of the sixteenth century, the most celebrated of the group was undoubtedly John Taverner. His music too was firmly rooted in the past and traces of thirteenth and fourteenth century techniques like *rota* and *hocket* are still to be found, together with such typically fifteenth-century devices as melodic sequences, head motives[4] and the use of a *cantus firmus*,[5] but his style was influenced by foreign contemporaries, especially Josquin, and he was probably the first English composer to make extensive use of a series of closely imitative points related to a clear-cut harmonic basis.

But the full force of the Late Renaissance style did not strike England until some half-century later than it had begun on the continent and its final adoption more or less coincided with the birth of the Church of England in 1549. Amongst composers of sacred music active in the mid-century were several whose names have long been familiar: Christopher Tye, John Merbecke, Osbert Parsley, Robert Parsons, John Sheppard, Robert White, Richard Farrant and William Mundy. By far the most important of them all was Thomas Tallis (*c.* 1505–85). These were the men who had to face the musical problems attendant upon the introduction of the new Prayer Book and produce musical settings for the new vernacular liturgy. They had, too, to survive the religious reverses and buffetings of the following ten years which saw the reign of Mary Tudor (1553–58) and the accession of Elizabeth.

As the century drew to its close a remarkable phenomenon occurred. By a curious and unexplained quirk of history a school of composers appeared so numerous and of such remarkable excellence that they rivalled, and many would even say surpassed, the famed contemporary Italian school. Indeed, though the Late Renaissance produced a number of distinguished musicians in most countries of western Europe, Italy's most serious rival in musical leadership was undoubtedly England. At this time there were five main branches of composition: sacred music for liturgical use, madrigals (some of which had sacred words but were intended to be sung in the home), solo songs with instrumental accompaniment (of these the lute songs form the most important part), keyboard works, and a small amount of instrumental chamber music (the *In Nomines* and *Fantasias*). Most composers showed particular interest or aptitude in one or other of these branches (e.g. Wilbye in madrigals, Dowland and Campian in lute songs, Bull in keyboard works) while many excelled in more than one branch (e.g. Morley, Tomkins, Weelkes and Gibbons in both sacred music and madrigals). Just as the genius of Palestrina transcended

[3] But see Paul Doe: *Tallis*, p. 47. (O.U.P.)
[4] See pp. 70 and 163.   [5] See p. 67.

that of all other Italian masters, so William Byrd towered far above all his English contemporaries; his supreme eminence was proclaimed by his fellow musicians and endorsed by posterity.

It is inevitable that comparisons should be made between Palestrina and Byrd. Palestrina was essentially a composer of church music; more specifically of Latin settings for use in the Roman rite. He wrote no instrumental music and his secular madrigals lack the lightness, grace and delicacy which characterize the *genre*. Berlioz even went so far as to say that Palestrina had only one style of writing and that his secular pieces were just as grave and austere as his sacred works: this criticism, though much exaggerated, is not without some justification. Certainly in his sacred music he was able to encompass the whole range of religious emotions; he could scale the heights of spiritual jubilation, explore the farthest reaches of human feelings and emotions, and plumb the utmost depths of grief and anguish. His music is at times impersonal and objective, at others intensely personal and subjective. It glows with passion or soars with mystical ecstasy. It can express tender and wistful beauty, ardent faith, unbridled exaltation and even, at times, the sublime.

Byrd was a much more versatile musician. He too was of a serious cast of mind and reached his greatest heights in his sacred music; but whereas Palestrina, in his liturgical music, set only Latin words, Byrd not only wrote Latin liturgical works many of which are in no way inferior to the Italian master's, but was also one of the earliest group of composers to write settings of English words for the Reformed Church: indeed, his *Great Service*, one of the earliest settings of the canticles in English, has never been surpassed and remains unique as the supreme achievement in its field. In addition he holds an honoured place among English madrigal composers: though his madrigals are mostly of 'gravitie and piety' he could occasionally unbend to write pieces of such grace and enchantment as *This sweet and merry month* and *Though Amaryllis dance in green*. In two other fields he was a pioneer — as a writer of art-songs with instrumental accompaniment and as the first to compose *idiomatic* chamber music for strings. Finally, whereas Palestrina was essentially a composer, not a performer, Byrd was himself a renowned virtuoso player on the virginal and organ. This helps to explain why, though earlier composers like Hugh Aston had written keyboard works, it was again left to William Byrd to show the immense scope and possibilities of keyboard writing.

SETTING LATIN AND ENGLISH TEXTS

To understand something of the changes brought about by the Reformation we have only to compare representative Latin works of the period with those set to English words. In most (though by no means all) Latin works, individual words or even separate syllables were set not to one note but to a group of notes (melismas), even at times an extended phrase or series of phrases. Not infrequently the individual syllables carried such lengthy melodic lines that consecutive syllables in a word became widely separated; the words thus lost their identity and significance and so ceased to have any coherent meaning. When this happened the music became little more than extended vocalisations on different vowel sounds and the words themselves were important only in so far as they generated the vocalisations — pegs on which to hang the music. At this point the music becomes almost entirely instrumental in conception, even though sung by voices, and is to be judged as instrumental music. Such music, untrammelled by the mechanics of conventional word-setting, is now free to express in its own terms the mood, feeling or meaning of the text, often at a far higher degree of intensity than can the words themselves. Taverner favoured this instrumental style of writing for voices and much of his music will yield passages like this:

Taverner: *The 'Western Wynde' Mass*
(tenor part from *Agnus Dei*)

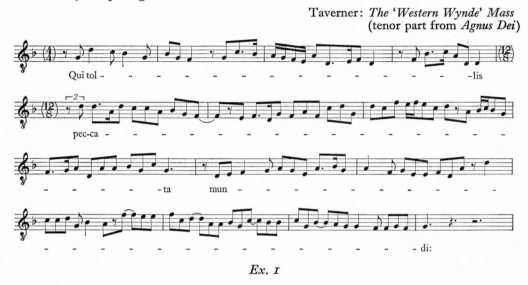

Ex. 1

Most of the history books agree in paying lip-service to Taverner but little of his music now survives in the standard repertory: his *Western Wynde* Mass is occasionally given an airing but it remains something of a museum piece. Perhaps his creative gifts have been overrated and his real importance is as a pioneer who helped to make possible the great achievements of the latter part of the century, achievements which inevitably made his own work seem stilted and rather shapeless by comparison.

Now let us look at one of the English anthems of the period, Christopher Tye's *Praise ye the Lord, ye children*. Instead of the words being just a peg on which to hang some music we feel that here they have been given pride of place and to some extent govern both the rhythm and the melodic shape of the music (note the initial climb up to the most important word 'Lord' and how the last note of the example, on the word 'high', is in fact the highest note thus far). In contrast to the almost wordless vocalisations of Taverner we see here the principle of 'for every syllable a note' being put into practice; the effect is totally different, though not necessarily better:

Tye: *Praise ye the Lord, ye children*

Ex. 2

Tallis: *Gaude gloriosa Dei Mater*

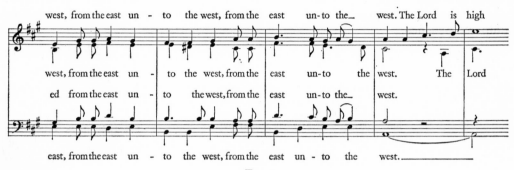

Ex. 3

After comparing two works by different composers we will next look at a Latin and an English piece by the same composer, Thomas Tallis, and the contrast will be equally remarkable. Here is a passage from the Latin motet, *Gaude gloriosa Dei Mater*: though the phrases are not as lengthy as those in the Taverner example there is still a feeling that this music is instrumental rather than vocal in essence (see previous page).

In the English anthem we again see that the adoption of Cranmer's principle makes the music subservient to the words; its function now is to heighten their expression and underline their meaning. Yet in the hands of a good composer directness and simplicity are by no means inimical to musical expressiveness, as in the next example. Furthermore, these simple settings enabled many more words to be sung in much shorter time than did the more elaborate Latin works which were nothing if not leisurely. Indeed, to an unmusical monk each one of the old Latin services must have been an additional penance.

Tallis: *If ye love me*

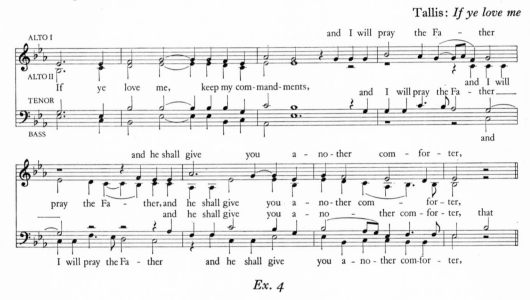

Ex. 4

Both in this and in the other English anthem quoted we see that the music begins in simple block harmony and then, after a few beats, dissolves into freely imitative counterpoint which in turn gradually builds up again into block harmony. This alternation of block harmony and imitative counterpoint is of very frequent occurrence in Late Renaissance music.

There is another important difference to note between Latin and English music. Latin is a language in which verbal stresses are comparatively weak and unimportant and a composer is therefore left rhythmically free to do more or less as he likes. In practice this usually leads to a somewhat suave, smoothly flowing style, rich in contrapuntal and harmonic beauty but lacking in rhythmic vitality. English, on the other hand, is a particularly accentual language and in most English works the verbal rhythm is so strongly marked that it can, in fact, be expressed reasonably accurately in musical notation. Thus, selecting a few words already used in this paragraph,

difference	might be expressed as	♫ or ♪
comparatively	as	♫
unimportant	as	♫
rhythmically	as	♫ or ♪
vitality	as	♫ or ♩
notation	as	♫ or ♩

It will be noticed that not only are these rhythms strongly marked but they are also usefully varied. It follows then that settings of English words are generally much more rhythmically live than are Latin settings and this is still more noticeable in contrapuntal passages where the simultaneous use of different words can lead to intricate and often exciting cross-rhythms. One of the notable features of English music in the sixteenth century and one which distinguishes it from contemporary Italian music is the skill with which English composers exploited the use of conflicting rhythms for expressive purposes.

If in addition to finding a rhythmical equivalent of a spoken word we can also hit upon a melodic formula for it which suggests the actual inflexions of a speaker's voice, then we shall have come near to translating that word into its musical equivalent. Thus by setting English words to their natural rhythms and then shaping these rhythms into melodic ideas based on the natural speech inflexions of the words themselves it is possible to arrive at a sort of musical projection which not only fits the words perfectly but seems, in fact, to grow out of them and heighten their meaning. In such writing the words dominate; the music is subservient. This domination of the word is seen most clearly in solo songs with lute or string accompaniment; in sacred music it is most apparent in passages for solo voice (as in Gibbons's *This is the record of John* and Morley's *Out of the deep*) and sometimes in homophonic passages. In polyphonic writing, word domination in the individual voice-parts is largely offset by using different words simultaneously in the various voice-parts: though adding enormously to the rhythmic interest, this contrapuntal style of writing often results in verbal confusion because the listener cannot distinguish what words are being sung in any one part; so the text gives way to the exigencies of the music—just as it had done in earlier Latin settings. Whenever this happens the music, now the dominant partner, inevitably begins to assume some at least of the attributes of instrumental, as opposed to vocal, style.

Facility in matching musical phrases to fit and underline the words is one of the chief glories of vernacular settings in the latter part of the sixteenth century, especially in England. During the next three hundred years words lost their pre-eminence and again became little more than a peg on which to hang musical ideas. This is no bad thing so long as the musical ideas are good enough in themselves to provide a satisfying and appropriate experience. To cite an extreme case, many modern composers have proved that the use of an entirely wordless chorus can become a powerful emotive element (e.g. Debussy's *Sirènes*; Delius's *Song of the high hills*; Ravel's *Daphnis et Chloé*; Vaughan Williams's *Flos campi*): here the music is conceived entirely instrumentally yet by using voices a new timbre is added to the orchestral palette; furthermore, voices have much stronger emotional overtones than have instruments. But what is perfectly valid in a concert hall has less validity in church where the chief justification for setting a prescribed liturgical text to music is to heighten the impact of the words themselves. The trouble with so much later church music, especially in the mid-nineteenth century, was that it failed on both counts: it not only failed to enhance the words in any way but the musical ideas themselves were so mediocre or meretricious that they were unable to communicate a true musical experience in their own right. It was not until the end of the nineteenth century that men like Stanford and Charles Wood made a determined attempt to restore to the words their former pre-eminence.

NOTATION AND PERFORMANCE

In the fifteenth and sixteenth centuries manuscripts and printed collections of sacred choral music for liturgical use were generally presented in one of two ways: choir-books or part-books.

Choir-books. In these the separate voice parts—cantus, altus, tenor and bassus—appeared side by side and one under the other on two opposite pages of the book:

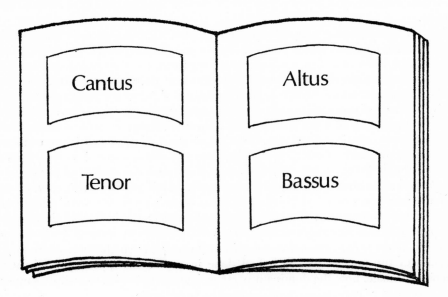

These books were so huge that the whole choir of from twelve to twenty people could stand in front of one book and read from it comfortably. The book was supported on a large lectern. Choir-books were often used in Italy and other continental countries but were much less common in England, though there are notable examples at Eton, Caius College, Lambeth and Edinburgh. On the other hand something similar to the choir-book scheme but on a very much smaller scale was particularly favoured in England for domestic use, where there was only one player or singer to each part. Here the upper two parts were written upside down so that the book could be laid flat on a small table and the performers could stand or sit on opposite sides. A more elaborate scheme enabled the performers to sit round the four sides of a square table with each reading his part the right way up. This lay-out, known in Germany as Tafel-Musik, was especially popular in England—but only for domestic music.

Part-books. Choir-books account for only a small part of the liturgical music used in the fifteenth and sixteenth centuries. Much more often, especially in England, the individual voice parts were written or (much more rarely) printed in separate books known as part-books. Thus for a motet in four parts at least four different choir part-books would be needed, a cantus part-book, altus part-book, tenor part-book and bassus part-book. In practice, most sets of part-books comprised eight or ten volumes (M⁶ATB or MAATB decani and cantoris) plus a separate organ-book. Each set of part-books would contain not just one work but a whole collection of pieces and obviously the same sequence of items would be retained in all the various part-books of the set. (It is interesting that the use of part-books still survives in chamber music where it is common for each member of a string quartet to possess a volume of Mozart's or Beethoven's collected string quartets, each volume containing only his own particular part—violin I, violin II, viola or 'cello.) In manuscript collections of choir music the selection would have been made by the choirmaster himself with the needs of his particular church or choir in mind. Composers, too, often collected several of their works together and issued them in separate part-books.

In England, apart from metrical psalters very little church music was printed, so nearly all part-books are in manuscript. It is the greater pity then that during the Cromwellian period of the seventeenth century there was great destruction of both choir-books and part-books; Dr. Peter le Huray computes the number destroyed at well over a thousand. Others were hidden or sent to private libraries for safe keeping. As a result, sets became broken up and part-books separated and dispersed. This explains why scholars like the Rev. Dr. E. H. Fellowes spent much time travelling from library to library in an effort to identify individual part-books and, where possible, associate them with part-books in other libraries until a complete set had been located: the separate parts could then be transcribed into score and the work published. Some works crop up again and again in different sets of part-books but very often a work occurs in only one set; if then one or more of the part-books of this set are missing the work remains incomplete. A skilful editor can often reconstruct a missing part with a fair measure of success but if two or more parts are missing reconstruction can involve so much editorial guesswork that it may be best not to make the attempt.

Using part-books, each singer would have only his own vocal line in front of him and would have no idea what others were singing in relation to his own part. Bar-lines were not used in polyphonic music at this time and so each separate part presented an almost unbroken succession of notes and rests, showing no metrical organisation and spaced rather to accommodate the words than to indicate relative note-lengths. This would have added to the difficulty of singing some later works in which rhythms could be highly complex with elaborate syncopations and cross accents.

Chromatically altered notes introduced another complication. Sometimes they were indicated in the part-books. More often they were simply left to the experience and taste of the singers who were guided by certain broad, if ill-defined, principles evolved over three centuries or more and known collectively as *musica ficta*. But the code of practice was very rough and ready and in chromatic or modulating passages no two singers would

[1] Meane: see pp. 57–8.

produce the same sequence of melodic intervals from the same part. Even when accidentals were marked they seem to have been sprinkled around haphazardly; in fact different manuscripts of the same work would vary widely in what accidentals were included and omitted. To illustrate the point, Dr. Peter le Huray has collated six different manuscripts of Hooper's 5-part anthem *Behold it is Christ* and has shown an astonishing variety of accidentals in a passage only four bars long.[7]

But all these problems are as child's play compared to those of underlaying the words. Modern editors and printers take immense care to ensure that syllables appear exactly under the notes to which they are sung and that when a syllable carries two or more notes these notes are indicated by a slur. We can scarcely conceive of a vocal part in which the notes on the stave and the text written beneath bear only a casual relationship to each other, yet in many Renaissance sources it is left to the singer to fit the words in as best he can. Just as accidentals vary from one manuscript to another so does the underlay. Again, Dr. Peter le Huray compares no less than eleven different underlays for four bars from the tenor parts of that same anthem.[8] Not only does the underlay vary from one set of part-books to another but even between Decani and Cantoris in the same set. Thus in one source a syllable might carry a lengthy melisma while in another words or verbal phrases are repeated several times to fill-in the melisma. In extreme cases, only the first few words were written in at the beginning of the part and the singer had to trust to memory for the rest and fit them in as he went along. The whole matter is so casual and underlays vary so much in their effectiveness and suitability that one suspects composers often left copyists to allocate words as they thought fit — or where they happened to have most room to write them in!

To make matters worse pronunciation had not yet been standardised. Words like 'patient' and 'gracious' could be treated as either two or three syllables ('pa-ti-ence', 'gra-ci-ous'), 'temptation' could be four syllables ('temp-ta-ti-on') while in many words of two syllables (like 'contrite', 'extreme', 'proclaim' and 'reveal') the accent could fall on either syllable. Small wonder that according to contemporary writers, choirmen were often confused by problems of underlay; not infrequently they cut the Gordian knot by simply leaving the words out altogether and vocalizing. It will be appreciated then that singing from part-books demanded considerable skill and musicianship from the singers, boys as well as men.

It is a strange fact that no full scores have survived of English liturgical music of the fifteenth and sixteenth centuries. Because of the rhythmic complexities of polyphonic music it is virtually certain that composers must have prepared a full score from which the separate choir part-books could be transcribed. How is it then that none has survived? Prof. Denis Stevens has put forward an interesting and feasible explanation.[9] In those days parchment and paper would have been costly items so people would have avoided wasting them on preliminary sketches, rough drafts, and even for documents whose period of usefulness was of short duration. Instead, they were in the habit of using waxed boards for such purposes. After use the wax could be smoothed over and the board would then be ready to receive the next imprint. An obvious advantage of waxed boards was that alterations were easily made. It is known that architects used such boards for their detailed plans and precentors used them for their weekly duty rosters. What more likely then that, according to Prof. Stevens, composers would have used them for their full

---

[7] Peter le Huray: *Music and the Reformation in England*, p. 103 (Jenkins 1967.)   [8] Ibid., p. 106.
[9] Denis Stevens: *Tudor Church Music*, p. 13. (Faber.)

scores which, to them, were merely rough drafts, a necessary preliminary to the preparation of the part-books.

The oft-repeated claim that the Late Renaissance was the 'golden age of unaccompanied singing' must be taken with some reservation, if not a pinch of salt. There is ample evidence that in western Europe, liturgical polyphony often had instrumental support; indeed, there is much to suggest that even in Palestrina's sacred music the voice parts would normally have been doubled by the organ. In England there seems little doubt that the use of instruments in public worship was well established and widely practised during most of this period though the extent to which they were used varied widely from time to time and even from church to church. It must never be forgotten that there were two warring factions in the Church—the traditionalists, who tended to favour elaborate music and the use of instruments, and the reformers, who did not. The reformers could again be subdivided into those who would permit a limited amount of choir music providing it was 'understanded of the people' and constructed more or less on the 'for every syllable a note' principle; and the extremists, following Calvin, who would admit little more than congregational singing of metrical psalms set to suitably 'grave' tunes. Of course all shades of opinion between these two extremes were represented and there were even some who favoured reform in the Church but were traditionalists musically. So these two main streams flowed side by side; as one widened the other would narrow and vice versa, but both never ceased to flow. Hence, even when the reforming party were in the ascendancy, as in the mid-sixteenth century, and instruments, especially the organ, came under bitter attack, there was never a time when they were completely silent—as there was to be during the Commonwealth. Conversely, when instruments became generally favoured, as at the beginning of the seventeenth century, there were still many churches in which almost the only music would have been metrical psalms and where the organ, long disused, had fallen into decay.

There is no doubt that the organ was used extensively in the fifteenth and early sixteenth centuries. Not only did it fulfil its customary role of giving support to the voices but it was especially useful in sustaining the long tenor *cantus firmi* which were exhausting for singers even when divided between two individuals or groups. In lesser services the custom grew of easing the burden on the choir by allocating parts of the Ordinary to be played on the organ, usually in alternation with the singers. Hymns and canticles were similarly treated. On great occasions too the organ came into its own; thus when Henry VII was received at York in 1486, the Te Deum 'was right melodiously songen with Organ as accustomed' (the last two words are significant). Probably on such occasions the organ decorated and embellished the vocal lines.

What did the organists play from? Though no full scores existed nearly all later sets of part-books included not only the voice-parts but also an additional 'organ-book' which gave a skeleton outline of the polyphony. The vast majority of organ-books gave only the top part and the bass in full; middle parts were omitted except for fragmentary indications of important leads in choruses or where the routine methods of filling-in the inner parts would conflict with unexpected happenings in the vocal lines. A few books offered only an unfigured bass (figured basses were not used until well into the seventeenth century). Certainly most organ-books left much to the skill and imagination of the player. Occasionally, even in full choir sections, the organ part was expanded into a short score of the vocal parts laid out on two staves, thick textures being suitably thinned or simplified. In verse anthems and Services, solo sections were normally provided with a

55

complete keyboard accompaniment, often highly contrapuntal, returning to the normal top-part-and-bass scheme when the full choir entered. Just as no two copies of the same vocal part ever quite agreed, so no two organ scores of the same work were exactly alike. Accidentals inserted in one would be omitted in another. Signs indicating ornaments occur from time to time but their meaning is obscure. Elaborate ornaments, fully written out, in the 'Batten' organ book (1634) suggest that organists were expected to add turns, runs, and other embellishments to the written score in a manner which we associate with the Baroque rather than the Renaissance. If organ parts were ornamented in this way, were the vocal lines similarly ornamented? Nobody knows—but it is extremely likely, especially in sections for solo voices. There is ample evidence that on the continent vocal parts were elaborately ornamented: it is well known, for example, that Allegri's *Miserere* depended for its ethereal effect entirely on its *abbellimenti*; furthermore a highly decorated version of Palestrina's *Benedicta sit* was published by Bassano (1591) during the composer's lifetime and presumably with his consent.[10]

Organ-books included all types of liturgical music—music for the Mass, responses, festal psalms, canticles, motets and anthems. This has led some scholars to believe that they were prepared for rehearsal purposes but if so, surely elaborate ornamentation would defeat its own ends. Much more likely, then, as now, the organ was used to support the singers and, if necessary, bolster up an incompetent choir or hide its deficiencies. In spite of rosy-tinted accounts by emotional visitors, the vast mass of evidence makes it obvious that in most provincial cathedrals and choral foundations the general standard of singing must have been deplorably low and the organ would have been essential to keep body and soul together. Only the Chapel Royal maintained a reasonably high professional standard. Some cathedrals bravely tried to sing unaccompanied: thus at Chichester, a Chapter resolution of 1616 implies that there, at any rate, full choir items were sung unaccompanied. Yet at this very time absenteeism was rife, 'Lawlessness, drunkenness, inefficiency and neglect of duty were repeated failings among the staff'[11] and within three months of the Chapter ruling the choirmaster, Thomas Weelkes, after repeated warnings, was fired for being 'a common drunkard and a notorious swearer and blasphemer'. One is left wondering what the unaccompanied singing sounded like, especially if they tackled some of Weelkes's own more elaborate pieces!

The organ was by no means the only instrument used in church worship. Persistent, though often tantalisingly vague, references to other instruments occur throughout the fifteenth to early seventeenth centuries, usually in such terms as 'and other excellent musicall instruments'. For ceremonial and other special occasions the town waits were engaged to supplement normal musical resources. The waits were originally the town watchmen who combined the functions of police force, soldiery, fire brigade and, to a lesser extent, municipal bandsmen. Their instruments were primarily intended for outdoor use and so would have been loud and somewhat coarse. The commonest was the shawm, a primitive double-reed instrument, precursor of the oboe and made in various sizes: soprano in c′, alto in f, tenor in c, bass in F and great bass in C. The trumpet too was obviously suitable though its tone probably sounded more like a modern bugle. The king had his own band, similar to that of the London waits; thus when Cardinal Wolsey visited St. Paul's in 1527 the Te Deum 'was solemnlie songen

[10] Quoted in the *New Oxford History of Music*, Vol. IV, p. 332. (O.U.P.)
[11] David Brown: *Thomas Weelkes*, p. 31. (Faber.)

with the King's trumpetts and shalmes'. With the trumpets went the slide-trumpet or sackbut, an early form of trombone.

During the sixteenth century the role of the waits gradually changed; they were relieved of their more menial duties and became primarily professional musicians. With their social upgrading they began to approximate more to European musical craft guilds; they became proud of their professional skill and jealous of their rights. Because they were increasingly engaged for banquets and social functions they had to learn to play instruments more suited to indoor performance, like cornetts and recorders. So far all their instruments were wind but towards the close of the sixteenth century they added viol-playing to their other accomplishments.

The cornett and sackbut were particularly favoured in church. The cornett must not be confused with the modern cornet. It was made of wood or ivory, provided with fingerholes like any other woodwind instrument but played with a cupped mouthpiece. It was supposed to resemble the human voice: it was similar in compass to the higher voices, had a bright clear tone and wide dynamic range, and needed very little breath. The sackbut covered the range of men's voices so that the two groups of instruments together could play full-scale Masses and motets. Cornetts and sackbuts seem to have been used at Canterbury as early as 1532 and to have been provided for at Carlisle in 1541. They were certainly used at Worcester in 1575 and at Christmas of that same year the city waits of Norwich played in the cathedral. These particular instruments grew so quickly in popularity that eventually the Chapel Royal and some cathedrals engaged their own bands of players; at Canterbury in 1634 they were actually placed on the foundation. All this in 'the golden age of unaccompanied singing'.

With the coming of the verse anthem with its obligatory accompaniment one would assume that viols found their way into church. Certainly records exist of their use at Exeter and Christ Church Cathedral, Dublin, while at Ely the choirboys were taught to play the viol. Otherwise, however, there is not much evidence of their use and verse anthems scored for viols were usually provided with an alternative organ accompaniment for use when the anthem was sung liturgically. On balance, therefore, it would appear that they never established themselves in church as did the other instruments.

While on matters relating to performance some reference must be made to the use of boys' voices in English Renaissance music. Just as men's voices can be said to be of four ranges — counter-tenor, tenor, baritone and bass — so at this period boys' voices were thought to be of two types — meanes (or means) and trebles. The normal voice for a boy was the meane, roughly equivalent to the modern mezzo-soprano, with a range (in modern pitch) of

Normal compass of the 'meane'

Nearly all liturgical works were scored for meanes and it was they, not trebles, who normally sang the top part in choir music. So the normal tone colours of a cathedral choir would have been MATB. By contrast, the treble voice had a range of

Normal compass of the 'treble'

Either it was a very rare voice or perhaps it was considered too bright or even too strident for use in day-to-day worship. Certainly treble voices were used very sparingly and of all the enormous bulk of known church music of the period, no more than about twenty-two works are scored for them; of these, nine come from the same manuscript, the Tenbury organ-book MS 791. These works are carefully marked 'with trebles' to draw attention to their unusual scoring and most of them are 'festal' works. It appears that treble voices were used only when effects of great brilliance were required—much as Bach used his clarino trumpets.

SACRED AND SECULAR: DUAL-PURPOSE MUSIC

In Elizabethan and Jacobean England a great many works with sacred texts were designed not only for performance in the church but in the home as well. To explain how this came about some further reference to the social background is necessary. The fifteenth and sixteenth centuries saw a remarkable expansion of the English middle classes—in numbers, wealth, influence and social importance. Squires, lawyers, yeomen, merchants, and the more well-to-do tradesmen built themselves spacious houses, lived in some style, and saw that their children, certainly their sons, were given a sound education. Partly through genuine religious conviction, partly perhaps through self-interest, the middle classes became predominantly Protestant. In their progress towards gracious living the larger houses tended to model themselves on the great houses of the nobility. Art was encouraged, rich tapestries adorned the walls, furniture was made by master craftsmen and portraits were commissioned from distinguished painters. To such people there was a genuine need for music in the home and even if they could not afford the elaborate musical establishments maintained by great families like the Kytsons at Hengrave, the Fanshawes at Ware and the Jermyns at Rushbrooke, they nevertheless enjoyed having vocal and instrumental music performed round their own firesides. This domestic music making included not only secular music but a considerable amount of sacred music as well. Indeed there were many in whose hearts the flame of Puritan piety burned so fiercely that they looked upon secular pieces as 'Godless ditties' and hence profane or even lascivious; they held that even in the home the human voice was best employed in singing 'psalmes and hymnes and spirituall songs'. Even the less devout had yet to appear 'respectable' and 'God-fearing' in an age when Puritanism had already become a powerful social as well as a religious and political force; they too found it expedient to entertain their guests with sacred melodies and religious items as well as more obviously secular works. In other words there was a rising demand for sacred music for use in the home, both for private devotions and also for recreation.

In the fifteenth and first half of the sixteenth centuries musical settings for the Latin rite were so esoteric that they would have appealed mainly to those professionally involved in their performance together with a handful of cognoscenti associated with the cathedral, chapel or monastery: such music would have had little popular appeal to laymen in the congregation. Furthermore the extended polyphony of pre-Reformation composers like Cornyshe, Fayrfax, Taverner and Tye demanded highly skilled specialist singers; most of it would have been far too difficult for domestic performance even if people liked it enough to want to sing it. Far better suited to the home were the Latin hymns and sequences which had a more obvious 'tune' and were set syllabically: these would have been sung in both church and home. In addition syllabic motets and litur-gical movements set syllabically would generally have been within the competence of amateurs. But of all sacred music performed in the home most popular of all would have been the carols. Today most of us associate carols specifically with Christmastide but before the English Reformation a carol was 'a song on any subject, composed of uniform stanzas and provided with a burden'.[12] In addition to a wide range of secular carols ranging from political to 'amorous' there was a wide selection for every season of the Church's year (including the commemoration of Saints), carols enshrining Church dogma and others of religious or moral counsel. Finally, to add variety to the repertory a few secular songs had been provided with religious words and these too appear to have been popular.

The changes brought about in sacred music by the English Reformation were just as marked in the home as in the church. For instance, somewhere about 1547–48 a new and simple, though strongly Protestant, form of sacred music was introduced—metrical psalmody, modelled on the metrical psalms being published by the Calvinists in Geneva. But whereas the Calvinists intended their psalm translations to be used in corporate worship, it must be emphasized that in England metrical psalms were at first intended solely for private devotional singing in the home. To this end they were cast into ballad metre so that instead of needing specially composed new melodies they could be sung to the popular old ballad tunes. So 'godly solace' replaced 'amorous and obscene songs' while still retaining the original simple and much-loved ballad tunes. Their success was spectacular and Sternhold's original publication unleashed a torrent of metrical psalters which was to continue in full spate for over two hundred and fifty years. Soon after the introduction of metrical psalms, composers began to write or adapt tunes 'of more solemn note' to carry them. Before long, tunes were being printed in the psalters but most of these early tunes were uninspired and uninspiring and only the *Old Hundredth* has retained its popularity through the centuries.

Other changes brought about by the Reformation were even more far-reaching. As we have seen, the suppression of the monasteries drove large numbers of church musi-cians to find a livelihood in secular music, often as teachers, and this in turn gave fresh impetus to the expansion and development of secular music. More people than ever before learnt to sing and play well enough to take part in corporate music-making and soon musical ability became a valued social accomplishment. As the century advanced more efficient methods of music publishing, printing and marketing made a wider range of vocal and instrumental music available for family music-making—even though it was still very expensive to buy. These then were the uniquely favourable conditions which made possible the rise of the English madrigal school towards the close of the century. In contrast to this, church music was still mostly circulated in manuscript copies and very little of it was printed.

As domestic performers grew in numbers and technical accomplishment so the Reformation introduced simpler and more immediately pleasing music into the Church. Cranmer's known desire for syllabic settings meant in practice that anthems were generally much shorter and often more obviously tuneful: thus they had greater popular appeal than the earlier music and soon became welcome additions to the household repertory. Furthermore, because they often made considerable use of block harmony they were much easier to sing. The fact that they were in English instead of Latin was

[12] Greene: *The Early English Carols*, p. xxiii. (O.U.P., 1935.)

yet another reason why they were more suited to home performance than the old pre-Reformation liturgical works.

Some description has already been given of the choir-books, part-books and organ-books which were used by church musicians in carrying out their duties; these are the basis of our knowledge of the sacred music of the period and may be termed the 'liturgical' sources. Quite separate from these are a number of 'secular' sources — manuscript and (later) printed collections of consort songs, madrigals and other pieces specifically intended for music-making in the home. What confuses the issue is that for the reasons given early in this section, many of these songs and madrigals had texts which were biblical, religious or of high moral sentiment even though their function was purely secular. Just as a number of church anthems were taken over for use in the home so a number of consort songs and madrigals with sacred words were introduced into the church. In this they differ markedly from the Italian *madrigali spirituali* which, because they were in the vernacular, could never have been introduced into the services of the Roman Church except, occasionally, in translation. Since so many sacred pieces were equally suitable in both church and home, composers soon began to write with this dual purpose in mind.

So, then, later sixteenth and early seventeenth century works with sacred texts can be divided into three groups according to their provenance: those found exclusively in liturgical sources, those found exclusively in secular sources, and those found in both, suggesting that they had a dual-purpose role. As one would expect, Service music, such as canticles, preces, responses and festal psalms, together with anthems composed for some special religious or state occasion are found only in the liturgical sources. On the other hand, those anthem-type pieces found exclusively in secular sources may for some reason have been regarded as unsuitable for liturgical use; maybe they were scored for some unusual group of voices which would have been inconvenient or unmanageable for an MATB cathedral choir, perhaps their style was considered too madrigalian or perhaps the text itself was too unliturgical. Of the large numbers of anthems found in both types of source the great majority seem to have been composed with their dual function very much in mind. For example, many verse anthems exist in two versions: in the secular sources the accompaniment is scored for viols while in liturgical sources it is set for organ. Often the texture suggests that it was originally conceived in terms of one medium and then, somewhat less happily, adapted to the other. Certainly it was much to a composer's advantage to write works which would win acceptance in both church and home; not only would his pieces receive more performances but his name would reach a far wider circle.

THE ORGAN IN BRITAIN

If we accept that an organ consists essentially of three things — 'a wind supply; a wind-chest with holes which can be opened or closed by valves; and pipes planted over these holes'[13] — then organs of a sort have been in existence for well over two thousand years. They have been associated with Christian worship from early times and were already established in England by the year 800. Several instruments with metal pipes existed in England in the tenth century, some of them built under the supervision of St. Dunstan (*c.* 909–988), but the first organ of which any detailed record exists was a prehistoric

[13] W. L. Sumner: *The Organ*, p. 15. (Macdonald.)

monster erected in Winchester Cathedral in the tenth century: it had four hundred pipes needed two players, and was blown by seventy strong men! 'Like thunder the iron tones batter the ear . . . everyone stops with his hand to his gaping ears, being in no wise able to draw near and bear the sound . . . The music is heard throughout the town.'[14] It probably sounded like a broadside of factory hooters. These primitive organs had no keys, the players merely pushing in and pulling out the sliders that admitted wind to the pipes. With such cumbersome mechanism probably only one note could be played at a time and when such an instrument was used to support the voices in plainsong it must have dealt death and destruction to rhythmic freedom.

During the Middle Ages three types of organ emerged:—

(a) a few large and intractable machines like that at Winchester; these were already becoming obsolete;
(b) the much more common 'positive' organ, roughly equivalent in size to a very small village church organ today. There were often two such 'pairs' of organs in large churches, one near the choir and one on the screen. Though normally left in one position they could be moved to another part of the building or even transported to another church. (It is worth noting that the plural form 'organs' or 'payre of organs' was often used where now we should employ the singular form; here the word 'pair' doesn't mean two but is a figure of speech, as when we say a pair of scissors, shears, steps, or trousers);
(c) tiny 'portative' organs which were carried by a strap round the player's neck. These little portable organs were later fitted with reeds instead of flue pipes and were then known as 'regals' (of which Henry VIII had no less than eighteen 'pairs'). The regal was admirably suited to the performance of concerted music as well as to accompanying singing.

During the twelfth and thirteenth centuries sliders gradually gave place to primitive keyboards. At first the 'keys' were clumsy wooden levers a yard long, several inches wide, and with up to twelve inches depression; the general appearance would have been not unlike the keyboard of some carillons. The man who pounded these keys was aptly known as *pulsator organorum*. From 1400 onwards organ-building became a highly specialised craft and rapid strides were made, though England lagged far behind the continent. The invention of roller-boards gave the builder more freedom in the disposition of his pipes and the ungainly levers were refined into a normal keyboard. These early keyboards had their black and white notes the reverse of modern practice. On the continent a second manual and coupler were added as early as 1386 but two-manual instruments are not known in England till 1606 (King's College, Cambridge). Builders learned how to produce different timbres by using different shapes, materials and scales of pipes and the various ranks were now controlled by stop levers. Whereas continental builders generally used metal for their pipes, English makers showed a strong preference for wood. Architects and designers came to realise that organ cases could be made an integral feature of church design and furnishing; soon craftsmen lavished their utmost skill on building and decorating them till they became works of art in themselves. Often quite small instruments of five or six stops would be displayed in sumptuous cases. The earliest example to survive in Britain is the magnificent case still in use at Old Radnor;

[14] Ibid., p. 21.

it was built during the first half of the sixteenth century. By 1500 the modern organ had been born.

Some mystery surrounds the introduction of pedals into Britain. On the continent they were in use at least as early as 1365 (Halberstadt Cathedral) though they were probably only pull-downs. By the mid-fifteenth century Netherlandish builders were experimenting with independent pedal organs and by 1455 the organ at the Nieuwe Kerk, Delft, possessed a trumpet on the pedals. It seems all the more inexplicable then that English organs were not equipped with pedals until as late as the 1720s and even then they faced a century and a half of bitter opposition before winning universal acceptance.[15] In the *Musical Times* of September 1960, Benjamin Maslen argued plausibly that pedals had in fact been introduced into England in the sixteenth century but were not then known as pedals; he adduces that, instead, they were known by such names as 'playne keyes' (1519–26), 'bases' (1554–59) and 'claves' (1598–1606). Since no British organ at this time had pedal pipes it is certain that if pedals existed at all they would only have been pull-downs. The real weakness in Maslen's argument is his difficulty in explaining why, if pedals had become established in the sixteenth century, no attempt should have been made to revive them in Restoration times from 1660 onwards, especially as so many organs, though silenced by the Puritans, neglected and dilapidated, would still have been intact. Furthermore, in 1660 there would still have been a number of pre-Commonwealth organists about capable, presumably, of playing on pedals. Cecil Clutton and Austin Niland, after weighing the evidence, reject Maslen's arguments though conceding that one or two isolated examples of pedals may possibly have been built.[16]

In the mid-sixteenth century a shadow comes over the picture. After the Reformation a strong body of opinion within the Church was opposed to the use of organs. As early as 1536 the Lower House of Convocation listed organ-playing among the '84 Faults and Abuses of Religion'. In 1550 there was a threat to remove some organs and two years later the organ in St. Paul's was silenced till Mary came to the throne in 1553. More serious still, on 13 February 1563 the Lower House of Convocation considered a resolution demanding the total abolition of organs; it was defeated by only one vote. Many London organs were removed; others were silenced and must have become dilapidated and unplayable long before the wholesale destruction of Cromwell's time. These dark days must have been discouraging for organ builders; few new instruments were built and technical progress was therefore retarded. However at the turn of the century there was a revival of interest. Some important new organs were built and for the first time in England a second manual was added (though without any coupler mechanism). This was originally and correctly called the 'chaire' or 'chair' organ, the word *chair* being corrupted into *choir* early in the nineteenth century. A fine two-manual organ was built at King's College, Cambridge, (1606) and its glorious case ('undoubtedly one of the most beautiful organ cases of all time')[17] remains to this day a noble monument to its designer, Thomas Dallam. But this brief flickering of interest was soon to be altogether extinguished during the Commonwealth and some important builders—including Robert Dallam, Thomas Harris and (probably) Bernard ('Father') Smith—fled to countries where their skill could be exercised unhindered.

[15] See pp. 334–5.
[16] Cecil Clutton and Austin Niland: *The British Organ*, pp. 60–1. (Batsford, 1963.)
[17] Ibid., p. 183.

And now from the general to the particular. Having attempted to set the development of church music in England within the general context of European musical development, some assessment must next be made of the work of individual composers.

CHAPTER IV

The Earliest Anglican Composers

MANUSCRIPT AND EARLY PRINTED SOURCES

For much of the English sacred music which has reached us from the middle third of the sixteenth century we are particularly indebted to three sources: the so-called 'Wanley' manuscripts (*c.* 1549–52); the Lumley part-books (also about 1549–52); and John Day's *Certaine notes* (published in 1565).

The Wanley Part-books (Bodleian Mus. Sch. e420–2). These are by far the most important of the Edwardian sources. Most of the music is scored for men's voices in four parts though boys' voices are used in one or two settings. Of the four part-books in the set only the two alto and bass remain; the tenor has long been lost. The manuscripts were probably written between 1549 and 1552 but much of the music dates from *c.* 1546–48 (i.e. two or three years *before* the introduction of the first Prayer Book) and some items may be as much as ten years earlier still. Unfortunately the Wanley manuscripts do not record the name of a single composer but from other sources the following have been identified:—

a Communion Service by Heath
an Evening Service by Whytbroke
Let all the congregation by Caustun
O eternal God by Robert Johnson
two anthems by Okeland
two anthems by Sheppard
three anthems by Tallis:
   If ye love me
   This is my commandment
   Hear the voice and prayer
two Masses by Taverner adapted to English words.

Most notable is the inclusion of no less than ten English settings of the Office for the Holy Communion. The appearance of English adaptations of two of Taverner's Masses is interesting. He himself died on 25 October 1545 but some years earlier he had been converted to Protestantism and his zeal was such that in 1538–39 he himself took an active part in the suppression of four friaries. The English adaptations of his Latin works included in Wanley are therefore very probably from his own pen and indicate that he clearly foresaw the pattern of future events and was preparing for them. Certainly he deserves to be considered among the earliest Anglican composers even though he died four years before the introduction of the first *Booke of the Common Prayer*.

The Wanley books also include liturgical settings for the daily offices, Litany and

64

occasional services, and also about thirty anthems. Except for Tallis's anthems and one or two other pieces the Wanley collection is of only slight musical interest.

The Lumley Part-books (British Museum MSS Royal App. 74–6). Here again, of the four part-books Triplex, Contratenor and Tenor survive but the Bass is missing. The earliest section dates from about 1549 but the manuscripts also contain a setting of the 1552 Kyrie. Apart from this there are no settings of the whole or parts of the Communion service—in contrast to Wanley's ten settings. The contents are much less interesting than Wanley; metrical psalms and canticles, a Litany, four prose psalms set to plainsong and six given full settings.

John Day's 'Certaine Notes'. This is the earliest and most important printed collection of Elizabethan sacred music. It was ready for the press and indeed partly printed in 1560 but publication was delayed till 1565 probably because the political and religious climate was so uncertain. Six anthems are common to both the Wanley part-books and Day, and Heath's Communion Service, included in Wanley, reappears greatly modified to accommodate the wording in the 1552 Prayer Book. All the items are simple 4-part settings and about half are for men's voices. There are two very complete Services (including Venite) for men's voices and another for MATB; two Evening Services for men, sixteen anthems, a Lord's Prayer, Litany and some Offertories. It is curious that Day includes nothing by Tye or Mundy, both eminent at that time, but a great deal by Caustun, a very minor figure.

In addition, two collections of Latin works are of outstanding importance—the Peterhouse and the Gyffard part-books.

The Peterhouse Part-books (Peterhouse 40, 41, 31, 32). These manuscripts were written between about 1540 and 1547 and give a good sample of the Latin music in use at the eve of the English Reformation. Again the tenor book has been lost. They contain antiphons by Aston, Fayrfax, Ludford, Tallis and Taverner; Mary-antiphons by Bramston, Chamberlayne, Hunt, Martyn, Mason, Merbecke, Norman, Pasche and Pygot; Jesus-antiphons by Erley and Mason; and one for St. Augustine by Sturmys. Most of these men were very minor figures who wrote only for the pre-Reformation Church; we need not discuss them.

The Gyffard Part-books (British Museum Add. 17802–5). These part-books are later in date: they were intended for use with the Sarum rite and so were almost certainly written during the revival of the old liturgy under Queen Mary (1553–58). They contain Masses by Appleby, Knyght, Mundy, Okeland, Sheppard, Tallis, Tye and Whytbroke. Other composers represented include Blytheman and Whyte.

Biographical details are scarce for most sixteenth-century composers. In particular, dates of birth are frequently unknown: sometimes documentary or circumstantial evidence enables us to guess them within a year or two but occasionally the question is so open that it is not even certain what generation the composer belongs to (e.g. Thomas Caustun, Robert Parsons and Richard Farrant). Research is complicated by the fact that several musicians working at different times in different places had the same names (two William Byrds, John Hiltons, Robert Johnsons and Robert Parsons—to name but a few). Even when the Christian names are different, confusion still arises because many manuscripts give only surnames (Thomas and William Byrd; John and Richard Farrant; Christopher, Edward, Ellis and Orlando Gibbons; John, Thomas and William Mundy; John, two Roberts and William Parsons; Giles, John, Nathaniel and Thomas Tomkins; Matthew and Robert White, and many more).

If it is difficult to discover the age of composers it is even more difficult to date their works. A little detective activity is usually sufficient to date manuscript collections within a year or two, though the manuscripts may have taken some years to compile and even then subsequent additions can confuse the issue. But even when the collection as a whole has been satisfactorily dated, individual works included in it may well have been in circulation for some years; indeed, the compiler of the collection is most likely to select pieces which have already proved their value and found wide favour. As a corollary to the problem of dating works it becomes very difficult to trace historical developments and to decide who really were the pioneers. Who was the influence and who the influenced? Who the innovator and who the copyist? Thus it is impossible to give a straightforward answer to such an obvious question as 'Who wrote the first verse anthem?' It could have been Mundy, Farrant or Byrd—or perhaps some other composer whose pioneering effort was subsequently lost.

But whatever the problems and uncertainties there is no doubt that when, in 1549, the first Prayer Book was introduced, the leading composers of the day were Christopher Tye and Thomas Tallis. Lesser men included Thomas Caustun, Robert Johnson, John Merbecke, Osbert Parsley, Robert Parsons and Robert Stone (remembered now only for his unpretentious but effective setting of the Lord's Prayer). A generation later came another group of composers of whom John Sheppard and William Mundy were the most important. This later group also included Robert White and Richard Farrant. All these men, except perhaps Robert Stone, merit some discussion, beginning with the two leading figures, Tye and Tallis.

CHRISTOPHER TYE (*c.* 1500—73)

Tye served in the choir of King's College, Cambridge, till 1541 when he was appointed Master of the Choristers at Ely Cathedral. Sometime later he seems to have been given the additional appointment of organist at Ely and also, about the same time, to have been a Gentleman of the Chapel Royal in London. (This was not unusual; singers in the Chapel Royal choir seem often to have retained provincial appointments and to have travelled to and fro in order to fulfil their spells of duty at court. Probably the cathedral authorities felt that to have a musician distinguished enough to hold a Court appointment enhanced the prestige of their own cathedral.) In 1560 Tye took orders in the Reformed Church and was inducted into the living of Doddington-cum-March in the Isle of Ely; he resigned his musical appointments at the cathedral early the following year though he had probably ceased carrying out his musical duties from the time of his ordination. Later he added other benefices to that of Doddington, where he died early in 1573.

Time has dealt sadly with Tye's music, much of which is now incomplete; but enough remains to show that his best work is to be found in his large-scale settings, especially those with Latin texts. He was one of the first English composers to grasp the implications of the imitative techniques which had originated in France and the Low Countries and to apply them expressively in his own work.

His Latin church music comprises three Masses and about twenty motets. In providing settings of the Mass it was the custom in England at this time to include only four movements—Gloria, Credo, Sanctus and Agnus Dei: the Kyrie was generally omitted. Gloria and Credo began at 'et in terra pax' and 'Patrem omnipotentem' respectively, the celebrant singing their intonations. Frequently too the Credo was shortened by omitting some of its clauses, especially in the latter part after 'et resurrexit tertia die'.[1] Tye's superb 6-part *Missa Euge bone* is typical: its Sanctus is notable for the solemn grandeur of the opening chords and for the imaginative use of high voices at 'Pleni sunt coeli et terra' ('Heaven and earth are full of thy glory'). Like Taverner and Sheppard, he also wrote a *Western Wynde* Mass in which the old melody is treated as the basis of a set of choral variations. The air itself appears only in the alto part and is sung no less than twenty-nine times; altos can be thankful that it is often elaborated and rhythmically varied. The 'Peterhouse' Mass is much the simplest and shortest of the three though it is imitative in style: by using a common opening for the various movements he gives the whole Mass some overall unity and cohesion.[2]

Of the motets, the two 5-part psalms *Miserere mei Deus* and the jubilant *Omnes gentes plaudite* represent the composer at his best. In the first, G-sharp is subtly introduced to give confidence and radiance to the words 'quoniam in te confidit anima mea' ('for my soul trusteth in thee'). Another fine piece is the 7-part *Peccavimus cum patribus* designed on an exceptionally large scale. The Jesus-antiphon *Sub tuam protectionem* is a good example of how Tye could use his mastery of imitative technique to serve wholly artistic ends. Three of the short motets are based on a *cantus firmus* — a term which needs some explanation.

A *cantus firmus* is a pre-existent melody which is made the basis of a polyphonic composition by adding to it contrapuntal voice parts. Usually, though not always, it is written in long notes (sometimes very long notes) which contrast effectively with the florid style of the added parts. Often the long notes are all of the same length: usually, too, the *cantus firmus* is given to the tenors (see Example 5 on following page). Most *canti fermi* were ancient plainsong melodies but some secular airs (like *L'homme armé* and *The Western Wynde*) were also used. In Germany some of the Protestant chorales were pressed into use as *canti fermi* — as in organ chorale preludes. In polyphonic music the older melody was almost inevitably lost under the vocal lines that overlaid it; furthermore, not only was it embedded deep in the contrapuntal texture but often it was either an obscure, little-known plainsong melody or a long-forgotten secular tune that nobody in the congregation was likely to recognise. If, instead of appearing in long notes, the *cantus firmus* was elaborately floriated or rhythmically varied, recognition would have been even more unlikely. By 1549, when the English Church was established, the possibilities offered by using a *cantus firmus* technique had already been virtually exhausted; so it was that in the second half of the century the *cantus firmus* became increasingly rare and, when used, was often introduced as an intentional archaism.

Turning now to Tye's English works, a setting of Nunc dimittis, in an English translation taken from the 'Marshall' Primer of *c*, 1535, appears in the Wanley part-books. It is therefore one of his earlier works and this explains the elaborately melismatic underlay of the parts by which single syllables can carry a large number of notes. This melismatic style was unusual in settings of English words and was soon to be discouraged by Cranmer's 'for every syllable a note' recommendation of 1544. Tye also wrote a setting of *Deus misereatur*. There is considerable doubt about the authenticity of a paired Magnificat

[1] For a scholarly and convincing explanation for the omission of the Kyrie and for the various cuts made in Credo and even Gloria see Denis Stevens: *Tudor Church Music*, pp. 25–7. (Faber.)
[2] See 'head-motif', pp. 70 and 163.

Hugh Aston: *Missa Te Deum — Agnus Dei*

Ex. 5

and Nunc dimittis described in one source as 'Dr Tye's Magnificat and Nunc dimittis to Mr. Parsley's Morning Service'; stylistically it is more likely to be by Parsley.

Like most of the English anthems of the time, the majority of Tye's are simple and functional rather than inspired or expressive: the more complicated ones were almost certainly written for the Queen's Chapel. Of the 4-part settings, *Blessed are all they* and *Save me, O God* are almost entirely chordal: harmony is stilted and cadences rarely leave the home key. Other 4-part anthems like *From depth I called; Give alms* and *O God be merciful* are imitative in style but the imitations are often mechanical and there is too much repetition not only of words but of whole musical phrases. A similar anthem, *Praise ye the Lord, ye children*, has already been quoted.[3] *Deliver us, good Lord* and *I have loved* are not only more elaborate but also far more expressive and the latter has a vivid pictorial passage to portray trickling tears and sliding feet! As the number of voice parts increases so does Tye's inventiveness. Of the 5-part works, *I lift my heart* is a poignant appeal for divine mercy; *My trust, O Lord* has an insistently recurring phrase to express the idea of 'world without ending'. The best of his English anthems is undoubtedly the 6-part *Christ rising* in which firm, massive writing gives immense dignity and splendour to the triumphant Easter test.

Mention must be made of a curious metrical version of *The Actes of the Apostles* which he wrote and then set to music. This was never intended for liturgical use; rather was it 'to synge and also to play upon the Lute, very necessarye for studentes after theyr studye, to fyle theyr wyttes, and also for all Christians that cannot synge, to read the good and Godlye storyes of the lyves of Christ hys Apostles'. It might have been better for the Christians who couldn't sing to stick to their Bibles rather than read the Godlye storyes in Tye's halting paraphrase because his doggerel verse was deplorably bad and is now quite unusable. Fortunately he got only as far as Chapter XIV. On the other hand, some of the music is well worth preserving and so new words have been adapted to it by modern editors: one of the most successful of these adaptations is the justly popular *Laudate nomen Domini* ('O come, ye servants of the Lord'). Other adaptations of music from the *Actes* include *O God of Bethel* (or *Once, only once*); *The Lord will come, and not be slow* and *A sound of angels*.

THOMAS TALLIS (*c.* 1505–85)

Tallis was born in the opening years of the sixteenth century (probably about 1505). The first we hear of him was in 1531 when he was *joculator organorum* of Dover Priory. In 1537 he was *conduct* of the choir in the city of London church St. Mary-at-Hill and a year later he left there, presumably to go to Waltham Abbey where he remained until 23 March 1540 when Waltham became the last of the monastic foundations to be suppressed under Henry VIII's notorious dissolution of the monasteries. Evidence suggests that at Waltham he was master of the choristers or organist. Tallis's next post was at Canterbury Cathedral as a lay-clerk. Here too his stay was brief because within two or three years he was elected a Gentleman of the Chapel Royal, which in those days was situated at Greenwich. He retained this appointment until his death in 1585. He married in 1552 but had no children. The fact that in 1557 Queen Mary granted him a lease of Minster manor in the Isle of Thanet is some indication of her regard for him, while in 1575 Queen Elizabeth granted a monopoly to print music and ruled music paper to Tallis and his young colleague William Byrd jointly, an enterprise which caused them much anxiety, trouble and, at first, financial loss but which gave to the nation the important volume of *Cantiones, quae ab argumento sacrae vocantur* containing thirty-four motets, seventeen by Tallis and seventeen by Byrd. At first sight seventeen seems rather a peculiar number to choose but the volume was dedicated — with the customary fulsome flattery — to the Queen, no doubt as a token of gratitude for her bounty in granting them the monopoly, and, as Prof. Denis Stevens has pointed out,[4] the number seventeen

---

[3] See Ex. 2 on pp. 48–9.
[4] Denis Stevens: *Tudor Church Music*, p. 43 (footnote). (Faber.)

was no doubt intended as a delicate allusion to the fact that the monopoly was granted, and the collection published, in the seventeenth year of her reign (1575). Tallis and Byrd must have been on terms of closest friendship at this time; in addition to their publishing business and their collaboration as composers they were joint organists of the Chapel Royal. The warmth of their friendship is further demonstrated by Tallis's becoming godfather to Byrd's second son who was named Thomas after him. Tallis died at Greenwich on 23 November 1585 and was buried in the parish church of St. Alphege.

Tallis is undoubtedly the most significant Elizabethan composer born earlier than Byrd. Like other musicians of his time he was brought up in the Roman Catholic faith and spent the earlier part of his professional life in its service. By the time the Church of England became established Tallis was already well into his forties. He served the Reformed Church faithfully and was by far the most distinguished of that group of composers who, in its earliest days, supplied it with English settings of cathedral standard; indeed evidence suggests that most of his English works date from this time and two of them, *Hear the voice and prayer* and *If ye love me*, appeared at least as early as the Wanley part-books. But his sympathies remained with the older faith and he continued to write Latin settings to the end of his long life. Among these (as with Tye) are to be found his finest works.

TALLIS: THE LATIN WORKS

Tallis's surviving Latin pieces include three Masses, a 4-part Magnificat, a 5-part Magnificat with paired Nunc dimittis, two sets of Lamentations, some thirty motets and a number of Office hymns. Of the three Masses, the festal *Missa Salve intemerata virgo* is a parody Mass based on an antiphon of the same name. 'Parody', in this sense, has no connotation of satirical imitation, caricature or comedy; instead it is a technical term referring to the practice, common at this time, of borrowing musical material from a motet and incorporating it into the structure of a Mass, the Mass then taking its name from the motet. So in Tallis's *Missa Salve intemerata virgo* each movement begins with bars 1–3 and 13–15 of the antiphon sung by counter-tenor and bass. But the relationship between antiphon and Mass is very much closer in this work than in most such couplings. Except for one short passage the entire antiphon has been absorbed into the Mass; furthermore, no less than three-quarters of the Mass is derived from the antiphon, leaving only one-quarter to be newly composed.

An unnamed 4-part setting is typical of the 'short' Masses of the period. These short Masses have no title associating them with a particular feast. They are more or less syllabic in style ('for every syllable a note') and are therefore mainly chordal in texture. The form imposes so many restraints that the composer's imagination is almost inevitably shackled and such settings often lack the expressiveness of more extended settings. Tallis's setting is even more syllabic than Taverner's *Playn Song Mass* and seems rather conventional and uninspired. Here again the various movements open with the same theme and harmonic progressions; in Gloria and Credo these openings are exactly similar. When the same theme, or motto, appears at the beginning of several movements it is known as a 'head-motif': if a head-motif is used in a parody Mass it usually consists of the opening notes of the parent motet.

Only the Gloria and practically all of the Sanctus have survived complete of a mighty

7-part *Missa Puer natus est nobis*, laid out on a vast scale and probably written for Christmas Day 1554 when Philip of Spain was still in London: it would then have been sung by the combined English and Spanish chapels. Such a service would have had a great feeling of 'an occasion' and Tallis would have been sensible of the honour, the challenge and opportunity — hence the opulence of seven vocal parts and the generally lavish scale. This theory is strengthened because the work clearly shows the influence of Gombert who had been associated with the music of the Spanish Imperial Chapel for many years. It is a *cantus firmus* Mass based on the first four phrases of the plainsong Introit *Puer natus*. This Mass not only ranks amongst Tallis's best work but is the culmination of a half-century of large-scale English Masses; it is therefore the greater tragedy that the Credo and Agnus Dei seem to be lost.

In his Magnificats Tallis followed the usual practice of his day by providing polyphonic settings only for the even-numbered verses; the odd-numbered verses were sung to plainchant. His two settings differ markedly in style. The earlier 4-part version, with its faburden tenor, lengthy melismatic phrases and florid upper parts, looks back to the 'differentiated' style of the Eton choir-book composers at the turn of the century. Its texture is a mixture of styles: the faburden origin of Magnificat settings would have determined the use of the differentiated style but at times this gives way to patches of freely imitative writing. The paired 5-part setting of Magnificat and Nunc dimittis has an interesting background. According to the Service-books of the old rite, polyphonic settings of Nunc dimittis could have been sung only once a year — on the feast of the Purification (this explains why Latin settings of this canticle are so rare). Even then Magnificat and Nunc dimittis could never have appeared together in the same service: in other words, paired settings were unknown. It was the 1549 service of Evening Prayer that first brought the two canticles together, but of course in English. However, Elizabeth, though resentful and suspicious of the recusants' allegiance to the Pope, shared with them a fondness for a Latin liturgy adorned with ornaments and ceremonial. Within a year of her ascending the throne, Walter Haddon published a Latin translation of the 1559 Prayer Book under the title *Liber precum publicarum* (1560) and this the Queen introduced into her own chapel. What more natural than that her senior composer should set the two evening canticles to music? The canticles share a common opening and in general the words are treated syllabically. In contrast with the earlier Magnificat both canticles are constructed on a series of imitative points typical of late Renaissance style. In Magnificat a sixth voice is added to colour 'Esurientes implevit bonis'.

Both on the continent and in England it became fashionable to write polyphonic settings of the Lamentations of Jeremiah. Of the sixty or so settings by continental composers the most famous are those by Palestrina, Victoria and di Lasso: in England, in addition to the famous settings by Tallis and Byrd others by Parsley, White, Ferrabosco and Mundy are highly regarded. All these settings are similar in structure and include, somewhat curiously, an elaborate and often very beautiful setting of the Hebrew letters which introduce each section — Aleph, Beth, Gimel, Daleth, Heth, etc.; these extended vocalisations serve as a kind of instrumental prelude to the following strophe and their flowing melismas are in marked contrast to the often declamatory style of the verses. Tallis's lovely setting of 'Beth', with its inverted pedal and sighing underparts, shows what artistry a great composer could bring to the setting of these letters:

71

Tallis: *Lamentations*

Ex. 6

For his two 5-part settings of the Lamentations Tallis chose the first two lessons of
Tenebrae for Maundy Thursday, though with minor textual deviations. They are among
the finest large-scale works of the mid-century and their scoring for the dark-hued tone
of men's voices without boys adds to their richness and underlines their penitential
character. They were probably never intended as part of any ritual office and may even
have been written for private devotional or recreational use.

Since the Lamentations are non-liturgical they must be classed, technically speaking,
as motets. Of the other motets, space does not permit a detailed discussion though the
following observations are of general application. Since Tallis's long life spanned the
transition from early to late Renaissance (virtually from mediæval to modern), pieces
written in the Henrician and Marian periods generally employ 'differentiated' techniques
while his Elizabethan works more often adopt the typical imitative polyphony of the
Late Renaissance. In the differentiated style there is the normal clear-cut division
between full chorus (usually in five parts or more) and a group of two, three or four
soloists: these solo sections are often so highly florid and melismatic as to make
considerable technical demands on the singers. It is also generally true that in the
pre-Elizabethan Latin works the composer's musical ideas are given freer rein and are
less trammelled by the words than are his later Elizabethan pieces; usually, too, the vocal
lines are more melismatic and wide-ranging. Elizabethan motets are more restrained in
style and are most often syllabic; melismas (groups of notes to one syllable) occur far
less frequently but the few that are admitted are used perceptively and expressively to
colour the words. In addition, an almost madrigalian interest in word-painting takes on
a new significance. But in both categories there are, of course, many exceptions.

Most of the pre-Elizabethan motets fall into one or other of three groups—votive
antiphons, responds and hymns. Up to about 1540 antiphons followed tradition by being

in two 'movements', the first usually in triple time, the second in duple: each movement had two solo sections for different groups of voices and ended with a section for full choir. After 1540 it became increasingly common to use duple time throughout. With a few exceptions (like Taverner's *Ave Dei patris*) sixteenth-century antiphons did not employ a *cantus firmus*. Five votive antiphons by Tallis are known, four on a large scale, the other short. Two of the large-scale antiphons, *Ave rosa* and *Salve intemerata*, are probably among the composer's very earliest pieces; the latter was absorbed into the parody Mass described above. On the other hand, because *Ave Dei patris* is in duple time throughout, a date after 1540 seems likely: this work survives only in a sadly incomplete form. The mighty 6-part *Gaude gloriosa* is not only the greatest of Tallis's votive antiphons in length, inspiration and craftsmanship, but it marks the ultimate which the form was to reach. In sheer physical length it takes no less than twenty-seven minutes to perform. All nine invocations are elaborately set, either for varying groups of solo voices or for full choir. The texture of the full choir sections is usually dense and all six voices are kept busy, but there are some important exceptions. Thus, typical of Tallis's mastery is the way verse 2, 'Gaude Virgo Maria', opens with only two voice parts; then more are gradually added until the whole choir bursts in on the word 'omnia' ('all'). There are some other effective examples of pictorialism. Themes have real character and many are notable for bold and vigorous use of rising intervals. Much of the writing is highly florid and often individual syllables carry lengthy melismatic phrases; these vocalisations become largely instrumental in effect. The whole motet is a work of the utmost grandeur. The one small-scale antiphon, the 4-part *Sancte Deus*, gains additional brilliance from being scored for two meanes; it culminates in endless peals of joy.

Tallis and John Sheppard were the only composers to write polyphonic settings of the Responds. In all six of Tallis's the plainsong melody appears in equal semibreves as a *cantus firmus*, usually in the tenor but once in the treble (*Dum transisset*) and once in the counter-tenor (*Homo quidam fecit coenam*). *Candidi facti sunt* (*a 5*) has a quasi-canon between top and bottom parts. The loquacious babbling of many tongues is felicitously suggested in *Loquebantur variis linguis* by writing seven rapidly moving parts within a restricted compass. The 5-part *Dum transisset* and *Honor virtus* achieve a monolithic massivity and loftiness. The 6-part *Videte miraculum*, with its wonderful opening expressing awed amazement, is to be counted amongst the composer's best works.

Again, Tallis and Sheppard were the only musicians of their time to write many settings of Latin hymns. As in Magnificat, only even-numbered verses were set in polyphony; the first and other odd-numbered verses were sung to the traditional plainsong. Tallis's eight hymns are all *a 5* with the plainsong in the highest voice. All except *Deus tuorum* have the first verse or two in triple time and then change to duple. The texture varies from imitative polyphony to chordal writing (homophony). Sometimes imitative points are derived from the plainsong and in *Iam Christus astra ascenderat*, treble and counter-tenor have the *cantus firmus* in canon.

The Latin motets which seem to be of later date and were probably written during Elizabeth's reign would not, of course, have been designed for specific liturgical use in the Roman rite; instead, they were intended to be sung before or after the daily offices in the Queen's Chapels. Thus they had much the same function as the English anthem and composers were now free to set any text which appealed to them in the manner they

73

considered most appropriate without regard to liturgical propriety or traditional forms. With only three exceptions all these motets are in five voice-parts; indeed Tallis and most of his contemporaries accepted 5-part writing as the norm, much as a nineteenth-century composer would naturally think in terms of 4-part harmony.

Only a few of these motets can be selected for brief comment. *Absterge Domine* has been criticised for being broken up by too many cadences—though supplicatory texts were often so treated. Certainly it must have been very popular as no fewer than four different English versions of it appeared in pre-Restoration manuscripts—*Discomfit them, O Lord*; *Forgive me, Lord, my sin*; *O God, be merciful*; *Wipe away my sins*. *In ieiunio* also has rather too many full-stops though it is remarkable for the freedom and boldness of its modulations which in a short span embrace keys as remote from each other as A flat and E major. The opening of *Derelinquat impius viam suam*, with its angular vocal lines and its imitative entries at a variety of unusual intervals, is intended to depict the ways of the wicked and the thoughts of the unrighteous. The two *Salvator mundi* settings are pure gems: the first in particular is a beautiful and polished piece of throughly-composed polyphony in which the imitative points are cunningly dovetailed, almost inevitable cadences are neatly side-stepped, and the final cadence seems endlessly deferred; (such construction is in marked contrast to the cadential fragmentation of *Absterge Domine*).

In the 1560s, psalm-motets seem not only to have taken over the function of the pre-Elizabethan votive antiphons but even to have retained their form and charac-teristics—triple time followed by duple; varied groups of solo voices contrasted with full choir. *Domine quis habitabit* and *Laudate Dominum* are of this type. The latter is excep-tionally brilliant for Tallis: it owes much to the Flemish-Italian style with some cross-rhythms in the 'et veritas Domini' section; it is also exceptional in that the setting includes Gloria Patri. In contrast to Tallis's Marian hymns, *O nata lux* makes no use of a plainsong *cantus firmus* nor does he set just the even-numbered verses; indeed, the motet consists of the first two verses only, treated polyphonically.

Of the three motets not in five voice-parts, the 7-part *Suscipe quaeso* is laid out for precisely the same forces as the great 7-part Mass and may well have been intended for the same occasion; it is in two separate movements. Technically, one of the most astonishing of Tallis's works is *Miserere nostri*. This too is in seven parts arranged as a canon six-in-two with a free tenor. The top two parts are in ordinary canon at the unison while the four lower parts (not counting the free tenor) are involved in a separate and very elaborate canon in which the *discantus* part is sung by the *contratenor* in double augmentation (notes four times as long); by the first *bassus* in triple augmentation (notes eight times as long) and inverted; and by the second *bassus* in augmentation (notes twice as long) and again inverted. To solve such a recondite puzzle at all bespeaks immense skill; to make it at the same time a moving setting of the text shows Tallis's complete mastery.

But even the achievement of *Miserere nostri* is totally eclipsed by that extraordinary technical and artistic *tour de force* the famous motet in forty real parts, *Spem in alium*. This mighty masterpiece is laid out for eight choirs each singing in 5-part polyphony. Paul Doe makes the interesting and likely suggestion that the employment of forty parts may have been intended as a tribute to Queen Elizabeth on her fortieth birthday in 1573.[5] Certainly the work is unique in the annals of English church music, though

[5] Paul Doe: *Tallis*, p. 41. (Oxford Studies of Composers.)

Italy and Spain also produced a few pieces on a Gargantuan scale. In effect it is rich and powerful and the physical disposition of the various choirs gives it a three-dimensional plasticity. In the opening section the first twenty voices enter successively with the same imitative point; then the other twenty introduce fresh material. After a short section in which all forty sing together, another theme is sung in imitation by twenty-eight parts leading to another short section for full choir. Then follows a thrilling passage in which huge blocks of sound are hurled across the spaces as groups of choirs answer one another and the work closes with a tremendous peroration for the full forty voices. Not only is *Spem in alium* a stupendous feat of technical virtuosity but it is also, like *Miserere nostri*, a magnificent work of art, immense craftsmanship being harnessed to achieve imaginative and aesthetic ends.

TALLIS'S ENGLISH CHURCH MUSIC

We have already noted (p. 20) that as soon as the boy-king Edward VI succeeded Henry VIII, Protestant reform was at last released from restraints; Cranmer and his associates went rapidly ahead with the preparation of a liturgy entirely in English and within two years the Act of Uniformity commanded the use of their work as enshrined in the first *Booke of the Common Prayer*. The Chapel Royal was at the very centre of all this ferment and innovation and it was inevitable that some of its musicians—including Tallis, Tye, Sheppard and Caustun—should be amongst the first to try their hands at composing syllabic settings of English words, long before the Act enforced the use of English in worship. It was some of these early and experimental settings which found their way into the Wanley part-books, including morning and evening Canticles, Communion settings (many adapted from existing Latin Masses), anthems and metrical psalms. It is likely too that some of the items in the 'Lumley' part-books (British Museum MSS. Royal App. 74–6), containing polyphonic settings of English texts, antedate the 1549 Prayer Book.

Of Tallis's Service settings, only one survives complete—the 'Short' Service in the Dorian mode. Soon after the institution of the Reformed services it became customary in the Holy Communion service for the choir to leave after the Creed, probably because Puritan thought discountenanced music during the more solemn part of the service. The choir was therefore not present to sing Sanctus and Gloria and so composers omitted these movements from their Service settings. Tallis's *Dorian Service*, being one of the earliest, is hence one of the very few to include these movements. Since it also includes a full setting of Venite it is unusually complete. It is a dignified setting of almost classical purity; as it is in note-against-note harmony throughout it covers the ground quickly and is therefore useful in both cathedral and larger parish church. Not surprisingly, however, the limitations of the style inhibited the composer of *Gaude gloriosa*, the Lamentations and the 40-part motet and the outcome is too stilted and pedestrian to do him justice. There was also a far more elaborate 5-part 'Great' Service: this too included Venite, Sanctus and Gloria, but only the bass part has survived. The terms 'Short' and 'Great' applied to Services need some explanation. 'Short' Services were simple and straightforward, written usually in 4-part harmony and mainly in block chords, and with little, if any, repetition of words (more or less 'for every syllable a note'): such settings had, as their name implies, the virtue of brevity and had the further advantage of being easy for a choir to learn. Conversely, 'Great' Services, as one would expect, were generally of considerable length involving a good deal of verbal repetition; mostly they were scored for at least five voice-parts and were elaborate in style and highly polyphonic in texture. Tallis's 'Dorian Mode' setting is a typical short Service; Byrd's 'Great' Service is considered to be the finest example of its genus.

An incomplete 5-part Te Deum has been conjecturally reconstructed by Fellowes and sounds authentic: this rather dull setting is to some extent redeemed by its rhythmic vitality. The 4-part Benedictus, together with the anthems *Hear the voice and prayer* and *If ye love me* were all written for men's voices; they are amongst the earliest of Tallis's English settings and all antedate the first Prayer Book. In these, chordal sections alternate with imitative writing, there is very little repetition of text, and melismas rarely occur except at cadences. Benedictus has one unusual moment of drama: the phrase 'from on high hath visited us' ends on a chord of C major; there is a moment's silence—then the whole choir enters in the remote and unrelated 'key' of A major to lend harmonic colour to the words 'to give light':

Tallis: *Benedictus*

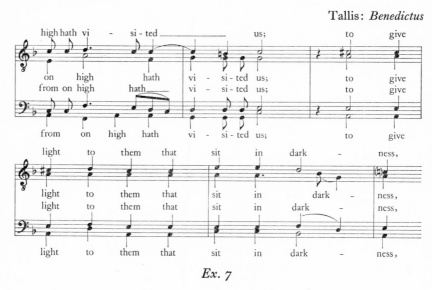

Ex. 7

The original version of Cranmer's *Letanie with Suffrages* (1544) had been set to a 'devout and solemn note', probably by John Merbecke.[6] For his Litany, Tallis took these tones and set them as the highest voice part in a 5-part texture. Tallis's setting ends at the Lord's Prayer; it follows therefore that any musical setting of the later antiphons and suffrages is not by Tallis but is an editorial adaptation devised either from the earlier part of his Litany setting or from his Responses. Tallis wrote two different 5-part settings of the Responses: to most people these are familiar only in Stainer's sadly debased 4-part versions known as Tallis's 'Ferial' and 'Festal' responses (Tallis himself would probably disown both!). The simplified so-called 'Ferial' set is useful in parish churches and is now hallowed by a long period of regular use, but the 'Festal' set is not suitable in parish churches as it goes too high for a congregation to sing comfortably. Tallis's original 5-part settings are often to be heard in cathedrals and larger churches.

[6] See p. 80.

Of the remaining English anthems which may well have been written before or around 1549, *Remember not, O Lord God* consists almost entirely of a series of simple 4-part chords whereas the exciting *Christ rising*, in 5-part polyphony, is unusually elaborate for an English anthem of its time. The 4-part *Out from the deep* has a poignancy and emotional intensity out of all proportion to the simplicity of the means employed. *Purge me O Lord* began life as a secular part-song *Fond youth is a bubble*.

Several anthems survive in so incomplete a form that we can have little idea of what they were like or when they were written. Of those probably composed at some later date, *O Lord in thee* and *Verily, verily* are largely chordal but *O Lord, give thy Holy Spirit* (*a 4*) is in the polyphonic style of the Latin motets and has some telling points of harmony. The part-writing of *Blessed are those* is so suave that Paul Doe suspects it to be an English adaptation of a Latin psalm. Indeed, some of the most familiar of Tallis's English anthems are actually adaptations of various Latin motets. Nearly all these adaptations are pre-Restoration; many of them probably date from the composer's lifetime and may even have been made by him or at least with his knowledge and approval (like *With all our hearts and mouths* from *Salvator mundi*). The English anthems listed below are all adaptations of Latin motets:

Absterge Domine	Discomfit them, O Lord
	Forgive me, Lord, my sin
	O God, be merciful
	Wipe away my sins
Mihi autem nimis	Blessed be thy name
O sacrum convivium	I call and cry
	O holy and sacred banquet
O salutaris hostia	O praise the Lord
Salvator mundi (1)	Arise, O Lord, and hear
	With all our hearts and mouths
Salvator mundi (2)	When Jesus went into

The fact that so many adaptations were made indicates that there must have been some demand for large-scale anthems in the polyphonic style: substituting English for Latin words was the quickest and easiest way of satisfying this demand as a stop-gap measure until such time as the politico-religious situation became clarified and composers could know for certain what music was needed and what music would be permitted in the new Church — that is if the new Church itself survived.

Our traditional system of singing the psalms to Anglican chants is of seventeenth-century origin. In the sixteenth century evidence suggests that where the psalms were sung at all they were sung to familiar plainsong tones, occasionally harmonized. On major feasts, however, psalms were sometimes sung to a sort of harmonic formula which the composer adapted as necessary to fit the individual verses. These 'formula' psalm-settings, a rather cumbrous forerunner of the Anglican chant, were written out in full. Tallis was the first composer, so far as is known, to write a sequence of such festal psalms and the ten examples he left together formed a Christmas cycle: unhappily only the second, third and fourth have survived complete.

So much for Tallis's choir music, but to the man in the pew Tallis is chiefly notable as a composer of hymntunes. From its very beginnings the Anglican church took over from continental reformers the curious custom of singing metrical paraphrases of the psalms: considering the liberal and, indeed, catholic outlook of the early English reformers this universal acceptance of such a strongly Calvinistic element seems a little unexpected. However, many collections of these metrical psalms were published of which the most important was that of Sternhold and Hopkins; this appeared in innumerable editions from 1549 onwards. Amongst later metrical psalters was one compiled by Archbishop Parker between 1560 and 1567 to which Tallis contributed nine tunes. Two of these tunes are now universally popular—the eighth, which appears reduced to half its length in modern hymnals, is the famous 'Canon' now always associated with Bishop Ken's hymn 'Glory to thee, my God, this night'; the ninth is *Tallis's Ordinal* now wedded to the words 'O Holy Spirit, Lord of Grace'. Others of the nine are found in modern hymnbooks though usually with their tenor and treble parts interchanged. The first is found at AMR 106 (EH 78); striking use is made of this tune in Charles Wood's *Passion according to St. Mark*: the second is found at EH 3; the third at EH 92, a lovely melody which inspired Vaughan Williams to write his profoundly moving *Fantasia on a Theme by Thomas Tallis*; the fifth is found at S of P 483 and the seventh at EH 496. Regrettably, these other tunes have never achieved the enormous popularity of the eighth and ninth.

THOMAS CAUSTUN (*d.* 1569)

Turning now to the other composers active at this time little is known about Caustun other than that he was a Gentleman of the Chapel Royal in 1552 and remained there till his death on 28 October 1569. He was the chief contributor to John Day's 'Certaine Notes' (1560) and the same publisher's edition of Sternhold and Hopkins' metrical psalter, called 'Whole psalmes in foure partes' (1563). That Day published two complete Services, an evening Service, six anthems and twenty-seven psalm settings would suggest that Caustun was one of the most admired and respected composers of the period, yet other collections compiled about the same time include nothing of his. As he possessed only very moderate talent and as the quality of his work falls markedly below that of his more illustrious contemporaries, it is likely that Day employed him to edit the collection and Caustun, like so many editors, succumbed to the temptation to include much too much of his own music, even to the exclusion of music by Tye and Mundy. Editors of modern hymnbooks often fall into this same trap.

Other services by Caustun exist in manuscript. The two full Services and Evening Service for men's voices in chant form have little to say but his Service 'for children' (i.e. MATB) is an effective 'short' Service still useful in cathedrals. Of his anthems, the longest and best is the 4-part *Most blessed Lord Jesu*, interesting in that two of the parts have an open key signature while the others have one flat. *O most high* has a mysterious and surprisingly original opening. Two other anthems are merely arrangements: *In trouble and adversity* was adapted from Taverner's instrumental *In nomine*; *Turn thou us* was originally a solo song with accompaniment for three viols.

ROBERT JOHNSON (*c.* 1490–*c.* 1560)

Johnson was a Scottish priest who, having been accused of heresy, fled to England 'lang before the Reformation'. A complete Service, a separate Te Deum and Jubilate, about a dozen Latin motets and half a dozen English anthems are known, as well as two or three secular songs and some instrumental music. His importance is largely historical because although he was almost certainly the oldest member of this group (some fifteen years older than Tallis) yet he seems to have been far more aware of new and far-reaching developments in France and the Netherlands than were most of his English contemporaries; indeed, there is reason to believe that French influence reached England by way of Johnson and perhaps one or two other Scottish composers.

The following examples give some idea of how progressive was his thinking. To begin with, nearly all the Latin works by other composers mentioned in this chapter either have liturgical texts or were intended to be used liturgically—antiphons, responds, tracts, sequences, Canticles, lessons, and so on: it was Johnson who, only ten years or so before the English Reformation, introduced from France and the Low Countries the early-Renaissance motet, both the text and the function of which were essentially non-liturgical. Again, his *Gaude Maria*, with its 'paired' parts and systematic use of close imitation, suggests the influence of his Flemish contemporary Nicolas Gombert (1490?–c. 1556) and is technically far more 'modern' than works by Sheppard, a much later composer who still clung to the old *alternatim*[7] style and plainsong-based polyphony. An even more striking example is Johnson's Morning, Communion and Evening Service; in this he at times reaches out towards a rhythmically free semi-*parlando* style akin to that adopted for some settings of metrical psalm verses by Claude Le Jeune (1528–1601), another Flemish or French musician nearly forty years his junior. In many ways, then, Johnson was strikingly in advance of most of his English contemporaries and in some respects his work foreshadows the late-Renaissance style of the late sixteenth century.

JOHN MERBECKE (*c.* 1510–85)

It seems likely that Merbecke, or Marbeck, was born at Windsor somewhere about 1510 and spent the rest of his life there, holding various appointments including that of organist of St. George's Chapel. In the earlier part of his life he wrote Latin works for the Roman (Sarum) rite and he appears to have been on terms of personal friendship both with Cranmer and with Stephen Gardiner, Bishop of Winchester, who was largely responsible for the 'Six Articles' designed to prevent the spread of Reformation principles and practices in England. But Merbecke found himself more and more in sympathy with the reformers until eventually he was completely won over to Calvinism and became a zealot in its cause. Hardly had Henry VIII set up his 'Great' Bible in the churches than Merbecke set to work on a monumental 'Concordance', the first in English, which occupied him for several years. Then in March 1543 disaster struck. Reforming zeal had led him and two of his colleagues at Windsor to copy out and distribute Calvin's essay denouncing the 'Six Articles'. The three men were arrested for heresy and committed to the Marshalsea: Merbecke suffered an even heavier blow when his vast Concordance was confiscated and destroyed. The trial took place on 26 July 1543 and all three were condemned to death. No time was lost in sending his colleagues Testwood and Benett to the stake but Merbecke, through the intervention of one of his chief accusers, his old friend Bishop Gardiner, was reprieved and, after a further short spell in the Marshalsea, was granted a full pardon by Henry VIII on 4 October. Even more surprising, he was actually reinstated in his post at St. George's, Windsor.

Why did Gardiner, his chief accuser, intervene? Why was Merbecke pardoned by the

[7] See p. 83.

king with the full knowledge of Cranmer? One possible explanation could be that at this time Merbecke was collaborating with Cranmer in providing a musical setting for the Litany, published 16 June 1544. This setting was largely an adaptation of the traditional Latin plainsong. Although there is no direct evidence to link Merbecke's name with the music of the Litany there are several unmistakable similarities between this and his *Booke of Common praier noted*, issued by the same publisher, Richard Grafton; these similarities are strong enough to suggest common authorship. If this is true, the preparatory work would have been in hand at about the time of the heresy trial and might explain the unusual leniency of the authorities.

But even reinstatement at Windsor did not bring back from the bonfire the Concordance and with astonishing courage, determination and perseverance Merbecke set to work and rewrote the whole immense book. When at last this double labour had been completed we can imagine his feelings when no publisher could be found willing to risk issuing a work so costly to produce. Dauntless, and with astounding persistency, he began writing yet a third version, considerably shortened and compressed and in this reduced form the work was eventually published. Some idea of the scope of the original can be estimated from the fact that the reduced version contains over nine hundred folios, each in three columns. It was published in 1550, the same year as his *Booke of Common praier noted*, a remarkable double achievement proving him to have been a scholar and theologian of no mean distinction as well as a composer.

His *Common praier noted* may have been commissioned by Cranmer and Northumberland; certainly it must have had their approval. Apart from this (see pp. 29–30) he appears to have written very little music—only a Mass, two motets and a carol have reached us. His Mass for Lent, *Per arma justitiae*, was almost certainly an early work, perhaps as early as 1531. It is curiously fifteenth century in style and feeling, not only because it was probably the only large-scale Mass based on a *cantus firmus* to be written by an Englishman at this time but also because it was written in the old 'differentiated' style instead of the later imitative style. This quaint throw-back must have been thought oddly conservative and old-fashioned by his contemporaries; neither is it very inspired. Of the two Latin works much the more successful was his large votive Mary-antiphon *Ave Dei patris filia* of which four out of the five voice-parts still survive. This was much more modern in style than his Mass and employed late-Renaissance techniques like imitation and contrapuntal homophony. The extended 5-part Jesus-antiphon *Domine Jesu Christe* also uses imitation but the music never really takes wings because the entries are not overlapped; so each short sub-section falls limply back to earth with a cadence in all parts simultaneously. A devotional 3-part Christmas anthem with English words, *A Virgine and Mother*, is stilted and undistinguished. It is presumably a later piece than the Latin works.

It follows from what has been said that Merbecke was a very minor composer and his fame, which is historical rather than musical, rests squarely on his *Booke of Common praier noted* and especially on the Holy Communion section which is the only part of it that most people know.[8] Though he lived for another thirty-five years after this book was published he composed no more music. Perhaps his growing identification with Calvinism led him to despise elaborate sacred music even though he was professionally responsible for its performance. This likelihood is strengthened by a passage in the introduction to his Concordance: 'I have consumed vainly the greatest part of my life

[8] See p. 30.

in the study of Musike and plaiyng the organs.' (Taverner similarly regretted his 'vain ditties' later in life.) But if Merbecke wrote no more music he continued to write profound theological works, one of which bears the irresistible title *A Ripping up of the Pope's Fardel* (1581).

OSBERT PARSLEY (1511–85)

Parsley was an almost exact contemporary of Tallis. For half a century until his death he was a singing-man at Norwich Cathedral—one of the few church composers not associated in some way with the Chapel Royal. Little of his music survives. His two Morning Services are well constructed but undistinguished and his Evening Service is known only in an organ score. His setting of the Lamentations is unusual in that for a *cantus firmus* he uses the liturgical reading-tone; but by placing the oft-repeated tone in the top part (triplex) some feeling of monotony is almost unavoidable. Perhaps his best memorial is the 5-part *Conserva me Domine* which makes enterprising use of canonic imitation.

ROBERT PARSONS (d. 1570)

Parsons became a member of the Chapel Royal in 1563 and was drowned in the River Trent at Newark in 1570 while still, presumably, a young man. His compositions include songs with contrapuntal accompaniment for four viols (many intended for the choirboy plays[9]), concerted instrumental pieces of the 'In nomine' and 'Browning' type, as well as sacred music in Latin and English. The few Latin pieces of his which survive show greater maturity and seem more deeply conceived than his English settings: they were almost certainly later works written during Elizabeth's reign and intended for those places of worship where Latin was still permitted.[10] Outstanding is the lengthy votive antiphon *O bone Jesu* with its arresting opening in block harmony, vigorous cross rhythms and chains of dotted notes (characteristic of Parsons). In this a series of psalm verses set polyphonically are interspersed with exclamations in block harmony—'O Adonay', 'O Heloy', 'O Emmanuel', 'O Raby'. The motet *Libera me Domine* uses the Sarum form of the plainchant as a *cantus firmus*: it differs significantly from the version used by Byrd in his setting of the same text. Parsons also composed several settings of Latin hymns: these are of considerable merit but regrettably the tenor part is missing. These hymns were intended to be sung *alternatim*, even numbered verses only being set in polyphony. No Mass setting by Parsons is known.

At a time when Protestantism frowned upon elaboration in church music, when too slavish adherence to the 'for every syllable a note' doctrine resulted in a good deal of music which was merely functional and often uninspired, Parsons' sacred works with English texts are remarkable for their unusual length and complexity; this suggests that they were written for the Chapel Royal where, as we have seen, the Queen adopted a far more liberal policy. But though at first they sound most noble and impressive, the almost unvarying rate of four harmonic changes per measure and the heavy preponderance of cadences in the same key soon become wearisome. By far the most impressive of his English pieces is his First Service, written between 1549 and 1553, one of the longest and most elaborate of all Edwardian and Elizabethan settings. In this Parsons

[9] See pp. 88–9.   [10] See pp. 22 and 71.

seeks to achieve expressive ends by varying the density of the texture; some sections are scored for only three or four voice-parts while at climactic passages the number of parts increases to as many as eight. He also calls for some antiphonal singing between Decani and Cantoris. Two other Services of his are incomplete — the second Morning Service 'for meanes' (including Venite) and a Morning and Communion Service with two counter-tenor parts. Both are for 5-part choir and are laid out on the same monumental scale as the First Service.

His anthems too are monumental. Of these *Deliver me from mine enemies* is the best known: it is for five voices with an optional canonic sixth and the highly contrapuntal texture gives rise to an unusual degree of dissonance, passing and suspended. His other anthems include two 5-part settings of *Holy, Lord God Almighty*.

JOHN SHEPPARD (*c.* 1523–*c.* 1563)

Of the next generation of composers Sheppard (sometimes Shepard, or Shepherd) and Mundy were the most important. Only about fifteen years of Sheppard's life are documented — from 1542 to 1557. In 1542 he succeeded Appleby as instructor of the choristers at Magdalen College, Oxford. He resigned a year later but was reappointed in 1545 at an annual salary of £8 plus extra emoluments and he continued to hold the post of 'Informator' at various times between then and 1556. He was never a Fellow of the college. In 1552 he was appointed a Gentleman of the Chapel Royal and seems to have held both posts in double harness for three or four years. In 1554 he supplicated at Oxford for the degree of Doctor of Music; at this time he was reported to have been 'a student in music for the space of twenty years'. In 1555 he was twice in trouble with the college authorities for the sadistic treatment of boys: on 2 June he pleaded guilty to keeping a boy (not a choirboy) in chains all night; a fortnight later he was accused of dragging a new choirboy in chains the whole way from Malmesbury to Oxford. He appears to have left Oxford early the following year and in 1557 is mentioned in Chapel Royal records as having presented some songs to the Queen. No later documentary evidence is known but there is some indirect evidence that he died about 1563. The date of his birth can only be guessed at — probably (in view of his 'twenty years a student' in 1554) between 1520 and 1525.

Though his life was comparatively short he was a prolific composer and his known works include five complete Masses; some fifty or so Latin works, mostly liturgical and usually built round a plainsong *cantus firmus*; two complete English Service settings; two settings of Te Deum, Magnificat and Nunc dimittis; and an Evening Service, together with several isolated Canticles and Service movements. There are also fourteen English anthems of which six have survived complete.

Of the Masses, his 4-part *Western Wynde* setting is the least interesting and certainly not to be compared with Taverner's fine work: because the tune nearly always appears in the highest voice its frequent repetition becomes monotonous. Other Masses include a 6-part festal setting, a Mass for men's voices *Be not afraide*, and a 4-part Lady-Mass called *Playnsong Masse for a Meane* which employs a head-motive. One of the most forward-looking of all his works is the 4-part *French Mass*, probably so called because he took for his model the shorter Masses of Gombert (1490?–*c.* 1556) with their short points of imitation; at times he introduces brisk triple rhythms with even terser imitative points. In these works he adopts an extraordinarily cavalier attitude towards the liturgical text. Thus in the Credo of the *Western Wynde, Be not afraide* and *French Masses* he omits the section 'Deum de Deo . . . de Deo vero'; he even goes so far as to omit clauses from the Gloria. In the Gloria and Credo of his *Masse for a Mene* (i.e. with boys singing the top part) he reverts to an older style of composition in which plainsong and polyphony alternate; hence the alternative name *Playnsong Masse*. Sheppard was perhaps the last composer to use this *alternatim* form extensively.

Responds were elaborate chants sung after lessons in the daily Offices. Sheppard wrote many such and in his hands they became one of the most interesting and virile forms of liturgical music. Responds too alternated plainsong and polyphony but the principle of *alternatim* was applied in two different and opposite ways. In responds with a long tradition of polyphony, like *Audivi vocem; Gloria in excelsis* and *In pace*, the old style of *alternatim* was retained in which solo sections were set polyphonically and sung by a group of solo voices, the full choir singing the alternate plainsong verses (in unison of course). In the last decades of the Sarum rite this method was reversed, the soloist singing the plainsong verses answered by the choir singing in polyphony. In polyphonic sections the plainsong normally appears in the tenor in notes of equal value (i.e. mono-rhythmic) and the polyphony itself is often derived from, or alludes to, the plainsong. The tenor part-book of the set which is our sole source for many of Sheppard's responds (Oxford, Christ Church MSS. 979–83) has been lost, but when the tenor is a mono-rhythmic *cantus firmus* it is easy to reconstruct with certainty and eight responds have been satisfactorily completed; *Non conturbetur* II; *Dum transisset* I; *Reges Tharsis*; *Impetum fecerunt*; *Spiritus Sanctus procedens* I and II; *Verbum caro* and *Gaude, gaude, gaude Maria* (with prose *Inviolata*). This last is not only Sheppard's finest piece but is also one of the supreme masterpieces of the last years of the Sarum rite: it is high time a practical edition was published for the use of choirs. Only the verse 'Gabrielem archangelum scimus' and the Gloria patri are sung to plainsong; all the rest of this long work is a fully polyphonic 6-part setting of both the respond and its prose—the only such example to survive. The third verse has an ethereal high 4-part texture for boys' voices where trebles and meanes break into 'gymel'. Gymel (gimel, gemell, *gemellum*), in sixteenth-century usage, was the division of a single part temporarily into two parts of similar range; thus it meant much the same thing as the modern term *divisi*. Gymel was most often employed in passages for solo voice and so implied a duet. When, as in this section of *Gaude, gaude*, two parts simultaneously divide, the resulting 4-part texture is termed 'double gymel'. Subsequently, when the two voice-parts again become one the word *semellum* ('single') is used.

Mass responds were almost entirely limited to Alleluias and most Alleluias were composed for the Lady-Mass; Sheppard's four Lady-Mass Alleluias were among the last to be composed. A fine and highly florid 6-part setting of the Easter Gradual *Haec dies* was sung probably at Vespers rather than at Mass: the plainsong, in long notes, is given to the first bass.

An important group of works written in the *alternatim* style are Sheppard's ritual antiphons. In *Laudate pueri* it is the even verses and their Alleluias that are treated polyphonically. These verses all receive different settings except that they have the same bass part in common; this bass is derived not from the plainsong itself but from its faburden. Thus the work becomes a set of variations on a ground bass. The word 'faburden' (faburdon, faux-bourdon) meant different things at different times; in this context it means the plainsong transposed up a third and slightly modified. Similar in every way to *Laudate pueri* but of unusual interest is *In exitu Israel*, a composite effort by Sheppard, Mundy and (Thomas?) Byrd in which all three wrote variations on the same ground: in this curious collaboration Sheppard wrote seven verses, Mundy four, and Byrd three. Another fine antiphon by Sheppard is the 6-part *Media vita* to be sung with Nunc dimittis during the last four weeks of Lent; it is severe in style, noble in expression. The votive antiphon *Gaudete caelicolae*, in imitative counterpoint, is short and spirited.

Of Sheppard's other Latin compositions two are outstanding — the gloriously sonorous 6-part Te Deum for men's voices and a Magnificat 'in medio chori'[11]; both are based on the plainsong. His lively setting of the Easter *Salve* is for men's voices in four parts. Tallis and Sheppard between them wrote almost all the Latin hymns of this period. Fifteen by Sheppard are known (for from five to eight voices) but only two are complete. One of these is a splendid setting of *Aeterne rex altissime*. In these hymns the plainsong is usually in the top part, not the tenor. Whereas most of Sheppard's work is characteristically animated and vigorous his psalm settings, like *Beati omnes*, are restrained, almost inhibited, and do not represent him at his best.

His English works, though few, deserve to be better known. The First Service is basically in four parts but extensive use of antiphony between Decani and Cantoris demands double choir; furthermore on both sides parts sometimes divide so creating five or more parts. The Second Service is a large-scale piece dividing into as many as seven parts. This too is to be sung antiphonally and the texture is more imitative and melismatic than that of the First Service. His other Service music is mostly too incomplete for editorial reconstruction. It includes two settings of Te Deum, Magnificat and Nunc dimittis, two Creeds, other isolated movements, and what appears to have been a long and brilliant Evening Service 'for trebles', almost in the style of the much later setting by Weelkes.

Like Tye, Sheppard left fourteen anthems but many again are too incomplete for reconstruction. One of the best is *Christ rising* for men's voices; it is of great richness and nobility. *Haste thee, O God*, one of the longest, is also very fine. In addition, Sheppard also left thirty-three settings of metrical psalms.

WILLIAM MUNDY (*c.* 1530–91)

If Tallis was the most distinguished of the older group of composers whose work bridged the English Reformation, Mundy can perhaps be regarded as the foremost of the younger group. He was born about a quarter-century after Tallis, and in 1542–43 was a chorister at Westminster Abbey where he became head boy. His father, Thomas, was for some time sexton at St. Mary-at-Hill, London (where Tallis had been choirmaster), and there in 1548 his son joined him as parish clerk, a post which included some musical responsibilities. He seems to have stayed at St. Mary-at-Hill until at least 1559. Then, after a short spell as a vicar-choral of St. Paul's Cathedral, he was sworn a Gentleman of the Chapel Royal on 21 February 1563. There he stayed till he died in 1591.

Like Tallis, he found his greatest inspiration in setting Latin texts where he was free to adopt a florid polyphonic style; his English pieces are few in number and in them he obviously chafes under the shackles of the imposed 'simple' style. Of his Latin works, twenty-five are complete or lack only one part which can be fairly satisfactorily

[11] See p.86.

reconstructed from the others. There are a few, however, of which **only** one of the parts survives.

In his two Masses 'apon the Square' Mundy is one of the few composers (the others are Appleby, Byrd and Lupus Italus) to include a setting of the Kyrie. In both, too, he begins the Credo at 'factorem coeli' instead of at 'Patrem omnipotentem'; it is notable that from this point onwards the words are given complete although it was customary at that time for composers to make several omissions in the text. The meaning of the term 'Apon the Square' remains obscure; it seems to refer to the melody on which the Kyries were based and may even have something to do with the square notation in which this melody was originally written—but then most Gregorian melodies had earlier been written in square notation. Other Latin Service music includes two Alleluias for the Lady-Mass and a fine Magnificat.

Among the best of Mundy's Latin pieces in the old florid style are the two very long votive antiphons *Maria virgo sanctissima* and *Vox patris caelestis*. Both are cast in the conventional mould for this type of work with the first half in triple metre and the second half in duple. Furthermore, both works are cumulative in construction, beginning with a passage in two voice-parts later expanding into three. Then the texture thickens still more and sections in four or even five parts culminate in a lengthy stretch of full 6-part polyphony. The second half, in duple time, similarly begins in only three or four parts, again building up to massive 6-part counterpoint. The composer used this same cumulative device in some of his psalm-motets: e.g. the 5-part *Adhaesit pavimento; Memor esto* and *Noli aemulari*, and the 6-part *Eructavit cor meum*. These psalm-motets, instead of being in the old highly florid style of the votive antiphons, are written in the imitative style of Josquin and Gombert. Being non-liturgical, they are treated more subjectively than are his liturgical settings; notice, for example, how *Memor esto* divides into double gymel at the words 'Cantabiles mihi erant justificationes tuae'. It must be admitted though that often the relationship between words and music is only slight and superficial. *Noli aemulari*, like some of Tallis's psalm-motets, retains the bisectional layout of the old votive antiphons, the first part being in triple and the second in duple time. *Exsurge Christe*, found in the Gyffard part-books, is a collect against heresy which pleads for the confounding of schismatics and for renewed zeal for apostolic truth. Mundy also wrote some outstanding examples of Latin hymns but, as usual, the tenor part is missing.

His known music for the English rite includes three Services and a Te Deum, all for men's voices; together with three fairly complete Services and an additional five settings of the evening Canticles, all for full choir. Of his several anthems, only five survive complete. The First Service, written some time before 1552, is contrapuntal in style and is mainly for five voice-parts, though occasionally it breaks into six or seven parts: there is a good deal of antiphony between Decani and Cantoris. The Second Service is similar though somewhat simpler in style and is scored for only four voices. The Service for men's voices 'in three parts' is mostly in six parts because the voices divide: this too is in the highly imitative style of Gombert. Two other men's voice Services survive only in fragmentary form but appear similar in style. Mundy added evening Canticles to a morning Service by Robert Parsons; this is more chordal than most of his Services and he effectively alternates homophony and polyphony. The most forward-looking of Mundy's Services is one known as *C fa ut* which is not only unusually tonal but is also notable for its repetition of phrases and enterprising use of sequence. But of all his

Service music the most impressive work by far is undoubtedly the 9-part Magnificat and Nunc dimittis 'in medio chori', probably composed for some special occasion at the Chapel Royal. Not only is it one of the most ambitious English sacred works of the century but it is also one of the very few (about twenty-two in all) which call for high treble voices. Allowing for the usual upward transposition of a minor third, top B flats abound and there are some thrilling passages for high voices (trebles, means and altos). Nobody knows for certain what 'in medio chori' means but it probably refers to a group of soloists 'in the middle of the choir' strategically placed between Decani and Cantoris to give an additional spatial dimension (Vaughan Williams' *Mass in G minor* provides a modern example).

None of his anthems is comparable in scale. Of the five which have reached us the most popular is the short unaccompanied 4-part *O Lord, the maker of all things*. It is in two sections AB, the second of which is repeated, and it strikes a happy balance between chordal writing and polyphony. A shorter piece *O Lord, the world's saviour* is similar in texture but is less distinguished. The longest anthem is the 5-part *O Lord, I bow the knees of my heart* but its close-knit polyphony suggests that it may be merely an English version of a Latin composition now lost.

Though William Mundy was highly regarded in his own day, much of his music now seems somewhat stilted, partly because his grasp of new techniques was not sufficiently assured for him to use them freely in the service of the words: often, indeed, there seems to be little connection between words and music. Perhaps his greatest importance is to be found in two anthems so far unmentioned, *Ah helpless wretch* and *The secret sins* (the latter for long attributed to Gibbons but almost certainly by Mundy). These are amongst the very earliest examples of a form destined to become of immense importance in the whole future development of English sacred music — the 'verse' anthem. In 'verse' anthems and Services, passages for full choir alternate with passages for solo voice, as they did in the mediæval antiphon: the difference is that in Tudor and Jacobean 'verse' passages the solo voice or voices are always accompanied by obbligato instruments, usually viols or organ but sometimes by other instruments such as the cornett. Sometimes an accompaniment originally written for viols was transcribed for organ. The important thing is that this accompaniment, whatever its form, is 'obbligato', in other words, the music would not be complete without it. Mr. Philip Brett has pointed out that this method of writing, which is peculiarly English and a product of the native tradition, sprang largely from the secular consort song written for solo voice with an accompaniment for three or four viols.[12] Such songs, by composers like Edwards, Parsons, Farrant, Strogers, Whythorne, Nicholson and Patrick, were popular long before the invasion of the Italian madrigal and everyone would have heard them at the choirboy plays.[13] Mr. Brett's theory is strengthened by the fact that composers of the early verse anthems showed a marked preference for metrical texts, often with a refrain or some kind of repeat structure. From this time onwards, pieces sung throughout by the choir as a whole, without using solo voices, are called 'full' Services and 'full' anthems to distinguish them from 'verse' Services and anthems. In this context 'full' must not be confused with 'complete' which usually implies that a Service includes all the required music for Morning, Communion and Evening services.

Mundy's verse anthems are both short. *Ah helpless wretch* is, typically, strophic in

[12] Philip Brett: *Consort Songs*, Musica Britannica, Vol. XXII, 1967, p. xv.
[13] See pp. 88–8.

form; the words are taken from William Hunnis's 'The poore Widowes Mite' (1583). Stanzas 1 and 2 are set for counter-tenor soloist, the chorus taking up his last line or lines. Stanzas 3 and 4 repeat the music of stanzas 1 and 2 but stanza 5 is set to new music in triple measure, the chorus repeating each line after the soloist. Often the vocal phrases are linked by short instrumental interludes. *The secret sins*, also for counter-tenor solo, is similar in structure. Only, perhaps, in these verse anthems does Mundy show some awareness that melody can fulfil an expressive function.

ROBERT WHITE (*c.* 1533–74)

The date of White's (or Whyte's) birth is unknown but was probably somewhere about 1530–35. After taking a Mus.B. at Cambridge in 1560 he was appointed Master of the Choristers at Ely Cathedral (*c.* 1562). There is some evidence to suggest that five years later he held a similar appointment at Chester. Then in 1568–69 he went to Westminster Abbey, still as Master of the Choristers. He is another of the very few composers who do not appear to have been employed at the Chapel Royal. He married Ellen Tye, daughter of the composer Christopher Tye. Then late in 1574 tragedy struck; he, his wife, and several of their children died of plague, leaving two little girls as the only survivors.

As composer and musician he enjoyed the highest regard of his contemporaries. Nearly all his best works were written for the Sarum rite and must therefore date from Queen Mary's reign, 1553–58. These include an *alternatim* Magnificat *a 6*, much in the instrumental style of Taverner; four *alternatim* settings of the Compline hymn *Christe qui lux es*; a 4-part *Libera me*; two large-scale 5-part votive antiphons *Regina celi* and *Tota pulchra es* constructed on their own plainsongs in the manner of responds; and two superb settings of the Lamentations, one for 5-part choir, the other for six voices. This last is on a grand scale and is one of the most expressive and profoundly moving of all sacred works written in the mid-sixteenth century. The density of the texture is effectively varied and the broad-flowing melodic lines are subtly moulded to reflect the shifting mood of the text; indeed the music is markedly subjective for its time.

Of his other Latin works, settings of twelve complete psalms were almost certainly written after 1588. The fact that they have no liturgical function would have precluded their use during the Marian period; furthermore, in their wide emotional range, melodic distinction and, at times, surging vitality they show that sureness of touch which usually comes only with maturity. Basically they are in five or six voice-parts but some sections are more lightly scored while in others division of parts can result in a 7-strand texture. In some he retains the old convention of using triple time for the first main division and duple for the second. At times, as in the following example, his style is nearly as florid as Taverner's (See Example 8 on the next page): at others it is simple and almost syllabic. Though these psalm-motets all reach a high level of excellence, the finest are undoubtedly those in sombre or penitential mood. An examination of all these Latin works suggests that scholars, publishers and choirmasters have failed to give White his just due.

He appears to have written very little, if anything, for the English rite. There are no Services and only five anthems are known. Of these *O Lord, deliver me* is only an English adaptation of *Manus tuae fecerunt me* and *Praise the Lord* similarly comes from

White: *Exaudiat te Dominus*

Ex. 8

Domine, non est exaltatum. There is also reason to suspect that *The Lord bless us* and the psalm *Lord, who shall dwell*, both lengthy 5-part works, may be English adaptations of Latin originals now lost. Finally, there is some evidence that *O Lord, how glorious* was composed not by White but by Edmund Hooper.

RICHARD FARRANT (before 1535–81)

Farrant's date of birth is unknown but he was born presumably some time before 1535. Nothing is known of his early life nor do we know the date of his appointment to the Chapel Royal, though it seems to have been about 1552. In 1564 he took the most unusual step of resigning from the Chapel Royal in order to become Master of the Choristers at St. George's Chapel, Windsor. In 1569 he was reappointed to the Chapel Royal, apparently as Master of the Choristers, though still retaining his post at Windsor (he must have had an easy-going Dean and Chapter at Windsor). He continued to hold both appointments jointly till his death. Church music formed only part of Farrant's interests and perhaps the lesser part because he was much involved in theatricals. At this time it was the custom for boys to take women's parts on the stage and the London theatres teemed with boys (Shakespeare's 'little eyases'[14]). The leading boy-companies were the choirboys of St. Paul's, the Chapel Royal and Windsor. During Farrant's time his Windsor and Chapel Royal boys had their own theatre at Blackfriars and so popular were their performances that London's highest and most fashionable Society fought for seats—which were appropriately expensive. In particular, the boys were in great demand at Elizabeth's Court. Furthermore, there was a lucrative business in hiring out boys to perform at banquets and entertainments in the city. No wonder Farrant grew rich. No wonder too that puritan hackles rose! For many of these entertainments Farrant

[14] See *Hamlet*, Act 2, Sc. 2, ll 361–76.

was author, composer, director, producer and, no doubt, a principal actor. This may explain why he wrote so little sacred music.

The four items to have reached us are all in English and consist of a Service and three anthems. The Service includes Morning, Communion (Kyrie and Creed only) and Evening Canticles and was known as the 'High' or 'Short' Service; another name, the 'Third', implies that two others have been lost. Of the anthems, *Call to remembrance* and *Hide not thou thy face* are 4-part miniatures of rare beauty and perfection. They are more subjective in feeling than are most of the works hitherto discussed and the writing is strongly tonal with clearly defined modulations. A similar anthem, the ever-popular *Lord, for thy tender mercy's sake*, is often ascribed to Farrant but seems more likely to be by the elder John Hilton.

But Farrant's greatest claim on posterity is his anthem *When as we sat in Babylon* which must have been one of the very earliest verse anthems. Unfortunately the voice parts have been lost and only organ scores exist. As with so many other early verse anthems the text is a metrical psalm. The verses are set strophically for solo voice and the last phrase of each solo is repeated by the chorus: the last verse receives independent treatment.

CHAPTER V

Characteristics of
Late Renaissance Style

We have seen (pages 42–43) that during the earlier part of the sixteenth century western European composers found themselves possessed of an expressive, flexible and highly sophisticated musical language which can conveniently be labelled 'late Renaissance': this polished style had taken something like four hundred years to evolve. True, it had reached its full flowering in Flanders and Italy rather earlier than elsewhere, its impact in France was slight, while in England its adoption was somewhat belated; indeed, it was largely in the work of those composers discussed in the last chapter, and their contemporaries, that the style finally emerged in England in its classic form.

It was in the latter part of the sixteenth century there came that extraordinary galaxy of great composers—di Lasso (Flanders); the Gabrielis, Marenzio, Gesualdo, Palestrina and Anerio (Italy); Victoria (Spain); Handl, Hassler and Praetorius (Germany); Byrd, Morley, Dowland, Tomkins, Wilbye, Weelkes and Gibbons (England), to name but a few. To what extent, one wonders, do these men owe something of their pre-eminence to the historical accident that they happened to be born at the climax of this long evolutionary period when, at last, a highly refined musical language had been perfected?

Since to all late Tudor and Jacobean church composers the late Renaissance style was their natural means of expression, it will be useful to examine the characteristics of this style in general terms first, before going on to discuss the work of individual musicians.

MELODY

A good 'tune' with simple accompanying parts for the other voices was quite foreign to the genius of Renaissance polyphony; instead, melodic interest was shared fairly equally between all the voices taking part. This, in fact, is precisely what the word 'polyphony' (i.e. 'many-voices') implies. One important exception was music constructed on a *cantus firmus* where the voice carrying the *cantus firmus*, usually the tenor, inevitably had an independent identity of its own and so could not take its normal part in the contrapuntal discussion going on between the other parts. Even then the *cantus firmus* was not necessarily intended to be 'brought out' at the expense of the other parts; though thematically different from the surrounding melodic strands it merged unobtrusively into the texture. Indeed when, as often happened, the *cantus firmus* was sung in very long notes, it tended to lose its own melodic identity and had instead a bonding effect on the surrounding polyphony—much like long-held horn notes in an orchestral texture. Only in chordal writing—as in some Latin hymns, carols, simple motets and anthems, and homophonic sections of polyphonic works — do we approach the modern conception of a 'tune' supported by harmony.

Instead of a lyrical melodic line divided into balancing phrases of 2, 4 and 8 bars, sixteenth-century melodies were far more dependent on the text both for the length and shape of their phrases. The text to be set was broken up into its constituent clauses or subsections,[1] each of which was then set either contrapuntally or harmonically. In general the melodic lines moved mainly by step; often the phrases were arch-shaped, rising to a point of climax and then falling back again:

Ex. 9

---

[1] See pp. 45 and 101.

Leaps of a third and of wider intervals were freely used to give shape and variety to the more common stepwise movement but it was realised that wide leaps and excessive disjunct motion, particularly in the upper parts, could easily spoil the smooth flowing of the vocal lines. To guard against this, various conventions seem to have been fairly generally observed, especially by the Italian school of church musicians:

1. Melodic leaps of a fourth or more were usually followed by progress in the opposite direction, generally by step:

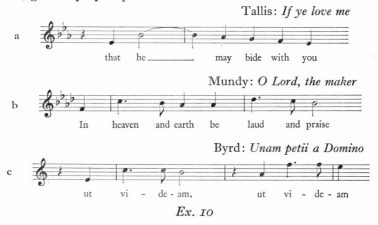

Ex. 10

2. Further, unless the leap came at the start of a phrase (as in the above examples) it was also customary to approach it by notes within it, so making a zigzag with the leap in the middle:

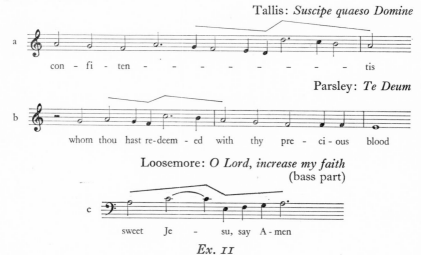

Ex. 11

3. Upward leaps of a minor sixth occurred frequently. Upward leaps of a major sixth or seventh were much less common. Downward leaps of all three intervals were very rare. Such leaps were nearly always approached and quitted by notes within the leap, usually by step:

Byrd: *Save me, O God*
(tenor part)

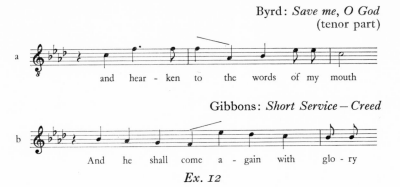

Gibbons: *Short Service — Creed*

Ex. 12

4. The augmented fourth or 'tritone' (three whole tones from, say, F to B or B to F) was considered to be *diabolus in musica* and was shunned by all composers of the period, both here and on the continent.

5. Two successive leaps in the same direction were infrequent:

White: *Christe, qui lux*   Morley: *Nolo mortem peccatoris*

Ex. 13

though a fifth was often given its intervening third:

Tallis: *Salvator mundi*   Philips: *Ascendit Deus*

Ex. 14

and an octave its intervening fourth or fifth:

Tomkins: *Fourth Service — Te Deum*

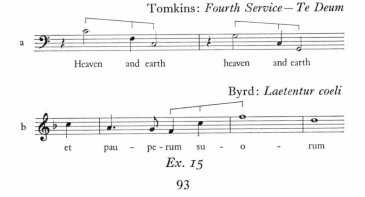

Byrd: *Laetentur coeli*

Ex. 15

6. The bass part was usually far more disjunct in its movement than the higher parts and upward and downward leaps of a fourth, fifth and octave abound:

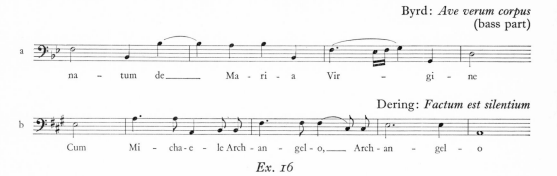

Byrd: *Ave verum corpus*
(bass part)

Dering: *Factum est silentium*

Ex. 16

7. Usually, the shorter the note values the more conjunct the movement (thus quavers were nearly always approached and quitted by step); conversely, slow-moving notes enjoyed far more freedom of movement.

8. Any leap was considered harmless if it came between the end of one phrase and the beginning of the next:

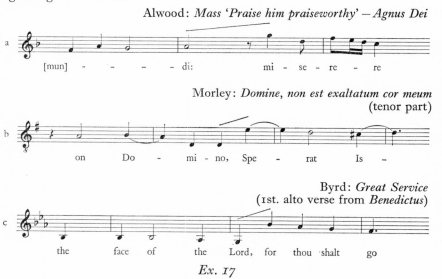

Alwood: *Mass 'Praise him praiseworthy' — Agnus Dei*

Morley: *Domine, non est exaltatum cor meum*
(tenor part)

Byrd: *Great Service*
(1st. alto verse from *Benedictus*)

Ex. 17

These, then, are a few of the principles which, consciously or unconsciously, regulated the melodic ideas of a late Renaissance composer. It remains to be said that, except in the matter of the tritone, English composers permitted themselves far greater liberties than did Palestrina and most other continental church composers. Independence of mind and love of adventure, typical of their age, is shown on almost every page by their daring and often exciting disregard for conventions. Of course, when the words demanded it they were just as capable of writing smoothly-flowing melodic lines as were the Italians, but they were also capable of bursting the fetters of convention in order to give freer rein to the imagination, encompass a wider range of emotions and achieve greater subtlety of expression.

RHYTHM

In a previous chapter[2] we saw how richly varied and intricate the rhythms of spoken words can be; Elizabethan and Jacobean composers were highly sensitive to these rhythmic implications and often attempted to give them musical expression:

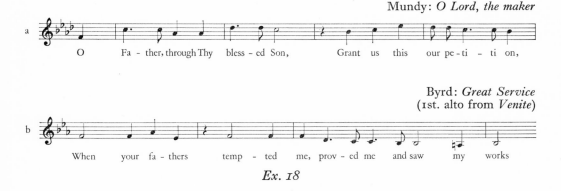

Mundy: *O Lord, the maker*

Byrd: *Great Service*
(1st. alto from *Venite*)

Ex. 18

The inflections of the spoken word are also infinitely varied and subtle and again composers sometimes tried to translate these delicate nuances into musical terms. A typical example is the fine solo narration in Gibbons's anthem *This is the record of John* where the rhythms, repetitions, sequences and melodic shapes vividly suggest the tones of the questions and answers:

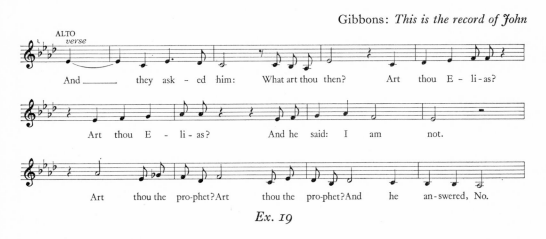

Gibbons: *This is the record of John*

Ex. 19

Often one feels that some of the later writers, especially Byrd, revelled in complex rhythms for their own sake:

[2] See pp. 50–1.

Byrd: *This day Christ was born*
(tenor part)

Weelkes: *Hosanna to the Son of David*
(tenor part)

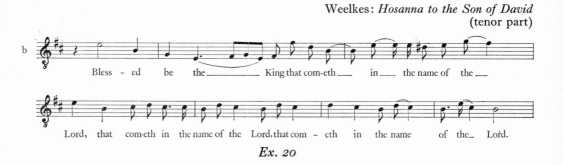

Ex. 20

The first is the tenor part of a 6-part anthem in which Byrd exhibits remarkable virtuosity in handling highly complex cross-rhythms and also dramatic changes of metre and pulse. In the second, also a tenor part from a 6-part work, the basic metre is more stable than in the Byrd anthem but the voice parts all become rhythmically complex.

A fascinating feature of poetry is the interplay between the irregular accents of the word rhythms and the regular stresses of the basic metre; sometimes the two coincide, often they are in opposition, and it is part of the poet's business to strike a just balance between the two. Similarly, in sixteenth-century church music (except for the simplest types of chordal music, carols and hymn-tunes) a conflict arises between the free and natural rhythmic accentuation of each individual melodic strand and the basic metrical beat, felt rather than heard, which is established by the interaction of these strands on each other. Before we can recognise departures from a norm we must first recognise the norm itself; that is why displaced accents, syncopations and cross-rhythms cease to exist at all unless there is a strong basic pulse from which we clearly feel them to be departures. In other words, this metrical pulse must be firmly established because it is the only yardstick by which we can measure the rhythmical freedom of each melodic strand. One effective way of securing this basic pulse is by harmonic means; each change of chord has the effect of a stress and by arranging the chord changes in some suitable pattern an underlying pulse can be imparted to the music. This is known as 'harmonic rhythm'.

Since bar-lines were not written in the part-books at this time, the singer was left free to group his part in twos, threes or larger groups, depending on the rhythm of the words and the shape of the musical phrase. His part proceeded rather like plainsong except that relative note-lengths had to be observed and the basic beat kept more strict for the sake of unanimity.

Gibbons: *Almighty and everlasting God*

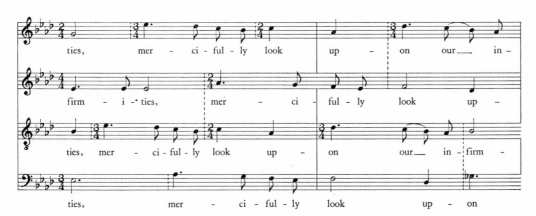

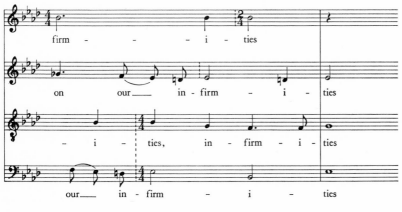

Ex. 21

When a rhythmical 'point' was treated imitatively or when rhythmically complex melodic strands were woven together contrapuntally (as in the Byrd and Weelkes anthems quoted above), the rhythms were offset against each other, resulting in an intricate pattern of cross-rhythms sometimes known as 'rhythmic counterpoint'. In Ex. 21 on the previous page the continuous bar-lines are editorial; the broken bar-lines indicate the accentuation of the individual voice parts. The lapping and eddying of the cross-rhythms now become clearly apparent. Only when actually sung in this way does such a passage come to life: so often choirs find Tudor music dull because they will persist in singing it in a lumpy four-square manner. This example is comparatively simple: it is, however, typical of its period and similar passages abound in the work of the later Tudors. Five- and six-part anthems yield more complex examples, of course, and such anthems as *This day Christ was born* (quoted above) and *Sing joyfully*, also by Byrd, show the expressive possibilities of highly intricate cross-rhythms in the hands of a master.

Rhythmic counterpoint was used even more extensively by the madrigal composers and here again Byrd's contributions to the literature include such splendid examples as *Though Amaryllis dance in green* and *The match that's made*.

MODES AND TONALITY

The old church modes survived well into the sixteenth century, no doubt because plainsong melodies were still the basis of composition, but although Italian composers, including Palestrina, remained faithful to the modal system and conformed to it fairly strictly, in other parts of Europe the winds of change had already been blowing for some time. It had long been the custom to alter certain notes chromatically for one reason or another—to avoid a tritone, to form a cadence, to avoid the harmonic interval of the diminished fifth under certain circumstances, or to change the last chord from minor to major. Any singer worth his salt was expected to know when to make these chromatic alterations and it would therefore have been considered a gross insult to his intelligence to write them into his copy. So tones became semitones and semitones became tones without any accidental or visual indication being marked (a major headache for modern editors!): such conventional but unwritten modifications were known as *musica ficta*.[3]

At first *musica ficta* merely made for smoothness in modal part-writing but more and more it modified the modes themselves in the direction of our modern major and minor scales (together with their implications of key and modulation) until by the last quarter of the sixteenth century modern tonality had all but superseded the ancient modes. This was especially true in England where composers from Tallis onwards had a strongly developed sense of key and key relationships. Later composers were quick to realise the new and exciting possibilities of modulation and their experiments were often bold and strikingly modern in effect. By this time, of course, *musica ficta* had given way to a more exact notation using sharps and flats. Men like Byrd, Gibbons and Weelkes amongst the church composers and Wilbye amongst the madrigalists showed a remarkable grasp of the structure and relationships of the key system and could move confidently and easily from one key centre to another. Here, for example, is an oft-quoted passage from Byrd's *'Second' Service*:

[3] See pp. 53–4.

Byrd: *'Second' Service—Magnificat*[4]

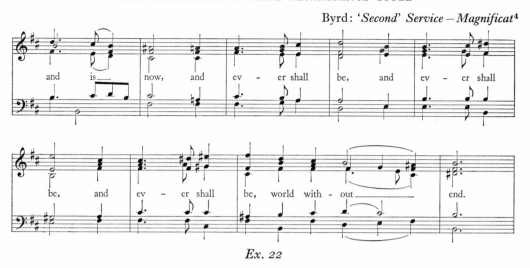

Ex. 22

COUNTERPOINT AND HARMONY

Counterpoint, as we have seen, is the weaving together of two or more melodic lines—the horizontal aspect of music; harmony is the chordal effect produced by the combination of these melodies at any given point in time—the vertical aspect of music. If we look at the following example horizontally we shall find some well known tunes combined together in 5-part counterpoint (not very academically!); if we look at it vertically we shall find that on the strong beats we have the following harmonies: D major, D major, A major, D major:

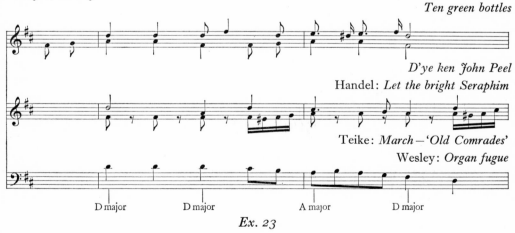

Ten green bottles

D'ye ken John Peel

Handel: *Let the bright Seraphim*

Teike: *March—'Old Comrades'*

Wesley: *Organ fugue*

D major   D major   A major   D major

Ex. 23

So the counterpoint produces harmony as a kind of by-product; indeed, it is almost impossible to have counterpoint without it making some sort of harmony. The converse does not hold good: it is quite possible, especially in keyboard music, to have harmony without counterpoint.

[4] This short score transcription taken from E. H. Fellowes: *William Byrd*, p. 129. (O.U.P.)

99

In the early days of the sixteenth century composers were much more interested in the combining of melodies than they were in the incidental harmonies so produced. Music was a sort of tapestry of interweaving strands which went serenely on their way untroubled by harmonic considerations. As the century advanced, however, musicians became increasingly aware of harmony as a component of contrapuntal writing until, by the end of the century, the underlying harmonic basis actually governed the progress of the individual strands. Though music was still fundamentally linear in con ception the interweaving parts were now written with an eye to some basic harmonic. scheme and even the melodic lines themselves carried inherent harmonic implications This is, exemplified by comparing one of Taverner's vocal lines with one of Gibbons's:

Taverner: *The 'Western Wynde' Mass*
(Counter-tenor part from *Gloria*)

Gibbons: *God is gone up*

Ex. 24

A young student, asked to 'harmonize' these melodies at the piano, might well quail before the Taverner example; it is just an undulating series of notes, vaguely A minorish, but devoid of any strong harmonic feeling. On the other hand, the second example 'harmonizes' itself; the harmonic implications are as strong and as clear-cut as they would be in a Bach fugue-subject or a theme by Beethoven. The pendulum had, in fact, already begun to swing from purely linear thinking towards vertical thinking, a swing that was to continue for another three hundred years. During this period composers achieved varying degrees of synthesis or compromise between the two styles: those, like Byrd, in the earlier part of the period still placed the emphasis on counterpoint; Bach, in the middle, struck a much more equal balance between the two, whilst the nineteenth-century writers thought more and more in terms of vertical harmony to the point where counterpoint, if it existed at all, was entirely subservient.

Because renaissance composers thought first and foremost in terms of counterpoint and (except in purely chordal writing) only incidentally in terms of harmony, it often happened that the horizontal movement of the individual voice-parts gave rise to passing harmonic clashes. Such clashes are so typical of the period that they will be discussed more properly in a later section.

The harmonic basis of sixteenth-century counterpoint is fairly easy to codify. Very briefly we may say that:

(a) except when used as passing notes, the intervals of the second and seventh above the bass were always discords requiring preparation;

(b) the fourth, augmented fourth and diminished fifth were always discords if they occurred between the bass and some other part and had therefore to be prepared and resolved accordingly. Between two upper parts they were permissible provided they were supported by the bass (as in a common or $\frac{6}{3}$ chord);

(c) major and minor thirds and sixths could be used freely;

(d) augmented fifths, augmented sixths and diminished fourths were used only experimentally;

(e) consecutive fifths and octaves were extremely rare.

FORM AND TEXTURE

The form of late Tudor and Jacobean church music was very simple and was, with few exceptions, largely governed by the words themselves. We have seen that the text was broken up into short clauses, as:

Sing we merrily unto God our strength. — Make a cheerful noise — unto the God of Jacob. — Take the shawm, — bring hither the tabret, — the merry harp with the lute. — Blow up the trumpet in the new moon, — e'en in the time appointed, — and upon our solemn feast-day. — For this was made — a statute for Israel — and a law of the God of Jacob.

Each of these sections was then set to music either contrapuntally or in block harmony. The contrapuntal sections could be treated in one of three ways:

(a) imitation (or 'fugato')
(b) canon, or
(c) free counterpoint.

In the first, one voice sang the words to an appropriate musical phrase and its 'point' was then taken up by other voices in turn, entering in a free sort of imitation. When the last voice had had its turn, the section would close in a partial or full cadence. Then the next 'point' would be introduced and taken up successively by the other voices as before, the previous point having dropped out of the picture. Composers soon learned to conceal the joins by dovetailing the entry of new points.[5]

Adopting the second or 'canonic' method, the imitation of one voice by another was much more exact and extended. Canons can be at the unison, octave, fifth or some other interval. If two voices take part in the canon it is called a canon 'two-in-one' (i.e. one melody for two voices). It is possible to have canons in three-in-one, four-in-one, etc. (a round, such as *Three Blind Mice*, is actually a canon four-in-one). Sometimes two different canons are carried on simultaneously, two voices to each; such a canon is called four-in-two. There are many other types of canon, too involved to discuss here: with some notable exceptions it is fairly safe to say that their artistic value varies in inverse

[5] See also p. 74.

ratio to their technical ingenuity. Two outstanding examples of canonic writing at this time are Tallis's astonishing 7-part canon *Miserere nostri*[6] and Byrd's 8-part *Diliges Dominum*; this last consists of four 2-part canons sung simultaneously, the second voice of each pair singing the first voice part through backwards! (Such retrograde canons are called *cancrizans* or *per recte et retro*.)

The third method, free counterpoint, can be taken loosely to include any texture which is contrapuntal in style yet not imitative.

All these types of texture, polyphonic and chordal, were available to the composer: he could adopt one or other of them for an entire work or he could ring changes on them from section to section. The sections themselves were often overlapped to avoid any break in the onward flow. By such a method of composition the music could obviously be kept going all the time there was any text left to set. Composers showed considerable imagination in securing variety and contrast within the obvious limitations of their medium. There were three main ways of doing this:

(a) by contrasting sections of polyphony with sections of chordal writing,
(b) by exploiting the difference in tone colours between high and low voices or between high and low registers of the same voices, and
(c) by contrasting the sonority of the full choir with sections of thinner texture — making frequent use of 2- and 3-part passages in 4-part works and 3- and 4-part passages in 5- and 6-part works.

As the modal system, weakened by *musica ficta*, gradually gave place to the major and minor key relationships, a fourth method of obtaining variety became increasingly important — that of modulation to nearly related keys, eventually returning to the home key. It was further found that this return could be so timed as to strengthen the feeling of finality of the concluding sections of the piece.

'Form' in the modern sense of the word was almost unknown at this time. Occasionally, if a work consisted of two or three short movements, one of them would be given a note-for-note repetition at the end, resulting in an ABA or ABCB shape (e.g. Weelkes's *Gloria in excelsis*). Almost unique is Gibbons's fine anthem *Hosanna to the Son of David*, an example of true ABA form within the movement itself, the second section being derived from material in the first.

UNDERLAYING THE WORDS

The nineteenth-century ideal of making voice-parts 'blend' together, so sacrificing much of their individuality in favour of an over-all harmonic synthesis, was quite foreign to the sixteenth-century musician who delighted in giving his parts as much individual freedom as possible by making them rhythmically independent of each other. To this end, anything which would disturb metrical regularity and break down what in these days we call 'the tyranny of the bar-line' was grist to the composer's mill; syncopations and cross-rhythms were, in fact, the very life-blood of renaissance polyphony.

It had been noticed that a change of syllable imparts a slight feeling of accent to a note; if, therefore, a syllabic change is arranged so that it falls on a normally unaccented note, that note will now carry a slight accent. Tudor composers seized upon this as yet another way of adding rhythmic interest and variety, deliberately contriving irregular

[6] See p. 74.

syllabic groupings; thus, if four quavers had to carry two syllables, the division would be one-plus-three or three-plus-one rather than two-plus-two:

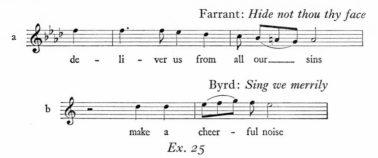

Ex. 25

To those unfamiliar with the idiom the following examples will all seem a little unusual, but with increasing familiarity it will be found that the underlaying is, in fact, easier to sing than the more orthodox regularity of nineteenth-century settings, whilst the displaced syllable not only gives an attractive lilt to the phrase but also gives it a light forward thrust:

Ex. 26

WORD-PAINTING

Certainly from the time of Josquin, if not earlier, composers had delighted to indulge in a certain amount of 'word-painting'. With the coming of the madrigal this form of pictorialism took on such significance that it became almost an essential feature of madrigal style and no composer, certainly no English composer, could resist obvious gestures on such words as 'high', 'fall', 'ascending', 'descending', 'joy', 'sighing', etc. Madrigal technique inevitably influenced sacred composition and what earlier had been merely an occasional indulgence now became a somewhat overworked mannerism, ranging from the ingenious to the naive. The following examples from the later sixteenth and early seventeenth centuries tell their own story:

Ex. 27

On a far higher plane aesthetically are those passages where, instead of attempting to illustrate individual words, the composer paints a more general picture or evokes some particular mood or emotion. Amongst many such passages two in particular spring to mind—first, Gibbons's lovely setting of the words 'Peace in heav'n' in the middle of *Hosanna to the Son of David* where for the space of four bars earthly tumult is hushed and the serenity of heaven gleams through. This is achieved by the simplest of means— low voices answering high in quiet 3-part chords—yet in its context this passage is unforgettable. Even more beautiful, perhaps, are the closing pages of the second part of Byrd's *Ne irascaris Domine* (often sung in its English translation *Bow thine ear*) where the constant reiteration of the pathetic phrase 'desolata est' ('desolate and void') not only gives us a vivid picture of almost inconceivable ruin and devastation but also depicts, with searing intensity, the hopeless and inarticulate longing of the exiles.

PITCH AND NOTATION

In the sixteenth century pitch was a good deal higher than it is now and the note which was then called F was very nearly as high as our modern G sharp. To perform the music at the pitch intended by the composer, and often to bring it within comfortable range of voices, it is therefore necessary to transpose it up a minor third.

There has also been an important change in notation due largely to the influence of keyboard composers. The sixteenth century breve, semibreve and minim were the equivalent of our modern semibreve, minim and crotchet respectively. Whereas we usually think of a semibreve as having four pulses, in those days it had only two—and they could be very fast! To the unwary, therefore, the white notes of renaissance music suggest a slow ponderous mode of performance entirely at odds with what the composer himself intended. Modern editors almost invariably compensate for these changes by transposing the scores up a minor third and halving the note values. Most of the examples given in this chapter have been so treated.

TUDOR AND JACOBEAN 'FINGERPRINTS'

Each century has its own musical style and mannerisms, a *lingua franca* shared by all the composers of the day. These mannerisms include little tricks of melody or harmony, regularly recurring clichés which are the stock-in-trade of their time, characteristic solutions of basic problems, some typical cadences, and other tell-tale fingerprints which give the music of each century its own particular character and flavour. Even the most casual listener to late renaissance music cannot fail to notice a number of such finger-prints, the more common of which may be briefly mentioned.

(a) Common Melodic Idioms. Certain melodic ideas occur again and again, due largely to the fact that they work easily in imitation; the rhythm and even the intervals may vary slightly between one piece and another but the basic shapes themselves were common property:

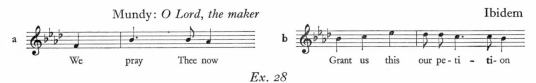

Mundy: *O Lord, the maker*   Ibidem

a   We   pray   Thee now   b   Grant us   this   our pe-ti - ti-on

Ex. 28

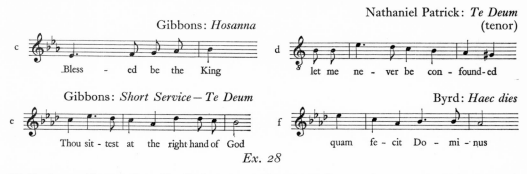

Ex. 28

(b) Cadence Formulae. Similarly, most cadences made use of one or other of a number of conventional endings, such as:

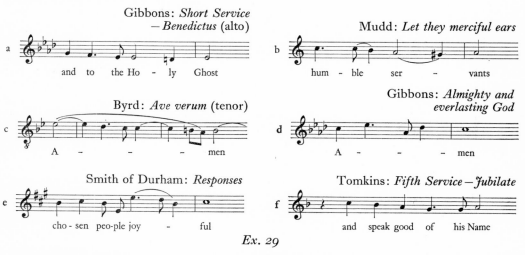

Ex. 29

(c) The Nota Cambiata. One of the most distinctive and ubiquitous of these mannerisms was the *nota cambiata*. This was normally a four-note figure which consisted essentially of the leap of a third, normally downwards, from an unessential note. It usually occurs in one of the following forms, the first being the commonest:

Ex 30

An extension of the idiom led to the so-called 'changing-note' figures:

Ex. 31

The *nota cambiata* was used variously as a melodic motif (as in Ex. 29e), as a cadence formula in an inner part, and sometimes as a constructional element in a web of polyphony, as in the following examples:

Morley: *Five-part Service*
(Amen of *Nunc dimittis*)

Gibbons: *Hosanna to the Son of David*

Ex. *32*

(d) Decorated Suspensions. English composers were, in general, much more enterprising, indeed daring, in their treatment of the suspension than were their Italian contemporaries and such ornamental resolutions as the following were of everyday occurrence:

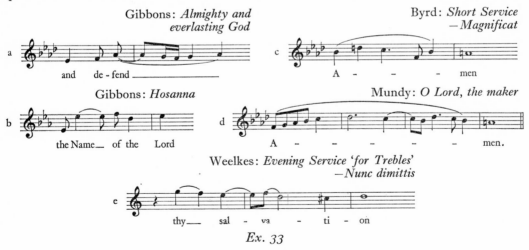

Ex. *33*

It was common practice for one suspension to resolve upon another and by an extension of this principle whole chains of suspensions could occur, usually arranged in the form of a sequence:

Tomkins: *Fourth Service — Te Deum*

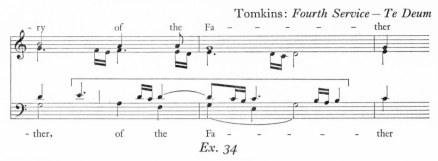

Ex. 34

(e) False Relations. Mention has already been made of incidental harmonic clashes brought about by the horizontal movement of the voice-parts. Typical of such clashes (there are other types as well) is the 'false relation' which can be found on nearly every page of Tudor music. It arises when a chromatically altered form of a note appears in close proximity to the natural form of the same note in another voice part: thus, if the tenors sing F in one chord and the trebles sing F sharp in the following chord, false relation is said to occur:

Ex. 35

A particularly beautiful cadence, involving false relation of the leading-note, was so much favoured by the Tudors and Jacobeans that it is often known as the 'English cadence'. The false relationship arises from the use of the descending form of the scale in one voice against the ascending form of it in another:

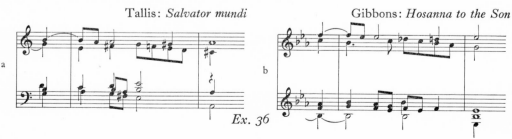

Ex. 36

Weelkes: *Evening Service for*
Trebles — Magnificat

Gibbons: *Short Service*
— Te Deum

Ex. 36

(f) Simultaneous Clashes. Sometimes, instead of the false relation existing between notes in two successive chords, it arises between two notes heard simultaneously in one chord and the effect produced, one of the most typical of the period, is both quaint and attractive. The resulting clash adds welcome piquancy to the smoothness of the counterpoint:

Tallis: *Candidi facta sunt*

Tallis: *In jejunio*

Farrant: *Call to remembrance*

Byrd: *Ave verum corpus*

Weelkes: *Evening Service for*
Trebles — Nunc dimittis

John Amner: *Remember not, Lord,*
our offences

Ex. 37

109

CHAPTER VI

William Byrd

It is a curious and unexplained freak of English history that the closing years of the sixteenth century and the first quarter of the seventeenth saw an extraordinary flowering of both literature and music. Of the poets and writers of the period we may mention Spenser, Sidney, Lyly, Lodge, Green, Bacon, Southwell, Daniel, Drayton, Campian, Nashe, Donne, Burton, the Fletchers, the Herberts, Wither and Walton: dramatists included Chapman, Marlowe, Dekker, Jonson, Heywood, Middleton, Marston, Tourneur, Webster, Beaumont, John Fletcher, Massinger, Ford, Shirley and, of course, Shakespeare himself. An even longer list of musicians can be compiled, the least of whom wrote effectively and in excellent taste whilst the best can worthily rank amongst the great composers of the century.

Just as the literature of the period can be conveniently grouped under two headings, dramatic and non-dramatic, so the choral and vocal music of the time can be divided into two main categories — sacred and secular. The latter consisted mainly of madrigals, though a number of balletts were written (notably those of Morley and Weelkes) whilst the solo song with lute, string, or vocal accompaniment developed into an important art-form in the hands of such men as Byrd, Dowland, Campian and Rosseter. Just as many of the poets were also dramatists and several dramatists were poets, so most church composers excelled in the writing of madrigals whilst a number of madrigalists made notable contributions to church music; whether we look upon such composers primarily as church musicians or as madrigalists is largely a matter of emphasis and proportion. This double interest in sacred and secular music resulted in a good deal of cross-fertilisation between the two: from church music, with its traditions of plainsong and polyphony, the secular field gained a wealth of technical skill and resource, an inner logic and strength, and an almost classical instinct for emotional restraint; at the same time, secular techniques, most of them imported from Italy and the Netherlands, gave to church music a stronger feeling for metre, increased flexibility in the handling of words, and such technical developments as the use of the solo voice with independent accompaniment.

At this time, when England could boast perhaps the greatest galaxy of literati the post-classical world has ever seen and when poetical genius appears almost to have been the birthright of every Englishman, one name stands alone, matchless and supreme, above all others — William Shakespeare. Music too had its Shakespeare, a transcendent genius who completely eclipsed all his illustrious contemporaries in every branch of composition practised at that time, both sacred and secular; a man acknowledged in his own day as 'a Father of Musick'[1] who was 'never without reverence to be named of the musicians',[2] loved and venerated by all who knew him, Latin scholar, man of letters,

[1] Cheque book of the Chapel Royal recording his death.
[2] Thomas Morley: *A plaine and easie Introduction to Practicall Musicke*; Edited R. A. Harman, p. 202 (Dent).

and one of the most outstanding and influential figures of that brilliant age: his name was William Byrd.

Far too many people who ought to know better indulge in that impossible, fruitless, and utterly silly game, 'Who is the greatest ——?' In arranging their hierarchy of composers they forget to take into account the capriciousness of historical accident. Had Beethoven been born in 1543, when keyboard writing was in its infancy and the orchestra unknown, he would now be just as unfamiliar to the general public as is William Byrd; by the same token, had Byrd lived two hundred and fifty years later there is every reason to believe that he would be universally acknowledged as one of the world's greatest composers. He 'was certainly the finest Elizabethan composer of Latin church music and one of the most versatile among the late renaissance masters anywhere'.[3] After Shakespeare, Byrd is without doubt the most imposing figure of the English Renaissance, towering above all his contemporaries. 'When discussing him, comparison can be made only to the other "princes" of music, Palestrina and Lassus, and, indeed, he has been called the English Palestrina.'[4] Speaking of him as a song-writer, Denis Stevens says, 'Compositions by Edwards, Parsons, Farrant, Nicholson, Patrick and Strogers demonstrate the excellence and variety of this basically simple combination of voice and string quartet, which was brought to its highest peak in the works of Byrd' who 'left far more songs for voice and strings than any other Elizabethan composer'.[5] As a pioneer of keyboard writing, Willi Apel says of him, 'Although Byrd seems to have been the first to cultivate the harpsichord extensively, he reached an artistic high-point which dwarfs all the other virginalists, except Gibbons.'[6] Fellowes, admittedly a somewhat insular partisan, sums all this up when he says that Byrd is 'recognised as standing supreme in English music. It may even be right to place him at the head of the sixteenth-century composers of all countries. This is not to say that he actually excelled such contemporaries as Palestrina, Lassus or Victoria as a composer of polyphonic music for the Church, even if some might be found who would endorse Peacham's opinion that in this branch of composition also, Byrd was at least their equal. But Byrd is outstanding because of his amazing variety of achievement. He excelled in every branch of composition known in his day and led the way into certain fields not previously explored, whereas most of the great musicians of the sixteenth century confined their outlook mainly to a single branch of composition. Byrd's wonderful versatility enables him to invite comparison with all the specialists of his time . . . It used to be said that the peaks of musical development are represented by three B's: Bach, Beethoven and Brahms. Representing the peak of pre-Bach development there stands a fourth B—William Byrd.'[7]

Byrd was born probably in 1543. Nothing is known of his parentage or early life though Fellowes's conjecture that he may have been one of the Children of the Chapel would explain certain circumstances of his later career. On 27 February 1563 he was appointed organist of Lincoln Cathedral and five years later he married Juliana Birley at St. Margaret's-in-the-Close. In February 1570 he was appointed a Gentleman of the Chapel Royal but continued in office at Lincoln until the end of 1572 when he went to London as joint organist of the Chapel Royal with Tallis, doubtless to ease the burden for the older man. Reference has already been made (p. 69) to the licence granted to

[3] Gustave Reese: *Music in the Renaissance*, p. 787. (Dent.)
[4] Paul Henry Lang: *Music in Western Civilisation*, pp. 286–7. (Dent.)
[5] Denis Stevens: *A History of Song*, pp. 81–2. (Hutchinson.)
[6] Willi Apel: *Masters of the Keyboard*, p. 61. (Harvard University Press.)
[7] E. H. Fellowes: *William Byrd*, pp. 243–5. (O.U.P., 2nd Edition).

them by the Queen on 22 January 1575, which gave them a twenty-one-year monopoly for the printing of music and music-paper; also to the first fruit of this monopoly—the 1575 set of *Cantiones Sacrae* to which both contributed.

Byrd was a lifelong Catholic who scorned to hide his convictions even when their public profession was unwise or even, at times, dangerous. After the Queen had reigned for twenty years, surrounded by intrigue, plots and counter-plots (real or imaginary), her attitude towards religious issues underwent a marked change; she suspected the Catholics of sedition and treason (not without foundation) and tolerance soon gave way to persecution. Some suffered martyrdom, some were imprisoned, most were fined or deprived, all were registered as 'recusants' (i.e. they refused to attend the services of the Reformed Church) and had from time to time to pay levies to redeem their recusancy. Byrd went to live at Harlington, West Middlesex, in 1577 and almost from the beginning he and his wife appeared frequently in the county Sessions Rolls as recusants; however, they appear to have been dealt with very leniently, perhaps because Byrd was known to enjoy the Queen's favour. At times he laid himself open to the suspicion of taking part in Popish plots but his innocence seems to have been clearly established and he continued his work at the Chapel unmolested. It may be wondered why the Queen retained 'a stiff Papist' in her service to direct the music of the Chapel Royal; also, if Byrd was sincere in his beliefs, how could he reconcile his conscience with taking a leading part in daily Protestant worship? The first question is easily answered: for the prestige and glory of her Court she was anxious to attract all the greatest men of her realm even if, in return for their services, she had to wink at their religious convictions (providing they were unswerving in their personal loyalty to her and kept well clear of Popish plots!). Discussing Byrd's apparent duplicity, Fellowes says, 'he was an earnest Catholic but he was no bigot; and we may judge from the beauty and sincerity of his music written for the Reformed Church that the musical services with which his musical duties associated him were by no means devoid of spiritual significance to him. Why then need he sacrifice such a position seeing that his livelihood largely depended on it?'[8]

From the Sessions Rolls it appears that his first wife, Juliana, died early in 1587; sometime later he married again. When Tallis died in 1585, Byrd became sole proprietor of the printing monopoly and in the next few years several collections of his works were published—*Psalmes, Sonets, & songs* (1588), *Songs of sundrie natures* (1589), the first book of *Cantiones Sacrae* (1589), and the second book of *Cantiones Sacrae* (1591). In 1593 he moved from Harlington to Stondon Massey, Essex, where he seems to have been very prosperous. Both from Harlington and Stondon he must have ridden over to Greenwich or Whitehall almost daily to attend to his duties at the Chapel Royal. It is a pity that the middle period of his life, when he was at the zenith of his powers, was clouded by a series of complex, prolonged, and time-wasting lawsuits relating to various properties in which he was interested. Early in 1606, very probably, his second wife, Ellen, died. He retained his position at the Chapel till the end of his long life though the last few years seem to have been spent virtually in retirement at Stondon. He died on 4 July 1623.

Byrd was a very prolific writer and the catalogue of his surviving works includes:

Cantiones Sacrae (with Tallis) 1575
Cantiones Sacrae (First book) 1589
Cantiones Sacrae (Second book) 1591

[8] Ibid., p. 37.

Gradualia (First book) 1605
Gradualia (Second book) 1607
Psalmes, Sonets, & songs of Sadnes and pietie (1588)
Songs of sundrie natures (1589)
Psalmes, Songs, and Sonnets (1611)
Three Masses
Motets and other Latin works
Preces and Responses
A Litany
Festal psalms
Two complete Services
Two evening Services
Fragments of a Te Deum and Benedictus
Anthems and other sacred music with English words
Madrigals
Consort songs
Canons and rounds
Music for viols
Keyboard works (nearly 150 pieces)

We are concerned here only with Byrd's setting of sacred texts but even this field is much too vast for adequate discussion; comment must be limited to a mere handful of representative works. We have seen with what tenacity he clung to the older faith so it is not surprising that he preferred to set Latin texts nor that much of his finest music is to be found amongst his Latin settings.

THE LATIN MASSES

The three Masses for the Roman rite — one 3-part, one 4-part and one 5-part — have an interesting background. All the part-books were issued without a title-page, no doubt because, for safety's sake, they were printed and distributed clandestinely. (It is now known that Thomas East was the printer.) So it has always been anybody's guess when they were printed and various dates have been suggested: Fellowes thought perhaps 1605,[9] the British Museum catalogue opted for 1588. Some smart detective work by Peter Clulow eventually shed new light on the problem and he has convincingly deduced that the 4-part Mass was issued in 1592–93, the 3-part in 1593–94, and the 5-part *c.* 1595.[10] It must have needed great courage to handle 'Popish' publications in those days of bigoted Protestantism: only a few short years before, Edmund Campion had been tortured, racked three times, then hanged, cut down while still alive, disembowelled, and finally quartered, merely because he refused to recant his Catholic beliefs,[11] and many other Catholics suffered a similar fate. Yet not only were Byrd's Masses published; Clulow has shown that a second edition of the 3- and 4-part settings appeared, still without title-pages, some four to six years later. We don't know how many were printed in either edition nor how they were distributed; no doubt the numbers were quite small

[9] Ibid., p. 52.
[10] Peter Clulow: *Publication Dates for Byrd's Latin Masses* (Music and Letters, Vol. 47, No. 1, 1966).
[11] Evelyn Waugh: *Edmund Campion*, pp. 160, 191, 197. (Longmans, 3rd Ed., 1961.)

and it is likely that the printer sold them at his own discretion to known sympathisers as an under-the-counter line; perhaps some of them went abroad. Certainly post-Reformation settings of the Mass published by a notorious recusant would have been even more obnoxious to the reform party than pre-Reformation settings and they would have sought out and destroyed copies whenever possible: thus the destruction, both then and during the Commonwealth, is likely to have been especially thorough.

All three Masses share certain characteristics which were unusual at this time:

(1) in each a setting of the Kyrie is provided; (due to liturgical considerations the polyphonic Kyrie had almost dropped out of use in England since the early part of the fifteenth century);[12]

(2) Byrd again makes use of the old 'head-motif' technique:[13] in the 3-part Mass the head-motif appears at the beginning of all movements except the Sanctus; except in its Credo, the 4-part Mass makes use of two motifs; and in the Mass *a 5* paired motifs are again used except in the Sanctus;

(3) Nowhere does he make use of a *cantus firmus*.

In the 3-part Mass the Kyrie, which is very simple, begins in F and ends in A; Gloria in excelsis is broken up into short phrases separated by minim rests; in the Credo there is a hint of word-painting at 'qui ex patre filioque procedit' which is given to two voices alone in canon; the Sanctus is perhaps the finest movement and builds up to a powerful climax; Benedictus, like the Kyrie, is short and simple, and Agnus Dei is full of tenderness and spiritual contemplation.

The Mass *a 4* is more extended. All its movements except the Sanctus open with treble and alto voices alone and its Kyrie is the longest of the three. Gloria in excelsis is another good example of Byrd's choral orchestration, much of it being written for changing groups of three voices; in the Credo there is a delightful melisma on 'coelis' which suggests the flight down from heaven; the 'crucifixus' section is given to three voices in block chords by way of contrast with the polyphonic texture of the rest of the movement, and a change of mood at 'Et unam sanctam' introduces an energetic conclusion; in the Sanctus the 'Pleni sunt coeli' section is set for the three upper voices, the bass being held in reserve to lead off the final 'Osannas'; Benedictus is rather more flowing in style. The gem of the whole work is the Agnus Dei, a sublime setting worthy to stand beside anything of Palestrina's: there is a beautiful sequential passage for the bass in the second 'miserere nobis', and the gently lapping phrases of 'Dona nobis pacem' bring the work to a heart-searching close of almost unearthly loveliness (see Example 38 opposite).

The 5-part Mass is one of Byrd's most powerful and noble works. It is by far the longest of the three and is rather more modal in feeling than the others. Except for Sanctus and Benedictus the various movements begin almost identically. The use of five voice-parts enables him to use them selectively in 3- and 4-part groupings, reserving the full weight of the 5-part choir for climactic passages, as at 'Gratias agimus' and 'Quoniam tu solus' in the Gloria and 'Crucifixus' and 'Et unam sanctam' in the Credo. The Kyrie is simple and straightforward; in the Gloria where the verbal phrases are short, the musical phrases too are short and end usually with a cadence; the texture of the Credo is more smoothly flowing though the 'Et resurrexit' passage affords a marked

[12] See p. 67 (footnote).
[13] See pp. 70 and 163.

114

Byrd: *Mass for Four Voices — Agnus Dei*

Ex. 38

contrast and is interesting for its rapidly shifting sequence of keys; (typically, a triple measure is introduced for 'tertia die'). Benedictus is surprisingly short and its 'Osanna' is identical with that of Sanctus. As in the Mass *a 4*, Byrd seems to have lavished his most profound music on the Agnus Dei: the first section is in three voice-parts and the second in four, keeping the full choir for the final section; the last few bars bring the whole Mass to a close of sublime serenity.

THE MOTETS

Byrd's other Latin works, loosely called motets, comprise forms as various as antiphons, festal psalms, hymns, sequences, Propers of the Mass, and other liturgical movements. Most of the motets are to be found in the printed collections of 1575, 1589, 1591, 1605 and 1607: these, covering a time span of thirty-two years, are so spaced that they offer a good guide to the composer's development. In the first, *Cantiones quae ab argumento sacrae vocantur* published jointly with Tallis, Byrd, still a young man of thirty-two, was out to establish himself; hence the seventeen motets include a wide variety of forms and styles. All show immense fluency and contrapuntal resource but some of them are somewhat prolix and diffuse. We see the composer forging his technique and experimenting, not always successfully, with new harmonic sonorities. Some of these experiments, like those in *Domine secundum actum meum*, sound surprisingly harsh compared with his mature style; others by their beauty and appropriateness give us a foretaste of things to come. His youthful preoccupation with technical considerations is further evidenced by the intricate canons found among these pieces: they are cunningly devised and one of them, *Miserere mihi, Domine*, is an outstanding example of the form. But canons often bear the same relationship to music that crosswords and acrostics do to literature and by their very ingenuity can draw attention to themselves to the detriment of the music as a whole; unless handled with the greatest artistry they sound artificial and self-conscious. In his later works Byrd seems to have recognised this danger; 'possessing marvellous skill in canonical writing, it is characteristic of his fine nature that he so seldom gave way to the temptation to display it'.[14] Many of the motets in this first set were apparently not intended for liturgical use as their texts had been selected from non-liturgical sources. Often, in fact, Byrd seems to have chosen his texts more for their 'expressive' possibilities than for their liturgical usefulness and this in itself was something new, even revolutionary. Composers of his generation were showing an increasing interest in 'expressiveness' in their treatment of words, in marked contrast to the unemotional and quasi-instrumental styles of the early and mid-Renaissance. Here again they were following a trend which had spread from the continent.

Undoubtedly the finest piece in the 1575 collection is the 5-part *Emendemus in melius*, which is no doubt why Byrd placed it first of his seventeen contributions. The maximum effect is obtained by means which look deceptively simple, but in a fine analytical essay Dr. Joseph Kerman has shown how the melodic line achieves a subtle synthesis of Gregorian chant and renaissance style, coupled with a sensitive feeling for the overall melodic form and shape; how the texture similarly shifts back and forth between chordal writing, half homophony, half polyphony, and imitative texture, with decorative melismata and suspensions; how the rhythm is cunningly controlled and varied; how bold is Byrd's tonal scheme, touching keys as remote as A flat and E minor; and how harmony and dissonance are nicely calculated to underpin the structure. Finally, and most important, he shows how all these various devices are made to interact and interlock in order to project the text with the utmost force and drama.[15] Nos. 10 and 11 in the set, *Aspice, Domine* and the ever-popular *Attollite portas*, are large-scale imitative settings in which the avant-garde quest for expressivity is especially apparent. *Aspice, Domine* has a plaintive passage divided between high and low voices to suggest 'desolata civitas', a sudden entry of the full choir in 6-part polyphony at 'plena divitiis' and agitated rhythms at 'non est qui consoletur eam'. *Attollite portas* is animated and brilliant: the words 'Quis est ipse Rex gloriae?' are sung three times in succession by three different pairs of voices, each pair a fourth lower than the previous pair; at the opening of the Gloria three lower

---

[14] E. H. Fellowes: *William Byrd*, p. 179. (O.U.P., 2nd Ed., 1948.)
[15] Joseph Kerman: *On William Byrd's 'Emendemus in melius'*. *Musical Quarterly*, Vol. XLIX, 4, October 1963, pp. 431–449.

voices echo the three upper voices in a passage which includes some striking semitonal clashes and consecutive seconds almost in the manner of Bach:

Byrd: *Attollite portas*

Ex. 39

The next motet, *O lux beata Trinitas*, begins similarly with the three lower voices answering the three high voices: it is in three sections of which the third, 'Deo Patri sit gloria', is a strict and lengthy canon three-in-one between 1st M, 1st A and T. *Laudate, pueri*, another brilliant 6-part setting, is also in three main sections though the piece is through-composed and the sections are dovetailed. Each section is repeated to different words and in each repeat the two alto parts are interchanged and so are the two bass parts. No. 19, *Siderum rector*, which Byrd called a hymn, is one of the most immediately attractive items in the book. It begins in 5-part block harmony but becomes increasingly polyphonic towards the end. The words are sung through twice, first by the three upper voices with the tune in the 1st meane part, then by the full choir with the tenors taking over the same tune: the Gloria section is also sung twice, first by the lower voices with a new melody in the tenor, then by the full choir, the 1st meanes now having the previous tenor tune.

Diliges Dominum is a highly ingenious canon which Byrd, as a young man, must have revelled in solving. Technically it is a canon eight-in-four cancrizans; that is, it consists of four 2-part canons sung simultaneously, so arranged that in each pair one voice part is the same as the other sung backwards. Put in another way, two 4-part choirs could sing the work starting from the two ends at the same time, meeting in the middle, and passing through each other; at the conclusion they would both have sung precisely the same thing. This sounds an astonishing technical feat but in practice such a canon is not so difficult to write as its description suggests. It has to be admitted though that for all its canonic intricacy the motet as a whole is more contrived than inspired and in performance sounds dull and stilted. In contrast, No. 29 *Miserere mihi, Domine* is a moving and deeply expressive penitential motet which happens also to be a highly complex canon. Both this and No. 33 *Libera me, Domine* make use of a plainsong *cantus firmus* in long notes. *Miserere mihi* is in six parts. As soon as the plainsong Miserere has been sung through in the bass part the canon is introduced, this time four-in-two to the same words. The top two parts sing a modified version of the *cantus firmus* in canon whilst at the same time the two lowest voices are also in canon, the middle parts being free. This is canonic writing at its best.

In addition to the volume shared with Tallis, Byrd himself published two collections of *Cantiones Sacrae* dated 1589 and 1591. These dates give no clue to the actual date of composition as it was his custom to gather his manuscripts together from time to time as they accumulated and publish them corporately as a set; hence the pieces in these two sets could have been written at any time between 1575 and the date of publication. Many of them circulated in manuscript long before they were published, often in very inaccurate copies; indeed, in the title of *Psalmes, Sonets, & songs* of 1588 he actually says 'whereof, some of them going abroad among divers, in untrue coppies are heere truely corrected'. These many 'untrue coppies' have been a headache to scholars and editors ever since. For more accurate dating we must look in other directions — internal evidence, biographical evidence, contemporary records and publications, dates of manu-script copies, methods of notation, watermarks, etc. — a field for the specialist.[16] But although the 1589 and 1591 sets include some earlier pieces, the sets as a whole show a style which is more taut and concise than that of 1575 and yet at the same time more flexible and expressive. The level of inspiration is almost consistently higher, the technique more assured, the harmony less experimental, the part-writing smoother and with less polyphonic padding. Some motets are almost madrigalian in their brilliance. As with the 1575 set, none of the pieces in the 1589 or 1591 collections has any specific liturgical function.

Though there are only sixteen complete motets in the 1589 publication, eight of them have two separate sections or 'movements', *Tribulationes civitatum* has three and *Deus, venerunt gentes* has four, making a total of twenty-nine all independently indexed. All are 5-part works.

Defecit in dolore, first in the collection, was probably one of the last to be composed and shows the economy and precision of Byrd's mature style. The next two motets, *Domine, praestolamur* and *O Domine, adiuva me,* are earlier compositions. The latter is a less happy example of that 'amorphous' style half way between block chords and imitative polyphony seen at its most fruitful in *Emendemus in melius* and best described perhaps as block harmony polyphonically decorated. It was this balancing of block chords with fluid part-writing which was later to become the basis of baroque texture. *Tristitia et*

---

[16] For a scholarly attempt to date Byrd's motets see Dr. Joseph Kerman: *Byrd's Motets: Chronology and Canon. Journal of the American Musicological Society,* Vol. XIV, No. 3, 1961.

anxietas expresses the suffering and yearning of a sin-stricken soul: it is a work of great beauty, often achieved by unusual harmonic effects like these:

Byrd: *Tristitia et anxietas*

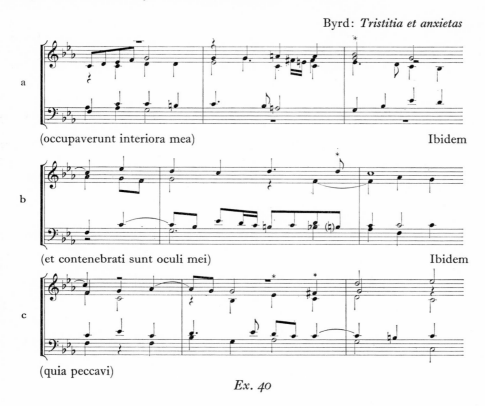

(occupaverunt interiora mea)   Ibidem

(et contenebrati sunt oculi mei)   Ibidem

(quia peccavi)

Ex. 40

The first catches us unawares by its unexpectedness; the second is much harsher and depicts the agony of blindness: the third shows Byrd's enterprising use of the highly expressive augmented sixth chord; there are only five examples known of it in his works and he seems to have been the only English composer to use it up to this time (though probably some of the Italians had used it long before). *Vide, Domine* (No. 9) is remarkable for its advanced harmony and powerful modulations into remote keys, especially at the words 'desolata Civitas electa' where we actually experience the bitter nostalgia of the exiles: its beautiful close is worth quoting, if only to show the poignant effect produced by the two striking chords marked with an asterisk:

Byrd: *Vide, Domine*

Ex. 41

Vigilate (No. 16), another late work, seems almost madrigalian in its vivid touches of realism—the descending phrase on 'sero', the cock crowing at 'an galli cantu', the breathless haste of 'ne cum venerit repente', and the sleepy head-nodding phrase on 'dormientes':

Byrd: *Vigilate, nescitis enim*

Ex. 42

No. 17, *In resurrexione tua* is short and full of rhythmic vitality. It is interesting that both in this and in *Laetentur coeli* the word 'exultet' is treated in similar fashion, with exciting imitations and cross-rhythms in short notes. No. 18, *Aspice, Domine* is the only motet in the book to be constructed on a plainsong *cantus firmus*; partly for this and partly because of its harsher dissonances it seems an early work more akin to those in the 1575 book.

The gem of the whole collection is probably *Ne irascaris* and especially its second part *Civitas sancti tui* to which several English texts were adapted during Byrd's lifetime. Of these, *Bow thine ear, O Lord* is now the most familiar. *Ne irascaris* is a good example of the composer's skill in using choral tone colours expressively; thus at the very outset there is a section for low voices in close harmony in their lowest register, a passage which is at once echoed by the high voices. The second movement, *Civitas sancti tui*, falls into three main sections; the first and third, both richly polyphonic, are bridged by a short passage in block harmony. In the first of these sections there is another lovely example of the augmented sixth (see Ex. 40c p. 119) used here to intensify the plea for Divine mercy:

Byrd: *Ne irascaris Domine*

Ex. 43

The harmonic middle section is of the rarest beauty; the utter devastation of the stricken city is lamented first by a quartet of high voices, then by the underparts an octave lower, in chords so simple that their appearance on paper gives little conception of their overwhelming sadness and burning poignancy:

Byrd: *Ne irascaris Domine*
(Second part: *Civitas sancti tui*)

Ex. 44

The F major chord produces an extraordinarily desolating effect, an effect which in the low voice repetition is immensely enhanced by the B minor chord which follows. Certainly this is one of those rare and sublime moments in music when our ordinary human experience is completely transcended. Immediately afterwards the voices take up a gently sighing phrase on the word 'Ierusalem' to which an appropriately bitter-sweet touch is added by the beautiful false-relation in the fifth bar:

Byrd: *Ne irascaris Domine*
(Second part: *Civitas sancti tui*)

Ex. 45

The closing words 'desolata est' ('desolate and void') are sung to a falling phrase of the utmost tenderness which is repeated upwards of thirty times, its very reiteration producing a cumulative effect of absolute and infinite desolation. This passage inevitably brings to mind the Agnus Dei of the 4-part Mass.

The 1591 anthology of Cantiones Sacrae again includes several early pieces which had long been circulating in manuscript, as well as items which may have been written especially for this publication. It comprises thirteen 5-part and eight 6-part motets, some of which again consist of two or three shorter pieces independently indexed. The first item in the book *Laudibus in sanctis*, a paraphrase of Psalm 150, was a late work. It is really a cluster of three motets, spaciously designed on a large scale, which together form one of Byrd's most extended pieces. The second movement, *Magnificum Domini*, is notable for its complex rhythmic counterpoint in a fast-moving triple measure; at the end of the third movement, *Hunc arguta*, there is a grand broadening into long notes, providing a splendid peroration to the whole triptych. (It is interesting to record that both here and in *Cantate Domino* (No. 29) Byrd uses the crotchet as his unit of measurement rather than the minim, thus anticipating later practice.) *Quis est homo* (No. 3) and *Salve Regina* (No. 6) were also recently composed at the time of publication and show the structural logic and economy of means characteristic of Byrd's maturity.

In the 5-part section of the book there are two outstandingly fine penitential works — *Haec dicit Dominus*, scored for men's voices ATTBB and thereby gaining immeasurably in effect, and *Miserere mei* which is largely homophonic in structure. The particular virtue of this latter piece lies in the ease and beauty of its modulations, a virtue which it shares with the similar piece *Emendemus in melius* in the 1575 anthology. *Recordare, Domine* (No. 17) is in the diffuse and verbose style of *Aspice, Domine* in the 1589 book and is probably an early work; its second part *Exsurge, Domine* also overstays its welcome though it is partly redeemed by many passages of singular beauty.

Of the 6-part motets, the masterly *Domine, non sum dignus* gives a graphic description of the healing of the nobleman's son: it abounds in subtle touches of expressive and descriptive writing. The words of the penitential motet *Infelix ego* (No. 24) are neither liturgical nor biblical. Byrd's setting is again rather long drawn out — and hence an early composition. The ending is exceptionally fine and this may explain its wide popularity in Byrd's own day. On the other hand *Domine, salva nos* (No. 31) is one of the most deeply moving works in the whole set, an extended exercise in that vein of wistful melancholy in which Byrd excelled. In contrast to these profound penitential compositions are the two brilliant pæans of joy *Cantate Domino* and *Haec dies*. This last, both in style and mood, has much in common with the Christmas 'carroll' *This day Christ was born* (see pp. 135-7): three twos are contrasted with, and sometimes pitted against, two threes and the changes of rhythm are many and various. The following passage is typical (see Example 46 opposite.) The result is tremendously exciting in performance and yet one feels that the piece is entirely madrigalian in conception; *fa la las* could easily replace the 'et laetemurs' without changing a single note whilst fair Diana, complete with her entourage of shepherds and nymphs, would not feel the least bit out of place amongst the exulting throng.

Art historians find it neat and tidy, if not always very accurate, to divide their biographical chapters into three phases: they are apt to write of the early or student works, the middle or mature period, and the late or final period in which their subject stands upon the summit of his previous achievements to peer into new and uncharted regions. If some such classification were applied to Byrd his two volumes of *Gradualia* (published 1605 and 1607) might well represent his final period. Perhaps the chief change is in his response to his text: whereas in the *Cantiones Sacrae* volumes the words frequently inspire him melodically and even harmonically phrase by phrase, embracing at times an almost madrigalian pictorialism, so now his response has become far more refined and subtle. His expression is generalised rather than particularised and he prefers to evoke a mood rather than paint individual words. Often the earlier brilliance is replaced by a golden mellowness, an inner luminosity which glows sometimes with the soft radiance of

Ex. 46

an old master, sometimes with the mystical fire of ecstasy. We are reminded again and again in these pages of the great Spanish mystic Victoria. Byrd's immense technique has now become almost unconscious, his harmony richer and more expressive, and his construction even more terse and economical. Indeed, this concision is sometimes carried to the point where it inhibits the composer's imagination. Furthermore, for reasons soon to be discussed, there is often some loss of structural unity and cohesion.

Volume I (1605) is in three parts: Part 1 provides thirty-two 5-part motets for the principal Feasts of the Virgin Mary—(1) In Festo Purificationis, (2) In Nativitate S. Mariae Virginis, (3) Pro Adventu, (4) Post Nativitatem Domini, (5) Post Septuagesima, (6) In Annuntiatione B. Mariae, (7) In Assumptione B. Mariae Virginis, (8) In Festo Omnium Sanctorum. Part 2 gives twenty 4-part works and Part 3 has eleven 3-part works for other feasts and holy days, mostly associated with the Blessed Virgin, a total of sixty-three motets. The three Parts were numbered independently, probably because they went to the printer separately. Volume II (1607) also has three parts scored respectively for four, five and six voices but the forty-six motets are here numbered consecutively: they provide Mass and Office settings for other principal holy days. Within these three sections, as in Part 1 of Volume I, groups of texts proper to the various feasts are given headings from the liturgical calendar. Most of the *Gradualia* motets are constructed in a number of short sections or 'movements'; even so, most of them are considerably shorter than the *Cantiones Sacrae* motets.

In a most important article which adds immeasurably to our understanding of the *Gradualia*, James Jackman has demonstrated that in addition to those liturgical events specifically provided for under the various headings, a whole range of Mass Propers for a further series of occasions could be compiled by a curious and unique system which Byrd devised.[17] The system works at two levels. Firstly, complete motets can be selected and rearranged in a new sequence; thus a summer Lady-Mass could be made up as follows:

Introit:	*Salve, sancta Parens* (I.1.6)
Gradual:	*Benedicta et venerabilis* (I.1.7–8)
Alleluia:	*Post partum, Virgo* (I.1.18)
Offertory:	*Ave Maria* (I.1.14)
Communion:	*Beata viscera* (I.1.11)

Secondly, many of the short sections or movements within the motets are designed to be interchangeable with similar sections in other motets. By transferring such sections from one piece to another on a do-it-yourself basis it is possible to assemble a complete motet for almost any occasion not otherwise provided for. Thus the Introit for the post-Christmas Lady-Mass, *Vultum tuum* (I.1.16) lacks its psalm verse and doxology 'Eructavit cor meum . . . Gloria Patri', but these can be extracted from *Salve, sancta Parens* (I.1.6). This same extract, 'Eructavit cor meum', can similarly be used to complete the Gradual for the same Mass.

Salve, sancta Parens itself raises a problem. The first section ends with a full cadence, fermata and bar-line. Next comes a self-contained 'alleluia' section which similarly ends with a full close and bar-line. These full closes, fermati and bar-lines have the effect of musical parentheses. Then follows the 'Eructavit cor meum' movement which seems so much in demand. Now it so happens that *Salve, sancta Parens* is the Introit both for the

---

[17] James L. Jackman: *Liturgical Aspects of Byrd's Gradualia. Musical Quarterly*, Vol. XLIX, 1 (1963), pp. 17–37.

Nativity of the Virgin Mary on 8 September when no 'alleluia' is called for, and also for the Lady-Mass for Paschal time when an 'alleluia' is prescribed. Hence Byrd has obligingly made the 'alleluia' detachable. Similarly the 'alleluia' section in *Diffusa est gratia* (I.1.22) is anomalous when the motet is used as Gradual, verse and Tract for the Annunciation (where Byrd has placed it) but is obligatory when used as Gradual, verse and Alleluia for the Assumption: again it has been put in musical parentheses so that it can be included or omitted. The same applies to the 'alleluia' sections in *Beata es, Virgo* (I.1.10), *Beata viscera* (I.1.11), *Ave Maria* (I.1.14), *Ecce Virgo* (I.1.15) and *Vultum tuum* (I.1.16); under the liturgical headings where Byrd has placed them these motets do not need their 'alleluias' but they could need them when used for other occasions. In *Constitues eos* (II.39) this optional treatment is extended to the words 'in omni progenie et generatione' which are not wanted when the motet is used as a Gradual and verse for SS. Peter and Paul but are requisite when it is used as an Offertory for the same Feast; as usual the optional passage is marked off with fermati and bar-lines. But the psalm verse 'Pro patribus . . .' needed for the Gradual must be omitted for the Offertory. Hence it would be a liturgical *faux pas* to sing both the 'Pro patribus' section and 'in omni progenie . . .' in the same performance.

There are many other traps for the unwary. Thus one Responsory is divided into two separate motets, *O magnum mysterium* and *Beata Virgo* (II.8–9); so is the Tract for the Blessed Sacrament Votive Mass which becomes *Ab ortu solus* and *Venite comedite* (II.13–14): these motets should therefore always be paired. Conversely *Diffusa est gratia* consists of a Gradual and a Tract, while in *Timete Dominum* (I.1.30) and *Oculi omnium* (I.2.2) a Gradual and verse and Alleluia and verse are given continuous settings. Again it was Byrd's custom to attach the Alleluia to the end of the Gradual; if however the Gradual was likely to be used after Septuagesima (when the Alleluia and verse is replaced by the Tract) then he made the Alleluia detachable. If not, there was no sectional break between the Gradual and Alleluia. Those responsible for performing *Gradualia* motets would do well to consult James Jackman's article if they wish to be sure of observing liturgical propriety.

The wide range of permutations and combinations available justifies Byrd's claim in his preface, addressed to 'True Lovers of Music', to have 'set forth . . . the Offices for the whole year which are proper to the chief Feasts of the Blessed Virgin Mary and of All Saints . . . also the Office at the Feast of Corpus Christi, with the more customary antiphons of the same Blessed Virgin . . . also all the hymns composed in honour of the Virgin'.[18] Incomplete texts can be completed and indeed of the seven Masses in Vol. I, Part 1, only those for the Nativity of the Virgin and for All Saints are liturgically complete; the other five lack one or more parts which can be found elsewhere in the *Gradualia* sets. Furthermore, in the Mass motets both the tonality and the vocal scoring are made to correspond so as to facilitate likely transferrals: thus no inartistic juxtaposition of unrelated 'keys' will arise, neither will a section of 6-part writing be incorporated into an otherwise 4-part Mass. Sometimes Byrd directs the repetition of a complete motet: for example, instead of following the Offertory *Felix namque* (I.1.19) with a setting of the Communion text, he directs that an existing setting *Beata viscera* (I.1.11) should be sung. Occasionally, as in *Beata Virgo* (II.9), Byrd's instruction to sing the first section through again results in a clear-cut ABA form, very rare at this time.

Byrd's economical plan of not resetting texts already used in other motets has some

[18] Oliver Strunk: *Source Readings in Music History*, p. 329. (Faber, 1950.)

disadvantages. Firstly, for convenience of transference the individual sections are often so short that the composer's imagination becomes constrained within too narrow limits and the writing sometimes seems rather cramped and stilted: longer movements give him more space to develop his ideas. Secondly, by writing a series of interchangeable motet 'elements' there is an inevitable sacrifice of constructional unity within the motet as a whole, even at times a feeling of disjointedness, however lovely the individual sections may be in themselves.

Not all the motets in the *Gradualia* volumes pertain to Byrd's main liturgical purpose. Some are complete and independent motets included simply for the delectation of 'True Lovers of Music'. Of the sixty-three motets in Volume I fifteen are irrelevant to the overall scheme—(I.1.26–28; I.2.9–11, 15–17 and 20; and I.3.6–10): in Volume II only two of the forty-six are irrelevant, *Laudate Dominum* (II.45) and *Venite, exultemus* (II.46).

Byrd almost certainly intended the *Gradualia* to be sung in the private chapels of wealthy Catholic families but, alas, his venture could hardly have appeared at a worse time. Publication of the first volume happened to coincide with the Gunpowder Plot and the relative leniency which Catholics had enjoyed for the previous year or two ended abruptly in a series of savage reprisals. Though the position had eased again slightly by the time the second volume appeared, circumstances were still not very propitious. Fellowes states 'in 1610 there was a demand for a second edition of both books'.[19] But the 1610 version is not a true second edition; it is merely the first edition re-issued with new title pages. This, coupled with the fact that so few copies of the two sets have survived, suggests that circulation was extremely limited. It seems likely that in the tide of anti-Catholic feeling engendered by the Gunpowder Plot, Byrd himself withdrew the first edition, re-issuing it in 1610 when times were safer.

Of the 109 motets only a few can be singled out for brief comment and these on a somewhat arbitrary basis. In the first book of 1605, two stand somewhat apart from the others, *Adoramus te, Christe* and *Turbarum voces*. The first is not a motet at all but a solo song with accompaniment for viols, like some of those in *Psalmes, Sonets, & songs* of 1588 of which Byrd wrote 'originally made for instruments to express the harmonye and one voyce to pronounce the dittie'. It certainly seems an early work. Why did Byrd include it in this collection? Did it get there by accident? Certainly as far as we know it is unique in being his only solo song with sacred words in Latin. The 3-part *Turbarum voces in passione Domini secundum Joannem*, though not representative of the composer at his best, is of considerable historical importance; it is a dramatic setting of the crowd's shouts in the Passion according to St. John, the roles of the Evangelist and of Christ being sung to the traditional plainsong Passion tones. Only three other early settings of the Passion story by English composers have survived, two from the middle of the fifteenth century by an unknown composer and one by Richard Davy dating from the close of the same century. It seems likely that these earlier settings 'were composed in a traditional manner which was already well-established and that they may even have been based on earlier continental models which have not survived'.[20] They were conceived ritualistically rather than realistically. Of the many dramatic settings of the Passion story which were written in the sixteenth century the three most notable are those by di Lasso, Victoria and Byrd; thus Byrd was one of the pioneers in the development of a form which culminated in the supreme achievements of J. S. Bach.

[19] E. H. Fellowes: *William Byrd*, p. 79. (O.U.P., 2nd Ed., 1948.)
[20] Basil Smallman: *The Background of Passion Music*, p. 23. (S.C.M. Press, 1957.)

Of the other works in the 1605 book of *Gradualia* we may briefly mention *Diffusa est gratia*, a splendid work in six movements; the brilliant and joyful *Gaudeamus omnes*, and the wondrously tender *Justorum animae*. One of the most beautiful pieces in the collection is *Ave verum corpus* (often sung in translation as *Jesu, Lamb of God, Redeemer*), important if only for the fact that it is one of the very few of Byrd's best works which come within the capacity of a reasonably competent parish church choir (at least as far as notes are concerned—interpretation is another matter!). This lovely work, which is mainly homophonic, is remarkable for three things: (a) the beauty and shaping of its phrases, (b) its striking modulations and shifts of key, and (c) the wide variety of suspensions and effective discords he uses. Such a passage as the following instances all three:

Byrd: *Ave verum corpus*

Ex. 47

Attention is drawn to the glorious tenor phrase at (a), the surprising effect of the C major chord at 'Cuius latus' following a cadence on D major (b), and the rare and pungent passing discord at (c). The following passage, like that quoted from *Civitas sancti tui* (Ex. 44, p. 121), looks very simple on paper but no one could forget the yearning beauty of its phrases and the ineffable sadness of the false relation (F–F♯) used to colour the word 'miserere':

Ibidem

Ex. 48

Of the others, the 5-part *Assumpta est Maria* and *Tollite portas* are both superb pieces and so is the 4-part *Ave Regina*. Of the 3-part motets *Haec dies; Regina coeli*, and *Alleluia: Quae lucescit* are outstanding.

The forty-six motets in the second book of *Gradualia* (1607) are very similar in style to those in the first. It would be tempting to quote the extraordinary chromatic harmony with which *O quam suavis* opens, or the fine 'Alleluia' at the end of *Hodie Simon Petrus*, or the stirring diatonic climbs of eleven and twelve notes which illustrate 'qui ascendit' in *Psallite Domino*, but space is too short. This last example is a flashback to the old madrigalian pictorialism and there are several others — like the rattling of chains at 'terrarum catenas' in *Solve iubente Deo* and a running commentary on a wrestling match in the 'Mors et vita duello conflixere mirando' section of *Victimae Paschali* a curious piece of 2-part writing: see, too, how the earth shakes at the beginning of *Terra tremuit*:

Byrd: *Terra tremuit*

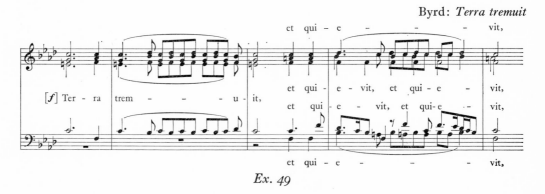

Ex. 49

Of the 4-part works *Alleluia: Cognoverunt discipuli* and *Puer natus* are particularly fine. Discussing *Viderunt omnes fines*, Fellowes states that Byrd's rubric 'Chorus (viderunt) sequitur' 'is equivalent to the *da capo* at a later period. The motet may thus be regarded as in "Aria" form.'[21] But Fellowes not only supplied the word 'viderunt' himself but has completely misinterpreted the rubric which merely signifies that the Alleluia verse *Dies sanctificatus* should follow immediately without any break. Among the best of the 5-part pieces are those brilliant pæans of joy *Haec dies* (a third setting), *Ascendit Deus* and *Psallite Domino*. All the 6-part works show remarkable power and invention, pride of place being given, perhaps, to *Venite, exultemus*.

In addition to the printed collections some thirty motets survive in manuscript. Most of them appear to be early works which pre-date the two books of *Cantiones Sacrae*. The most important of these is *De lamentatione*, a setting of verses 8–10 of the second chapter of the Lamentations of Jeremiah. This work is obviously influenced very strongly by Tallis's essay in the same genre (see pp. 71–2) and is similarly laid out for five men's voices, usually in the lower part of their compass. It is elaborately contrapuntal throughout and there are some intricate cross-rhythms (as at 'Cogitavit Dominus dissipare murum filiae Sion'). As was the custom at that time, the Hebrew letters which introduce the verses (in this case Heth, Teth, and Jod) are set in complex polyphony. As we have seen (p. 71) these lengthy choral *melismata* fulfilled much the same function as did instrumental interludes at a later time. Of the other motets, the most familiar is the

[21] E. H. Fellowes: *William Byrd*, p. 90. (O.U.P.)

5-part hymn *Christe, qui lux*. Byrd intended that the first verse, omitted in the manu-script, should be sung in unison to the plainsong melody and his harmonized setting begins at the second verse. The melody is given first to the basses and then in sub-sequent verses it is given to every voice-part in turn, rising through the choir until at last the highest voices sing verse six. The voices not singing the melody are in note-against-note block harmony with it and each verse is differently harmonized. Because the notes on paper look so simple to sing the piece is popular with choirs, but unless sung with great artistry and subtlety of phrasing it is likely to become just a dreary succession of trudging chords.

ENGLISH SERVICE MUSIC

Byrd's English liturgical music consists of a full set of Preces and Responses, two other versions of the Preces, a complete 4-part setting of the Litany with the plainsong in the tenor, some festal psalms (mostly in extended chant form), two complete Services, two Evening Services, fragments of Morning Canticles and some anthems. This is all that is known to survive.

The Short Service comprises seven movements—*Venite, Te Deum, Benedictus, Kyrie, Creed, Magnificat* and *Nunc dimittis*—with the unusual addition of an extra *Kyrie*. It will be noticed that in the Communion Service only the Kyrie and Creed are set (the Kyrie being the responses to the Ten Commandments, not the tripartite 'Lord have mercy, Christ have mercy, Lord have mercy'): this fashion was subscribed to by most of the reformation composers except Tallis. Denis Stevens suggests that 'the extreme Protestantism of Edward VI's reign may have been partly responsible for the musical setting of only Kyrie and Creed since the remaining movements (Sanctus and Bene-dictus, Agnus Dei, and Gloria) occurred during the latter and more solemn part of the Communion service, when music was probably frowned upon'.[22] By Byrd's time the custom had already become established of setting all the various movements in the same mode or key: this had the advantage of giving an overall sense of unity and balance yet it did not lead to any feeling of monotony because only two or three movements appeared in any one service and these were well spaced out by the liturgy. The *Short Service* is mainly *a 4* but in the Creed there are sections for five and six voices. Though written fairly closely in accordance with the 'for every syllable a note' theory, its simplicity is deceptive. The structure of the work is basically A, B1, B2, C1, C2, etc., each phrase being sung first by Decani and then repeated by Cantoris to different words; Byrd probably borrowed this scheme from Tallis's Short Service. The phrases are carefully moulded to the words and are the more telling for being sung antiphonally. The lovely setting of Magnificat in this Service is notable for its enterprising modulations and for its brilliant Gloria.

The Great Service, one of Byrd's most extended and sublime works, stands with the 5-part Mass at the very summit of his achievements. It is in the 'Great' Service tradition of Parsons, Sheppard and Mundy and is acknowledged to be the finest Service ever written for Anglican use. It includes the same movements as the *Short Service* except that it has only one Kyrie. It is laid out for two choirs, each of five parts, and, as its name implies, is a lengthy work, elaborately polyphonic and remarkable for its rhythmic freedom and intricacy. Like the *Short Service*, it adheres fairly closely to the syllabic

[22] Denis Stevens: *Tudor Church Music*, p. 52. (Faber, 1961.)

ideal but Byrd permits himself considerable latitude in the repetition of verbal phrases and even of individual words. To give some cohesion to the work as a whole, Byrd employs a 'motto theme' at the beginning of Venite which not only reappears (slightly modified) at the beginning of Benedictus, the Creed, Magnificat, and Nunc dimittis, but is at times woven into the fabric of some of the movements (as at 'Thou art the everlasting Son', 'Thou sittest at the right hand of God' and 'let me never be confounded' in the Te Deum): this is a late survival of the old 'head-motif' technique which dates back to the fourteenth century and is seen in the Masses of Dufay, Ockeghem, Josquin, Dunstable, Fayrfax, Taverner, and many others. Another unifying element is the use of similar scalic passages in the closing bars of Benedictus, the Creed, and Nunc dimittis. A striking feature of this Service (and to a lesser extent of the *Short Service* too) is Byrd's extraordinary flair for choral 'orchestration'. From his total available forces he selects groups of voices or even, in so-called 'verse' sections, groups of solo voices to give tonal colour to the words he is setting: (in a true verse Service the verse sections would, of course, have an obligatory accompaniment). Thus, in Te Deum the words 'Thou sittest at the right hand of God, in the glory of the father' are given to four high solo voices (in modern editions Tr1, Tr2, A1 and A2) to suggest the brightness of celestial glory, whereas the succeeding section 'we believe that thou shalt come to be our judge' is given the more sombre colouring of A1, A2, T1, T2, B1 and B2. At the thought of being 'numbered with thy saints' we return to the tone colour of empyreal brilliance, then immediately afterwards the prayerful versicle 'O Lord, save thy people' is sung by a low-voiced quartet, A1, A2, T and B. In Benedictus, at the words 'And thou child shalt be called . . .' there is a lovely quiet passage given to the unusual group A1, A2, A3 and T. In the Creed a darker tone, A1, A2, A3, T and B tinges the words 'who for us men . . . came down from heaven'. When, in Decani-Cantoris antiphonal settings, the two sides of the choir joined together to sing 'full', it was the custom in England for both halves of the choir to sing the same voice-parts, so maintaining the same number of parts but doubling the number of singers: in Italy, on the other hand, the two sides were brought together on an additive basis, so doubling the number of voice-parts and thickening the texture. It is significant that in the *Great Service*, Byrd often builds his climaxes on an additive basis, Italian fashion, so increasing the number of real voice parts to six, seven, eight and even ten: thus, in Te Deum, the words 'Also the Holy Ghost, the Comforter' are in seven parts and an eighth voice is added for the succeeding section 'Thou art the King of Glory'; the Creed proliferates into ten parts at the words 'He suffered and was buried . . .'. Both Benedictus and Magnificat have particularly fine Glorias, surpassed only by that of Nunc dimittis, of which the last few bars are given here; the endless repetitions of the words 'world without end' seem to suggest that Byrd was indeed loathe to bring to a close this wonderful peroration to the whole work (see Example 50 opposite).

Unless one actually hears this music, these brief notes are just as inadequate to convey any impression of it as would be a verbal description of the *Mona Lisa* without seeing the picture: readers unfamiliar with it are therefore urged to take the first opportunity of hearing a performance or a recording. Even if we cannot wholeheartedly subscribe to W. G. Whittaker's eulogy, 'this is the greatest piece of music of the sixteenth century by any composer whatsoever',[23] there is no doubt that the *Great Service*, like some vast cathedral in sound, should be just as familiar to every knowledgeable musician as the

[23] W. Gillies Whittaker: *Musical Quarterly*, Vol. XXVII (1941), p. 478.

Byrd: *Great Service—Nunc dimittis*

Ex. 50

'48', the *B minor*, the last quartets, *Die Winterreise, Gerontius, Das lied von der Erde* or
Le sacre, and every Anglican, whether musical or not, should be proud that such music
is part of his heritage. It is certainly a far cry from the majesty of this glorious and noble
work to that slovenly and pathetic grinding of some dreary chant which passes for church
music with so many worshipping Anglicans.

The Evening Services. The two Evening Services, both 5-part, are known respectively as the 'Second' and 'Third' Services. The Second is of considerable historical interest as it appears to be the earliest known example of a 'verse' Service.[24] Most of Byrd's secular songs are in the consort song idiom and his experiments with the solo carol with chorus, and his treatment of the Psalms (e.g. *Teach me, O Lord*), led directly to the verse Service and anthem. After a brief organ introduction a solo counter-tenor sings 'My soul doth magnify the Lord' and the chorus responds 'And my spirit rejoiceth . . .' There is an interesting passage at 'He hath scattered the proud' where the meanes' rhythm is offset against the rest of the choir singing in block harmony. At 'He hath put down' the solo voice is heard again, introduced briefly by the organ as before, the chorus re-entering at 'He hath filled the hungry'. The canticle ends as it began with a passage for solo voice. The Gloria, for full choir, is bold, original, and modern in feeling: attention has already been drawn to its striking key changes (Ex. 22, p. 99). The Nunc dimittis also begins with a short introduction for organ and a solo counter-tenor sings the first half-verse answered by the chorus. The section 'To be a light to lighten the Gentiles' is imaginatively set for a quartet of high solo voices, giving extra effect to the full entry of the choir immediately afterwards at 'glory be to the Father'. The choral sections of this Service are mainly in block harmony and the organ accompanies throughout.

The Third Service is mainly in triple measure ('Master Bird's Three Minnoms'[25]) except for a fine passage in four-time at the words 'He remembering his mercy . . .' As in the Second Service, the chorus sections are basically note-against-note though here they are laid out antiphonally, Decani and Cantoris. At 'He hath filled the hungry . . .' the tenor is in canon with the treble.

Fellowes has drawn attention to the many examples of Byrd's artistry and restraint in these Services and instances how:

(a) in the Magnificat of the *Short Service* the highest note is used once only—on the word 'exalted';

(b) in the *Great Service* Creed, the chord of B flat is used in only one passage and then with striking effect to underline the words 'crucified' and 'suffered'; and

(c) in the Third Service Magnificat, the triad on the flat seventh is again used only once—on the word 'mercy' in 'He remembering his mercy . . .'

SACRED MUSIC WITH ENGLISH WORDS

In his book *English Cathedral Music*, Fellowes speaks of the psalms and sacred pieces from *Psalmes, Sonets, & songs* and *Songs of sundrie natures* as being written 'for the English rites of the Church',[26] and in his book on Byrd he devotes an entire chapter to 'English Anthems'. It must be said at once that most of the sacred pieces in these publications are not anthems and were almost certainly never intended for liturgical use. Careful reading of the full titles of these collections confirms that they were secular books published for the domestic market:

Psalmes, Sonets, & songs of Sadnes and pietie . . . heere published, for the recreation of all such as delight in Musicke. (1588)

[24] See p. 86.
[25] Barnard: *First Book of Selected Church Musick*, 1641.
[26] E. H. Fellowes: *English Cathedral Music*, p. 71. (Methuen, 4th Ed., 1948.)

Songs of sundrie natures, some of gravitie, and others of myrth, fit for all companies and voyces . . . and published for the delight of all such as take pleasure in the exercise of that Art. (1589)
Psalmes, Songs, and Sonnets: some solemne, others joyfull, framed to the life of the words: Fit for Voyces or Viols . . . (1611)

In fact, though Byrd wrote nearly seventy anthem-like pieces, most of them are consort songs and sacred madrigals found only in these secular publications. He wrote very few true anthems for liturgical use, either full or verse. One or two of the verse anthems are found in both liturgical and secular sources; thus *Christ rising*, published in the 1589 set, was circulating in manuscript ten years earlier and can be considered a true anthem. It is one of the composer's best English anthems and it was probably because it was so popular that he decided to include it in his printed set. A quartet of viols introduces the Sarum chant *Alleluia: Christus resurgens* which is then taken up by two meanes. The development of this theme in the initial fourfold statement 'Christ rising' is imaginative and expressive:

Byrd: *Christ rising again*

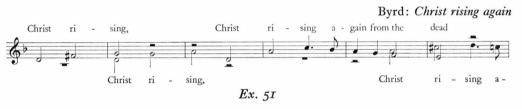

Ex. 51

The piece is full of deft and dramatic touches and the contrast between 'For as in Adam all die' and the triumphant 'So by Christ shall all men be restored to life' is just as effective in its way as Handel's. There is some reason to believe that *Christ rising* was one of the first, even perhaps the very first, verse anthem ever to be written. Other verse anthems in the printed collections include the 'carowles' *An earthly tree* (1589), *From virgin pure* (1589), and *O God that guides* (1611), all having a single verse and concluding chorus; and *Have mercy upon me* (1611) with four verse sections and choruses: of these the first and last named are also found in liturgical sources. In the printed collections, verse anthems clearly show their derivation as an amalgam of two other styles also represented in the collection – the solo song with string accompaniment (i.e. consort songs) and the madrigal, with its intricate polyphony and interplay.

About another dozen unpublished verse anthems are known. These are exclusive to liturgical sources and so were intended for liturgical performance. Of these only four have survived complete: *Behold, O God* and *Thou God that guid'st* are bread-and-butter settings of doggerel prayers for the royal health; *Alack, when I look back* is strophic with long solos and short choruses, and *O Lord, rebuke me not* has longer chorus sections which repeat sections of the previous verse. Most of the verse anthems are set for one or two solo voices with brief interjections by the chorus; often the chorus adds a fairly extended coda. As pioneer works Byrd's verse anthems are of great historical importance but, except for *Christ rising* and the carols, they are rarely performed in these days.

Liturgical sources yield nine original full anthems of which *How long shall mine enemies; O Lord, make thy servant Elizabeth* and *Prevent us, O Lord* are either very early works or perhaps they are misattributed: Dr. le Huray hints that they could well be by Mundy.[27] Some of the others, like *Arise, O Lord* and *Save me, O God*, have some similarities to motets in the 1575 *Cantiones Sacrae* but are smaller in scale. By far the best of these full anthems was one of the last to be composed, *Sing joyfully*. Whereas Tallis's finest work is nearly always associated with penitential words, Byrd's range of expression embraced the whole gamut of human emotion; it is all the more interesting therefore that in his Latin pieces he, too, seems to have been particularly inspired by prayerful and penitential words while his best English pieces are all expressions of praise and joy. Of these latter, two of the most popular are *Sing joyfully* and *This day Christ was born*. Both Barnard[28] and Boyce[29] included *Sing joyfully* in their collections. It is a 6-part work in three main sections of which the first is elaborately polyphonic. The opening phrase is set for the four highest voices, the other two being held in reserve for the second phrase, 'Sing loud unto the God of Jacob', which is rather more homophonic. An intricate example of rhythmic counterpoint to the words 'the pleasant harp and the viol' rounds off this first section:

Byrd: *Sing joyfully*

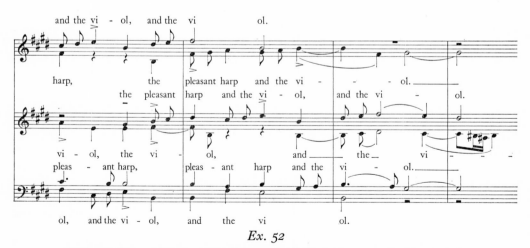

Ex. 52

[27] Peter le Huray: *Music and the Reformation in England*, p. 242. (Jenkins, 1967.)
[28] Barnard: *First Book of Selected Church Musick*, 1641.
[29] William Boyce: *Cathedral Music*, 1760, 1768, 1773.

The middle section begins homophonically with a conventional bugle-call setting of 'Blow the trumpet in the new moon' (see Ex. 27c), redeemed by its effective disposition for antiphonal voices: the succeeding phrase is again polyphonic in texture and its final cadence is notable for the exciting close imitation between bass and 1st alto:

Ibidem

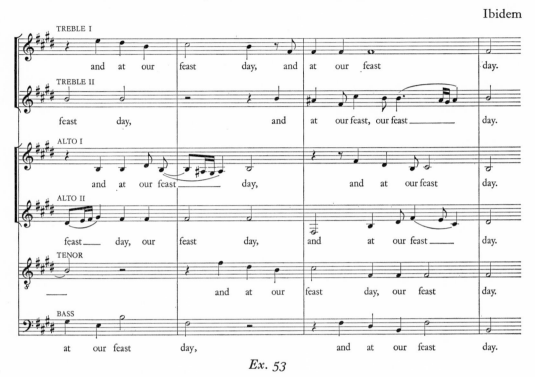

Ex. 53

The last section opens more broadly in block harmony with the words 'For this is a statute for Israel', breaking once more into exciting cross-rhythms for the final clause 'and a law of the God of Jacob'.

In addition to the original anthems, several more were adapted from early motets or consort songs, probably by Byrd himself, certainly with his knowledge. Nine anthems were adapted from early motets. *Ne irascaris* seems to have been one of his popular pieces and this appeared with no less than four different sets of English words, three similar in mood to the original but one a joyous Christmas text!

Just as motets and anthems which proved popular in church were likely to be absorbed subsequently into the domestic repertory, so enterprising choirmasters undoubtedly transplanted suitable secular works into the choir stalls. This two-way traffic makes it even more difficult to distinguish what works Byrd conceived as liturgical and what as secular. Modern choirmasters continue the old custom of introducing Byrd's secular pieces into worship. One of the best of such transplants is *This day Christ was born*, a brilliant sacred madrigal from the 1611 book. In *Sing joyfully* cross-rhythms are offset against a fairly steady basic pulse but in *This day Christ was born* even more complex cross-rhythms are imposed against a frequently shifting metrical pattern of $\frac{4}{4}$, $\frac{3}{2}$, $\frac{3}{4}$, $\frac{6}{8}$ and $\frac{9}{8}$, creating a rhythmic labyrinth in which many a choir has come to grief. This too is in six parts, sometimes seven, and begins with energetic polyphony based on this theme:

Byrd: *This day Christ was born*

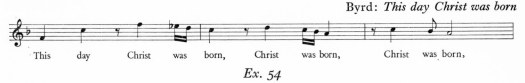

Ex. 54

(The rhythmic significance of the rests will not be overlooked.) A short contrapuntal section on the words 'This day the angels sing in earth' leads to a vigorous imitative treatment of the phrase:

Ibidem
(Bass)

Ex. 55

The little melisma colouring the word 'glad' here dominates the counterpoint. The words 'This day the just rejoice' usher in a new section which exploits the rhythmic opposition of three twos against two threes; the words are first set in 3-part block harmony for high voices, then in 4-part harmony for low voices, and finally in fairly complex 6-part polyphony—with another little touch of word-painting on the second syllable of 'rejoice':

Ibidem

Ex. 56

A return to four-time on 'saying' introduces an extended 6-part imitative passage 'Glory be to God on high' followed by a light, quick 'Alleluia' section which ends the piece. The many pulse changes are unexpected and exciting but the total effect is somewhat scrappy and disjointed: both in style and feeling this piece betrays its madrigalian origin.

Tallis and the other composers mentioned in Chapter IV all remained Catholics at heart and their genius responded far more readily to the Latin words of the Roman rite than to their mother tongue; in consequence they wrote comparatively few English settings and those they did write are markedly inferior to the best of their Latin works. Similarly there is no doubt that the general level of Byrd's English writing, apart from the *Great Service*, falls considerably below that of his Latin work and at first sight it would seem that here again the explanation is to be found in the strength of his Catholic convictions; but then how are we to account for the fact that the *Great Service* is one of his finest works? There is another possible reason. Byrd, we know, was a deeply religious man and found his greatest inspiration in the service of the Church. If therefore we accept that most of his English sacred works were addressed to the hearth instead of to the altar we shall see why they failed to call forth the most profound expression of his genius whereas the *Great Service*, designed as a liturgical work, shows him at the height of his powers. The difference is as much one between secular and liturgical use as between Catholicism and Protestantism.

It is a thousand pities that most of Byrd's music is far too difficult for even the best parish choirs while much of it is a severe test for all but the very finest professional choirs. 'Getting the notes right' in itself is no mean feat but that is only the beginning of the story: when all notes are correct and safe the hardest tasks still have to be faced — securing complete rhythmic freedom in the individual vocal lines, shaping every phrase in every part, securing perfect blend and balance throughout the texture and, most important of all, realising the mood and spirit of the words. Note and rhythmic accuracy must become so natural and effortless that they no longer need conscious thought and the singers are left free to concentrate on matters of interpretation. For example, such a motet as *Haec dies* must be sung nimbly and very lightly — not at all in the 'church anthem manner' — with an effortless ease which gives no hint of its formidable technical difficulties. Of course the more a choir sings renaissance music the more they become steeped in its style, textures and idioms and the easier they find it.

CHAPTER VII

Some Late Renaissance Composers

Byrd occupies a central and somewhat solitary position in the 'golden' period of late renaissance music. The generation which included Tallis, Tye and Merbecke were some forty years older than he was, whilst Thomas Morley, his junior by fourteen years, comes about half way between him and that important group of composers—including Tomkins, Wilbye, Weelkes and Gibbons—who were born some thirty years after him and brought this wonderful period of English music to a fitting close.

THOMAS MORLEY (?1557–c. 1602)

Much of Morley's biography remains in doubt. Even the date of his birth is uncertain though if an inscription in the Sadler MS.[1] is to be relied on he was born in 1557, probably in Norwich. Certainly he came from a Norwich family. His father was a brewer who appears, at least for a time, to have combined this role with that of head verger of Norwich Cathedral. At the early age of seventeen Thomas was granted by the Dean and Chapter the reversion of the post of Organist and Master of the Choristers. Not only does this imply that he was a precociously musical boy but it carries an almost irresistible assumption that he had been a 'singing-child' at the cathedral. By 1583 he was sharing duties and salary with the old organist Edmund Inglott and by 1586 he seems to have been effectively in charge. In July 1588 he took the Oxford degree of B.Mus., presumably externally, and soon afterwards moved to London, where his rise to fame was meteoric. By September 1591 he had 'long since' been organist of St. Paul's Cathedral[2] and this could mean that he was appointed to St. Paul's while still at Norwich—hence his move to London. It was probably soon after settling in London that he became a pupil of William Byrd under whose tutelage he 'became not only excellent in musick, as well in the theoretical and practical part, but also well seen in the Mathematicks, in which Byrd was excellent'.[3] In 1592 he was sworn a Gentleman of the Chapel Royal.

An interesting entry in the register of St. Giles, Cripplegate, dated 14 February 1589, records the burial of 'Thomas ye sonne of Thomas Morley, Organist' and many have taken this to mean that at that time Morley was organist of St. Giles itself. More likely, however, the word 'organist' refers not to the actual appointment he held but rather to his profession generally (it could as easily have been 'merchant' or 'clerk'). Whether or not he was organist of St. Giles before he went to St. Paul's is a matter of conjecture but is on the whole unlikely: it could well be that while he was organist of St. Paul's he lived in the neighbouring parish of St. Giles. Very little is known about his wife, Suzan.

There is some reason to believe that about this time Morley became involved with

---

[1] Bodleian MS. Mus.e. 1–5.
[2] *Nichols' Progresses*.
[3] Anthony Wood: *Athenae Oxoniensis*.

some subversive Catholic organisation and even visited intriguers in Flanders, later turning informer against his previous associates; however, no details are known and the evidence is far too tenuous for us to form any opinion. Sometime towards the end of the century he went to live in the parish of St. Helen's, Bishopsgate. For many years controversy has raged over whether or not Morley and Shakespeare were friends. The known facts are as follows:

(1) For some time Shakespeare and Morley both lived in the same parish of St. Helen's, Bishopsgate: both were eminent men and would have been notabilities in their small local community;

(2) In a Roll of Assessment for subsidies dated 1598 both names appear and both men's goods were valued at £5 and assessed at 13s. 4d.;

(3) Both men decided to appeal against the assessment;

(4) Some of Morley's *Consort Lessons* of 1599 were almost certainly intended as incidental music for the stage and could, in fact, have been associated with some of Shakespeare's plays;

(5) *As you like it* was written about 1599–1600. In Act V, Sc. 3 appears the poem *It was a lover and his lass* though it is probable that Shakespeare himself did not write the words. Morley's setting of these same words, published in 1600, is one of the most deservedly popular of all Tudor songs. Three questions spring to mind: did Shakespeare like Morley's song so much he decided to incorporate it into his play? Or did the play come first and these stanzas appealed to Morley so strongly that he decided to set them to music? Or did Shakespeare himself invite the composer to provide the words with a musical setting? (In passing, it is worth pointing out that Morley's wordless melody called *O mistress mine* has no connection whatsoever with the well known song in *Twelfth-Night* (Act II, Sc. 3): it is cast in an entirely different form and has a different metre. Any attempt to wed the two does violence to both.);

(6) A passage in *The Taming of the Shrew* (Act III, Sc. 1, 74–79) is very probably based on the Table of the Gam(ut) in Morley's *A Plaine and Easie Introduction* (1597).[4]

It will be seen that there is no direct evidence connecting the two but there is a balance of probability that they were at least acquaintances, if not friends.

The twenty-one year licence for the printing of music and music-paper granted to Tallis and Byrd lapsed in 1596 and Morley began to seek ways and means of having it renewed in his own favour. In 1595 he had dedicated his volume of Balletts to the all-powerful Sir Robert Cecil: three years later he presumed upon this to enlist Cecil's aid in securing the monopoly. By dint of a good deal of wire-pulling on Cecil's part letters patent were granted to Morley giving him a monopoly to print songs and song-parts 'howsoever to be songe or playd'. But this by no means satisfied him and again Cecil's aid was invoked. As a result, when the licence finally appeared in the Decrees and Ordinances of the Stationers' Company it had been miraculously enlarged to include virtually all vocal and choral music, sacred and secular, in any language, as well as manuscript paper — a typical piece of Elizabethan chicanery. However, the Stationers' Company and one or two private individuals already held various patents for the

---

[4] Thomas Morley: *A Plaine and Easie Introduction to Practicall Musicke*; Ed. R. A. Harman, p. 11. (Dent, 1952.)

printing of psalters, metrical psalms, etc.; when these came into conflict with Morley's patent, bitter quarrels ensued and Morley proved a determined and unyielding adversary: even the Bishop of London himself found him completely intractable and unapproachable. Partly because of this, the whole question of monopolies was thrashed out in the House of Commons in 1600 and it was then decided that on the expiration of Morley's licence, no further monopolies would be granted. The whole of this business seems pretty shady and reflects little credit on Morley.

In his *Plaine and Easie Introduction to Practicall Musicke*, published in 1597, he complains of serious and persistent ill-health and seems to have been confined to his home. Again, in the Address to the Reader in his *First Booke of Ayres* (1600) he speaks of 'God's visitation in sicknesse'. It was probably this illness which led to an early death at the age of forty-five or thereabouts for on 7 October 1602 a George Woodson was appointed to succeed him at the Chapel Royal and since Chapel Royal appointments were normally held for life it seems safe to infer that he must have died some time before this, especially as nothing more is heard of him after this date. Whatever physical incapacity he may have suffered towards the end of his life he was certainly not idle for between 1593 and 1601 he issued a series of important publications culminating in the 'Oriana' collection which he devised and edited.

Morley's work can be considered under four headings:

1. Secular vocal music, including canzonets, madrigals and balletts;
2. An important theoretical treatise called *A Plaine and Easie Introduction to Practicall Musicke*;
3. Latin and English Church Music;
4. Music for a consort of strings.

He will always be regarded primarily as a secular composer because of the large number and general excellence of his works in this field. He was one of the leading figures of the great English Madrigal School and was one of the most characteristically 'English' of all the madrigalists, yet he was very knowledgeable on Italian music and rejoiced to model his music on Italian patterns; this is reflected in their titles:

Madrigal: from the Italian *madrigale*, a part-song written in imitative counterpoint (often of considerable intricacy). Morley was the very first Englishman to apply the term to settings of English words.

Canzonet: a diminutive from the Italian *canzone*, a light-hearted madrigal in dance-song style; and

Ballett: from the Italian *balletto*. Since balletts were originally intended for dancing they were generally homophonic in texture and had a strongly-marked metrical rhythm. They were strophic settings, the same music being repeated for the various stanzas, and an essential part of their structure was a *Fa la la* refrain; for this reason they were sometimes known as 'Fa las'.

(It should be noted that the later madrigal composers used these and several other terms very loosely and no hard and fast definitions are possible.)

It is the more surprising then that in his *Plaine and Easie Introduction* he calls the Italian language a 'barbarism'[5] and inveighs against 'our countrymen who will highly esteem

[5] Ibid., p. 204.

whatsoever cometh from beyond the seas (and especially from Italy) be it never so simple, condemning that which is done at home though it be never so excellent'[6] (an attitude which is still to be met with!). Some of Morley's most popular madrigals include *Ho! who comes here?; Now is the month of maying; My bonny lass she smileth; Fire! fire!; About the maypole,* and *Hard by a crystal fountain.* This last comes from *The Triumphes of Oriana,* that famous collection of madrigals by various composers which Morley inspired and edited and which was itself modelled on a similar Italian collection, *Il Trionfo di Dori,* published by Gardano of Venice in 1592.

Morley's *Plaine and Easie Introduction* (1597) is the most important English theoretical treatise of the Renaissance. It is a delightful, friendly book to read and the genial, sunny disposition and warm personal charm so clearly revealed in its pages seem oddly at variance with other known traits in his character. This book too shows a considerable knowledge of Italian music and methods.

His instrumental music occupies an important place in the history of English chamber music but does not concern us here; again, many of the individual pieces bear Italian titles.

Compared with his secular output, Morley wrote little for the Church and it is to be regretted that, with few exceptions, the standard of his church music falls well below that of his best secular pieces; indeed, many of his sacred pieces appear to be early works. Four Services are known. The 'First' is a verse Service, mainly *a 5*, which includes not only the Morning and Evening Canticles but Venite, Kyrie and Creed as well. He extends Byrd's idea of interspersing passages for solo voice amongst the choral sections by writing sections for trios and quartets of solo voices, while the Te Deum begins with a solo counter-tenor singing the Sarum intonation with an independent organ accompaniment. The rhythmical fluidity of this work owes much to the influence of his teacher, William Byrd. The other Morning and Evening Service is a full 5-part setting but the only known text of it, in Durham Cathedral library, is incomplete. The two Evening Services are *a 4* and *a 5* respectively: the *a 4* version is a syllabic setting, mainly homophonic in texture but relieved by the occasional use of simple points of imitation. The 5-part setting is perhaps even more simple but the fact that it is mostly in three time ('Three Minnoms') gives opportunities for interchanging rhythms: it is very closely modelled on Byrd's 5-part 'Three Minnoms' setting.

Morley was apparently the first to write a setting of the Burial Service. It is unusually complete and includes not only the opening sentences but also the graveside sentences *Man that is born of a woman; In the midst of life; Thou knowest, Lord,* and *I heard a voice from heaven.* The sombre beauty of this deeply conceived work is in striking contrast to the brilliance and gaiety of most of his secular pieces. So eminently suitable was it for its purpose that it held its place in popular affection at least into the eighteenth century, when Boyce included it in his *Cathedral Music* and Charles Burney warmly commended it; only in this last century has it been largely superseded by Croft's fine setting. The opening of *Man that is born of a woman* is typical of the work as a whole: it is 'in a minor key, and chiefly in simple counterpoint, but with a grave . . . harmony and modulation'[7] (see Example 57 on the next page).

---

[6] Ibid., p. 293.
[7] Charles Burney: *A General History of Music.* (First published 1776–89: republished Dover 1957), p. 92n.

Morley: *Man that is born of a woman*

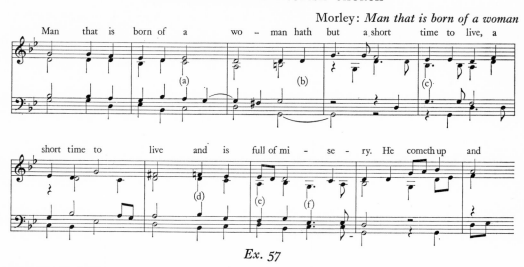

Ex. 57

We note the effective passing-note in the tenor of the second bar (a), the simple imitations on 'hath but a short time' (b) which give rise to the effective E flat inversion in bar 5 (c), the dramatic harmonic change from D major to B flat in bar 7 (d), and the grinding minor (e) and major (f) ninths in the next bar to colour the words 'full of misery'.

Morley's 5-part setting of the Preces and Responses is now regularly sung in nearly all cathedrals. Whereas in similar settings by Tallis and Byrd the priest's reciting note is treated mainly as the dominant of the harmony, Morley establishes it as the tonic, a subtle harmonic change which results in quite a different aural effect. The choral writing is very simple and is in syllabic block harmony except for 'The Lord's name be praised' which is given more elaborate treatment:

Morley: *Preces and Responses*

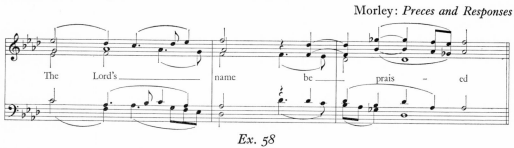

Ex. 58

Ten of Morley's motets are still in existence, four of which originally appeared as examples in his *A Plaine and Easie Introduction*. He is known to have written at least two others but only fragments of them have survived. Dealing first with the *Introduction* pieces, the lovely Agnus Dei is in the Dorian mode (transposed) but the hard edges of the mode have been softened by freely interchanging the major and minor forms of the sixth note; the elusive modality which results adds much to the beauty of the piece. *Domine fac mecum* is in triple measure except towards the end where it suddenly and effectively breaks into fours. In its construction Morley employs a device of which he was very fond; indeed, it can almost be said to be characteristic of him — the development of melodic material by repeating each phrase of the text either in exact sequence or in sequential imitation. *Eheu, sustulerunt Dominum meum* opens with a series of despairing sighs on the word 'Eheu', suggestive of the Magdalene's suffering and desolation: her grief is further expressed in the tendency of the phrases to begin on a high note and sink to their cadence. The ending is particularly fine: biting false relations lead to a poignant climax on the word 'nescio', intensified by the double passing notes over the G minor harmony; after the climax the melodic sequence sinks back to a quiet close:

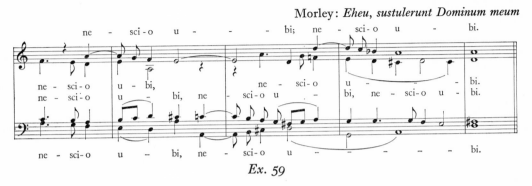

Morley: *Eheu, sustulerunt Dominum meum*

Ex. 59

O amica mea is an interesting essay in musical construction as the whole piece is virtually a proliferation from one melodic concept, most of the imitative points being derivatives of this one basic pattern:

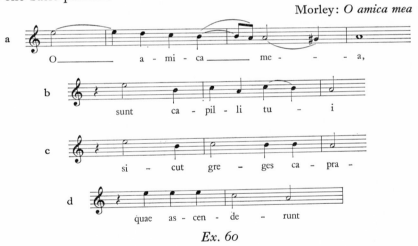

Morley: *O amica mea*

Ex. 60

The final cadence itself is clearly a rhythmic variant of (a) above—even to the final G sharp; it therefore locks the whole piece together in a most satisfying manner:

Ibidem

Ex. 61

In thus confining himself to the use of one distinctive phrase throughout the work Morley does not entirely escape the danger of monotony, yet the consistent use of thematic variation as a structural element curiously foreshadows the symphonic ideals of later centuries. In the second part of this motet, *Dentes tui sicut greges*, new material is introduced and again treated sequentially but the phrase-outline from the first part continues to take a prominent part in the discussion and the whole work ends with a final statement of the basic theme:

Ibidem
(Second part—*Dentes tui sicut greges*)

Ex. 62

Of those motets which were not printed in the *Introduction* we must briefly discuss the very long *Domine, non est exaltatum cor meum*, a prentice work written when the composer was only nineteen. It breaks most of the conventions of renaissance part-writing and this can be interpreted in two ways: some believe that Morley, as a forward-looking young man with new ideas, impatiently threw off petty rules and conventions so as to achieve heightened intensity of expression: others suspect that he had not yet mastered his technique and so perpetrated what the older theorists used to call 'infelicities': clumsy part-writing, a weak bass, unconvincing harmony, unsatisfactory balance of voices, suspensions heard against their own resolutions (though this may have been deliberate—Morley was somewhat addicted to this habit throughout his life), unresolved passing notes, too much reliance on well-worn clichés, etc. The following examples are typical:

Morley: *Domine, non est exaltatum cor meum*

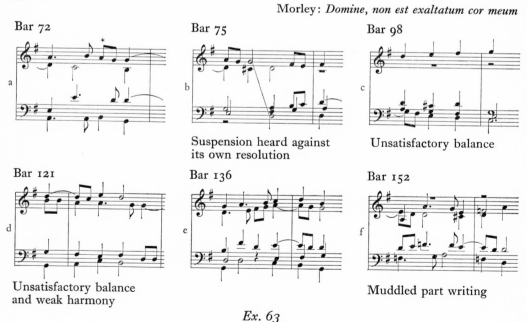

Ex. 63

Had such passages also appeared in his later work we could assume they were a deliberate element in his style; on the contrary, his mature works are technically highly polished. One suspects then that the examples quoted are signs of immaturity and it may be some encouragement to today's students to reflect that at this stage Morley too might well have failed his exams. *Domine, Dominus noster*, written in the same year, shows similar weaknesses but is somewhat redeemed by a very good ending. By way of contrast with these early pieces *Gaude Maria virgo*, with its second part *Virgo prudentissima*, is much more typical of its composer. It is vigorous and brilliant in style and the first part ends with an impressive climax based on a descending scalic figure on the word 'permansisti'. The whole work deserves to be far better known.

Psalm 130 must have had some special significance for Morley as it inspired two of his best works, one in Latin and one in English. The Latin setting, *De profundis clamavi*, is in six parts; the first and third verses only of the Psalm are set, interspersed with other material. The work opens with a beautiful phrase, expressive of the deepest contrition, which plunges downwards a minor 6th on the second syllable of 'profundis'; the mood of this opening is sustained throughout. Morley uses a rich harmonic palette which normally engages five of his six voices, full 6-part polyphony being reserved for climactic moments such as the full choir entry on 'oculos meos' and the great climax at the end of the 'Si iniquitates observaveris' section. *Laboravi in gemitu meo*, also 6-part, is unequal. There are some splendid passages in it but there are also occasional patches of turbid part-writing and at least one rather ugly false relation (in bar 53), suggesting that it may be an early work. Morley lightens the texture at times and there is some effective 3-part writing. But its most serious fault (and a somewhat rare one in renaissance sacred music) is that the mood of the music seems to be at variance with the mood of the words; one is left with the feeling that it really needs to be sung twice as fast to some such words as 'Gloria in excelsis' or 'Alleluia'.

Only a handful of English anthems survive but these include his two best sacred pieces, *Nolo mortem peccatoris* and the magnificent verse anthem *Out of the deepe* (the English version of Psalm 130). Indeed, it may be true to say that Morley is the first composer we have encountered whose English music is better than his Latin. It may seem strange that an English anthem should have a Latin title but there is a simple explanation: Morley set two stanzas of a poem begnning *Father, I am thine only son* and each stanza concludes with the Latin refrain 'Nolo mortem peccatoris'; he conceived the happy notion of using this refrain as a short prelude to the whole anthem which thus begins and ends with these same words. The setting is entirely syllabic, almost in the style of the early Elizabethans, and is probably another of the composer's early works. It is scored for men's voices only ATTB, their darker tone colour fitly matching the prayerful agony of the words.

A set of festal psalms are not very remarkable but the four surviving verse anthems are both interesting and important. The penitential *O Jesu meek* is somewhat loosely constructed and the 5-part refrains are brief. In *How long wilt thou forget me* the musical ideas are much more distinguished and are developed with far greater economy. It is a superb example of the verse anthem form and if, as seems likely, both it and *O Jesu meek* were written before Morley left Norwich, then the verse anthem had already reached a high standard of development by the time Gibbons, 'a pioneer in this hitherto untried field',[8] was a little boy of four or five! *Let my complaint* is on a somewhat smaller scale

[8] E. H. Fellowes: *English Cathedral Music*, p. 103. (Methuen, 1948.)

with only one solo voice and 4-part choir. But the real gem of the group, generally regarded as Morley's finest sacred work, is *Out of the deepe*, set for tenor or counter-tenor soloist and 5-part choir. The beginning of this anthem has often been quoted; it is a splendid example of that virtue which we so admire in the work of the late sixteenth and early seventeenth-century Englishmen — their knack of inventing a melodic phrase which exactly catches the rhythm, inflections and mood of the words and is yet beautiful in itself, highly organised and balanced:

Morley: *Out of the deepe*

Ex. 64

Of this passage Fellowes said, 'The value of the bar's rest before the impassioned appeal for a hearing, and the repetition of the words "Lord, hear my voice", slightly prolonged in the second statement, show a subtlety of touch only to be met with in work of the highest class.'[9] Musically, the phrase is an arch constructed from three melodic fragments, *a*, *b* and *c* (of these, *c* is clearly recognisable as an inversion of *a*) and the highest point of the arch coincides with the verbal climax. Verse 2 begins with a choral statement of fragment *b* which is then extended sequentially. Verse 3 is given to the soloist and a touching effect is produced when the choir wonderingly echoes the soloist's question 'O Lord, who may abide it?' The chorus and soloist then sing alternately verse by verse, the chorus having the even-numbered verses. The other solo passages all exhibit the same mastery of vocal declamation as does the one at the beginning. The work closes with a particularly lovely 'Amen', the sustained note in the top part having the effect of an inverted pedal:

[9] Ibid., p. 84.

Ibidem

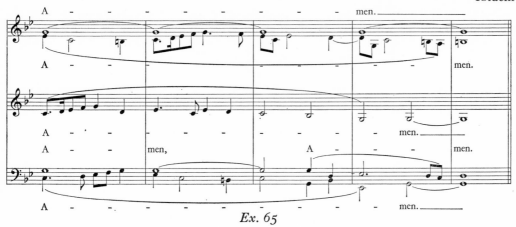

Ex. 65

We feel that in this piece Morley is at one with the Restoration composers of a century later.

THOMAS TOMKINS (1572–1656)

Tomkins was born in 1572 in Pembrokeshire, probably at St. David's where his father was first a vicar-choral and later 'Master of the Choristers and Organ Player'. Like the Bach family, Tomkins's family was highly musical and most of his forebears, brothers, nephews, sons and descendants were professional musicians. Thomas's own childhood at St. David's seems to have been somewhat shadowed by financial hardship. When he was six or seven his father secured his appointment as one of the two or three choristers at St. David's, partly to give the boy a good musical training and partly to supplement the family income. An elder brother, also called Thomas, perished in the *Revenge* in Sir Richard Grenville's foolhardy action against the Spaniards in 1591.

Three years later the father, who had by this time been ordained, was appointed a minor canon at Gloucester Cathedral and the family moved to that city. From 1594–96 it would seem that young Thomas was sent to London to study under William Byrd: that he was an apt pupil can be inferred from his appointment in 1596 to the post of Organist and Master of the Choristers at Worcester Cathedral. The following year he married Alicia, the widow of his predecessor Nathaniel Patrick; (it was not unusual at this time for a newly-appointed cathedral organist to take over his predecessor's widow or daughter as part of his perquisites!). However, the marriage appears to have turned out very happily. It seems clear that Thomas's reputation had already made some impact in London musical circles because he was honoured by an invitation to contribute a madrigal to *The Triumphes of Oriana*, published in 1601. It is likely too that he composed one of the anthems, *Be strong and of good courage*, sung at the Coronation of James I in 1603.

In July, 1607, Tomkins took an external B.Mus. degree at Oxford, affiliating to Magdalen College for the purpose. Two years later his father was made Precentor of Gloucester Cathedral—no doubt a well-deserved reward for faithful service—and in

1611 his own little son Nathaniel was made a chorister at Worcester. During the following year Henry, the popular Prince of Wales, died of typhoid fever and for his obsequies Tomkins wrote the deeply moving verse anthem *Know ye not*, remarkable for its advanced chromaticism (which points forward to Purcell's *Hear my prayer, O Lord*). About this time the verse anthem was fast growing in popularity and the importance it placed on an independent organ accompaniment made it necessary to rebuild the organ in Worcester Cathedral. Generous contributions from many sources enabled Tomkins to design a two-manual instrument of thirteen stops which was built by Thomas Dallam in 1613–14: it must have been a splendid instrument for its time. There is also evidence to suggest that in addition to the organ a group of instrumentalists shared in the work of accompanying, at least on important occasions.

Though Tomkins now grew to be a man of some substance and influence in Worcester, he knew that his real future lay in London. Sometime between 1617 and 1620 he was sworn a Gentleman of the Chapel Royal and in 1621 he became one of the organists of the Chapel under Orlando Gibbons. As was customary at that time, he still retained his post at Worcester and during his spells of duty in London he handed over his work at Worcester to his deputy, John Fido. In that same year he contributed some tunes to Ravenscroft's *The Whole Book of Psalms* and in the following year published his own *Songs of 3. 4. 5. and 6. parts* which attracted wide attention. The *Songs* are particularly interesting because though they are collectively dedicated to the Earl of Pembroke, each song also bears an individual dedication to various relatives and friends of the composer, thus giving us a fairly clear picture of his social background and the breadth of his interests. The collection includes madrigals, madrigals with *fa la la* refrains (but not homophonic ballets) and four pieces with sacred words which are usually listed amongst the anthems, though it is more than likely that Tomkins, following his master's example, intended them as sacred madrigals for use in the home.

The death of King James in May 1625 was followed by the death of Orlando Gibbons a month later; as the next senior organist, Tomkins, assisted by three older members of the Chapel, seems to have been mainly responsible for the music of Charles I's coronation which took place the following February. Unhappily the special music which he composed for this occasion has not survived. It is pleasant to record that his old father and stepmother were still alive to rejoice in their son's success though they both died the following year, 1627.

Tomkins had now completed thirty years of faithful and devoted service at Worcester; at the same time, the reflected glory of his brilliant achievements in London no doubt shed added lustre on his home cathedral. So it came about that in 1627, the year in which his parents died, the Chapter decided to reward him with the grant of a lease of property and land. Attending to this property and dealing with his parents' affairs in Gloucester must have kept him very busy at this time. In the following March the Crown decided to honour Tomkins (probably in belated acknowledgement of his work for the coronation) and he was appointed to succeed Alfonso Ferrabosco (ii) as composer-in-ordinary to King Charles. Very typically, however, the post had already been promised to Ferrabosco's son and we can guess how chagrined Tomkins must have felt when his royal appointment was revoked. Perhaps it was some consolation to him that in the following year his son Nathaniel was made a canon of Worcester Cathedral.

The next few years seem to have been fairly uneventful though no doubt overclouded by the ever-increasing unrest and friction between Royalists and Parliamentarians. As a loyal servant of the Court he could hardly fail to be distressed by the political and ecclesiastical intrigues by which the king was surrounded. In 1640 he was consulted by the Dean and Chapter of Gloucester about building a new organ. Two years later his wife died after forty-five years of happy and devoted companionship.

Worcester, a Royalist stronghold, became an obvious target for the Parliamentarians and in a foray by some of Essex's men, both the cathedral organ and Tomkins's house were damaged. After the outbreak of civil war in 1642 further damage was done to the house, this time by a stray cannon shot when Waller attacked the city in 1643. In this same year an assistant was appointed to train the choristers; this suggests that the ageing man was finding his work something of a strain and was obliged to relinquish some of his duties. With advancing years and increasing infirmity he seems to have turned more and more towards composition and most of his keyboard works were written at this time. After the siege of 1646, Worcester surrendered and soon afterwards the cathedral organs were removed and the cathedral itself closed. One can imagine the utter horror, helplessness and desolation he must have felt as he watched his life's work crumbling to ruin. In 1647 Tomkins wrote two memorial works, *Earl Strafford's Pavan* (Strafford had been executed in 1641) and *Pavan: Lord Canterbury*. When, in 1649, the king himself was martyred, Tomkins gave expression to his feelings with a *Sad Pavan: for these distracted times*.

It was in 1654 that Tomkins's son Nathaniel, who was a widower, married a wealthy widow who owned a small manor at Martin Hussingtree, a village halfway between Worcester and Droitwich. The couple invited the old man (now aged eighty-two) to live with them and so Tomkins sold his home and furniture, wound up his affairs and retired to the country. Two years later he died and was buried in the churchyard at Martin Hussingtree, mourned, admired and loved by all who knew him.

TOMKINS'S CHURCH MUSIC

Unlike Morley, Tomkins was first and foremost a church composer and from his student days till the end of his life he poured out a steady stream of Services, anthems and liturgical music. He was a prolific writer and on the whole he maintained a consistently high quality. None of this music was printed in the composer's lifetime except some psalm-tunes and the three or four pieces with sacred words in the madrigal collection *Songs of 3. 4. 5. and 6. parts* (1622) though for many years before his death he had planned to bring out a collected edition and he had even done much of the preparatory work in readiness, assisted no doubt by his son Nathaniel. But the religious and political temper of those times was inimical to the printing of 'Popish' music and as Tomkins grew older so it became less and less likely that he would ever see his church music in print. However, after

> good King Charles had returned to his throne
> the old Church of England came back to its own

and Nathaniel thought the time propitious to go ahead with his father's plan. He had always been a devoted son and now that the old man had died he 'knew that his bounden duty was to create an imperishable musical memorial to his father's skill and piety. At that time Nathaniel was the only person who could adequately perform such a task for he had inherited most, if not all, of his father's manuscripts, and had lived with him long enough to understand and carry out his wishes.'[10] The collection was eventually published in 1668 under the title *Musica Deo Sacra*. Because Nathaniel approached his task in a spirit of dedication he took immense pains to achieve accuracy and it is no small tribute to his skill and industry that except for accidentals and the underlay of the words, modern editors find comparatively little to correct in either vocal or organ parts. *Musica Deo Sacra* includes:

5 Services	29 full anthems
preces and responses	6 anthems for men's voices
2 antiphonal psalm settings	19 3-part anthems
41 verse anthems	5 metrical psalm-tunes

In addition to the music included in this printed collection a few other works have survived:

2 Evening Services (incomplete)
17 anthems (most of them incomplete)

Nowhere does Tomkins set a Latin text; he is thus the first composer in this record to set English texts exclusively.

Tomkins was in no sense a pioneer or an experimenter and the cataclysmic changes brought about in Italy by Monteverdi's *seconda prattica* (1605) scarcely stirred a leaf in the Cathedral Close at Worcester. He was prepared to accept the tools of his trade from his older contemporaries, especially Byrd; to use them with imagination, artistry and astonishing resource; and eventually to lay them down in pretty much the same state as he had found them. Throughout his long working life his techniques neither changed nor developed though as he grew older he seems to have preferred the 'verse' to the 'full' style of writing. Much of his work betrays madrigalian characteristics but they are always kept strictly in check and his sacred music is consistently more weighty, more developed and more restrained than his madrigals. He did not excel, and rarely indulged, in feats of technical dexterity like canonic writing, and he deliberately shunned harmonic or rhythmic extravagances which would draw attention to themselves—though he often used them to brilliant and dramatic effect in his madrigals. Within the limits he set himself he achieved quite remarkable variety of structure, texture and rhythm, but his greatest strength was undoubtedly his sensitive and imaginative response to the mood of his text.

TOMKINS: THE SERVICES

The five Services in *Musica Deo Sacra* have several characteristics in common:

(1) In all his Services, Tomkins tries to give the various movements some structural logic and cohesion by employing thematic links to lock the whole work together.
(2) For the same reason he resorts to the old device of using head-motifs.[11]
(3) Within each movement he often achieves an inner logic by making distinctive use of a semi-sequential method of melodic extension.

[10] Denis Stevens: *Thomas Tomkins, 1572–1656*, p. 69. (Macmillan, 1957.)
[11] See pp. 70 and 163.

(4) Instead of contrasting the tone colours of high and low voices, as Byrd so often did, he usually prefers the spatial alternation of Decani and Cantoris. The full choir is reserved for beginnings and endings and for occasional clauses of special significance.

(5) Except for one or two isolated movements all the Services have an organ accompaniment: in the first three, the organ merely doubles the voices but in the two verse Services the organ part is, of course, independent.

(6) Madrigalian pictorialism often shows itself in his treatment of such phrases as 'and hath raised up', 'and ascended into heaven', 'heaven and earth', 'he hath put down', and 'the sharpness of death' (where, in all Services, sharps inevitably appear in the score!).

(7) Only the First Service includes Benedictus; in the Second, Third and Fifth he sets Jubilate in preference, and in the Fourth he omits both.

The First is a 'short' Service for four voices, known as 'C fa ut'. It was the only one to achieve popularity in the composer's lifetime. A head-motif of about a dozen beats in length appears at the beginning of the morning and evening Canticles:

Ex. 66

At the words 'he hath put down' in Magnificat there is an interesting sequence which, by means of some slight subdivision of the treble part, achieves both tonal and spatial contrast:

Tomkins: *First Service*
— Magnificat

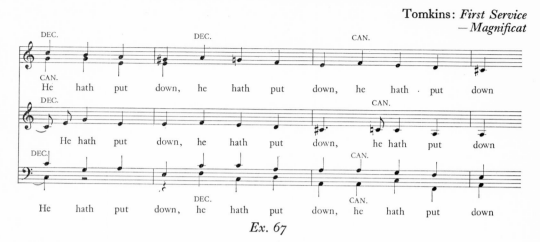

Ex. 67

The Second is also a 4-part 'short' Service in which Tomkins makes extensive use of sequential writing. Both Venite and Kyrie are unaccompanied and Jubilate is set instead of Benedictus. Instead of the opening words of Te Deum being intoned to the old plainchant formula by priest or cantor, they are set chorally to a phrase which later becomes the head-motif of Magnificat: another head-motif is shared by Jubilate and Nunc dimittis. Two short sections for solo voices appear in Te Deum; meanes are subdivided in the first and counter-tenors in the second: since, however, the accompaniment merely doubles the voices and is not independent, they are not truly verse sections. Such passages provide welcome variety of tone colour. There is a more extended verse-type passage for divided meanes and counter-tenors in Jubilate. Though simple and straightforward, this Service has many passages of great beauty and originality such as this one from Magnificat where the harmony is enriched by the inverted pedal G:

Tomkins: *Second Service*
— Magnificat

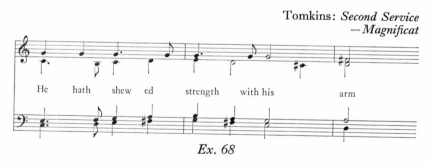

Ex. 68

Both the First and Second Service owe much to Tallis's Short Service.

The Third Service is a 'Great' Service scored in ten parts (Decani and Cantoris MAATB) with a solo quartet (MMAT). In spite of the impressive appearance of the ten vocal lines as they are spread down the pages of *Tudor Church Music*,[12] a closer examination shows that the ten apparent parts often coalesce to form five real parts; the advantage is that the composer, somewhat unusually for him, was able to select different voice groupings within the framework of his ten parts, so drawing on a far

[12] *Tudor Church Music*, Vol. VIII, p. 82 et seq.

wider range of tone colours. Again, in the 'short' Services already discussed hardly any attempt is made to overlap antiphonal phrases; in the Third Service, however, where antiphonal singing occurs, careful dovetailing helps to secure far greater smoothness and fluidity: (Denis Stevens suggests that more antiphony and more verse sections were actually employed than are marked in *Musica Deo Sacra*[13]). Jubilate again replaces Benedictus. Magnificat and Nunc dimittis share an implied head-motif; they both begin quietly with a verse-type section. Some idea of the scale of this Service can be gained from the fact that the Te Deum alone takes eight minutes to perform.

The Fourth Service—a verse Service with independent accompaniment. Stevens says that, 'The organ part in the Fourth and Fifth Services is an integral part of the texture, and even though Tomkins gave no more than a sketch of what he would have played, it is clear that he favoured a greater degree of elaboration than was common among his contemporaries, chief of whom in the realm of the verse Service were Gibbons and Byrd.'[14] Certainly no other composer up to that time had written organ accompaniments nearly so florid as those accompanying the verse sections in these Services. The Fourth Service is mainly *a 5* but there is some division of parts, reaching as many as eight in the Te Deum at 'in glory everlasting'. Only three Canticles are included: Te Deum, Magnificat and Nunc dimittis. The Te Deum opens with a paraphrase of the ancient Sarum intonation. For the head-motif common to Magnificat and Nunc dimittis, Tomkins used the opening phrase of the Magnificat in Byrd's Second Service: this charming and delicate tribute to his 'much reverenced master' is dismissed by Fellowes as 'a curious example of plagiarism whether committed consciously or not'![15]

The Fifth Service, also a verse Service, is distinguished by four features:

(1) the series of verse sections for bass voice, remarkable for their range and expressive quality; they were probably written with some particular singer in mind;
(2) the more dramatic style of the choral writing;
(3) a typically Elizabethan fondness for cross-rhythms based on the $\frac{6}{4} : \frac{3}{2}$ relationship;
(4) an unusually close thematic link between the Glorias of the evening Canticles. 'Glory be to the Father, and to the Son, and to the Holy Ghost' in Nunc dimittis is almost identical with the same passage in Magnificat save that whereas in the latter it appears in the key of G minor, in the Nunc dimittis it is lifted into the serene radiance of B flat major, thus forming a perfect coda to the evening Canticles. Furthermore, it is worth pointing out that this B flat version is an almost exact transposition of 'As it was in the beginning . . .' in the Nunc dimittis of the Second Service.

It is unimportant but curious that in all these Services Tomkins adopts Byrd's treatment of the word 'scat-ter-ed', faithfully preserving the older composer's dotted rhythm and often, like Byrd, using widely leaping intervals.

Fragments of two other Services survive in manuscript but they are too incomplete to have any practical value. It is necessary to add that so-called 'faux-bourdon' Services by such composers as Morley, Tomkins and others are entirely spurious. That alleged to be by Tomkins[16] is a corruption of fragments from his two Psalm settings—Psalm 47

[13] Denis Stevens: *Thomas Tomkins, 1572–1656*, p. 78. (Macmillan, 1957.)
[14] Ibid., p. 79.
[15] E. H. Fellowes: *English Cathedral Music*, p. 90. (Methuen, 1948.)
[16] Edited by Burgess and Shore. (Novello: *Parish Choir Book*, Nos. 889 and 1037.)

(Whitsun) and Psalm 15 (Ascension) — interlarded with plainchant verses. Such a curious hybrid would have been quite unknown to Jacobean composers. Of course there is no objection to such Services *per se*; it is simply that they are misattributed: it would be more honest to say 'based on' or 'derived from' instead of 'by'. Because of minor changes in the liturgy we can no longer use Tomkins's very fine 5-part Preces and Responses in their original form, but a suitably modified edition has been published [17] and now they are sung regularly in almost every Anglican cathedral.

TOMKINS: THE ANTHEMS AND FULL ANTHEMS

The Anthems. Of the items printed in *Musica Deo Sacra*, some twenty or so were written for special occasions: 11 settings of Collects; music for the Burial Service; 2 coronation anthems; 2 Saint's Day anthems (St. George: St. Stephen); Preces and Responses; 2 special anthems for Christmas and Easter.

The editors of *Tudor Church Music* speak with some feeling of the 'strange and uncouth' underlaying of the words in *Musica Deo Sacra* and other scholars endorsed their remarks. Certainly Nathaniel appears to have been very casual in this matter though Denis Stevens is probably right when he says 'In order to secure a really musical and singable underlay, Nathaniel would have had to sing through, not once but several times, every voice-part of every work in *Musica Deo Sacra*, and amend the printer's copy accordingly. Nathaniel, in spite of his genuine devotion to his task, might understandably have baulked at such a proposition . . . He evidently placed his trust, not unwisely, in the ability of singers to adapt the text in a convincing and artistic manner to the varying lengths of the musical phrases.'[18] But even the most able singers would have been hard put to it to relate the words to the music in the nineteen 3-part anthems for men's voices *a cappella*. Indeed, so difficult would their task have been that Dr. Bernard Rose advances an interesting and well argued theory that some of them 'rather than being composed as anthems, had originally either secular texts — were in fact 3-part madrigals, for that is their style — or no text at all, being in the nature of counterpoint exercises; and that some person unknown (the printer?) added the texts which they now have'.[19] But then why should Nathaniel have included 'counterpoint exercises' in a collection of *Musica Deo Sacra* or why should a conscientious editor allow a printer a free hand to add any text which occurred to him? It is all rather inexplicable.

Full Anthems. The unaccompanied 3-part anthems just mentioned are set for different combinations of voices. Though almost certainly intended for men's voices, most of them would sound equally effective sung by boys, women or mixed voices. They may well have been written for his own family. With three exceptions they are all setting of psalm texts. The seven penitential psalms, in particular, seem to have inspired Tomkins to highly imaginative and expressive writing and it is a pity these pieces are so rarely heard.

Of the eleven 4-part anthems, six were also composed for men's voices. That Tomkins should write so much for men suggests that his boys at Worcester must have been of very poor quality, a suspicion which is considerably strengthened when we learn that

---

[17] Atkins and Fellowes: *Six Settings of the Preces and Responses by Tudor Composers*. (O.U.P.)
[18] Denis Stevens: *Thomas Tomkins, 1572–1656*, p. 70. (Macmillan, 1957.)
[19] Proceedings of The Royal Musical Association, Vol. 82 (1955–6).

in 1619 cornetts were engaged to double the meane parts. Was he spending too much time in London to ensure that they received a proper training? The 4-part anthems include *Turn thou us*, one of Tomkins's few excursions into multiple canonic writing. It is a canon four-in-one but the technical difficulties obviously taxed him sorely and the outcome seems laboriously contrived and stilted in expression. *The heavens declare the glory* and *O how amiable* both deserve to be sung more often and it is a pity that the latter has been overshadowed by a setting of the same words by Weelkes.

The fifteen 5-part anthems include what many consider to be Tomkins's finest sacred piece, *When David heard*. In this, tonal sequences, bold chromaticism, expressive repetitions, and a slow-moving harmonic basis combine to achieve breadth and nobility of style together with rare beauty and tenderness of expression: towards the end the words 'Absalom my son' are set to a particularly wistful passage based on the *nota cambiata* formula:

Tomkins: *When David heard that Absalom was slain*

Ex. 69

A companion piece to this is *Then David mourned*, perhaps even more deeply moving and grief-laden. As we have seen, composers of sacred music are often at their best in this pathetic vein and Tomkins has left many other fine examples, such as *Lord enter not into judgement; Withdraw not thou thy mercy* and *He that hath pity on the poor*: yet it has to be admitted that even at his best he rarely achieves that inner luminosity which characterises Byrd's finest work in this same style. *Arise, O Lord God* is a lovely setting in which the music subtly reflects the varying emotions in the text. *Almighty God, the fountain of all wisdom* is notable for its 'Amen', one of Tomkins's most bold and original passages (see Example 70 on following page). In almost all of his full anthems chordal writing is introduced from time to time to add point to the text and to provide variety of texture: *Why art thou so full of heaviness* is exceptional in that it is polyphonic throughout.

Of the full anthems *a 6*, *Who shall ascend the hill of God* shows the composer somewhat untypically making effective use of 'choral orchestration'. Beginning with varying groups of three, four and five voices, he reserves the full weight of the 6-part choir till he reaches the climactic point 'from the God of his salvation'. This feeling for vocal colour is again exemplified in the opening bars of *Woe is me* (Psalm cxx, v. 4) where the insistent minor seconds underline the nostalgia of the exile (Cf. John Blow's *Salvator mundi*).

Tomkins: *Almighty God, the fountain of all wisdom*

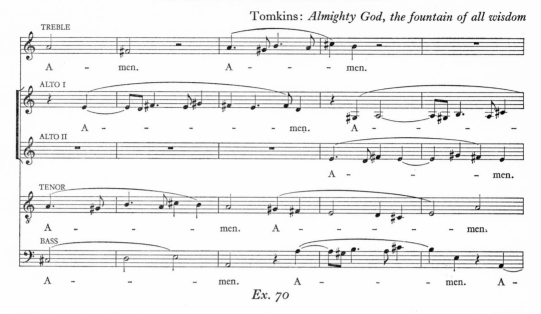

Ex. 70

However, since this latter piece appears only in the 'Songs' it seems likely that it was never intended to be sung in church; certainly the highly madrigalian *It is my well-beloved's voice*, from the same source, would be out of place in Worcester Cathedral for all that it has Biblical words and is usually listed amongst Tomkins's sacred pieces.

Anthems in more than six parts appear to be early works. Of these the most ambitious is the 12-part *O praise the Lord all ye heathen*, probably written for some state occasion or even, perhaps, for the composer's degree exercise in 1607. Here again he seems to have overreached himself. The counterpoint runs smoothly enough and again by means of selective scoring he obtains some effective tonal contrasts; but the harmonic rhythm moves slowly and lacks variety while the chordal pattern becomes far too repetitive. In performance, of course, the sheer weight of sound cannot fail to impress.

TOMKINS: THE VERSE ANTHEMS

Tomkins calls his verse anthems by the quaint title 'Songs to the Organ'. It is interesting to see the revaluation they have undergone in recent years. Writing in 1928 the editors of *Tudor Church Music* were able to say 'His Full Anthems are almost all of real musical interest and value, and in those of the later style [i.e. verse anthems] his touch becomes sure, if never quite inspired . . . The tentative experiments of Gibbons in this kind reach fuller maturity in Tomkins, but in neither case do they make much appeal to modern taste; and the space occupied in *Musica Deo Sacra* by "Songs to the Organ" tends to obscure the composer's worth and to impair his fame.'[20] Few church musicians would agree with this nowadays. The modern view is aptly summed up in the words of Dr. Bernard Rose, 'The Full Anthems, fine as some of them are, are very much in the old contrapuntal style of some of his predecessors and older contemporaries while in the main lacking the intimate eloquence of many of them.

[20] *Tudor Church Music*, Vol. VIII, pp. xvii, xviii.

The large scale Full Anthems are an exception, particularly the great twelve-part *O praise the Lord all ye heathen* and *O sing unto the Lord a new song* which is in seven parts.'[21] In fact it is now generally agreed that it is in the verse anthems, not the full anthems, that his great gifts are most fully revealed, neither would many people in these days consider that 'the tentative experiments of Gibbons in this kind reach fuller maturity in Tomkins': 'tentative' is hardly the word which leaps to mind when listening to such a polished gem as Gibbons's *This is the record of John.*

Forty-one verse anthems by Tomkins are known. Most of them are intended for the greater feast days or Saints' days and many are settings of the appropriate Collects. Perhaps their chief importance is that by placing increasing emphasis on the role of the organ as an accompanying instrument with a vital and independent life of its own, they contributed not only to the art of organ accompaniment but also created technical demands which led to the advancement of organ building and a reawakening of interest in the organ itself. We have already seen that a new organ became necessary in Tomkins's own cathedral in 1613 and many other organs were rebuilt or enlarged during the first forty years or so of the century, so leading directly to advances in organ construction. In verse sections the organ is on a par with the solo voices and makes its own independent contribution to the texture, supporting, enriching and decorating. Just as the new and intricate verse accompaniments encouraged the rise of the virtuoso player, so the vocal lines demanded a high standard of solo-singing: hence, though verse anthems seem to have become generally fashionable at about this time, the style inevitably reached its finest flowering in the one place where the country's best singers and players were gathered together — the Chapel Royal — and in the pages of those composers most closely associated with it — Byrd, Tomkins and Gibbons.

Except for *Rejoice, rejoice* (which may not be his), all Tomkins's 'songs to the organ' begin with a verse and end with a chorus, but there is astonishing variety in between. Often the short choruses repeat the words of the soloist, so confirming and underlining them; sometimes the chorus even repeats the music of the solo sections. Occasionally, however, instead of repeating the soloist's words the choir continues with the next clause of the text (as in *My shepherd is the living Lord*). In one anthem, *O pray for the peace of Jerusalem*, the same words are sung three times, verse-chorus-verse. There is no hard and fast rule and Tomkins shows remarkable ingenuity in the way he varies the relationship between verse and chorus. By far the most elaborate is *Behold, I bring you glad tidings*, a Christmas anthem in which one solo voice is answered by a 10-part choir: it was almost certainly written for the Chapel Royal, probably the only choir at that time capable of singing it. Even now few choirs can meet the demand for four alto lines! *Almighty God, whose praise*, a setting of the Collect for Holy Innocents Day, opens with a very lengthy verse section for five solo voices: the five are rarely heard together and Tomkins secures variety and contrast by careful selection and grouping of the different timbres and registers. *Stephen being full of the Holy Ghost* employs six soloists in various combinations; by allowing the chorus to tell the story and using solo voices to represent the various speakers the narrative acquires a new dramatic force (a force which may owe something, perhaps, to the old Dramatic Passion settings).

Four anthems are scored for consort instruments though the instruments are not specified: *Above the stars; Know ye not; Rejoice, rejoice*, and *Thou art my king, O God.* The verses in this last, and in *O Lord, let me know mine end, Sing unto God* and *Give*

[21] Dr. B. Rose: Proceedings of the Royal Musical Association (Vol. 82, 1955–6).

sentence with me make almost virtuoso demands on the soloists and the bass duets in *Give sentence* are perhaps the most forward-looking passages in all his output. Such writing is much more typical of the Baroque than the Renaissance:

Tomkins: *Give sentence with me, O God*

Ex. 71

Most of Tomkins's work was strongly diatonic but when he wished to achieve effects of great poignancy, no composer showed a better grasp of the expressive possibilities of unconventional and chromatic modulation: the full anthem *When David heard* is the most striking and sustained example but many shorter examples are to be found in the verse anthems. Here is one from *Hear my prayer, O good Lord* (See Example 72 opposite). Similar passages can be found in *Almighty God whose praise this day; Hear my prayer, O Lord; Praise the Lord, O my Soul; My beloved spake*, and elsewhere.

Tomkins seems to have had a penchant for the bass voice and some of his best solo passages were written for it. The tenor fares badly, however, and of all the verse anthems he is given only one, *Praise the Lord, O ye servants*.

CHARACTERISTICS OF TOMKINS'S STYLE

There are several characteristic 'fingerprints' which appear so frequently in Tomkins's

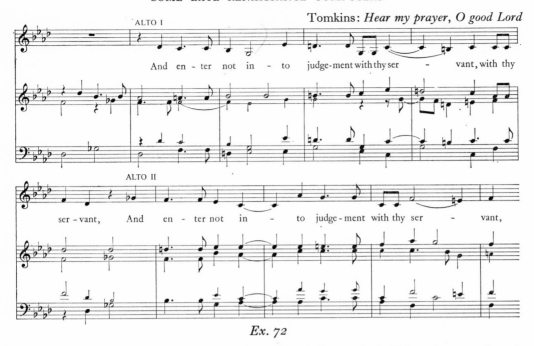

Ex. 72

music that they seem peculiar to him and are regarded as typical of his style, even though they occasionally appear in the work of other composers.

(1) Dr. Bernard Rose has drawn attention[22] to his trick of following a minor triad with its dominant chord, returning immediately afterwards to the same triad but this time with its third sharpened, either in the same or in another voice-part:

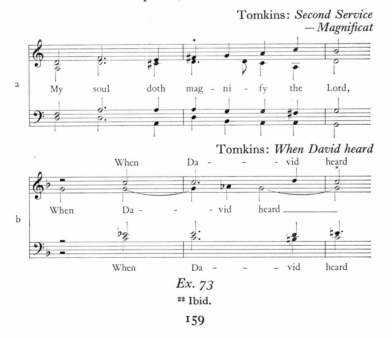

Ex. 73

[22] Ibid.

(2) He had a curious fondness for repeating the last two words or so of each phrase. Of this Fellowes says, 'A rather irritating mannerism in Tomkins's work is his habit of frequently repeating the final tag of a verbal phrase. For example, in his anthem *Great and marvellous* the first sentence ends with the repetition of the two words "thy works". A few bars later the voices are singing "True and just are thy ways, thy ways". Another anthem begins "O God, wonderful art thou, art thou". Such examples could be indefinitely multiplied. The same mannerism is found in his secular work. For instance, in his fine madrigal *Oft did I marle* the soprano voice sings without a break "but fire and water there may mell, may mell, where love and hate together dwell, together dwell". Again in the Ballet *Cloris, when as I woo*, all the voices in block harmony sing "If as a maid you use it, you use it, say No and ne'er refuse it, refuse it".'[23] Commenting on Fellowes's stricture, Denis Stevens says, 'It is perfectly true that Tomkins frequently does this, but he is in excellent company because Byrd, Gibbons, and Weelkes also provide plentiful examples of the same alleged fault.'[24] Nevertheless the fault does seem much more glaring and frequent in Tomkins's work and many will feel that Fellowes's criticism is not without substance.

(3) We have already mentioned Tomkins's enterprise and skill in the writing of florid organ accompaniments. Dr. Rose has pointed out[25] that one interesting feature of these accompaniments is Tomkins's partiality for flourishes of semiquavers (demisemiquavers in modern notation), either in the form of octave runs (a) or else as a measured trill (b):

Tomkins: *O Lord, let me know mine end*

Tomkins: *Thou art my king, O God*

Ex. 74

One reason why Tomkins's anthems are still so little known and so rarely heard in our cathedrals is simply that most of them are not available in print. Until recently only a mere handful had been published in modern editions and it is an almost incredible fact that in spite of the tremendous resurgence of interest in sixteenth- and seventeenth-century music, nobody had thought it worthwhile to reprint *Musica Deo Sacra*, either in a library edition or (of far greater value) in a cheap practical edition for choirs. Recently, however, Dr. Bernard Rose was asked to prepare an edition for the British Academy and the first two volumes, containing eleven and fourteen respectively of the verse anthems, appeared in 1964 and 1967. But though much of the music is still not readily available in print, broadcasts and gramophone records are gradually making it

[23] E. H. Fellowes: *English Cathedral Music*, p. 91. (Methuen, 1948.)
[24] Denis Stevens: *Thomas Tomkins, 1572–1656*, p. 93. (Macmillan, 1957.)
[25] Bernard Rose: Proceedings of the Royal Musical Association, Vol. 82 (1955–6).

better known and there is no doubt that the more we hear of it the more the work of this fine musician grows in our estimation and affection.

THOMAS WEELKES (*c.* 1575–1623)

No one knows when or where Thomas Weelkes was born but in his first published madrigal collection of 1597 he offers 'the first fruicts of my barren ground, unripe, in regard of time'; in the dedication of the 1598 set he again speaks of 'my yeeres yet unripened', and in February 1602 the Oxford University Register records that he had studied and practised music for sixteen years. It follows from all this that he was probably born somewhere between 1573 and 1578: Fellowes narrows this down to 1576[26] but Walter Collins thinks it may have been a year or two earlier.[27] Certainly the first we hear of him is in 1597 when he published his *Madrigals to 3. 4. 5 & 6 voyces* followed in 1598 by *Balletts and Madrigals to five voyces*. This latter collection is dedicated to Edward Darcye, Groom of the Privy Chamber, but in spite of the usual fulsome dedication (the same in which he writes of his 'yeeres yet unripened') there is no evidence to indicate that he was actually in Darcye's service. About this time (1598) he was appointed organist of Winchester College at a meagre stipend of 13s. 4d. per quarter, plus his lodgings and daily commons. Two further collections of madrigals appeared in 1600 — one in five voice-parts dedicated to Henry Lord Winsor, Baron of Bradenham; the other, a collection of 6-part pieces, dedicated to George Brooke.

It was probably in the autumn of 1601 that he left Winchester for Chichester where he was appointed organist of the cathedral: either then or subsequently he received various other appointments connected with the cathedral music — lay singing-man, master of the choristers and Sherborne clerk. It would appear that from this time onwards his interests as a composer were centred mainly in church music. His last collection of madrigals, *Ayeres or Phantasticke Spirites*, was published in 1608 and it seems likely that most of his church works were composed during his early years at Chichester. It would have been soon after taking up his new post that he contributed the splendid 6-part madrigal *As Vesta was from Latmos Hill descending* to Morley's *The Triumphes of Oriana*. Weelkes and Morley must have been close friends at this time because when Morley died, Weelkes commemorated him in the madrigal *Death hath deprived me of my dearest friend* which was published as 'A remembrance of my friend, M. Thomas Morley' in *Ayeres or Phantasticke Spirites*.

In 1602 Weelkes took his B.Mus. degree from New College, Oxford. On 20 February 1603 he married Elizabeth Sandham, a wealthy Chichester girl. This was obviously a shotgun wedding as their first child, Thomas, was baptized on 9 June in the same year. Young Thomas was admitted as a chorister to sing in his father's choir on 1 August 1614 and he left on 2 August 1617, presumably when his voice changed. There were two other children, Alles (Alice), baptized 17 September 1606, and Katharine. In the 1608 collection he described himself as 'Gentleman of his Maiesties Chappell', a title he would hardly dared to have claimed if he was not entitled to it, though his name has never been traced in the records of the Chapel Royal. Probably for a time he was a Gentleman Extraordinary rather than a regular member. Only two more works of his were published in his lifetime; they were both sacred pieces, *Most mighty and all-*

[26] E. H. Fellowes: *English Madrigal Composers*, p. 191. (O.U.P.)
[27] Music and Letters, Vol. 44, No. 2, April 1963, p. 123.

knowing Lord and *O happy he*, and they appeared in Sir William Leighton's *The Teares or Lamentacions of a Sorrowfvll Soule* (1614).

Very little is known of Weelkes's private life. At various bishops' visitations in 1609, 1611, 1613 and 1615 Weelkes, in company with other members of the choir, seems to have been pretty constantly in trouble because of his behaviour and neglect of duties (though if he really was a member of the Chapel Royal this might explain why his duties in Chichester were neglected). Finally, in January 1617, the bishop ordered his removal from his various offices for being 'a common drunkard and a notorious swearer and blasphemer' and for neglecting his duties in order to spend more time in the ale-house. He continued to receive the meagre wages of singing-man and organist till his death but the loss of his appointments as master of the choristers and Sherborne clerk must not only have led to financial hardship but to social opprobrium as well. Compared with the fame and esteem enjoyed by composers like Byrd, Tomkins and Gibbons, Weelkes seems to have earned scant recognition in his lifetime; perhaps his personality counted against him and certainly in later life he seems to have been 'undisciplined and unclubbable', a victim of chronic alcoholism. Little is known about the closing years of his life except that his wife died in September 1622. Towards the end of 1623 he himself paid one of his periodic visits to London and stayed at the house of Henry Drinkwater, who lived in the parish of St. Bride's, Fleet Street. During this visit he was taken ill and died. He was buried in that church on 1 December.

WEELKES: THE MUSIC

Weelkes ranks with Morley and Wilbye as one of the best of the English madrigalists; indeed the finest work of these men compares not unfavourably with that of the greatest foreign madrigalists. Weelkes was master of all the techniques available to an English madrigal writer at that time and within the framework of conventional harmony he could produce powerful and massive works like *Mars in a fury* as well as pieces of such gossamer lightness as *On the plains, fairy trains*. But what distinguished him above most of his contemporaries was his daring use of novel, and especially chromatic, harmonies to give emotional colour to the expression of care, sadness, grief or lamenting. One of the most notable examples of his harmonic freedom is the superb madrigal *O care, thou wilt despatch me*. Even in 3-part works he does not hesitate to use boldly chromatic harmony, as in *Cease sorrows now*. Such pieces seem to suggest Italian influence, especially perhaps that of Gesualdo; certainly they represent a considerable advance on the work of most of his English contemporaries.

These last two madrigals are comparatively early works. Some time before his last madrigal collection was published in 1608 his interest seems to have veered to church music and after that date he wrote little else but sacred works. It is, then, the more disappointing that though his imaginative insight and technical mastery produced much magnificent music for the Church, yet he set his face against the radical harmonic experiments which made some of his madrigals so outstanding: indeed, in the whole range of his anthems, full and verse, it is doubtful if more than a dozen or so truly chromatic chords could be found. Perhaps he considered the church the wrong place for technical experiments and sensuous harmony.

In fact Weelkes exhibits two opposite and at times conflicting aspects of his role as a composer. Much of the writing in his full anthems represents a strongly conservative element, a determination to identify himself with the renaissance style. Their idiom and texture is almost severely orthodox and he seems to enjoy his own mastery in writing 5- and 6-part polyphony in the conventional manner: anthems like *Rejoice in the Lord; O Lord God almighty* and *O how amiable* seem to have been about fifty years behind the times. In contrast to this conservatism there was one direction in which his church music shows him to have been a daring innovator far ahead of his time — his ceaseless quest for structural logic and cohesion. He was remarkably enterprising in his experiments with returning and enclosed forms and in this he was more closely akin to the Baroque than to the Renaissance. The structure of many of his anthems can be represented by such formulae as ABA, ABACA, and often the recapitulations are interestingly varied. Yet the very conception of 'recapitulation' would be inimical to the thought processes of a true renaissance composer, whose primary concern was with the clause-by-clause requirements of his text and whose musical vision was limited to the clause he was actually engaged upon at any one time. Long-range structural repetition did not come within his purview.

But the overall formal pattern of Weelkes's structures does not tell half the story. Far more intricate and subtle are the many methods by which he achieved internal unity, integration and balance. One such method, used in some of the Services, was his elaborate use not only of head-motifs but of tail-motifs as well, to a far greater extent than any of his predecessors and older contemporaries. (Just as a head-motif is a common opening or beginning shared by two or more movements and appearing in one, more than one, or all voice-parts, so a tail-motif is a common ending shared by two or more movements, similarly varying in the number of voice-parts involved: like the head-motif, it may be a thematic fragment of only three or four notes, a longer phrase, a harmonic pattern of a few underlying chords, a short section of polyphony such as an 'Amen', or even a fairly extended section such as a complete Gloria. The repetition may be literal or so varied that it becomes difficult to recognise.) Like Tomkins, but to an even greater extent, Weelkes went so far as to introduce secondary head-motifs and penultimate tail-motifs. Thus in four of the Services he locks two Canticles together by giving them both the same Gloria and Amen. The First Service is even more tightly knit by a series of internal cross-references so numerous and intricate that only a bar-by-bar analysis would reveal them all.[28] Furthermore, not only does Weelkes integrate the several movements of his Services in this way but often there is a direct linkage between a Service and an anthem, certain passages being common to both, suggesting that he intended the two to be sung during the same service. Thus the latter half of the Gloria of the Nunc dimittis in the Fourth Service is sung to different words in *Alleluia, I heard a voice. O how amiable* contains the last seven bars of the Eighth Service Magnificat while the head-motif of the same Service becomes the Amen in *All people clap your hands*. The Magnificat of the Ninth Service shares a 10-bar section with *O Lord, grant the king a long life* (both 7-part works) while the Amen of Nunc dimittis is almost identical with the Amen of the same anthem. Numerous other examples could be cited. Obviously problems associated with structural unity and cohesion had an irresistible fascination for Weelkes and governed much of his musical thinking.

Except for the two minor pieces included in Leighton's *The Teares or Lamentacions of a Sorrowfvll Soule*, none of his church music was published. This is little less than

---

[28] For a thorough discussion of the whole matter see David Brown: *Thomas Weelkes*, pp. 183–191. (Faber, 1969.)

a tragedy because the manuscripts seem to have been particularly ill-fated; out of twenty-three verse anthems only five have survived intact while of the ten Services, none is complete. Full anthems have fared rather better and twelve out of seventeen are intact. Where the texture is fairly simple and only one part is missing it is fairly easy for competent scholars to reconstruct the missing part: especially is this true of the outer parts which are usually duplicated in the organ book. One may cite the interesting case of the 6-part anthem *Gloria in excelsis Deo*. When Fellowes first published this work, 33 bars of the 2nd meane part were missing and he therefore reconstructed them from the other five parts. Subsequently the missing voice-part came to light and so a new edition, edited by Dr. Walter S. Collins, was published.[29] Comparing Fellowes's reconstruction with the original we find that only in 14 bars does this version differ significantly. But his reconstruction of the Evening Service 'for Trebles' was far less defensible. He based his work on the erroneous and rather unlikely assumption that no less than six vocal parts were missing and that three of those extant were imperfect. He therefore laid out the score for two 5-part choirs and two 5-part groups of soloists, all TrTrATB, singing antiphonally. The result is a gorgeously sonorous work with overtones of Giovanni Gabrieli—but it is as much Fellowes as Weelkes! Some time later three of the missing voice-parts were discovered; these proved the work to be much smaller in scale than Fellowes had supposed and only one 5-part choir and one group of soloists is needed. A new and far more accurate edition incorporating the newly found parts has been published by Dr. Peter le Huray.[30] In this latest form the piece is nothing like as sumptuous as it was in Fellowes's edition but it is more typical of its composer and of the period he lived in.

WEELKES: THE SERVICES

Ten Services by Weelkes are known:

1. 'The First Service to the organs in Gamut', also described as 'in verse for a meane'. It includes Te Deum, Jubilate, Offertory, Kyrie, Creed, Magnificat and Nunc dimittis.
2. 'The Second Service to the organs in D-sol-re' (same movements as No. 1).
3. Evening Service 'to the organs in F-fa-ut'.
4. Service 'for trebles' (Te Deum, Magnificat and Nunc dimittis).
5. Evening Service 'in medio chori'.[31]
6. Evening Service 'in verse for two counter-tenors'.
7. Short Service for four voices (Venite, Te Deum, Jubilate, Magnificat and Nunc dimittis).
8. Service for five voices (Te Deum, Jubilate, Magnificat and Nunc dimittis).
9. Evening Service for seven voices.
10. Jubilate.

The first six are verse Services, the remainder are full, though even some of the full Services seem to have brief passages for solo voices. All except No. 10 include the evening Canticles while Nos. 3, 5, 6 and 9 are evening Services only. Only Nos. 1 and 2 include

[29] Thomas Weelkes: *Gloria in excelsis Deo* (Ed. Collins). (O.U.P.)
[30] Thomas Weelkes: *Evening Service 'for Trebles'* (Ed. Peter le Huray). (Stainer and Bell.)
[31] See p. 86.

Communion settings but they are unique in that in addition to the usual Kyrie and Creed they each include a setting of the Offertory sentence. Of all thirty-five movements in the ten Services only the morning Canticles of No. 7 have survived intact; all the others are, to a greater or less extent, incomplete. Nos. 2, 3, 5 and 8 exist only as organ scores: of No. 10 only tenor and bass chorus parts are known and of No. 6 alto, tenor and bass. History has dealt more kindly with the evening Canticles of No. 4 and the whole of Nos. 7 and 9, and sufficient material from them exists to make reconstruction comparatively easy and satisfactory. Of the other Services, the chorus parts of Te Deum, Magnificat and Nunc dimittis in No. 1 can be credibly reconstructed but not, alas, the verse sections, although a performing edition has been published.[32] Finally, though only an organ score of No. 8 exists it happens to be unusually complete and presents much of the vocal writing in short score: with some imaginative guesswork in matters of detail, therefore, performing versions have been issued.

Of those Services or parts of Services which can be made singable, the evening Canticles of No. 4 'For Trebles' are the most immediately appealing. The chorus sections strike a happy balance between chordal writing and polyphony and are exceptionally lyrical; the high treble voices, so rarely employed at this time, are here used with telling effect. But the real charm of the work is to be found in its verse sections, scored for TrTrTBB. Two pairs of solo voices (treble and bass) answer one another in 'For he that is mighty'; 'He hath showed strength' is for solo tenor and 'He remembering his mercy' is set as a 24-bar canon for two solo trebles. In Nunc dimittis both the first and last verses are set as gracious duets for two trebles. The highly imaginative and brilliant use of boys' voices in this Service is characteristic of Weelkes: so too is his trick of letting the organ anticipate the leading verse singer's next motive; in other words, each imitative point is first announced by the organ. This is certainly one of the most exquisite Service settings of the whole period.

The Seventh is a conventional 'Short' setting, though within the limits of its type Weelkes shows considerable resource. Its chordal structure is often relieved by allowing one voice to anticipate the others by a couple of beats[33] and on two occasions brief imitative points are admitted. Like the Short Services of Tallis and Byrd it is mostly intended to be sung antiphonally between Decani and Cantoris. This is the only Service by Weelkes—and one of the very few of the whole period—to include a full setting of Venite. The Eighth, though a 5-part full Service, includes a few sections for solo voices, apparently in four parts though often arranged in two pairs answering each other. This light and transparent texture contrasts well with the more massive style of the chorus entries. All four Canticles are very closely integrated thematically.

The Ninth is in every sense of the word a 'Great' Service, even though not so called. It is laid out for a large number of voice-parts though except for the Gloria of Nunc dimittis, Weelkes does not employ more than seven simultaneously. Even so, with this one exception, seven is the largest number of voice-parts he ever used; furthermore, the verse sections themselves seem to demand no less than four altos. The scale is large and spacious, the counterpoint masterly, and the total effect grand and noble. This work comes nearer than any other of its time, both in scale and inspiration, to Byrd's Great Service; indeed, there are many close resemblances to the Byrd Service (compare, for example, the Amen of Weelkes's Nunc dimittis with that of Byrd's Magnificat, and 'He

[32] Thomas Weelkes: *Magnificat and Nunc Dimmitis, Service No. 1* (Ed. David Brown).
[33] See pp. 166–7.

remembering his mercy' in both settings) though Weelkes's harmony is often more boldly dissonant. The Nunc dimittis is a superb example of an integrated structure, largely achieved by deriving most of the imitative points from the same basic 4-note motif; the whole movement is, in fact, built on a leitmotivic system. This Canticle is undoubtedly the finest of all Weelkes's liturgical works. The great length of this Service, the large forces employed and its formidable technical demands suggest that it must have been written for the Chapel Royal.

For a detailed and most interesting survey of the other Services too incomplete for reconstruction see Chapter II in David Brown's monograph.[34] In general terms it may be said that in the verse Services Weelkes's employment of the solo voice, his idiomatic organ accompaniments and his elaborate use of antiphony show a noted advance on the work of his predecessors and significantly widen the scope of the traditional cathedral Service.

WEELKES: THE FULL ANTHEMS

To the twelve full anthems that have survived intact, the editors of the Musica Britannica edition of Weelkes's anthems[35] have added four more by the conjectural reconstruction of missing parts: these are *O Lord God Almighty; Rejoice in the Lord; Laboravi in gemitu meo* and *Deliver us, O Lord*—though this last is almost certainly not by Weelkes. The best-known of all Weelkes's anthems, tuneful and long popular with parish choirs, must also be taken away from him; this is *Let thy merciful ears*, now known to be by (Thomas (ii)?) Mudd.

Weelkes's full anthems show some special features which may be considered characteristic of his style:

1. His love of thickness in sound. He wrote normally for 5 voices, often for 6, more rarely for 4 or 7. Whereas most renaissance composers obtained variety and thinned the texture by reducing the number of voice parts from time to time, he preferred to keep his singers continually active (except in imitative openings and antiphonal passages). Sometimes the result is an over-thick texture which tends on occasion to become wearisome. Such passages lack the transparency and linear clarity which we associate with some of the best work of the period, yet its very power and massivity can occasionally have expressive significance.

2. Whereas in his Services he uses antiphony between Decani and Cantoris more, probably, than any other English composer of his day, it is remarkable that he never used double choir markings in his anthems (with one possible but very doubtful exception in *O Lord God Almighty*). On the few occasions when he does use antiphony, it is not from side to side of the building but between contrasting groups of voices.

3. Another hallmark of his style is his fondness for beginning with a single voice-part, followed immediately by the rest of the choir entering simultaneously on the tonic chord:

[34] David Brown: *Thomas Weelkes*. (Faber, 1969.)
[35] Brown, Collins and le Huray: *Thomas Weelkes: Collected Anthems* Musica Britannica, Vol. XXIII. (Stainer and Bell, 1966.)

Ex. 75

In *Lord, to thee I make my moan* this device is used for the head-motif itself which stands at the beginning of all three main sections; it thus becomes a unifying structural element:

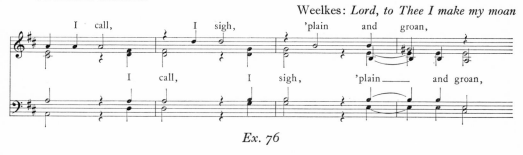

Ex. 76

4. In later sections of full anthems he is fond of writing two simultaneous entries of a motive in parallel 3rds or 6ths. Some notable examples occur in *Laboravi in gemitu meo*.

5 Most of Weelkes's anthems end with elaborate and florid Amens for full choir, characterised by their thick counterpoint and subdominant emphasis. Usually these Amens are based on one or more of the motives heard in earlier sections. In *All people clap your hands* the Amen brings together three of the motives heard earlier.

Beginning at the lower end of the scale, *Rejoice in the Lord* is the only 4-part full anthem known. The two highest parts are missing though the top part can be taken from the organ copy and the second part is easy to reconstruct. It is a simple little piece in which two short imitative passages alternate with block harmony, but it scarcely does its composer justice.

Of the 5-part anthems, *All people, clap your hands* is in two main sections: because the 'Amen' is derived from fragments of both sections it fuses them together and aptly summarizes the whole piece. *Lord, to thee I make my moan* comes off well in performance though its text counts against it: some of its harmonic asperities seem almost deliberate archaisms. The two top parts of *O Lord God Almighty* are missing but are easy to reconstruct. It is a setting of the prayer for the royal family in the Book of Common Prayer and is one of only two anthems designed exclusively for liturgical use. Such a text could not inspire even Weelkes and here again the false relations and biting harmonic clashes suggest the mid-sixteenth rather than the seventeenth century. This otherwise pedestrian anthem is partly redeemed by the splendour of its Amen. Both the words and some of the musical ideas of *O mortal man* are taken from an anonymous 4-part Scottish anthem of about 1580. Weelkes follows his model by giving the piece an AABCC form but improves on it by making C share certain melodic and rhythmic ideas with A, so resulting in an overall ternary structure.

Two of the 5-part anthems can be bracketed together — *O how amiable* and *Deliver us, O Lord our God*. Not only do they have much musical material in common but, with only minor changes, they actually share a passage some four and a half bars in length; (furthermore, as we have seen, the Amen of *O how amiable* is virtually the same as the last seven bars of the Eighth Service Magnificat). These two anthems are more polyphonic in texture than most of those already discussed. Here again *O how amiable*, one of the longest of the full anthems, is so antique in style as almost to suggest deliberate pastiche; it is nevertheless an effective work which reaches its climax in its Amen. The interesting thing is that *Deliver us* is almost certainly not by Weelkes at all but by William Cox, a canon of Chichester Cathedral. It is known that Weelkes copied out Cox's anthem and it is likely that while doing so he found that some of Cox's ideas fired his own imagination, so leading to the composition of *O how amiable*. *O happy he* was one of the two pieces published in Leighton's *The Teares of Lamentacions of a Sorrowfvll Soule* and so was intended for private, not liturgical, use. It is one of the composer's least impressive efforts.

Undoubtedly the gem of the 5-part anthems is the justly popular *Alleluia, I heard a voice*, the only anthem of its time known to have existed in both 'full' and 'verse' forms. Seven bars of introduction disclose two motives which are later developed in the main Alleluia section (A). After a short bridge passage in block harmony a new theme (B) is developed for sixteen bars to the words 'and to the Lamb for evermore'. Then follows a full restatement of the Alleluia section (A) in which, however, the final cadence is sequentially deferred. The last group of Alleluias form a coda based on material from (B). The overall shape is therefore: Introduction — A-B-A — Coda (B). We have seen that Weelkes intended certain anthems and Services to go together: this one is paired with the Fourth Service 'for Trebles'. Not only are there obvious thematic links between the anthem and the Nunc dimittis but the main Alleluia section is exactly the same, note for note, as the end of the Gloria of Nunc dimittis.

Of the 6-part works, two are found only in secular sources and are therefore more properly considered as madrigals — the laments *O Jonathan* and *When David heard* (with its famous second part *O my son Absalom*). Both *O Jonathan* and *O my son Absalom* begin similarly with an all-consuming grief powerfully expressed in a broken, 'silence-laden' texture. *O Jonathan* has some other passages of great poignancy but towards the end it becomes merely conventional. David's lament on the death of Absalom inspired many superb settings, including those by Josquin des Prez, Jacob Handl and Heinrich Schütz on the continent and by East and Tomkins in England. Tomkins's setting has already been discussed (see p. 155) and no greater compliment can be paid to Weelkes than to say that his version is in no way inferior. It is shorter, more massive, but just as deeply moving. We have quoted a passage from the close of Tomkins's setting (Ex. 69, p. 155); here is the corresponding passage by Weelkes; the stabbing 'O's', the disjointed phrases and the sighing intervals vividly depict the incoherence of unbearable grief:

Weelkes: *When David heard that Absalom was slain*

Ex. 77

Such an unrestrained, even dramatized, outpouring of emotion bespeaks the madrigalian origin of the piece; good taste and a true understanding of the nature of public worship inhibited composers from giving such free rein to emotional expression when writing music specifically for use in church. It was the next generation of composers—Porter, Portman, Child and the Lawes brothers—who, strongly influenced by Italian music and especially Italian opera, introduced the truly baroque conception of dramatic, passionate and 'pathetick' expression into their liturgical music.

If David's laments are found only in secular sources, *O Lord, grant the king a long life*, like that other prayer for King James *O Lord God Almighty*, is found only in liturgical sources. Weelkes has a marvellous flair for building up emotional tension and in this work, after 32 bars of solid 6-part writing he unexpectedly introduces an additional bass part to increase impressiveness and reinforce the climax. Weelkes left only one Latin anthem, *Laboravi in gemitu meo*, but it is outstandingly good. He modelled it on Morley's setting of the same text and its conservative idiom is in the true tradition of the great stream of Latin music from Taverner through Tallis to Byrd. It is a most impressive work, more rhythmically enterprising than most of Weelkes's anthems and it includes dotted-note motives (somewhat rare in his church music), effective syncopations and a highly florid ending where paired entries burst in simultaneously in parallel 3rds and

6ths. These various circumstances lead David Brown to suggest that it was probably Weelkes's B.Mus. exercise and was therefore composed in 1602.

Two more 6-part anthems remain to be considered. *Gloria in excelsis Deo* is one of the most popular and exciting of all the full anthems. It has a middle section in English, 'Sing, my soul, of God the Lord . . .', after which the Latin opening section is repeated in full, so giving a simple aria-form ABA structure. When the opening section returns Weelkes gives his singers (if not his hearers) variety by interchanging the two highest parts. Another superb anthem is *Hosanna to the Son of David*, remarkable for its simplicity of means. Thus, except for a brief modulation in bars 23–4 the whole piece is built out of only three chords. The great cry 'Hosanna' is immediately repeated at the beginning and end and sung three times in the middle: on each of its seven appearances it is hurled forth in block harmony using precisely the same sequence of three chords though each time the disposition of the parts, including the top part, is richly varied. The last two shouts of Hosanna are made even more dramatic by being preceded by a rest in all parts. It is a short anthem and if we count the Hosannas as 'A' the structure becomes ABACA, the B and C episodes being elaborately polyphonic in contrast to the block harmony of A. In the polyphonic sections the entries crowd excitingly together. Instead of an Amen, the Hosannas are completed by a coda on the words 'in excelsis Deo'.

Only one 7-part anthem is known but it shows Weelkes at the height of his powers: *O Lord, arise into thy resting place* is fully polyphonic and is designed in large paragraphs which pile one on another till at last they tumble over in a riot of Alleluias, a magnificent peroration to a great anthem. It is the more surprising then to discover that this anthem bears many striking resemblances to Tomkins's *O sing unto the Lord*, also a 7-part work. These resemblances include an identical series of initial entries, a cadence, melodic ideas and an especially close correspondence in their final Alleluias. It is impossible to know which setting was composed first and who was indebted to the other. However, we have already seen how Weelkes's work is a tangled network of self-quotation, cross references and thematic linkages between different sections in the same work and even between different works. We have also seen that *O mortal man* is closely modelled on a Scottish anthem; *O how amiable* is largely derived from material in Cox's *Deliver us, O Lord*; and *Laboravi* is a skilful reworking of material in Morley's setting of the same text. It looks therefore as if at times Weelkes needed some kind of catalyst, some outside stimulus to spark off his own creative gifts: this catalyst could be a piece by some very minor composer in which case the ideas borrowed would be transmuted by his superior skill, or it could be a work by a distinguished composer like Morley in which event we are confronted by two masterworks sharing some common ideas but treating them quite differently. Hence, on balance there is a strong probability that Tomkins's *O sing unto the Lord* came first and that Weelkes used it as a taking-off point for *O Lord, arise*.

WEELKES: THE VERSE ANTHEMS

Of twenty-three known verse anthems only five are intact: to these the editors of the Musica Britannica volume have been able to add another three partially reconstructed. (These do not include the verse anthem version of *Alleluia, I heard a voice*.) As usual, Weelkes is much preoccupied with problems of achieving structural logic, unity and cohesion. Most of the verse anthems follow the same basic plan: verse sections alternate with chorus sections and the whole is rounded off with an Amen coda based on material from earlier sections. Usually there are three or four verses each followed by a chorus, but there can be as many as six or seven. He often tries to give coherence by repetition and extension, by recapitulating complete sections or parts of sections, by recalling motives or distinctive rhythms, and by extensive use of head-motifs to link verse to chorus, verse to verse or chorus to chorus. Thus when, at times, he makes the chorus repeat the last phrase or so of the soloist's text, they often repeat his last musical phrase as well. One peculiarly Weelkesian trait has already been mentioned—his method of allowing the organ to anticipate the verse singer's motives. This device becomes an important structural feature in *If King Manasses* where the organ anticipates almost every phrase of the verse parts.

He shows a marked preference for high voices, especially for a duet of trebles (as in the famous Service) or counter-tenors. Solos for meanes are frequent (in contrast to their rarity in restoration music), bass solos are uncommon and tenor solos exceedingly rare. Chorus sections are usually for five voices (MAATB) but six voices are not unusual. Accompaniments were all written for the organ, suggesting that the verse anthems were intended for liturgical rather than private use.

Weelkes was not very discriminating in his choice of texts and only too often took refuge in Sternhold and Hopkins' metrical psalms: but he was careful to disguise their wooden accents by the astonishing fluidity of his rhythms. His settings were mostly syllabic and melismas are infrequent. To such a brilliant madrigalist, word-painting was second nature and even in his sacred pieces he was quick to seize upon whatever opportunities his text offered.

Most of Weelkes's church works have a strong feeling of the minor key but, as in the madrigals, each section ends on a major chord (the *Tierce de Picardie*). No example of true canon is to be found in the verse anthems and such devices as augmentation and diminution are very rare; yet this same composer wrote one of the most famous examples of augmentation in history in the refrain of his Oriana madrigal *As Vesta was from Latmos hill descending*.

All laud and praise and *What joy so true* may be considered typical of his style and methods. At the beginning the organ embellishes the vocal theme in advance. Verse sections are lengthy and are set as a solo, duet or trio of high voices. Chorus entries are relatively brief and repeat the last two lines of each stanza of the text. Rather more interesting is the large-scale *If King Manasses*. Here again the verse sections are fairly lengthy. Towards the end the texture changes from 5-part to 6-part by the addition of an extra part for meanes and the last verse entry is itself in six parts, arranged in two antiphonal groups of three. The third verse-passage is one of the composer's few solos for bass voice. His treatment of the refrain 'sweet Jesu, say: Amen' is reminiscent of Loosemore's setting of the same words in his well-known anthem *O Lord, increase my faith*. The last two chorus sections show Weelkes's full 6-part polyphonic style at its best: the Amen, in particular, makes a grand ending. It is a pity that the words of this anthem are so impossible; who could keep a straight face when singing or listening to:

> A worthless worm some mild regard may win
> And lowly creep where flying threw it down,
> Where flying threw it down—threw it down.

Give ear, O Lord is not only one of the greatest verse anthems of its time but is another example of the composer's experiments in formal construction. The text, by William Hunnis, Master of the Chapel Royal choristers, has three stanzas each of which is treated as a verse; the first is scored for two altos, the second for two meanes, and the last for a meane, two altos, tenor and bass. Every stanza ends with a refrain 'Mercy, good Lord, mercy' and this refrain is then taken up by the choir. Every time the refrain is sung, either by soloists or choir, the same melodic motif is used, a kind of leitmotif representing 'mercy'. Since each solo section ends with this leitmotif it becomes also a tail-motif; the choir then takes it over, so ensuring a smooth transition from verse section to full chorus, yet on each occasion the basic motive is developed quite differently. The Amen brings the work full circle with a restatement of the 'mercy' theme just before the final cadence. Thus we have an unusual combination of rondo structure and air-and-variation technique. Incidentally this is the only one of the verse anthems to be found in a secular source. One of Weelkes's finest verse anthems is the massive 6-part *Give the king thy judgements*. The text is short and so there are many verbal repetitions but the sections are cunningly dovetailed to reduce the number of full cadences, fermata and double bars between sections. The first and last choruses are identical but voice parts are interchanged. The third verse is patterned on these choruses, using the same words as the first and musical ideas from the first and second. The whole is cyclic in form and tightly locked together.

Three anthems with parts missing have been reconstructed by the Musica Britannica editors. Only the meane part of *O Lord, how joyful is the king* has been lost. It was written for a service held annually on 5 November to commemorate the frustration of the 'Gunpowder treason'. Not only is it the longest of the verse anthems (it has seven verses and choruses) but it is also one of the most original and deeply felt. Here again Weelkes shows great resource in hiding the sing-song rhythm of the Sternhold and Hopkins text. *In thee, O Lord, have I put my trust* lacks the two higher parts of the 4-part choruses. It is unusual in two ways: (a) all solos are for bass voice, and (b) considerable use is made of sequential repetition. First and last verses begin identically. *Plead thou my cause* is almost complete except for the second verse-section, a short bass solo: the third verse is one of Weelkes's rare solos for tenor.

Of the verse anthems which have defied reconstruction, one in particular tantalizes by its incompleteness—the long and elaborate *Christ rising/Christ is risen*, of which only a single organ part survives. Here choruses and verses seem to break in on each other in a way that suggests some attempt to fuse or combine full and verse anthem forms. There is also a remarkable coda, 16 bars long, in a key a tone lower than that of the rest of the anthem. For an important discussion of the other incomplete verse anthems, the reader is referred to David Brown's excellent monograph.[36]

Most mighty and all-knowing Lord was the other Weelkes work published in Leighton's *Teares and Lamentacions*. It was erroneously printed among the songs 'of 4 parts with voices' and so has often been regarded as a full anthem. It is now clear that the piece was never intended for choral performance at all; it was, in fact, a simple consort song accompanied by viols—one of the composer's very few works with string accompaniment.

Perhaps in this section too much emphasis has been placed on Weelkes's structural procedures. Certainly they were a new departure, far in advance of anything being

[36] David Brown: *Thomas Weelkes*. (Faber, 1969.)

attempted by his English contemporaries, yet they were never an end in themselves. His best work has a beauty and power which makes an immediate impact on the listener.

ORLANDO GIBBONS (1583–1625)

It is notoriously difficult to assign precise dates to the beginning and ending of movements and phases in the arts, yet there is some justification for the claim so often made that the great era of English renaissance music closed in 1625 with the death of Orlando Gibbons. Admittedly a few renaissance composers outlived him, indeed Tomkins outlived him by thirty years, yet it is probably true to say that those who typified the old polyphonic school wrote little church music of major importance or striking originality after 1625. The Renaissance was a spent force. Styles and fashions were changing rapidly and the torch now passed to those composers who were to bring about the gradual transition from Renaissance to Baroque.

Gibbons himself was certainly 'born among the Muses and Musick' [37] because, like Weelkes, he came of a highly musical family. His father, William Gibbons, was one of the 'waytes' first Cambridge, then of Oxford. As we have seen (pp. 56–7), the waits were professional musicians employed by civic authorities, skilled in singing and competent performers on both wind and stringed instruments. Orlando's three brothers were also professional musicians. Edward, the oldest, was Master of the Choristers at King's College, Cambridge, and later Succentor at Exeter Cathedral; Ellis, the second brother, contributed two madrigals to *The Triumphes of Oriana*, while Ferdinando, third on the list, followed in his father's footsteps by becoming a town wait.

Orlando's father, William, seems to have been born and brought up in Oxford but sometime before 1566 he moved to Cambridge where he settled and reared a numerous family. Some fifteen years later he was back in Oxford and it was here (not Cambridge as stated on the monumental tablet in Canterbury Cathedral) that his famous son was born (baptized in St. Martin's Church on Christmas Day, 1583). In 1588, the year of the Armada, the family returned to Cambridge, this time for good, and William died there in 1595.

Orlando would have been four years old when this last move took place. From February 1596 until early in 1599 he sang as a chorister in his brother's choir at King's College and in 1598 he matriculated as 'a sizar from King's' to become a student in the College. From then onwards he seems to have been commissioned to compose music for special occasions. On 21 March 1605 he was admitted a Gentleman of the Chapel Royal at the early age of twenty-two—an indication that his gifts must have been outstanding even in this period when fine musicians seem to have been as multitudinous as rabbits. In 1606 he took his Mus.B. degree at Cambridge and was incorporated at Oxford a year later. About this time he married Elizabeth Patten by whom he had three sons and four daughters.

Soon he was recognised as one of the best composers of his day as well as the finest organist in England. By 1615 he was one of the two organists of the Chapel Royal and numerous other honours and royal favours were bestowed upon him, many of which carried with them valuable emoluments. In 1623 he succeeded Parsons as organist of Westminster Abbey, though still retaining his post at the Chapel Royal. Soon after his

[37] Boyce: *Cathedral Music*, Vol. I, p. viii.

appointment King James died (27 March 1625) and was succeeded by Charles I: by virtue of the offices he held Gibbons would have been mainly responsible for the music associated with these State events. On 1 May 1625 Charles married Henrietta Maria in Paris by proxy, the king himself remaining in London. Then his bride, attended by a retinue of some four thousand courtiers and servants, set sail for England. Her spouse, not willing to be outdone, moved his whole court—including the entire Chapel Royal with its staff, choir, vestments, books and ornaments—to Canterbury to await her arrival, and he himself met her at Dover on 13 June. It was during this waiting period, while the Chapel Royal was in Canterbury, that on Whitsunday, 5 June 1625, Gibbons had 'an apoplectic seizure' and died: he was buried in Canterbury Cathedral the next day. A rumour that he died of plague was hotly denied by his doctors but is very likely to have been true.

The family musical tradition was continued by Orlando's second son Christopher (1615–76) who was a chorister at the Chapel Royal, became organist of Winchester Cathedral in 1638, and in 1660 followed his father by becoming organist of both the Chapel Royal and Westminster Abbey.

GIBBONS'S CHURCH MUSIC

Gibbons wrote important music for the keyboard and for stringed instruments. His collection of *Madrigals and Mottets of 5. Parts* (1612) ranks as one of the supreme achievements in this branch of composition: it also gives some clue to the composer's own personality for the texts he has chosen all reflect a somewhat austere cast of mind. He shuns the more frivolous, even *risqué*, love poetry used by most of the madrigalists and chooses instead words of a more philosophical cast—*The silver swan; I weigh not Fortune's frown; What is our life?* and *Trust not too much.* How he must have warmed to the words that he himself set:

> O that the learned poets of this time
> Who in a love-sick line so well can speak,
> Would not consume good wit in hateful rhyme,
> But with deep care some better subject find.

But Gibbons, like Byrd, was primarily a church composer, though whereas Byrd was at his best when writing for the Latin rites, Gibbons, like Tomkins, was a true Protestant and confined himself exclusively to the setting of English texts. He was not very prolific and his known works consist of two sets of preces and psalms, two Services, ten full anthems, about twenty-five verse anthems and seventeen hymn-tunes. The two preces settings are almost identical.

Of the ten handsome volumes of *Tudor Church Music* published 1922–29 by Oxford University Press for the Carnegie Trust, Volume IV (1925) devoted to Gibbons is in some ways one of the least satisfactory, both from the viewpoint of scholarship and of evaluation. Thus, of the three psalm settings given, the incomplete *Awake up, my glory* is almost certainly not by Gibbons but by William Smith of Durham,[38] and of the thirty-nine anthems included, no less than seven are now known to be the work of other composers:

[38] John Buttrey: *William Smith of Durham.* (Music and Letters, Vol. 43, No. 3, July 1962.)

Arise, O Lord	Leonard Woodeson
Have mercy	William Byrd
Have pity	Christopher Gibbons
O Lord, increase my faith	Henry Loosemore
Out of the deep	(William Byrd?)
Sing we merrily	Palestrina
Why art thou so heavy	Henry Loosemore

It is almost certain, too, that *The secret sins* is by William Mundy. To discover that Gibbons did not write *O Lord, increase my faith* is as great a shock as the realisation that Weelkes did not write *Let thy merciful ears*.

Like Weelkes, but to an even greater extent, Gibbons was a composer of transition. In Italy the death of the Renaissance was greatly hastened by the birth of the Baroque. Monteverdi was the giant in whom the Renaissance achieved its ultimate consummation yet who, at the same time, was not only one of the first composers to conceive the new music but also gave impetus and direction to it. More than anyone else, he was responsible, consciously or unconsciously, for formulating the principles which were to govern its development. These cataclysmic changes taking place in Italy spread out in widening circles across western Europe. As usual, their impact was late in reaching England and was not fully felt until the Carolinian period (1625–49); nevertheless, even in the lifetime of Weelkes and Gibbons change was in the air. Gibbons himself was no Monteverdi, though he was unquestionably the greatest English composer of his day and is considered second only to Byrd among composers of the late Renaissance. He was brought up in the renaissance tradition and his madrigals and full anthems testify to his total mastery of the style; as the *Tudor Church Music* editors put it, he 'is a noble climax to the school whose tradition reaches back to Fairfax, Aston and Taverner'[39] (and, one could add, to Dunstable). The age of polyphony had, in fact, largely worked itself out; its problems had been solved, its potential realised, its possibilities almost exhausted. Already, in the work of Byrd, Morley, Weelkes and others, the seeds of its own dissolution are apparent within it.

Byrd and his contemporaries had already breached the walls of pure polyphony when they first introduced the use of solo voices with obligatory accompaniment, but skilled as they were in the technique of choral writing they had not yet acquired facility in writing for the solo voice: their verse passages demanded only a narrow vocal range and their measured style often sounded somewhat ponderous and even, at times, tentative. Byrd himself used no more than two solo voices in verse sections. It was the lute-song writers of the early seventeenth century who discovered how to exploit the solo voice effectively and how to write for it expressively. Gibbons profited much from their example and his verse writing begins to approach more closely to the baroque principles of accompanied recitative. He achieves much greater flexibility and plasticity in fitting music to his text; the use of shorter note values enables the words to flow at a speed corresponding more nearly to that of real speech; he tends to use a wider vocal range, a more elaborate vocal line slipping at times into free declamation, and he employs up to as many as eight soloists: these factors together help him to project the text more emotively and dramatically than his predecessors. That these two words can be applied is in itself a measure of the shift which had already taken place towards baroque thinking.

[39] *Tudor Church Music*, Vol. IV, Orlando Gibbons, p. xxiii.

Another indication of the disintegration of the old style was a growing awareness of the possibilities of musical form. Instead of the text generating its own series of imitative points, there is now an increasing interest in structural and harmonic organisation for its own sake. This search for musical form soon imposed its own demands on the words which now began to take second place to the music. We see this process well advanced in the work of Weelkes. Gibbons too was interested in organising his structures into formal patterns and made effective use of returning and enclosed forms of the ABA, ABACA type though he showed little interest in the complicated system of internal and external cross-references favoured by Weelkes. Perhaps it is true to say that Weelkes placed greater emphasis on the architecture of music, the words taking second place, whereas Gibbons took his stand on the text itself, realising both its sounds and its emotions in musical terms so that text and music seem perfectly wedded to each other. It is in this declamatory, dramatic style of writing that Gibbons shows himself not only 'a noble climax' to the Renaissance but also a forerunner of the Baroque, 'prospecting a new path which is to lead to Blow, Pelham Humfrey, and Purcell'.[40]

GIBBONS: THE SERVICES

Both aspects of Gibbons's work are typified in his two Services; the full Service in F shows his effortless command of the polyphonic idiom whereas the verse Service in D minor, though not among his best work, shows greater freedom and tonal variety in verse sections than was customary, coupled with an effective scheme of structural organisation.

The full Service in F strikes a happy balance between the 'Short' and 'Great' Services of Byrd and others: it is 'Short' in that it covers the ground quickly with very little repetition of words, and 'Great' in that instead of being mainly chordal in construction, it is ingeniously contrapuntal to such an extent that only rarely does the same word occur simultaneously in all voices. It begins with a full setting of Venite, probably amongst the last settings of this Canticle to be written because within a few years the custom of singing

Gibbons: *Short Service*
— Te Deum

Ex. 78

[40] Ibid., p. xxiii.

Ex. 78 (continued)

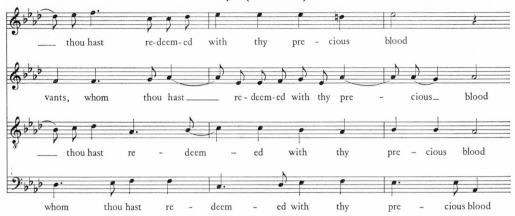

it to a simple chant became universal. Te Deum provides many good examples of the way in which Gibbons can compress fairly intricate counterpoint into the 'for every syllable a note' concept of the 'Short' Service; Example 78 is typical (Incidentally, the underlay of the middle parts presents serious problems to modern editors.) In the Magnificat occurs this curious but highly characteristic phrase:

Gibbons: Short Service
—Magnificat

Ex. 79

It is not known whether these semiquavers indicate a run or a portamento but in any case, the octave rise to an unstressed syllable represents a bold departure from general Tudor practice and from Gibbons's own normal practice; it needs considerable care in performance if an ugly false accent is to be avoided. Gibbons seems partial to such flourishes and several more are to be found in his anthems.[41] Perhaps they show the influence of Italian opera and anticipate the *cadenza* of later times; more likely such ornamental 'filling-in' notes were often supplied by singers even when not indicated by the composer and Gibbons merely regularised the position. Nunc dimittis is chiefly remarkable for its Gloria in which the meane and alto parts are in canon at the fourth below throughout, accompanied by the two lower voices. Such an extended example of canon was rare at this time when most polyphonic music was built on a succession of short phrases, yet it is deftly handled and never sounds contrived. The 'Amens' are especially fine.

The Second Service in D minor, though inferior to the Short Service, is in many ways more interesting. A 'verse' Service similar to those of Byrd and Tomkins, it is more extended and advanced than theirs. It has only four movements— Te Deum, Jubilate, Magnificat and Nunc dimittis—and no part of the Communion service is included.

[41] See Ex. 86, p. 184.

Fellowes speaks disparagingly of the lengthy Te Deum, pointing out that verse sections are often thin in texture and that the treatment of 'Thine honourable, true, and only Son' is conventional, perfunctory and repetitious.[42] One particularly harsh false relation, which has no relevance to the words at this point, seems a quaint throwback to the style of Tye and Tallis:

Gibbons: *Second Service*
— Te Deum

Ex. 80

Perhaps Gibbons himself agreed with Fellowes because he also wrote a much shorter version of the morning Canticles. In this Second Service he follows Weelkes in setting Jubilate instead of Benedictus—a somewhat unusual choice at this time. It is sung alternately by soloists and choir, each verse of the text being sung through in its entirety by one or two solo voices followed by the entry of the full choir repeating the last few words of the verse section. In Magnificat a different scheme is adopted; after a fairly extended organ introduction the Canticle verses are set alternately for verse soloists and chorus. The evening Canticles both end with the same 'Amen' which thus becomes a tail-motif helping to lock them together. The whole Service is notable for its imaginative scoring and telling contrasts of tone colour; e.g., high solo voices answered by the choir's lower voices in Magnificat, and the charming duet for meanes at the end of Nunc dimittis.

GIBBONS: THE FULL ANTHEMS

Of the ten known anthems in the polyphonic tradition some rank not only amongst Gibbons's finest work but occupy an honoured place among the greatest works of the whole period. Those in four voices are mainly penitential in mood and include some of the composer's most expressive writing. *Almighty and everlasting God*, though only a small-scale work, shows Gibbons at his best. The beautiful phrase 'mercifully look upon our infirmities' is typically Jacobean in its matching of musical and verbal rhythms and so are the graceful imitations to which it gives rise (vide Ex. 21, p. 97). *Deliver us, O Lord* and its second part *Blessed be the Lord God* are somewhat stark and austere, due largely to the frequent use of open fifths, doubled thirds and false relations. The many bare fifths and occasional thin harmony suggest that another alto part may be missing. In the second part, *Blessed be the Lord God*, there is a striking sequence (one of Gibbons's infrequent excursions into homophony) which sinks slowly through a series of bold key changes only to leap upwards a sixth for its final statement; furthermore, the unexpectedness of this sudden upthrust is capped by making the third note rise instead of fall:

[42] E. H. Fellowes: *Orlando Gibbons and his family*, p. 69. (O.U.P., 1951.)

Gibbons: *Blessed be the Lord God*

Ex. 81

Some of Gibbons's anthems are no longer usable because their words are of such poor quality—metrical hymns and psalm paraphrases which are no more than doggerel. The lengthy penitential 5-part anthem *O Lord, in thee is all my trust* suffers in this way and is rarely sung, though the music has a quiet dignity that is very moving and many passages of considerable beauty.

Turning now to the 6-part full anthems, the famous *Hosanna to the Son of David* represents the composer in his most brilliant style. It provides a good example of that interest in musical shape and formal construction which we have already noted. The closely imitative opening (see Ex. 32b, p. 107) is followed by a contrasting passage which begins quietly in block harmony to the words 'Peace in heaven and glory in the highest places'. This in turn leads to a complete note-by-note restatement of the opening section sung to different words; this is then extended to form a powerful and satisfying coda. Thus we have a clear ABA form, remarkable for the satisfying balance it strikes between form and content. It is worth pointing out that no matter how an editor arranges his bar-lines, the opening phrases are in triple time and when phrased in this way

Gibbons: *Hosanna to the Son of David*

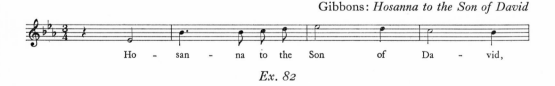

Ex. 82

the cross accents suggest even more vividly a bustling crowd. It is inevitable that this fine anthem should be compared with the equally famous setting, beginning with the same words, by Thomas Weelkes. Of the two, Gibbons is much the more contrapuntal. As the imitations lap, overlap and curl round each other we sense the suppressed excitement of the waiting, jostling throng; we hear their shouts of acclamation being tossed back and forth, hushed only momentarily by the vision of heavenly peace. Weelkes's crowd is more disciplined; they lift their voices simultaneously in great shouts of 'Hosanna' and sometimes the impact of these outbursts of praise is heightened by a silence beforehand, all six parts having a rest at the same time. Homophony and polyphony alternate. Whereas Gibbons's texture is rich and sonorous, Weelkes aims for extreme brilliance, exploiting the highest register of the two treble parts in a way which suggests trumpet fanfares.

To return to the 6-part anthems, *Lift up your heads* is similar in mood and scope to *Hosanna*. Its final cadence is particularly fine, its effectiveness being much enhanced by the daring introduction of a flattened 7th just before the final *nota cambiata*:

Gibbons: *Lift up your heads*

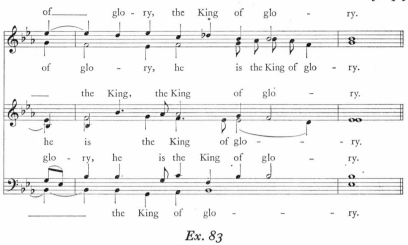

Ex. 83

The remaining 6-part anthem is the supremely beautiful *O Lord, in thy wrath*, another penitential piece similar to those in four parts but, of course, richer in texture: it has an austere tenderness and the boys' pathetic cries 'O save me' answering each other across the spaces of some great cathedral are almost unbearably poignant.

Gibbons's biggest anthem is the well-known 8-part *O clap your hands* with its second part *God is gone up*. This monumental work is accounted one of the great treasures of Anglican church music: it is sublime in conception, masterly in execution, and massive and noble in performance. It is a pity, but inevitable, that its technical demands place it beyond the reach of all but the most competent choirs: it also needs a fair body of tone to make its full effect.

GIBBONS: THE VERSE ANTHEMS

Of the twenty-five verse anthems known, only sixteen are complete or can be completed and one of these, *The secret sins*, is probably by Mundy, not Gibbons. Most of them are 'occasional' pieces written for some specific Church or State event and this probably explains why only two of them are found in secular sources. Since most of them are found only in liturgical sources it is the more surprising that no less than ten are scored for instruments—viols, and possibly cornetts. As many of these anthems were almost certainly written for the Chapel Royal it seems equally certain that by this time stringed instruments were in use there, at least on important occasions. Hence when, in the 1660s, Charles II appointed twenty-four string players to the Chapel Royal, the idea was not so revolutionary as some historians would have us believe.

Gibbons's verse anthems vary widely in quality but few people in these days could subscribe to the evaluation given to them by the editors of *Tudor Church Music*, Vol. IV:

When we turn to his work in the new style, i.e. verse anthems, we trace in all directions the groping and hesitation of the pioneer . . . Only the shallow student will complain if in the pioneer work he finds the prentice hand. It would be easy to take a few works . . . and enlarge on their crudities.

To begin with, as we have seen, Gibbons was no pioneer: Byrd's magnificent verse anthem *Christ rising/Christ is risen* was written five years or more before Gibbons was born! Secondly, works like *Behold, thou hast made my days; See, see, the Word is incarnate* and *This is the record of John* scarcely show the 'prentice hand'; they are masterpieces in their own right and are amongst the finest verse anthems of the whole period. This *Tudor Church Music* assessment was drastically revised in the Appendix, published in 1948, but the harm done half a century ago took a long time to live down.

But even if Gibbons was not one of the first to write verse anthems, he made an important contribution to the form by introducing a more declamatory and virtuosic style of writing for solo voices. Whereas in Byrd's anthems the soloist's vocal line often sounds merely like one strand detached from the accompanying web of instrumental polyphony, Gibbons at his best writes a well-organised and highly effective melody in its own right; although this melody generates its own accompaniment, the accompaniment remains subservient to the solo voice. In other words, the emphasis is shifting from true polyphony to monody.

There is a tendency for Gibbons's verse anthems to be longer than Byrd's. Whereas in Byrd the sections are usually fairly short and the entries of the full choir often have the effect of merely interrupting the progress of the 'verse', Gibbons's verse and chorus sections are much more complete in themselves so that in practice the anthem consists of a series of miniature movements alternately verse and choral. When, as often, the verse sections have an accompaniment for strings, we can already see in embryo the cantata-like verse anthems of Purcell and his contemporaries. The accompaniments, whether for organ or strings, are often as elaborately contrapuntal as the choral sections; this is where Gibbons's renaissance background shows itself. In general, he is at his best when writing for a solo voice rather than a group of solo voices.

It has been mentioned that most of the verse anthems are occasional pieces: *Almighty God, who by thy Son* is typical. It is a setting of the Collect for St. Peter's Day and can therefore be used only once a year—a pity, since it is a very fine work. When Dr. Maxie, Dean of Windsor, was dying in 1618, he asked Gibbons to set the funeral text *Behold, thou hast made my days*, from Psalm 39. This too is an excellent piece. It is scored for counter-tenor solo, 5-part choir and instrumental accompaniment and there are thematic linkages between the three verses and their choruses, almost in the manner of Weelkes.

Glorious and powerful God begins with a bass solo with string accompaniment which could almost have been written by Purcell: the counter-tenor then takes over and the remaining verse passages are arranged as duets between counter-tenor and bass. The chorus sections, 5-part, are particularly good and the work ends with an unusual but very lovely 'Amen'. Another outstanding verse anthem is *O God, the king of glory* and Fellowes has drawn attention to its powerful ending where, after a swift interchange between verse and full choir, a drop of a 7th in bass and treble and a clashing major and minor 3rd bring the work to an exultant close:[43]

[43] E. H. Fellowes: *English Cathedral Music*, p. 103. (Methuen, 1948.)

Gibbons: *O God, the king of glory*

Ex. 84

Two anthems which are among the best musically, suffer from impossible words. *O all true faithful* (*British*) *hearts*, a 'thanksgiving for the King's happy recovery from a great dangerous sickness', includes couplets like:

> For he our David from the snares of death
> Hath freed; prolong his days, enlarge his breath.

Ouseley, the Victorian editor, solved the problem by inviting his friend the Reverend H. R. Bramley to write new words for it, adapting the music where necessary. These words, *O thou the central orb*, are the ones now generally sung to Gibbons's music (but they have become even better known in their modern setting by Charles Wood). This anthem is yet another instance of the composer's instinct for musical shape and structural balance. The original poem consists of three stanzas all ending with the same refrain:

> Rejoice in him, give thanks, his great name bless,
> For a remembrance of his holiness.

He treats the stanzas freely as verse sections but the refrain, which alone is sung by the full choir, remains exactly the same each time so producing an AB CB DB structure: the whole piece is rounded off by a florid Amen coda.

Even more curious is the text of *See, see the Word is incarnate*, which presents a potted biography of Christ describing his birth, ministry, passion, resurrection, and the consequences of the resurrection. Yet these words inspired Gibbons to write one of his greatest anthems. Though verbal repetition is reduced to a minimum such a lengthy text inevitably results in a lengthy anthem. The surprising thing is that in spite of its length it coheres extraordinarily well; seams are concealed, joins dovetailed and there are very few total breaks in its onward surge. To secure even greater cohesion, effective use is made of recapitulation and chorus sections are thematically linked. This superb dramatic piece deserves to be far better known.

The most famous of all Gibbons's verse anthems is undoubtedly *This is the record of John*, one of the best verse works of the whole period. The declamatory narration stands as a superlative example of the composer's felicity in matching music and words and both rhythmically and melodically, the music seems a perfectly natural projection of the text:

Gibbons: *This is the record of John*

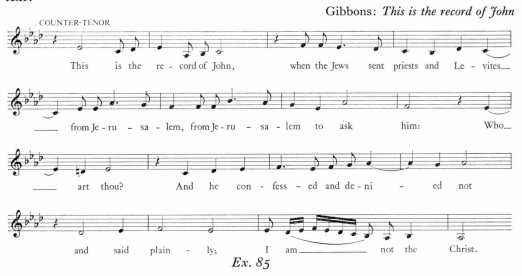

Ex. 85

The strong denial at the end gives us a vivid picture of the heavily-bearded, skin-bedecked figure of the fanatical Baptist, his eyes blazing with anger that he should be mistaken for the Christ, emphatically shaking his head and protesting vigorously. (The treatment of 'Jerusalem' is identical with Byrd's in *Civitas sancti tui*—see Ex. 45, p. 121.) In the final verse section, note how the highest note is reserved for the word 'crieth' in 'that crieth in the wilderness'. This powerful piece fully merits its great popularity.

GIBBONS: THE HYMN-TUNES

To the ordinary churchgoer, Gibbons will be esteemed mainly for his hymn-tunes. Seventeen from his pen are known, of which sixteen were written for George Wither's *Hymnes and Songs of the Church* (1623). Most of these, after a long period of neglect, have found their way into modern hymnbooks and are becomingly increasing popular. They include the tunes now usually sung to 'Drop, drop, slow tears', 'Eternal ruler of the ceaseless round', 'Forth in thy name, O Lord, I go', 'Jesu, grant me this, I pray' and 'Love of the Father, Love of God the Son'.

CHARACTERISTICS OF GIBBONS'S STYLE

1. Gibbons is one of the most humanistic of the renaissance composers. Not for him the ecstasy of contemplation, the mystical glow of religious fervour, preoccupation with liturgiology, ritual and dogma, or the cool timelessness and impersonal austerity of the

Latin language. In contrast to Tallis, Tye and Byrd (and even more the Continentals — Palestrina, Victoria and di Lasso), Gibbons is at his best when dealing with human situations and emotions, especially when expressed in action — *Lift up your heads; O clap your hands; Hosanna to the Son of David; This is the record of John*. Even his penitential works seem more subjective and we sense a close personal identification in such settings as *O Lord, in thy wrath rebuke me not* and *O Lord, in thee is all my trust*.

2. He is one of the most contrapuntal writers of the whole period. In his polyphonic works he uses fewer chordal passages than almost any other composer and the part-writing is overlapped to such an extent that it is most unusual for the same word to occur simultaneously in all voice parts, except at a cadence point. Even the verse anthems were essentially polyphonic and the instrumental accompaniment consisted normally of a tightly imitative texture derived from the vocal phrases.

3. He and Weelkes were among the first composers of their day to be consciously concerned with form and structure and we have noted several of his experiments in giving unity and cohesion to his longer pieces. Though simple, and in the light of our experience often obvious, these experiments do in fact represent an important and considerable step forward from the conventional stringing together of musical phrases based on clauses of the text.

4. His fondness for little bravura flourishes of which the following are typical (see p. 177):

Ex. 86

Such flourishes are still more abundant in his accompaniments, especially when written for strings.

5. As we have seen, Gibbons is essentially a member of the great school of polyphonic composers and it is largely by his works in this idiom that he is reckoned amongst the very greatest English masters of the period. Yet through the contributions he made to the development of the verse anthem and his more advanced treatment of the solo voice he can also be considered a transitional composer who 'sowed the seeds of a new kind of crop to be harvested after the Restoration'.

SOME LESSER COMPOSERS

We come next to a group of composers of more modest talents, yet though they may be minor figures they are still far from negligible. Their best work is sometimes of surprisingly high quality and would not disgrace more eminent composers of the period and even their less satisfactory pieces usually show considerable technical facility and often imaginative detail. In what way then is their music unsatisfactory? Various faults occur, sometimes singly, sometimes in combination, but the three most common are these:

(1) too many full cadences, so fragmenting the piece;
(2) too restricted a range of keys and harmonies; often a whole work is centred round one tonic together with its relative minor or major and there is not enough enterprise in modulation;
(3) a naïve delight in word-painting for its own sake; this frequently gets out of hand and verges on the ludicrous. Often quaint and eccentric texts are chosen for no better reason, one suspects, than the opportunities offered for bizarre pictorialism.

Yet the best work of these men certainly deserves a place in today's music lists.

JOHN AMNER (Before 1590?–1641)

Of these lesser composers Amner was one of the most original. He was organist and master of the choristers at Ely Cathedral from 1610 till his death. His known works include two sets of Responses, a Short Service (MATB), two complete verse Services, an evening Service, and over forty anthems and sacred part-songs. Most interesting is his published collection of *Sacred Hymnes. Of 3. 4. 5. and 6. parts for voyces and vyols* (1615), probably intended for domestic use in the house of his patron, the Earl of Bath. It includes some twenty works, the longer of which are divided into separate subsections to produce a total of twenty-six short pieces. Many of these, like *St. Mary, now but erst the sound of many*, suffer from a text so tortuous or naïve that it could not possibly be sung seriously in these days. The pieces are each marked 'motect' or 'alleluia'. They are mostly syllabic in style but those called 'alleluias' include an extended 'Alleluia' section which is often highly florid.

Of the 'motects', Dr. le Huray draws attention to the expressive little 4-part *Woe is me* and the extraordinarily fine *Remember not, Lord, our offences* with its superb Amen:[44]

[44] Peter le Huray: *Music and the Reformation in England, 1549–1660*, p. 337–8. (Herbert Jenkins, 1967.)

John Amner: *Remember not, Lord, our offences*

Ex. 87

Of the verse anthems, two Christmas settings are the most elaborate: *Lo, how from heaven* has some good music but again the text is rather quaint; the other, *O ye little flock*, is lavishly scored for solo voices, 6-part choir and six viols. It is very long and has three movements each culminating in a powerful chorus. The second of these choruses is perhaps the most exciting of all Amner's 'Alleluias'. He is one of the few composers of his day to include settings of Sanctus and Gloria in excelsis in his Service settings: usually only Kyrie and Credo were included (see p. 75).

No true assessment of this composer can be made until more of his music is available in print. The indications are that he is a more considerable figure than earlier evaluations suggest.

ADRIAN BATTEN (1591–*c.* 1637)

Batten was baptized at St. Thomas's Church, Salisbury, and later became a chorister at Winchester Cathedral. In 1614 he was appointed a vicar choral of Westminster Abbey and ten years later became both vicar-choral and organist of St. Paul's Cathedral. He wrote only church music and his works are found solely in liturgical sources. He is known to have written two sets of Preces, a Litany, festal psalms, seven Services (one for men's voices only) and nearly seventy anthems — though some twenty of them have been lost.

He is now chiefly remembered by his simple 4-part pieces like *Deliver us, O Lord our God; Haste thee, O God* and *O praise the Lord, all ye heathen*. Of the larger full anthems the 5-part *Hear the prayers, O our God* is one of the best; the 8-part *O clap your hands* offers some dramatic antiphony and a texture which strikes a happy balance between polyphony and block harmony.

The verse anthems are rarely heard now, largely because the solo passages are so lacking in distinction: Batten was too often content to write a somewhat characterless series of notes rather than a real melody. Word-painting too is carried to excess, as in *O Lord, thou hast searched me out*, while in the larger anthems and Services the other faults listed above are only too apparent — an inability to move far from the home key and too many full cadences in that key.

A large and important source book of renaissance music at St. Michael's College, Tenbury, is known as 'Batten's Organ Book' but no evidence exists to show that Batten was in any way concerned in its compilation.

MICHAEL EAST (*c.* 1580–1648)

For most of his working life East was organist and master of the choristers at Lichfield Cathedral. He is regarded primarily as a madrigalist but of his seven published collections the sixth (1624) consists entirely of anthems: a few more anthems are to be found in the miscellaneous sets of 1610 and 1618 and an Evening Service survives in manuscript. The trend of events generally is reflected in East's work by the proportion of full anthems (4) to verse anthems (10); all the verse anthems are scored for strings.

East preferred to work on a large canvas. Most of his anthems are long, are in two or more sections and are laid out for five or six voices. He is especially fond of long instrumental introductions and *ritornelli* and he makes skilful use of the contrasts between voices and instruments. He too suffers from a basic inability to leave his home key, a weakness which is underlined by too frequent cadences. Many anthems include passages of naïve word-painting, like 'a reed shaken with the wind' in *As they departed* and in such pieces as *Blow out the trumpet* and *I have roared* he succumbs to the obvious invitation.

Fellowes especially admired *When Israel came out of Egypt* though there seems little to choose between this and his other verse anthems. East's most deeply felt work is undoubtedly the 6-part full anthem *When David heard*. Of all contemporary settings of this much-used text his alone eschews chromatic writing and in its diatonic simplicity generates great expressive power.

THOMAS RAVENSCROFT (*c.* 1590–*c.* 1635)

He was a chorister at St. Paul's Cathedral. In 1607 he took his Mus.B. at Cambridge and from 1618–22 was music master at Christ's Hospital. Ravenscroft was a versatile musician who wrote a somewhat pedantic treatise on musical theory, published collections of songs and catches associated with 'Hunting, Hawking, Dauncing, Drinking, and Enamouring', but who is most renowned, perhaps, for his 'Psalter' of 1621.

Only eleven anthems are known of which two are full and the rest are verse anthems for voices and a consort of viols. As only two of Ravenscroft's anthems are to be found in choir part-books, most of the others may well have been written for his schoolboys at Christ's Hospital. In general they are richly scored in five or six parts.

Of the innumerable music editions of Sternhold and Hopkins' metrical psalter, Ravenscroft's *Whole Booke of Psalmes: with the Hymnes Evangelicall, And Songs Spirituall* (1621) was one of the most important. It was also the last harmonised edition to be published. It included more tunes than any other psalter except Day's. Of the 105 harmonisations twenty-eight had appeared before but fifty-one were by Ravenscroft himself. In addition to tunes by William Parsons and Tallis taken from Day's Psalter of 1563, and by Allison, Bennet, Blanks, Cavendish, Dowland, Farmer, Farnaby, Hooper, Kirby and Morley taken from psalters by Este and Barley (most of which he reharmonised), he included new tunes by Cranford, Harrison, John Milton (the poet's father), Richard Palmer, Martin Peerson, Stubbes, John and Thomas Tomkins, and Ward. As was customary at that time, the melody always appears in the tenor, not the soprano, part. Whereas in earlier psalters tunes in double common-metre (D.C.M.) had preponderated, Ravenscroft favoured single common-metre (C.M.) tunes. He also took over Este's idea of naming tunes after towns and places and applied it to all his tunes: so we have 'Bristol', 'Durham', 'Lincoln', 'Norwich', 'Salisbury' and others. By introducing Scottish and Welsh tunes into an English book for the first time, he gave them a far wider circulation. Some established themselves so firmly that they have retained their popularity ever since and are still in frequent use today: amongst these may be mentioned 'Dundee' and 'York' (from the Scottish Psalter of 1615) and 'St. David'. Tunes which Ravenscroft himself composed probably include 'Bristol' and the truly magnificent 'Old 104th'.

WILLIAM SMITH (1603–45)

There were two minor canons of Durham Cathedral called William Smith: John Jebb (1805–86) in his *The Choral Responses and Litanies of the United Church of England and Ireland* (1847) stated that the composer 'was Organist of Durham Cathedral from 1588 to 1598' and this misattribution was accepted and perpetuated by Atkins and Fellowes in their edition of his Preces and Responses and in the 3rd, 4th and 5th editions of *Grove's Dictionary*. In fact the composer was born in April 1603 and at the age of nine he attended Durham School where he was twice listed among the King's Scholars. He married in 1625 and two years later he became a minor canon of Durham Cathedral and was also Sacrist till 1634 after which he was Precentor. At various times he was given the benefices of Witton Gilbert, St. Mary-le-Bow, and St. Magdalene in Gilliegate, doubtless to supplement his cathedral stipend. His wife died in 1640 and he married again. A son of the second marriage lived only six months and the composer himself died on 19 April 1645.[45]

His appointment to Durham Cathedral coincided with the classic battle about cathedral music between John Cosin, Prebendary of Durham 1624–34, Master of Peterhouse 1635–40, and later Bishop of Durham 1661–72 (translator of 'Come, Holy Ghost, our souls inspire'), and his colleague at Durham, Prebendary Peter Smart. This famous battle, bitter and prolonged, deserves a few lines here. Cosin favoured elaborate ceremonial and complex liturgical music for choir, soloists, 'organs, sackbuts and

[45] For this information I am indebted to Dr. John Buttrey's article, *William Smith of Durham*, Music and Letters, Vol. 43, No. 3, July 1962. (O.U.P.)

cornetts' while Smart was a dyed-in-the-wool Protestant zealot who would countenance only simple services and 'grave' psalm tunes, and who campaigned fanatically against Cosin's 'Popish' practices. The opening salvo, in 1628, came from Smart in a virulent sermon attacking Cosin, for which the High Commission of York at once suspended him. He retaliated by taking legal action against the Dean and Chapter at Durham but lost his case. The next year he preferred the same charges, still unsuccessfully; he was discredited and fined £500 (a very large sum in those days). He refused to pay (perhaps he couldn't) and so suffered imprisonment for his beliefs. With the coming of the Long Parliament in 1641 his fortunes changed dramatically. He was released and his imprisonment declared void. It was now the turn of his arch-enemy, Cosin, to be arraigned before the House of Lords and stripped of his benefices because of his 'Popish innovations'. In 1642 Cosin fled to Paris: there he stayed until the restoration of Charles II when he was made Bishop of Durham. Such, then, was the controversy at the very centre of which William Smith would have found himself, especially as his music was mostly of that elaborate type favoured, and no doubt requested by, Cosin but to which Smart took such violent exception.

'Smith of Durham' is now known almost solely by his very fine set of 5-part Preces and Responses which are sung regularly in nearly all Anglican cathedrals and choral foundations. His other works are all liturgical and include five sets of festal psalms and seven anthems, four of which are settings of Collects:

> *O God, which for our sake* (1st Sunday in Lent)
> *Grant, we beseech thee* (Ascension)
> *Almighty and everlasting God* (Purification)
> *O God, which has taught all the world* (Conversion of St. Paul)

All of these are in verse style.

The festal psalm *Lord, thou art become gracious unto thy land* is one of Smith's very few settings for full choir. It is a lengthy piece, smoothly written and dignified in style but, yet again, has far too many closes in the home key.

JOHN WARD (?–c. 1640)

Very little is known of Ward's life other than that for much of it he was a musician in the service of Sir Henry Fanshawe of Ware Park, Hertfordshire.

He is known chiefly as a madrigal composer but his church music includes two Evening Services and a Te Deum, Kyrie and Creed, all in the verse style, three full anthems and some sixteen verse anthems and sacred songs. Like Ravenscroft's anthems, most of these are laid out somewhat opulently in five or six parts with accompaniment for viols. *Let God arise* seems to have been popular and is found in both liturgical and secular sources, but his other sacred works seem scarcely to have been known in his own day.

COMPOSERS OF TRANSITION

These chapters on renaissance music come to a close with a group who may be called 'composers of transition'. This term needs some justification. As we shall see, in England the Renaissance and the Baroque overlapped by something like half a century, the Renaissance waning as the Baroque waxed. Inevitably, then, composers working during this period showed an admixture of the two styles, beginning with those who were still firmly rooted in renaissance traditions and thought basically in terms of imitative polyphony yet who found themselves increasingly influenced by the new and exciting developments taking place in Italy, elements of which to a greater or lesser extent became incorporated consciously or unconsciously into their own work. Gradually the balance altered until by the end of this period of overlap most composers had become essentially baroque in thought and feeling though many of them could not, even then, shake off entirely the old and long-established styles which had become almost ingrained.

Since, however, the earlier group are still essentially renaissance composers in spite of their baroque innovations, it seems better to discuss them here rather than in the chapters devoted to baroque music even though this involves using a few technical terms which will not be explained until Chapter IX. Two of these men, Philips and Dering, were composers of considerable stature while Robert Ramsey can hardly be dismissed as a 'minor composer'.

PETER PHILIPS (c. 1560–1628)

Philips, or Philipps, was a Catholic who for reasons of security fled to the continent in 1582 and spent the rest of his life abroad, living first in Rome where he studied intensively for three years under his contemporary Felice Anerio and then, after five years of extensive travelling in the service of Thomas, Lord Paget, settled in Antwerp. In 1597 he moved to Brussels to become organist of the Royal Chapel, a post he retained till his death some thirty years later. In 1610 he took holy orders and held several ecclesiastical preferments; these appear to have been sinecures because he continued to carry out his full-time duties in Brussels.

Philips's works include motets, madrigals and instrumental pieces. Most of his secular vocal works were written in the earlier part of his life; after publication of his 6-part madrigals in 1603 he apparently devoted himself henceforth to the composition of sacred works. The key to Philips's position as a composer is to be found in his three years of study at the English College in Rome (1582–85) where Felice Anerio became musical director. At that time Venice was the centre for the *avant-garde* in church music while Rome set itself up as a bulwark of conservatism and reaction. In Rome, Palestrina had been enshrined as a model of perfection, a musical deity, and his younger contemporaries and successors — like the Anerios, Soriano, Nanini and Allegri — struggled to preserve the old renaissance style (which now became known as *stile antico*) against the encroachments of the new baroque style (called *stile nuovo* or *stile moderno*). But as they fought their rearguard action they failed to perceive that because they had themselves been 'contaminated' by the new ideas, they were subtly changing the very substance of what they had committed themselves to preserve. For if the *stile antico* is compared with the truly polyphonic style of, say, Palestrina, several changes will be apparent — the essentially harmonic approach to part-writing, a far greater proportion of chordal writing and sustained chordal effects, more dependence on harmonic colouring, the use of strongly accentual rhythms and a wide dynamic range: yet all these changes are to some extent disguised by the seemingly traditional imitative polyphony with its various 'points'. The resulting style, however backward looking, is just as much a hybrid in its way as the more obviously experimental work of men like Viadana, Banchieri and Grandi in Italy, and East, Peerson and Ramsey in England. But the rushing tides of change were to force still further concessions from the traditionalists: even the works of established masters like di Lasso and the deity, Palestrina himself, were republished with a continuo accompaniment added.

Philips, as a student under Felice Anerio, became closely identified with the Roman *stile antico*. Nearly all his best sacred works were originally conceived as *a cappella* motets in the old imitative style though it is not without significance that his sixty-nine 5-part motets published by Phalèse in 1612 under the title *Cantiones Sacrae* were re-issued in 1617 with an added *basso continuo* part.[46] Similarly the 8-part *a cappella* motets of 1613 were re-issued with a *basso continuo* in 1625. His first works designed to have a continuo accompaniment were the 2- and 3-part motets issued in 1613 and these are the earliest known example of the use of a *basso continuo* by an English composer: but even here one often senses that the accompaniment was something added, an afterthought, rather than an integral part of the conception.

His best works abound in imaginative detail. Thus in *Surge Petre* the upward leap of a fifth in the opening point is exactly imitated by two voices, the other two rising a fourth instead of a fifth; but when immediately afterwards the command is repeated, increasing urgency is given to it by making the leap a whole octave. At the beginning of *Alma redemptoris mater* the opening motif is sung in normal imitation by three voices, the other two singing it in inversion. *Elegi abjectus esse* opens with two meanes and tenor in strict imitation, the bass has a tonal answer but the alto is free. In *O beatum et sacrosanctum diem* the broken triads at 'in sono tubae' are almost identical with a setting of similar words, 'in voce tubae', in *Ascendit Deus* by Jacob Handl (1550–91). Philips's own *Ascendit Deus* has a similar passage at the same point though the correspondence is not so exact. This brilliant motet ends with a vigorous 'alleluia' section of a type which became increasingly common in English church music of the next century and a half. Philips's most popular work, *Cantantibus organis,* is another rousing piece full of excitement and vitality. He was at his best in this vein.

Pater noster is something of a throw-back as it is constructed on a plainchant *cantus firmus*: a feeling of deliberate pastiche is underlined by the use of degree inflection and false relations to colour the word 'libera'. In *Regina coeli*, Philips draws on plainchant for his opening theme which is then subjected to paraphrase treatment. *Ave Maria* and *Salve Regina* are also paraphrase works. *O Beatum* and *Tibi laus* are mainly chordal and the predominantly duple measure is varied by sections in triple time: the latter work ends brilliantly with a chattering section to the words 'et superexaltatum' which demands rapid repetition of notes and is great fun to sing.

Drama and suffering are subtly suggested in *Ave verum corpus*: double suspensions portray the agony of 'immolatum in cruce' and the eloquent 'miserere mei' section forms an emotional climax to the whole piece. A particularly interesting work is *O virum mirabilem*, a setting of the antiphon to Magnificat at 2nd Vespers of the Feast of St. Francis: the many repetitions in all voices of 'Francisce' suggest humanity crying out to the Saint, begging for his intercession. Another superb work is *O crux splendidor*: it is even more conservative in idiom than most of Philips's work but it has that inner radiance and intensity which one associates with the Spanish school (incidentally the opening has much in common, both in mood and style, with the beginning of King John of Portugal's setting of a very similar text, *Crux fidelis*). Some may think the madrigalian 'alleluias' at the end rather weaken its impact.

[46] *The British Union–Catalogue of English Music*, Ed. Schnapper, p. 780. (Butterworth, 1957).

These motets are all 5-part works.

In 1613 Philips brought out a book of 2- and 3-part 'motets' scored for two meanes, or two meanes and bass, with a *basso continuo* part for the organ. They were an imitation of some motets by Viadana published in his *Cento Concerti Ecclesiastici* of 1602 and are an adaptation for voices of the style of the baroque trio sonata. The madrigalian lightness and rhythmic buoyancy of these songs established them as an important form. Within a few years collections of similar pieces were issued by Dering, Childs and the Lawes brothers, following Viadana's model.

MARTIN PEERSON (*c*. 1572–1650)

Born in March, Cambridgeshire, Peerson was from 1613 till his death organist of St. Paul's Cathedral. He was a fairly prolific composer and his output included some splendid string fantasias, keyboard pieces (some were included in the Fitzwilliam Virginal Book) and madrigal-type part-songs for 4, 5 and 6 voices, as well as eight full anthems, thirteen extended verse anthems and about a dozen Latin motets, though he was a staunch Protestant. He seems to have been one of the first Englishmen to use the term 'basso continuo'. His collection of secular and sacred madrigals *Mottects or Grave Chamber Musique* (1630) contains 'Songs of five parts of severall sorts, some ful, and some Verse and Chorus. But all fit for Voyces and Vials, with an Organ Part; which for want of Organs, may be performed on Virginals, Base-Lute, Bandora, or Irish Harpe'. Though the organ part is clearly optional the mere fact that it exists at all destroys the true spirit of the madrigal and is a measure of the decline to which this beautiful form had fallen. On the other hand this same collection has an importance in musical history out of all proportion to its intrinsic merit because, so far as is known, it was the very first publication in England to be provided with a *figured* bass-line. (Admittedly Peter Philips used figuring many years before Peerson but his works were published abroad.) Actually Peerson's continuo is not purely and simply a figured-bass within the usual meaning of the words; rather it is a short score showing the top part in addition to the bass, sometimes with a few additional notes. Curiously, it does not distinguish between vocal and instrumental sections.

Of his sacred pieces with English words, only three appear in choir part-books: *Blow out the trumpet; Bow down thine ear* and *I will magnify thee*. This implies that most, if not all, of his English sacred works were designed for domestic use and so are not really anthems at all. If so, this would help to explain the odd texts he so often chose and would also account for his intensely subjective and 'pathetick' style, largely brought about by the use of chromatic intervals and progressions. *Blow out the trumpet* won considerable esteem for its composer during his lifetime mainly because of the novelty and extravagance of his word-painting; the drumming rhythms of the 'sound an alarum' section must have been a special treat for connoisseurs of the bizarre.

The verse anthems are laid out on a lavish scale with five or six solo voices, choir, instruments and organ. The instruments and continuo are used throughout to accompany both soloists and full choir; this was fairly common practice during the period of transition. *O Lord, in thee* is a rare instance at this time of an anthem founded on a psalm-tune: it is one of the first in that long line of 'hymn-anthems' which have always proved popular. Such pieces are a specialised adaptation of the air-and-variations form.

RICHARD DERING (*c.* 1580–1630)

Just as we blithely bracket together composers as disparate as Bach and Handel, Haydn and Mozart, Bruckner and Mahler, Debussy and Ravel, so Philips and Dering seem to be immutably yoked together — and perhaps with better reason, for much that was written above about Philips applies with equal force to Dering, though Dering (or Deering) flourished a generation later. He was born somewhere between 1575 and 1585. He was an illegitimate son of Henry Dering of Liss, Hampshire. When, in 1610, he supplicated for a B.Mus. degree from Christ Church, Oxford, he stated that he had been studying music for ten years. It seems likely that he was the 'Mr. Dearing' who in 1612 was in the service of the British ambassador to Venice, Sir John Harrington. At some stage in his early life he was converted to Roman Catholicism but it is not known if his conversion took place while he was in Italy. It may be that he was converted while still a student and then, thinking life would be safer and less restricted abroad, decided to emigrate. There seems little doubt that most of his adult life was spent on the continent and from about 1617–25 he was organist of the Convent of the Benedictine Nuns in Brussels. It was not until 1625 that he returned to England and took up an appointment as organist to Queen Henrietta Maria and 'musician for the lute and voice' to Charles I. He died five years later. As Philips and Dering were both distinguished organists and composers, especially for the Roman rite; as they were both English recusants living in exile in the same foreign city; and as they even published their works through the same firm, it seems fairly certain that they were closely acquainted: in fact it is more than likely that Dering obtained his appointment through Philips's influence.

His long exile meant that most of his music was published on the continent, including four sets of *Cantiones sacrae* issued by the Flemish publishing house Phalèse of Louvain. Indeed his long neglect by students of English church music may largely be due to the fact that he was a recusant exile who wrote and published most of his music abroad. Furthermore, very little of his music has so far been available in print though at long last a collected edition is now in preparation.

Dering is one of the most important of this group of 'composers of transition', partly because of the sterling merit of much of his work but more because he appears to have been one of the first to introduce elements of the Italian *stile nuovo* (what Monteverdi called his *seconda prattica*) into English church music. This strengthens the likelihood that he had lived in Venice where he would have heard at first hand the new and exciting music being composed by Monteverdi, Caccini, Donati, Grandi, Peri, Saracini, Viadana and others. As we have seen, Venice was at this time the centre for the *avant-garde*. We have noted the time lag between new developments abroad and their acceptance in England: during his sojourn abroad, and especially if he had lived in Venice, Dering would have imbibed the new ideas directly and immediately, so placing himself stylistically well in advance of his English contemporaries.

One obvious way in which foreign influence separates him from his English colleagues is his provision of a continuo accompaniment to his printed works resulting in a curiously ambivalent transitional style in which a chorus *a cappella* is combined with a *basso continuo*. The bass is unfigured and it was left to Peerson to use figuring for the first time in England. As we shall see in Chapter IX, the use of *basso continuo* in itself implies a marked swing towards harmonic, as opposed to contrapuntal, thinking, a swing which is reflected in the high predominance of chordal textures in Dering's music. The

G

increasing use of chordal textures in late renaissance/early baroque music was brought about not only by purely musical considerations but also by a changing attitude towards the words themselves. The text now had to be heard clearly and unequivocally; obviously this was more likely to be achieved if all the voices were singing the same word at the same time rather than singing different words simultaneously, as in a polyphonic texture.

Of course Dering's early training, like that of Weelkes and Gibbons, was in the late renaissance polyphonic tradition and he too was skilled in the art of writing smoothly-flowing polyphony; yet even in his motets the influence of Luzzaschi, Gesualdo, Viadana and Monteverdi is apparent, both in mood and idiom. Whereas typical renaissance sacred music was essentially objective and impersonal, a generalised and at times classic expression of universal religious emotions and moods, so the new music was far more subjective and personal, an eloquent outpouring of an individual's religious impulses, passionate and dramatic in expression. This passion and drama is conveyed by a much more fragmented texture with frequent full closes, often followed by a startling change of key or a sequential repetition often in some quite unexpected key: sometimes chordal passages are separated by silences (always effective in a large building). There is an increasing delight in simple rhythmic patterns, no doubt suggested by the madrigal and

Dering: *Contristatus est Rex David*

Ex. 88

194

especially by such dance-song types as the *canzonet* and *ballett*. Even more striking is a far greater freedom in the treatment of dissonance: whereas the sixteenth-century composer prepared and resolved dissonances according to fairly strict 'rules', his early seventeenth century successor would use far more daring dissonances without preparation. Most of these points are illustrated in a passage from Dering's *Contristatus est Rex David* (see Example 88 opposite).

At (a) we have a rest preceding a chordal passage which is itself arranged in a ballett-like rhythmic pattern (b); at (c) an unprepared discord involves the melodic leap of an augmented 2nd in the second treble part. A similar passage occurs in *O vos omnes* at the words 'Attendite universi populi'. Of course, a brief silence before a full choir entry was no new thing (there are some spine-tingling examples in Tallis's 40-part *Spem in alium*) and passages in dance-rhythm are not uncommon in late sixteenth-century sacred music. It is Dering's distinctive and more frequent use, often resulting in 'affective' or dramatic fragmentation, coupled with his daring and much freer use of discord which makes his music quite unlike that of more typical English renaissance composers. (Incidentally there is an even more moving 'O Absalom' passage at the end of his anthem *And the king was moved*.) Even in a comparatively conservative motet like *Factum est silentium* at one point the second tenor leaps down from D to A sharp: the same interval occurs in *Vox in Rama* and in *Ave verum corpus*.

Now look at Ex. 88 again: in the last two bars we see some parallelism between the upper voices. This is characteristic of the composer and is found in most of his available works. In the following example, from the 5-part *O bone Jesu*, doubling two melodic lines at the 3rd and/or 6th results in two streams of chords in contrary motion, a device which three centuries later was to be greatly developed and elaborated by Vaughan Williams (see p. 426):

Dering: *O bone Jesu*

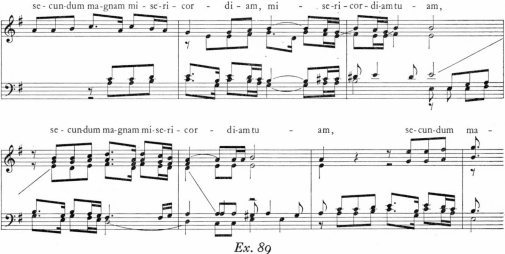

Ex. 89

It must be noted that by bracketing two or three parts together in parallel motion, each individual part loses its independence: such a sacrifice is diametrically opposed to true renaissance style where all parts enjoy an independent existence — like the parts in a string quartet.

One of Dering's best and most characteristic pieces is the 6-part Christmas motet *Quem vidistis pastores* in which there is highly effective interplay between high and low voices. The middle section 'collaudantes Dominum' breaks into triple measure (one edition marks it minim = 76, another has minim = 138: the latter is probably nearer the truth). The work ends with a brilliant 'alleluia' section. Whereas most composers of the sixteenth and early seventeenth centuries seem to have found sombre and penitential texts more congenial, Dering excelled in works of great brilliance. Two other 6-part works in similar vein to *Quem vidistis pastores* are *Factum est silentium* and *Cantate Domino*: such pieces show him at his best. *O vos omnes* may be thought rather less successful because the brilliance and sumptuous richness of the part-writing seem at variance with the agony of the text; yet degree inflection, augmented intervals above the bass, and chains of false relations impart a subtle poignancy. There are also instances of a descending leap of a diminished fifth followed by a semitone rise. Several leaps of a major sixth occur. The lovely 5-part *Jesu, dulcis memoria* accurately reflects the composer's Janus-like position, its smoothly-flowing polyphony and telling use of degree inflection testifying to his renaissance background and training, its clear-cut harmonic basis, harmonically derived vocal lines, frequent chordal passages, dancing rhythms, and the use of a *basso continuo* clearly pointing forwards to the baroque style. Another powerful dramatic work is *Vox in Rama*. *Ave verum corpus* too reaches a high level of inspiration and the shifting harmonies of the closing bars brings about an ending of the most tender melancholy.

Following in the footsteps of Viadana and Peter Philips, Dering too composed a number of 2- and 3-part Latin songs with *basso continuo* accompaniment. They were probably first heard in Queen Henrietta Maria's private chapel at Somerset House from 1629 onwards and they soon enjoyed immense popularity. They were published posthumously in 1662 by John Playford under the title *Cantica sacra*.

Dering wrote a few sacred pieces with English words, including two verse anthems, but these are less distinguished. Clearly, a proper assessment of this composer cannot be made until much more of his music becomes available in print.

A curious footnote. Oliver Cromwell, arch-Puritan and iconoclast, had two choirboys specially trained so that they could join him in singing Dering's 2- and 3-part Latin sacred songs. Dering, a staunch Catholic, was the Protector's favourite composer.

ROBERT RAMSEY (Fl. 1610–44)

Ramsey is by far the most obscure of this group of composers. More or less ignored by his contemporaries and successors and largely overlooked by scholars since, it is only in the last few years that serious attention has been given to his work and his English sacred music, edited by Edward Thompson, published.[47] Dates of his birth and death are not known and other biographical details are scanty. All that is known about him is that after seven years' study he took his Mus.B. at Cambridge in 1616, was organist of Trinity College, Cambridge, 1628–44, and master of the children there from 1637–44. That and no more. The implication is that his working life extended from about 1610 to at least 1644. In that year he probably died. His surviving music is all vocal and most of it is sacred, with texts in English and Latin. His English works include a fairly complete

[47] Edward Thompson: *Robert Ramsey I*: *English Sacred Music* (Early English Church Music, Vol. 7. Stainer and Bell.)

4-part Service (included by Tudway in his collection of cathedral music, 1714–20, and admired by Ouseley and Fellowes), seven full anthems, a verse anthem, and a 3-part dramatic dialogue with accompaniment. Another ten English works are known but are too fragmentary for editorial reconstruction. Latin works surviving complete or capable of completion include two settings of Te Deum and Jubilate, a Litany, three motets and the 'commencement song' *Inclina Domine* written for his degree in 1616.

It is possible to trace a fairly clear line of development from Ramsey's early works through to his later pieces. The earliest anthems are markedly madrigalian in form and texture with typical touches of expressive pictorialism (as at 'he went up to his chamber' in *When David heard*). Even so, baroque influence shows in his affective use of the diminished fifth to colour the word 'desolate' in *How doth the city* and to depict the fate of the mighty in *How are the mighty fallen*. In this last anthem Ramsey attempts to heighten the affectiveness by some bold modulations, violent false relations and clashing major and minor thirds, but often the result sounds merely forced and restless. In *When David heard* there is an unforgettable moment when the three lower voices sing 'thus he said' to a cadence in D major which is echoed by the three highest voices: then there is a beat's silence before the full choir enters on the totally unexpected chord of B flat major for the dramatic cry 'O my son Absalon'.

Edward Thompson has suggested a date between 1620 and 1630 for items in some part-books at Peterhouse. These 'middle period' anthems are less polyphonic, more chordal, though their form is still derived from imitative points. The text is often repeated merely to satisfy musical needs—balancing of phrases, antiphonal effects and the like. Aggressive false relations and clashing major and minor thirds everywhere abound and at times almost suggest early renaissance style, but the baroque craving for heightened emotion and affectiveness is manifest in Ramsey's jagged melodic lines and extensive use of diminished fourths, fifths and octaves as melodic intervals. The following passage from *Almighty and everlasting God, we humbly beseech* is typical (see Example 90 on the next page). Notice the angular melodic lines (a), the diminished fourth (b), and the clashing thirds (c).

God who as upon this day, the Collect for Whitsunday, has a curious passage near the end which, however contrived on paper, sounds like a chain of exposed consecutive fifths: it is repeated a fourth lower. In *Grant, we beseech thee* the madrigalist in Ramsey responds predictably to phrases like 'ascended into heav'n' and 'thither ascend'. This group includes *My song shall be alway*, the only verse anthem to have survived in a reasonably complete condition (Edward Thompson has reconstructed the missing tenor part). It is scored for bass soloist, 4-part choir, and organ accompaniment. The solo is largely built on sequences; nearly every phrase is at once repeated at a different pitch and so the text emerges as:

> My song, my song, shall be alway, shall be alway,
> of the loving kindness of the Lord, of the loving kindness
> of the Lord: with my mouth, with my mouth, will I be ever
> showing thy truth, will I be ever showing thy truth, from
> one generation, from one generation, to another.

Perhaps the most important work in the Peterhouse part-books is the 4-part Service which includes Te Deum, Jubilate, Kyrie, Litany, Creed, Magnificat and Nunc dimittis.

Robert Ramsey: *Almighty and everlasting God, we humbly beseech*

Ex. 90

Thompson points out that it shows little Italian influence but bears a close kinship with Gibbons's Short Service.

Thompson suggests a date after 1630 for the 5-part *O come, let us sing* and the extraordinary scena *In guiltie night*. In the former, extensive use of dotted-note figures generates the same kind of rhythmic vitality and forward thrust that we find in Restoration full anthems; another foretaste of Restoration style is the jingling 'alleluia' section with which the piece ends. This anthem is surprisingly forward-looking for its time. Incidentally, though Ramsey was a notable innovator and experimenter, it is worth recording that none of his church music is provided with a *basso continuo*.

In guiltie night is not an anthem: it is a dramatic scena in the form of a 'dialogue' between Saul (tenor), the Witch of Endor (soprano), and Samuel's ghost (bass), with unfigured continuo; it ends with a short 3-part chorus. The work is a series of recitatives very much in the *stile nuovo*. The influence of Italian monody may be either direct (Dr. Thompson suspects that Ramsey may have spent part of his early life in Italy) or indirect—through Lanier, Porter, the Lawes brothers and others—but it is certainly strong. Diminished intervals, expressive harmonies, broken phrases and similar affective devices are used to build up dramatic tension. Because the music is used only to heighten the drama there is no repetition of text merely to satisfy musical needs. Here again Ramsey seems to lean forward half a century: though his recitative has not the plasticity of line, melodic beauty, and sense of overall shape which we find in the best work of Purcell and Pelham Humfrey, the piece is nevertheless typically Restoration in style and feeling. The following extract shows that the process of transition is already far advanced:

Robert Ramsey: *In guiltie night*

Ex. 91

For the following information about Ramsey's Latin works I am indebted to Dr. Edward Thompson personally. He points out that three motets and the 'commencement song' *Inclina Domine* have survived complete and that the other liturgical music is sufficiently complete to make reconstruction feasible. Of all Ramsey's music only the 8-part *Inclina Domine* can be accurately dated; it is an early work, written in 1616, and is notable both for its effective use of choral recitative and its exciting antiphonal harmonic clashes.

In Dr. Thompson's opinion the other Latin works were probably 'middle period' works composed between 1620 and 1630. Of these the two 6-part motets *In monte Olivete* and *O vos omnes* are similar in style to *How are the mighty fallen* which comes from the same source, the secular part-books in the Euing Collection at Glasgow University Library. These works are not found in any liturgical source whereas the 5-part *O sapientia* is found only in the liturgical Peterhouse manuscripts and not in any secular source. Ramsey's Latin works reflect the spirit of the *nuove musiche* to a much greater extent than his English settings though even here he never provides a *basso continuo*.

Of all his output, Latin and English, the most interesting and forward-looking pieces are his 4-part and 5-part settings of Te Deum and Jubilate with Latin text. The Te Deum settings in particular make considerable use of *concertato* textures in which verse passages are set against full sections, though there is no independent accompaniment for strings or organ. Another distinctive feature of these settings is Ramsey's use of choral recitative. Rhythms are complex and harmonies daring. In the 5-part Te Deum, solo passages and verse sections are unusually elaborate. What a world of difference there is between the flash and fire of these passionate, dramatic Latin Canticles which could almost be by Monteverdi himself and the demure and rather colourless 4-part English Service. This contrast highlights the conflicting elements which were never effectively reconciled during this period of transition.

CHAPTER VIII

Church Music and the Puritans

It is well known that the Puritans discountenanced elaborate music in their public worship. After the brilliant period of the Elizabethans and Jacobeans during which church music achieved new heights in beauty, richness, expressiveness and technical mastery, it was suddenly hurled to the lowest depths it had ever reached. Yet this Puritan attitude was no new thing; as we saw in Chapter II, from the very earliest days of the Church there were some who had grave misgivings about the power which music could exert.

Nevertheless the popular image of them as stern, sour, moralising, intolerant, drably garbed zealots, bitterly opposed to all forms of personal vanity and worldly pleasure, especially music and dancing, bears little resemblance to reality. In his book *The Puritans and Music*,[1] Dr. Percy Scholes amassed an impressive collection of evidence to show that secular music, far from languishing during the Commonwealth period, flourished as never before. He points out, for instance, that during this period:

1. England's first full-time music publisher, John Playford, set up in business in 1648 and issued a series of books including, amongst others:

    1651 *The English Dancing Master* — new and enlarged editions 1652 and 1657. (Interesting because the Puritans are popularly thought of as being opposed to all forms of dancing.)
    Musick and Mirth (Rounds and catches for three voices — another volume which suggests good humour and frivolity.)
    A Musicall Banquet, in three books, consisting of Lessons for the Lyra Viol; Allmans, and Sarabands, Choice Catches and Rounds, etc.

    1652 *A banquet of Musick, set forth in three several varieties of musick; first Lessons for the Lyra Viol, the second Ayres and Jiggs for the Violin, the third Rounds and Catches, all of which are fitted to the capacity of young practitioners.*

    Catch that Catch can, or a choice collection of catches, rounds and canons for 3 or 4 voices, collected by John Hilton. Though we of the twentieth century can hardly call ourselves squeamish or prudish, the words of many of these catches, completely acceptable in Puritan England, would be considered quite unprintable today!
    A Book of new lessons for the Cithern and Gittern.

    1653 *Ayres and Dialogues for one, two, and three voyces by Henry Lawes.*

    1655 His famous *An Introduction to the Skill of Musick, in two books; first a brief and plain introduction to musick, both for singing and for playing the Violl, by J. P.; second the Art of setting or composing musick in parts . . . formerly*

[1] Percy Scholes: *The Puritans and Music.* (O.U.P. 1934, reissued 1970.)

> *published by Dr. Tho. Campion, but now republished by Mr. Christopher Sympson.* (Second edition 1658, third edition 1660.)
>
> 1657 *Ayres and Dialogues to be sung to the Theorbo-lute, or Basse Viol by John Gamble.*
>
> 1659 *The Division Violist or an introduction to playing upon a ground, by Christopher Sympson.*

2. Opera was first introduced into England during the Commonwealth by the play-wright Sir William Davenant, a noted Royalist and Catholic, who had been imprisoned in the Tower for two years under threat of execution but was finally reprieved through the intervention of Puritan friends (including Milton). Davenant's productions included:

> *The First Dayes Entertainment* (1656)
> *The Siege of Rhodes* (1656)
> *The Cruelty of the Spaniards in Peru* (1658)
> *The History of Sir Francis Drake* (1659)

The First Dayes Entertainment was given at Rutland House but later productions were mounted at 'Drewry' Lane.

3. Music teaching and the teaching of dancing became flourishing and highly respected professions. Playford, in his *Musicall Banquet* of 1651, lists eighteen of London's most eminent teachers 'for the Voyce or Viole' and another nine for the Organ or Virginall, adding 'cum multis aliis'. Nicholas Hookes, in his *Amanda* (1653), gives a curious list, in execrable verse, of musicians prominent in Cambridge, and Anthony Wood, the Oxford chronicler, gives detailed accounts of the musical life in his city and describes his own musical training. Furthermore, youths continued to be legally apprenticed to the study and trade of music.

4. The rising popularity and rapid growth of music clubs and meetings became a new social force in musical life. Many professional musicians maintained a series of regular weekly concerts in their own homes; such meetings paved the way for the public concerts of Banister, Britton and others later in the century.

5. The town waits seem to have been everywhere maintained with little interruption or curtailment of their activities except that they were forbidden to perform on Sundays.

6. The harp, representing Ireland, was one of two emblems (the other being the cross of St. George of England) which were displayed over the Speaker's chair in the Puritan Parliament and which appeared on many coins issued during the Commonwealth. Cromwell also had the harp emblem incorporated into his own personal standard. A frigate commissioned in 1656 was called the *Harp* and the emblem also appeared on the naval 'Jack' until the Restoration, when its use was discontinued in deference to the king's wishes.

7. The Puritan Parliament paid arrears of salary due to Charles I's musicians: they gave consideration to a scheme for offering financial relief to dispossessed church musicians, and appointed a 'Committee for the Advancement of Musicke'.

8. Several Puritan writers show their love and knowledge of music, including Milton, Marvell, Bunyan and George Wither. Milton was himself a capable performer and there is some evidence to suggest that so was Bunyan.

9. Such prominent Puritans as Bulstrode Whitelocke (Member of Parliament, a

Commissioner of the Treasury, Keeper of the Great Seal, and Ambassador to Sweden) and Francis North (Lord Guilford) actually took music lessons and became accomplished performers. Cromwell himself was so fond of music that he maintained a small musical staff under John Hingston which included two boys specially trained to sing Richard Deering's Latin motets! He had the organ of Magdalen College, Oxford, removed to his own palace of Hampton Court and his daughters received music lessons from Hingston.

So Scholes achieves the purpose of his book—to prove beyond all doubt that the Puritans enjoyed dancing, secular music and other worldly pleasures in moderation, so long as the sanctity of Sunday was not violated. But then who were the Puritans? In general terms they were a legacy of the Reformation and consisted of those who felt, for one reason or another, that the reformers had not gone far enough. The word 'Puritan' itself is useful but imprecise: it is an umbrella word which covers groups varying from moderate reformers still enfolded within the established Church to dangerous extremists like the Fifth Monarchy men; it embraces sects as disparate as the Presbyterians, Baptists, Anabaptists, Separatists (or Brownists), Quakers, Independents, and the 'lunatic fringe' of such groups as the Seekers and Levellers. With so many contending factions, uniformity would obviously be impossible—though most desired it and would even have sanctioned military action to enforce it (on their own terms). Even unity would be difficult to achieve. The one thing which they all had in common was an implicit trust in the Bible as the one only, sufficient and infallible instrument of personal salvation. In practice this meant that 'they demanded express Scriptural warrant for all the details of public worship, believing that all other forms were popish, superstitious, idolatrous, and anti-Christian'.[2]

The struggle between them and the established Church swayed back and forth with shifting emphasis and varying intensity over three main areas of conflict:

1. The organisation of the Church. In general the Puritan sects rejected the threefold order of Bishops, Priests and Deacons and were opposed to the prelacy and to senior clerical appointments. The 'Root and Branch Bill', given its first reading in the Commons on 27 May 1641, is a typical expression of this attitude: it was 'An Act for the utter abolishing and taking away of all archbishops, bishops, their chancellors, commissaries, deans and chapters, archdeacons, prebendaries, chanters, and canons, and all other their under officers'. In place of the existing order there should be a new system of government by Presbyters, at least half of whom would be 'elders', i.e. laymen, elected and set apart to assist in matters of administration and discipline.

2. Theological doctrine and dogma. Puritan theology incorporated many of the tenets of the Continental reformers—the Bible as the only authority on which to base life and religion, justification by faith without works, the certitude of salvation for the elect, and Calvin's doctrines of predestination and the inadmissibility of grace. Insistence on the Bible as the only basis for worship led to a rejection of all that was considered man-made—prescribed forms of worship; fallible traditions and customs; the lives, example and writings of non-Scriptural saints and divines; and the material wealth and worldly power of the Church. In the central act of Christian

[2] Article 'Puritans' in *The Oxford Dictionary of the Christian Church*. Ed. F. L. Cross (O.U.P.) 1957.

worship the English Prayer Book had already changed the concept of 'Eucharist' to that of 'Holy Communion'. The Puritans refuted both the doctrine of transubstantiation and the idea of the Communion as a propitiatory sacrifice; instead, they laid emphasis on the commemorative character of the 'Lord's Supper' (the use of this title is significant) and instead of an altar, a 'Holy Table' was placed table-wise amongst the people.

3. Forms of worship and clerical vestments. In their reaction against the beauty, richness and complexity of ritual and ceremonial in the Church of Rome and, to a lesser extent, in the Church of England, the Puritans threw out everything which was not specifically enjoined in Scripture. Not only did they abandon prescribed forms of service; they abolished the sign of the cross and attacked church ornaments and 'superstitious vanities', communion rails, vestments, surplices, rochets, organs, choirs, and elaborate music. Even beauty in coloured glass, wood and stone was abhorrent to the extremists. Henceforth all worship must be centred on 'The Word of God'—in Bible readings, psalm-singing and, most of all perhaps, in preaching (the exposition of 'The Word').

This then was the general pattern of Puritan thought, a pattern subject to considerable variation within the many dissident sects. So far as church music is concerned, virtually all Puritans were hostile to what we have called 'the cathedral tradition' and their hostility extended to several aspects of parish church music.[3] In *The Puritans and Music*, Scholes is not primarily concerned with church music. Insofar as he treats it at all he appears so anxious to whitewash the Puritans that he glosses over an exceedingly ugly piece of authorised vandalism and smilingly holds out for our inspection a few organs (such as King's and Christ's Colleges, Cambridge; York Minster; St. Paul's and Lincoln Cathedrals) which somehow survived the holocaust. The stark fact remains that buildings were pillaged, art treasures destroyed, robes burnt, and organs hacked to pieces. In Ryves's *Mercurius Rusticus* (1642–43) it is recorded that:

[at Westminster Abbey] the soldiers of Westborne and Caewood's Companies . . . brake downe the Organs,[4] and pawned the pipes at severall ale-houses for pots of ale; [at Exeter] they brake downe the organs, and taking two or three hundred pipes with them in a most scornefull and contemptuous manner, went up and downe the streets piping with them; [at Canterbury] they violated the monuments of the dead, and spoyled the organs; [at Chichester] they leave the destructive and spoyling part to be finished by common soldiers; brake down the organs, and, dashing the pipes with their pole-axes, scoffingly said, 'Harke how the organs goe'; [at Winchester they] burnt the Books of Common Prayer and all the Singing books belonging to the Quire: they threw downe the organs, and brake the Stories of the Old and New Testament, curiously cut out of carved work.

A Durham Cathedral chronicler describes how
on Midsummer Day of that year [1641], and not till then, did they use any violence

---

[3] See pp. 20 and 231–2.
[4] The plural forms 'organs' or 'payres of organs' were often used where now we should employ the singular form. See p. 61.

or harm to the organs in this church; but then they fell on them and broke them, and tore up all the keys of the great organs . . .

The desecration of Norwich Cathedral in 1643 is vividly depicted by its Bishop, John Hall, who wrote:

Lord, what work was here, what clattering of glasses, what beating down of walls, what tearing up of monuments, what pulling down of seats, what wresting out of irons and brass from the windows and graves, what defacing of arms, what demolishing of curious stone work that had not any representation in the world but only the coat of the founder and skill of the mason, what toting and piping upon the destroyed organ pipes, and what hideous triumph on the market day before all the country, when, in a kind of sacrilegious and profane procession, all the organ pipes, vestments, both copes and surplices, together with the leaden cross which had been newly sawn down from over the green yard pulpit, and the service books and singing books that could be had, were carried to the fire in the market place, a lewd wretch walking before the train, in his cope, trailing in the dirt, with a service book in his hand, imitating, in an impious scorn, the tune, and usurping the words of the Litany, used formerly in the church; near the public cross all these monuments of idolatry must be sacrificed to the fire, not without much ostentation of a zealous joy in discharging ordnance to the cost of some who professed how much they had longed to see that day. Neither was it any news, upon the Guild day, to have the Cathedral, now open on all sides, to be filled with musketeers, waiting for the major's return, drinking and tobaccoing as freely as if it had turned ale-house.

Many similar accounts exist in contemporary records. Those given here are actually quoted by Scholes in *The Puritans and Music* but he lightly brushes them aside with two arguments. First, he suggests that most of them come from royalists, dispossessed clerics, or people with axes to grind. Thus, speaking of Ryves, he says 'I mention these facts merely as a hint that we should take at any rate a small pinch of salt with any story Ryves tells us about the Puritans as, *though it is doubtless correct as to its main fabric*, it has probably nevertheless some small decorative trimmings of a Cavalier colour' (my italics). His second argument is, perhaps, more valid: 'It should be remembered, too, that all the organ destructions he [Ryves] mentions took place in the early days of the war: they are not merely prior to the official order of Parliament for the destruction of organs, but also to the creation of the disciplined New Model Army (1644); the material of the army when these deeds were done was still that of which Cromwell had to complain to Hampden, "Your troops are most of them old decayed serving men and tapsters and such kind of fellows".' We all know that louts and rowdies are quick to seize upon any excuse to let off steam and do damage and it is not unlikely that marauding bands of mercenaries enjoyed smashing up churches. But is this the whole story? As early as 1580 a Puritan pamphlet unequivocally demanded 'Let cathedral churches be utterly destroyed . . . very dens of thieves, where the time and place of God's service, preaching and prayer, is most filthily abused; in piping with organs, in singing, ringing and trolling of the Psalms from one side of the choir to another, with squealing of chanting choristers . . . Dumb dogs, unskilful, sacrificing priests, destroying drones, or rather, caterpillars of the Word . . . Dens of lazy, loitering lubbards.'[5] Further, if most organs had already been destroyed in the early days of the Civil War, why was it necessary for Parliament to issue, on 9 May 1644, *Two ordinances of the Lords and Commons assembled in Parliament for the speedy demolishing of all organs, images and all matters of superstitious monuments in all Cathedralls, and Collegiate or Parish-Churches and Chapels, throughout the Kingdom of England and the Dominion of Wales; the better to accomplish the blessed reformation so happily begun, and to remove all offences and things illegal in the worship of God*, and what practical effect did these ordinances have? Scholes remains silent on both points, yet the purpose of the ordinances seems explicit and must ever stand as a damning indictment against the Puritans. In any case, how can we blame a few common soldiers for running wild when we read how their leader behaved at Peterborough cathedral:

> The first that came was a foot regiment, under one Colonel Hubbard's command; upon its arrival some persons of the town, fearing what happened afterwards, desired the chief commander to take care the soldiers did no injury to the church; this he promised to do, and gave orders to have the church doors all locked up. Some two days afterwards comes a regiment of horse, under Colonel Cromwell, a name as fatal to ministers as it had been to monasteries before;[6] the next day after their arrival, early in the morning, these break open the church doors, pull down the organs, of which there were two pair. The greater pair, that stood upon a high loft over the entrance into the choir, was thence thrown down upon the ground, and there stamped and trampled on, and broke in pieces, with such a strange, furious, and frantick zeal, as cannot be well conceived, but by those that saw it.[7]

It is no extenuation of this crime to say that ten years later Cromwell had the organ of Magdalen College, Oxford, taken down and installed in his own home at Hampton Court: domestic organs were common enough in the wealthy homes of those days and it must be remembered that there was no objection to the organ itself as a musical instrument so long as it was not used in public worship.

But hacking organs to pieces was the least damaging of Puritan measures against church music; far more pernicious in the long run was the destruction of music libraries and part books, and the disbanding of choirs.

It is not easy for us to appreciate how much irreparable harm was done by the burning of choir music libraries. Most of the music would still have been in sets of hand-written part-books containing a series of services and/or anthems selected by the choirmaster. Since music copying was laborious and expensive[8] usually only one set, just sufficient for the choir, would exist. Each set would therefore be individual and unique so that if it should be destroyed its contents would vanish forever, unless any of the pieces happened to be used in other churches. Of course popular pieces or works by famous composers would be sung by most choirs and would therefore find their way into a good many sets of part books, so providing modern editors with a fair number of manuscript sources (not all of which agree). The few printed part-books which then existed were

---

[5] Quoted by Bishop Stephen Neill in *Anglicanism*, p. 114. (Penguin Books.)
[6] A reference to Thomas Cromwell, Henry VIII's agent in the Dissolution of the Monasteries.
[7] Gunton's *History of the Church of Peterborough*, published 1688.
[8] See full title of Barnard's *Selected Church Music* on p. 288.

issued in very limited editions and here again wide-scale destruction by the Puritans led to the total disappearance of some works and to the survival of maimed and incomplete sets of others. Even those sets of parts which escaped Puritan bonfires often became split up and separated: thus, such a useful printed collection as Barnard's *Selected Church Musick* (1641), issued in ten separate part-books, has nowhere survived complete; fortunately in this case it has been possible to transcribe the entire work because Hereford possessed eight of the ten parts (since purchased by Christ Church, Oxford) and the two missing parts were found to exist elsewhere. Often those who loved choral music tried to forestall the coming of the vandals by hiding the part-books away or giving them into the custody of private families till better times should come; this accounts for the many manuscripts and printed scores discovered in private libraries during the present century. So widespread was the destruction, in fact, that except for a mere handful of works the vast bulk of Tudor and Jacobean church music virtually disappeared for nearly three hundred years. It was not until the late nineteenth and early twentieth centuries that scholars, of whom perhaps Dr. E. H. Fellowes was the most notable, undertook the prodigious task of finding, transcribing, collating and editing what survived; through them and through later scholars much that remained scattered and forgotten has now been restored to its rightful place in Anglican worship.

The disbanding of choirs also had far-reaching effects on the development of English music. Organists, choirmasters and professional singers, finding themselves out of work, did much as their modern counterparts would do—turned to music-teaching and whatever other opportunities secular music could provide. These opportunities would include such things as taking service with private families, organising Music Clubs on a professional basis, taking part in Davenant's operatic ventures, going into the up-and-coming trade of music publishing, and joining the town waits or tavern musicians: the less successful probably soon gave up the struggle and found other ways of making a living. But private teaching would have been the stand-by of most of these displaced musicians and it says much for their technical skill and ethical conduct that they built up the credit and influence of their profession till it acquired a high social status. Incidentally, it is interesting that in Playford's list of teachers (see p. 202), nine are teachers of the 'Organ or Virginall'; this at a time when church organs had been silenced, implying that in wealthy homes the instrument was still much favoured. As more people learned to play and sing so there was a growing demand for instruction manuals and we have already seen how the publisher, Playford, met this demand. There was also a growing need for 'domestic' music and composers who previously would have written for the Church now found themselves writing for this new market. So the country's finest musicians, no longer wanted by the Church they had served so well, directed their skills into secular channels, vastly enriching music in the home and bringing about that acceptance of music as an essential social grace which we read about in Pepys, Evelyn, and others. But the cost was high. Choirs are not pieces of furniture to be scrapped and replaced at will; not only does it take years of expert training to produce a good one but choirs develop their own styles, traditions and loyalties, which are often jealously guarded. Furthermore, tradition plays an important part in the training of choirboys: once established it is self-perpetuating, little boys learning from seniors, accepting, conforming, and eventually passing on to others the tone, style and customs peculiar to their choir, thus considerably lightening the choirmaster's work. Once the choir has been disbanded and the chain of tradition broken, it takes at least five years of unremitting effort to build a new tradition, assuming that the choirmaster himself is trained and steeped in the spirit of cathedral music. But if the choirmaster has lost his own roots too, then the whole process of re-establishment is likely to be more difficult and lengthy, a problem the Restoration church had to face.

So far attention has been entirely focused on the negative attitude of the Puritans towards church music but there was one form of it which they not only accepted but to which they made a significant contribution: this was metrical psalmody. Metrical psalmody was essentially a product of the Reformation. Dr. C. S. Phillips, in his book *Hymnody Past and Present*, says:

> From the moment of its inception the Reformation movement of the sixteenth century showed signs of division into two camps—a Right and a Left, to borrow the phraseology of continental politics. The Right is represented by Lutheranism and (in a still more marked degree) by our own Church of England; the Left by the various bodies that are grouped together as 'Reformed' or 'Calvinistic' . . . The difference between Lutheranism and Calvinism is to be seen in their respective attitudes towards hymnody as well as in major matters. The former, while encouraging the use of German metrical translations of the Psalms, was willing at the same time to give free play to the poetic gifts of its members in the production of original hymns, and even to permit the adaptation of Catholic material for a similar purpose. Zwingli and Calvin, on the other hand, with their rigid insistence on 'The Bible and nothing but the Bible', frowned on anything save the metrical psalms. Thus the hymn-singing of the 'Reformed' churches was virtually confined to these. The metrical psalters of these various Churches were naturally closely interconnected, despite their differences of language . . . It should be added that, while in doctrine, organisation and ritual the Church of England was more Catholic than the Lutheran, in the sphere of hymnody it followed for a long time the Calvinistic churches in its preference for metrical psalms over hymns.[9]

The first metrical psalter was that of Sternhold and Hopkins (later known as the *Old Version*) which first appeared in its complete form in 1562 and soon established itself as the standard collection for all English Protestants. This book, for all its popularity and influence, had four serious defects:

(1) in order to challenge the profane and obscene ballads on their own ground, no less than 134 psalms were rendered into the familiar ballad metre (C.M. or D.C.M.). The monotony of this jog-trot and uninspiring rhythm was in marked contrast to the splendid richness and variety of metres in Calvin's Genevan Psalter;

(2) the verse was often of poor quality, halting and laboured. 'Their piety was better than their poetry; they had drank more of Jordan than of Helicon.'[10];

(3) the tunes provided were generally as dull and uninteresting as the words to which they were set. Few of them have survived in modern hymnals;

(4) the original idea of providing every psalm with its own 'proper' tune was abandoned. Of the 150 psalms only forty-seven had tunes of their own: the rest drew

[9] Dr. C. H. Phillips: *Hymnody Past and Present*, pp. 123–4. (S.P.C.K.)
[10] Fuller: *Church History of Britain* (1655).

on these same tunes. Since most of the psalm-versions shared the same metre it was reasoned that they could therefore share the same tunes. Accordingly a small pool of tunes was provided: these were known as 'common' tunes—as distinct from 'proper' tunes specially written to carry a particular poem.

Fortunately this meagre musical fare was soon to be supplemented by the publication of various collections of psalm-tunes. Of these, we may briefly mention those of

John Day (1563), the first to be harmonized in four parts (melody in the tenor);

William Damon (1579 and 1591), from which we get *Southwell* (A. & M. 122, E.H. 77) and *Old 120th* (A. & M. 259, E.H. 464);

John Cosyn (1585), harmonized in five parts;

Thomas Este (1592), an important publication in which the settings were composed by ten leading musicians of the time. Interesting too because Este was the first to call tunes by the names of places. Modern hymn-books are indebted to Este for *Cheshire* (A. & M. 342, E.H. 109) and the sturdy *Winchester Old* (A. & M. 62, E.H. 30);

William Barley (*c.* 1599);

Richard Allison (1599), in which for the first time the tune appears in the treble instead of the tenor;

Robert Tailour (1615), whose five-part settings are all elaborately contrapuntal in the style of Tudor anthems; and

Thomas Ravenscroft, whose *Whole Booke of Psalmes* (1621) is particularly important. It includes many new tunes, D.C.M. giving place to the four-line (C.M.) tunes. He adopts Este's practice of calling tunes by place-names and extends the idea to all his tunes. From this book we get *Bristol, Lincoln, Salisbury* and *St David*; also *Dundee* (from the Scottish Psalter of 1615).[11]

But Sternhold and Hopkins was not the only metrical psalter of this period: there were many others, of which we may notice Archbishop Matthew Parker's psalter (for which Tallis wrote his nine tunes), William Hunnis's *Seven Sobs of a Sorrowfull Soule* (1583), and George Sandys' *A Paraphrase upon the Divine Poems* (1637), notable for its adventurous metrical schemes as well as for twenty-four tunes by Henry Lawes. Nor must we forget the important Scottish Psalters of 1564, 1615 (all unison settings) and Millar's scholarly edition of 1635 in four-part harmony. George Wither's *Hymns and Songs of the Church* (1623) has two claims to fame: it was the first true hymn-book to be published in English, because instead of limiting himself to psalm paraphrases he drew on both Old and New Testaments for his subject matter, producing free compositions of considerable literary distinction; secondly, to accommodate Wither's unusual metres, Orlando Gibbons wrote fifteen fine tunes, many of which have now established themselves among the great hymn-tunes of Christendom. It must not be assumed that all these psalters were intended for public worship; it is likely that some of them (like those of Hunnis, Sandys and Wither) were designed more for private or family worship.

It will be seen that though all English Protestants adopted metrical psalmody, they had a wide range of books and editions to choose from. Features which would pass for virtues with one sect would be regarded as vices by another. Cosyn's five-part harmony, Tailour's anthem-like settings, and Ravenscroft's musicianship would appeal to the

[11] See p. 188.

more conservative and 'High Church' groups while more zealous reformers would protest against anything more elaborate than the unaccompanied unison singing of simple 'common' tunes. During the period of the Civil War, Commonwealth and Protectorate therefore, the more musicianly psalters fell into desuetude whilst Sternhold and Hopkins, dull and unimaginative, tortuous and heavy-footed, ruled the musical waves. For a typical example of the literary style of the *Old Version* we need look no further than the *Gloria Patri*:

> All laud and prayse be to the Lord,
> O that of might art most:
> To God the Father and the Sonne,
> And to the holy Ghost.
> As it in the beginning was,
> For ever heretofore:
> And is now at this present time,
> And shall be evermore.

It seems strange that folk with such a profound reverence and genuine love for the English Bible should yet turn away from it for their psalm-singing, preferring these lumbering metrical travesties to the matchless beauty of Coverdale's English. Practical considerations no doubt came into this: at a time when few people could read and books were expensive, rhymed jingles would be easier to memorise than Biblical prose. Even so, public worship still made great demands on the memory; hence the practice which grew up of 'lining-out'. Each line of words was first read or intoned by the minister, precentor, or some other officer, then taken up and sung by the congregation. At the end of the first line the precentor would call out the next which, in turn, would be repeated by the people — and so continuing. This practice would have added greatly to the length of each psalm, especially at a time when it was thought a mark of reverence to sing slowly.

Though metrical psalmody has certainly bequeathed a number of fine hymns to modern collections, the cold fact remains that the period of Puritan supremacy can be regarded only as a disaster for the true development of English church music.

CHAPTER IX

The English Baroque—I

On 8 May 1660, Charles II was proclaimed king and on 29 May, his birthday, he entered London in triumph amidst tumultuous rejoicing. What a day that must have been!

Cromwell had destroyed the two main pillars of seventeenth-century England—the king and the established church. Then, on the strength of his success as a soldier, political power was suddenly thrust upon him and he found himself, with neither training nor preparation, as supreme head of state (a situation not unfamiliar in our own day). But without the two stabilising influences he had himself destroyed he found it increasingly difficult to control the forces—political, military and religious—he had unleashed: often he was driven to the expedient of using the army to impose his will on a recalcitrant parliament. Subjected to intense pressures and trying in vain to resolve the struggle between parliament and army, he was forced to the bitter realisation that only within the framework of monarchy could order and tranquillity be restored to a shattered nation. More and more the republican dictator found himself exercising the functions of a king though without the title and trappings. When his supporters demanded that he should accept the crown he refused it, somewhat reluctantly, realising that to accept meant the negation of all that he stood for and the betrayal of many who had supported him. When, in 1658, it was apparent that he would again be offered the crown, he would almost certainly have accepted had not death intervened. But the country as a whole had had more than enough of Puritan rule and when the weak and ineffectual Richard succeeded his father there was so much strife and bitterness between the army and parliament, and even amongst the Puritans themselves, that the royalist cause triumphed: it could only be a matter of time before Charles was recalled from exile.

But the monarchy was only one of the mainstays of the nation; the other also must be put on its feet. Accordingly three important steps were taken to help re-establish the Church of England:

1. Even before the king set foot in England, Common Prayer was read before the Lords (10 May 1660) and no time was lost in re-issuing the Prayer Book. This short-lived edition of 1660 was virtually a reprint of the edition of 1604 put out under King James's seal after the Hampton Court Conference;
2. Another conference was called to try to iron out some of the thorny doctrinal and liturgical problems existing between the High Church party and the Puritans. This was the disastrous Savoy Conference of 1661 but it led to the issuing of our present Prayer Book in 1662;
3. The king came down heavily on the side of the High Church party, immediately re-established the Chapel Royal and took steps to restore it to its former glory. So well did he succeed that the history of church music over the next forty years is chiefly concerned with the doings of a group of Chapel Royal choirboys—Pelham

Humfrey, Robert Smith, Michael Wise, John Blow, Daniel Roseingrave, Thomas Tudway, William Turner, Henry Hall and Henry Purcell—who are often referred to collectively as the 'Restoration School'. Of these some are comparatively unimportant, at least in the field of church music, so that in practice the term 'Restoration music' largely means the music of Humfrey, Wise, Blow and Purcell.

Even to the most casual listener the work of these composers is markedly different to that of the polyphonic period. In the past it has been customary to attribute this change to two causes: first, since choirs had been disbanded, organs and books destroyed and the great tradition broken, musicians of the restored Church found themselves in a musical vacuum and had therefore to create a style of their own; second, the king, having spent his exile in the court of Louis XIV (a teenager himself during this period), had grown fond of the gay metrical music of Lully and others and so had introduced their style into his own chapel, even to the extent of appointing (1662) 'four-and-twenty violins' in imitation of the 'vingt-quatre Violins du Roi' (to the delight of Pepys and the disgust of Evelyn). The first reason is an exaggeration: it takes much longer than twenty years for established traditions to pass from living memory and there must have been scores of people left who could remember the old music and how it was performed; furthermore, though many music libraries had been damaged, there were still enough books surviving to re-establish the old repertory in the provincial cathedrals and this is, in fact, exactly what happened; it was only in the Chapel Royal itself that new and experimental music was to be heard, largely because it was the only place with sufficient resources to perform it. In other words 'Restoration music' was a home-made product of this one institution, geographically localized: it did not become a national movement till a third of a century later.

As for the king's musical taste, it must be remembered that at this time French music itself showed strong Italian influence—that same influence which had already reached English composers directly long before Charles went to France—and what appealed to him was in reality the new Italian music received at second-hand and considerably modified by its transmission through France. In fact baroque music, having originated in Italy, soon spread across Europe and ultimately changed the whole course of Western music. France and Germany were amongst the first to fall under its sway but it was not until the 1630s that its full impact hit England. When it did, English musical thought too underwent a dramatic revolution resulting in an entirely new style, part Italian, part traditional, a style shared by all composers from Lanier and the Lawes brothers to Purcell and beyond. The so-called 'Restoration School' consisted of a later group of composers who shared similar thoughts, feelings and aspirations with several earlier groups, shortly to be considered; they were the final flowering of a movement which had its beginnings long before the Restoration—or even the king's exile. It is therefore high time we dropped the misleading term 'Restoration' and frankly recognised the period for what it really was, the English Baroque: the use of this name for it has the further advantage of identifying it with that great European art movement of which it forms a small part. It is typical of British insularity that we should try to cut up our musical history into tidy little bits and apportion them to various kings and queens—Tudor, Elizabethan, Jacobean, Commonwealth, Restoration, etc.—and then complain because the bits overlap or because some untidy composers do not seem to fit in properly: we lose sight of the fact that England was part of the far greater pattern of Western European music and so reflects all the main movements—renaissance, baroque, classical and romantic—even if these movements happen not to coincide with phases in English political history. The development of the baroque style is easily traceable in secular music but in church music the Commonwealth cut right into the middle of the period, all but severing its beginning from its maturity. It is difficult to agree with Dr. Ernest Walker that the Commonwealth 'enormously accelerated' the change to the Purcellian style;[1] on the contrary, the enforced cessation of cathedral music impeded and delayed inevitable progress by some twenty years. Had experiment and development been allowed to continue unhampered perhaps we should sooner have produced composers worthy to stand beside the great continental masters—Gabrieli, Schütz, Carissimi, Lully and others.

What then was the king's real contribution to all this? So impetuous was the onward sweep of the baroque tide that in the long run it is doubtful if either Puritans or kings could greatly affect the final outcome. Nevertheless the king's personal involvement stimulated development in two ways: first, he took a keen interest in the new music and encouraged his musicians to experiment with it; secondly, he personally introduced the string band into his Chapel and expected his composers to include string symphonies and *ritornelli* in their anthems, an innovation which was comparatively short-lived.

So far, no attempt has been made to define the word 'Baroque': this is because no simple definition can be found for a word used to describe composers as far removed in time and place and as apparently dissimilar in style as Monteverdi and Bach, Gabrieli and Handel, Purcell and the young Haydn. Instead, we shall consider in some detail the manifestations of the baroque spirit in music and from these considerations arrive at a deeper understanding of the movement as a whole. In England such men as Byrd, Morley, Weelkes and Gibbons already felt the winds of change from across the Alps but the true baroque style first appeared in the masques of Lanier, Coperario, Robert Johnson, Campian, and William and Henry Lawes. In church music it can be seen in the development of recitative; in the increasing emphasis on, and understanding of, the solo voice; and in the expressive use of 'pathetick' (i.e. emotional) melodic and harmonic devices.

Italy is to be thanked for another important innovation about this time—the introduction of the violin and its associated group of instruments. During the sixteenth century much rivalry existed between the new family of violins and the well-established consort of viols, but the many advantages of the violin—stronger tone, much wider compass, increased flexibility, variety of tone colours, and infinitely greater expressive powers—spelled doom to the older instruments and they gradually disappeared during the seventeenth and early eighteenth centuries, surviving longer in France and England than in other continental countries.

We must now examine in more detail what is meant by the word 'Baroque', see how the new style was grafted on to a strong native tradition, and compare the baroque style of the so-called 'Restoration' composers with the polyphonic style of the Elizabethans and Jacobeans.

---

[1] Ernest Walker: *A History of Music in England*, p. 175. (O.U.P., 3rd Ed.)

MONODY AND RECITATIVE

At the very end of the sixteenth century a group of literary and musical intellectuals in Florence, known as the Camerata, deliberately renounced the polyphonic idiom of their time, objecting that the singing of different words simultaneously must inevitably 'lacerate' the poetry (Cf. John Wesley: 'It is glaringly, undeniably contrary to Common Sense, namely, in allowing, yea appointing different words to be sung by different persons at the same time . . . Pray, which of those sentences am I to attend to?')[2] Instead, they evolved an entirely new type of music—solo melody with a chordal *basso continuo*[3] accompaniment. On the face of it there is little in this that is new: after all, renaissance composers had long since learned the art of writing for solo voices with instrumental accompaniment—as in their lute songs, consort songs, and their verse Services and anthems—but it must be emphasized that even when writing for a solo voice they still conceived the texture contrapuntally as a polyphonic web in which all the strands were of equal interest and significance, and in which the voice part was but one of the strands. The new Italian music was totally different. No longer was the texture conceived polyphonically. Where before there had been four or more strands in the texture there were now only two, a melody (at first usually sung) and an instrumental bass. Harmonic colouring was supplied by a succession of chords, at times widely separated in time.

There was also a significant change in the accompaniment itself. Renaissance composers used a variety of accompanying instruments such as the lute, theorbo, or a consort of viols; only in church music was a keyboard instrument—the organ—commonly used. But in the *nuove musiche* a keyboard instrument was obligatory, in secular as well as in sacred music, and since in homes and secular buildings organs were rare, the harpsichord (or 'virginals') became pre-eminently the accompanying instrument, though the organ continued to be used for sacred music. It was soon found that the harpsichord suffered from a serious defect; its lack of sustaining power resulted in a weak and insecure bass. To compensate, it became customary to use some sustaining instrument to strengthen the bass line—usually a viola da gamba or 'cello though at a later stage a violone or double-bass was sometimes substituted and even, at times, a bassoon. These two, the keyboard instrument and the sustaining bass, were together known as the *continuo*.

Two branches of the new style can be distinguished, though they are not always easy to differentiate or define—*Monody* and *Recitative*.

Monody is a term which is often used loosely. Sometimes it is used as a synonym for 'monophony' (a single melodic line with no additional parts or accompaniment—like plainsong or most forms of folksong); sometimes it is used to describe accompanied solo song generally. But to the historian the term has a special connotation: it refers to that particular type of solo song which emerged early in the seventeenth century and which owed its origins to the theories of the *Camerata*. The texts of the poems were usually 'dramatick', 'pathetick', or at least highly subjective, and an entirely new relationship between words and music was established. Monody was, in fact, a totally new conception of melody. Instead of having a purely musical function, melody must henceforward be entirely subservient to the words, imitating their rhythms and inflections, heightening their emotions, illustrating and colouring their meaning, and at times even giving an

---

[2] John Wesley: *Thoughts on the Power of Music* (Arminian Magazine), 1781.
[3] See pp. 219–21.

almost onomatopoeic equivalent of them. These principles had, of course, operated during the late Renaissance too but they had never before been allowed to take such complete command of the music: for example, in imitative polyphony a 'point' considered in isolation was often written in accordance with them but as soon as the succeeding voices entered, purely musical considerations took control. Even in longer melodies like the lute songs, there was always some give-and-take between words and music and when the two happened to come into direct conflict then it was usually the words that gave way. But in the new monodic style initiated by the *Camerata* and adopted later by the early baroque school, all this was changed and the composer meekly knelt at the poets' feet. Melody no longer had a reasonably independent life of its own but was tightly clamped to the rhythm and syllabic rise and fall of the words. At its worst it could degenerate into a stylized form of reading aloud, a sort of *Sprechgesang*. As Thurston Dart has written, 'Take away the words of an air and you are left with a tune; a declamatory song without its words is a mere string of notes.'[4] All this must have been flattering to poets and authors and accounts for Milton's admiration of Henry Lawes: it also explains why poets queued up for Lawes to set their verses. (Incidentally, perhaps it is significant that whereas the sixteenth-century songwriter usually wrote his own words, his seventeenth-century successor turned to established poets for his texts.) Even punctuation had to be scrupulously observed and was normally reflected by a cadence in the music: worse still, in setting poems with end-stopped lines, the music lamely halted at the end of each line of verse so that no matter how far the melodic inspiration might soar it had inevitably to collapse after every few words.

Whereas *monody* was usually a setting of a verse text, *recitative* was the application of the same principles to a prose text. It was particularly successful in carrying narrative passages where its strength was in its close approximation to ordinary speech and its ability to cover the ground quickly while its melodic weaknesses were less obvious. To achieve the utmost fidelity in approximating to ordinary speech, the normal principles of melody, phrase and rhythm were largely set aside and their place taken by a syllabic treatment of the text, reiterated notes, quick notes in irregular groupings, and small but subtle inflections: it is here that it parts company with late renaissance techniques. This *stile recitativo*, devised in theory as a metaphysical exercise by the *Camerata*, achieved its first practical expression in the very earliest operas—Peri's *Dafne* (1597), Caccini's *Euridice* (1600), Peri's *Euridice* (1600) and others. These early recitatives were usually declamatory or dramatic in style and rather slower and more dignified than we should expect.

Almost from the outset several different types of recitative emerged and during the seventeenth and early eighteenth centuries these in turn underwent modification and development until they reached the sophisticated and flexible forms so familiar in the works of Bach, Handel and Mozart. To treat this development adequately would in itself need a sizeable book. It must suffice here to mention one or two of these earlier forms and see what they later became. The earliest type of all was in some ways the least characteristic: this was the *recitativo arioso* which, instead of being a stylized form of ordinary speech, was much more lyrical and expressive. Very soon the lyricism became increasingly melodic, the phrasing more clear and the construction more organised; and so was born the *Aria* which itself appeared in many different forms—strophic arias, strophic-bass

---

[4] Thurston Dart: Article 'Song' in Grove's *Dictionary of Music and Musicians*, Vol. VII, p. 931. (Macmillan 1954, 5th Ed.)

arias, ostinato arias, *da capo* arias and the like. As the *arioso* developed into the aria, so true recitative became faster and less lyrical. In its simplest form only the two continuo instruments lightly supported the vocal declamation: this was the style that approximated most closely to natural speech and which later came to be called *recitativo secco*. This could vary considerably in speed and could, in fact, move very rapidly indeed, especially in opera. In slower passages the melodic line could be supported by a fuller and more elaborate accompaniment (*recitativo accompagnato*) and often this was scored for instruments as well as continuo (*recitativo stromentato*): the employment of a larger group of accompanying instruments inevitably involved some sacrifice of rhythmic freedom and made necessary a more measured style. (In Bach's *St. Matthew Passion* the narrative and dialogue is in *recitativo secco* except for the part of Christ which is in *recitativo stromentato*.) It must be pointed out that the very rapid *parlando* recitative such as we find in the operas of Mozart and Rossini was an eighteenth-century development of *recitativo secco*.

Though recitative quickly established itself on the English stage its appropriate application to liturgical music was obviously much more limited. However, here is an example of *secco* recitative from an anthem by Pelham Humfrey (1647–74):

Humfrey: *O Lord my God, why hast thou forsaken me*

Ex. 92

This example is quite unlike anything we have seen in earlier chapters.

The emergence of this new harmonic form of accompanied melody, whether as monody or recitative brought with it implications so far-reaching that it was to alter the whole course of musical history and a movement which began initially with a group of aristocratic literary and musical *dilletanti* in Florence soon engulfed the whole of western Europe.

'AFFECTIVE' MELODY AND HARMONY

Distinct from the mechanics of word-setting, melody had now to express human emotions, especially extreme and violent ones. Augmented and diminished intervals which had been shunned by the polyphonic writers, such as the diminished seventh and that *diabolus in musica* the tritone (three whole tones, as from B to F, G to C sharp), were now found to have a 'pathetick' quality ideal for expressing sighs and suffering, while falling chromatic semitones were redolent of pain, grief and weeping (see, for example, the bracketed intervals in Ex. 92, p. 222). Thus was greatly increased emphasis placed on the expressive dimension of melody so that it should stir the emotions and inflame the passions. Other devices were resorted to: attention could be focused on important words by setting them with various ornaments, roulades and flourishes (in some Italian music the melodic line was so overlaid with highly elaborate ornaments, many of them improvised, that the basic metrical pulse was obliged to give way to accommodate them); perhaps significant words would be underlined by some striking change of harmony; or again, the rhetorical repetition of words or phrases (often coupled with the cunning placing of rests) enhanced their 'dramatick' effect. Here is an example of this last technique:

Henry Purcell: *The Blessed Virgin's Expostulation*

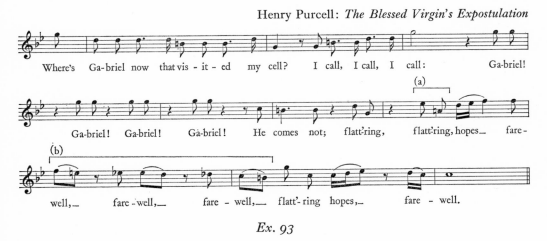

Ex. 93

The falling tritone at (a) and the falling chromatic semitones at (b) are both typical of this 'affective' style.

Finally, one of the most obvious characteristics of the style was an even greater passion for realistic word-painting than even the renaissance composers had had—and *that's* saying something! As far back as 1597 Morley had recommended that words like 'ascending', 'high', 'heaven', 'descending', 'depth', lowness' and 'hell' should receive appropriate musical illustration (and see Weelkes's madrigal 'As Vesta was from Latmos Hill descending' in *The Triumphes of Oriana*), but the early baroque composers carried this to extremes. Any word like 'running', 'flying', 'wind', 'sighing', 'thundering', 'trumpet', 'alone' and 'together' would be sure to receive lavish pictorial treatment. To us, much of this realism seems incredibly childish and ridiculous but there is no doubt that many composers chose texts, both secular and sacred, which offered the maximum opportunity for the exercising of their talents in this field.

Harmony too was used affectively, especially the treatment of dissonance. In renaissance technique, discords had either to appear on weak beats or in passing from concord to concord: they could appear on strong beats only as suspensions, resolving downwards. In the baroque era not only could the old discords be used much more freely and even resolve upwards, but the augmented and diminished intervals now appearing melodically could be frozen into new and exciting chord clusters strategically placed to underpin the melody and intensify drama and passion.

REGULAR BARRING AND ACCENTUATION

As we have seen, the polyphonic music of the previous age had had no regular barring: its rhythms were fairly free and arose naturally from the accentuation of the words. Furthermore, since in imitative counterpoint these rhythms were set one against another, a bar-line which suited one part would obviously not suit another. As there was often no regular metrical pattern, bar-lines as we know them were unnecessary and the individual part-books were accordingly left unbarred. In England it was not until towards the end of the sixteenth century that bar-lines began to be used for keyboard and lute music. The first vocal music to be printed in score and using bar-lines seems to have been a posthumous edition of Cipriano de Rore's 4-part madrigals, printed in Italy in 1577 but the idea was slow to spread and was not adopted in England until well into the seventeenth century. Even then these bar-lines were spaced irregularly and had no metrical significance; indeed different manuscripts of the same work were often barred differently. Such bar-lines served merely to guide the eye from time to time when scanning the score vertically. It was only in lighter music like balletts and solo 'ayres' that regular barring was used with something like its modern function of indicating the underlying metre. The rise of orchestral music in the early seventeenth century led composers to adopt the modern system of writing a full score with bar-lines, still often placed at irregular intervals, but again it must be emphasized that these bar-lines carried little or no metrical significance and the first pulse of a new bar was not necessarily a 'strong beat'. In practice the bar-lines were often set in opposition to the true scansion of the music and the stress pattern which seemed to be implied by the barring rarely coincided with the natural accentuation of the music.

It was not until the mid-seventeenth century that bar-lines began to carry their modern connotation of conferring a stress on the next succeeding pulse and almost all music, except certain types of recitative, now became subject to regular barring which imposed some basic metrical pattern — 1–2, 1–2–3, 1–2–3–4, etc. This meant that whereas in the old system melodic ideas could be freely shaped to fit the words, there now was an additional complication; verbal stresses had somehow to be reconciled with the metrical accents of the music. When the words took precedence, as in dramatic and declamatory settings, the music was so subservient that it almost ceased to have any independent life of its own (as in some kinds of recitative): when the music came first, as in most songs, part songs, choral and sacred works, the words had somehow or other to be fitted to the metre of the music, even if this involved placing unimportant words on strong beats. So began 'the tyranny of the bar-line' which was to dominate music for the next three hundred years.

THE KEY SYSTEM AND HARMONIC THINKING

Fundamental to the new music was a shift in emphasis from counterpoint to harmony, from a horizontal concept of musical construction to a vertical. One factor which contributed significantly to this development was the gradual decline of the old church modes and the rapidly growing importance of the major and minor scales with their feelings of tonality, a gravitational centre, and the ultimate realisation of all the implications of the classical key system—chords and their relationship within a key complex, chromatic notes, and the almost unlimited possibilities of modulation from key to key. Another factor was the rapid development of keyboard techniques which opened composers' ears to the exciting new sonorities of harmonic writing. Composers were also quick to realise that harmony could be a powerful ally in helping to establish a regular metre: by arranging for a harmonic change to occur on main beats the natural stress could be strongly reinforced. It was but a short step from here to the recognition that there could be such a thing as 'harmonic rhythm' independent of metrical rhythm: it was noticed too that the fewer and slighter the harmonic changes the more smooth and relaxed the music while the more frequent and violent the harmonic changes, the greater the emotional intensity. Thus, in the following example we see a gradual intensification of the harmonic rhythm:

Purcell: *Rejoice in the Lord alway*

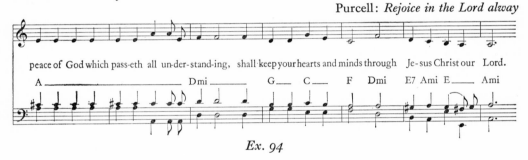

Ex. 94

FIGURED BASS AND CONTINUO PLAYING

There can be no clearer indication of this change of outlook than the rise of what is technically known as *thorough-bass* though popularly referred to as *figured-bass*. This was a system of writing keyboard accompaniments in a species of musical shorthand. So far as is known it was first used in February 1600 by Cavalieri in his allegorical oratorio *Rappresentazione di anima e di corpo* and later in the same year by Peri and Caccini in their operas, though it may well have been in use a year or two earlier. The composer merely wrote out the bass line, adding where necessary a few numerals under the notes to indicate what chord should be used to fill in the accompaniment. The numerals signified harmonic intervals above the bass note within the key of the piece: thus, in the key of C major a 6 under the note C would show that an A must occur somewhere in the chord; if the key were C minor, the same symbol would indicate an A flat. Normally only 2nds, 4th, 6th, 7ths and more advanced discords were marked; where notes were left unfigured, 3rds, 5ths and 8ves (the common chord) were assumed. Chromatic alterations were usually shown by placing a sharp, flat or natural in front of the figure (sometimes behind it); an unattached sharp or flat applied to the 3rd of the chord. A complex or chromatic chord would sometimes necessitate as many as three or four figures one under another. All this is, of course, a dangerous over-simplification of a very complex and highly specialised subject, but one thing is clear — such a system can be used only where musical thought is essentially harmonic.

As we have seen, the accompaniment needed at least two instruments, a keyboard instrument (usually a harpsichord but sometimes clavichord or organ) and a sustaining bass to give the texture stability and continuity. These two were together known as the *basso continuo* (though the same words are often used to designate what they played from, i.e. the figured bass part as written). Continuo is one of the fundamental and essential features of the baroque music of all countries, from the earliest experiments of the Italian pioneers to the crowning achievements of Bach and Handel. It was left to the skill, taste and discretion of the keyboard player to translate (or, to use the technical word, to 'realise') this shorthand notation into an accompanimental texture. Providing always that he retained the bass as written and kept to the harmonies indicated by the figuring, the actual arrangement and spacing of the chords, and the style, density and texture of the accompaniment were a matter for his personal skill and artistry. He could clothe the harmonic skeleton with any suitable keyboard figuration and was expected to add ornamentation wherever appropriate (and often, one suspects, where it was wildly inappropriate!). It will at once be appreciated that to those who have the requisite skill there is far greater satisfaction in accompanying from figured-bass than in playing a fully written-out accompaniment. The former is a challenge to the musicianship and ingenuity of the player. Furthermore, he feels that he has a stake in the actual process of composition; that the composer accepts him into partnership not just as a re-creator but as a co-worker in the act of creation itself. It is important to realise that for the next one hundred and fifty years or so composers (including Bach and Handel) had so much confidence in the skill and artistry of the continuo player that they tacitly invited him to extemporise his own accompaniment to the written vocal line. It could be argued that it was because the harmonic filling was of only secondary importance that composers were content to give the player such a free hand to improvise, on the assumption that as long as he kept to the prescribed bass and figured harmony he could not do much damage, but let it not be forgotten that Bach in his Third Brandenburg Concerto and Handel in his D minor Organ Concerto very probably expected the keyboard player to improvise an entire movement, while Mozart, Beethoven, and even Brahms in his Violin Concerto of 1878, left the soloist to improvise or compose his own cadenzas to their concertos. The corollary of all this is that when today we buy a song by one of these baroque composers, the printed accompaniment is not the work of the composer himself but has been realised from the figured-bass by a modern editor who may or may not know his business. However, providing the original bass and harmonies are retained, a sensitive performer need not scruple to rearrange the details to his own satisfaction.

The following examples will demonstrate the principles of figured-bass notation; first comes the bass itself as printed, then two possible realisations of it:

Figured-bass as printed

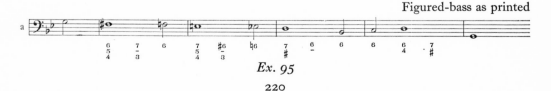

Ex. 95

Ex. 95 (continued)

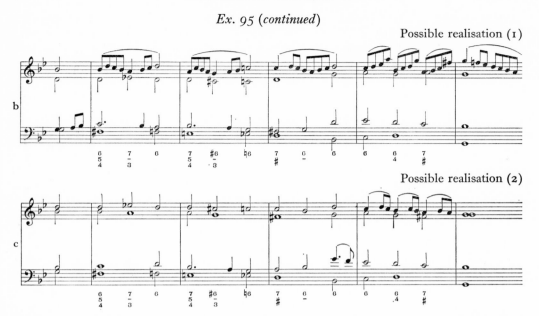

Thus the realisation will vary from player to player and even from performance to performance by the same player. For an exhaustive (and exhausting!) study of the subject readers are referred to the monumental treatise by F. T. Arnold.[5]

THE INFLUENCE OF HARMONY ON MELODY

While music was conceived polyphonically composers enjoyed great freedom in constructing their melodic lines. They had two principal objects in mind: first to find a phrase which was, as nearly as may be, the musical counterpart of the natural rhythms and intonation of the spoken word; and second, so to contrive this phrase that it lent itself easily to imitation and other contrapuntal processes. Of course this does not mean that polyphonic music had no harmonic component; on the contrary we are nearly always aware of some harmonic basis, but it seems to arise naturally as a sort of by-product from the weaving together of the various horizontal strands (see p. 99 and Ex. 23).

From the seventeenth century onwards composers surrendered much of this melodic freedom. Because their basic conception was now harmonic, not contrapuntal, their melodic ideas were to a large extent dictated by harmonic exigencies, a state of affairs which had already been foreshadowed towards the close of the sixteenth century (see p. 100). Indeed, harmony soon governed melody so completely that a mere glance at a melodic line is sufficient to identify its underlying harmonic basis (see p. 219, Ex. 94). This is what makes possible the time-honoured examination question 'At the keyboard, harmonize the following melody . . .'. By the time of Mozart and Beethoven it is commonplace to find that many of their themes are built out of, or around, the arpeggio of the key chord (e.g. Mozart's Piano Sonatas in B flat (K.570) and D (K.576); Beethoven's Piano Sonatas Op. 2 No. 1, Op. 10 No. 1 and Op. 57 (the 'Appassionata'); the Eroica, and

[5] F. T. Arnold: *The Art of Accompaniment from a Thorough-Bass.* (O.U.P., 1931.)

several themes in the 5th Symphony). Many of Brahms's themes are similarly constructed; e.g. *Sapphische Ode, Wiegenlied* and innumerable songs, and the opening themes of his Quartet No. 1 in C minor (Op. 51 No. 1), Symphonies No. 2 in D and No. 3 in F, and the Violin Concerto.

ENGLISH 'RECITATIVE MUSICK'

When the irresistible force of Italian monody reached England it encountered the almost immovable object of a strongly entrenched native musical culture; the outcome was a compromise. At first, naturally, many composers enjoyed playing with the new toy — Lanier, Coperario, Porter, the Lawes brothers and others — but they soon became selective, absorbing rather than adopting such elements of Italian technique as would fertilize the English tradition and rejecting those elements which were inimical to it: thus the rapid type of *recitativo secco* with its natural and irregular speech-rhythm never really caught on in England. Certainly in sacred music the English generally preferred a more dignified vocal line containing elements of both monody and recitative and supported by a fairly developed accompaniment for continuo with or without a group of strings. This vocal line was not always given to one solo voice but was often shared among three or four separate solo parts. In general it was strictly mensural — accurately notated with a time signature, bar-lines and precise note values. Indeed it has often been claimed that mensural recitative is peculiar to the English though in fact it was used extensively by Schütz and other continental composers. At first the process of absorption was painful

Pelham Humfrey: *A Hymne to God the Father**

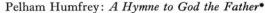

* Edited by M. Tippett and W. Bergmann. (Schott & Co.)

Ex. 96

and incomplete: the result was a vocal line which was often stilted, angular, more or less tuneless and sometimes almost laughably naïve, yet even so, it never suffered from that excessive ornamentation which disfigured much Italian music. It was left to the later baroque composers, especially Humfrey and Purcell, to blend and fuse the new elements into a smooth powerful melodic line, sung in strict tempo but flexible and responsive to verbal rhythms, having such musical shape and significance that once again musical needs override mere textual considerations. The preceding example, part of Pelham Humfrey's song *A Hymne to God the Father*, is typical of the English affective style at its best and illustrates many of the points raised.

THE GROWING IMPORTANCE OF THE SOLO VOICE

When Italian monody eventually found its way into English church music the ground had already been prepared for it by Byrd, Morley, Gibbons and others in their verse anthems. No sooner had direct Italian influence reinforced this existing native impulse than the Commonwealth period closed the door to church music and further development was possible only in secular fields. But here too the tendency was still towards individualism. Musicians who had formerly trained choirs now found themselves teaching private pupils. Whereas before they wrote motets and madrigals in 5, 6, 8, and even 40 parts, they were now called upon to write domestic music—solo songs, keyboard pieces and string trios. Thus the secularisation of music implied a shift from performance by groups to performance by individuals. Perhaps too religion itself had become a more individual matter; the reformed churches thought less in terms of the Church Universal and more in terms of a personal salvation, a personal 'call' and an individual awakening and response.

Anyway, whatever the reasons, not only did composers of the Restoration take over from the Jacobeans the idea of writing solo sections in their verse-anthems but they extended the length and increased the number of verses to such an extent that the roles of soloists and full choir were reversed: whereas before verse sections were employed to give some occasional relief from the weight of the full choir, now the choir itself was used but rarely and then only to provide a little variety or else to round off the whole piece with a joyful noise.

Increasing emphasis on solo singing could hardly fail to focus public interest on the singers themselves. In Italy this led to the rise of the 'star' singer—a phenomenon which has cursed music (especially Italian opera) ever since. Singers cultivated a dazzling display of vocal pyrotechnics and coupled it with a 'temperamental' personality which was cultivated just as assiduously. They were self-centred, conceited, pampered, and bitterly jealous of each other, yet they were so lionized by an undiscriminating public that they amassed fabulous fortunes and were fawned upon by a retinue of servants. They lorded it over composers and even dictated what sort of music should be written for them.

PROBLEMS OF FORM

As we have seen, Tudor composers constructed polyphonic works by the simple method of breaking up the words into a series of short phrases, setting each phrase to a musical 'point' and then treating the point imitatively. The points themselves rarely bore any direct relationship to each other, neither did melodic ideas used at the beginning normally recur towards the end (a few pieces like Gibbons's *Hosanna* being notable exceptions). On the other hand, cohesion was given to the piece by its mode. The mode acted as a centre of gravity, its fairly well defined range of permissible cadences giving the composer a comfortable feeling of security, knowing that he could never stray too far from his home cadence. By adopting this method of composition musical form presented no problems: as long as there were any words left to set the composer could continue to spin his contrapuntal web. But once modality and contrapuntal methods had been abandoned some other means had to be found to give coherence and shape. It was here that baroque musicians encountered difficulties. Though they well understood the techniques of modulating from one key to another their modulations tended to be transient, somewhat aimless, and had as yet no structural significance. They did not realise the elements of relief and contrast afforded by writing whole sections in related keys or appreciate the profoundly rewarding effect of returning to their basic key either at some climactic point, or to effect a recapitulation, or to round off a piece with a satisfying feeling of 'home-coming' to the original key.

Having therefore abandoned the old methods and not yet having developed the new, composers found it difficult to organise their music satisfactorily. Short movements they could manage: these were held together largely by the balancing of phrases and by such devices as sequence, repetition and echo effects; episodes in imitative counterpoint were used as a foil to passages in block harmony. For larger works they had perforce to be content with stringing together a number of short sections or movements, mostly in the same key, in such a way as to secure as much variety as possible—slow, fast; major, minor; solo, trio, full choir, etc. But composers still treated a key as they had previously treated a mode, looking on it as a safe and sure stronghold from which little sorties could occasionally be made into the unknown and rather mysterious surrounding territory, only to rush back to safety almost immediately; in other words, not only were most of the sections in the same key but so were many of the cadences within those sections, giving an overall feeling of monotony no matter how attractive each individual section in itself might be. Furthermore, the old mean-tone system of tuning keyboard instruments seriously curtailed the number of keys available to a composer: though closely related tonalities would have been more in tune than on a modern piano tuned in equal temperament, remote keys would have been impossibly out of tune.

Perhaps only one solution to the problem of musical form was entirely satisfactory at this time, at least in church music: this was the *ground bass* (not to be confused with 'thorough-bass'). The form itself was not new, indeed, the harmonic type of ground goes back at least as far as the thirteenth century ('Sumer is icumen in'). The melodic type of ground favoured by Purcell and his contemporaries is a specialised application of the familiar air-and-variations formula. A melodic motif (usually in 3 time) is announced in the bass. Strictly, this is then repeated over and over again while a more or less complex superstructure with its own melodic line is built above it. In performance the listener's attention is so held by this superstructure that the recurring bass theme passes almost unnoticed, yet it admirably fulfils its function of unifying the structure. Often, instead of adhering rigidly to the basic pattern, composers allowed themselves some flexibility; the ground would be transposed or lifted to the soprano line (as in a *passacaglia*) and octave transpositions of odd notes or part of the theme, inversions, and melodic extensions were freely used to add variety. To prevent a halting effect every time the bass theme reached its cadence point, the melodic phrases were usually of a different length to the ground bass itself; thus if the length of the ground were six bars and the melodic phrases were eight bars, their cadence points would coincide only at every twenty-fourth bar. Towards the end of his life Purcell used the form again and again in secular works and in his hand the ground bass achieved heights of expression never previously imagined and rarely since surpassed. The lament 'When I am laid in earth' from *Dido and Aeneas* is typical of his best work in this genre. It is all the greater pity therefore that he so rarely used the form in his sacred music (most of which was written in the earlier part of his life).

THE CHAPEL ROYAL AFTER 1660

The Chapel Royal under Charles II must have had one of the finest choirs England has ever produced. A Royalist captain, Henry Cooke, was appointed bass singer and Master of the Children (i.e. choirmaster); he was an old Chapel Royal boy himself, he enjoyed a considerable reputation as a singer, and he appears to have studied singing in Italy (in which case Italian ideas would have been injected directly into the nerve-centre of Restoration music). By virtue of invoking an ancient press-gang warrant, Captain Cooke was empowered to raid cathedral and collegiate choirs and carry off their best boys for service in London. At first this method could not have yielded much material because the other choirs themselves were being re-formed at the same time and nobody would have had any trained boy singers; indeed, during these early days the Chapel Royal boys were so weak and inexperienced that their part had to be doubled by cornetts. But Cooke showed unerring skill in selecting boys for his choir; contemporary writers agree on the superlative technique and quality of their singing and several of Cooke's boys themselves became distinguished composers. (Purcell, who joined later, was not chosen by Cooke but was accepted because of his father's position.) As for the men singers it must have been prestige alone that ensured a virtual monopoly of the finest singers in England—some of them well-known organists and choirmasters in their own right—for although their salaries appeared to be high, money was rarely forthcoming to pay them and the singers were often in dire financial need. (When Cooke himself died, £500 was owing to him in salary — a large sum in those days: see also the scandalous business of Lewis Evans, the harpist, in Pepys's *Diary*, 19 December 1666, and a further reference in Pepys, 29 July 1667.) Certainly these men had splendid voices, a virtuoso technique, and first-class sight-reading ability. One of them, the Reverend John Gostling, had a truly phenomenal voice of immense range and power, and because many of the bass solos in the Chapel Royal anthems were written with his particular voice in mind, the anthems themselves are now practically unusable. The men of the Chapel Royal were, in fact, England's nearest equivalent to Italy's opera stars and one can imagine that the fashionable congregation, more interested perhaps in entertainment than in spiritual edification, would have looked forward to some florid solos to titillate their fancies in just the same way that Italian opera-goers demanded some display of vocal gymnastics. Small wonder then that during the first two or three years while the boys were still inexperienced, verse sections were written almost exclusively for these wonderful adult voices, and when the verse-solos were grouped in trios and quartets the top part was taken not by a boy but by a counter-tenor, a voice which was then very popular. Once having started, the custom of using men's voices was continued even when experienced boys were readily available. This explains why the boys have so little to do in Restoration verse anthems.

H   225

USE OF STRINGED INSTRUMENTS

Much has been written about the use of strings in Restoration anthems but this was by no means a revolutionary innovation. As we have seen, Gibbons wrote an accompaniment for viols in some of his verse anthems (e.g. *This is the record of John*) and so did Byrd before him. It was a personal fad of the monarch himself to engage twenty-four 'violins' and make them available to play in the Chapel Royal. He had enjoyed the light, gracious music of the French court and it was at his personal request that composers provided opportunities for hearing the same sort of thing in his own Chapel. The term 'violins' actually included violas and 'cellos as well; it was, in fact, a full string orchestra. This orchestra appeared for the first time at his coronation on 23 April 1661 but did not take part in Chapel Royal services until 14 September 1662 (according to Pepys; Evelyn, probably inaccurately, gives 21 December). At first the whole group played together but in later years only five or six of them would be on duty at a time and even these were lax in attendance. If Thomas Tudway is to be relied on, the violins were played only when the king attended services in person; at other times the normal resources of the Chapel seem to have been adequate — lutes, viols and wind instruments in addition to the organ and choir.

Evelyn was no doubt voicing a considerable body of opinion when he complained 'Instead of the antient, grave, and solemn wind musiq accompanying the organ, was introduced a concert of 24 violins between every pause, after the French fantastical light way, better suiting a tavern or playhouse than a church.' It is not clear whether the objection is to the tone colour of the violin family 'as being more airie and brisk than viols' or to the purely instrumental movements they played — lengthy overtures, symphonies and *ritornelli* — interspersed among the sung sections. But violins themselves were no new thing in church; they had been used at the funerals of both Elizabeth (1603) and James I (1625). After Charles's death the twenty-four violins were heard no more; indeed, the use of stringed instruments in church generally dropped out of favour.

It is interesting to compare Purcell's treatment of strings with, say, Byrd's. The baroque composers showed a well-developed sense of idiomatic writing. Gone are the days when music was equally 'apt for viols or voyces', when its significance rested entirely on the interplay of its linear parts irrespective of their tone-colour. Baroque musicians recognised the inherent character of the various voices and instruments and deliberately used tone-colour as an expressive element. They were the first to appreciate the sheer beauty of unaccompanied choral singing unspoiled by instrumental support (this may seem a surprising claim because we have been brought up to think of the sixteenth century as the golden period of *a cappella* music, yet there seems little doubt that instruments usually doubled or replaced some or all of the voices). Further, their awareness of tone-colour led them to exploit the characteristic sonorities of strings, organ, choir, and soloists, often using them in contrasted blocks of tone. This style of construction was called *concertato* and is very typical of baroque thought. It follows, then, that the main function of the orchestra was not so much to accompany the voices (though this it did sometimes) as to alternate with them. Some of the string *ritornelli* were so lengthy that they could almost be extracted from their contexts and played as separate movements in their own right.

ANTHEMS AND SERVICES

Restoration anthems, like those of the late Renaissance, can be divided into two broad groups, full anthems and verse anthems. The full anthems follow pretty closely the well-defined path laid down by the Tudors and Jacobeans and show little advance on their predecessors. The most obvious difference is that now they are firmly rooted in the tonal system and are conceived harmonically. This strong feeling for 'key' sometimes leads composers to experiment in chromatic writing, as in Blow's *O Lord God of my salvation* and Purcell's *Hear my prayer*, though in this vein they were still not as venture-some as some of the Italians. The best of the full anthems tend to be those which are penitential in spirit and massive in construction.

It is in the verse anthem that progress is most striking: this is not surprising as the form would naturally have appealed to composers at this time. As we have seen, the easiest way they could write a lengthy piece was by stringing together a series of short sections or movements. But in setting Biblical words the text was already divided into verses each of which was just about the right length for one such section: thus their verse-by-verse treatment made a virtue out of necessity. It was in the verse anthem that all the various innovations that we have discussed had their freest play. With its lengthy orchestral introduction acting as an overture, its solos, trios, sections for full choir and orchestral interludes, it grew into a full-length cantata taking as long as twenty minutes or more to perform. Such schemes as the following are typical (both by Purcell):

The Lord is my light

1. Orchestral overture: slow, fast.
2. Verse trio: 'The Lord is my light'.
3. Short orchestral interlude.
4. Bass recitative: 'Though an host of men'.
5. Short orchestral interlude.
6. Verse trio: 'For in the time of trouble' (slow and rather chromatic).
7. Orchestral ritornello: repeat of second part of Overture (1).
8. Counter-tenor solo: 'And now shall he lift up mine head'.
9. Orchestral symphony.
10. Slow verse trio in 4 time: 'Therefore will I offer' leading to
11. Fast verse trio in 3 time: 'Alleluja'.
12. Orchestral symphony.
13. Full chorus: 'Alleluja'.

Praise the Lord, O my soul

1. Orchestral overture:
    (a) common time, dotted rhythm,
    (b) a faster movement in 3 time.
2. A 6-part verse, 'Praise the Lord' (high voices answered by low voices, then all together).
3. Orchestral interlude.
4. Another 6-part verse beginning as if repeating (2).
5. Orchestral interlude.
6. Slow verse trio: 'The Lord is full of compassion and mercy'.
7. Tenor solo: 'He hath not dealt with us'.
8. Ritornello (repeat of second section of Overture).
9. Bass recitative: 'For look how high the heaven is'.
10. 6-part verse: 'O speak good of the Lord' (high voices answered by low voices; then all six together).
11. Ritornello (derived from 5).
12. Full chorus: 'Praise thou the Lord'.

But in the nature of things a succession of bits and pieces lacks overall cohesion and it has to be admitted that even the best of the verse anthems often sound scrappy and disjointed. Some sections seem merely perfunctory; many are dull and cliché-ridden: worse still, the silly fashion grew of including a jaunty 'Hallelujah' section, however inappropriate it may be (a notorious example is Purcell's evening hymn *Now that the sun hath veil'd his light*). Yet taken as a whole the verse anthems explore new fields of expression, are often illuminated by startling flashes of inspiration, and include much music of rare beauty.

One thing is plain: these lengthy works can have no place in our regular worship today; we have neither the instruments, the time, nor the singers. Only in recitals can they be heard in full. When they appear in cathedral and church music lists what we actually hear is a sadly mutilated edition—the orchestral introduction and *ritornelli* either omitted or drastically cut, the orchestral texture losing its springy rhythms and sparkling vitality when transferred to the organ, and repeats omitted. As we shall see, in many editions even the part-writing is emasculated. Such a popular piece as Purcell's *Rejoice in the Lord alway* (to name just one example) is known to most of us only in such a maimed and debased version. Yet it would be a pity for the Church to lose such pieces altogether: perhaps the best solution is to accept the cuts and omissions as inevitable in church, but to insist on scrupulous fidelity to the composer's notes and note values.

Turning now to Service settings, the most surprising thing is that they seem quite unaffected by the new techniques. Instead of developing along similar lines to the verse anthem, they actually regressed, gaining almost nothing and losing much of their rhythmic freedom. After the advances made by Morley, Tomkins, Weelkes and Gibbons in the development of the verse Service, such composers as Rogers and Child reverted to the Short Service form, mainly in block harmony, adhering fairly strictly to the 'for every syllable a note' principle. Even when 'verses' are introduced, they are always for trio or quartet and can be sung unaccompanied. The solo voice was not used, and even short introductions and interludes for the organ disappeared. Most of these Services are distressingly dull. The reason is probably the persistence of Puritan modes of thought. Though no longer in power, the Puritans were by no means a spent force and some of their principles and ideas still had considerable influence on Christian thought (this is reflected in the Prayer Book of 1662). Though a composer might feel free to experiment and introduce innovations in an anthem, the Canticles seem to have been regarded as sacrosanct and only the plainest musical setting was thought suitable: dullness would have been deemed a virtue. This may also explain why only the Short Services of the Elizabethans were retained in the repertory; their verse Services fell into disuse and were eventually completely forgotten.

Restoration Services normally included the following movements: Te Deum, Jubilate, Kyrie, Creed, Magnificat and Nunc dimittis. That the psalm Jubilate should have been used in preference to the canticle Benedictus again attests to the strength of Puritan influence. It will be noticed that following the practice of the Tudors and Jacobeans only two parts of the Ordinary were set to music: this was because on Sundays, Mattins was followed by 'ante-Communion', both fully choral; then the choir (and probably most of the congregation) filed out after the Prayer for the Church militant. Occasionally a setting was provided for the Responses to the Commandments and even more rarely Gloria in excelsis was included. In a few isolated pockets like Durham, Ely and Westminster an attempt was made to preserve a full choral Mass, but in most churches the Communion service itself was more and more neglected until during the eighteenth century it was celebrated no more than four times a year (Christmas, Easter, Whitsuntide and Michael-mas)—if at all. So it remained until revived and revivified by the reforming zeal of the Oxford Movement.

CHURCH MUSIC OUTSIDE THE CHAPEL ROYAL

So far we have thought of Restoration music exclusively in terms of the Chapel Royal and those associated with it, but this unique institution, with its splendid resources and its royal mandate to be experimental and progressive, in no way represents the true state of church music in the country as a whole. What of the cathedrals, college chapels and parish churches throughout the rest of England?

In 1660 two problems confronted choirmasters, (a) to rebuild the choir, and (b) to find something for them to sing. It would not have been too difficult to get men singers: some who had been lay-clerks in pre-Commonwealth times would have been glad to get back into harness and many of the younger men would have received training as choirboys in the old days. As in the Chapel Royal, the chief difficulty would have been to build up a new boys' choir from raw recruits, especially as there was no tradition or continuity; this would have taken from three to five years. During this time cornetts were often used to strengthen the boys' line and give them confidence.

In spite of the destruction of choir music and books by zealots during the Civil War and after, a good deal of Tudor and Jacobean music still survived and this would have become the staple diet of choirs immediately after the Restoration. If a part-book was missing it is likely that one of the older lay-clerks would be able to sing his part from memory (not entirely accurately perhaps!) and his version would then be written out to complete the set. As the boys were inexperienced and as most choirs were small in numbers for financial reasons, only Short Services and the smaller anthems would have been within their competence, with perhaps a more ambitious anthem on special occasions. To this corpus would have been added recent works by a group of composers we are soon to consider—William and Henry Lawes, Porter, Portman, Child, Rogers, Christopher Gibbons, Cooke and Locke.

We do not know much about the standard of behaviour and devotion to duty of church musicians during the seventeenth century and we can only guess at the quality of their performance, but what we do know is far from reassuring. 'Respectability' had not yet laid its chilling hand on the Church and contemporary evidence suggests that many church musicians were pretty colourful characters—too colourful perhaps for the diligent and inspiring performance of their duties. Thus Richard Hutchinson, organist of Durham and a notorious frequenter of alehouses, broke the head of one of his singing-men with a candlestick, wounding him dangerously. In 1663 Mr. Mudd, organist of Lincoln, 'shewed the effects of his last week's tipling, for when Mr. Joynes was in the midst of his sermon Mudd fell a-singing aloud, insomuch as Mr. Joynes was compelled to stopp . . . and at length some neere him, stopping his mouth, silenced him'. At Gloucester, Stephen Jeffries (organist 1682–1710) was admonished 'for manifold neglect and unreasonable absence from the church without leave desired or obtained'; four years later (1688) he 'immediately after the sermon ended and the Blessing given play over upon the organ a common ballad in the hearing of 1,500 or 2,000 people, to the grate scandal of religion, prophanation of the Church, and grievous offence of all good Christians.' Just to show there was no mistake about it he regaled them with a repeat performance after Evensong the same day. (One trembles to think what the words of such a ballad might have been, especially at this period!) Yet Hutchinson and Jeffries retained their posts—as did that 'common drunkard and notorious swearer and blasphemer', Thomas Weelkes of Chichester, earlier in the century. In 1687 another well-known composer, Michael Wise, was murdered in a brawl with a city watchman. Such incidents are not isolated; they are typical of many.

In London the deplorable practice arose of allowing one singer to hold appointments simultaneously at Westminster Abbey, St. Paul's, and the Chapel Royal: he himself would appear at one of them (normally the Chapel Royal) while deputies would stand in for him at the others. An unscrupulous man could accept all three salaries and rarely appear at all in person, deputies representing him at all three. This practice survived well into Victorian times and even today some of the London choirs have approved deputies who are permitted to stand in for absent lay-clerks. But then why should we expect mere singers to be conscientious when a man like Hoadly, bishop of Bangor for six years and of Hereford for two, never once set foot in his diocese; and Bishop Blackburne, suspected by Horace Walpole of keeping a harem, 'was a great, roistering, ex-naval chaplain, who shocked even one of his vicars by calling for pipes and liquor in the vestry after a confirmation'.[6] Amongst the clergy 'pluralism, non-residence, nepotism, sinecures all flourished with disastrous results for the spiritual life of the Church'.[7] But amongst both clergy and musicians there were saints as well as sinners, conscientious men as well as the lazy and self-seeking.

THE ORGAN AFTER 1660

Immediately following the Restoration there came a boom in organ-building. Once they were freed from repression most people, including clergy as well as laity, reacted sharply against the austere and depressing worship imposed by the Puritans and delighted in introducing more colour, ceremonial and music. The organ, which had been under a cloud during much of the previous century, now came into its own. The trouble was that so many instruments were no longer playable: some, we know, had been mutilated by rowdies in the Civil War but a far greater number had lain silent and neglected for the best part of a century because of the antipathy of clergy or of influential parishioners. These instruments were now in an advanced stage of decay and lay shrouded in dust and cobwebs. In many cases an entirely new organ was the only answer but builders were so inundated with work that they just could not cope with the orders pouring in. Yet so urgent was the demand for organs that many of these old ones were hurriedly patched up and pressed into temporary service. Thus within three months of the king's return Pepys records attending the Chapel Royal where 'I heard very good music, the first time that ever I remember to have heard the organs and singing-men in surplices in my life' (8 July 1660): this was the old organ which had been dismantled during the Commonwealth and now re-erected, only to be replaced two years later by a two-manual organ, the first to be built by 'Father' Smith. (Does Pepys's emphasis on singing-men imply that at this stage Cooke did not yet consider his boys ready to sing in public?) At King's,

[6] Basil Williams: *The Whig Supremacy 1914–60*, p. 78. (O.U.P.)
[7] J. R. H. Moorman: *History of the Church in England*, p. 285. (A. and C. Black.)

Cambridge, pending the rebuilding of the organ, the College borrowed a small 'positive' from their organist (Loosemore) to tide them over.

The most notable builders at this time were Thomas Thamar, George Dallam, Ralph Dallam, James White, Robert Taunton, William Hathaway, and Lancelot Pease, not forgetting the returned exiles, Robert Dallam, Thomas Harris, and Bernard Smith. Within a few years supply had caught up with demand and most important churches could boast an adequate instrument. And now two really great builders emerged — Renatus Harris, son of old Thomas Harris; and Bernard Smith, later known as 'Father' Smith. During the Commonwealth Renatus had spent his youth in France and there is good reason to believe that Smith similarly had been trained in Holland:[8] both men were therefore influenced by continental ideas and brought new techniques and developments to English organ-building, grafting foreign ideas on to an English stock. They were bitter rivals, their work was quite dissimilar, yet they both in different ways laid the foundations upon which British organs were to develop during the next two centuries. The fact that technical progress was so slow and lagged behind the continent is due more perhaps to shortage of money and lack of imagination on the part of the clergy than to the builders whose more enterprising and ambitious schemes were often turned down. It was not until 1710 that Harris was able to build Britain's first four-manual organ at Salisbury (46 stops), and another sixteen years elapsed before (probably) the first English pedal-board was installed at St. Mary Redcliffe, Bristol (and then only one octave of pull-downs; independent pedal ranks were not introduced till about 1778). Pedals met with intense resistance from many English organists and even as late as 1851 Sir George Smart at St. George's Chapel, Windsor, and later still Spofforth at Lichfield refused to use them. The swell box was invented by an Englishman, Abraham Jordan, in 1712. During the eighteenth century some German builders settled here and made a significant contribution to organ development: Snetzler set himself up in business; Schrider worked for Smith and eventually succeeded him as head of the firm in 1708; Schwarbrick was first employed by Harris but later established himself as a master builder at Warwick.

MUSIC IN THE PARISH CHURCHES

If music in the cathedrals left something to be desired, that offered in the smaller churches must often have been execrable. Our knowledge is not very detailed and considerable research remains to be done.

On Sundays most churches had only two services with music — Morning and Evening Prayer. A few may have had ante-Communion after Morning Prayer but (outside London) Holy Communion itself would generally have been held at most four times a year and in some churches not at all. In the vast majority of churches the musical content of the Sunday Offices would have consisted almost solely of metrical psalms and Canticles. The Psalms appointed in the Prayer Book were usually read as a duet between the parson and the parish clerk, verse and verse about (the 'Reading Psalms') but in many churches a metrical paraphrase would be sung instead. The metrical psalms were also introduced as hymns at various other points in the service. True hymns, designed for congregational singing, can hardly be said to exist during the early years of the Restoration though a number of devotional poems and songs, personal rather than scriptural,

[8] Clutton and Niland: *The British Organ*, p. 71. (Batsford.)

had been issued for use in private and family devotions. Many of these reached a high literary standard contrasting very favourably with the halting doggerel of so many metrical psalters (e.g. George Wither's *The Hymnes and Songs of the Church*, 1623, with tunes by Orlando Gibbons). Some of these devotional poems found their way into public worship. Modern hymnody was a product of the eighteenth century and owed much of its enormous popularity and rapid expansion to the work of such pioneers as Isaac Watts (1674–1748) and later the Wesleys. The high quality of many of these hymns, the variety of their prosody and the catchy tunes to which many of them were set spelled eventual doom to all but the best of the metrical psalms, but before metrical psalmody was finally displaced it was given a new lease of life by the publication in 1696 of a new metrical psalter by Nahum Tate, the Poet Laureate, and Dr. Nicholas Brady which was authorised for use as an alternative to Sternhold and Hopkins. From now onwards Tate and Brady was known as the 'New Version' and Sternhold and Hopkins as the 'Old'. At first the new book naturally met with fierce opposition but its superior merits led first to its acceptance on terms of equality with the Old and eventually to its gradual supersession of the Old till it in turn had to make way for the nineteenth-century hymnbooks.

Reference has already been made to the way in which metrical psalms were sung. They were taken very slowly and deliberately, the parish clerk or someone reciting each line aloud before it was sung so as to aid the memories of illiterate worshippers. Often short interludes were played to provide a musical background to this 'lining out'. The first note of each line was treated as a 'gathering' note; that is, it was held long enough for all the congregation to gather on it before moving off in measured tread along the next phrase of the tune. The 78th Psalm performed in this way and followed by a two-hour sermon must have given the faithful a pretty fair foretaste of eternity. 'Amens' were not sung at this time.

In Tudor and Jacobean times organs of some kind were fairly common though in parish churches they would generally have been small positives or even little regals. Such a splendid instrument as that at Old Radnor would have been very rare in a village church. For various reasons—old age, lack of skilled maintenance, deliberate neglect, vandalism, or obedience to the Order of Council of 1644—few of these organs survived the Commonwealth in playing condition and since after the Restoration the cost of new instruments was prohibitive, there were in fact far fewer organs after the Commonwealth than before it. Many churches had therefore to find other ways of getting the congregation to sing. Two of these may be briefly mentioned; the third—the church gallery minstrels—calls for a section on its own.

Pitch-pipes. In poorer churches the singing was unaccompanied. A note would be blown on a pitch-pipe by the parish clerk and the people tuned-in to this note by singing some such phrase as 'Praise ye the Lord'. Then when all had found their note the singing began in earnest, led by the stentorian tones of the parish clerk himself. The pitch-pipes used were wooden, about 18 inches long, usually square in section, and fitted with a sliding stopper to raise and lower the pitch. Many of them are still preserved.

Barrel-organs ('Winch' or 'Dumb' organs). In small communities where organists were hard to come by there was much to be said for an instrument requiring no more skill than the turning of a handle. The music was set up in brass staples or pins projecting from a wooden cylinder about 3 feet 6 inches long and 9 inches in diameter which was slowly rotated, the projecting pins operating simple keys which admitted air to the pipes.

Barrel-organs varied much in size. They were usually built with either 8, 14, 17, 21, 27, 28 or 31 keys though larger ones were not uncommon. Only the very grandest instruments had a full chromatic compass: the smaller ones were tuned to provide two or three closely related diatonic scales and all tunes played had then to be transposed into one of these keys. To give tonal variety the better models were provided with up to seven or more stops while some exceptionally lucky parishes even had a drum and triangle to enliven their worship. The more ambitious instruments had a finger keyboard (hence 'finger organ') in addition to the barrels. Most churches possessed three or four barrels each playing ten or twelve tunes; often these barrels were mounted in a revolving frame to facilitate rapid changing. The tunes included psalm-tunes 'with their Givings-out and Interludes, Ec.' and later, chants and voluntaries: the tunes were often embroidered with runs, shakes, and other fashionable ornaments. Sometimes alehouse ditties were incongruously mixed up with the sacred pieces, suggesting that the barrel-organ heard in church on Sundays found another home during the week.

Barrel-organs have a long and interesting history. They were known in the Netherlands at least as early as the fifteenth century and in England, Thomas Dallam made a highly elaborate one in 1599. But it was in the eighteenth and first half of the nineteenth century that the instrument really came into its own and even great composers like Handel and Mozart did not scorn to write for it.

THE GALLERY MINSTRELS[9]

Useful though they were, pitch-pipes and barrel-organs were usually regarded merely as a stand-by, a temporary makeshift to fall back on in an emergency. Most churches up and down the country, in town and village alike, aspired to something far more impressive—a band of mistrels seated in a gallery at the west end of the church. Most of the galleries were specially built for the purpose. The minstrels included both singers and instrumentalists but the composition of the group was almost infinitely variable. There seems scarcely an instrument which did not appear in some minstrel gallery or other: serpent, ophicleide, bugle, vamp-horn (megaphone), guitar, banjo, drums, concertina and tinwhistle blended with more conventional instruments to the greater glory of God and often, one suspects, to the still greater confusion of his flock. Certain instruments appear to have been considered almost indispensable; these were the flute and bassoon (Brightling had no less than nine bassoons at one time) and the 'bass viol' ('cello). Clarinets and hautboys (oboes) were also especially favoured. Many of these instruments were home-made and 'cellos still survive hammered out of metal in the blacksmith's shop! Of course the early woodwind instruments were very simple and had few keys.

Members of the minstrel group were often referred to as 'musicianers' or 'musickers'. They were very proud of themselves; proud too of the group as a whole and they would practise regularly and work hard to gain the ascendancy over minstrels from neighbouring parishes. In some places their congregations would rally to their support and much the same friendly rivalry existed between the various groups of minstrels as existed more recently between neighbouring brass bands. But this same strong corporate spirit could occasionally bring them into conflict with the clergy or people or both; indeed, in many

[9] For a fuller treatment of this subject and many amusing anecdotes consult Canon K. H. MacDermott's *The Old Church Gallery Minstrels* (S.P.C.K.).

parishes the minstrels were a force to be reckoned with. They were often autocratic; they were not above putting the parson firmly in his place (during a service if need be) neither did they shrink from going on strike if necessary in order to get their own way. They were jealous of their rights and even a seat in the gallery was a privilege hedged round with protocol and taboos. They resisted change, even when it did not personally involve them, and their opinion had considerable influence in the parish. In some churches the minstrels looked upon the music as their own special prerogative and woe betide any member of the congregation rash enough to join in!

Most of the minstrels were yokels — ignorant, illiterate and musically self-taught — yet they possessed immense zeal and diligence and often by sheer perseverance the more intelligent players learned to read and write music: such men copied out all their own parts and took great pride in their collection. But as every choirmaster knows it is all too often the worst singers who are the keenest. Similarly minstrel performances were usually more notable for enthusiasm and vigour than for accuracy and artistry; indeed contemporary accounts are scathing in their criticism and make it plain that both the singing and playing were often so appalling as to be either pathetic or frankly ludicrous. Many writers comment on the 'shrill tone', 'screeching' or 'screaming' of the children and the uncouth voices of the men. It is not without significance that almost every tune-book published about this time had an introductory lesson on the rudiments of music designed to teach singers how to read a part — but then few village minstrels could even read the instructions. (Perhaps these lessons were intended more for musical members of the congregation in town churches.) It was the ambition of every choir to sing in 4-part harmony: the normal arrangement was for the tune to be given to the tenors and the other parts were allocated to two altos and bass; trebles sang the tenor tune an octave higher. But such complexity was far beyond most choirs and many had to admit defeat. So Playford, having published in 1671 his *Psalms and Hymns in Solemn Musick of Foure Parts*, found himself obliged only six years later to issue his *Whole Book of Psalms* in only three parts with the melody in the treble, so arranged that the tunes could be sung in only two parts, treble and bass, at a pinch. The band would have been much worse even than the choir. Home-made instruments would be very difficult to make or play in tune; balance would have been poor and one or two instruments would inevitably predominate; faltering technique, ragged ensemble and an inordinately slow speed would combine to destroy all rhythmic vitality.

If the music was bad the standard of behaviour was worse and there seems to have been a total lack of reverence. Instruments would be tuned during the sermon; loud exhortations, blame and praise from the leader of the minstrels would punctuate the service; raucous arguments in the gallery distracted the worshipper below; and discussions about the music between the parson, the parish clerk and the leader would be bellowed across the church during the service itself. Some of the instruments were found useful for chastising choirboys (or the 'charity children' who formed the top line) and the intermittent thwacks and the boys' yells were merely another irritation for the congregation to endure. All this was made worse because during the singing it was customary for the congregation to turn round in their seats and 'face the music', so they could not escape seeing as well as hearing all that went on. Of course there must have been many churches where a far higher standard both of music and of behaviour obtained but they would have been exceptional. For the rest, it is difficult to share Canon MacDermott's nostalgia for things now mercifully past.

ANGLICAN CHANTING

Though it took place a century or more later, the evolution of Anglican chanting bears certain resemblances to the development of the motet; in both, three somewhat similar phases are discernible:

(a) a unisonal plainsong melody;
(b) the same melody (usually in the tenor) with two, three, or more added parts;
(c) the plainsong melody replaced by a freely-composed part resulting in free counterpoint in 3, 4, or more parts.

In the cathedrals, choral foundations, and probably some of the 'high' churches, simple Gregorian psalm-tones sung in unison seem to have continued in use until well into Restoration times — at least they continued to appear in such printed collections as Lowe's *A Short Direction for the performance of Cathedrall Service* (1661), Clifford's *The Divine Services and Anthems usually sung in the Cathedrals and Collegiate Choirs of the Church of England* (1664: 2nd edition), and Playford's *Order of Performing the Divine Service in Cathedrals and Collegiate Chapels* which he included in the 1679 edition of his famous *Introduction to the Skill of Music*.

For the second phase, in which the plainsong melody is embedded as a tenor part in a 4- or 5-part harmonization, we find that as far back as the mid-sixteenth century Tallis harmonized the psalm-tones in 5-parts, leaving the original melody in the tenor. He also treated the Responses in the same way. In 1641 Barnard published a number of harmonized psalm-tones (including Tallis's) while the Lowe, Clifford, and Playford collections mentioned above included harmonized settings as well as unison chants. The addition of harmony inevitably involved some loss of rhythmic freedom because, as we have seen, harmony creates its own independent accents, especially at cadences. The important point is that early harmonized chants still tried to preserve as far as possible the rhythmic freedom and flexibility of the original plainsong; it was later, during the latter part of the seventeenth century, that these rhythms were finally reduced to the stilted chant formula so horribly familiar today. The last stages of complete ossification were brought about by the introduction of bar-lines and their misinterpretation as a series of fixed accents followed by an invariable stress on the final note. Whereas formerly the chant was free to accommodate the natural rhythm and accentuation of the words, now the words themselves were pushed together or pulled apart to conform to a rigid metrical scheme with a recurring pattern of heavy accents.

Once a stereotyped formula had been evolved the plainsong tone rapidly disappeared and chants became free compositions. This was the third phase. At first chants were single, that is to say they carried only one verse of the psalm, but during the eighteenth century double chants, carrying two verses of the psalm, became popular. The early chants were simple, dignified, and eminently appropriate to worship; several of them have continued in regular use till our own day. However, from about the time Boyce published his *Cathedral Music* (1760), chants shared in the general decline in church music and by the middle of the nineteenth century far too many of them consisted of pretty, meretricious little tunes, soupy harmony and fanciful modulations, festooned with passing notes: double chants gave even more scope than single ones for such excesses. The end product of all this was an irritating little part-song, seven or fourteen bars long, with a rigid, unyielding, regularly-spaced accent to which magnificent words had somehow or other to be tailored. This little song was endlessly repeated, its mechanical beats pounding with relentless monotony regardless of the true verbal rhythms. Anglican chanting reached its nadir in 1875 with the publication of the *Cathedral Psalter*, representing the very antithesis of all the principles of good chanting.

CHAPTER X

The English Baroque–II

Everyone knows that, apart from 1066 and all that, historical movements and eras overlap, interlock and interact and it is rarely possible to assign precise dates to them: thus Tomkins, who died in 1656, can be reckoned a renaissance composer while William Lawes is essentially a baroque musician even though he died eleven years before Tomkins. The period from about 1620 to 1670 was one of transition from the renaissance to the baroque: the two styles overlapped considerably and are even seen side by side in the work of the same man. Whereas William Lawes clearly foreshadows Purcell's work, William Child, after an uneasy flirtation with new methods, was content to fall back upon the old.

The greatest barrier to any study of English baroque church music is that so little of it is easily accessible. Despite splendid work done by several scholars in specialist fields, the fact remains that nobody has done for this period as a whole what E. H. Fellowes did for Tudor music: as a result, not only has much of the music never been published but a good deal of it has never even been transcribed into score from the vocal parts. What is not available cannot be performed and so even to modern cathedral organists such men as Nathaniel Giles, John Mundy, John Ward and Matthew Locke are not much more than names in history books whilst important composers like Humfrey and Blow are rather poorly represented in print. Attention has already been drawn to the inadequacy of most of the available printed editions and it is a sad fact that though we all pay lip service to Purcell's genius, few of the popular performing copies of his sacred works do him justice. Since so much of the music is inaccessible it is impossible to survey the field adequately or to arrive at any just appraisal of individual composers. All that can be done is to discuss such pieces as are in general use together with a few more which deserve to be better known. It it much to be hoped that scholars and publishers together will soon make far more of this music available in reliable performing editions.

In the last chapter we discussed some technical aspects of baroque music but it must be remembered that these appeared in their most developed forms only towards the end of the period—mainly, in fact, in the music of Purcell and Blow. But before considering these composers more fully we must first retrace our steps a little and pick up the threads after the death of Gibbons in 1625, examining more music of the transitional period and tracing the development of the baroque style in the work of those composers who were active in the middle of the century. At this time musicians were becoming increasingly independent of Church and Court. Except for Child, Rogers, Goldwin, and perhaps one or two others, they had far wider interests than most of the Tudor and Jacobean composers and church music formed only part (and sometimes the least important part) of their output. A new branch of composition attracted many—music for the stage, including masques and (later) opera—whilst most of them produced a good deal of chamber music after the Italian manner: string fancies, suites, sonatas and the like.

If we accept that Philips, Peerson, Dering and Ramsey constitute the earliest group of transitional composers (see pp. 189–200), then Walter Porter, Richard Portman, Henry and William Lawes, and William Child form a second group, though the two groups overlapped considerably. This second group have one thing in common —a tendency to look two ways at once. They could not help being profoundly influenced by the musical revolution then taking place in Italy and they naturally experimented in the new techniques; some composers even learnt to handle them with considerable facility. At the same time they could not entirely shake off the effects of their early training in renaissance techniques and of the polyphonic traditions which they inherited. None of them was big enough to achieve a satisfactory synthesis of elements so disparate, yet in trying to do so they evolved a style which was to govern the development of English music over the next century. There is no doubt that later restoration music owed far more to them than to the mere accident of a king's exile.

NICHOLAS LANIER (1588–1666)

Lanier stands somewhat apart from this group because not having been trained as a church musician he missed that thorough grounding in the disciplines of polyphonic technique which was the common lot of musicians of his day and he would therefore have accepted new ideas the more readily: perhaps this also explains why in later life he wrote nothing for the Church. Lanier was a man of wide culture —painter, art connoisseur, composer and singer. As a composer he was much attracted to the stage and wrote a number of masques. His chief claim to our interest is that he was probably the first to introduce operatic recitative into English music, an innovation which soon found its way into the verse anthem.

WALTER PORTER (c. 1595–1659)

This composer is interesting because in him the Italian influence is direct; he had been to Italy and studied under Monteverdi. In 1632 he published *Madrigales and Ayres. Of two, three, foure and five voyces, with the continued Base, with Toccatos, Sinfonias and Ritornellos to them. After the manner of Consort Musique. To be performed with the Harpesechord, Lutes, Theorbos, Base Violl, two Violins, or two Viols*, modelled on his master's seventh madrigal book. This publication is important for many reasons: it is one of the earliest volumes to be printed with regular barring; it is another very early example of figured bass in England, in fact Porter is probably the first to use the terms 'continued Base' and 'thorow Base'. In an introductory address 'To the Practitioner' he gives the earliest printed instruction explaining to the singer how to distinguish between vocal lines and the instrumental accompaniment; he says he has made 'the singing Base also a thorow Base in which you are not to sing but where there are words or this signe :||: of Repetition'. He also exhorts the performer to write out his continuo realisation rather than risk improvising it. By adding an organ accompaniment Peerson had already changed the entire character of the madrigal: Porter carries this decay a stage further by writing an obbligato instrumental accompaniment with 'Toccatos, Sinfonias and Ritornellos' which he says 'are good for the respiration of the Voyse'. His progressive outlook is further demonstrated by the preference for violins over viols expressed in his title.

Porter's *Madrigales* is also the first English publication to give the performer directions about speed and dynamics in Italian instead of English—a practice which has continued ever since. His reason for this is most interesting and sheds light on the origin of this custom: 'I have made use of these Italian words because they [the performers] shall not mistake and sing them if they were expressed in English, being mixed among the other words.' More simply, if these directions were given in English they might get mixed up with, or mistaken for, the text so that an unwary sight-reader could find himself singing 'Praise the slow Lord O my loud soul': by putting the performing directions in Italian it differentiates them from the text. Monteverdi's influence is obvious in a curious mannerism (to be revived half a century later by Jeremiah Clarke) which Porter explains thus: 'In the Songs which are set forth with Division where you find many notes in a place after this manner ⎯♩♩♩♩⎯ in rule or space, they are set to express the *Trillo*.' An instance occurs at (a) in Ex. 97 below.

The first piece in the set, *O prayse the Lord*, is usually listed as an anthem though it was almost certainly never intended to be sung in church. In spite of its *naïveté* it achieves something new in setting sacred words—the infusion of a theatrical element into the established verse anthem style. It is this 'theatrical' element which foreshadows the baroque cantata style of Purcell and distinguishes the restoration anthem from the Jacobean. This distinction could hardly be demonstrated more clearly than by comparing Porter's *O prayse the Lord* with Gibbons's *This is the record of John* (both written much about the same time). Gibbons's three chorus entries in solid 5-part polyphony bespeak his Tudor background as surely as Porter's quasi-operatic recitatives, encrusted with characteristic baroque *fioritura*, typify the new spirit. Here is the opening of *O prayse the Lord*:

Walter Porter: *O prayse the Lord*

Ex. 97

239

Porter was neither a great composer nor a strikingly original one; at best he was but a very pale shadow of Monteverdi: yet some of the new ideas he imported into English music must have startled his contemporaries and he would certainly have been considered among the *avant-garde* of his day.

RICHARD PORTMAN (d. *c.* 1655)

Of Portman's three Services and a dozen or so anthems only the Service in G (including Venite) and two anthems, *O God, my heart is ready* and *Rejoice in the Lord*, survive complete and even these are never sung now. Portman, a pupil of Orlando Gibbons, is chiefly famous as the composer of what is virtually the first genuine church cantata to be written in English, a miniature work called *Dialogue of the Prodigal Son* in which solo parts are given to the prodigal, his father and the elder brother; only two sections are allotted to the chorus.

HENRY LAWES (1596–1662)

Perhaps the best known composers of this early group are the two Lawes brothers, Henry and William, though their most significant work was done in fields other than church music. Henry, the elder, is much better known by Milton's sonnet addressed to him than by any music he himself wrote. The famous eulogy beginning

> *Harry* whose tuneful and well measur'd Song
> First taught our English Musick how to span
> Words with just note and accent,

does greater credit to Milton's reputation as a poet than to his perspicacity as a music critic for, as we have seen, practically every composer of the previous hundred years 'spanned words with just note and accent'—it was simply part of the accepted technique of word-setting. Lawes merely carried it to excess. By making his music follow the rhythm and inflection of the words too slavishly his vocal lines often became stilted and shapeless. Furthermore, to say that music is 'tuneful' is not necessarily complimentary and even 'well measur'd Song' hardly commends itself after the rhythmic subtlety and fluidity of the Lutenist school.

Henry is most often associated with works for the stage; in particular, he wrote the music for Milton's masque *Comus* (1634) and also collaborated with others in one of Davenant's operatic ventures. It was in some of his three hundred or more songs however that his ideas of 'just note and accent' were most consistently worked out, resulting in a kind of *aria parlante*, neither recitative nor aria but partaking a little of both. It was left to Purcell and his contemporaries to take over this way of setting words and bring it to artistic fruition. Henry's younger brother William fought on the king's side in the Civil War and was killed at the siege of Chester. Three years later Henry, partly as a memorial and partly as a lasting testimony to the love and admiration each had for the other, edited William's psalm settings and religious canons and added a further thirty psalm settings of his own in the same style; he invited four famous poets and eight well-known musicians amongst their circle of friends to write commendatory verses and elegies, and then issued the whole collection under the title *Choice Psalmes* (1648). Henry's own contributions, modelled on those William left in manuscript, are

240

not of great merit. In addition, he wrote about twenty liturgical anthems of which only six have survived complete or nearly so. Of these, *Zadok the priest* is a rather pedestrian setting written for the coronation of Charles II. His most popular piece appears to have been *My song shall be of mercy*.

WILLIAM LAWES (1602–45)

Of all this group of pioneers, William Lawes was by far the best musician. Dr. Lefkowitz, in his monograph on the composer,[1] declares he 'was a true representative of the seventeenth-century Baroque. His music establishes him as a leading figure in the acceptance and development of new styles and techniques in England. He was an artist who worked in advance of his times. Versatile, prolific and highly original, he must be considered a major composer of the first half of the seventeenth century—one of the great figures of English music.' It is in his chamber music, especially the remarkable 5- and 6-part fantasias for viols, that his talents show to greatest advantage; he also excelled as a song writer and in composing music for the theatre. Among his sacred pieces are a number[2] of psalm settings for two trebles and bass with thorough-bass accompaniment. It seems likely that Lawes patterned these psalm settings on similar works by William Child with whom he was closely associated at the Chapel Royal: Child had composed a number of such pieces 'after the Italian way' (i.e. in the style of similar works by Viadana, Philips and Dering) and no doubt William felt tempted to experiment in the same genre himself. These 'psalmes' were probably composed about 1637–38 and they formed the nucleus of his brother's memorial publication: as we have seen, Henry added thirty more in the same style. The word 'Psalmes' here carries a wide interpretation and includes paraphrases of Isaiah, the Lamentations of Jeremiah, and even four Latin texts. In selecting texts he seems to have preferred penitential words and for these he adopted a fairly contrapuntal style, often with *fugato* imitations. Tears and lamentation found conventional expression in descending chromatics or chains of dissonance though his treatment of them often shows originality and great artistry. On the other hand, joy and praise called forth solid block harmony, almost in hymn-tune fashion. Four of William's settings end with an extended *Hallelujah* section. These jigging *Hallelujah* choruses too can be traced back to an Italian model, Gabrieli this time, and we have seen that Philips, Dering and Ramsey all used *alleluia* sections to end some of their works. Once started, the fashion caught on and within a few years it became almost obligatory to end all anthems, certainly verse anthems, with a 'Hallelujah chorus' whether appropriate or not. Purcell was as much an offender as anyone.

Choice Psalmes also included ten religious canons and rounds by William Lawes; the next example, quoted from Lefkowitz,[3] gives an idea of the profound beauty and emotional intensity which he could compress into these miniature forms (see Example 98 on following page).

It must be emphasized that the *Choice Psalmes* were written for the Chapel Royal and Court of Charles I; they were never intended for public worship. At the time they were written Puritanism was already strangling choir music and such pieces could have been

---

[1] Murray Lefkowitz: *William Lawes*, p. 259. (Routledge & Kegan Paul, 1960.)

[2] Murray Lefkowitz, in his book *William Lawes* (Routledge & Kegan Paul) gives thirty on p. 238 but lists thirty-one on pp. 280–1; Peter le Huray in *Music and the Reformation in England, 1549–1660* (Herbert Jenkins) gives twenty-six on p. 349.

[3] Murray Lefkowitz: *William Lawes*, p. 248. (Routledge & Kegan Paul, 1960).

William Lawes: *She weepeth sore* (Round)

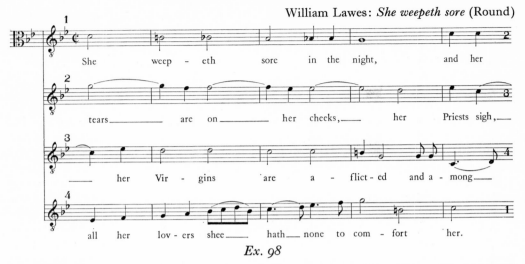

She weep - eth sore in the night, and her

tears_____ are on_____ her cheeks,_____ her Priests sigh,_____

_____ her Vir - gins are a - flict - ed and a - mong_____

all her lov - ers shee_____ hath_____ none to com - fort her.

Ex. 98

sung only in private chapels and in the home (see Pepys, 7 November 1660, 'After all this he called for the fiddles and books and we two and W. Howe, and Mr. Childe, did sing and play some psalmes of Will. Lawes's': also 12 April 1664, 20 April and 9 August 1664).

Christ Church, Oxford, possesses three manuscript part-books which contain twelve long verse anthems by William, based on 'common tunes'. Each anthem is built round a well-known metrical psalm-tune which recurs from time to time in its original simple form marked 'Cho:' ('chorus' or 'choir'). Each anthem begins and ends with a plain statement of the common tune; other statements of it are clustered mostly near the beginning and end of the anthem and only rarely in the middle, so buttressing its overall structure. The various appearances of the church tune are interspersed with a wide variety of solos, duets and trios. It seems highly probable that Lawes intended the congregation to join in singing those verses set to the common tune, resulting in an elaborate responsorial between soloists and congregation; if so, then these anthems are almost certainly unique in the history of Anglican church music. The solos, duets and trios are similar in style to Lawes' declamatory songs and suffer from the same defect — a too rigid adherence to the principles of Italian monody resulting in a shapeless, tuneless melodic line and a veritable orgy of word-painting. Lefkowitz believes these verse anthems may have been early works written sometime prior to 1631:[4] if so, they are remarkable productions whatever their faults. Another verse anthem, *Let God arise*, is for bass voice and of two others, only the words survive. All the religious pieces mentioned so far appear to have been written for private devotion and show strong secular influences: only one of his anthems seems to have been intended for public worship and that was *The Lord is my light* (a bowdlerized version of which appeared in Boyce's *Cathedral Music*). This is rather more dignified in style and contrapuntal in texture than most of his pieces and is pleasantly tuneful.

WILLIAM CHILD (1606–97)

Primarily Child was a church composer though he also wrote some songs and instrumental works. Some eighteen Services, over fifty anthems and a Latin motet are known

[4] Ibid., p. 256.

in addition to his published set of twenty psalms, but only about half the Services and a third of the anthems survive complete. Some of these are still occasionally to be heard. In 1632 he was appointed one of the organists both at St. George's Chapel, Windsor, and the Chapel Royal, and from then till he died most of his long life was divided between these two foundations except for the Commonwealth period during which he retired to a small farm and occupied himself in composition. He was a distinguished organist, alto singer and cornett player and was a close friend of Samuel Pepys.

Child suffered the penalty of being a minor composer working in a period of rapid transition. Steeped in the polyphonic tradition he reached out towards new ideas but was unable to integrate them into a consistent personal style: he was like a modern organist who, brought up on *Hymns Ancient and Modern*, attempts to improvise in the serial idiom. He began bravely enough by issuing, in 1639, *The first set of Psalmes of iii voyces, fitt for private chappells, or other private meetings with a continuall Base, either for the Organ or Theorbo, newly composed after the Italian way.* By 'after the Italian way' he means that his settings for two meanes, bass and continuo are in the baroque trio sonata style evolved by Viadana and developed by Philips and Dering: he has abandoned polyphonic texture in favour of a firm harmonic basis and a melodic line which is both affective and declamatory. Another secular influence is apparent—that of the English madrigal, revealed in his fondness for somewhat crude word-painting and more particularly in his use of dissonance and chromaticism. This influence persists as late as the church music of Purcell.

But these modest essays in the new style are not wholly convincing and he is much more at home in the *a cappella* idiom in which most of his works are written. Even his verse anthems and verse Services can be sung unaccompanied; there are no instrumental symphonies or *ritornelli* and the verse sections are all in three or four parts, making complete harmony in themselves. The solo voices merely alternate with the full choir, often in fairly rapid declamation, giving much the same sort of block contrast as when a string quartet alternates with full orchestral strings or an organist alternates two manuals. The full choir itself often sings from side to side so that altogether four blocks of tone are available—full, decani, cantoris, and solo group. This 'concertato' form of construction again hints at a secular influence in Child's work. After the rhythmic fluidity of renaissance music the regular metre of early baroque work imposes a rhythmic straight-jacket and makes much of his work seem heavy-footed.

Child's Services once enjoyed great popularity, especially those in D and E minor printed by Boyce: a verse Service in E flat appeared in Arnold's collection (1790) and two complete Services in F and G were printed by Goss and Turle in 1847. Most of these have long since disappeared from cathedral lists. Instead of pursuing the lines of development initiated by Morley, Gibbons and others, he contented himself with the simplest form of Short Service, mostly note-against-note in block harmony. His Services, like his anthems, can be sung entirely unaccompanied, including the verse sections, though in practice they were always accompanied on the organ: hence Burney's somewhat curious reason for admiring the Service in D which he says 'is extremely pleasing, the more so, perhaps, from being composed in a key which is more perfectly in tune than most others on the organ'. This Service, like the one in 'Gamut' (G major), was written before the Civil War. It used to be much esteemed for its several sections in 4-part canon but to us now they seem rather ponderous and contrived: the part-writing is more free in this than in much of his work but even so it often sounds laboured and at times naïve. His most interesting Service is probably his setting of the Evening Canticles in D minor; here all the verses are scored for boys' voices in four parts (four meanes) answered by a 5-part choir (MAATB).

His High Church sympathies led to the composition of a Te Deum, Jubilate, Sanctus and Gloria, all in Latin. He was, in fact, the first composer to set either Sanctus or Gloria for the English rite since the earliest years of the Reformation: in all his nine English Communion settings he again includes a setting of Sanctus, an innovation which most of his younger contemporaries were quick to adopt.

Among his better anthems were those written in preparation for the king's return from exile — *If the Lord himself; O pray for the peace of Jerusalem* and *O Lord, grant the king a long life* — together with the 7-part *Sing we merrily* (his B.Mus. exercise). Many of his anthems end with a short and conventional Hallelujah chorus and he has been pilloried for writing such passages as:

William Child: *O Lord, grant the king a long life*

Ex. 99

Musically the effect is unsatisfactory and lacking in dignity but a comparison with Morley's balletts will at once show that here again Child has tried to adapt a secular style to church needs.

Generally speaking, his short full anthems are more successful than his verse anthems—in fact one of his best pieces is the lovely 4-part Latin motet *O bone Jesu*: this reaches such a high level of inspiration that Fellowes even went so far as to question his authorship. Child was one of the very few English composers to experiment, often highly successfully, with the more extreme forms of Italianate chromaticism and there are some striking and highly effective examples in *Bow down thine ear*; *O God, wherefore art thou absent* and *Woe is me*. Yet contradicting what has just been written, perhaps the finest work of all is his superb verse anthem *Turn thou us* in which strength and beauty of line, original and interesting harmony and rhythmic vitality are skilfully employed for expressive ends.

Child is generally blamed for having a very conservative outlook. Dull and uninspired he often is but it is difficult to sustain a charge of conservatism. Admittedly he often chose to write in the *a cappella* manner, setting his face against the introduction of stringed instruments; admittedly, too, Tudor mannerisms sometimes crept into his work. But certainly in his younger days he introduced new secular elements which helped pave the way for the greater men who followed him.

BENJAMIN ROGERS (1614–96)

We come now to the third group of English baroque composers which included Rogers, Christopher Gibbons, Captain Henry Cooke, George Jeffreys, Locke, Creighton and Dean Aldrich: these too overlapped with members of the first two groups. Of the baroque composers discussed so far, Rogers's name is perhaps the most familiar to many church musicians. This is partly because unlike some of the others he was first and foremost a church composer; even more because some of his works have always held their place in cathedral music lists. Much of the earlier part of his life was spent as a singer at St. George's Chapel, Windsor, where at the age of eighteen he came strongly under the influence of the organist, William Child. From 1664 to 1685 he was organist of Magdalen College, Oxford. Before 1660 he wrote mainly instrumental pieces; most of his church music was written after the Restoration. He also wrote glees and organ music. So closely did Rogers model himself on Child, uncritically accepting the older man's ideas, prejudices and limitations, that in many people's minds the two are now firmly bracketed together. Rogers's Services, like Child's, are mostly written in the Short Service form and can be sung unaccompanied. He adhered to the 'for every syllable a note' formula even more literally than did Child and the combination of block harmony with an insistent four-in-a-bar makes his Services dull and uninspiring though redeemed to some extent by a simple and pleasing melodic line. Four of them—in D, F, A minor and E minor—used to be very popular in the nineteenth century and the Service in D (the 'Sharp Service'), included in Boyce's *Cathedral Music*, has recently been re-issued in a scholarly edition.[5] Rogers even follows his exemplar in abandoning the traditional plainsong intonation of Te Deum and substituting a nondescript tonic-dominant phrase (see Example 100 on the next page).

It is curious that Rogers's Services should have remained in the cathedral repertory while William Lawes's sacred pieces are still unknown. The explanation is that where choral services have to be maintained without sufficient time for thorough rehearsal, choirmasters are naturally attracted to 'safe' Services which are easy to sing and pose

[5] Rogers: *The Sharp Service*, Ed. Bernard Rose. (Novello.)

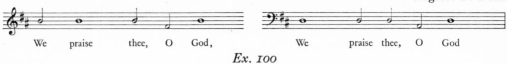

Rogers: *Te Deum*

We praise thee, O God,   We praise thee, O God

Ex. 100

no problems, so releasing precious rehearsal time for more challenging items. Such settings are also popular with the less musical clergy because they cover the ground quickly and the service ends sooner. Neither reason is a very good one.

Like his Services, Rogers's anthems were once in great favour but have now all but dropped out of use. They included four Latin settings, *Audivit Dominus; Deus misereatur; Exaltabo, te, Domine* and *Jubilate Deo*, and were mostly in 4-part harmony. The three that have proved most enduring are all short pieces: *Lord, who shall dwell;*, *Teach me, O Lord*, and *Behold now, praise the Lord* with its 'poor gabbling Hallelujahs'. Most of them are solid, dignified and devotional but lacking in imagination. They make few demands on singer or listener; the harmony is smooth and conventional, their rhythm four-square, and the melodies graceful and pleasant but rather obvious.

One piece of his continues to be performed however—the *Hymnus Eucharisticus* sung on the top of Magdalen College tower every May-day at 5.00 a.m. (its first stanza 'Te Deum Patrem colimus' is also sung as a daily grace in Magdalen College hall).

CHRISTOPHER GIBBONS (1615–76)

It is manifestly unfair to measure Christopher against his illustrious father, Orlando; not surprisingly he was vastly inferior both as a player and composer. His best work is to be found in his string fantasias. In his anthems the renaissance style of his father and the baroque style of his contemporaries are often found side by side but he had neither the imagination nor the technique to fuse them into a satisfying whole even though his most uninspired works are occasionally lit by flashes of real power and inspiration. His music is rarely heard now.

HENRY COOKE (*c.* 1616–72)

We come now to a man who was in many ways a key figure in the development of English music of the baroque era. He was important as an inspired choir-trainer, musical director and teacher rather than as a composer and his compositions are of only minor significance. He seems to have studied in Italy, he sang 'after the Italian manner' (Evelyn: 28 November 1654), taught his boys to sing Italian songs in Italian, and both his own and his choirboys' anthems are markedly Italianate in style. He was one of Davenant's collaborators in *The Siege of Rhodes* and he composed some coronation music as well as more than thirty anthems. Pepys wrote 'a strange mastery he hath in making of extraordinary surprising closes, that are mighty pretty' (13 February 1667), but then Pepys was not a very reliable music critic. Fuller-Maitland, in his article in 'Grove', more prosaically dismisses his part-writing as 'ungrammatical', but then to a musician trained under nineteenth-century theorists most restoration works would seem ungrammatical. More certainly Cooke succumbed to a temptation to which cathedral organists are often prone—a tendency to fill their music lists with their own works. A silly legend that he so resented the supposedly superior ability of his pupil, Pelham Humfrey, that he collapsed and died in a frenzy of professional jealousy can be laid at the door of that gullible old gossip Anthony à Wood of Oxford: at any rate Cooke seems to have approved of Pelham sufficiently to accept him as a son-in-law.

Cooke appears to have been the first to write verse anthems scored for violins and continuo. Certainly one of them, *Behold, O God, our defender*, was written as early as 1661 for the coronation of Charles II. Though musically undistinguished and somewhat embryonic in form, this piece nevertheless establishes a pattern for the restoration verse anthem. It begins with an opening 'symphony' for 4-part strings which leads into a verse section, the last phrase of which is taken up by the chorus. The strings play short *ritornelli* between full and verse sections and also introduce the final 'alleluia' chorus. Thus we have three 'blocks' of tone—strings, solo voices and full choir—used as though they were three separate manuals of an organ and so alternated as to provide effective variety and balance, the strings opening and the chorus closing the work. Both this anthem and *We will rejoice* are scored for 4-part strings though Cooke normally scored for strings in three parts. Most of his longer anthems suffer from the generic defect of his time, that of having far too many cadences in the home key, but this fault is less obvious in his shorter pieces.

GEORGE JEFFREYS (*c.* 1610–85)

There is some evidence to suggest that he served in the Chapel Royal prior to 1643. In that year he was appointed one of two organists to Charles I at Oxford. Three years later he went to Kirby Hall, Northamptonshire, as steward to Lord Hatton and there he spent the rest of his life. Many of the texts he set, and presumably wrote himself, are so strange as to suggest that he must have been very eccentric.

As a composer he was versatile and prolific and his known works include string fancies (*c.* 1629), music for the stage (1631), about thirty-five anthems and sacred songs with English words (only four of which are found in liturgical sources) and over seventy with Latin words, as well as a Morning, an Evening and a Communion Service. Some of these pieces are of the 'trio-sonata' type of psalm settings for two trebles, bass and continuo like those of Child and the Lawes brothers. His anthems appear to have been written between 1648 (*Turn thee again*) and 1669 (*A music strange*). The titles of some of these anthems are revealing—*A music strange; Busy time*, and *Whisper it easily*—and the texts make astonishing, often hilarious, reading.

But his importance is that the process of transition initiated by Philips, Peerson, Dering and Ramsey is in him completed. He is the most 'advanced' composer of the group, the one most wholly immersed in the *stile nuovo*; in other words, the most truly baroque. Much of his writing seems far in advance of its time and his use of dotted and back-dotted rhythms, 'affective' intervals and chains of daring modulations often suggests Humfrey, Blow or Purcell. Almost inevitably his longer pieces show structural weaknesses and there are many dull patches, but almost every known work has some striking feature—a highly original texture, expressive chromaticism, a bold key-change, an unexpected cadence or an unusual melodic line.

The trouble is that only a handful of his works are available in modern editions. Here, surely, is a composer who merits thorough investigation.

MATTHEW LOCKE (1622–77)

The most significant composer of the group was unquestionably Locke though he was not primarily a church composer. Either alone or with others he wrote music for a succession of masques and stage works including *Cupid and Death* (1653), *The Siege of Rhodes* (1656), *The Stepmother* (1663), *Macbeth* (?) (1663), *The Empress of Morocco* (1671), *Psyche* (1673) and *The Tempest* (1674). Of these, *Cupid and Death*, written in collaboration with Christopher Gibbons, is best known. It is especially notable for his attempts to achieve emotional expression by means of elaborate and often highly effective *melismata* placed not, as one would expect, on important words but on unimportant words like 'a', 'the', 'or' and 'to': often, by thus holding back the more important word which follows, the melisma throws additional emphasis on it when at last it does appear. *Psyche* contains an 'echo' chorus, a form which had long been popular on the continent (e.g. di Lasso's *O la, oche bon eccho*). *The Tempest* is remarkable for its violent dynamic markings, tremolo sections and harmonic acerbities. Locke wrote a considerable amount of chamber and instrumental music. His *Little Consort of Three Parts* (1651, published 1656) is for viols or violins and his *Consort of Four Parts* is a set of six suites each of which has a fantasia, two dances and an 'ayre'. In these works, as in his vocal music, the Italian influence is very marked: even his music for 'sagbutts and cornets', played during Charles II's royal progress to Whitehall on 22 April 1661, seems to lean heavily on the brass writing of Giovanni Gabrieli. In 1673 Locke published *Melothesia, or Certain General Rules for playing upon a Continued Bass . . .* , one of the first books on this subject to be published in England.

Locke's sacred works include a Kyrie and Creed in F, thirty anthems (six with instrumental accompaniment), sacred songs, twelve Latin pieces and six psalms; an Evening Service in D minor may also be his. Very few of these works are available in print — not enough, anyway, to arrive at a realistic appraisal of his work. What is available suggests that his church music is less distinguished than his secular, particularly his music for the stage; it also shows a marked similarity in style and technique with the

Locke: *When the Son of Man shall come*

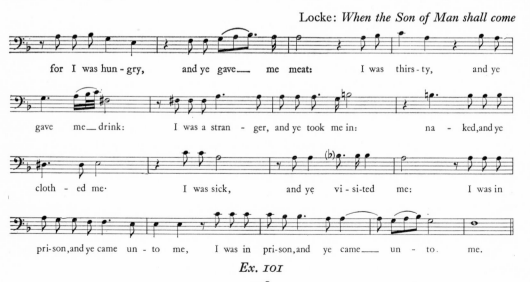

Ex. 101

248

work of Henry Lawes, especially on those occasions in his recitatives when excessive fidelity to 'just note and accent' betrays him into writing a somewhat rambling and aimless melodic line. Here, for instance, is part of the bass recitative in *When the Son of Man shall come* (see Example 101 opposite).

But Locke is superior to Lawes in that even his dullest pages are often relieved by some striking phrase or gracious turn of melody. Not all of Locke's sacred music was intended for public worship. The musical chronicler Roger North (*c.* 1651–1734) says that 'He set most of the psalmes to musick in parts, for the use of some vertuoso ladys in the citty': of these, *Praise our Lord, all ye Gentiles* (SSA) is perhaps the most popular.

Of works designed for liturgical use his large-scale pieces are the best; most, if not all, of these would have been intended for the Chapel Royal. *Not unto us, O Lord*, for example, laternates sections for double choir with verses for counter-tenor, tenor and bass; much of the 8-part writing is gloriously rich and massive. In many of these large-scale works, like *O be joyful* and *The Lord hear thee*, he experimented with various groupings of voices and instruments. *Sing unto the Lord, all ye saints* is interesting because in addition to 4-part verse, 4-part chorus and strings, it is also scored for oboes and flutes. Furthermore, instead of the instruments merely alternating with the voices on the 'blocks of tone' principle, (i.e. *concertato*) they are often combined with the voices to increase the sonority and expressiveness of the texture. Formal problems too are more successfully dealt with and this anthem is less scrappy than most. Locke's largest and most elaborate work is *The king shall rejoice* (1666) laid out for three 4-part choirs, 5-part strings and a group of viols (shades of Gabrieli!).

O give thanks unto the Lord is an effective anthem in which the bass soloist sings a series of florid recitatives in strict tempo: each recitative is answered by the upper voices singing their refrain 'for his mercy endureth for ever'. Locke seems to have a partiality for the bass voice; such bass solos as these and the one quoted opposite (Ex. 101) must have been written for some outstanding singer (the famous bass John Gostling did not join the Chapel Royal choir until 1678). The Latin piece *Omnes gentes* also has a highly florid bass solo. Only one of Locke's anthems appeared in Boyce's collection; this was *Lord, let me know mine end*, an attractive piece and one which would probably be far better known had not a later composer, Maurice Greene, provided the same text with a setting of such beauty that these words are now almost exclusively identified with it. In *How doth the city sit solitary* Locke attempts a deeper emotional expression not altogether unsuccessfully. His Kyrie and Creed in F were first performed on 1 April 1666: the Kyrie nearly led to a mass walk-out by the Chapel Royal choir because he had broken with tradition by writing different settings for each of the ten responses.

Apart from his music, Locke goes down in English musical history as one of the most quarrelsome, acrimonious and abusive men of all time.

ROBERT CREIGHTON (*c.* 1639–1734)

A gap of about twenty years separates Creighton from Locke, almost a whole generation in fact, but no one would think so to look at his music. He became Professor of Greek at Cambridge and twelve years later was appointed canon residentiary and precentor of Wells Cathedral. Creighton was for long remembered by two Services, one in E flat and one in B flat, and an anthem. The two Services have now all but dropped out of use leaving only the anthem *I will arise* to represent him. It is a pedantic, somewhat stilted little work, probably because most of it is in canon 3 in 1. It is dangerously easy to write a contrived canon as a technical exercise but so very difficult to write one which is also inspired music, artistically satisfying.

HENRY ALDRICH (1647–1710)

Aldrich, another cathedral dignitary, also shares with Creighton the distinction of being amongst the very few composers discussed here who had no connection with the Chapel Royal. This kindly and modest Dean of Christ Church, Oxford, Vice-Chancellor of his university from 1692–95, was a man of immense talent in widely diverse fields. He was a famous theologian; he wrote standard text-books on Logic, Heraldry and Architecture; as a practical architect he designed All Saints Church, Oxford, and the Peckwater Quadrangle at Christ Church; he prepared extensive notes for a massive book on the history, theory and practice of music (a mine of information for scholars); and he composed a quantity of music, most of it for the church. Strangely, it is as a musician that Aldrich achieved his greatest fame though he was probably less gifted in this field than in any other. Perhaps his best musical memorial is his Service in G, a simple setting in Short Service form, because until fairly recently it was in the repertory of nearly every cathedral choir: yet it is a dull piece of work, competent but unimaginative, distinguished only by the fact that it includes Sanctus and Gloria in excelsis—unusual at that time. Two of Aldrich's anthems, *Out of the deep* and *O give thanks*, were published in Boyce's collection: these too are uninspired but they were popular until well into the present century.

In addition to his creative work as a composer, Aldrich had a curious and highly pernicious passion for tinkering with the music of others. This particular form of vandalism included re-writing, enlarging, and sometimes completely recasting the original. For example Wise's *How are the mighty fallen* was enlarged and retitled *Thy beauty, O Israel*; Tallis's Versicles and Responses were adapted to complete his Litany; while Farrant's 4-part *Hide not thou thy face* emerged smiling with four more brand-new additional parts! His favourite victim was the Italian composer Carissimi who suffered all sorts of indignities at his hands. Perhaps we should end with one last word in his favour: he was an inveterate collector of old, rare and curious music books, both printed and in manuscript, and he amassed a priceless antiquarian library which ultimately he bequeathed to his College. It has been of immense value to scholars ever since.

THE 'RESTORATION' COMPOSERS

The fourth group of English baroque composers consists of Captain Cooke's almost legendary choirboys—Pelham Humfrey, Robert Smith, Michael Wise, John Blow, Daniel Roseingrave, Thomas Tudway, William Turner, Henry Hall and Henry Purcell. Together these constitute the most clearly defined and certainly most important group of baroque church musicians. It is this group only who may fittingly be called 'Restoration' composers. Although the early pioneers were of considerable historical importance, with the exception of William Lawes and Matthew Locke they left behind them little of genuine artistic worth: they experimented in new techniques but could not attain sufficient mastery of them to turn them to expressive ends; they chased theories and their work became artificial and stilted. Yet they prepared the way for the greater men who followed them and it was this present group of composers who, seizing upon the new ideas and opportunities offered, brought to fruition the seed planted by the early baroque musicians and lifted English music to new heights of expression.

PELHAM HUMFREY (1647–74)

Humfrey was one of the first boys to be admitted to the reconstituted choir. Whilst still a child he distinguished himself as a composer and no less than five of his anthems were included in the second edition of Clifford's *Divine Services and Anthems* (1664). He also joined with his fellow choristers Blow and Turner in the composition of *I will always give thanks*, known as the 'Club Anthem' because each boy contributed one of its three movements. When Humfrey left the choir in 1664, Charles II personally sent him to study in France (probably under Lully) and Italy, making him a grant of £450 out of Secret Service funds. During his absence abroad he was appointed a royal lutenist (1666) and a Gentleman of the Chapel Royal (1667). On his return in 1667, Pepys described him as 'an absolute Monsieur, as full of form, and confidence, and vanity, and disparages everything, and everybody's skill but his own'.[6] But if he adopted French fashions in his clothes and manners it is Italian influence rather than French which is so apparent in his music. Humfrey married Cooke's daughter and when Cooke died in 1672, Humfrey succeeded him as Master of the Children, thus becoming one of Purcell's teachers. His training in Italy ensured the continuance of Cooke's Italianate traditions. He died at the early age of twenty-seven and was buried in Westminster Abbey.

In addition to church music Humfrey wrote a large number of songs; many of these were part of the incidental music to stage plays. Of his church music eighteen anthems are known to survive, thirteen of which are extended works with string symphonies: there is also a Service in E minor. This last is in 4-part harmony and has mainly 3-part verses (AATB in Magnificat); like the Services of Child and Rogers, it can be sung unaccompanied. It is a workaday setting of no great merit. Boyce printed seven of Humfrey's anthems (1768 and 1773) but omitted their instrumental interludes: the mere fact of their appearance in such an important publication gave them wide currency and it is therefore the greater pity that Boyce's selection hardly represents the composer at his best.

It is in his treatment of the solo voice that Humfrey is conspicuously successful. Though he was by no means the first to introduce recitative into English church music (some claim that he was) he was certainly the first to use it as a means of artistic expression. He was able to accept the pedantic principles of affective monody, scrupulously observing verbal rhythms and inflections, yet he was able to reconcile them with the broader and superior claims of musical shape and balance (a fine example from one of his songs will be found on p. 222, Ex. 96). Humfrey had a fondness for chromatic melodic intervals, especially the diminished and augmented fourth, which he used naturally and effectively though rather too often; these soon became the stock-in-trade of his younger contemporaries and were done to death. Another virtue of Humfrey's style is the sheer beauty and excellence of his string writing; this applies not just to the

[6] 15 November 1667. Captain Cooke was one of Pepys's personal friends. Pepys took a keen interest in the music of the Chapel Royal and his Diary abounds in references to the Chapel, to Cooke, the boys, the men and the music they sang.

1st violin part but to the others as well (e.g. the opening symphony of *By the waters of Babylon* and the *ritornelli* in *O give thanks*; notice also the striking violin obbligato that accompanies the opening bass solo in *By the waters*). No longer 'apt for viols or voyces' such idiomatic passages clearly show that Humfrey was himself an accomplished violinist. There is a general impression, for which Pepys and Tudway are largely responsible, that because Humfrey had studied under Lully (itself unproven) he introduced the light and rather frivolous French style into his church music, so exercising a harmful influence on Purcell. This is nonsense. Humfrey's sacred music (like Lully's) is serious and often full of deep and tender melancholy as in *Haste thee, O God; Like as the hart; O Lord my God* and *Thou art my King* (all in minor keys be it noted). Even his more cheerful pieces are marked by a sober restraint. Of course his stay in France left some marks on his music: his fondness for breaking into iambic metre from time to time derives from Lully whilst the opening symphony of *O give thanks*, beginning in four-time with dotted rhythms and then breaking into triple measure, is not unlike a miniature overture of the 'French' type favoured by Lully.

Humfrey had a far better grasp of musical form than had most of his older contemporaries. His verse anthems, like theirs, were in several sections beginning with a 'symphony' and ending with a chorus but instead of the various sections being self-contained entities succeeding one another haphazardly, he imposed some overall shape and continuity. Proportions were cunningly balanced; his string *ritornelli* were often thematically linked or repeated; some sections would return later in the work, sometimes reappearing several times rondo-fashion; more importantly, the psychological tension induced and released by departing from and returning to the main key began to be used purposefully to make the structure more taut and cohesive (Humfrey was one of the first English composers really to grasp the psychological potentiality of key relationship and tonality). For an example of his skill in securing overall cohesion take *O Lord my God, why hast thou forsaken me*: it is in no less than ten sections yet the work holds together far better than anthems of similar scale by Cooke, Locke and others. In both *Thou art my King* and *Rejoice in the Lord* he makes extensive use of recurring ritornelli and returning sections to unify the structure.

By the waters of Babylon is not only one of Humfrey's best pieces but ranks among the finest anthems of its time. It is sufficient here to draw attention to the beautiful second violin sequence in the opening symphony, the eloquence and yearning of the opening bass recitative, the dramatic power and sensitive word-painting in the altercation between the bullying Babylonians and their captives, and the final fugal chorus with its falling chromatic subject. Another long anthem, *The king shall rejoice*, also has some fine writing for strings; a curious feature is that the choir frequently repeats words just sung by the soloist, almost as though he is 'lining out' for them. Of the anthems given by Boyce, *Hear, O heavens* is perhaps the best: its mood of lamentation resolving into hope and trust is tellingly conveyed and the verse trio beginning 'Wash ye, make you clean' is cunningly laid out for the three voices. Occasionally he indulged in a little harmonic experimenting; his less successful essays often sound somewhat crude—as in these two passages from *Thou art my King, O God* (see Example 102 opposite).

But it is as a pioneer of effective recitative that Humfrey deserves his place not only in the history books but, far more importantly, in the modern cathedral repertory as well. We should feel ashamed to acknowledge that much of this composer's best music has never yet appeared in print.

Humfrey: *Thou art my King, O God*

Ex. 102

ROBERT SMITH (c. 1648–75)

He seems to have been a remarkably early starter and by the time he was sixteen no less than six of his anthems were deemed worthy of inclusion in Clifford's collection: alas, the music has not survived. On leaving the choir he turned to secular music and wrote mainly songs and incidental music for stage productions. Like several of the Chapel Royal boys, he died young.

MICHAEL WISE (c. 1648–87)

When Wise left the Chapel Royal he became first a lay clerk at St. George's Chapel, Windsor (1663?), then organist of Salisbury Cathedral (1668). Eight years later he was appointed a counter-tenor at the Chapel Royal, thereafter dividing his time between Salisbury and London. A few months before his death he was appointed master of the choristers at St. Paul's Cathedral. His stormy and quarrelsome career came to a violent end in an affray with a night-watchman, though whether in London or Salisbury seems uncertain.

About thirty-six anthems and a number of Services are known. In general he is much more conservative than other composers in this group: to give but one example, there are no symphonies or *ritornelli* for strings in any of the surviving manuscripts, though there are occasional clues that some of the present brief 'symphonies' and *ritornelli* may have been later substitutions for more extended string passages, now lost. (The word 'symphony' in this context refers to an instrumental introduction before the singing begins whereas *ritornelli* are instrumental interludes *between* sung sections.) Wise's vocal writing is usually fairly simple and, as with most restoration composers, chorus sections are normally brief. In verse sections he preferred duets and trios to single voices. What is more interesting, he was the only one of the group to write extensively for boy soloists (see p. 225). Treble verses are common in his anthems. *I will arise* ('The prodigall') has a solo verse followed by a duet and then a trio, all for trebles, while in *Prepare ye the way of the Lord* there is a curious canonic duet for trebles. It is interesting to record that while Wise favoured the treble voice so much his contemporary and friend, Pelham Humfrey, wrote not a single solo or verse part for a boy soloist.

Three early verse anthems, dated 1669 or before, soon became popular and established the composer's reputation—*Have pity upon me; Blessed is he that considereth the poor* (included in Boyce) and *By the waters of Babylon*. Wise is at his best in these small-scale pieces; generally speaking the more ambitious he is the less successful the outcome. Thus in *O praise the Lord* the florid sections are fussy and conventional while the concluding Hallelujah section sounds uninspired and empty. *I will sing a new song* is another large verse anthem. Far more satisfying is *How are the mighty fallen*, especially the very fine bass recitative 'Ye mountains of Gilboa':

Wise: *Thy beauty, O Israel*

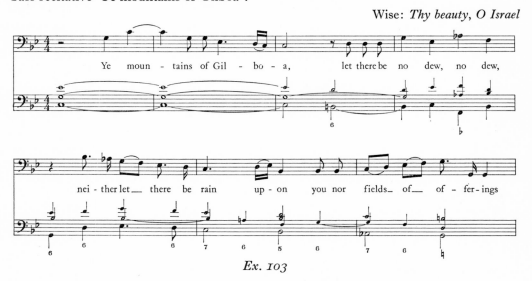

Ex. 103

Incidentally, the version of this anthem printed by Boyce under the name *Thy beauty, O Israel* had been extensively revised and re-written by Henry Aldrich.

The other four anthems which Boyce issued are those by which Wise is chiefly remembered today—*Prepare ye the way; Awake, put on thy strength; The ways of Sion do mourn* and *Awake up, my glory*. In all of these Wise attempts to give the piece some structural unity and cohesion by using a chorus or verse section as a sort of refrain which recurs from time to time, either with the same or with different words: the basic plan varies from one anthem to another but the principle holds good. (Pelham Humfrey does the same thing in *Rejoice in the Lord*.) Wise's verse sections are usually set for three voices, often treated imitatively. *Prepare ye the way* does all the expected things with 'Ev'ry valley shall be exalted . . . and hill shall be made low', and there is an amusing canon for two trebles on the words 'And the voice said Cry'; the second voice asks 'What shall I cry?' and the first one tells him, the second dutifully crying what he's told phrase by phrase! In *Awake, put on thy strength*, the Hallelujah section occurs no less than four times but some relief is provided by transposing its second appearance down a minor third. *The ways of Sion do mourn* is one of Wise's best anthems. It opens with a bass and treble duet beginning with a curiously haunting chromatic phrase (not unlike that used by Purcell in *Hear my prayer*): the threefold repetition of 'do mourn' to this drooping figure seems the very epitome of lamentation:

Wise: *The ways of Zion*

The ways of Zi - on do mourn,— do mourn,— do mourn

Ex. 104

This duet is lengthy and at times the gap between the two voices seems uncomfortably wide. The highlight of the work is the lovely treble solo 'Is it nothing to you'; it will be noticed that the voice is kept within the lower part of its range (a 'meane') and no use is made of a boy's high notes. *Awake up, my glory* is mainly a verse trio for treble, alto and bass, except for nine bars of chorus at the end. It is a simple, engaging little piece with a tuneful melodic line and a good deal of rather obvious imitation.

Of Wise's Services the two most popular were a complete setting in D minor and an Evening Service (Magnificat and Nunc dimittis) in E flat. This latter is a typical Short Service, almost entirely in block harmony, yet it is effectively written and is still to be heard in most Anglican cathedrals.

DANIEL ROSEINGRAVE (*c.* 1650–1727)

Having served as a choirboy under Cooke at the Chapel Royal, Roseingrave was successively organist of Gloucester (1679–81), Winchester (1682–92) and Salisbury Cathedrals (1692–98). Then he moved to Dublin where he was organist simultaneously of St. Patrick's Cathedral and of Christ Church. His youngest son, Ralph, succeeded him at both cathedrals in Dublin.

Only two anthems by him are known—*Haste thee, O Lord* and a fine 5-part verse anthem *Lord, thou art become gracious* which deserves to be heard much more often. It includes some poignant chromatic writing, a highly expressive verse quartet, an exciting treble solo and a brilliant final chorus.

THOMAS TUDWAY (*c.* 1650–1726)

The music of Blow and Purcell will be the subject of a separate chapter and so we come next to Thomas Tudway. Like most of his fellow choristers at the Chapel Royal he became a professional musician and was appointed organist of King's College Chapel, Cambridge, in 1670, becoming Professor of Music in the university in 1705. When he was well into his sixties he was commissioned by Lord Harley (afterwards Earl of Oxford) to make a collection of English cathedral music. The task of selecting and editing occupied him from 1714 to 1720 and resulted in six large, thick volumes of manuscript.[7] It is interesting to find that Tudway included works by Tomkins and other renaissance composers even though the bulk of his collection consisted of music by his contemporaries, especially his boyhood friends at the Chapel Royal. He also included an Evening Service, eighteen anthems and a Latin motet of his own in addition to pieces by nonentities like Finch, Lugg and Wildbore. We are indebted to him for some valuable biographical notes on composers represented in his collection, many of whom were

[7] British Museum, Harley MSS. 7337–42.

known to him personally. The second volume has a long and important preface addressed to Lord Harley in which Tudway shows himself a thorough-going conservative; he deplores the introduction of the string orchestra into church music and considers 'theatricall performances' highly improper in religious worship. Because Tudway's collection was never printed it had nothing like the influence and authority of Boyce's later collection; nevertheless it still remains an invaluable source-book for scholars and historians.

His own compositions have no musical value and are never sung now, though from a historical viewpoint they are not without interest. For example, both *I will sing unto the Lord* and *Sing, O heavens* have the direction 'trumpet stop' written into their organ parts. He seems to have been fond of the organ and his verse anthem *Is it true that God will dwell* is probably one of the earliest to have *ritornelli* specifically designed for the organ instead of strings. It was written for the opening of Sir Christopher Wren's new St. Paul's Cathedral in 1697. Except for a short 'Hallelujah' section at the end, *I will lift up mine eyes* is one long and very flowery tenor solo, notable for its use of demisemiquavers (very rare in English church music at this time), whilst *My heart rejoiceth* is so long that it must be considered not an anthem but a cantata. (As a concession to popular demand, he managed to stifle his conscience sufficiently to score this work for instruments.) Boyce showed some discernment in not including any of Tudway's music in his *Cathedral Music* collection.

Fellowes quotes a solo passage from a highly florid Evening Service in B flat to prove how 'exaggerated' and 'lacking in dignity' it is compared with those by Purcell, Humfrey and Blow.[8] In his revised 5th edition of Fellowes's book (1969), Prof. J. A. Westrup makes the same point and gives a much longer and fuller quotation to show that the organ accompaniment is just as florid as the tenor solo.[9] But the criticism misfires somewhat because this particular Service is almost certainly by Blow himself.

WILLIAM TURNER (1651–1740)

Originally a chorister at Christ Church, Oxford, Turner was probably one of the boys press-ganged by Cooke into the Chapel Royal choir. Whilst there he was one of the contributors to the 'Club Anthem' (the others being Humfrey and Blow). When his voice changed he developed into an outstanding counter-tenor and sang for a time at Lincoln Cathedral. In 1669 he was sworn a Gentleman of the Chapel Royal and soon afterwards added other singing posts at St. Paul's and Westminster Abbey. In 1696 he graduated Mus.D. at Cambridge. After nearly seventy years of happy married life he and his wife died within four days of each other and were buried in the same grave in the west cloister of Westminster Abbey.

For one who spent most of his life in cathedral choir stalls Turner wrote surprisingly little church music—a couple of Services and some sixteen anthems. He seems to have been more interested in songs and catches and stage music. Of the anthems only two seem to have established themselves in the repertory, *Try me, O God* and *Lord, thou hast been our refuge*. This last is a fine anthem; it contains a lovely short chorus 'For a thousand years in thy sight'. He had a natural felicity in writing for strings (he was almost

[8] E. H. Fellowes: *English Cathedral Music*, p. 152. (Methuen, 4th Ed. 1948.)
[9] E. H. Fellowes: *English Cathedral Music*, pp. 155–6. (Methuen, 5th Ed. edited by Prof. J. A. Westrup, 1969).

certainly a violinist himself) and it is often the string sections of his anthems which are the most interesting and rewarding. The opening symphonies of *Hold not thy tongue, O Lord* and *God sheweth me his goodness* are especially good and both rhythmically and harmonically they anticipate Purcell himself to a quite remarkable extent—no small tribute! *Behold now praise the Lord* is distinctive in that it is constructed on a ground bass throughout: the ground is stated twice during the opening symphony. *O praise the Lord* also makes use of a ground bass.

Some anthems were *pièces d'occasion* such as *The Queen shall rejoice* (coronation of Queen Anne) and *The King shall rejoice* (St. Cecilia's Day 1697). This last was Turner's most ambitious work. The St. Cecilia's Day festival was held in St. Paul's Cathedral and was sung by the combined choirs of St. Paul's, Westminster Abbey and the Chapel Royal. Musically it must have been a very splendid occasion and it inspired Turner to write at such great length that his anthem became a full-scale cantata. He enhanced its brilliance by adding two trumpets to the string ensemble and showed an excellent grasp of the possibilities of instrumental colour in the way he contrasted trumpets and strings. The work is also notable for a remarkable treble solo in which, perhaps for the first time in English church music, the high range of a boy's voice is fully exploited. There is an urgent need for this work to be published and recorded.

HENRY HALL (*c.* 1655–1707)

The last of Cooke's famous choirboys to be mentioned in this chapter, Hall was successively organist of Exeter and Hereford Cathedrals and took deacon's orders in 1698. Tudway included an uninspired Te Deum in E flat, a Benedicite in C minor, a Cantate Domino and Deus misereatur in B flat and five anthems in his collection. Other anthems by Hall are extant. None of his music is available in print or is easily accessible: cursory examination suggests that, as with other composers of his time, his anthems reach a far higher level than his Services. He is one of many composers of this period whose music awaits an intensive study.

It is worth repeating that the real problem of discussing and evaluating the work of the English early baroque composers is the inaccessibility of much of their music. Representative works of important composers like Locke and Humfrey (and until recently, Ramsey) have never yet been published and sometimes not even scored from the manuscript parts. It is much to be hoped that the learned societies will turn their attention to this challenging and fascinating period of our musical history.

CHAPTER XI

The English Baroque – III: Blow and Purcell

Our brief survey of the work of Cooke's choirboys omitted two names and those the most illustrious of them all – John Blow and Henry Purcell. Purcell is universally acknowledged to be one of England's very greatest musicians and he is unquestionably the most considerable composer between Byrd and Elgar. In the more limited field of sacred music, however, even Purcell himself must yield pride of place to Blow, and so it is fitting that the work of these two should be considered in a separate chapter.

JOHN BLOW (1649–1708)

Blow was ten years older than Purcell. He was born at Newark and probably attended the Magnus Song School there. When he was six years old his father died. He was one of the first group of boys selected by Cooke for the royal choir and even as a child his compositions attracted sufficient attention for three of his anthems to be included in Clifford's collection of 1663 when the boy was only fourteen. In the following year his voice broke and there followed an extended period of training (probably some form of musical apprenticeship). At some point he studied under Christopher Gibbons.

It must have been gratifying to a youth of nineteen seeking his first job to be appointed organist of Westminster Abbey, even if the salary was the somewhat modest one of £10 a year. Four months later (January 1669) he received a Court appointment as 'musician for the virginals'. On 16 March 1674 he was sworn a Gentleman of the Chapel Royal and when, in that same year, Pelham Humfrey died, Blow succeeded his friend in the important and influential offices of Master of the Children of the Chapel Royal and Composer-in-ordinary for voices in the royal household. This eventful year also saw his marriage to Elizabeth Braddock, daughter of the choirmaster at Westminster Abbey, by whom he had five children: nine years after their marriage Elizabeth died in childbed. On 10 December 1677 he became the first person ever to receive the Lambeth degree of Doctor of Music; this honour is doubly interesting because it was conferred on him by the Dean and Chapter of Canterbury, the Archbishopric then being vacant. About this time he became one of the three organists of the Chapel Royal. In 1679 Blow resigned from Westminster Abbey where he was succeeded by his pupil, Henry Purcell. The legend that Blow, perceiving his pupil's superior genius, was so magnanimous as to stand down in the younger man's favour is as charming as Peter Pan – and alas, about as true. No one knows why Blow resigned: one likely explanation is pressure of work at the Chapel Royal and at Court; another, that there was some clash of personalities. Other important appointments came to him: in September 1687 he succeeded Wise as Almoner and Master of the Children at St. Paul's Cathedral; then on Purcell's early death in 1695 he again took up his old post at Westminster Abbey so that he now held important positions at the Abbey, St. Paul's and the Chapel Royal simultaneously. Finally, in 1699 he became the first holder of the office of Composer for the Chapel Royal. He died on 1 October 1708 at Westminster and was buried near Purcell in the north aisle of the Abbey.

Blow was a prolific composer; in fact he wrote far too much with the result that his output is extremely unequal. At best he is not unworthy of comparison with the greatest church composers of all time; at worst he churned out dull, unimaginative things which could just as well have been written by the least of his contemporaries. In connection with his various royal appointments Blow was expected to provide music for official 'odes' commemorating a wide variety of special occasions including royal marriages and deaths, events at Court, St. Cecilia's Day celebrations, and the like. The texts for most of these were manufactured by official poetasters and were of such sickening banality that no composer could be blamed if they failed to call forth his best work. Blow's settings were usually as barren as the texts, uninspired and cliché-ridden: it is significant that on the two occasions when he had better texts to set—Cowley's *Awake my Lyre* (Act Song for Oxford University) and Oldham's *Begin the Song* (St. Cecilia Ode for 1684)—he produced two remarkably fine works. This recalls the famous passage in the Latin dedication of Byrd's *Gradualia* where he says 'there is a certain hidden power, as I learnt by experience, in the thoughts underlying the words themselves; so that, as one meditates upon the sacred words and constantly and seriously considers them, the right notes, in some inexplicable manner, suggest themselves quite spontaneously'.[1] Blow was first and foremost a church composer but he also wrote innumerable songs, part-songs and instrumental pieces (including some for the organ and harpsichord) as well as his official odes. Apart from a Sonata for two violins and continuo he seems to have had little interest in chamber music; neither did the professional stage appeal to him though it would have brought him much greater popular success and financial reward than writing church music (his work in this field was limited to a few incidental songs). His short opera *Venus and Adonis* was written for performance by amateurs at Court; hence its composer looked upon it as 'A Masque for the Entertainment of the King'. It is important for three reasons: it is the first true English opera to survive complete; it was the precursor of Purcell's *Dido and Aeneas*; most of all because it still makes delightful listening today.

Blow's church music offers a wide field of study. In his article in Grove's *Dictionary*, Mr. H. Watkins Shaw has reprinted and revised Dr. Heathcote Statham's list which now shows eight complete Services and several other Canticle settings, eleven Latin anthems, and about a hundred English anthems of which nearly a quarter have orchestral *ritornelli*. The anthems of both Blow and Purcell generally fall into one or other of the main categories—verse anthems, sometimes with strings and continuo, sometimes with organ accompaniment; and full anthems which, though often provided with an organ accompaniment, are now nearly always sung *a cappella*. This latter form, having its roots in Tudor polyphony, continued to hold its own side by side with the newer verse anthem. Since both Blow and Purcell were responsible in turn for the music at Westminster Abbey and the Chapel Royal simultaneously, historians have been tempted to associate the more solemn dignity and massive strength of the full anthems with the Abbey and the sprightly tunes and dancing rhythms of the verse anthems with the more secular

[1] Translated by E. H. Fellowes in his book *William Byrd*, p. 80. (O.U.P.)

atmosphere of the Chapel Royal. There is some basis of truth in this but the division was by no means hard and fast.

BLOW: THE VERSE ANTHEMS

Though Blow's verse anthems include many fine passages and some highly imaginative writing, they do not (with one or two exceptions) represent his best work. They suffer from many of the weaknesses inherent in the form itself, especially a scrappy disjointedness which neither he nor Purcell could entirely eliminate. We find the usual over-indulgence in ingenuous word-painting, the inevitable Hallelujahs, the mannerisms, the clichés of the period: even his recitative has neither the expressive power nor the emotional depth of Pelham Humfrey's. Added to this is the fact that Blow was limited in his range of emotional expression: he excelled in conveying tenderness, sadness, grief, penitence, strength and nobility, but was less successful in expressing such emotions as joy and thankfulness where he was inclined to fall back on stock formulae.

Perhaps the best known of all the verse anthems, though by no means the best, is *I beheld, and lo, a great multitude* which illustrates some of the points made above. In the editions still used by most choirs, based on the version published by Boyce, the instrumental interludes have been either omitted or drastically cut. The opening verse for ATBB uses the voices in pairs, $AB_1—TB_2$, mainly in parallel 3rds and 6ths, and the two pairs answer each other imitatively. In the ensuing chorus there is some highly effective antiphony between full choir and verse soloists. A little judicious monkeying with his text at this point enables him to drag in a Hallelujah section for verse trio. Presently the alto, tenor and bass soloists each have a fairly long solo (incidentally the composer almost certainly intended the bass solo to be divided between the two verse singers, the opening section 'Therefore are they' going to the 1st bass, his colleague taking over at 'And all the angels'). Of these solos the tenor is the best and offers some effective word setting. The echoing of the last phrase in both the alto and tenor sections is reminiscent of Humfrey. In the last bass section a typical example of rather naïve word-painting occurs at 'fell down, down, down before the throne'. The final chorus, 'Blessing and glory', sung responsorially between verse soloists and full choir provides an effective climax and the concluding Hallelujahs here seem to be more apposite than usual.[2]

And I heard a great voice of much people is also known under the title *I was in the spirit*, words which were adapted to it some years later. There are some fine passages; take for instance the grand sweep of the opening tenor phrase with its powerful upward-springing tenth:

Blow: *And I heard a great voice*

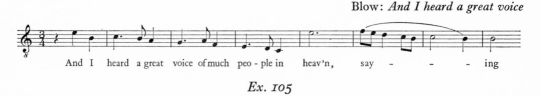

Ex. 105

[2] An excellent performing edition, edited by H. Watkins Shaw, is published by O.U.P. and this is the one to use.

There is a thrilling moment when this phrase suddenly appears unexpectedly much later in the work. Yet the piece is sadly maimed by the Hallelujahs which pustulate on every page: there is a particularly bad one just before the bass verse 'And the four and twenty elders' which sounds like a Revivalist hymn. *O sing unto God* is an extraordinarily florid affair abounding in baroque *fioritura*. Semiquaver runs and dotted rhythms are prominent and Blow has no scruples about making his soloists negotiate demisemiquavers. The bass recitative 'The chariots of God' is a poor thing but the counter-tenor solo in 3 time which follows, 'Though art gone up', is full of melodic charm; the way each vocal phrase is echoed by the organ is wholly delightful. The opening trio now returns in modified form (Blow groping towards musical shape) and the piece ends somewhat inconclusively with a short section sung responsorially between verse-soloists and chorus. Mercifully there are no Hallelujahs! It is probably an early work.

I said in the cutting off of my days is a splendid verse anthem, even if one does tire of quite so much 3-part verse. A brief introduction for strings leads into a short tenor solo of no great distinction though it is partly redeemed by an accompanying obbligato for 1st violins. Then follows an extended symphony for strings, some 40 bars in length, leading to a short section for verse trio based on the first phrase of the earlier tenor solo. Now follows a series of short verse sections (ATT): 'I am depriv'd' (slow), 'But the Lord was ready' (fast), 'therefore will I sing' (fast), and 'Hallelujah'. The full choir takes up the Hallelujahs, again with an obbligato for 1st violins, and this brings the first part of the anthem to an end. Now follows a sort of 'Trio' section consisting of another lengthy string symphony; a tenor recitative with one or two striking phrases—'The grave cannot praise thee'; and a verse trio 'But the living, they shall praise thee' interspersed with instrumental interludes. At the conclusion of the Trio, a return is made to 'therefore will I sing' in the first part of the anthem which is then repeated from that point onwards, ending with the 'Hallelujah' chorus. This lengthy repeat together with the violin obbligatos at the beginning, middle and end, lock the many short sections together and give this very long anthem an overall unity.

Another impressive verse anthem is *O Lord, I have sinned*, written for the funeral of General Monck in 1670. Here Blow's instinct for pathos and profound sadness responds

Blow: *O Lord, I have sinned*

Ex. 106

to the words and the occasion, resulting in much that is deeply moving. Occasionally the music is rather too affective for twentieth-century tastes and such a passage as the preceding example (106) needs to be sung supremely well if it is to avoid mawkishness (the falling chromatic intervals are reminiscent of Humfrey's recitatives).

No wonder the orthodox Dr. Burney was shocked and castigated Blow for his 'crudities in the counterpoint . . . and licences in the harmony which look and sound quite barbarous. Indeed, these crudities are so numerous as to throw doubt on his learning, as well as genius'. There speaks the voice of eighteenth-century harmonic rectitude!

A short anthem for treble solo and choir, *O pray for the peace of Jerusalem*, is well within the capacity of many choirs though the solo boy has to be fairly agile (vocally I mean). The form of this little piece is interesting: it is in two movements—first the solo, which is quite long, and then a short concluding chorus in which melodic ideas already given fairly full treatment in the solo are briefly recapitulated.[3] *The Lord is my shepherd* contains much fine music *qua* music, but the jaunty 3 time, the dotted rhythms and the catchy *ritornelli* seem oddly at variance with words so intimate and profound. It is difficult for us now to accept this sort of thing:

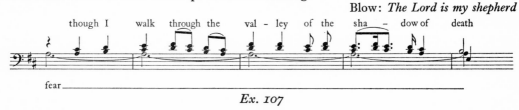

Blow: *The Lord is my shepherd*

though I walk through the val - ley of the sha - dow of death

fear

Ex. 107

When the Duke of York was crowned James II on 23 April 1685, Purcell was organist of Westminster Abbey and so would have been ultimately responsible for the music performed. But Blow was ten years older than Purcell, held many high musical appointments at Court (including that of 'Composer') and had himself been organist of the Abbey: naturally, then, Purcell showed some deference to his old teacher, colleague and friend and Blow took a prominent part in the proceedings. (The Master of the King's Music, Nicholas Staggins, seems to have been a complete nonentity.) Charles II had died unexpectedly on 6 February and there were only ten weeks in which to prepare for James's coronation, yet there can surely have been few coronations in British history for which so much magnificent music was expressly written. A full account of the service, its ceremonial and music is given in Sandford's *History of the Coronation of James II*. Nine items were sung:

1.	I was glad	Purcell
2.	Let thy hand be strengthened	Blow
3.	Come, Holy Ghost	Turner
4.	Zadok the Priest	Lawes
5.	Behold, O God our defender	Blow
6.	The King shall rejoice	Turner
7.	Te Deum	Child
8.	God spake sometime in visions	Blow
9.	My heart is inditing	Purcell

Purcell's two pieces include the mighty *My heart is inditing*; Blow's three contributions

[3] A good practical edition of this by H. Watkins Shaw is published by Novello (Anth. 1286).

included the equally mighty *God spake sometimes in visions* and these two works are not only amongst the finest verse anthems their composers wrote but in their field are probably unsurpassed in the whole era of the English baroque. *God spake sometimes* is a vast anthem laid out for huge forces. The chorus sections are all in eight parts, arranged TrTrAATBBB, this disposition of the lower voices giving increased richness and sonority. Verses are sung by varying groups of soloists though there are no self-contained solos for individual voices (nor are there in Purcell's companion piece *My heart is inditing*). Instead of the strings alternating with the choir, as was usual, they accompany it throughout, adding still more parts to an already rich texture. Professor Anthony Lewis, in his introduction to the anthem in *Musica Britannica*, Vol. VII, says: 'His handling of the strings—always a particular feature of English contemporary style—shows not only a clear grasp of their capacities but also a noteworthy ability to dispose the *ritornelli* so as to give contrast, breadth and formal unity to his work . . . Blow's music has the expected contrapuntal mastery, harmonic vigour and invention, and constantly renewing rhythmic energy, yet the outstanding importance of this great anthem in his achievement and in English music of the period as a whole lies in its firm sense of construction over a lengthy span. Intensity, rather than spaciousness, was the characteristic of much European music of this era, and Blow therefore showed uncommon qualities in being able to assume the grand manner with conviction.'[4]

BLOW: THE FULL ANTHEMS

But to appreciate Blow's true genius we must turn from the verse to the full anthems, especially those in melancholy or penitential mood. In such works the old polyphonic tradition of Tallis, Byrd and Tomkins lives on, though modified by new influences. Typical of these we may cite the 8-part works *God is our hope and strength* and *O Lord God of my salvation*, rich tapestries of counterpoint shot with iridescent harmonies, unforgettable for their massive dignity and nobility. Blow's harmony has called forth much comment: Boyce's praise for 'his success in cultivating an uncommon talent for modulation' so incensed the self-righteous Dr. Burney that he expresses himself amazed that 'so excellent a judge of correct and pure harmony could tolerate his [Blow's] licenses . . . and the additional praise he has bestowed upon him is as unaccountable as any thing in Blow's compositions'. For some reason Burney made John Blow the whipping boy for all the sins of the restoration group. Since then Blow has been blamed and sometimes overpraised for his harmonic originality, many writers failing to see that most of his more daring discords (such as the simultaneous clash of the major and minor 3rd) are merely a continuation and extension of the Tudor principle that each part adheres to its own independent scale scheme (e.g. ascending and descending forms of the melodic minor used to avoid augmented intervals) regardless of what the other parts are doing. The matter may best be summarized in Dr. Walker's words: 'As for the two and a half closely printed pages of "Dr. Blow's crudities" which the usually amiable Burney indignantly sets forth, they may be divided into three fairly equal classes—things explicable on the above lines, other kinds of things, not altogether successful but about which it is pedantic to trouble overmuch, and things that show really brilliant harmonic originality, rising at times to something like prophetic genius.'[5]

[4] *Musica Britannica*, Vol. VII. The Royal Musical Association. (Stainer and Bell.)
[5] Ernest Walker: *A History of Music in England*, p. 393. 3rd Ed. revised by J. A. Westrup. (O.U.P.)

One of Blow's greatest and most deservedly popular anthems is *My God, my God*, one of the most poignant utterances in all Anglican music. In such pieces as this Blow shows a strong affinity with William Byrd and the Spanish mystic, Victoria; there is that same spiritual fervour and glowing luminosity: in their best works these men have gained access to a world which few can enter and themselves but rarely. Here are the opening bars:

Blow: *My God, my God*

Ex. 108

The texture remains fugal but there is a steady building up of emotional intensity. Crotchets give way to quaver movement at 'and art so far from my health' and the unbroken minor tonality veers towards major at 'and in the night season'. The climax is reached when, after a momentary silence, the full choir enters in block harmony for the first time at the words 'O thou worship of Israel'. As this phrase dies away there is a lacerating moment when the basses quietly usher in a repeat of the opening and the work ends with a two-fold statement of the despairing question 'Why has thou forsaken me?'. This anthem is in only four parts (TrATB) and looks easy to sing, but it requires quality in individual voices and the utmost sensitivity and artistry in all voice parts: a good choir is essential.

Most of his other 4-part full anthems pose fewer problems and could be sung by any competent parish church choir though musically some of them are not very distinguished. One which deserves to be far better known is *My days are gone like a shadow*. This is a deeply felt little work of considerable beauty though it abounds in typical Blow 'crudities': what agonies poor Burney would suffer in such a passage as the following—with a special twinge as the B flat collides with the B natural:

Blow: *My days are gone like a shadow*

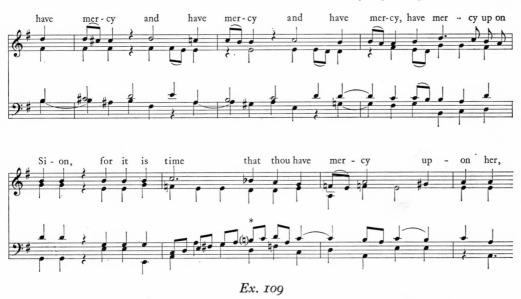

Ex. 109

Be merciful unto me, O Lord is very similar in style: it too is full of fascinating harmonic detail.

The group of Latin anthems yields one which must rank amongst Blow's very greatest works—the glorious 5-part setting of *Salvator mundi* ('O Saviour of the world'). This begins with an extraordinary series of imitative entries which generate a chain of minor 2nds, repeated notes reinforcing and emphasizing the intensity of the discords:

Blow: *Salvator mund*

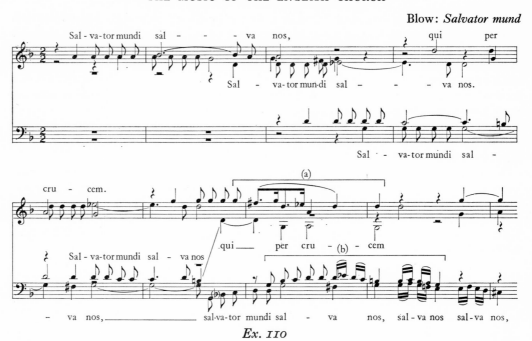

Ex. 110

In this example note the sheer beauty of the phrases marked (a) and (b). A falling chromatic phrase, also treated imitatively, underlines the agony of 'qui per crucem' ('who by thy cross') and leads to a most lovely cadence in which even the lower voices have gracious phrases to sing — (c) and (d):

Ibidem

Ex. 111

266

The opening is now repeated, its astringency wondrously mellowed by making the repeated 2nds major instead of minor; it ends quietly on a chord of D major. There is a momentary silence. Then for the first time the whole choir enters together in block harmony, triumphantly, in the remote key of B major, repeating the words 'qui per crucem' but thinking no longer now of the agony of the cross but of its victory—'who by thy cross and precious blood hast redeemed us'. At the same moment the rhythm changes to 3 time. Though short, this passage is overwhelmingly powerful:

Ibidem

Ex. 112

After this great outburst there is an ethereal passage in which the three upper voices quietly introduce the 'auxiliare nobis' section, to be taken up at once by the lower voices. Again notice the beautiful tenor phrase (e):

Ibidem

Ex. 113

A new phrase, 'te deprecamur', is treated imitatively and builds up till, at its climax, the choir comes to rest on a shattering discord before resolving into the final cadence. This anthem alone would prove Blow to be a highly imaginative artist and it will always remain one of the supreme monuments of English church music. It deserves careful study.

BLOW: THE SERVICES

Although Blow's various Service settings conformed to the fashion of his day and were all in short form, they nevertheless reached a far higher standard than the better known settings by people like Rogers and Child. It is all the more regrettable then that such a well written setting as the Service in G should not be sung more often. (He wrote three Services in G; the one referred to was written sometime before 1676, was included by Boyce, and is now available in a reliable edition by Mr. Watkins Shaw.[6]) Within his restricted terms of reference Blow manages a happy balance between block harmony and freely imitative counterpoint resulting in a texture not unlike that of Byrd's Short Service; this similarity grows stronger in such a passage as the following with its clashing major and minor 3rd and false relations:

Blow: *Evening Service in G*
— Magnificat

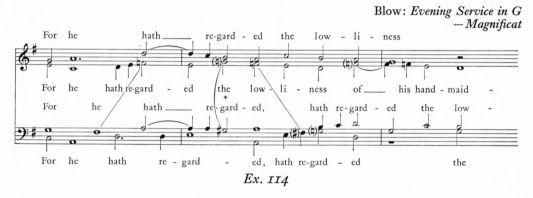

Ex. 114

This Service includes all the alternative Canticles—Benedictus, Jubilate, Magnificat, Cantate, Nunc dimittis, and Deus misereatur—and also, more notably, settings of Sanctus and Gloria in excelsis. The 'Glorias' are canonic, that of Jubilate, for instance, being four-in-one, of Magnificat three-in-one, and of Nunc dimittis two-in-one.

Most of the other Services are more chordal in style and the part-writing is less free, yet the complete settings in A and E minor are sturdy and vigorous and have several unusual harmonic twists which clearly betray their author's identity. In the Service in A there is a particularly grand 'Amen' to Deus misereatur, built over a firmly descending bass. The four smaller-scale settings of the Morning and Evening Canticles in F, A minor, G minor, and D minor are all somewhat conservative in style. The first is outstanding and shows a genuine feeling for words which is expressed by the simplest means (e.g. the quaver 3rds on 'rejoiced' in Magnificat): the last is probably the most familiar of all Blow's Services and is usually called 'Blow in the Dorian Mode'—better known to generations of choirboys as 'Blow in the door'. This is a pastiche of Tudor style and is full of conscious archaisms, yet it is undeniably effective and is a useful setting for small choirs on ferial occasions. An Evening Service in B flat is briefly discussed on p. 256 in the section headed 'Thomas Tudway'.

[6] Published by Stainer and Bell.

HENRY PURCELL (1659–95)

Purcell was one of six boys and two girls. His father, also Henry (not Thomas, as given in many reference books), was a tenor in the Chapel Royal choir who later succeeded Henry Lawes as musician for the lute and voice and was given various other royal appointments. Confusion has been caused because Henry's brother, Thomas, was also a Gentleman of the Chapel Royal. With his father and uncle already in the choir young Henry was accepted by Cooke as a chorister in 1669 and there he stayed till his voice broke in 1673. In 1672 Cooke died and was succeeded by Pelham Humfrey whose French and Italian leanings undoubtedly influenced the boy. During his time at the Chapel Royal, Purcell, like many of the boys, gained a reputation as a composer. On leaving the choir he seems to have continued his association with the Chapel and studied under John Blow. He was also apprenticed to John Hingston, formerly Cromwell's director of music, and his training included being 'keeper, maker, mender, repayrer and tuner of the regalls, organs, virginalls, flutes and recorders and all other kind of wind instruments whatsoever, in ordinary, without fee':[7] he also did some music-copying for Westminster Abbey. He seems to have been an apt pupil: at fifteen, after only one year's training he became official organ tuner at the Abbey; at eighteen he succeeded Locke as composer for the king's violins (a much coveted position), and two years later he followed Blow as organist of Westminster Abbey. In 1681 he married and the following year he returned to the Chapel Royal as one of its three organists (the other two being William Child, senior organist, and John Blow) yet still retaining his post at the Abbey. There is some evidence to suggest that he sang both bass and counter-tenor in the Chapel Royal choir and that in the latter capacity he was outstanding. Only a fortnight after his appointment his father died (31 July 1682) and in the following October his infant son also died.

By now he was very active as a composer and in addition to a considerable quantity of sacred music he wrote the Fantasias for strings (and later the Sonatas of III Parts) as well as incidental music and songs for the stage. One of his less satisfying chores at this time was the provision of elaborate music for a stream of official 'odes' and 'welcome songs'. If the king left his capital to spend a few days at Winchester or Windsor, his return to London had to be celebrated by an ode, while royal marriages, deaths and birthdays (especially, in later years, Queen Mary's birthday) called forth a whole series of such odes. The words have to be seen to be believed; they consist of the most revolting, crawling sycophancy expressed in execrable rhyme: one wonders how the recipient managed to endure, let alone accept, such fulsome rubbish without acute embarrassment. As we have seen, Blow seems to have treated such words with the music they deserved: Purcell more readily accepted any words as a peg on which to hang music and, though bad verse did not inspire him to his greatest heights, it is surprising how often he lavished such fine music on it that the result becomes a work of art. 'Like Schubert, he had the power of transfiguring the second-rate.'[8] On a far higher level are the odes for St. Cecilia's Day, an annual festival which seems to have been inaugurated in 1683. This may be because versifiers like Christopher Fishburn and Nicholas Brady wrote better rhyme than the general run of court poetasters but much more likely because it is more

[7] Lafontaine: *The King's Musick*, p. 255. (Novello.)
[8] J. A. Westrup: *Purcell*, p. 46. (Dent.)

inspiring to praise the art of Music itself than to grovel at the feet of a dissolute old roué like Charles II on his return from a spree at Newmarket.

In December 1683 John Hingston died and Purcell followed him as keeper of the king's wind instruments, so theoretically adding another £60 a year to his income — though it was only rarely that Charles's musicians received even part of their salaries. In 1685 the king died and Purcell, as organist of Westminster Abbey, was largely responsible for the music at the coronation of James II. Soon after his coronation James appointed Purcell harpsichord player in his private music but the new king seemed no more anxious to pay his servants than the old had been and in 1687 we find Purcell demanding satisfaction from the Treasury. Nor did he fare much better under William and Mary: having again been responsible for the music at their coronation in 1689 he had to wait more than a year before he received his fees. In this same year a son, Edward, was born to Purcell; the boy survived and he too eventually became an organist.

From now till the end of his short life Purcell almost ceased to write church music, preferring to lavish the full flowering of his genius where it would be better rewarded in fame, popularity and fortune — music for the stage. In that same eventful year, 1689, he wrote one of his most important works, the chamber opera *Dido and Aeneas*. Other operas or semi-operas followed (*Dioclesian* 1690, *King Arthur* 1691, *The Fairy Queen* 1692, *The Indian Queen* 1695, *The Tempest* 1695); in addition he wrote songs and incidental music to about forty other stage productions, some of them in collaboration with Dryden. In 1692 appeared the splendid ode *Hail, bright Cecilia* and for the same festival in 1694 he composed his Te Deum and Jubilate in D. He seems to have been genuinely attached to the virtuous and kindly Queen Mary and punctiliously wrote an ode for her birthday each year: that for 1694 was the justly famous *Come ye sons of Art*. On her death he wrote the anthem *Thou knowest, Lord, the secrets of our hearts*, short, simple, but immensely moving, especially when accompanied by the awesome sonority of four trombones. He followed this with two beautiful elegies on her death. Within nine months of her obsequies *Thou knowest, Lord* was again sung by combined choirs in Westminster Abbey, this time for the funeral of its composer. He died on the eve of St. Cecilia's Day, 21 November 1695, aged thirty-six.

Purcell was fortunate in that his genius was universally recognised in his own lifetime. Not only did he enjoy public acclaim but, far more important, even his fellow musicians acknowledged his supremacy and paid generous tribute to him. After his death his fame lived on right through the eighteenth and nineteenth centuries, yet though everyone paid him lip service and he was habitually referred to as 'England's greatest composer', most of his music remained unknown — and what was known was often completely misunderstood. There were three main reasons for this:

1. Printed editions were few, expensive, and wildly inaccurate. Editors, trained in the new rigid disciplines of eighteenth and nineteenth century musical theory, assumed that all departures from its many rules must be errors, misprints or 'crudities' which they took upon themselves to 'correct'. Baroque progressions and cadences, with their lovely freedom of part-writing and highly original harmonies, were forced to conform; rhythms were altered and accidentals deliberately inserted or omitted. Because strings were no longer available *ritornelli* were omitted or drastically cut: repeats too were often left out.

2. The idea grew up that for music to be 'sacred' and performed 'reverently' it must

necessarily be slow and so the lilting rhythms of baroque music were drawled out like psalm-tunes, their dotted notes slurred by slovenly lay-clerks, and the sparkling, dancing string interludes played at quarter speed with jelly fingers on heavy woolly diapasons.

3. So few singers were capable of singing Purcell's highly exacting virtuoso solo parts. Admittedly the bass, John Gostling, had a freak voice but there was still all the difference in the world between the astonishing brilliance, agility and clarity of the restoration counter-tenor and the sepulchral wordless hooting of the nineteenth-century cathedral alto. Vocally, no doubt, the alto voice and the counter-tenor amount to much the same thing: but there is a world of difference in mental approach.

No wonder Mendelssohn fled when he heard Purcell's Te Deum in D at St. Paul's in 1829!

Corrupt texts, a lack of a sense of style, and inadequate voices are still to be found in our cathedrals but modern standards of scholarship and the easy availability of first-class performances on gramophone records have given us a new and deeper understanding not only of baroque music but of renaissance music as well. In this process of reappraisal many long cherished beliefs have suffered hard knocks. For example, with our new knowledge of the great Elizabethan musicians it is no longer realistic to call Purcell England's greatest composer: there cannot be degrees of comparison between things which cannot possibly be compared and Purcell is now accepted as one of our several great musicians. With a better understanding of how his music should be performed, many people were shocked to find the verse anthems so thoroughly secular in feeling: we just have to accept that the Chapel Royal was little more than an exclusive concert hall (certainly on Sundays and at big services); its main function was not the worship of Almighty God but rather the delectation of his fashionable flock. Nor does Purcell seem to have been a particularly religious man. Of course it is easy to pick out a number of his works in which he expresses deep religious feelings (*Thou knowest, Lord* for example) but then a dramatist or an actor can create a saint or a villain without being either, and a great composer can similarly encompass all manner of moods. It may be questioned whether, if stripped of their words, the music of even his most profound religious pieces is any more moving than some of the airs in his stage works (e.g. Dido's lament). Certainly he had no compunction about switching from composing church music to writing for the stage—a lure which Blow resisted. Is it, perhaps, too far-fetched to see some resemblance in temperament between Purcell and Handel on the one hand and between Blow and Bach on the other?

One other aspect of this reappraisal must be briefly considered. It has often been claimed that Purcell is a highly original composer—and so he is if we first define what meaning we attach to 'original'. To most people the word suggests an innovator and to us with our recent history of Wagner, Debussy, Stravinsky, Schönberg, Haba, Boulez, Stockhausen and others, it is clear that Purcell was in no way an innovator: he invented no new forms, no new systems or technical procedures, opened up no new paths. Everything he did had been done before or was being done elsewhere: he simply did it so much better than most of the others. Where he is truly original is in his ability to breathe new life into established forms and styles. How he does this is not easy to define. In part it can be attributed to his contrapuntal, and hence his harmonic, freedom which shows itself in the unexpectedness of his progressions and also in the astonishing variety of his cadences.[9] Parts rarely lead where one expects and in few composers of the 1650–1850 period is it so difficult to guess what chord will follow a turn of the page; for the same reason it is extremely difficult to improvise, or even to write, 'in the style of Purcell'. It is one of the tragedies of English music that instead of his successors developing and extending this freedom of part-writing, they were happy to be suffocated in the folds of a rigid harmonic system with its paraphernalia of prescribed part-progressions, 'correct' chord sequences, and its miserly handful of permissible cadences. It was left to a twentieth-century composer, Benjamin Britten, to go back to Purcell, take up the threads of his originality, and pursue the new lines of development to which they led.

As we have seen, the majority of Purcell's anthems were written before he reached the age of twenty-six. Some of them may have been works of his childhood or student years and only a few of them represent the composer's maturity. This explains why the general level of his sacred music falls somewhat below that of his greatest secular works written in the last six years of his life. Yet it is unreal to place too great emphasis on the general inferiority of his church music: these things are relative and even the lesser works of genius often outshine the best works of lesser men. Purcell wrote some very fine full anthems but it must be remembered that to his contemporaries such pieces would have seemed a deliberate harking back to an outmoded style. It is in the verse anthems that his development can best be traced. The later verse anthems developed along lines similar to his secular odes and welcome songs though there are one or two significant differences; thus in his church music he seems deliberately to have eschewed the use of either a ground bass or of solo arias, though both are used extensively in his secular choral works. Clearly traceable is a gradual progress from the daring harmony, contrapuntally derived dissonance, and frequent modality of the earlier works towards a more tonally directed harmony and a simplified harmonic texture in the later works; thus he reflects a change which was taking place in European music generally, a movement towards the eventual rigidity and inevitability of late eighteenth-century harmonic practice. That Purcell himself was well aware of the growing trend is shown by the way he re-wrote some of his early works so as to conform more closely with the emerging principles of tonally directed harmony. For example, in *Hear me, O Lord*, the interesting and often experimental harmonic ideas of the first version give way to tonal harmony operating through a circle of 5ths in the second version:

Purcell: *Hear me, O Lord* (First version)

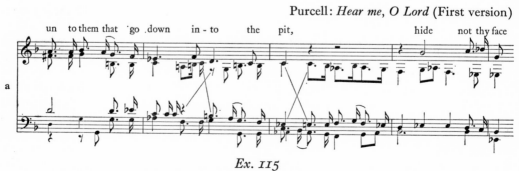

Ex. 115

[9] See Dag Schjelderup-Ebbe's book on Purcell's Cadences. (Oslo University Press).

Ex. 115 (continued)

Purcell: *Hear me, O Lord* (Second version)

It is a trick of historical perspective that what Purcell no doubt considered to be very modern and forward-looking in compositional technique inevitably seems to us somewhat obvious and conventional while what he probably regarded as undeveloped and transitional now strikes us as highly colourful and original and essentially 'English', pointing the way towards harmonic and contrapuntal freedoms whose immense possibilities and potentialities would have to wait two hundred and fifty years for a Benjamin Britten to perceive. Not that in Purcell's music even the most trite harmonic progression necessarily sounds stereotyped: often, as we shall see, the contrapuntal decorations are so arranged that the basic harmony is effectively disguised.

Of the many characteristics, technical devices and mannerisms which are summed up in the one word 'Purcellian' there are two in particular which, though by no means peculiar to him, are yet especially associated with him. First must be mentioned his inordinate fondness for dotted-note rhythms, especially in verse sections in aria style, usually in triple time; such passages as the following everywhere abound:

Purcell: *My heart is fixed*

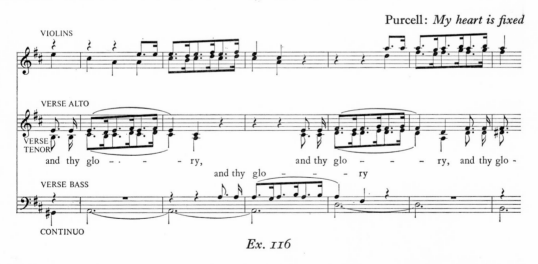

Ex. 116

Secondly, nine out of ten of his final cadences are the common dominant-tonic $(V-I)$ progression (the familiar 'Amen') yet often so richly decorated with innumerable auxiliary notes (often chromatic), passing notes, suspensions and anticipations as to be effectively disguised. In most of these cadences one or more notes of the final (tonic) chord are anticipated against the dominant harmony of the previous chord, resulting sometimes in a sharp clashing of the two harmonies:

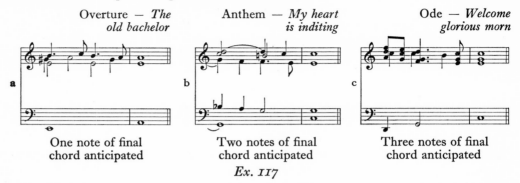

Overture — *The old bachelor*

Anthem — *My heart is inditing*

Ode — *Welcome glorious morn*

a   One note of final chord anticipated

b   Two notes of final chord anticipated

c   Three notes of final chord anticipated

Ex. 117

Purcell, like Blow, wrote so much church music that all we can do here is to mention a few of the more significant anthems and Service settings.

PURCELL: THE FULL ANTHEMS

Only thirteen full anthems are listed in Zimmerman's Catalogue and these, except for *Thou knowest, Lord*, were all early works written about 1680–82 and in some cases perhaps even earlier, yet these thirteen include several noble examples of the form representing some of Purcell's greatest sacred music. Of course, even the so-called 'full' anthems often contain verse sections for three or more voices: what distinguishes them from the verse anthem proper is that they have no independent accompaniment or instrumental *ritornelli* and are capable of being sung unaccompanied, even the 3- and 4-part verse sections always making complete harmony. Actually in Purcell's day they were given organ support but today they are always sung unaccompanied. Many of these early pieces seem to have been modelled on the full anthems of the Tudors, even to the extent of introducing conscious archaisms, though of course the idioms, progressions and part-writing bespeak a later origin.

Pride of place must go to the tremendous 8-part motets *O Lord God of hosts* and *Hear my prayer, O Lord*, written in genuine 8-part polyphony — not glorified 4-part works arranged for double choir. The first opens with a section for full choir in which a theme and its inversion are treated imitatively. A pathetic 3-part verse 'Thou feedest them with the bread of tears' is sung first by low voices then repeated by high voices and leads into a second section for full choir. Another deeply moving verse 'Turn us again', this time in five parts, leads to the massive final chorus, 'O let us live and we shall call upon thy name'. *Hear my prayer, O Lord* is always listed in the reference books as incomplete. This may give a wrong impression because the piece ends quite satisfactorily, indeed very impressively, as it stands. However, in the autograph manuscript in the Fitzwilliam Museum, Cambridge, not only did Purcell fail to close this anthem with his customary double bar and flourishes but he also left a number of blank pages after it; it therefore seems certain that he had originally intended to add another movement or movements. This fine work (sung at the coronation of King George VI) is almost entirely built out of the two phrases (a) and (b) heard at the outset, the second curling chromatically upwards; these phrases are often inverted. Here are the opening bars:

Purcell: *Hear my prayer, O Lord*

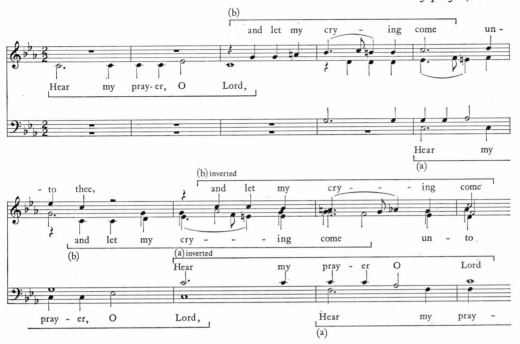

Ex. 118

From this quiet opening the work builds up steadily in power, range, sonority and emotional intensity to a mighty climax (see Example 119 on following page). As the trebles climb to their highest note in the whole work the basses move steadily down an octave scale, the two together producing a great impression of broadening out. The powerful, jagged second tenor line would certainly lose marks in a harmony examination!

Similar in style is the 6-part *O God, thou hast cast us out*: this has a verse (also in six parts) which includes some effective antiphony between low- and high-voice trios. Of the three 5-part pieces, *Remember not, Lord, our offences* can be reckoned amongst Purcell's masterpieces. It is a deeply moving setting chiefly remarkable for its imaginative chromaticism; just before the end there is a particularly effective modulation into F major. The other 5-part full anthems are less important: *Lord, how long wilt thou be angry* is consciously archaic; *I will sing unto the Lord* is mainly in block harmony and Professor Westrup has traced in it the influence of secular song.

The 4-part anthems include some lovely things. *In the midst of life* is a fine work and the sliding chromaticism of 'the bitter pains of death' seems an exact projection of the words. Purcell, like other great composers, was eminently successful in devising music which evokes in the listener much the same emotional response as does a reading of the words he is setting. This emotional matching of music with words is a far deeper and more satisfying thing than the mere mechanical imitation of rhythms and inflections sought after by the monodists though, as Humfrey proved, the two are not necessarily

Ibidem

Ex. 119

incompatible. Another example is the verse section 'My soul thirsteth for thee' in *O God, thou art my God*. This anthem concludes with a fine swinging 'Hallelujah' section in block harmony which has since been adapted as a hymn-tune to the words 'Blessed city, heavenly Salem' (A. & M. Revised 620). Two more outstanding examples are Purcell's grave and noble settings for the Burial service. The first of these, a setting of the funeral sentences *Man that is born of woman*, is solemn and profoundly moving, but even more wonderful is the kontakion-like setting of *Thou knowest, Lord*, written at the end of his life. Twice before had he set these words, the second time as a verse anthem, but it was in this third setting that the mature composer turned from the contrapuntal complexity and harmonic ingenuity of earlier years to an artless, daring simplicity, almost Handelian in the way he achieves maximum effect by the very simplest means. Except for the last phrase there is no counterpoint and the whole piece is in simple 4-part block harmony; phrases are separated by rests, cunningly placed, and the feminine endings 'holy', 'mighty', 'Saviour', and 'eternal' end on a half-beat:

Purcell: *Thou knowest, Lord*

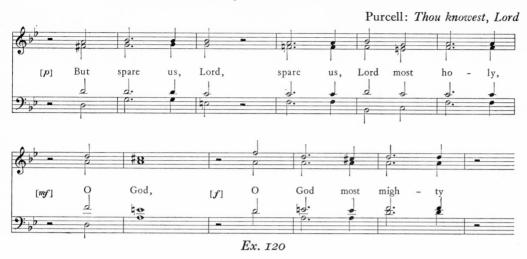

But spare us, Lord, spare us, Lord most ho - ly,

[*p*]

[*mf*] O God, [*f*] O God most migh - ty

Ex. 120

The ending is intensely poignant, the music itself sinking slowly to its close and the agony of death subtly suggested by the false relations and by the unexpected drooping 4th on the repetition of the word 'pains':

Ibidem

for a - ny pains of death, for a - ny pains of

for a - ny pains, for a - ny

for a - ny pains of death

death to fall, to fall from thee. A - men.

pains of death,

to fall, to fall from thee. A - men.

Ex. 121

The voices were doubled by four 'flatt mournful trumpets': these were slide trumpets, not unlike small trombones. They first appeared in England about 1691 and Purcell is the only composer known to have used them, but the peculiar sonority of a quartet of trombones was well understood in Germany and had been effectively employed nearly a century earlier by composers like Osiander (1534–1604), Praetorius (1571–1621), Schein (1586–1630) and Scheidt (1587–1654).

277

PURCELL: THE VERSE ANTHEMS

Turning now to the verse anthems, space will allow only a few to be picked out for brief discussion. In very general terms it may be said that Purcell's essays in this form are open to two main criticisms—scrappiness (an inherent weakness of the form) and secularity. Many strong arguments have been advanced to refute, minimise, explain or excuse this last charge, all with some substance, but the fact remains that many sections in the verse anthems would not sound the least bit incongruous if introduced into *King Arthur* or *The Fairy Queen*, while the virtuoso solo parts written for singers like Gostling were frankly intended to amaze or titillate a sensation-seeking congregation. Yet in the very same anthems there are other parts which are nobly conceived and profoundly moving. Small wonder then that such widely disparate elements cannot always be satisfactorily fused together and that the total effect can be somewhat disjointed.

Amongst the early pieces in verse form, the wedding anthem *My beloved spake* well illustrates these points. After a lengthy overture for strings the solo quartet begins with a tenor phrase which, for all its charm and novelty, ends rather lamely:

Purcell: *My beloved spake*

Ex. 122

Later in the piece a graceful lilting chorus 'and the time of the singing of birds is come' is wholly secular in feeling while the ATBB quartet which follows, 'And the voice of the turtle', though only six bars long, is full of wistful beauty and tenderness. (Incidentally, Turle's well-known double chant 'from Purcell' has been extracted—painfully—from this):

Ex. 123

A string symphony leads to a tenor recitative which is effective though not outstanding. Then to hold the work together Purcell repeats the opening verse section. Strings introduce, and end, another verse, 'My beloved is mine and I am his', and the work concludes with a conventional Hallelujah chorus (this one is better than most and seems more appropriate).

It is a good thing to give thanks is a long anthem, beginning with a typical 'French' overture. The second part of the opening verse, 'to tell of thy loving kindness', is fairly florid (with suitable melismata to underline the words 'loud instrument') and a later bass solo 'O Lord, how glorious' is even more elaborate. The Hallelujah section sounds like peals of bells, the effect being enhanced by echo effects indicated by the composer himself. One of the *ritornelli* has an interesting bass which moves throughout in dotted rhythm: it occurs twice. Some of the early verse anthems have an accompaniment for organ, not strings: these include *Who hath believed our report; Out of the deep; Bow down thine ear; O Lord, thou art my God; Turn thou us, O good Lord; Blow up the trumpet in Sion*, and *Save me, O God*. This last concludes with a notable canon 5 in 1 'And mine eyes have seen his desire'. *Blow up the trumpet* is scored very lavishly for ten solo voices and 10-part choir but is musically undistinguished. A greater work is *Behold now, praise the Lord*, the final chorus of which is also in ten parts, three of the parts being instrumental. This is probably the first anthem Purcell wrote with an accompaniment for strings and it begins with an overture in the French style.

Turning now to those anthems written between 1682 and 1687 (approximately), nearly all of them include sections of great beauty, passages of striking originality, unexpected modulations and harmonic twists, masterly examples of contrapuntal skill, and supreme artistry in setting words; yet often these are embedded in much that is commonplace and stereotyped—the monotony of ATB trios, the ubiquitous dotted rhythms, and unending strings of 3rds (themselves often dotted).

An unusual feature of *O praise God in his holiness* is that the second part of the overture is repeated as the accompaniment to the opening verse for ATBB quartet. Strings of 3rds appear at 'Praise him in his noble acts' and 'the sound of the trumpet'. The bass solo 'Praise him on the well-tuned cymbals' has a violin obbligato moving almost entirely in dotted notes. At the end, the words 'Let everything that hath breath' are sung antiphonally between 4-part verse and 4-part chorus, while the addition of two string parts above the voices leads to some splendid 6-part imitative polyphony. A particularly unequal anthem is *In thee, O Lord, do I put my trust* which is unusual because both its overture and the final chorus ('Alleluja') are built on a ground bass, a form which, as we have seen, Purcell used but rarely in his church music. But the bass of this last chorus is only two bars long and is so firmly rooted in the tonic that its constant repetition becomes monotonous and the movement remains earthbound (this may be because it is probably amongst his earliest experiments in this form). In contrast to this, the verse 'For thou, O Lord God' is a splendid example of word setting and the passage 'thou art he that took me out of my mother's womb' reaches great heights of expression. Similarly, the most striking feature of *Awake, put on thy strength* is the few bars of deft tone-painting when 'sorrow and mourning shall flee away'.

Let God arise was long thought to be a very early work, perhaps because the accompaniment is for organ instead of strings, but stylistic considerations led Dr. Zimmerman to conclude that it was written some time after 1683. Certainly the piece is highly Italianate in style and contains much florid writing for two tenors. *The Lord is my light* exemplifies Purcell's weaknesses rather than his strengths—the lengthy verse trios, dotted rhythms (especially in the tenor recitative 'And now shall he left up mine head'), and the chains of dotted 3rds in the 'Alleluja' verse—neither has *I was glad* much to distinguish it. *My heart is fixed* suffers from a veritable rash of dotted notes (see Ex. 116) but the final chorus is effectively planned with an independent accompaniment for the orchestra. *O Lord, our Governor* has verses for the unusual sonority of three trebles and two basses.

In contrast to these last three, *Praise the Lord, O my soul, and all that is within me* is a splendid work. Admittedly the overture consists almost entirely of dotted notes but here one feels that they are an essential structural element rather than a conventional figure. In the first and last sections Purcell effectively deploys four groups—high voice trio, low voice trio, all six soloists together, and strings (the full choir sings only the last seven bars!). The verse trio 'The Lord is full of compassion and mercy' is a lovely thing. After a repeat of the second part of the overture, the highlight of the anthem is reached— the deeply moving bass recitative 'For look, how high the heav'n is': the beautiful ending of this deserves quoting:

Purcell: *Praise the Lord, O my soul*

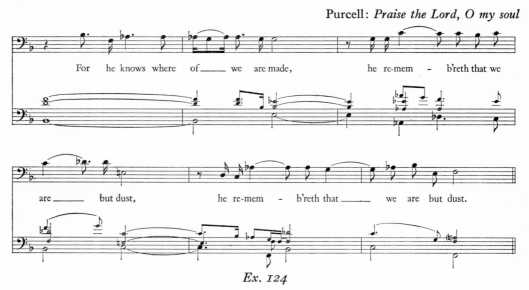

Ex. 124

Not to be confused with this is an anthem of similar name, *Praise the Lord, O my soul, O Lord my God*, chiefly notable for an awesome alto and bass duet 'When thou hidest thy face' which compresses into a mere six bars a wealth of religious experience and emotion. *Rejoice in the Lord alway* is too well-known to need discussion here, yet it is nearly always sung from a badly mutilated edition and comparatively few people have heard the anthem as Purcell wrote it, complete with its lengthy string *ritornelli*. In any case, it does not represent the composer at his best.

With few exceptions those anthems believed to have been written from 1685 onwards show no advance on Purcell's earlier work. *My song shall be alway* has a lengthy solo for either bass or treble—but which of the two seems uncertain. If for the latter, it is the composer's only anthem with an extended treble solo and Professor Westrup advances good reasons for believing it to have been written not for a Chapel Royal chorister but for the castrato Siface who visited England in 1687:[10] on the other hand it could have been written for Gostling. *I will give thanks unto thee, O Lord* and *They that go down to the sea in ships* both have formidable bass solos designed to show off Gostling's virtuosity.

[10] J. A. Westrup: *Purcell*, p. 217. (Dent—'Master Musicians' series.)

To a generation capable of negotiating the vocal lines of Schönberg, Webern, Boulez and others, Purcell's parts can no longer be considered difficult but even so their range would still defeat most singers. Discussing the following passage from *I will give thanks*, Fellowes says 'Such a tit-bit might have been the talk of London Society for days':

Purcell: *I will give thanks*

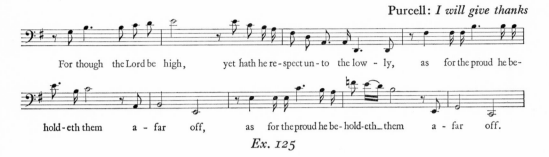

For though the Lord be high, yet hath he re-spect un-to the low - ly, as for the proud he be-

hold-eth them a - far off, as for the proud he be-hold-eth them a - far off.

Ex. 125

but since few choirs today can boast a John Gostling these anthems are rarely—if ever—heard. If, for a moment, the extravagant virtuosity can be disregarded it will be found that the verbal declamation is extremely sure and accurate. *Unto thee will I cry, O Lord my strength* includes the following passage in which, in addition to the usual dotted 3rds, Purcell writes a series of unprepared 7ths:

Purcell: *Unto thee will I cry*

al - le - lu-ja, al - le - lu - ja,

al - le - lu - ja,

al - le - lu - ja,

Ex. 126

Boyce included the charming piece *Thy word is a lantern* in his collection. Two passages of particular note are (a) the sliding chromatic harmonies at 'I am troubled above measure', and (b) the brief but lovely alto solo 'The ungodly have laid a snare for me'—a good example of Purcell's sensitivity in setting words in declamatory style. Boyce also included *O give thanks*, which is rather uninspired, and *O sing unto the Lord*, one of Purcell's happiest creations. This last is a very long anthem yet almost throughout it sustains a high degree of excellence, many of its component sections serving as models of their type. Most unusually, the composer here uses his string orchestra to accompany solo declamation and the powerful bass recitative 'Declare his honour' with its string interjections bears a striking resemblance to 'Thus saith the Lord' in *Messiah*. The alto and treble duet 'The Lord is great', constructed on a ground bass, is rather weak and has too many parallel 3rds and 6ths but in contrast, the following verse and chorus 'O worship the Lord' is a masterly example of pathetic expression; it builds up a considerable intensity of emotion, soon to be released in the rollicking bass aria with chorus

'Tell it out among the heathen'. Even the concluding Allelujas, shared between verse, chorus and strings, here sound an inevitable, fitting, and indeed noble peroration to the whole work.

But perhaps the greatest of all Purcell's anthems is *My heart is inditing*, written for the coronation of James II on 23 April 1685. This work is so vast in conception, monumental in scale and extended in length that it is really a considerable cantata rather than an anthem and was obviously intended to match in splendour and magnificence the great ceremony it adorned. Like John Blow's monumental anthem written for the same occasion, *God spake sometimes in visions*, it is laid out for eight verse soloists, 8-part choir and strings (it is interesting to note that both works are scored for an unusual disposition of the lower voices—TrTrAATBBB—and neither work includes any passages for a solo voice). The overture is long enough to stand as a separate work for strings. The great choruses in 8-part polyphony, often with additional independent string parts, are richly developed and even the verse sections are laid out for six or more voices. Thus the work is an interesting hybrid owing something to both the verse and full anthem: though technically a verse anthem, much of the chorus work is in the style of the old polyphonic full anthem though having an accompaniment for strings. Halfway through, the overture is repeated, followed by a verse 'Hearken, O daughter' sung first by an octet then repeated by a sextet, culminating in a grand series of massive discords. A short *ritornello* leads to the last chorus which gains in strength and contrast by being mainly in block harmony. The whole is rounded off by a brilliant Alleluja coda in swinging 3 time which seems to set all the bells ringing, and the great work ends with tremendous united shouts of acclamation. This is one of the greatest monuments of English church music and those unfamiliar with it should lose no opportunity of getting to know it.

PURCELL: THE LATIN ANTHEMS

In addition to full and verse anthems, Purcell wrote at least three Latin anthems—*Beati omnes qui timent Dominum; Jehova quam multi sunt hostes*, and the incomplete *Domine, non est exaltatum* (which begins canonically). Just as Blow's Latin setting *Salvator mundi* must rank amongst his finest works so *Jehova quam multi* is recognised as one of Purcell's greatest sacred pieces and is deservedly popular in our cathedrals. It is scored for 5-part choir with organ continuo and opens with a chorus of great emotional power, beginning in block harmony then breaking into imitative counterpoint. A fine declamatory tenor solo is followed by the chorus 'Voce mea ad Jehovam clamanti' which, beginning in C, builds to a loud and exultant cadence on the chord of D major. Immediately afterwards the choir, now hushed almost to a whisper yet singing with great inner intensity, begins the slow section 'Ego cubui' in the unexpected key of B flat. This transition is a magical touch and the whole passage is breathtaking in its beauty, especially the drooping figure on 'et dormivi' ('I laid me down and slept') so suggestive of sleep (see Example 127 opposite). A bass solo follows, ending with a superb example of verbal declamation at its best ('Qui percussisti omnes . . .') and the work concludes with a somewhat conventional chorus.

PURCELL: THE SERVICES

Only three Services are known: a very complete setting in B flat which includes all the

Purcell: *Jehova quam multi sunt hostes*

Ex. 127

alternative Canticles, the popular Evening Service in G minor, and a festival setting of Te Deum and Jubilate in D, probably written for St. Cecilia's Day, 1694. The B flat setting is largely in block harmony and, except for the Benedicite, has little to commend it: the Gloria of Magnificat is a canon 3 in 1, and of Nunc dimittis a canon 4 in 2. On the other hand the G minor setting of Magnificat and Nunc dimittis is one of the most interesting and original Service settings of the whole period. Not only are its melodic lines distinguished and memorable but its extensive use of dotted-note rhythms is very rare in Canticle settings of the time. Above all it is notable for its remarkably effective dialogue between high voice (TrTrA) and low voice (ATB) trios. There is some evidence to suggest that the Gloria to Nunc dimittis, the best part of the whole Service, was written not by Purcell but by Thomas Roseingrave (1690–1766) who achieved fame as an organist and composer; it followed the fashion then current by starting as a canon 4 in 2. Both these Services make effective use of verse passages for men's voices. The Te Deum and Jubilate in D are so long and elaborate and are laid out for such large forces — choir, solo voices, strings and trumpets — that they must be counted amongst the forerunners of such works as Bach's Mass in B minor, Beethoven's Mass in D, and the Requiems of Berlioz and Verdi, intended not for normal liturgical use but rather for festival or concert performance.

Some of Purcell's sacred songs are occasionally sung as anthems, especially the *Evening Hymn* ('Now that the sun hath veiled his light'), but it must be remembered that they were never intended for public worship. Hymns and chants said to be by Purcell must be treated with some reserve; many of the ascriptions are spurious or doubtful and several of the tunes have been drastically altered or have been adapted from other works. Dr. Zimmerman's *Catalogue* provides the safest guide.

DANIEL PURCELL (1660–1717)

Henry's younger brother, Daniel, is sometimes found in music lists as the composer of an attractive Evening Service in E minor: the origin of this is an organ copy in short score without words. The vocal score was edited and the words fitted to it in the last century by Sir John Stainer.

CHAPTER XII

The Eighteenth Century

GENERAL

From the first Prayer Book of 1549 to the death of Purcell in 1695 the history of English cathedral music was one of growth, experiment, innovation and development; of achievement, new influences, change and fresh achievement. By the time of Purcell's death all the main forms had been evolved—full anthems with or without accompaniment; full anthems with verse sections; verse anthems accompanied by organ or strings, often with solo passages in either declamatory or 'aria' style; 'great' Services; 'short' Services with or without accompaniment; verse Services; hymns and chants. Then from about 1700 till amost 1900 very little further progress was made: not only was development almost at a standstill but in some ways there was even regression and decline. Regression is most clearly noticeable in matters of technique: it can be seen in the strong swing towards harmonic thought until a point was reached where, except in fugal writing, counterpoint had only a decorative rather than a structural function (and even in fugal choruses, thematic material and even structural events were largely dictated by harmonic considerations); it can be seen in the almost total rejection of the modal system with its wide variety of cadences and its associated range of emotional responses; it can be seen in the way the richness of the renaissance and baroque harmonic palette was surrendered in exchange for the more limited harmonic resources of the classical key system; it can be seen most of all in the way the words, instead of inspiring and shaping the music (which in turn illuminates the words), were now ruthlessly sacrificed to the demands of a 'good tune' in four- and eight-bar phrases. Decline is equally apparent in aesthetic matters: composers on the whole seemed less concerned with the inner meaning and implications of the words they set and the place of those words in worship, and more concerned with writing superficially attractive music which would make an immediate appeal to their fellow men, the words coming off second best.

So far, every reference we have made to the classical key system has been somewhat disparaging yet we all know that much of the world's greatest music—including that of Bach, Haydn, Mozart, Beethoven and the Romantics—was not only written in it but was only possible because of it. Some explanation therefore seems called for. In various aspects of life, and especially in the arts, we often find that evolution involves not only gain but some loss: we surrender certain advantages in order to reap the greater advantages which the change seems to offer. Now we have already seen what price was paid for classical harmony: what, then, were the advantages gained? First, it offered a relationship of chords one to another within a key, especially the strong relationship existing between the dominant, tonic and subdominant (an obvious example is the way a dominant 7th seems to demand resolution on to the tonic). Second, it offered a relationship between every key and certain other keys, based on a circle of 5ths. Of course, both these relationships had been known and understood for a couple of centuries but it was only now that their full implications were realised. These implications are associated with a curious aural phenomenon—a psychological polarity which every listener feels towards the key in which a piece begins and which demands that, whatever modulations may occur subsequently, the piece must end in this same key. This polarity was found to be so strong that once a key was firmly established at the outset, no matter how many other keys were introduced or for however long, the listener was still instinctively waiting for the return to the original key. Once this principle was fully understood it became possible to delay the return to the main key more and more, thus building up suspense and making possible the construction of ever longer movements, culminating in the immense structures of Bruckner and Mahler. An old problem had at last been solved.

The outcome of all this was a major revolution in the whole concept of musical construction. What before had often been instinctive was now consciously organised; sections were carefully balanced against sections according to key relationships. The old contrapuntal styles and forms—polyphony, imitation, canon, fugue, contrapuntal variations, chorale preludes, etc.—gave place to the new architectural forms—sonata and rondo (though sonata form had to some extent been foreshadowed in the 'aria'). These new forms were found to be particularly well suited to abstract instrumental and orchestral music. Most fundamental of all, key and modulation, defined and controlled by harmony, implied an essentially vertical conception of music as opposed to the horizontal conception of the polyphonic writers. Of course this revolution did not occur dramatically at some particular point in time: it was a process spread over nearly two centuries, a process reflected in and accelerated by the emergence of the figured bass. We have seen that for many years both methods of construction existed side by side and were even found in the same work. Purcell, as we have seen, appeared to glimpse the immense possibilities opening up before him and moved a long way towards them. Bach was perhaps the watershed between the two styles and in him the rival claims of counterpoint and harmony seem to be most justly balanced.

So, then, the classical key system opened up the whole world of symphonic thought and made possible some of the greatest music of all time: all it asked in return was more control over part writing, some restriction of harmonic freedom and some limitation of cadence structure—surely a modest price to pay for such boundless riches? Yet this price spelled disaster for the church musician. He got the worst of the bargain and the very concessions demanded of him were, in fact, his life-blood while what he received in return was of no use to him. He was concerned only with the setting of words, and his texts, usually brief, were subdivided into short verses or clauses, each verse having its own individual mood and emotion which had to be reflected in the music set to it. Such settings demanded piecemeal treatment. What good to him then were the large-scale architectural forms, so essential to the symphonist? They could have no place in church. Furthermore, attempts to provide short texts with extended settings inevitably resulted in endless and meaningless repetition of words. (It was left to Stanford at the end of the nineteenth century to try to effect some *rapprochement* between church music and symphonic forms.) Denied the large-scale forms, harmonic thinking had to content itself with balancing small-scale sections and subsections against each other and this is where the fondness for regular four- and eight-bar phrase lengths had its origin. Also, since counterpoint was now at a discount, interest tended to centre more and more in the top part which therefore became increasingly melodic and 'tuneful', at the expense of the lower voices which merely provided supporting harmonies. These tendencies, in various stages of advancement, are well exemplified in such well-known anthems (or parts of anthems) as Greene's *Thou visitest the earth*, Attwood's *Come, Holy Ghost* and *Turn thee again*, Crotch's *Comfort, O Lord*, Goss's *O Saviour of the world*, and Walmisley's *From all that dwell*: (it is symptomatic that the first four of these should be in triple time).

These then are some of the reasons for the decline in church music during the eighteenth and nineteenth centuries, yet the plain fact remains that a composer of genius would have found his own solution to the problems. Alas, the genius never appeared. We produced no great musicians and few second-rate ones. Most church composers were competent and sincere men who did their best to uphold the traditions of their art—but competence and sincerity are not enough in creative art and most of their work seems very uninteresting compared with what had gone before. Only a few could rise at times to works not unworthy of a place in the English cathedral music tradition.

The eighteenth and nineteenth centuries were notable for the number of famous foreign musicians who either paid frequent visits to this country, stayed here for a time or, as in Handel's case, settled here and became naturalized: these included, among others, Handel himself, Haydn, Spohr, Weber, Berlioz, Mendelssohn and Gounod, all of whom were rapturously received. The English have always had a touching reverence for foreign music and musicians, cordially welcoming even the least inspired work of foreigners to the detriment and neglect of far better native work (Morley complained about this as early as 1597). At a time when the stream of native music had dwindled to a trickle, it is hardly surprising that such distinguished foreigners should have had some influence on English music and of course church music was naturally more influenced by those continental masters who had earned recognition as composers of sacred works—like Handel, Spohr, Mendelssohn and Gounod. Yet the influence of these composers has often been grossly exaggerated, mainly, one suspects, in order to excuse or even explain the extraordinary dearth of native talent. It is beyond a musician to try to explain why the last half of the sixteenth century could produce fifty or more first-rate musicians, some of world class, while the eighteenth and nineteenth centuries yielded precious few who could even rise to second-class. The fact remains and just has to be accepted: it seems silly to try to pin the blame on foreign musicians.

But if cathedral music was in the doldrums the parish church fared much better. It can well be said that the eighteenth century was the golden age of English hymnody. Until almost the end of the seventeenth century the view was still largely held that only scriptural words should be sung in church—in other words the metrical psalms and Canticles (especially those of Sternhold and Hopkins). Hunnis, Wither, Playford and others made various attempts to introduce genuine hymns but the time was not yet ripe. Then a year after Purcell's death an entirely new metrical psalter, the work of Nahum Tate and Nicholas Brady, received official blessing: from now onwards this was referred to as the 'New Version' while Sternhold and Hopkins became the 'Old'. Tate and Brady guardedly admitted a few freely-composed hymns into a 'Supplement' (1700) which included 'While shepherds watched'. Larger supplements and other collections quickly followed. However, the great wave of hymn-singing which was about to break over the nation had its origins in an entirely different quarter—the Nonconformist churches and the Evangelical movement. Here, inspired by Isaac Watts and immensely popularised by the Wesleys, hymn-singing was found to satisfy a human need long unfulfilled. So strong and powerful did this movement become that the Established Church could no longer remain aloof: prejudice was gradually overcome and as the century advanced hymns increasingly took the place of metrical psalms. Hymn collections poured from the presses and composers were kept busy providing tunes. Of the vast number of hymns written (Watts alone produced about six hundred and Charles Wesley some six thousand five hundred!) only a fraction have survived in use but this fraction includes some of the noblest and most inspiring examples in our language. Some idea of the richness of English hymnody at this time can be gained by listing such writers as Addison, Doddridge, Newton, Cowper, Haweis and Toplady, evangelicals like Hill and Kelly, and high churchmen like Heber and Milman. Known composers include Clarke, Croft, Handel, Carey, Lampe, Hayes, Boyce, Webbe, Hatton and Shrubsole but many of the finest tunes appeared anonymously in innumerable collections.

That lowliest form of musical life, the Anglican chant, does not perhaps call forth the utmost in technical skill and the highest flights of imagination from its composer; nevertheless it has a secure place in public worship and in the affections of worshippers. Nor is it to be despised. To write a good chant is by no means as easy as it looks — as the hundreds of bad ones testify. Not only must it have a shapely melodic line with satisfying, clean supporting harmonies effectively laid out for voices, but it must be able to stand up to constant repetition. Some of the best chants were produced in the eighteenth century. At first they were mainly single but double-chants rapidly grew in popularity.

MANUSCRIPT AND PRINTED COLLECTIONS

To return to cathedral music, a word must be said about manuscript and printed 'collections' which became of considerable importance about this time.

In 1641 the Reverend John Barnard, a minor canon of St. Paul's Cathedral, had published. *The First Booke of Selected Church Musick, consisting of Services and Anthems. Such as are now used in the Cathedrall, and Collegiatt Churches of this Kingdome. Never before printed. Whereby such bookes as were with much difficulty and charges transcribed for the use of the Quire, are now, to the saving of much labour and expence, publisht for the generall good of all such as shall desire them, either for Publick or Private exercise ...* Barnard cared deeply for the great traditions of English cathedral music and lamented the growing strength of Puritan opposition to it. It was clear to him that cathedral music would soon be proscribed, perhaps for evermore, so partly for his own satisfaction and partly for the benefit of posterity he collected together a representative anthology of Services and anthems and published them in ten part-books (no organ score was issued). He included Services by Tallis, Strogers, Bevin, Byrd, Gibbons, Mundy, Parsons, Morley, Giles, Ward (Evening), Woodeson (Te Deum), with Preces, Psalms, Responses and Litanies by Tallis, Byrd and Gibbons; forty-two full anthems by Tallis, Hooper, Farrant, Sheppard, Mundy, Gibbons, Batten, Tye, Byrd, White, Giles, Parsons and Weelkes; and twelve verse anthems by Byrd, Mundy, Morley, Gibbons, Batten, Ward and Bull. Only two years after this collection was issued, cathedral choirs were silenced and a further compilation, in which Barnard proposed to issue the work of living composers, was abandoned: fortunately it still exists in manuscript.[1] Judging by the extreme rarity of *Selected Church Musick* it was probably a very limited edition and those copies which survived the vandalism of the Civil War were worn out by regular use after the Restoration. Barnard's collections are immensely important for

[1] Royal College of Music: MSS. 1045–51.

two reasons: they are the only known source for some works which otherwise would have perished, and secondly, they give us a clear idea of what music was being sung at that time. Of course after the Restoration these printed sets would have become the staple fare in those provincial cathedral and chapel choirs lucky enough to possess them.

Three years after the Restoration another minor canon of St. Paul's, James Clifford, inspired perhaps by Barnard's work, published a collection of the words of anthems used at that time in the cathedral. This was followed by a second edition in 1664 which gave the words of some hundreds of anthems from Tye to his own day, including some by Humfrey and Blow who were then only schoolboys. What a pity that Clifford did not give the music as well! Certainly from Barnard and Clifford we get an accurate picture of the cathedral repertory before and after the Commonwealth. Early in the eighteenth century Tudway, as we have seen, made his famous collection for Lord Harley; this was never published. By far the most important of the various collections was that of William Boyce, issued in three splendid volumes (1760, 1768 and 1773), which had enormous influence. In 1790 the indefatigable Samuel Arnold published four volumes of *Cathedral Music* intended as a continuation of Boyce.

In days when church music publications were few, scattered and costly, anthologies containing a good selection of Services and anthems must have been a godsend. As Barnard himself explains on his title page, 'whereby such Bookes as were heretofore with much difficulty and Charges, transcribed for the use of the Quire, are now to the saving of much Labour and expence, publisht for the generall good of all such as shall desire them, either for publick or private exercise'. Yet their very convenience and popularity constituted a danger. By their nature any such publication can present only a small selection from all the material available; the actual choice of items will inevitably reflect the editor's own criteria, taste and predilections. Furthermore, pressure of space will mean that much of real value must be excluded. But the choirmaster who has just invested in a set of copies and can find sufficient for his needs within their covers is hardly likely to concern himself with what has been omitted. When therefore a collection is widely used (as was Boyce's) it can profoundly influence musical taste, either for good or ill, and give a historical perspective which may be considerably distorted: music not included is in grave danger of falling into oblivion, composers not represented by their best work are liable to be misjudged, so are those who intentions have been nullified or misrepresented by editorial bungling, while inferior pieces may be given a popularity and a permanence out of all proportion to their merits. The better and more useful the collection the more likely these things are to happen.

THE END OF THE ENGLISH BAROQUE

The baroque period was rather shorter-lived in England than it was on the continent. Having reached its zenith in Purcell it was now in decline and those composers active at the beginning of the century — Jeremiah Clarke, John Goldwyn, William Croft, John Weldon and (a little later) Maurice Greene — were its last remnants. Their work comes as an anticlimax after the glories of Blow and Purcell and their talents now seem very slender. Yet historians and critics seem to discuss only the same mere handful of their pieces and these turn out to be the ones Boyce happened to include in his collection and which have therefore been republished in modern editions. But what of all the other works of these composers? It is well known that Boyce's artistic perception was by no means faultless and his selection did not always represent composers by their finest achievements. It is therefore unfair to pronounce judgement on them till all their manuscripts have been transcribed and their works are readily available for study. Here surely is a promising field for scholars.

JEREMIAH CLARKE (*c.* 1673–1707)

Clarke is now best known as the man who wrote 'Purcell's' *Trumpet Voluntary* (arising from a misattribution which was later cleared up by Mr. Charles Cudworth). He was a Chapel Royal chorister under Blow and was later organist of Winchester College (1692) and St. Paul's Cathedral (1695) where, in 1703, he was appointed almoner and master of the choristers. In 1700 he and his fellow-chorister, William Croft, were sworn in as Gentlemen-extraordinary of the Chapel Royal, becoming joint organists in 1704. Three years later, in a fit of depression, Clarke shot himself. The quaint account of his end which appeared in Bumpus's *A History of Cathedral Music*, though almost certainly apocryphal, is well worth repeating:

> Being disappointed in love, so the story goes, he determined to destroy himself. Riding into the country and alighting from his horse, he went into a field, in a corner of which were a pond and some trees, when he began a debate in his mind whether he should end his days by hanging or by drowning. Not being able to resolve the *knotty* question, he left it to the decision of chance, and tossed up a halfpenny; but the coin, falling on some clay, stuck sideways. Though the decree of chance did not answer his expectations, still, it seemed to ordain that neither hanging nor drowning was advisable. He therefore quietly remounted his horse, rode back to London, and blew out his brains with a 'screw pistol' at the sign of the Golden Cup, his house in S. Paul's Churchyard.

Clarke wrote instrumental music, keyboard music, choral works, and songs and duets for the theatre, in addition to twenty anthems, two morning Services (Te Deum and Jubilate), and a Sanctus and Gloria, mainly for men's voices, printed in Arnold's *Cathedral Music*. Of the three anthems printed by Boyce, *Praise the Lord, O Jerusalem*, written for the coronation of Queen Anne, is the least satisfactory; it is very fragmentary in construction and the various short sections in different rhythms have little to commend them. *How long wilt thou forget me?* has considerable melodic charm and its somewhat excessive triple time is effectively broken by the forceful recitative 'Lest mine enemy say'. Since almost the whole of this lengthy piece is for treble solo and the full choir enters only for a few bars at the end, the anthem is most useful and effective for boys' voices (no great damage is suffered by letting the organ replace the underparts at the end, or even by omitting the last chorus entirely). *I will love thee* is the best of the three and fully merits a place in music lists. In several ways it shows considerable originality. For example, the sequence of keys is most unusual; the piece begins and ends in B minor, the second section plunges straight from B minor to G minor and is followed by a third section in E minor—daring, if not wholly convincing! There is an extraordinary dramatic chorus 'the earth trembled and quaked' in which Clarke exploits that curious *tremolo* effect apparently invented by Monteverdi and introduced into England by Walter Porter (see p. 239). But far more interesting than the *tremolo* itself are the chords on which it occurs—accented and reiterated diminished 7ths here used in a way which inevitably seems to anticipate Haydn:

Jeremiah Clarke: *I will love thee*

The earth trem - bled and quak'd, the earth trem - bled and quak'd

Ex. 128

The very florid and exciting duet 'thunder, hailstones and coals of fire' clearly identifies the composer with baroque expression while the final chorus could almost have been written by Purcell himself. Other anthems once popular—*Bow down thine ear, O Lord God of my salvation*; *The Lord is my strength*, and *The Lord is full of compassion*—have fallen by the wayside. Perhaps Clarke's most enduring memorial will be his hymn tunes, which include *Brockham, Tunbridge, King's Norton* and *Uffingham* in addition to the ever-popular *St. Magnus* ('The head that once') and *Bishopthorpe* ('Immortal love').

WILLIAM GOLDING (*c.* 1670–1719)

William Golding or Goldwin was a pupil of Child. His Service in F is no better than others of its time and his anthem *I have set God alway before me*, printed by Boyce, is uneventful. However, he seems to have inclined towards the old-fashioned type of polyphonic full anthem and here he was much more successful. The 5-part *Hear me, O God* and the 6-part *O Lord God of hosts* well deserve an occasional hearing, while the ground basses of his 2-part verse anthem of the same name are strongly Purcellian in style. Such works suggest that his untranscribed manuscripts at Ely and Christ Church, Oxford, might well yield works of even greater merit.

WILLIAM CROFT (1678–1727)

William Croft or Crofts was one of the few outstanding musicians of the century. As we have seen, he was a fellow chorister with Clarke at the Chapel Royal under Blow. The two young men were both sworn Gentlemen-extraordinary of the Chapel Royal in 1700 and became joint organists four years later. In 1708 Croft succeeded Blow at Westminster Abbey and as Master of the Children and composer to the Chapel Royal. It was this last office which called forth some notable occasional pieces including funeral and thanksgiving anthems, an Ode to Peace, and various Odes to Queen Anne. He took the Oxford Mus.Doc. degree in 1713.

Croft is famed for one glorious work of near genius—his setting of the Burial Service. He also wrote three other Service settings, well over sixty anthems, many of which reach a high standard of excellence, and some splendid hymn tunes. The Services include a

Te Deum, Jubilate, Sanctus, Kyrie and Credo in A (to which Stephen Elvey later added an Evening Service in similar style); a Te Deum, Jubilate, Sanctus and Gloria in B minor; and a Te Deum, Jubilate, Cantate Domino and Deus misereatur in E flat. A curious feature of this E flat Service is that in Jubilate he forgot to set the verse 'O go your way into his gates', having left a space for it intending to fill it in later. It will be noticed that Croft set both Sanctus and Gloria in excelsis—somewhat unusual at this time. To say that his Services rank amongst the best written in the eighteenth century is no great praise and even the once popular Service in A is now rarely heard. In 1724 he published thirty of his anthems and the Burial Service in a two-volume edition called *Musica Sacra*. This collection has the distinction of being the earliest known example of English sacred music to be 'engraved and stamped on plates' in full score with the various voice-parts set out one under another and with a figured bass for the organ. The preface is historically important because in it he justifies publishing his music in full score by pointing out the great advantages of scores over separate part books and pleading eloquently that choirs should sing from scores in preference to separate voice parts. It also shows Croft to have been a man of integrity and breeding and, above all, of true modesty, a man who had given a great deal of thought to the purposes and function of sacred music. Given this quiet, humble and introspective cast of mind it is not surprising that his more brilliant and elaborate works are on the whole the least successful.

The verse anthems in particular show all the weaknesses with which we are only too familiar—the perfunctory Hallelujah sections (*Praise the Lord, O my soul; The Lord is king; I will alway give thanks*), the strings of parallel 3rds and 6ths. (*Give the king thy judgements; Rejoice in the Lord; God is gone up*), excessively florid writing (*The heavens declare; I will alway give thanks; O give thanks*), and his fondness for word-painting (e.g. 'little hills', 'flourish', 'long', and 'wondrous' in *Give the king thy judgements*). Highly florid writing often spreads to the organ accompaniments which were now becoming much more idiomatic. Composers were beginning to indicate what registration they wanted and we find Croft calling for 'Loud organ with the left hand' in *Sing unto the Lord*, '2 Diapasons upon the left hand' in *O Lord, thou hast searched me out*, and for a cornet stop in the right hand against two diapasons in the left in 'Let the Mount Sion rejoice' from *We wait for they loving kindness*. Croft is also probably the last composer to inherit as part of his natural idiom the clash of major and minor 3rd sounded together (Te Deum in E flat; *O Lord, rebuke me not*).

More ambitious anthems include *Rejoice in the Lord, O ye righteous* and *O give thanks*. They are both very long, extremely florid and have an orchestral accompaniment including sections with an obbligato for trumpet or hautboy, yet all the bustle and excitement cannot hide the poverty of invention and the basic emptiness of the music. *Give the king thy judgements* and *The heavens declare* are similarly florid and here again the rushing about is merely an elaboration of well-worn clichés. The lengthy bass and tenor solos in *O Lord, thou hast searched me out* well display his gift for writing attractive melodies yet these melodies often seem merely a decoration added to the words instead of an intensification of the words themselves. Similarly the simple *O praise the Lord, all ye heathen,* in ABA form, offers little except melodic charm and freshness. Perhaps the best of the verse anthems is the long and impressive *O Lord, I will praise thee.*

To see Croft's work at its best we must turn to his full anthems, especially those of the graver kind which he seems to have found more congenial. Structurally he adopts a sandwich form: chorus – verse – chorus. *Be merciful unto me* and *Put me not to rebuke* (with its realistic suggestion of flights of arrows) are both dignified and expressive settings. *Sing praises unto the Lord* (4 and 5 parts) and the 5-part *Cry aloud and shout* are robust settings if not greatly inspired. He wrote both a verse and a full setting of *O Lord God of my salvation*: the full choir version (in 4 and 6 parts) is very fine and deserves to be heard more often. On the other hand it is difficult to account for the immense popularity which *God is gone up* still enjoys: in the first part the rather wooden rhythm announced at the beginning, 'One two-and-three four-and-one', is continued without any break whatsoever throughout the entire movement and becomes wearisome in the extreme; in the second part the parallel 3rds and 6ths sound trivial. *Hear my prayer*, beginning in 5 parts and ending in 8, is a good anthem not unworthy to stand beside some of the best of the Restoration period, but perhaps the finest of all is the splendidly austere and solid *O Lord, rebuke me not* (*a cappella*) which should surely be sung in every cathedral. The opening section in 6-part polyphony is followed by an affective trio for ATB. The last two sections are both fugues for six voices. the first of them having a double subject. Choral fugues were something of a novelty at this time though within a few years they were to become as fashionable and inevitable as were the Hallelujah choruses of the preceding period.

Croft's place in musical history is most likely to be assured by his setting of the Burial Service and by his hymn tunes. Both Morley and Purcell wrote settings of the Burial Sentences but it is Croft's which has established itself as the most sublime and classic expression in music of these profound words and it is Croft's which is now used on all national occasions of public mourning and at many funerals where music is performed. It is typical of the composer's innate modesty that there should be one omission in his setting; he declined to compose new music to the sentence 'Thou knowest, Lord' on the grounds that Purcell's setting of these words was unapproachable, adding that he 'endeavoured, as near as possibly he could, to imitate that great master and celebrated composer, whose name will for ever stand high . . .' Accordingly he incorporated Purcell's setting into his own at this point. The most obvious characteristic of Croft's work is its apparent simplicity. After all the froth and hot air of some of the more fanciful verse anthems, the serenity and calm confidence of these few simple chords in block harmony comes as a shock, but we must not forget that after the wind, the earth-quake and the fire came the still small voice. In music it is surprising how often it happens that when the wind and fire of a composer's most elaborate works have passed by, he is found to be at his very greatest when at his simplest. The passage here quoted from Croft's setting is typical: notice how the music accurately reflects the accents and rhythms of the words, the careful use of chromatic intervals without overdoing them, the effective drop of a tritone lending colour to the word 'misery' without being too melo-dramatic, the poignant effect produced by repeating the last four words to an echoing phrase which sinks to its cadence, and the way the cunningly placed rest in bar 5 adds to the significance of this repetition. Such writing shows great artistry (see Example 129 on following page).

There can be no finer testimony to Croft's pre-eminence as a composer of hymn tunes than to say that he wrote, amongst others, *Eatington, Croft's 136th* (or *148th*), *Binchester* (usually sung to 'Happy are they') and *St. Anne* ('O God our help'); there is also good reason to believe that he wrote *St. Matthew* and, not quite so certainly, *Hanover* ('O worship the king'). These sturdy, eminently singable tunes, still sounding as fresh as the day they were written, have inspired generations of Christians of all denominations

Croft: *Burial Sentences*

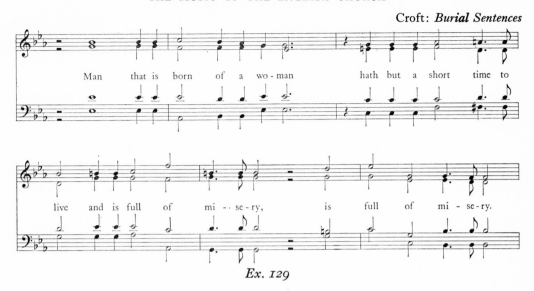

Man that is born of a wo - man hath but a short time to

live and is full of mi - - se - ry, is full of mi - se - ry.

Ex. 129

throughout the world and in particular have become an integral part of the Anglican heritage.

JOHN WELDON (1676–1736)

John Weldon was two years older than Croft and outlived him by nine years. He was one of Purcell's pupils, becoming organist of New College, Oxford (1694) and of the Chapel Royal in 1708, combining with this latter post the organistship first of St. Bride's, Fleet Street, and (in 1726) of St. Martin-in-the-Fields. Whereas Clarke and Croft were scholarly musicians who, in spite of their limitations, more or less consciously maintained the traditions of the past, Weldon was much more a child of his time and his slighter talents were content to produce music which was tuneful, elegant and pleasing (in this we see the seeds of a corruption which was to gnaw away the very vitals of church music in the next century). *O God, thou hast cast us out* and *O praise the Lord* typify these characteristics. *Who can tell how oft he offendeth* is ostensibly in seven parts though the seven voices are scarcely ever heard simultaneously. The little piece *O praise God in his holiness* once enjoyed great popularity: its block harmony, four-square rhythm, pleasant tune and wretchedly dull underparts lead one to consider it more as a glorified hymn-tune than as an anthem. In the first section of the verse anthem *In thee, O Lord, have I put my trust*, the rising demisemiquavers on the word 'thee' were intended as a little upward 'scoop' on the 'th' to enhance the affectiveness of the passage. The alto and bass duet 'Bow down thine ear' is attractive enough in a mild sort of way though the two voices spend a lot of time trotting along in 3rds and 6ths with each other. Of more solid worth is *Hear my crying* which at times becomes truly expressive in spite of some rather mechanical imitation. There are two verse passages, one in four parts and one in six, and the work ends with a choral fugue (another early example). The words 'When my heart is in heaviness' are imaginatively set and near the end there is a striking passage showing not only bold use of a diminished 7th (a) but also, very rare at this time, an inverted German 6th (b):

294

Ex. 130

Weldon's best piece is virtually unknown. It is a lengthy solo cantata in several sections, with choral interjections, called *The Dissolution*. Both its words and its length preclude it from liturgical use but it would be an interesting item in a sacred concert or recital. The words are very curious and abound in vivid imagery; how any baroque composer's heart would have leapt at such a challenge to his skill in word-painting! Here is a sample:

> I see a flaming Seraph fly
> And light his flamboy at the sun,
> Then hasting down to the curst globe his blazing torch apply.
> See the green forests crackling burn
> The oily pastures sweat with intolerable heat,
> The mines of hot Vulcan's turn
> Their horrid jaws, extended wide,
> The sulphurous contagion spread.
> Why do the aged mountains skip?
> And little hills like their own sheep,
> Like lambs, which on their grizzly head once wanton play'd?
> Expanded vapours struggling to the birth
> Roar in the bowels of the earth;
> And now the earth's foundations crack asunder,
> Burst with subterraneous thunder;
> Dusky flames and livid flashes
> Rend the trembling globe to ashes.

A little later the chorus enters with the thought-provoking couplet

> Was it for this the statesman wracked his thought?
> Was it for this the soldier fought?

This curious piece is notable for some very fine declamatory passages; indeed, the work as a whole reaches a far higher level than most of his anthems and is often strongly Purcellian in style.

MAURICE GREENE (1696–1755)

Born a year after Purcell's death and younger than Weldon by nearly twenty years, Greene was the last composer for the English church to show the direct influence of his Restoration background. Not only was he the best composer of the group under discussion but, like Croft, he was one of the few musicians of any stature in the whole century. He combined four important appointments—organist of St. Paul's Cathedral, organist and composer to the Chapel Royal, professor of music at Cambridge (a sinecure in those days), and Master of the King's Music. In 1743 he published his *Forty Select Anthems* and during the last five years of his life he spent much time collecting together in score a representative selection of English sacred music which was ultimately incorporated into Boyce's collection.

He was for many years a very close personal friend of Handel's and all writers on Greene have shaken their heads sadly at the harmful influence the older man had on him, turning his talents aside into a false imitation of his German model and preventing his genius from finding its fullest and freest expression in the native tradition. But is this true? If so, to what extent? When it comes to showing just how Handelian influence manifests itself in Greene's music these writers are noticeably vague. Handel, of course, was a genius and nobody can imitate the essence of genius; he possessed that inner driving force which alone can give life and significance to mere details of style and technique. All that Greene or anyone else could imitate were the external features of Handel's idiom—a few harmonic formulae, melodic twists, cadence patterns, particular decorative devices, a fondness for fugal writing, and so on. But to what extent were these Handel's own? Such things are merely the trappings, the inessentials, of composition and do not in themselves make a composer: we have to look much deeper than this to discover wherein lies the uniqueness of a great composer's utterance. Most of these features were simply the musical fashions and mannerisms of the age, the late baroque, and were the *lingua franca* of all musicians working at that time, not only the big people like Couperin, Rameau, Telemann, Bach, the Scarlattis and Vivaldi, but also the smaller fry like Steffani, Marcello and Manfredini in Italy; Kuhnau, Walther, Kellner and Stamitz in Germany; and Pepusch (a German), Greene, Boyce and Arne in England. In other words, Greene's traits were very much those of his time and it could well be that even if he had never set eyes on Handel his works would still not be very dissimilar to what they are now. That English historians have placed exaggerated importance on Handel's supposed influence stems from that typically insular outlook which treats England as though it were a cultural as well as a geographical island, completely cut off from European thought and development, and fails to appreciate that English music is part and parcel of the general European scene, exhibiting (sometimes belatedly) the same trends, ideals and techniques. The truth of the matter is that, setting these external features aside and making due allowance for Greene's fondness for a pretty tune, he has basically far more affinity with Croft than he has with Handel; he is in fact the last of the true English baroque church composers and he shares their strengths and weaknesses (plus a few additional weaknesses of his own). Perhaps if he had copied Handel a little more and Croft a little less, posterity might have been spared the large crop of fussy, florid verse anthems such as *O sing unto the Lord with thanksgiving; Praise the Lord ye servants,* and *I will give thanks.* Indeed, a list of baroque weaknesses can be drawn up for Greene as for Croft—the usual Hallelujahs (*Sing unto the Lord; My soul truly waiteth; Let God arise*); the parallel 3rds and 6ths (the 6-part chorus in *Behold, I bring you glad tidings*, 'O sing praises' in *O sing unto God*, and parts of *Blessed are they that dwell*); the excessive use of dotted-note rhythms ('Among the gods' in *O Lord, give ear*, 'O that men' in *O give thanks*, and 'He giveth rain' in *I will seek unto God*).

As is usual with verse anthems, those by Greene are very uneven in quality. Within any one anthem inspiration flickers fitfully, distinction rubs shoulders with the common-place, and sections of considerable power or beauty appear beside others which are meretricious or (even worse) dull. Thus the gracious little tenor aria and chorus 'Thou visitest the earth', familiar to us as a harvest anthem, has been extracted from a much larger work *Thou, O God, art praised in Sion*: this begins with an alto and tenor duet followed by a particularly florid and empty alto aria 'Blessed is the man'. A short recitative leads to another duet, 'Thou stillest the raging', which, predictably, contains a good deal of word-painting. This in turn is followed by 'Thou visitest'. Greene seems to have favoured the alto voice; not only has he written many elaborate solos for it but it often gains prominence by being the highest voice in verse sections (another Restoration fashion which lingered on).

Where Greene differs markedly from his predecessors is in his vastly increased use of ornaments. In his more florid writing, especially in solo passages, the melodic line is often encrusted with acciaccaturas, appoggiaturas, shakes, turns and mordents; further-more the performer was expected to add still further embellishments of his own as the spirit moved him—*roulades*, runs, trills, slides and the like. This rich ornamentation was also applied to the organ accompaniment (see, for example, the opening solo of *O Lord, grant the king* and the 'For thy loving kindness' section of *O God, thou art my God*). The accompaniments themselves are often much more florid in Greene than was usual in the work of his predecessors. Thus, in 'Let his seed endure' from *O Lord, grant the king* the organ bass is largely in semiquavers; *O Lord God of hosts*; *Praise the Lord, O my soul*; and *O sing unto the Lord with thanksgiving*, amongst others, include an organ bass in running quavers, while 'The Lord delighteth' from this latter anthem has an exceptionally elaborate organ bass. Several accompaniments are constructed almost entirely in dotted-note rhythms (e.g. the opening duet of *O God, thou art my God* and 'The Lord shall go forth' in *Sing unto the Lord*). Greene followed Croft in developing the art of writing idiomatically for the organ: this is shown not so much in his demands for specific registration, such as the 'trumpet stop' in *O sing, sing*, as in such delightful obbligati as that at the beginning of *Acquaint thyself* in which he shows a genuine feeling for the instrument.

The proliferation of ornaments in Greene's music is again typical of the times in which he lived and is a characteristic manifestation of the spirit of the *Rococo*. It is seen at its best in Bach's keyboard works, particularly some of the organ chorale preludes (e.g. the coloratura setting of *Allein Gott* in A; *Komm, heiliger Geist* in G; two of the *Nun komm* settings; *O Mensch, bewein* and *Schmücke dich*). It is also seen in some of Handel's operatic arias and it is here that Greene most nearly approaches Handel's style: many of the more lengthy solos in Greene's anthems are virtually arias similar to many in Handel's operas (which, in their turn, were derived from Italian opera). In such 'arias' the composer is primarily concerned with writing an attractive melody. Though some attempt is usually made to correlate the mood of the music with that of the words, the words themselves are relegated to second place and are repeated as often as necessary, regardless of meaning and significance, in order to accommodate the demands of the melody. Of course the repetition of words had always been a feature of church music and we have seen how Cranmer set his face against it; yet generally speaking the older composers either repeated complete sentences or phrases or else repeated particularly significant words so as to give them special emphasis for expressive purposes: even then the music was fitted to the words—not the other way about. But in the eighteenth century fragments of phrases and even unimportant words are repeated, not to secure added significance or expressive emphasis but merely to fill out the melody. Example 131 below is typical. In Ex. 131(b) the repetition of 'Hear, O Lord' is highly effective in that it emphasizes the earnestness of the plea whereas the repetitions of 'hear my complaint' are merely there to carry the melodic phrases. It is only when there is obvious scope for word-painting or dramatization (like the typical *roulades* on such words as 'praise', 'thanksgiving', 'sing', 'power' and 'raging') that there is any obvious connection between words and music. This concern with tunefulness for its own sake, and especially the ornamented, operatic type of tunefulness favoured by composers of the late baroque, results in music which is essentially secular in feeling, even though set to sacred words. This applies just as much to some of Bach's arias (and even Haydn's) as to some of Handel's and Greene's; it is simply a characteristic of the period. The following examples from Greene's anthems are typical of this floriated aria style; the third is especially Handelian:

Greene: *O sing unto God*

Greene: *Hear, O Lord, and consider*

Greene: *The Lord is my shepherd*

Ex. 131

One reason why many of Greene's anthems have dropped out of use is that to our way of thinking the rather facile prettiness of his melodies ill becomes the power, the beauty, the profundity, even the simple dignity, of his texts.

Chorus sections are usually short; sometimes solo voices and chorus are used in alternation as in 'Behold, God is my salvation' in *O Lord, I will praise thee*; the duet 'Help us, O God' in *O God, thou hast cast us out*, and the fine 'like as smoke vanisheth' in *Let God arise*. Some of the choruses are fugal in texture but the form sits heavily on Greene. Most of his fugues sound contrived and mechanical, largely because the entries so often follow each other at exactly the same distance. When this distance is one bar, as it usually is, all the entries occur with mechanical regularity on the same beat of successive bars, producing an effect of monotony.

Perhaps the best of the verse anthems are *Arise, shine*; *The Lord, even the most mighty God*; *God is our hope and strength* and, especially, *Acquaint thyself with God* (which demands an outstanding counter-tenor soloist). *O God of my righteousness* deserves an occasional hearing if only for the beauty of the aria 'I will lay me down in peace'.

In common with those of his predecessors, Greene's full anthems are usually rated much more highly than his verse anthems. One wonders why. As composers became increasingly concerned with melody *per se* there was a corresponding loss of interest in choral writing which showed itself in a marked decline in contrapuntal skill: the vertical habits of harmonic thought which the new style brought into being meant that composers no longer conceived music instinctively in terms of counterpoint. Instead of the various voice-parts in the polyphonic texture having complete independence, they were now often yoked together in consecutive 3rds or sixths. This, as any student knows, is an easy way out and there is no doubt that the excessive use of this device disfigures much eighteenth-century choral writing, including Greene's full anthems and the chorus sections of his verse anthems. Technical weakness also shows itself in fugal writing where, as we have seen, the imitations are often laboured and mechanical. There is no doubt that verse anthems were much nearer to Greene's heart than full anthems; this is attested both by their numerical preponderance and by the high level reached in their best sections. In them he seems more personally committed and there is no doubt that the finest of them show far more genuine inspiration than do the full anthems. It is difficult therefore to subscribe to the view that 'He was at his best with the full, or unaccompanied, anthem'.[2] Perhaps prejudice plays some part in such an assessment because most of us instinctively feel that the massive effect of a full choir singing in four, five or eight parts is somehow more 'religious' than florid solo arias which inevitably seem to smack of the operatic stage: they also seem to shed too much limelight on individual 'star' performers and this seems undesirable in public worship—though the parson and the organist get their share and take no harm. But though more consonant with our preconceived notions of what is 'religious', the fact remains that Greene's full anthems are not always deeply inspired and they contain a good deal of weak and dull writing. Even the popular and greatly admired *O clap your hands*, with its exciting homophonic acclamations 'For God is the king of all the earth', takes a long time to get going and hangs around much too much in its home key with cadence after cadence in tonic or dominant. The consecutive 3rds appear at 'O sing praises': they also appear at 'My lips shall speak' in *Let my complaint*. Another particularly fine anthem which has earned the econiums of criticis is *Lord, how long wilt thou be angry?*, but again it is spoiled

[2] E. H. Fellowes: *English Cathedral Music*, p. 180. (Methuen 1948).

by its clockwork imitations, the entries of such phrases as 'And upon the kingdoms' and 'that have not called' all following one another at a bar's distance. *O sing unto the Lord* and *I will sing of thy power* are broad and dignified even if undistinguished; the latter can be sung unaccompanied. The 8-part *How long wilt thou forget me?* is usually described as massive, though stolid might be a better word: in any case the mood created by the rich texture is suddenly shattered by the introduction of a particularly feeble and incongruous little verse section for treble duet in triple time, 'but my trust is in His mercy'.

In the best parts of these full anthems we sometimes get a curious impression of pastiche—as of Gibbons seen through a glass, darkly. That Greene was capable of deliberate pastiche is demonstrated by a group of six full anthems for five voices *a cappella* in Tudor style, one in each of the six principal modes—Dorian, Prygian, Lydian, Mixolydian, Aeolian and Ionian.[3] These curious pieces have no great intrinsic value; what is more, they lay bare for all to see those basic flaws in the composer's choral writing which we have discussed. Yet that any composer living at that time should interest himself in modal music sufficiently to attempt such an exercise is, in itself, remarkable.

In the final analysis, critical opinions on specific works are largely subjective. Just how subjective is strikingly proved by the following pronouncements on Greene's anthem *Lord, let me know mine end*. Fellowes says 'Greene's sense of proportion seems to have been dimmed through lack of self-criticism, with the result that many movements become boring owing to their extreme length. In *Lord, let me know* the figured-bass accompaniment is an unbroken succession of single crotchets extending through 128 bars of common measure marked *Largo*. No break is even made in the middle section which is written for treble duet. The final passages of this anthem, however, are very beautiful.'[4] Walker describes it as 'the finest masterpiece produced by a native-born Englishman in the whole period . . . full, from the first bar to the last, of nobly expressive solemnity—the sombre, never-ceasing, funeral march rhythm of *Lord, let me know* is superbly conceived—and the workmanship is of a very high type.'[5] Phillips says '*Lord, let me know*, a moving text, brings to birth one of the finest works of any period where the accompaniment plays an integral part,—a rarity for its time—where the counterpoint sends the wondering questions from one voice to another, where the rests are used as movingly as the notes and where the slowly dying end, traditionally sung *morendo* for twenty bars or so, sounds like the coda of some great symphony.'[6] Most of us will agree wholeheartedly with the last two writers.

Greene's Morning and Evening Service in C, a most unequal work, is never heard now. Some of the chorus sections show an astonishing poverty of invention (see, for example, the Gloria of Nunc dimittis) and since these are laid out for six and even eight voices. his lack of contrapuntal skill merely exacerbates their shortcomings. A large-scale Te Deum in D and two oratorios, *Jephtha* and *The Force of Truth*, are not worth resurrecting.

WILLIAM BOYCE (1711[7]–79)

Boyce was a chorister at St. Paul's Cathedral and later studied under Greene and

---

[3] Dr. Maurice Green: *Six Full Anthems for Five Voices*, Ed. Walter Slater. (Faith Press.)
[4] E. H. Fellowes: *English Cathedral Music*, p. 180. (Methuen, 4th Ed., 1948.)
[5] Ernest Walker: *History of Music in England* (Revised Westrup), p. 180. (O.U.P.)
[6] C. H. Phillips: *The Singing Church*, p. 173. (Faber.)
[7] Donovan Dawe: *New light on William Boyce*. (Musical Times, September 1968, pp. 802–7.)

Pepusch. He was successively organist of St. Peter's, Vere Street; St. Michael's, Cornhill, and All Hallows, Thames Street. In 1736 he followed Weldon as composer to the Chapel Royal and in 1758 became one of its three organists. In 1749 he received the Doctor of Music degree at Cambridge and six years later succeeded Greene as Master of the King's Music. When only twenty-seven years old he was appointed conductor of what is now called the Three Choirs Festival and in this connection it is interesting to record that he was one of the earliest to 'conduct' in the modern way, using a roll of parchment for a baton; (the general practice at this time—and for many decades afterwards—was for the harpsichord player to direct the performance from the keyboard or the leading violinist to nod or indicate the time with his bow). Throughout his life Boyce suffered from defective hearing. By 1769 his deafness had increased to such an extent that he gave up most of his public duties and retired to Kensington where he devoted the rest of his life mainly to composition and editorial work. As a person he seems to have been outstandingly kind, generous, modest, and helpful to others; he was universally liked and respected by his colleagues and students.

Boyce was a widely accomplished musician and a versatile composer: his works included music for the theatre, twelve trio sonatas, twelve overtures, eight highly interesting 'symphonies' and some concerti grossi, keyboard pieces, songs, forty-three court odes, cantatas, over sixty anthems and several Services. His output is uneven in quality: the keyboard works and songs are of no importance (even the famous *Heart of Oak* was a poor thing as the composer left it—it was later improved by others) yet many movements in the symphonies and overtures still sound fresh and engaging. Boyce was another composer who lived under the shadow of Handel yet remained essentially English in style: such a song as *Tell me, gentle shepherd* is undefinably yet unmistakably 'English', and so are many of his orchestral pieces.

Several of the less distinguished anthems by Greene and Boyce are so similar in style that they could equally well have been written by either composer. Such pieces were meant to entertain rather than to uplift and in them we see that corruption and debasement of the true baroque style which came to be called the *Rococo*. But in his best pieces, Boyce shows himself a superior musician to Greene and at times reaches such heights that Fellowes even went so far as to question his authorship, hinting that as none of Boyce's sacred music was issued in his lifetime, the two volumes of 1780 and 1790, published posthumously and 'printed for the author's widow', may accidentally have included some Restoration anthems which Boyce had intended to include in his *Cathedral Music* and which were therefore found in his handwriting.[8] But such a theory is quite untenable. Boyce's style is markedly different from that of the Restoration composers and could never be confused with theirs; furthermore, the editor of the posthumous volumes, Dr. Philip Hayes, was a sufficiently competent scholar to check his manuscripts carefully and recognise immediately the work of other hands (always assuming, which is itself most unlikely, that Boyce copied out other people's works without adding the composer's name). So, then, the authenticity of his works cannot seriously be doubted and he remains the outstanding composer of the century.

A number of typically Restoration traits linger on in Boyce's music. Thus the all too familiar Hallelujah choruses, which had bedevilled the verse anthem for more than a century, blaze up again—for the last time. Word-painting still has an irresistible fascination: such words as 'sing', 'praise', 'thanks' and 'glory' almost invariably carry

[8] E. H. Fellowes: *English Cathedral Music*, p. 185. (Methuen, 4th Ed., 1948.)

elaborate roulades; texts like 'The floods are risen' and 'unto the going down' are fitted with their obvious musical counterparts, and in such passages as 'The waves of the sea are mighty and rage horribly' in *The Lord is king* the quest for realism makes both singer and organist go rushing wildly about in semiquavers. Even when the words do not call for it, there is still a good deal of fussy, empty-sounding florid writing which does little more than show off the skill of the singers:

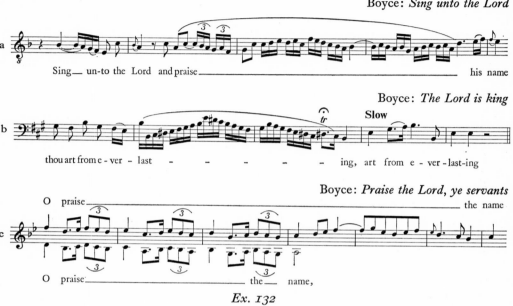

Ex. 132

In the last example we see our old friends, the consecutive 3rds: passages in parallel 3rds and 6ths had by now become a well-established eighteenth-century fashion; (see also the 8-part *O give thanks*). Purcellian dotted notes have all but dropped out of the picture though they still appear sometimes in the accompaniment (as in the alto solo 'I will wash mine hands in innocency' in *Be thou my judge* and the last part of *O be joyful*: they also occur in the final chorus of *I have surely built*). In fugato passages Boyce usually arranges his entries much more freely than Greene, though parts of *Wherewithal shall a young man* and *O give thanks* are more mechanical.

It was in the field of organ accompaniment that Boyce made his most notable contribution to the development of the English anthem, taking over ideas already introduced by others but extending their use and employing them far more expressively. We may instance the following:

1. The use of obbligati. This device, with which Greene had made some tentative experiments, became an important feature in many of Boyce's anthems (e.g. 'The poor shall eat' in *O praise the Lord*; 'One thing have I desired' in *The Lord is my light*, and the charming example at 'For the Lord hath pleasure' in *O sing unto the Lord*). The opening of *Teach me, O Lord* has a particularly delightful and idiomatic obbligato:

Boyce: *Teach me, O Lord*

Ex. 133

2. 'Trumpet' fanfares. More often than not, the organ obbligato takes the form of fanfares played on a trumpet stop. Boyce was especially fond of this effect and missed no opportunity of introducing it. Obvious examples are the opening of *O praise the Lord* and *O sing unto the Lord*, the duet 'For the Lord himself' in *If we believe* and the 'riches and plenteousness' section of *Blessed is the man*.

3. Unison introductions. Several movements begin with a few bars of organ introduction in unison. The instruction 'Loud organ in octaves' occurs in *Sing praises to the Lord* and in *O sing unto the Lord*, while in *Praise the Lord, ye servants* it is made even more explicit, 'Loud organ in octaves without chords'.

4. Accompanimental figuration. A particularly significant development in some of Boyce's music is his consistent use throughout a movement of some little recurring motif as an integral part of the accompaniment. These accompanimental figures become a structural feature of the entire movement, locking it together, much as they do in a Schubert song: indeed, in print such a Boyce movement looks not unlike some Schubert songs. Thus, in the following example, the accompaniment of *The Lord is King* is built largely on a short phrase (a) which is developed as at (b) and shown in Example 134 on the next page. Other notable examples occur at 'The Lord is high' in *Sing praises*, 'O turn away mine eyes' in *Teach me, O Lord*, and 'In them hath he set' in *The heavens declare*.

Boyce's anthems, like Greene's, are so unequal in quality that often a good anthem will be marred by some mediocre section or a poor anthem partially redeemed by a

Boyce: *The Lord is king*

Ibidem

Ex. 134

movement of considerable merit. In the first group we may mention the lamentable chorus 'For the kingdom is the Lord's' and the feeble Hallelujahs in *O praise the Lord*, 'O turn away mine eyes' in *Teach me, O Lord* (which is delightful as music but weak as a setting of the words) and the somewhat sickly trio 'If I forget thee' in *By the waters of Babylon*. It is often the movements in 3-time that are the weakest, sounding superficially melodious and rather smug. In the second group are the delightful duet for two trebles 'The sorrows of my heart' in *Turn thee unto me*, 'Examine me' in *Be thou my judge*, the solo 'For the Lord hath pleasure' in *O sing unto the Lord* and the beautiful ending of *If we believe that Jesus died*.

Of all these anthems, only four appear to retain their popularity. The 4-part full anthem *By the waters of Babylon* begins with a fine chorus: note the effective rests at 'As for our harps' and the desolate chords at 'when we remembered thee, O Sion'. Curiously, the taunt 'Sing us one of the songs' is here given to two trebles, so losing much of its sting. The setting of 'If I forget thee' hardly does justice to the words but the final chorus makes amends.

I have surely built thee an house is a splendid anthem notable for the accuracy and expressive beauty of its declamation. The opening is typical and the soloist actually builds his house up the common chord:

Boyce: *I have surely built thee an house*

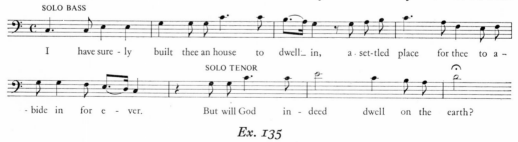

Ex. 135

This is strongly Purcellian (not Handelian) in style, as is the following alto solo with its typical break into three semibreves and the reversed dotted rhythm near the end:

Ibidem

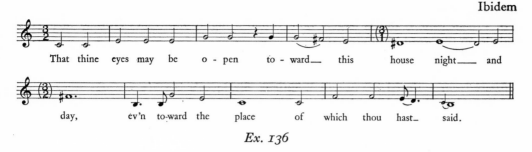

That thine eyes may be o - pen to - ward___ this house night___ and
day, ev'n to-ward the place of which thou hast_ said.

Ex. 136

There is a magnificent tenor recitative 'If there be in the land famine' and an extraordinary one for bass 'And the Lord said to Solomon' with a striking accompanimental
figure. Only the 'chearfull' Hallelujahs at the end spoil this very fine work.

The 5-part *O where shall wisdom be found?* is one of the really great anthems of the
Anglican tradition. Again Boyce's verbal accentuation is superb. Particularly effective
is the emphatic repetition of the word 'where' in the opening questions, 'Where, where
shall wisdom be found?' followed later by the answer 'Then, then did he see it'. An
entrancing touch of sensitive word-painting occurs when the silver is weighed. The
words 'Whence then cometh wisdom?' generate a contrapuntal climax culminating in a
beautiful phrase in block harmony 'seeing it is hid from the eyes of all living'. Then, for
the first time, the full choir bursts in, 'God understandeth the way thereof'. The reversed
dotted rhythms of the succeeding trio have a strong Purcellian flavour as has the sudden
shift into D flat for the 'lightning'. Then suddenly, in hushed tones and mysterious
harmonies, the final answer is given:

Boyce: *O where shall wisdom be found?*

And un-to man he said, Be-hold, the fear of the Lord,
that is wis - dom; and to de-part from e vil is un-der-stand - ing.

Ex. 137

which is then taken up in a somewhat tame and conventional concluding chorus.

The 5-part *Turn thee unto me* begins with a deeply expressive chorus containing some
beautiful imitative counterpoint. Then follows one of Boyce's very typical duets for two

trebles in 3-time, full of grace and charm if not very profound. The concluding chorus is of weaker calibre and is largely built round a highly florid and entirely unsuitable roulade on the word 'confounded'.

With all their faults these four anthems represent a very durable and valuable contribution to Anglican worship.

Apart from a Burial Service in E minor, all Boyce's Service settings were of the morning Canticles and the Ante-Communion Service: he wrote no evening settings. The Morning Services in C and A once enjoyed considerable popularity but are rarely heard now. Of far greater interest is the verse-Service in A which rises well above the level of most eighteenth-century Services.

But it is as the editor of the great three-volume collection of *Cathedral Music* that Boyce will always be most revered. The collection had a complicated genesis. It was first planned by Maurice Greene. Independently, the organist of Lichfield Cathedral, John Alcock, was at work on a similar compilation. As soon as he heard of Greene's project, Alcock generously passed all his material over to Greene. At the latter's death the work was still incomplete and the task was bequeathed to his pupil, Boyce, who eventually finished the work and issued the volumes in 1760, 1768 and 1773. They are superb specimens of engraving and are especially remarkable for the inclusion of elaborate designs of birds, fishes and curious figures produced by a single unbroken line drawn without lifting the pen from the paper. As we have seen, this collection guided the English cathedral repertoire for upwards of a century.

MINOR FIGURES

So far we have discussed only the more important composers of the period. What of the others?

Perhaps it is true to say that no century has produced so much incredibly dull music as the eighteenth. English church music is generally reckoned to have reached its nadir in the mid-nineteenth century and there is no doubt that the bulk of church music written at that time can be variously described as weak, meretricious, amateurish, puerile, vulgar, sentimental, mawkish, and so on, yet the mere fact that such words can be applied to it shows that at least it makes some sort of impact, however unfavourable. It is often said that many Victorian anthems descended to the level of domestic ballads — yet let us not be too contemptuous even of these: many ballads were surprisingly tuneful (who has not found himself at some time or other humming *Where my caravan has rested*; *Homing* or *Until?*) and even at worst they were rarely, if ever, merely dull. Similarly, though Victorian church music had many faults and could often be fatuous or inappropriate at least it avoided the most heinous of all faults — sheer dullness; some of its weakest and most inappropriate tunes have a curious habit of sticking in the mind. In contrast to this much eighteenth-century work, especially Service settings, makes absolutely no impact at all. Here we find Dullness decked out in her full panoply of 4-part block chords and tonic and dominant cadences enshrined as tribal deity of the minor composers. Had Pope included musicians in his *Dunciad* what unlimited scope he would have had!

In approximate chronological order the list includes Charles King (1687–1748), Thomas Kelway (1695–1749), James Kent (1700–76), John Travers (1706–58), Thomas Kempton (died 1762), William Hayes (1705–77), James Nares (1715–83), William

Jackson (1730–1803), Thomas Dupuis (1733–96), Benjamin Cooke (1734–93), Philip Hayes (1738–92), Samuel Arnold (1740–1814) and Robert Cooke (1768–1814).

Most of these musicians are remembered chiefly as writers of Services, especially King, who was described by his pupil Greene as 'a very Serviceable man!' Actually he wrote only six but they enjoyed immense popularity until well into the present century. Kelway wrote a full Service in F and Evening Services in A, A minor, G minor and B minor: this last is still to be heard. Kent wrote several anthems and a Service in D: his fame rested chiefly on the Service and on *Hear my prayer*, an anthem renowned for its duet for two solo trebles. He was a wretched composer. Kempton's Morning and Evening Service in B flat is one of the best of Services of the period and is still sung sometimes. It is a pedestrian work and clings tenaciously to the orbit of its home key. (A lay clerk at Canterbury Cathedral used to declare that his favourite piece of music was the 'Mad Scene' from Kempton in B flat.) William Jackson of Exeter is known by one work, his Service in F. The following passage from Te Deum shows his complete subservience to the grip of two- and four-bar phrase lengths, the words being packed in or stretched out as occasion demands:

Jackson in F: *Te Deum*

Ex. 138

One needs only to compare such a passage with almost anything written by Gibbons and his predecessors to see the extent of the decline.

Benjamin Cooke's fame hangs on one work, his Service in G ('Cook-in-g' as choirboys call it): though hardly inspired it certainly has more vitality than most others of its time. Samuel Arnold's Evening Service in A was intended as a pendant to Boyce's Morning Service in the same key. It is still frequently sung in cathedrals and parish churches and is fairly tuneful—though its melodic line can be curiously aimless and, at times, wretchedly obvious:

Arnold in A: *Magnificat*

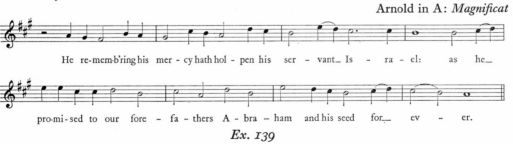

Ex. 139

In very general terms and with few exceptions, all these Services are in short form, more or less in block harmony with occasional passages in 3rds and 6ths; the words are made to fit into two- and four-bar phrases and the pieces are designed to be sung antiphonally—Decani and Cantoris. The writing is academic, uninspired and un-inspiring. Since in most of them the organ merely doubles the voices it follows that they can effectively be sung unaccompanied. The reason why these unimaginative settings are still sung in most cathedrals and many parish churches has already been discussed (pp. 245–6): the main attraction is that they are easy to sing and need little rehearsal, so releasing precious rehearsal time for other things.

Two composers stand out a little above the others. John Travers deserves mention for his anthem *Ascribe unto the Lord* which contains a florid, but remarkably fine, baritone solo 'Let the heavens rejoice' accompanied by an equally fine organ obbligato for the 'mounted cornett' stop (a mixture). His Service in F was once a stand-by in every cathedral but has virtually disappeared now. James Nares's Services in C and D long ago dropped into oblivion but the one in F managed to survive until quite recently; however, he is still represented by three attractive anthems—*O Lord my God; Try me, O God*, and *The souls of the righteous*. This last, for boys' voices, is particularly effective; it has a most attractive melody and considerable charm. The solo section 'In the sight of the unwise' is a sensitive setting and the succeeding duet provides excellent contrast. Except for the ending, the last chorus for full choir is weak: when used as an anthem for boys' voices the underparts of this chorus can be omitted.

Almost all the composers mentioned in this section wrote chants which are still the mainstay of most modern chant books.

CHAPTER XIII

Church Music under the late Georgians

Both Italian monody and the baroque styles profoundly influenced the whole course of English music, yet the 'Classical' style, as exemplified in the work of Haydn and Mozart, had comparatively little effect. This is largely because the classical style was fundamentally an instrumental style whereas the English musical genius has always been essentially choral. In the last chapter we traced the gradual evolution of the eighteenth-century anthem from its baroque/Restoration origin and saw how various composers gradually modified it until, by the time of William Boyce, it had changed considerably though still retaining many distinctively baroque features.

The next group of composers we have to consider were all working at the close of the eighteenth century but by and large they seem to have remained untouched by the epoch-making developments in Vienna and elsewhere. Battishill was at heart an Elizabethan and looked backwards; Samuel Wesley was a disciple of J. S. Bach who was himself one of the last survivors of an era already past; William Crotch continued in the English tradition. Only Attwood had any direct contact with the new style. He was for a time a pupil of Mozart's but even his best work was but a dim shadow of his master's worst. The only visible sign of his studies under one of the world's most phenomenal musical minds was to write a few anthems that sound vaguely like Mozartean minuets. Indeed, a passion for music in triple time became a besetting sin of the next generation of church musicians — hymn-tune writers as well as cathedral composers. Not of course that there is anything wrong with triple time in itself — some profoundly moving music has been written in it — yet (perhaps through association of ideas) most of us instinctively feel it to be basically a dance rhythm and therefore less appropriate to carry grave and sober thoughts. The strong rhythmical pulse which is inherent in it — ONE, two, three, ONE, two, three — so often traps composers into writing facile tunes with feminine cadence points. This weak melodiousness is superficially attractive, even 'pretty', and is much beloved by congregations, but sensitive people will feel that it is often inappropriate to its context and unworthy of the words to which it is set. Many otherwise excellent pieces are weakened by the intrusion of such a movement. We sense this in some of Greene's work and still more in some of Boyce's.

On the credit side, some of the Restoration fashions and conventions which had by now become threadbare with use were at last abandoned. After Boyce, the Hallelujah choruses which had for so long disfigured English anthems almost completely dropped out of use and so did the typical Purcellian dotted-note *roulades*.

JONATHAN BATTISHILL (1738–1801)

Discussing this period of Anglican music Fellowes wrote 'Only three names are to be found here that rise even to the level of mediocrity: Jonathan Battishill, Thomas Attwood and Samuel Wesley.' However, farther down the same page he says that Battishill's *O Lord, look down* 'is worthy of a place among the best unaccompanied anthems in the entire repertory of English Cathedral music'.[1] And so it is. In trying to reconcile Fellowes's two statements it must be remembered that he was a pioneer in the revival of interest in Tudor music and his knowledge, enthusiasm and proselytizing zeal for it made him somewhat unsympathetic towards the music of later periods; hence his judgement becomes less sure and he sometimes underestimates achievements. This is especially true of his attitude towards the eighteenth and early nineteenth centuries.

Battishill was primarily a secular composer and his output includes stage works, songs, ballads and glees. His church music consists of ten anthems and about the same number of chants. Of the anthems, eight are of comparatively poor quality and are never heard now, whereas the other two are outstanding examples of the form, one of them being a minor masterpiece. *Call to remembrance* is in two sections. The first opens in E minor with a fine 5-part chorus in imitative counterpoint: this is followed by a 7-part verse section in which a high voice trio is answered by a low voice quartet: this section is beautifully written and the musical phrases seem exactly to reflect the mood of the words:

Battishill: *Call to remembrance*

Ex. 140

The second part of the anthem, 'O remember not the sins', moves into the major key and (typically) triple time: the power and depth of the opening give way to the grace and charm of a melodious verse trio (accompanied) which is later taken up by the choir, beginning in five parts and building up to seven. This cumulative effect is further enhanced by a series of effective pedal points. (This use of pedal points was something of an innovation at the time but the device soon became very popular.) The whole anthem is remarkably effective but there is no doubt that the second part lacks the depth of the first and is also rather too long.

Even finer is *O Lord, look down*, one of the really great anthems of the English church. It is the more remarkable in that it is constructed in one closely knit movement in which all the lovely and expressive detail is subordinated to the profound over-all effect. It opens with imitative counterpoint in the minor key, beginning with three voices, then four, and building to six (Battishill was fond of reinforcing tone gradually by thickening the texture in this way). At the climax there comes a magnificent passage in which the

[1] E. H. Fellowes: *English Cathedral Music*, p. 192. (Methuen, 4th Edition 1948.)

composer deliberately exploits the reverberation of a vast building, hurling block chords into the void and giving them time to evaporate in space. Then, as these blazing chords recede into silence, comes the repeated question, wondrously set, 'are they restrained?' This passage is one of the most deeply moving in all cathedral music and is a brilliant essay in the effective use of unaccompanied voices:

Battishill: *O Lord, look down from heaven*

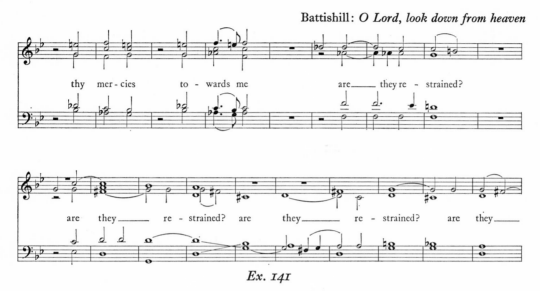

Ex. 141

Both this anthem and the first part of *Call to remembrance* are astonishingly Elizabethan in conception and feeling; they have the same power and massive grandeur as Tudor polyphony at its best.

THOMAS ATTWOOD (1765–1838)

Compared even with Greene, Boyce and Battishill, Attwood was a man of very modest attainments; in fact his work is discussed here not because of its merits but because much of it is simple enough to have become staple fare in our parish churches. He was a chorister at the Chapel Royal under Nares and Ayrton. In 1783 the Prince of Wales sent him to study in Naples and two years later he went to Vienna where he studied under Mozart (who thought very highly of him). After returning to England in 1787 he received a whole series of Court appointments while in 1796 he became organist of St. Paul's Cathedral. He was one of the first professors appointed to the newly formed Royal Academy of Music in 1823 and in 1836 became organist of the Chapel Royal. During the earlier part of his life he was interested mainly in music for the stage and Grove lists thirty-two operas or musical plays. Later, however, he turned his attention to sacred music and wrote twenty or so anthems, five Services and some excellent double chants. In general, the more pretentious he is, the less successful: thus his coronation anthems *I was glad* and *O Lord, grant the king a long life* betray his training in stage music and are often flamboyant and theatrical, depending for much of their effect on a fussy orchestral accompaniment. The inspirational level of these pieces can be gauged from the fact that in the first the national anthem is woven into the orchestral introduction as a counter-melody, while in *O Lord, grant the king* the introduction is built round Arne's *Rule, Britannia!*

When Attwood is content to work within his own limitations he shows a real talent for writing shapely and charming airs supported by suave, mellifluous harmony. It is all very gracious, elegant and well-bred though of course there can be no place for power or passion in such music. Its very mildness is its own undoing and after a time one craves for some jagged outlines or dissonant harmonies to ruffle its smiling surface. Many of these smaller pieces show a genuine awareness of the importance of musical form, even though the forms he uses are of the utmost simplicity. Thus *Turn thee again* is in straightforward A–B–A form with coda added (in this case extra contrast is provided by setting 'B' in the mediant minor of the main key). *Turn thy face* is in simple binary form, each of the two sections being sung first by a soloist then repeated by a small chorus, resulting in an A–A–B–B plan. This appreciation of the importance of constructional forms may well be one of the few things he acquired from his work with Mozart.

The little hymn-tune for two trebles *Songs of praise the angels sang* is almost too pretty for serious consideration. Of far more substance is the 4-part accompanied Epiphany piece *O God, who by the leading of a star*. This is well written and effective, even if not inspired, and makes a useful addition to the somewhat slender repertory for Epiphany. *Teach me, O Lord* is very similar in style to *Turn thee again* (both are in triple time) but lacks the latter's formal tidiness: the exposed tenor and bass notes are much enjoyed by bad singers.

SAMUEL WESLEY (1766–1837)

Samuel was the second son of the Reverend Charles Wesley and hence nephew of John Wesley, founder of the Methodists. Both he and his brother showed unusual musical precocity. At six he learnt the organ; at eight he had written an oratorio; by nine he was a virtuoso violinist, and at eleven he published *Eight Lessons for the Harpsichord*. Within the next few years he had distinguished himself as a classical scholar, cultivated a sensitive taste in English literature and acquired a useful knowledge of modern languages. Round about 1784 he joined the Church of Rome, attracted more apparently by the music at the Portuguese Embassy than by Roman doctrines (in which he had little interest): indeed, just before he died he disclaimed the conversion, saying that it was only the Gregorian music which had enticed him and that he had never been able to accept the tenets of the Roman faith. Nevertheless his flirtation with the 'Scarlet Woman' led him to write a series of Masses and motets one of which, the *Mass de Spiritu Sancto*, was accepted by the Pope. At the age of twenty-one he fell into a builders' excavation and sustained some damage including, probably, concussion. Lengthy periods of mental disorder from which he afterwards suffered were always attributed to this accident but it seems most unlikely that there was any connection between the two. Madness is next to genius, they say, and Samuel with his superior mental attainments seems always to have been unstable and subject to fits of severe depression. He was acknowledged to be the greatest organist of his day and was particularly famous for his masterly powers of extemporisation, but his ill health prevented his holding any major post and he occupied various minor appointments. He was one of the first Englishmen to recognise the genius of J. S. Bach and was tireless in his championship of Bach's music. Not only did he play the organ works in his own recitals but he edited and published the '48' and also an arrangement of the organ trios; further, he promoted the publication of Forkel's *Life of Bach* in English.

Wesley was a prolific composer in many fields and his output included orchestral works, chamber music, choral works, songs, duets, glees, piano and organ music as well as sacred works. Some of this output is far in advance of its time. Take the orchestral music for example; it includes symphonies, overtures and piano and organ concertos. One of these symphonies (in B flat) has been revived in recent years; it represents an enormous advance on Boyce's so-called 'symphonies' most of which consist of a fairly extended 'prelude' or 'prelude' and fugue, followed by a couple of short dance movements. Wesley's superb work is, in fact, a real symphony, one of the earliest to be written by an Englishman, and it is clearly influenced by Haydn's 'London' symphonies. Continental influence is also obvious in his chamber music which includes a quintet, string quartet and sonatas.

In addition to Masses and motets for the Roman liturgy, his church music includes Services, anthems and psalm-tunes for the English church. Only a few of them are, even now, available in print and it is high time that more of his work was published and recorded. After discussing Attwood's work, Samuel Wesley's comes as a complete contrast. Instead of scented elegance and smooth charm he conveys a strong feeling of massivity and grandeur. Even in 4-part writing, as in *Dixit Dominus* and *Thou, O God, art praised in Sion*, he still achieves this massive effect while in works with additional voice parts it is even more in evidence. Whereas Attwood's best pieces are his small-scale works, Samuel excels when working on a large canvas. It is not surprising then that the two compositions by which he is best known (both reckoned among his finest) are fairly lengthy. The 5-part *Exultate Deo* is often sung to its English words *Sing aloud with gladness*. It is a brilliant fast-moving piece which sounds best when taken at a swinging one-in-a-bar. It is a gloriously wide-spanned movement which is virtually constructed from two phrases:

Samuel Wesley: *Exultate Deo*

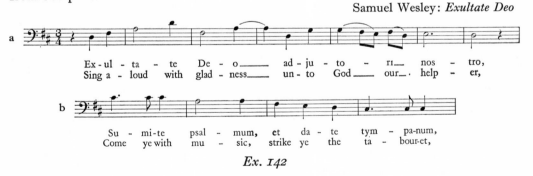

Ex. 142

The organ part presents a problem: throughout the anthem it merely doubles the voices and is therefore better omitted; but at the very end the organ, now solo, is given an important coda. The usual practice is to sing the anthem almost to the end unaccompanied. Then, after twenty-two pages (275 bars) of swift-moving unaccompanied 5-part polyphony with plenty of top A's for the boys, fairly heavy organ is suddenly brought in for the last phrase, quickly building to full organ for the coda. The effect is electrifying — but it demands a first-class choir which can keep pitch well and even then there is an anxious moment for everyone when the organ suddenly comes in. The real weakness of the piece is that the two short phrases given above are simply unable to carry the weight put upon them. They neither grow nor develop, they never undergo any rhythmic or intervallic transformation; they are merely repeated over and over again in various keys, on and on, until one has wearied of them long before the end.

The same criticism can be levelled at what is probably Samuel's finest church work, the splendid 8-part motet *In exitu Israel*. Here there are four main themes which recur again and again, chasing each other around in different keys. The result is curiously static. There is a great deal of bustle and activity but the piece has little forward movement: it seems permanently engaged in a sort of thematic Ring-a-ring-o'-roses. Nevertheless the total effect is very powerful. The unison passages are particularly effective, especially the thrilling 'Jordanis conversis' entry two-thirds of the way through. Only once does this anthem fall from its high level: near the end, at the beginning of the coda, there is a weak, melodious passage reminiscent of Haydn that sounds incongruous in this powerful and vigorous work. Immediately afterwards, however, comes a tremendous restatement of the opening theme in full 8-part harmony which, in augmentation and in the minor key, brings the work to a splendid close with discords which would have made poor Attwood shudder.

'Carmen Funebre' (*Omnia vanitas*) is a setting of Latin words alleged to have been spoken to Samuel by his dying father ('Vanity, vanity, all is vanity'). Like the other two motets it is constructed in one long single movement. After the fragmentary seventeenth and eighteenth century anthems with their innumerable little sections and sub-sections, these far-flung, tautly-constructed movements seem altogether more satisfying; indeed, Samuel Wesley has the distinction of being the first English choral composer to write really long integrated movements. Again, too little thematic material is made to go too far and there is also some rhythmic monotony, but in spite of such faults the work is undeniably impressive, especially the closing pages. The powerful entry in block harmony at bar 93 not only echoes but intensifies the rhythm of the opening bars. Another fine piece which deserves to be much better known is his 6-part *Tu es sacerdos*.

Most of Samuel's unpublished sacred works have English texts and are set as solo anthems, duets or trios. Some include short chorus sections. In general they lack the rugged grandeur of the big Latin works and are content to be tuneful and gracious. The solo anthems *Who can tell how oft he offendeth* and *My delight shall be in thy statutes* are attractive little pieces in triple time somewhat after the manner of Greene. *I will arise* is only twenty-three bars long but has one or two points of rhythmic interest. Far more interesting is *How are thy servants blest, O Lord*, a recitative with violin obbligato followed by a 3-part 'Alleluia — Amen' chorus.

Of the 2-part works *The Lord is my shepherd* is not very inspired. *Mansions of Heav'n* ends with a chorus in which the phrase 'He comes array'd in robes of light' is sung in unison to good effect. The most lengthy of these unpublished works is probably *Hear my prayer, O Lord*. The opening section is rhythmically somewhat repetitive. Then come two more extended sections 'Hold not thy peace' and 'O spare me a little'; the whole is rounded off by the chorus repeating the phrase 'O spare me a little' and then breaking rather surprisingly into *vivace* for 'before I go hence'. *O be joyful* for 4-part chorus and strings has a long counter-tenor and bass duet 'be ye sure', and a counter-tenor solo 'For the Lord is gracious'.

This shall be my rest for ever and *Behold how good and joyful* are trios for counter-tenor,

tenor and bass. The latter work has common chord arpeggios for 'Behold, behold' and breaks into triplets on the word 'dwell' towards the end. There is no certainty that *Be pleased, O Lord, to deliver me* for two trebles and bass is by Samuel Wesley, though the quite astonishing key signature of six sharps (astonishing for its time, that is) could well have been suggested by his enthusiasm for the '48'. It has no organ part; in any case, an organ tuned to mean tone temperament would have been dreadfully out of tune in the key of F sharp major.

His Latin setting *Salve regina* is also scored for counter-tenor, tenor and bass. It has two main sections and is very effectively laid out for the three voices; there are some bold and exciting modulations. It is perhaps the most interesting of the unpublished works and could well prove popular if it was issued in print.

Wesley's Morning and Evening Services, once very popular, are never heard now: they are not greatly inspired. Perhaps the best of them was the Short Service in F (Te Deum, Jubilate, Kyrie, Sanctus, Magnificat and Nunc dimittis).

WILLIAM CROTCH (1775–1847)

Crotch goes down as one of the most astonishing infant prodigies in the whole history of music: compared with him Mozart was a late developer! At two he could play from memory, improvise, and supply a satisfactory bass to a melody. At four he gave several organ recitals and a series of daily piano recitals in London. At eleven he was assistant organist of King's College, Trinity College and Great St. Mary's Church, Cambridge, and at fourteen he had his first oratorio performed. At fifteen he was appointed organist of Christ Church, Oxford, and became Professor of Music there only seven years later. Subsequently he became first Principal of the Royal Academy of Music. Crotch's gifts were by no means limited to music. He was renowned for his drawings and paintings, could rapidly sketch a person's likeness, could write shorthand, and could play the violin 'in almost every imaginable position'. What is more, he could write music with both hands simultaneously, as well as design elaborate fireworks and pyrotechnic set-pieces!

It is the greater pity then that as a composer he did not fulfil his early promise. Very few of his works have stood the test of time: those that have are short, easy pieces which now are far more likely to be heard in a small parish church than in a cathedral. *Comfort, O Lord, the soul of thy servant* may be taken as typical. It is the second part of a longer anthem *Be merciful unto me* which is never sung in its entirety. The *Comfort, O Lord* section could equally well have come from Attwood's pen with its gracious melody (of course in triple time), inevitable harmony and, especially, its ternary construction — A–B–A.

A far better work is *How dear are thy counsels*. This is a pleasantly tuneful, cleanly-written little piece of considerable charm. As in *Comfort, O Lord*, the opening section returns towards the end so giving a simple but quite satisfying A–B–A form. The fact that the words are made to fit the tune rather than the other way round is shown by the upper leap of an octave to the weak syllable of the word 'coun-SELS': choirs always find it difficult to put the accent back on the low note and then sing the top note rather lightly. The best of all Crotch's anthems, *My God, my God, look upon me*, is never sung now, being eclipsed no doubt by Blow's infinitely superior setting of the same words. But Crotch's version is worth reviving. It has a pathetic yearning tenderness which exactly reflects the desolation of the words and would make an acceptable alternative to the better-known setting. The bigger anthems are somewhat disappointing: often they include attempts at realism like the rather naïve trumpet fanfare in *The Lord, even the most mighty God* and the passage 'though the earth be moved' in *God is our hope and strength*.

Crotch's most notable achievement was an oratorio called *Palestine* which stands high above the multitude of similar works being poured out at this time. Though never performed now, two movements from it are often extracted and used as anthems, *Be peace on earth* and *Lo! star-led chiefs*. This last is a jolly affair in which three of the principal motifs are in triple counterpoint (i.e. they fit together in such a way that any one can be top, middle or bottom). The accompaniment was originally orchestral but it can be made very effective on the organ. This tuneful little work is another useful Epiphany anthem and is well within the scope of a competent parish choir.

CHAPTER XIV

The Nineteenth Century

THE STATE OF THE CHURCH

The decline in musical standards which we have followed in previous chapters merely reflected a far more serious decline in the whole state of the Church itself. By the beginning of the nineteenth century things had reached rock bottom and slackness, apathy and neglect had gnawed their way into most aspects of church life. While bishops drew salaries of £30,000 and even £50,000 (Winchester), half the curates were living on less than £60. Yet most of the bishops shamefully neglected their duties, preferring to indulge themselves to the full in the luxury, high life and worldly pleasure which affluence and prestige procured. Amongst the parochial clergy the richest livings were mostly in the gift of private families; these plums were dropped into the laps of favoured hangers-on who accepted them as profitable sinecures. Pluralism and nepotism were the order of the day and the more wealthy clergy lived as country squires, attending church on Sunday and spending the rest of the week huntin', shootin' and drinkin'—that is if they happened to live in their parishes, which was unusual. Absenteeism was considered normal and in 1827 three-fifths of the clergy were non-resident. Many of them were either sons of the landed gentry or else social climbers (a state of affairs reflected in Jane Austen's novels). Holy Communion was still administered quarterly (if at all) and many country churches were so little used that they became increasingly mouldy and dilapidated. Even where Sunday services were still held regularly they had often degenerated into a dialogue between a curate and the parish clerk, interrupted by the efforts of the gallery musicians.

The Evangelical Revival of the previous century, led by men like the Wesleys, John Berridge, George Whitefield, John Fletcher, Henry Venn, the redoubtable Countess of Huntingdon and others, battled against worldliness both in Church and society. Their message was one of personal conversion and salvation based upon Bible study and achieved through strict self-discipline. They were fundamentalists in their approach to the Bible. Their fear or suspicion of all forms of pleasure and self-indulgence coupled with a strict Sabbatarianism gave the word 'puritan' its modern dour connotation— utterly at variance with the spirit of the Cromwellian puritans. But the Hanoverian Church remained complacent and apathetic and, in the end, Wesley's followers and the Countess's chapels were driven to separate, leaving the main body of the Church to slumber on, even though many Evangelicals remained within its fold. The horrors of the French Revolution and especially its attitude to the Church had hardened opinion in this country against all expressions of dissatisfaction and dissension. The Church came to be looked upon as a solid bastion against new and possibly dangerous ideas and any suggestion of reform at once aroused the suspicion of an incipient revolution. This attitude of mind delayed reform for more than a generation.

But if public worship and pastoral work were in the doldrums, churchmen were certainly active in other directions, especially the Evangelicals. To them, spiritual ministration and liturgiology were of far less importance than 'preaching the Word' and performing good works: the emphasis was on 'being good and doing good'. So was born the great age of 'practical' Christianity. To this the 'Hackney Phalanx' of high churchmen also made a useful contribution, especially in educational fields. Many new religious societies came into being—the Church Missionary Society (1799), the British and Foreign Bible Society (1804), the National Society for the Education of the Poor (1811), the Church Building Society (1818), the Church Pastoral Aid Society (1836), and the Additional Curates Society (1837). Social evils were tackled by Acts of Parliament—the East India Bill (1813), the repeal of the Test and Corporation Acts (1828), the Catholic Emancipation Bill (1829), and the Abolition of Slavery (1833). Foreign missions were so strong in the field and well supported at home that the Church overseas was far more virile and spiritual than it was at home.

Nevertheless there were many who recognised that the true strength of the Church did not rest in its societies, committees and charitable works. At the very centre of all religion and religious enterprises there must always be the public worship of Almighty God. This, together with pastoral care and the Christian training of young and old, depends upon the adequate provision of a selfless, utterly dedicated, well-trained and well-organised priesthood, free of social barriers and distinctions. As soon, therefore, as the scare caused by the French Revolution died away, reformers again raised their voices. A bitter attack on conventional Christianity was launched in *The Black Book, or Corruption Unmasked* in 1820–23 and followed up in *The Extraordinary Black Book* of 1831. Sydney Smith and Thomas Arnold of Rugby were two of the most outspoken reformers. In 1833 Arnold issued his *Principles of Church Reform* in which he propounded the conception of a truly Christian State run rather on the lines of a good public school. In that same year, on 14 July, Keble preached his famous sermon on 'National Apostasy' which triggered off the greatest reform in the established Church since the Reformation itself—the Oxford Movement.

This is not the place to discuss the complicated history of the Oxford Movement (1833–45). It is sufficient to say that it was essentially a High Church movement and its emphasis was on worship, ritual and ceremonial, sacerdotalism, and dogma: in some ways it looked back to the pre-Reformation Church. It was an intellectual movement and its ideas were propagated mainly by a series of ninety *Tracts for the Times* written by Newman, Pusey, Keble, Froude and others. The immense impact which the Oxford Movement had on church music will be discussed later.

Reform was much in the air at this time. Having passed the Reform Bill of 1832 which gave fairer representation in Westminster, Parliament turned its attention to the Church. A body called the Ecclesiastical Commissioners was set up in 1835. These Commissioners began by grasping the biggest nettle firmly and recommending a much more fair and equal redistribution of the bishops' incomes. They also proposed two new sees, one at Manchester and one at Ripon. The following year they turned their attention to the cathedrals. In place of innumerable non-resident canons drawing fat salaries yet holding other preferment they suggested that each cathedral should have a dean and four residentiaries—all other canonries to be honorary. The incomes of poorer clergy were then augmented from the money thus saved. Parliament also dealt with tithes (the Tithe Act, 1836), church rates, and ecclesiastical courts.

But the desire for reform did not stop short at Church administration, organisation, finance, institutions, ordering of services, and ceremonial. The Church found itself rocked to its very foundations by two powerful attacks on its fundamental beliefs and doctrines — one from within and one from without. From within, the attack came from theologians themselves. The infallibility of the Bible was first questioned by German scholars and their work was made known in England by Herbert Marsh and later by Pusey in his *Inquiry into German Rationalism* (1828). The poet Coleridge also attacked the fundamentalist's approach to the Bible in his *Letters on the Inspiration of the Scriptures*. In his challenging book *History of the Jews* (1829), H. H. Milman treated the 'Children of Israel' merely as one of many eastern tribes and called Abraham 'an Arab Sheikh'. The new textual criticism of the Bible raised many doubts and these were expressed by seven Oxford scholars in *Essays and Reviews* (1860). Mention must also be made of the 'heretical' writings of Bishop Colenso.

The attack from without was neither deliberate nor, probably, conscious — but it was devastating. The advances of scientific enquiry blasted great holes in the long-cherished beliefs of the fundamentalists and indeed in the simple faith of church people. Lyell's *Principles of Geology* (1830) and *Vestiges of the Natural History of Creation* (1844) made utter nonsense of the Biblical account of 'creation'. Even more devastating were Darwin's books *The Origin of Species* (1859) and *The Descent of Man* (1871) which proved beyond all reasonable doubt that far from being made in God's own image, man was merely a glorified ape. Or was God but a glorified ape?

If the Church had been slumbering in 1800 it was certainly very wide awake by 1850 and was doing its utmost under new leadership to set its own house in order and meet the criticisms and attacks levelled against it on every side. Convocation, which had been dormant since 1717, was again called into being in the teeth of considerable opposition: the Southern province met in 1854 and the Northern in 1861. After that they continued to meet regularly. Throughout the remainder of the century the Church increased greatly in vigour and vitality, powerfully influencing nearly all aspects of British life and thought.

CATHEDRAL MUSIC

In the earlier part of the century the cathedrals suffered from the pervading neglect and dereliction of duty so general in the Church. Deans and 'residentiaries' were only too often non-residentiary. Thus the Dean of Carlisle was also rector of St. George's, Hanover Square, London, and his Deanery was merely a house where he spent his summer holiday! In ten months the Dean of St. Paul's had not attended on as many days while one of his canons never attended above thirty days in the year. Such men had little interest in their cathedrals and even less in the standard of worship offered in them. Precentors and minor canons were often appointed who had no skill, training or interest in the performance of their musical duties. For example, the Dean and Chapter of Bristol appointed a Precentor who was so hopeless that they had to abandon the choral performance of parts of the service. The position is trenchantly summarised by the Rev. John Jebb, writing in 1843:

As to the dignities, it is notorious that they have been generally bestowed without the slightest reference to the performance of their peculiar duties. Men have been contented to possess the contemptible distinction of holding places of prominent

319

ecclesiastical rank, the names of which have become, through their incompetence, practical falsehoods. They have aided, by their neglect, in fixing a secular sense on the ecclesiastical term 'sinecure', which is far from meaning an exemption from duty, but merely from those which are peculiarly parochial: though indeed, in strictness, every Priest who ministers before God has, during his ministration, the cure of souls. As Canons they have been content to defeat the wills of their founders and do nothing. The name of Precentor, for instance, is often assumed by men utterly ignorant of Choral Music and the ecclesiastical Chant, nay perhaps absolutely hating it, or else considering it as a matter beneath the notice of Dignitaries, or Clergymen, or gentlemen, and are content to delegate to inferior ministers, whom they despise, employments which have been exercised by Prophets and Kings inspired by the Holy Ghost. In like manner there have been Chancellors utterly neglectful or incapable of the functions of scholars or divines. And so of other offices. The result is a system of delegation of the most sacred capitular offices, as in the Cathedral of St. Paul, to Minor Canons, to men who have the responsibility without the authority.[1]

Since senior clergy had no interest whatsoever in cathedral worship and its music they saw little point in wasting money on it. As a consequence choirs were so reduced in size that it became impossible for them to fulfil their proper function. St. Paul's, which at one time had had forty-two choirmen, was now reduced to six. As for conditions at Westminster Abbey, Jebb has given us a vivid description:

The Church of Westminster, though most richly endowed, and so situated as to command every advantage required by so magnificent a foundation, though connected in a peculiar manner with the chief Estates of the Kingdom, as the place of Royal Coronations, the Chapel of the House of Lords, and the frequent scene of the Councils of the Church, though made famous by the gravest religious and historical associations, has long claimed the pre-eminence of setting the most perfect example that perhaps any Collegiate Church in the Realm affords, of coldness, meagreness, and irreverence in the performance of the divine offices. Of the richly endowed Prebendaries, instead of the simultaneous residence of at least four, as required by the ancient regulations, but one at a time usually attended, except during the height of the London season: the Prebends being of course considered as mere sources of revenue to individuals, or as appendages to Parochial incomes. The residences were in many instances alienated to laymen. The Choir, till of late years, wretchedly few in number, were permitted to perform their duties by deputy, and these were discharged in a manner which at best was barely tolerable, without life or energy. The Lessons were commonly read with the same degree of solemnity as the most ordinary document by a clerk in a Court of Law. The service was opened in a manner the most careless: no decent procession was made; and the striking of a wretched clock was the signal for beginning to race through the office: there was a squalid neglect in all the accessories of divine worship; the books were torn and soiled, and the custom of the place apparently enjoined on the Choir boys the use of surplices more black than white. The whole aspect of the Church plainly indicated the mechanical performance of a burthensome duty.[2]

[1] Rev. John Jebb: *The Choral Service of the United Church of England and Ireland*, 1843, p. 63.
[2] Ibid., pp. 130–2.

If this was the state of affairs in the most famous church in the country, things were far worse in some of the provincial cathedrals. It was not uncommon to find choirs with only one man singer (who was presumably expected to sing alto, tenor and bass simultaneously by triple stopping). This accounts for the large number of solo and duet verse anthems produced by Greene, Boyce and others: Sebastian Wesley's popular anthem *Blessed be the God and Father*, composed for Easter Day at Hereford Cathedral, was originally written for boys' voices and one bass singer—the Dean's butler! It also helps to explain why the music of such composers as Attwood and Crotch is so much easier to sing than that of the sixteenth- and seventeenth-century writers.

Choir practices were practically unknown. The repertory was reduced to a mere handful of Services and anthems which were used in rotation (often irrespective of suitability) and as new boys came in they just 'picked up' the treble parts from their seniors. No money was forthcoming for the maintenance of libraries and the addition of new music. Even at the Chapel Royal, Attwood had to dip his hand into his own pocket to pay for the copying of his anthems. Boyce suffered heavy financial loss over his *Cathedral Music* because so few copies were bought. When Samuel Wesley published his Service in F, Exeter was the only cathedral to subscribe to it and the plates were eventually melted down and used for a set of quadrilles. One organist, referring to his Chapter, wrote 'They never spend a pound to purchase music; and if they did, the choir is in such a wretched state, we could not sing it.'

The organists themselves were too often hopelessly incompetent: like the senior clergy, they were appointed for no better reason than that they happened to know the right people. Some of them could scarcely play—much less could they organize, train, control, discipline and inspire a choir. Deputy organists were appointed because of their 'long connection with the cathedral' or their 'unexceptionable character'. Even when a good man was appointed, circumstances were against him:

> Painful and dangerous is the position of a young musician who, after acquiring great knowledge of his art in the Metropolis, joins a country Cathedral. At first he can scarcely believe that the mass of error and inferiority in which he has to participate is habitual and irremediable. He thinks he will reform matters, gently, and without giving offence; but he soon discovers that it is his approbation and not his advice that is needed. The Choir is 'the best in England', (such being the belief at most cathedrals) and, if he give trouble in his attempts at improvement, he would be, by some Chapters, at once voted a person with whom they 'cannot go on smoothly'.[3]

Those who suffered most were the choirboys. Many of them were boarded out with a 'Master' or with clergy or other officials living near the cathedral who, instead of supervising their education and upbringing, ruthlessly exploited them as sweated labour, making them boot-boys, pantry-boys or garden-boys or (worse still) hiring them out to other unscrupulous employers. In all but a few places their treatment seems to have varied between scandalous neglect and brutal ill-treatment. They were given no proper musical training either in singing or in reading music: in any case this last skill was not needed because any intelligent child would rapidly learn by rote the few Services and anthems in use. Much worse, the old Almonry schools had fallen on evil days and offered

[3] Dr. S. S. Wesley: *A Few Words on Cathedral Music*, p. 11 (footnote). Reprinted by Hinrichsen Edition Ltd.

little in the way of schooling; consequently the boys' education was often shamefully neglected and when their voices broke they were still almost illiterate. Thus the only academic teaching that even the Chapel Royal boys received was from a part-time 'Writing Master' who attended from 12.30 till 2.00 p.m. on Wednesdays and Saturdays — a mere three hours per week! Even their general health and cleanliness was often neglected; in some cases they were dressed in rags and set to do the lowest menial chores. We know about child labour in the mines and factories; we scarcely expect to find it in the quiet beauty of an English cathedral close.

Sebastian Wesley, writing in 1849, sums up the position thus: 'No cathedral in this country possesses, at this day, a musical force competent to embody and give effect to the evident intentions of the Church with regard to music.'[4]

REFORMERS OF CATHEDRAL MUSIC

These many and varied abuses in cathedral music stimulated a number of people to attempt to bring about reforms. Of these, five proved to be particularly influential in their work for the improvement of choral foundations and to these five the twentieth century owes an immeasurable debt.

The Rev. Dr. John Jebb (1805–86) undertook a survey of all the choral foundations in England and Ireland, publishing the results in his famous book *The Choral Service of the United Church of England and Ireland, being an enquiry into the Liturgical System of the Cathedral and Collegiate Foundations of the Anglican Communion* (1843). The two extracts already quoted will give a fair idea of its pungency. Such a factual and well-documented report was a damning indictment of cathedral administration. Two years later he published *Three Lectures on the Cathedral Service of the United Church of England and Ireland*, originally delivered in Leeds in 1841. Such an attack from such a source obviously carried great weight and contributed in no small measure to the immense improvements effected later in the century.

Sebastian Wesley, great Samuel's greater son, was a formidable and lifelong fighter for better conditions. The year after Jebb's *Choral Service* appeared, Wesley published a hard-hitting preface to his Service in E for which he was branded as 'a Radical Reformer, a rater of the Clergy, and particularly of the dignitaries of the Church'.[5] In 1849 he followed up this with *A Few Words on Cathedral Music and the Musical System of the Church, with a Plan of Reform*. The 'few words' occupy some ninety pages and include two of his father's motets! He is sometimes belligerent in his castigation of cathedral authorities, sometimes eloquently persuasive (as in his plea for financial provision for composers) and generally well-reasoned in his arguments. The whole pamphlet is an appeal for greater understanding of, and respect for, the music of worship; a severe indictment of the niggardliness of capitular bodies; an insistence on a far higher standard of professional competence from all those appointed to musical posts; and a fairly detailed, though too idealistic, basic 'Plan' which it was hoped cathedrals might adopt as a general standard. The main points of the 'Plan' were:

1. That every choral foundation should provide for at least twelve choirmen at a minimum salary of £85 p.a. Ideally this salary should be raised to £100–£150 so

---

[4] Ibid., p. 5.
[5] *Morning Post*, 26th February, 1844.

that choirmen would not be obliged to supplement their stipends by taking up other employment. These singers should be selected by a panel of three, consisting of the cathedral organist himself assisted by the organists of the two nearest cathedrals.

2. In addition to its twelve professional choirmen, each choir should have three extra men in reserve who could step in in case of illness or other cause; these should be paid a retainer of £52 p.a.

3. In larger towns the voluntary services of enthusiastic and competent amateurs could be enlisted to supplement the professional choir.

4. 'The Cathedral Organist should, in every instance, be a professor of the highest ability' elected by the organists of the seven nearest cathedrals and paid a salary of £500–£800 (higher at Westminster Abbey and St. Paul's). 'It will be said how many Curates there are in the Church at a salary of £60–£80 per annum? But it is not here a question of men standing at the threshold of their professions. The artists pointed to are the *bishops* of their calling — men consecrated by their genius, and set apart for duties which only the best talent of the kind can adequately fulfil.'

5. A College should be founded for the training of cathedral musicians — organists, choirmasters, singers and composers. The expense of maintaining it should be shared amongst all those choral foundations likely to benefit from it.

6. There should be some common fund, administered by a 'Musical Commission' for the management of choirboys, the provision of printed music, and repairs to, or improvements of, organs.

7. Every cathedral should have its own full-time music copyist.

A few years after this the Cathedral Commission sent out a questionnaire to precentors and organists on the subject of cathedral music. This incited Wesley to publish an outspoken *Reply to the Inquiries of the Cathedral Commissioners, relative to the Improvement in the Music of Divine Worship in Cathedrals* (1854). Apart from his published writings his whole life was dedicated to securing improvements in the salary, conditions and status of cathedral organists and singers: he served on various committees and deputations and both in conversation and correspondence the subject was never far from his mind. He had the burning zeal (and the tough hide!) of the true reformer.

While Wesley planned reform from the top — administration, finance, and the status and training of cathedral musicians – Miss Maria Hackett (1783–1874) concerned herself with the humblest musicians in God's temple — the choirboys. Appalled at their treatment and righteously angered by the callous indifference of the senior clergy (who were sometimes the worst culprits) she devoted her time and substance to ameliorating their condition. At first her interest was centred in the boys of St. Paul's Cathedral and she opened her campaign in 1811 with a letter to the Bishop of London, quoting documentary evidence to show how they had been deprived of their rights. The Bishop sent her letter to the Dean — who did nothing. For the next two years she peppered the cathedral authorities with well-documented and logically-argued letters — but to no avail. Then in July 1813 she wrote as follows to the Chancellor (the official most directly responsible):

Rev. Sir. As you have never condescended to take the slightest notice of my representations concerning your neglected charge at St. Paul's, I am at liberty to interpret your total silence into a tacit acknowledgement that the documents respecting the

Cathedral School, which I transmitted to you in the month of September last, continue unanswered, because they cannot be controverted . . .

Her reply to a letter from Dr. Hughes is also worth quoting:

You refer the protection of the Choristers to the 'Residentiary of the day'. There is no Residentiary of the day. In your absence there is seldom anyone to whom an appeal can be made . . .[6]

Still getting no satisfaction she published in 1816 a mass of documentary evidence in support of her claims on behalf of the boys, to be followed many years later by her *Correspondence and Evidences respecting the Ancient Collegiate School attached to St. Paul's Cathedral* (1811–32). By now her interests had widened to include all choristers in choral foundations and she visited every cathedral in England and Wales to see conditions for herself. Her findings were published in her *Brief Account of Cathedral and Collegiate Schools* (1827), a scholarly work full of accurate and detailed factual information. A copy was sent to all the authorities concerned and many must have squirmed as they read it. She was an indefatigable correspondent and wherever she saw evils and abuses she addressed letter after letter not just to one but to all the officials concerned. Most of her letters were ignored: when finally someone was stung into replying, the reply was usually evasive. But this resourceful lady was not easily deterred and her letters would continue to pour forth, becoming increasingly insistent until the matter was righted. After her first fact-finding survey of the cathedrals it became her custom to visit them all again at least once every three years to keep a watchful eye on the choristers' welfare. Wherever she went she distributed a book, a purse and a new shilling to every boy, and their names were carefully recorded in her diary. She maintained these annual visitations for well over fifty years and had the joy of seeing her work bear abundant fruit in the vastly improved conditions and better education enjoyed by 'her dear children'. Her life's work was most gloriously crowned when, at the age of ninety, she was shown over a splendid new St. Paul's Choir School in Carter Lane. How richly she deserved her title 'The Choristers' Friend'.

The Rev. Sir Frederick Arthur Gore Ouseley shared the concern of Jebb, Wesley and others about the parlous state of the choral foundations. Being a man of considerable wealth he decided to make a unique contribution to the cause of English cathedral music by founding an entirely new choral foundation. This was the famous College of St. Michael at Tenbury, Worcestershire, which was completed in 1856. Its Statutes, modelled on those of the old Collegiate churches, made provision for a Warden; four resident Fellows, from whom should be chosen a Subwarden, a Precentor and a Librarian; a Headmaster, an Assistant Master, a Choirmaster, an Organist (junior to the Choirmaster) and a Bursar, any one of whom could be a resident Fellow; up to twenty non-resident Fellows; three Lay-Clerks (who would have been augmented by some of the other officers); a Sacristan; ten Choristers and ten Probationers. John Jebb was made one of the original Fellows. A parochial district was assigned and Ouseley endowed the living as well as the College. St. Michael's was the first choral foundation to be established since the Reformation. It had an unusually full complement of staff and singers and in

[6] These extracts are quoted from Sir Sidney Nicholson: *In Quires and Places where they Sing*, pp. 52–3. (S.P.C.K.)

many ways gave practical expression to Wesley's 'Plan'. It was intended to serve as a model to the whole Church in the efficient rendering of daily choral services, in the selection of a truly representative repertoire of the best sacred music, and in the well-ordered education of choirboys under ideal conditions. Its very existence challenged the slackness everywhere else. By a further act of munificence Ouseley bequeathed to St. Michael's the large and priceless library of manuscripts and early and rare printed editions he had amassed during his lifetime — said to be the most valuable and extensive private music library in England. Ouseley's great foundation still flourishes and his life is perpetuated in its fine school, its magnificent library, and the excellence of its daily choral services. Its Statutes were revised in 1921, 1927 and 1957; there are now seven Lay-Clerks and the school has been expanded to take seventy boys, of whom eighteen are on the Choral Foundation.

Sir John Stainer is generally thought of in these days as an inferior composer. It is a pity that he should be remembered more for the one thing he did badly than for the many things he did well. Thus, for his time he was an enlightened and accomplished scholar and musicologist whose work even now has some value. He was also a first-class choir trainer and organiser of cathedral music. A year after St. Michael's College, Tenbury, first opened in 1856, Stainer (then only sixteen) was selected by Ouseley to be its organist (the first organist, Hanbury, appears to have held office for only a few months) and he seems to have drawn lifelong inspiration from the vision of the older man. Various other appointments followed and in 1872 he became organist of St. Paul's Cathedral where he found conditions still far from satisfactory, even allowing for all the improvements brought about by Miss Hackett's campaign over the years. By his own skill, personality and tact, inspired perhaps by Ouseley's vision, and with the whole-hearted backing and support of an enlightened Dean, he completely reorganized the musical life of the cathedral, raising the standard of the choir until it was generally held to be the finest in England. He was also largely responsible for reintroducing at St. Paul's Cathedral the choral celebration of Holy Communion and insisting on a high standard for its proper rendering. Finally, Stainer attached great importance to the careful education and thorough training of the choristers and was instrumental in making St. Paul's Choir School a model for all other cathedral choir schools in the country — much to the delight of Miss Hackett.

As a result of the selfless labours of these and other pioneers and reformers, there was a vast improvement in all aspects of cathedral music in the last quarter of the century. This, in turn, prepared the way for the remarkable revival of English church music in the present century.

MUSIC IN THE PARISH CHURCHES

The beginning of the nineteenth century also found parish church music still at a very low ebb. Practice varied. In some churches the prose psalms, canticles and responses continued to be recited as a dialogue between parson and parish clerk but most churches managed to raise some sort of a 'choir'. In country churches the choir consisted then, as now, of voluntary singers though contemporary accounts suggest that their standard was often deplorably low: all too often congregations were held to ransom by autocratic and insufferably conceited yokels who bawled with raucous voices. In many churches, especially in towns, the choir consisted of, or was augmented by, the 'charity' children or the parish school children who were marched to and from all services. Their 'compulsory scream' provoked Jebb as usual to dip his pen in acid: 'Our parish system has been to compel all our children to sing, and that at the very top of their voices without the slightest regard to the antiphonal system, in such numbers effectually to drown such of the congregation as attempt to throw in a harmony . . . during the whole Sunday they are on drill; and they are considered not as the children of Christian parents, and as members of families, but as No. 1, 2, or 3, in such a Class in the School . . . When do we see the child of a poor person kneeling by her mother's side at Church?'[7]

There were still a few churches left where the custom of singing unaccompanied survived, pitch being set by a pitch-pipe, but by now most English churches (though not Scottish or Welsh) aspired to some kind of instrumental support. Most of the larger town churches had acquired a keyboard-organ and where a reasonably proficient player was available it had become customary to have a long voluntary before the first lesson in addition to those before and after the service; organ interludes were also introduced elsewhere in the service, sometimes between the verses of the metrical psalms. But such glories as a keyboard organ and someone who could play it were only for the more favoured parishes; humbler churches had to be content with a barrel-organ or the more usual band of 'musickers'. The organ, barrel-organ or band was still generally situated in a west gallery with the singers grouped around it. The congregation took little part in the singing: in many churches they remained completely silent throughout; at best they could hope to join only in the metrical psalms.

Here and there individual clergy and musicians aimed for something better. A few better-balanced and more competent choirs began to appear and more churches installed organs. As early as the eighteenth century the practice grew of singing the Canticles and sometimes even the prose psalms to Anglican chants, especially it seems in Yorkshire and the north Midlands, while more ambitious choirs introduced anthems after the third collect. In the early years of the nineteenth century more churches adopted this 'cathedral' type of service and at Leeds a surpliced choir of six boys and six men (apparently the first surpliced choir in a parish church) was introduced as early as 1818: they chanted both Canticles and psalms. (This, be it noted, was fifteen years before the beginning of the Oxford Movement.) Similar robed choirs were formed independently within the next few years at St. John's Church, Donaghmore, Limerick and St. James's Church, Ryde, Isle of Wight. Reform was in the air.

Yet these were isolated efforts: elsewhere the general picture remained depressing. Slow, dismal psalm-tunes in cold dingy churches had little to offer those victims of the industrial revolution who worked long hours under appalling conditions in mines, mills and factories and lived in drab depressing slums. In fact after three centuries of metrical psalms and nearly two centuries of the gallery musicians the Church had had more than enough: large-scale changes were inevitable, indeed long overdue, and were therefore the more likely to be drastic and rapid when they did come. All that remained to be seen was how they were to be brought about and what form they would take. In the event, the instrument which largely effected and directed the course of these changes was the Oxford Movement and there is no doubt that much of its impact and success derived from the fact that the time was ripe for it.

At first the Oxford Movement was not concerned with matters of ritual and ceremonial.

[7] Rev. John Jebb: *The Choral Service of the United Church of England and Ireland* (Parker, London, 1843), pp. 302, 303.

Soon, however, it gave rise to a new church party, the 'Ritualists' or 'Anglo-Catholics', who scandalized the country by introducing vestments and customs which everyone, thought the Reformation had swept away for ever. The outward and visible manifestations of Ritualism have been admirably summarized by Dr. Alec Vidler: 'altar lights, vestments, wafer bread, the mixed chalice (mixing a little water with the wine at the communion), making the sign of the cross, incense, genuflexions, preaching in a surplice instead of a black gown, surpliced choirs, much singing and chanting, the use of holy water, fixed stone altars instead of moveable wooden ones, crucifixes and statues, cultus of the Virgin Mary and Saints, reservation and adoration of the eucharistic sacrament, and auricular confession. Some of these things, for example surpliced choirs, were eventually adopted almost universally in the Church of England, but most of them continued to be peculiar marks of Anglo-Catholicism.'[8]

To many people brought up in the dreary traditions of early nineteenth-century worship so much colour and spectacle was a revelation and the new forms of worship rapidly grew in popularity, especially in industrial areas, in spite of fierce opposition from most of the bishops and entrenched clergy. However, the bishops were rendered almost powerless because the Ritualists were most careful to justify their actions by claiming that, far from introducing new ideas, they were merely restoring the ancient practices of the Church and fulfilling the clear intentions of the early Reformers as enshrined in the vague and contentious 'Ornaments Rubric' at the beginning of The Book of Common Prayer.

If we accept that one of the chief practical results of the Oxford Movement was a renewed interest in the Prayer Book services and a genuine zeal to perform them more conscientiously and reverently, then its effect on church music was to give rise to two opposed schools of thought — (a) those who wanted to restore to the congregation its full right of active participation in worship and especially in singing the responses, psalms and canticles; and (b) those who believed that parish churches should aim to achieve something of the glory of cathedral worship in which a highly trained choir offers music on behalf of the congregation. The situation was further bedevilled because church politics became involved, the high churchmen or 'Ritualists' favouring congregational participation while more moderate churchmen tended to favour the cathedral ideal.

The first group were quick to discover that it is extremely difficult if not impossible for a congregation to sing psalms effectively to Anglican chants, an art which demands much rehearsal and hard work: (many modern churchmen still delude themselves about this). Instead, partly from practical considerations and partly from their desire to establish links with the pre-Reformation Church, they sought to introduce the ancient Gregorian psalm-tones, the theory being that since the tones were unisonal whereas Anglican chants were in harmony, the tones must be easier to sing. Indeed, except in anthems, the Ritualists favoured unison singing throughout.

Perhaps the earliest of the pioneers in this field was Frederick Oakeley; indeed, in his authoritative book on this period[9] Bernarr Rainbow goes so far as to declare that the great revival in church music began in 1839 with Oakeley's appointment to the Margaret Chapel, London (later rebuilt as All Saints, Margaret Street) which, during his incumbency, became the mainspring of Tractarian worship in London. Another pioneer was Walter Kerr Hamilton of St. Peter's-in-the-East, Oxford, who, with his organist

[8] Dr. Alec Vidler: *The Church in an Age of Revolution*, pp. 157, 158. (Pelican.)
[9] Bernarr Rainbow: *The Choral Revival in the Anglican Church 1839–1872*. (Barrie & Jenkins, 1970).

Alexander Reinagle, produced in 1840 a *Collection of Psalm and Hymn Tunes* which included the first published set of Gregorian psalm-tones arranged for the Prayer Book psalms. Thomas Helmore at St. Mark's College, Chelsea, is especially associated with the Gregorian movement. In 1849 he published his famous *Psalter Noted* in which the musical setting of every psalm to its appropriate tone was printed in full, the words under the notes; with additions it was re-issued the following year as *A Manual of Plainsong* and this, considerably revised and modified, is still in regular use. Thomas Helmore's younger brother Frederick became the most famous church choirmaster in the country; he travelled widely forming choirs and coaching them intensively for a month or two, often in small villages like East Farleigh and Harrietsham in Kent and Ellingham and Bellingham in Northumberland as well as in many towns. He was even summoned by the Prince Consort to form choirs at Buckingham Palace and in the domestic chapel at Windsor Castle. He had remarkable facility in producing silk purses from sows' ears and he appears to have created astonishingly accomplished choirs from the most unlikely material. Other influential high churchmen were W. J. E. Bennett (St. Paul's Church, Knightsbridge, and later St. Barnabas', Pimlico) and William Dodsworth (Christ Church, Albany Street).

Robert Druitt, a medical doctor with Tractarian sympathies, published a pamphlet *Popular Tract on Church Music, with Remarks on its Moral and Political Importance* (1845). The next year, in association with three London incumbents — W. J. E. Bennett, W. Watts (Christ Church, Endell Street) and T. M. Fallow (St. Andrew's, Wells Street) — he formed a Society for Promoting Church Music, an early forerunner of the Royal School of Church Music. Its most important achievement was to produce a monthly journal *The Parish Choir* which ran from February 1846 to March 1851. It was dedicated to raising the standards of church music and choirs. Though fairly short-lived, this periodical was immensely influential; furthermore, its monthly music supplements also provided a comprehensive and inexpensive library of well-written simple music. It is notable, however, that on practical grounds *The Parish Choir* departed from the strict Tractarian line by advocating Anglican chanting in preference to Gregorian tones.

Another reason why 1839 was a significant year in the context of church music reform was that three Trinity undergraduates, Benjamin Webb, Alexander Hope and John Mason Neale, founded the Cambridge Camden Society. Though concerned at first with the architecture and fabric of church buildings, this well-supported and highly influential Society later came to include church music within its purview, declaring its unqualified enthusiasm and support for Thomas Helmore's advocacy of Gregorian chanting. A ripening friendship between Helmore and Neale led to their joint publication of *The Hymnal Noted* in which Neale's English translations of ancient Latin hymns were adapted by Helmore to their original Sarum melodies: the first part appeared in 1852, the second part in 1854.

Turning now from those who insisted upon congregational participation to those broad churchmen who frowned upon it, the movement to introduce cathedral-type worship into parish churches had its origins at Leeds Parish Church where in 1841 the vicar, Dr. Walter Hook, sought and followed Jebb's advice on what policy he should adopt regarding the music in his newly-built church. The outcome was the institution of a cathedral-type fully choral service sung by a re-established professional choir of men and boys, robed and seated in choir stalls facing each other. By the end of that year Hook had engaged England's most distinguished church musician, Samuel Sebastian Wesley, to be his organist at a guaranteed salary of £200 per annum for ten years (a handsome salary in those days). Sir Frederick Gore Ouseley was another who thought that the congregation ought to find spiritual refreshment and inspiration in just listening to the richness and beauty of a well-rendered choral service, neither expecting nor wishing to take an active part in it; he particularly loathed plainsong and Gregorian tones — which must to him have seemed very plain and bare. His great choral foundation at St. Michael's College, Tenbury, showed his determination to ensure that there should be at any rate one parish church in the land where daily choral services sung by a first-class professional choir should be maintained in perpetuity. Other influential musicians who shared the views of Jebb, S. S. Wesley and Ouseley included Edward J. Hopkins at the Temple Church, John Hullah (whose highly successful system of musical education revolutionized amateur music-making and vastly increased the technical competence of church choir members), Henry Smart (St. Luke's, Old Street) and George Macfarren.

Of these two schools of thought the second — the cathedral ideal — met with far greater success. Perhaps the reason for this was that the parish churches had no continuing musical tradition except for the dreary metrical psalms and they therefore had to find one. Their one and only ancient precedent — plainsong — was so strange, so remote and (to Victorian thinking) so stark that it appealed only to the intelligentsia. It had no point of contact with workers in mines and factories nor indeed with the large majority of worshippers; to them it was an exotic culture as unreal and unnatural as something from outer space. They vastly preferred the emotional tunefulness or vulgar robustness of Victorian hymns which at this time were rapidly growing in popularity. Furthermore, in practice it was found that singing prose psalms in English to Gregorian tones was just as difficult for congregations as Anglican chanting and, save in those few places where the congregation could be thoroughly rehearsed (as in schools and colleges), their contribution remained hesitant and half-hearted. The main justification for using Gregorians therefore proved a myth. Apart from some extreme Anglo-Catholic churches which insisted on retaining Gregorians more or less as a political banner, Gregorian singing has never really caught on in Britain. It is particularly sad that the plainsong movement should have acquired a political label because many churches whose worship could be greatly enriched by the introduction of some of the more beautiful office hymns, and even occasional psalm-tones, are thereby deterred.

The parish churches had therefore to seek elsewhere for some musical roots. Perhaps it was because cathedral music had retained its links with the past and presented a fairly continuous tradition that parishes began to look to cathedrals for their model. With the shining example of Frederick Helmore's splendid country choirs before them and the work being done at Leeds, there was a rush to introduce surpliced choirs and to clutter chancels with organs and cumbersome choirstalls. Anglican chanting, anthems and even Service settings were introduced. Because the need for change had for so long been kept in check and was now so insistent, the new ideas spread rapidly so that within a few years nearly every parish church in the land had its organ and surpliced choir. The rule of the gallery minstrels was at an end and ultimately many of the galleries themselves followed the minstrels into dust.

As hundreds of choirs sprang into being all over the country there arose a tremendous demand for music for them to sing. Up to this time printed music had been bulky to handle and costly to buy. Such a lavish production as Boyce's *Cathedral Music* was cumbersome to use and so expensive that comparatively few sets were sold — not enough to cover the costs of production. Arnold's collection was even more massive. Most organists solved the problem by making pirate manuscript copies of what they wanted (they still do!)—hence Wesley's insistence that every cathedral should have its own copyist; but for parish churches amateur copying was often inaccurate and professional copying too expensive. There was a crying need for cheap printed music in a handy format. Recognising this need, Alfred Novello, son of the founder (Vincent Novello) of the famous publishing house, began in 1846 printing music in the well-known 'Octavo Edition' at a price within reach of every choir. This was made possible by the invention of cheaper methods of paper-making, improved presses for music printing and the likelihood of vastly increased sales. Thus Handel's *Messiah*, which had previously cost two guineas, was issued at first (1846) in twelve sixpenny parts. By 1854 it was available complete at four shillings while a pocket-sized edition cost only one-and-fourpence. Many short choral pieces were issued for as little as a penny per copy.

Even had parish choirs been able to afford such important collections as Boyce and Arnold they would have found most of the music far too difficult to sing. The specialized technique required for singing freely-barred and cross-accented renaissance music was a lost art and in any case far beyond their capabilities while most baroque and Restoration works were much too lengthy and demanded first-rate solo singers. Only the simplest pieces, like those by Attwood and Crotch, were within their powers and of these there was nothing like sufficient to meet the growing demand. In any case most parish choirs wanted something 'tuneful' with a simple and obvious metrical beat, preferably in triple time. Here then were choirs clamouring for easy music, and here the presses waiting to print it: all that was needed was the music itself. Nature abhors a vacuum and soon everyone who could put pen to paper was busy churning out ear-tickling pieces for little choirs. The hallmarks of this music were banality, *naïveté*, mawkish sentimentalism and, only too often, technical incompetence: the Spohr of *As pants the hart* and the Gounod of *Nazareth* were taken as models though the copies never achieved such dizzy heights as the originals. 'There has probably been no form of any art in the history of the world which has been so over-run by the unqualified amateur as English Church music from about 1860 to about 1900. Many of our professional musicians at this time stood also at a low level of culture and intelligence and were quite content to flow with the stream so that our Service books, and still more our Hymn books, were filled with dilutions of Mendelssohn, reminiscences of Spohr and, worse than either, direct imitations of Gounod: as incongruous with the splendour of our Authorized Version and of our Book of Common Prayer as were some of the stained glass windows of the period with the strength and dignity of our Church architecture. This music was deplorably easy to write, it required little or no skill in performance, it passed by mere use and wont into the hearts of the congregation, it became a habit like any other, and it is only during comparatively recent years that any serious attempts have been made towards eradicating it.'[10] (These attempts have not been altogether successful. Even now, half a century after Hadow's lecture, much of this music is still to be heard in parish churches up and down the country and even more in nonconformist chapels. Within a few miles of where this is being written a parish choir still sings pieces by Caleb Simper—one of the worst of the group!) Perhaps Joseph Barnby (1838–96) was Gounod's most faithful disciple; Dykes, Sullivan, Maunder and, at times, Stainer wrote much that was as bad. Yet in spite of frivolous melodies, juicy harmonies, jog-trot rhythms and lamentable taste, in

[10] Sir W. H. Hadow: *Church Music*, pp. 23–5. (Longmans, Green, 1926.)

spite of a second-hand quasi-operatic style, brass band type accompaniments and a strong whiff of parlour balladry, this music usually avoided the most heinous fault of all—that sheer stultifying dullness which so often blighted eighteenth-century church music, especially the Service settings.

The repertory was still further enlarged by extracting movements from the large-scale sacred works of continental masters and singing them as anthems. Handel's *Messiah*, had of course, long been plundered in this way but now Mendelssohn's oratorios and Bach's cantatas were found to yield a number of attractive anthems, some very simple, others of greater degrees of difficulty. Excerpts from Haydn and Berlioz appeared. Less healthy was the admission of movements from the oratorios of Spohr and Gounod. More worthily, motets by foreign composers like Palestrina, Lassus, Victoria, Eccard, and King John of Portugal were provided with English words and used as anthems.

What most needs to be emphasized in all this is that the revival of choral music in the Anglican Church during the second third of the nineteenth century was essentially a parish church movement—as was the reintroduction of choral celebrations of the Holy Communion. The cathedrals seemingly would have slumbered on for ever and they resented and resisted the reforms going on around them. It was only because they were lashed by the reformers, harried by public protest (especially in the national press as well as in specialised journals like *The Parish Choir*), and put utterly to shame by the parishes, that they finally capitulated and made some attempt to improve matters. A lead was given to cathedral reform when William Kerr Hamilton, formerly of St. Peter's-in-the-East, Oxford, was appointed to Salisbury Cathedral as a minor canon in 1841 and soon afterwards became Precentor: thirteen years later he was consecrated Bishop of Salisbury. Here this ardent reformer was able to exert a wide and beneficent influence. Other cathedrals slowly came into line.

However, the general picture throughout the country was of a growing understanding of the value of music in worship, an enormous increase in the numbers of choirs and organs, the provision of robes, choir stalls and better facilities, revolutionary advances in the organisation and training of choirs and a truly phenomenal improvement in their competence and discipline. The tide had begun to flow and nothing could stop it. Whereas in the 1840s the introduction of a surpliced choir frequently met with fierce hostility, cries of 'No Popery!' and even rioting, by the 1870s the position was reversed and incumbents of churches without an adequate choir found themselves under pressure from their congregations to form one. It was a sad irony that this astonishing rise in the number and standard of choirs should have been offset by a corresponding fall in the quality of what they sang.

There was one other direction in which parish churches set the pace, the cathedrals dragging far behind: this was in the growth and development of hymn-singing, a subject which merits a section to itself.

THE GROWTH OF HYMNODY

We have seen that during the eighteenth century a determined battle raged between Psalmody and Hymnody. The evangelicals, perhaps the only lively party in the Church, favoured the use of hymns largely because hymns were subjective and personal. The traditionalists and some high churchmen still clung tenaciously to their metrical psalms ('God's own word as set forth in Holy Scripture') because psalms were considered impersonal and universal: to them hymns were suspect because of their strong evangelical and Methodist associations. Yet new hymns appeared in great numbers and some of them were so good, so eminently singable, so easily memorized, so popular, so varied and wide-ranging, that the metrical psalms steadily lost ground. The final triumph of hymnody was foreshadowed by the publication in 1827 of the first real modern hymnbook arranged for the Church's year, a book which came not from an evangelical but from a high churchman. This was Bishop Heber's *Hymns written and adapted to the Weekly Church Service of the Year*. Though the absence of tunes militated against its popular success, this splendid and truly 'literary' collection did much to overcome traditionalist opposition.

It was the Oxford Movement that eventually broke down the prejudice against hymns. We have emphasized that the Tractarians took their stand on Catholic antiquity. The more deeply they delved into early liturgical forms the more ancient and universal they found the practice of hymn-singing to be. This put an entirely different complexion on matters and what before was frowned upon for being an evangelical innovation now became accepted as an integral part of worship, yet there was one fundamental difference between the ancient Catholic hymns and the modern hymns of English evangelicals: whereas the latter tended to be an expression of personal experience and devotion, the former were essentially liturgical, i.e. concerned with doctrine and worship — the voice 'not of the individual believer but of the worshipping Church'.[11]

So the Anglo-Catholic party began to develop its own hymnody which was derived mainly from two sources: first, translations into English of the old Catholic hymns; secondly, the production of new hymns similar in subject matter, thought and expression to the old. The translators included Isaac Williams (whose best-known translation is 'Disposer supreme'), John Chandler ('On Jordan's bank', 'Conquering kings', 'In stature grows', 'As now the sun's declining rays' and 'Christ is our corner-stone), Richard Mant, John Henry Newman, Frederick Oakeley ('O come, all ye faithful'), W. J. Copeland, Edward Caswall ('Hark! a thrilling voice', 'My God, I love thee', 'Bethlehem of noblest cities', 'All ye who seek' and 'Jesu, the very thought') and Robert Campbell ('Ye choirs of new Jerusalem' and 'At the Lamb's high feast we sing'). Some of these men also composed original hymns which have since won an abiding place in the hymnbooks of many Christian denominations; we may mention 'Be thou my guardian' (Williams), 'Bright the vision' and 'For all thy saints, O Lord' (Mant), 'Lead, kindly light' and 'Praise to the holiest' (Newman), and 'They come, God's messengers of love' (Campbell).

It was that greatest of all translators, John Mason Neale (1818–66), who in 1849 pointed out that the work of his predecessors in this field was open to three serious objections:

(a) they had not, in fact, gone back to the truly ancient hymns of the Church (which were virtually inaccessible) but had been content to draw upon the seventeenth- and eighteenth-century neo-Gallican breviaries, especially the Parisian Breviary of 1680;

(b) they had made no attempt to reproduce the varied and unusual metres of their originals;

(c) even worse, their work showed 'great carelessness, haste and slovenliness'.

[11] L. F. Benson: *The English Hymn*, p. 498 (1915).

Whereupon this great scholar-poet published his *Hymnal Noted* (1852, 1854) which included ninety-four of his own translations of Latin hymns used in England in the Middle Ages, set to their original plainsong melodies. This uncompromising book, reflecting Neale's extraordinarily mediæval cast of mind, would have frightened off all but the most determined Anglo-Catholics and there would have been few organists and choirs capable of reading and understanding the plainsong notation in which these ancient melodies were printed.

Neale was the first to make English versions of some of the great Sequences and these appeared in *Mediæval Hymns and Sequences* (1851): he also issued other collections of Latin hymns and translations. Some idea of our indebtedness to him can be formed by recalling that his translations from the Latin included 'Ye choirs of new Jerusalem', 'Jerusalem the golden', 'Blessed City, heavenly Salem', 'Light's abode, celestial Salem', 'Jesu!—the very thought is sweet', 'O what their joy', 'The royal banners', and 'All glory, laud and honour'. But his work went far beyond this. In 1862 he published *Hymns of the Eastern Church* translated from, or adapted from, or even inspired by, ancient Greek hymns: to this source we owe 'Stars of the morning', 'The day is past and over', 'Come ye faithful, raise the strain', 'Christian, dost thou see them' and 'A great and mighty wonder'. The quality of his work varies: his translations are always extremely accurate and sensitive while his versification is usually smooth and easy (he had an almost phenomenal flair for rhyming). He can sometimes lapse into banal and even ridiculous phraseology from which a sense of humour would have saved him, but at best he reaches such heights of poetic expression that the translation becomes a far greater work of art than its Latin or Greek original. Neale also wrote a number of original hymns of which we may mention 'Around the throne of God a band', 'Art thou weary', and 'O happy band of pilgrims'.

In addition to the translators there were those who wrote original hymns from an Anglo-Catholic viewpoint. The best known of Keble's hymns are not really hymns at all but are stanzas detached, often violently, from poems in his devotional work *The Christian Year* — 'New every morning', 'Sun of my soul', 'Blest are the pure in heart', and 'When God of old'. F. W. Faber's hymns included 'My God, how wonderful thou art' and from Henry Collins came 'Jesu, meek and lowly' and 'Jesu, my Lord, my God, my All'.

Now that the High Church party had at last been won over to hymn-singing, from about 1850 onwards new hymnbooks sprang up like flowers in May. Since most of these combined ancient Catholic hymns with the more recent ones, these books merely competed against one another. The stage was reached when it was feared that there would be almost as many different books as there were churches.

Nor were the Evangelicals idle; the broad river of Protestant hymnody flowed on in the works of H. F. Lyte ('God of mercy, God of grace', 'When at thy footstool', 'Abide with me' and 'Praise, my soul, the King of Heaven'); Robert Grant ('O worship the King'), Henry Alford ('Come, ye thankful people, come' and 'Ten thousand times ten thousand') and the ladies, Harriet Auber ('Our blest Redeemer') and Charlotte Elliott ('Just as I am' and 'Christian, seek not yet repose'). Here again there was a plethora of books to choose from and by 1872 high and low churches between them accounted for no less than 269 different hymnals then in use in a sample section of 355 rural deaneries in the Province of Canterbury alone.[12]

[12] W. K. Lowther Clarke: *A Hundred Years of Hymns Ancient and Modern*, p. 58. (William Clowes.)

What was wanted more than anything else at this juncture was one really good standard hymnbook, combining the best of all worlds and accepted by the majority of churches. The first move towards this came from the Anglo-Catholic side. F. H. Murray, Rector of Chislehurst, initiated the idea in 1857 and with the help of others of like mind formed a committee which first met in 1859. The Secretary of the Committee was the Rev. Sir Henry W. Baker, Vicar of Monkland, Herefordshire. As a result of its deliberations and greatly helped by the practical goodwill and generosity of various hymnbook compilers and proprietors, a new book containing 273 hymns was evolved. It followed the scheme first used by Bishop Heber in his 1827 collection by providing each Sunday and the principal Holy Days, festivals and seasons with appropriate hymns based on the theme of the day as given by Epistle or Gospel and set out in the order of the Church's year. The musical editor was Dr. W. H. Monk and he it was who suggested the admirable title 'Hymns Ancient and Modern'. The new book first appeared in its complete form with tunes in 1861. Though Anglo-Catholic in origin and a typical product of the Oxford Movement, *Hymns Ancient and Modern* was destined to become by far the most popular and universal of all Anglican hymnbooks — 'nothing less than a national institution'.[13] So immensely successful was it that by 1868 no less than four and a half million copies had been sold. The supplement of 1868 added 113 hymns and in the Revised Edition of 1875 the total had grown to 473. In 1889 a further supplement was added to the Revised Edition and by the end of 1890 this 1889 version had already sold three and a half million copies. By now it had become remarkably comprehensive and included hymns of all periods from many different countries.

Because at its inception *Hymns Ancient and Modern* was essentially the book of the Anglo-Catholic party, Evangelical hymnody tended to crystallize into two other books — Bickersteth's *Hymnal Companion to the Book of Common Prayer* (1870) and the S.P.C.K.'s *Church Hymns* (1871). As the three books grew in popularity most other hymnals fell into desuetude though, as we have seen, at least 269 different books were still in use as late as 1872.

THE ORGAN

At the beginning of the nineteenth century English organs were very small and poorly equipped compared with continental instruments and even at this late stage very few had independent pedal organs — or even pedals. In fact the introduction of pedal organs in England was a saga of almost incredible obstinacy and stupidity. Pedals are known to have been in use on the continent in 1365 and independent pedal organs existed in 1455,[14] yet the first known pedal board in England was built at St. Mary Redcliffe, Bristol, in 1726, consisting of one octave of pull-downs with possibly an octave coupler, though the builder, John Harris, had previously worked on large continental pedal organs. St. Mary Redcliffe's strong claim to have had the first organ pedals in England can, perhaps, be challenged by St. Paul's Cathedral which may have had pedals six years earlier. But it was one thing for enterprising builders to introduce pedals and a few venturesome organists to play on them; it was quite another for pedal organs to be adopted universally as a normal department of the instrument. They met with fierce and entrenched opposition. By 1810 only two out of thirty-three cathedrals possessed

[13] Erik Routley: *The Music of Christian Hymnody*, p. 119. (Independent Press.)
[14] See p. 62.

any separate pedal pipes. At the Exhibition of 1851 Sir George Smart, who had played for two coronations, was invited to play upon an organ with pedals; 'I never in my life played upon a gridiron' was his withering reply. In 1860 the organist of Lichfield Cathedral, Samuel Spofforth, opposed the introduction of a fine pedal organ of ten stops and refused to use it when installed; Sir John Goss, organist of St. Paul's Cathedral until 1880, exhorted another organist to 'Charm with your fingers, not your feet'; and as late as 1884 Canterbury Cathedral had only one octave of short pedals. Nevertheless, despite this ostrich-like attitude, pedal organs became general during the latter half of the century, due largely to the influence of 'Father' Henry Willis's work, especially his instruments for the 1851 Exhibition and for St. George's Hall, Liverpool.

We have seen that the awakening of interest in parish church music in the middle of the century resulted in the establishment of robed chancel choirs and a tendency, encouraged by Jebb and others, to ape the cathedral-type service. This meant the erection of an organ as near as possible to the choir. In churches which already possessed organs, they 'were moved eastwards to accompany the newly robed choirs and were re-erected, often considerably enlarged, in chancels or side-chapels never designed to hold them. The results were often tonally and architecturally deplorable.'[15] Churches without organs felt called upon to keep up with the Joneses and large sums of money were raised to build oversize organs of poor quality in unsuitable positions. A further stimulus to organ building was provided by the 1851 Exhibition when fourteen instruments were erected in the Crystal Palace. Here Willis displayed a quite remarkable instrument of three manuals, seventy speaking stops and seven couplers, with pneumatic action and the world's first thumb pistons (also pneumatic). This instrument was destined to have immense influence on English organ building for the rest of the century: (some of its pipework is still to be heard incorporated into Winchester Cathedral organ).

Willis followed up his success at the 1851 Exhibition by building what has come to be regarded as the first 'modern' British organ—the large instrument of 100 speaking stops built in 1855 at St. George's Hall, Liverpool, later to be made world famous by the recitals of W. T. Best. For this instrument Dr. S. S. Wesley (the consultant) and Henry Willis devised the radiating and concave pedal board which has now become standard in Britain and Italy. It had also a modern console with inclined stop-jambs, pneumatic stop mechanism, pneumatic thumb pistons and composition pedals (including general pistons), and pneumatic lever action to all departments, couplers and swell pedal. Of course both these Willis organs had an independent pedal department.

From now onwards the organ became a very popular instrument both in church and concert hall. In days when there was neither radio nor gramophone and when most municipal orchestras were content to play tea-shop music, it was the organists who familiarized the public with great orchestral and operatic works by means of their transcriptions. W. T. Best alone published immense numbers of arrangements and there is little doubt that could he have lived long enough he would have cheerfully reduced every orchestral work ever written to an organ arrangement. Not only were orchestral works transcribed but so were operatic airs, instrumental pieces and popular ballads. Furthermore enormous quantities of original organ music poured from the presses and since, like the anthems, it was written to meet a sudden popular demand, most of it, again like the anthems, was of fifth-rate quality. So far as this music had any positive qualities at all it was 'romantic' in conception and since nearly all the orchestral and

[15] Cecil Clutton and Austin Niland: *The British Organ*, p. 155. (Batsford, 1963.)

operatic works transcribed were also of the romantic era it is not surprising that the organ developed as an essentially romantic instrument with the emphasis on stops which imitated orchestral instruments and effects—a sort of one-man band. This conception, fundamentally opposed to the very nature of the instrument, lasted for about a century (roughly from 1851 to 1954, the date of the opening of the Royal Festival Hall organ in London), and was developed by such builders as Schultze, Willis, Walker, Thynne, Hope-Jones and Arthur Harrison.

In very general terms the characteristics of the English romantic organ might be summarized as follows. First, the manuals were designed for contrast of tone and volume rather than for balance: whereas on the old baroque organs all the stops (except chorus mixtures) were of similar power and it was therefore easy to balance two manuals, now the swell flue chorus was considerably softer than that of the great; similarly the choir was often a miniature great. Secondly, the English favoured a thick muzzy mash of tone which showed itself in the large number of 8ft stops in large organs, especially powerful diapasons, most of them duplicating or obliterating each other, many of them having neither character nor definition. Feeble flute mutations and screaming mixtures produced quite different effects from the sparkle and sheen of continental organs. Even English reeds were often thick and tubby compared with their continental counterparts. The pedal organ was the most unsatisfactory department of all. In small organs one stop was usually made to suffice—a soft and muzzy 'bourdon' so devoid of definition that a manual had to be coupled to it to give it any musical significance. In larger instruments there were far too many fluffy-toned 16ft stops duplicating or cancelling each other out; worst of all were the large booming 'open woods' which utterly swamped the lower half of the manuals. Yet in spite of a superabundance of 16ft stops, pedal organs were hopelessly deficient in 2fts, light mixtures and even light 4fts to give edge and clarity. These faults are still very much with us. To make confusion worse confounded, instead of using separate manuals to give contrast, players almost invariably couple them together (so increasing the 8ft duplication) and then couple manuals to pedals. The resulting turgid mess of noise rolls round and round a reverberant building, confusing the congregation when accompanying and completely blurring the contrapuntal lines in solo playing. This wash of organ tone gives the unmusical a vague sense of holiness while sensitive musicians rush screaming from the building with their fingers in their ears. The English romantic organ was suitable for most nineteenth-century organ music (Franck, Guilmant, Widor, Vierne, and especially Max Reger, Rheinberger, and Karg-Elert) but was quite unsuitable for the performance of seventeenth- and eighteenth-century contrapuntal works, including the organ music of Bach.

The sudden surge of interest in organ-building created an unprecedented demand for players. Instruction manuals were in great demand and Rinck's famous organ tutor paved the way for others by Cooper, Best, Stainer (a best-seller) and Alcock. 1864 saw the formation of what is now the Royal College of Organists, a body which has done invaluable work in raising the standard of organ-playing and (later) choir-training. The latter part of the century also saw the rise of the first great school of virtuoso recitalists— Henry Smart, George Cooper, W. T. Best and John Stainer, leading on to such figures as Kendrick Pyne, Walter Alcock, Alfred Hollins, E. H. Lemare (a great arranger of Wagner), William Wolstenholme and (later) G. D. Cunningham: nor should it be forgotten that in addition to playing Handel's choruses, the *Ride of the Valkyries* and Lemmens's *The Storm*, these men did their utmost to stimulate public interest in Bach's organ works.

Small churches too poor to buy an organ or unlikely to obtain the services of an organist contented themselves with barrel-organs capable of playing a selection of hymns and psalm-tunes. On the other hand, 'as is shown by the pages of the *Musical Times* (London), there seems to have been a superfluity of organists towards the seventies of the last century and the smallest stipend or honorarium would attract a considerable number of applicants in most parts of the country. Many amateurs were content to give their services free. Thus, few barrel organs were required and many were destroyed or were rebuilt as "finger organs".'[16] Churches are still living in the past and have not yet realised that these halcyon days are over; that if they are to command the services of competent organists in future they must be prepared to pay adequately—and justly. Otherwise perhaps some of the present 'finger organs' will end up fitted with barrels.

CHARACTERISTICS OF VICTORIAN CHURCH MUSIC

In previous centuries the composers had almost all been connected either with the Chapel Royal or with various cathedrals or collegiate foundations. Furthermore their works were intended to be performed by professional choirs, however understaffed or incompetent these choirs may have become. With the upsurge of parish choirs in the middle of the century the pattern changed and cathedral musicians, instead of writing exclusively for cathedral resources, now produced a considerable bulk of music specifically designed for parish choirs; such pieces had to be short, simple and tuneful and in no more than four voice parts. The potential market was so vast that writing such music became not only a lucrative sideline but carried the additional attraction of regular and frequent performance in churches all over the country. On a higher level, there is no doubt that many of these composers, like Stainer himself, sincerely believed that they were fulfilling a genuine need and making a useful contribution to Christian worship.

Where many of them made a fatal mistake was in deliberately trying to write down to the level of the average worshipper. God was lost sight of in an attempt to satisfy the lower instincts of his flock: music was designed not to inspire but to entertain; it had to be easy to sing but flattering to the singers. This applied as much or even more to hymn-tunes as it did to anthems and Services. No higher praise could be bestowed than to say that a piece was 'melodious', 'tuneful', 'pretty' or 'charming'. And, of course, the tune fell obediently into a neat, balancing series of two- and four-bar phrases. Obviously, in such a situation the words counted for little and were crammed in, spaced out, or repeated as much as was necessary to carry the tune. Of course the repetition of words has always been established practice in choral music and examples can be found in the works of almost all the composers we have considered, but it is a device which needs to be handled with the utmost care and sensitivity. Since to the Victorian mind words counted for so little, this care was rarely taken and many amusing examples of verbal repetition can be found on the lines of

He's our best bul-, he's our best bul-
He's our best bulwark still

And catch the flee-
And catch the fleeting hour

[16] Ibid., p. 119.

and   Oh for a man-, Oh for a man-,
        Oh for a mansion in the sky.

Far more pernicious than these are the repetitions of one or more words which, by altering the structure of the sentence, make theological nonsense or result in downright heresy; such examples as the following spring to mind: 'As it was, it was in the beginning' (Barnby's Service in E); and 'that whoso believeth, believeth in Him' (Stainer's *Crucifixion*). Incidentally this quartet, 'God so loved the world', is a good example of the way slavish adherence to the four-bar phrase can make mincemeat of the words: in the clause 'that whoso believeth in Him should not perish but have everlasting life' not only is the meaning obscured by repeating the word 'believeth' but the musical section ends on the word 'Him' and there is a strong cadence and a break just where the words demand to flow on.

Victorian church musicians are notorious for their excessive use of chromatic harmony, yet not only was their chromatic harmony weak but there was also a certain fatal enervation even in their diatonic harmony. They simply could not resist the effeminate and 'pathetic' and this shows itself in many ways. We may instance their preference for the dominant seventh instead of the plain dominant as the penultimate chord in cadences; for example, compare the following:

Ex. 143

One's first impression is that (b) somehow seems richer and far more expressive than (a), but after many repetitions the C in the tenor begins to cloy and its drooping weakness becomes wearisome and irritating: by comparison (a) seems clean and strong, however often it may be repeated. In other words (a) wears much better than (b)—something felt instinctively by all the great composers, who used the dominant seventh very sparingly at cadences and then usually only for some special effect.

The following passage illustrates a number of other weaknesses which may be considered typical of the period:

Ex. 144

Notice: 1. the curiously naïve and rather bogus simplicity of the harmonic basis;

      2. the static bass part—merely a series of pedal points, like a village organist's extemporisation (Compare this with the bass of a Bach chorale);

      3. the excessive use of parallel thirds between the soprano and alto;

      4. the use of triple time;

      5. the rhythmic monotony;

      6. the characteristic diminished seventh chord at a climactic point (marked with an asterisk). Compare the hymn-tunes *St. Vincent* (A. & M. Std. 311 (iii)) and *Pax Tecum* (A. & M. Std. 537(i));

      7. the much-admired feminine cadence.

Again, if a Victorian composer had to harmonize the four notes of a scale descending from C to G he would almost certainly reject such strong and firm solutions as at (a), (b) and (c) and his instincts would incline him in favour of something like (d) or, even more likely, the spineless, nerveless (e):

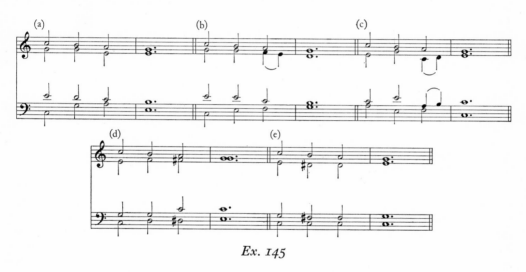

Ex. 145

Yet it would give an entirely false picture to attach too much importance to such music, most of which has either passed into oblivion already or has been doomed to a lingering death in revivalist hymnbooks. After all, all centuries have produced their quota of bad music. Of far greater significance are those composers who, in spite of the temptations, fashions and declining ideals around them, managed to keep the torch of true cathedral music burning, sometimes fitfully, often dimly, but at least with sufficient of the vital spark for it to blaze once more into full glory with the coming of the twentieth century. Amongst these minor composers were men like R. L. Pearsall (1795–1856), John Goss (1800–80), Thomas Attwood Walmisley (1814–56), William Sterndale Bennett (1816–75), Frederick Gore Ouseley, and George Garrett (1834–97). Standing far above all these was one really significant composer—S. S. Wesley (1810–76), the most important church musician since John Blow.

CHAPTER XV

Some Victorian Composers

SAMUEL SEBASTIAN WESLEY (1810–76)

S. S. Wesley was the first of several illegitimate children born of an irregular union between Samuel Wesley and his housekeeper, Sarah Suter: he was thus a grandson of Charles Wesley, the hymn-writer. Samuel Sebastian was admitted a chorister at the Chapel Royal, and from the age of fifteen held a number of organ appointments in London. He became organist of Hereford Cathedral at the early age of twenty-two. Three years later he moved to Exeter Cathedral but before taking up his new duties he contracted a runaway marriage with the Dean of Hereford's sister—a circumstance hardly calculated to advance the career of a young and ambitious cathedral organist. While at Exeter he took the Oxford Mus.Doc. degree. By now he was acknowledged to be both the foremost church composer and the leading organist of his day. In 1842 Hook persuaded him to go to Leeds Parish Church where he spent seven very active, fruitful, and comparatively happy years. From Leeds he was appointed organist of Winchester Cathedral and of the College. Here he stayed till 1865 when he made his last move—this time to Gloucester Cathedral where he remained in office till he died in 1876. As we have seen, he was much concerned with reforms in the administration, organisation and performance of cathedral music.

Wesley wrote about thirty anthems, a fairly complete and somewhat lengthy Service in E, a Short Service in F, some Chant Services, and various hymns and chants. Unlike the later Victorians he was essentially a cathedral composer. Many of his best-known anthems were written long before the general introduction of robed choirs into parish churches and even in the later part of his life he still seems to have thought in terms of cathedral rather than of parish church resources; indeed, several of his anthems are of great length and demand a first-rate choir. Admittedly the large scale-Service in E was written for Leeds Parish Church but then the choir there was of cathedral standard. Though it has been said that his pieces lack the massivity of his father's best work the fact remains that they usually reach a high level of inspiration, show marked originality and are technically assured; furthermore, he was so extraordinarily sensitive to the rhythms and inflections of words that in his recitatives he often displays an artistry so subtle as to be worthy of the Tudors. No wonder then that his work occupies an exalted place in the annals of English church music.

Before discussing some of Wesley's works in greater detail there are a few general considerations which apply to most of his output. First, he is distinguished above all his contemporaries and eighteenth-century predecessors by the sheer inventive power of his musical imagination in response to his feeling for the meaning and verbal-music of his text. This imagination shows itself in the sweep of his melodies, the richness of his harmonic palette, the boldness of his modulations, the accuracy of his word-setting, the grandeur of his climaxes and his idiomatic use of the organ. His verse anthems follow the same general pattern as those of his predecessors but in the longer ones individual sections are developed at much greater length, so becoming fairly extended movements in their own right. These longer movements make for greater structural integration and coherence, especially when compared with the typical seventeenth- and eighteenth-century verse anthem with its multitude of little short sections. Even so, some of the shorter anthems, like *The Wilderness* and *Blessed be the God and Father*, do not quite avoid sounding somewhat scrappy and disjointed.

Wesley's methods are clearly shown in his treatment of the solo voice; the short solo sections favoured by Greene and his contemporaries are now sometimes extended into full length arias remarkable for the beauty of their melodies, their dramatic power and their bold and exciting modulations, especially at climaxes. Typical of this style is the magnificent bass aria 'Thou, O Lord God' in *Let us lift up our heart* (see Ex. 153, p. 347):

S. S. Wesley: *Blessed be the God and Father*

Ex. 146

other examples are the trable solo 'Who can express' in *O give thanks* and the fine bass arias 'Say to them of a fearful heart' in *The Wilderness* and 'For our heart shall rejoice' in *O Lord, thou art my God*. His recitatives are particularly fine and show an unerring ear for verbal rhythms and inflections. Instead of adopting the speech-rhythm *recitativo secco* favoured by Handel, he preferred the measured recitative in strict tempo perfected by Humfrey and Purcell, yet he used it in a way distinctively his own. Within a strict metrical framework he not only achieved a remarkable plasticity of verbal phrasing, accurately converting speech rhythm and inflections into their corresponding musical notation, but he infused the whole with musical significance and vitality. So often, in other hands, recitative becomes merely perfunctory and quite devoid of any real musical interest. Wesley's recitative is seen at its best in his early but highly popular anthem *Blessed be the God and Father* (see Example 146 on the previous page).

Compared with most of the music written in the eighteenth and nineteenth centuries many of Wesley's melodies have a characteristic springing vigour and a feeling of grandeur and nobility about them. This is due in part to their exceptionally wide range and in part to his fondness for widely leaping themes, several of which are built on rising arpeggios:

Ex. 147

342

but his wide ranging parts sometimes lead him into difficulties and often he makes impossible, or at least ineffective, demands on voices. However good his musical ideas were in conception, he seems to have had singularly little notion of how to lay out his music for voices and his longer works set many problems of balance. Every choirmaster has to rearrange Wesley's voice parts to make them practicable and effective; in particular, the extremely low alto parts have frequently to be interchanged with the tenor. Such passages as the following are of common occurrence; not only is the tenor high against a very low bass with the alto (also low) between them, but later the alto, tenor and bass appear upside down with the bass above the tenor and the alto at the bottom:

S. S. Wesley: *Praise the Lord, O my soul*

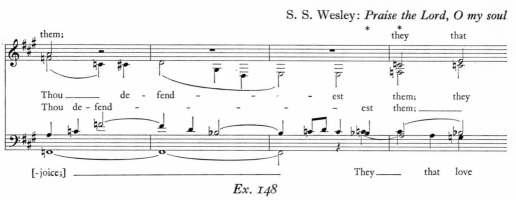

Ex. 148

This lack of vocal sense in his writing suggests that he was not at heart a choralist; indeed there is much in his work which hints that he was probably a rather poor choir-trainer – not altogether surprising, perhaps, because he was a brilliant organist and it is rather rare for one person to excel in both capacities.

Occasionally he was infected by the prevailing fashion of sentimentalism and his harmony became mellifluous and at times even reminiscent of Spohr, especially in his early works (e.g. the treble recitative 'But as he which hath called you' and aria 'Love one another' in *Blessed be the God and Father* and the concluding verse 'And sorrow and sighing' in *The Wilderness*). More often, his harmony was not only strong but striking – as in the following succession of chords (notice too the emotional *crescendo* generated by the bass descending as the melodic line rises):

S. S. Wesley: *Wash me throughly*

Ex. 149

At times he would unflinchingly plunge into a series of discords which must have seemed exceedingly harsh to his contemporaries; often such discords arise from the logical continuation of a harmonic sequence regardless of incidental clashes:

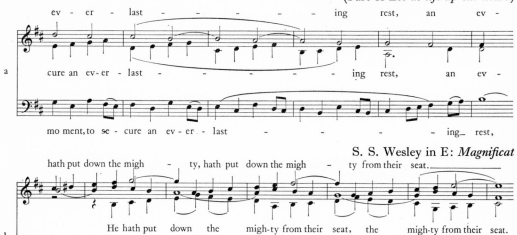

Ex. 150

Reference must be made to Wesley's extremely free use of key relationships, his masterly skill in modulation and his venturesome use of remote keys and enharmonic changes; indeed it is impossible to reconcile this last with his insistence on mean-tone temperament in the tuning of organs, especially as many of his own works would sound hideously out of tune on a mean-tone organ. (Wesley was the last great English organist to champion this method of tuning which was already outmoded in his own day.) To appreciate just how original and imaginative he was it is only necessary to play through some eighteenth-century Services by King, Kent, Travers, Kempton, Jackson, Cooke and others, and then play some of Wesley's Service in E. One enters a different world! It becomes clear that Wesley has reverted to the sixteenth- and seventeenth-century concept of a 'Great' Service, bringing to the old form the new harmonic concepts of nineteenth-century Romanticism and adding a fairly elaborate independent organ

Ex. 151

accompaniment. Who else living at that time would have dreamed of beginning the Gloria of a Service in E firmly and squarely in the remote key of E flat (D sharp)? At this point the organ interlude has led one to expect the tonality of B major: the sudden entry of full choir and organ in the totally unexpected key of E flat is probably the most dramatic single moment in church music since the B major entry in Blow's *Salvator mundi* (see Example 151 opposite).

A favourite trick of his is to add to the excitement of a climax by introducing a striking and unexpected modulation at its peak. This happens so frequently, both in choruses and verse passages, that one example must suffice:

S. S. Wesley: *The Wilderness*

Ex. 152

Another good example occurs in the same anthem at the end of the bass aria 'Say to them'.

The musical interest of Wesley's music is usually centred in the vocal writing: except in passages for solo voice the organ accompaniment rarely has much independent life of its own and usually merely doubles the chorus parts. Even when the organ accompaniment is independent it is rarely enterprising; generally it does little more than supply the harmonic background. Such a passage as 'for the Lord hath spoken it' in *O Lord, thou art my God* is exceptional and even here the rushing semiquavers seem curiously purposeless and ineffective. On the other hand his accompaniment of the solo voice represents a great advance on the old days of figured bass. His carefully written directions show a subtle use of recent technical advances for artistic ends. His effective use of crescendos, diminuendoes, punctuating chords on full swell, sustained chords and pedal points, together with his keen idiomatic sense of registration, show Wesley to have been a true Romantic. His restraint in the use of the pedals is especially laudable and their entries, always accurately marked, are the more effective for their careful placing.

One other aspect of his writing deserves a passing mention — his curious tendency to plagiarize his own works, no doubt quite unconsciously. Thus it often happens that a melodic phrase, a harmonic progression, a sequential formula or a series of key changes in one piece is similar to, or even identical with, a passage in some other. For example, bars 50–53 of *O give thanks* are identical with the phrase 'sojourning here in fear' in

345

Blessed be the God and Father, while the key sequence in the Gloria of his Jubilate in E is exactly the same as the key sequence in 'For in the wilderness' in *The Wilderness* (rising from E by major thirds). Compare also 'world without end' in the Magnificat in E with 'Ye are the blessed of the Lord' in *Ascribe unto the Lord*; 'See, we beseech thee' in *Let us lift up* with the chorus entry 'O hearken thou' in *Praise the Lord*; and 'the rebuke of his people' in *O Lord, thou art my God* with the organ interlude just before 'And a highway' in *The Wilderness*.

WESLEY: THE TWELVE ANTHEMS

With these general considerations in mind we can now glance quickly at some of the individual pieces. In 1853 Wesley published a volume of twelve anthems containing:

Ascribe unto the Lord	*O Lord my God* (Solomon's Prayer)
Blessed be the God and Father	*O Lord, Thou art my God*
Cast me not away	*The face of the Lord*
Let us lift up our heart	*The Wilderness*
Man that is born of a woman	*Thou wilt keep him in perfect peace*
O give thanks	*Wash me throughly*

Of these, two of the most popular were written at Hereford while the composer was in his early twenties — *The Wilderness* and *Blessed be the God and Father*. The former, first performed on 6 November 1832, is an unequal work and it has met with a mixed reception. While Gauntlett drew attention to the 'glorious pedal point' in the 5-part fugue, Wesley's detractor, J. W. Davison, spoke of 'modulation run mad' and Ernest Walker found in it a 'certain vein of rather weak elegance that Wesley afterwards altogether discarded'. Certainly the bass solo 'Say to them' is very fine indeed and the choruses are at least exciting. After the men's unison statements 'And a highway shall be there' etc., there is a dramatic moment when the high voices, in a remote key, reply 'But the redeemed shall walk there'. The last section is by far the weakest, not so much because of its tear-jerking melody and glutinous harmonies as because it is one of the few instances in the composer's output where the music seems inappropriate to the words: the idea that 'sorrow and sighing shall flee away' is surely a matter for thanksgiving and rejoicing. *Blessed be the God and Father* opens with an effective chorus which is often spoiled because choirmasters begin the *crescendo* at bar 12 instead of holding it back till the end of bar 15 where the composer marked it. The middle section never fails to earn the approbation of elderly ladies: Wesley originally conceived the section as a 2-part song sung antiphonally between Decani and Cantoris but later changed it to the present version where it is sung responsorially between a solo treble and the rest of the boys. The succulent sections in both these anthems betray the young musician caught up in the fashionable idiom of his day.

Another popular verse anthem, *Ascribe unto the Lord*, is more mature. There is an effective touch near the beginning where the chorus entry 'Let the whole earth' is first sung grandly in G major and then later repeated *pp* a fourth lower. The succeeding quartet sounds best when sung entirely by boys (but the boy altos have to be good!). Wesley himself used to take the fugal section 'As for the gods' very fast and rehearse it unaccompanied. In the description of the idols, the awkwardly placed alto lead 'They have hands and handle not' is usually given to tenors. After a lengthy stay in minor keys the sudden transition back to G major imparts a radiant confidence to the words 'As for our God, He is in heaven'. The final chorus is full of good tunes. The short verse anthem *O give thanks* is not outstanding. The second movement is a fully developed

S. S. Wesley: *Let us lift up our heart*

Thou O Lord God art the thing that I long for: thou art my hope,

thou art my hope, thou art my hope,— thou,

thou, e-ven from my youth, O Lord,— thou ——— O Lord,— art my

hope,— thou, thou Lord,— art— my hope.

Ex. 153

treble aria in A–B–A form, 'Who can express the noble acts of the Lord'; it is often extracted and sung separately as a unison anthem for boys' voices.

All who have written on Wesley seem agreed that *O Lord, thou art my God* is the finest of his large-scale verse anthems. Certainly it is by far the longest (it takes eighteen minutes to perform) and most elaborate: the first, third and last movements are laid out for double choir and there are lengthy passages in five and six parts. The second movement is a long and rather conventional bass aria 'For our heart shall rejoice'. Of course a composer of Wesley's stature can be depended on to produce some impressive passages when writing in eight parts and it cannot be denied that the anthem has many fine moments. Yet taken as a whole it is difficult to understand why this particular piece should have earned such encomiums. It is somewhat conventional and predictable and has few of those imaginative flashes which illumine this composer's best pages: the melodies are comparatively undistinguished and many listeners will consider the whole piece goes on too long. *Let us lift up our heart* is, in the writer's opinion, immeasurably superior. It is nearly as long as the previous anthem and begins similarly with an extended chorus for double choir, full of points of interest—the powerful accented passing notes in the bass at 'doubtless Thou art our Father' and the exciting shift into A major at the close of this passage; the detached chords on 'Behold, see, we beseech thee', and the break into flowing quavers at 'the mountains might flow down'. The succeeding quartet and chorus 'Be not very sore' has a glorious melodic sweep and a powerful ending; there is a weak point in it where the organ, for no very cogent musical reason, breaks into a few bars of somewhat ineffective quaver figuration. The bass (or counter-tenor) solo 'Thou, O Lord God' is not only the highlight of the anthem but must surely rank amongst the very finest of sacred songs. Its soaring melodic lines, wide compass, powerful harmonies, thrilling modulations and tremendous sense of climax may be thought too dramatic or even operatic by purists, but many people will feel that such superb writing is at least as good as the best pages of Blow, Purcell, and even Handel, in this vein. Its ending is shown in Example 153 on the preceding page. It is high time this aria was disinterred and taken into the standard repertory: for that matter it seems incredible that the anthem itself, perhaps Wesley's finest achievement, was out of print for many years. Only the last part was available, published as a separate anthem under the title *Thou judge of quick and dead*: this final section consists of two 4-part choruses, 'Thou judge of quick and dead' with its powerful unison passages, and a fugal movement the words of which are, perhaps, a little unfortunate, 'O may we thus insure a lot . . .' The whole anthem is now available in a modern edition.[1]

Turning next to the *a cappella* anthems in the 1853 collection, the 4-part *O Lord, my God* (Solomon's Prayer) is a poor thing and unworthy of its composer. Far more expressive is *Man that is born of a woman*, a setting of the graveside sentences in the Burial Service which Wesley intended should precede and culminate in the singing of Purcell's famous setting of the last sentence, *Thou knowest, Lord*. The piece is in block harmony throughout but the harmonies are subtly coloured. The ending is particularly fine: after an unexpected and overwhelming climax on the key word, 'Saviour', the music sinks back and poignant discords underline the 'bitter' pains of eternal death in a close of great beauty. *The face of the Lord* is more elaborate. The first of its three movements, laid out for TrATTB, is an excellent bit of writing entirely characteristic of its composer. The words 'Many are the afflictions of the righteous' are set most effectively to a

---

[1] Published by Ascherberg, Hopwood & Crew.

drooping phrase over a long-sustained pedal but the last page is spoiled by the rush of notes on 'delivereth him out of all', necessitated by the 2-bar phrases. The second movement, 'The righteous cry and the Lord heareth', is for double choir. It is less inspired and its harmony often seems weak and contrived; it is partly redeemed by a fine passage near the end where the phrases, again over a held pedal note, leap upwards to accent the word 'cry':

S. S. Wesley: *The face of the Lord*

Ex. 154

The last movement, TrTrATB, is short and conventional. The gem of this group is *Cast me not away from thy presence*, for six voices (TrTrATTB). On 23 December 1847, when Wesley was returning to Leeds from a fishing expedition to Helmsley, he was involved in an accident which resulted in a compound fracture of the left leg. During several months of convalescence which followed he wrote this anthem and there is probably a wry personal touch in the discords underlining 'the bones which thou hast broken'. The last dozen bars are particularly lovely.

The two short full anthems with organ accompaniment, *Thou wilt keep him in perfect peace* and *Wash me thoroughly*, fully deserve their unbroken popularity. The second in particular gives perfect expression to the wistfulness and heartfelt contrition of the words and is generally considered to be one of the most flawless gems in the whole corpus of English church music. The tender beauty and serenity of these anthems is in marked contrast to Wesley's own personality which was contentious, intractable and often avaricious; he bore a perpetual chip on his shoulder.

WESLEY: OTHER ANTHEMS

The 1853 collection includes most of his best anthems. It is not possible to discuss all those published later but two deserve mention. The 4-part *All go unto one place*, a funeral anthem for the Prince Consort (1861), is in two movements joined by a singularly feeble organ link. In the first movement Wesley makes effective use of unison and octave passages, and the words 'And now, Lord, what is my hope? truly my hope is even in Thee' are set as a refrain. The second movement is in block harmony and again exhibits that expressiveness and serenity characteristic of the composer's penitential writing. This anthem is eminently suitable for parish choirs. Another work of 1861, the verse anthem *Praise the Lord, O my soul*, was written for the opening of the organ in Holy Trinity Church, Winchester—which accounts for some of the florid organ writing. It is a fine piece, similar in style to *The Wilderness*, but is notorious for the particularly low tessitura of its alto part—which even tenors would still find uncomfortably low:

349

much of the ATB writing really needs recasting and rearranging for TBB. The anthem is in three movements the first two of which are in modified A–B–A form. The treble solo is a great favourite with choirboys. A brief chorale-like passage forms a bridge to the last movement, the well-known *Lead me, Lord* which is published and often sung as a separate anthem.

WESLEY: THE SERVICES

From the historical point of view Wesley's most important work by far is his full Service in E. We have seen how, from the Restoration onwards through the eighteenth and nineteenth centuries, Service settings declined in quality and interest. Now at last a composer appears who, at one bound, lifted the art of Canticle setting out of the mire and placed it in the forefront of the church composer's art. The Service in E is Wesley's most original work. Though entirely different in style and technique, it has something of the grand manner of the Tudor 'Great' Service. It is a lengthy setting; there is a good deal of verbal repetition and the melodic phrases are often spacious in outline. One obvious difference between this and a Tudor setting is that whereas in the earlier work the music is tailored to fit the words, Wesley usually fits the words to the music; since the music is to some extent constrained by the two- and four-bar periodicity inevitable at that time (though Wesley is far more free in his phrase lengths than other composers of his day) there will usually be some compression or expansion of words to fit the tune. Thus, Jubilate begins:

S. S. Wesley in E: *Jubilate Deo*

Ex. 155

However, the total impression is one of great power and brilliance. Bold modulations are frequent and are often resorted to for dramatic effect and, especially, for building up climaxes. A good example of this is the Gloria of this Jubilate which, as we have seen (Ex. 151), begins in the remote key of E flat. The section 'As it was in the beginning' returns to E major and breaks into 3 time. Then follows a series of passages in G sharp, C major, E minor and back to E major again: these are not merely passing modulations but are definite sections which later editors have dignified with double bars and new key signatures; various other keys are visited *en passant*. (Exactly the same sequence of keys occurs in *The Wilderness* at 'For in the wilderness'.) These powerful enharmonic modulations, almost Straussian in effect, bring about a tremendous emotional crescendo. As the climax is approached, Wesley piles on still more excitement by a totally unexpected swing back into $\frac{4}{2}$ time followed almost immediately by the most shattering key shift of all—two big D major chords—before eventually resolving on to the final cadence (see Example 156 opposite). Basically the Service is laid out for 5-part choir TrTrATB (Decani and Cantoris) but there are passages for various combinations up to eight parts, including solo voices and 'verse' groups. This Service soon became a model which many copied but few equalled: it initiated a line of development which led on,

Ibidem

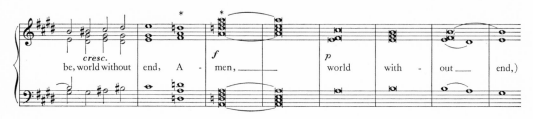

Ex. 156

with little basic change, through Walmisley, Garrett, Stanford, Charles Wood and others, to the work of Howells and Britten in our own day.

The Short Service in F is naturally much less venturesome because the restricted form gives a composer less scope for displaying originality; but even here the touch of the master craftsman is shown in the moulding of the melodic lines, in the way that chordal writing and contrapuntal passages are justly balanced, and in a number of imaginative details. It is one of the best Short Services of the century and is still to be heard in cathedrals. Though Wesley intended the organ to double the voices, the piece is now usually sung unaccompanied.

WESLEY'S HYMN-TUNES

Wesley wrote a large number of hymn-tunes. Of these, four have established themselves and appear in most hymnbooks: *Harewood* (usually sung to 'Christ is our Corner-stone'), *Hereford* ('O Thou who camest from above'), *Alleluia* ('Alleluia! sing to Jesus!') and, most popular of all, *Aurelia* ('The Church's one foundation'). A tune of his which deserves to be better known is *Wetherby*. Of his chants, the double chants in F and G are firmly enthroned in all Anglican hearts; the chromatic single chant in F (F sharp) minor may be thought by some to be too succulent for contemporary taste but it can sound quite lovely when sung to a short penitential or meditative psalm.

ROBERT LUCAS PEARSALL (1795–1856)

Pearsall was born into considerable wealth. He was a barrister by profession and an amateur musician. He travelled widely and spent much time abroad where he widened his musical studies. His chief importance is in the field of secular music. He is a classic example of an artist who lived out of his time—in his case the Elizabethan madrigal

351

period—and his best work is modelled directly on composers like Morley, Wilbye, and Weelkes. But he was no mere imitator and the best of his madrigalian part songs are outstanding. His anthems and his settings of the Lord's Prayer fall well below this exalted standard; they dropped out of use and scarcely merit revival. To church musicians Pearsall is now regarded as a 'one-work' composer but that one work is sung universally wherever choirs are accomplished enough to sing it—this is his beautiful 8-part *a cappella* arrangement of the ancient carol 'In dulci jubilo'. It consists of a set of choral variations on the old melody remarkable for their originality, polished part-writing and, above all, for their sheer musical beauty. In the last verse the brilliant effect of peal upon peal of bells is vividly suggested as the choir, now in five parts, sings 'There are angels singing . . . and there the bells are ringing'—a typically madrigalian touch.

JOHN GOSS (1800–80)

Goss was Wesley's senior by ten years. After spending his boyhood at the Chapel Royal he studied under Attwood. He was organist of Stockwell Chapel and St. Luke's, Chelsea, before succeeding his master as organist of St. Paul's Cathedral in 1838. In 1872 he was knighted and soon afterwards he retired from St. Paul's. Towards the end of his long term of office music declined to a particularly low level and it was left to his successor, John Stainer, to redeem it. Goss was honoured by being made a Doctor of Music at Cambridge in 1876.

As a composer he seems a very minor figure compared with Sebastian Wesley, yet in an age of false values, appallingly bad taste and shoddy workmanship he preserved high ideals and kept them untarnished. He maintained a well-ordered flow of clean, worthy, graceful music put together with professional expertise, unruffled by either inspiration or individuality. It is all disciplined, gentlemanly and likeable without ever uplifting or disturbing us, but the best of it has proved enduring and is still to be heard—and deservedly so—in cathedrals and parish churches.

One of Goss's best-known anthems is *The Wilderness* and it is instructive to compare his setting with Wesley's. Goss includes far more of the text (Isaiah xxxv) but writes a much shorter anthem. Wesley selects his text very carefully, eliminating unessentials, so that the meaning emerges more clearly; thus in the following passage, set in full by Goss, Wesley omits all the words shown in brackets:

> And a highway shall be there, [and a way and] it shall be called the Way of Holiness; the unclean shall not pass over it; [but it shall be for those: the wayfaring men, though fools, shall not err therein. No lion shall be there, nor any ravenous beast shall go up thereon, it shall not be found there;] but the redeemed shall walk there.

On the other hand Wesley repeats his text considerably more than does Goss: thus the opening words, set by the latter as 11 bars of recitative, becomes 46 bars of verse quartet in Wesley, while the thirteen words 'For in the wilderness shall waters break out as streams in the desert', set by both composers as a chorus, occupy 74 bars in Wesley as against 25 in Goss. Goss's recitative is just as careful and accurate as Wesley's but lacks the younger man's sheer musicality. The two opening phrases, both set for bass soloist, are characteristic of their composers:

352

Goss: *The Wilderness*

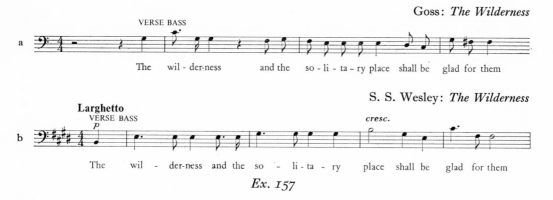

Ex. 157

Whereas Goss's line begins high with a strong accent on 'wilderness' and then droops down, ending in a conventional cadence, Wesley builds up strongly through the notes of the common chord culminating in a powerful accent where it surely belongs — on the word 'glad' — and rounds off with a cadence which is more individual and arresting. Goss's trio section 'Say to them' ends with a feeble coda (the *moderato* section) but the short tenor recitative 'Then the eyes of the blind' is excellent. Even finer is the recitative for men's voices 'And a highway shall be there' which rises to a sustained high D on the word 'redeemed':

Goss: *The Wilderness*

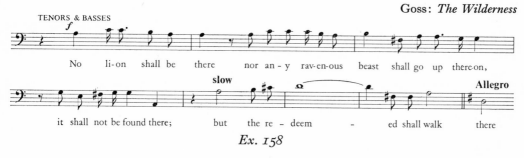

Ex. 158

The last chorus is pleasant enough though strictly conventional. As so often with Goss it is the little coda section at the end (complete with slower speed, pauses, simultaneous rests, dominant sevenths and *p* markings), meant to be soulful, which is so weak.

Of the other verse anthems, *Fear not, O land* and *Stand up and bless the Lord* (both 1863) are commonplace. *Brother, thou art gone before us* (1865) has a fine first movement which has been adapted to different words and published separately as a beautiful little anthem, *Lord, let me know mine end*. The middle section is mildly interesting for the prominence given to the melodic interval of the tritone — but Goss is no Pelham Humfrey and his use of it is not so much affecting as effete. *The Queen shall rejoice* is remembered mainly for its treble solo. An anthem which was once exceedingly popular is *Praise the Lord, O my soul*, written for the Bicentenary Festival of the Sons of the Clergy on 10 May 1854. At this first performance, sung in St. Paul's Cathedral by two hundred and fifty voices accompanied by organ and wind instruments, it was no doubt quite impressive, especially the male voice recitative 'They that put their trust': (this recitative follows the English pattern, favoured by Wesley, by being in strict tempo). When the anthem is

M

transferred to the parish church, however, the accompaniment of the concluding choral fugue, shorn of its wind instruments, sounds merely empty and bombastic. Even *The glory of the Lord*, written as late as 1869, is unequal in quality and quite devoid of inspiration.

The truth is that Goss does not show himself to advantage in the verse anthem form and for his best work we must turn to his unaccompanied anthems. Most of these are for 4-part choir, look simple on paper and are quite short: it is worth noting too that Goss is not so shackled to triple rhythm as some of his predecessors. Even of these simple anthems the majority reach little more than a pleasant mediocrity and such a piece as *O taste and see*, once universally popular, has now all but disappeared. But in a mere handful of works Goss soared to unaccustomed heights and wrote music of truly spiritual value. Of these, *O Saviour of the world* (1869) is a thoughtful setting which begins quietly and builds up twice to effective climaxes on the words 'hast redeemed us'. The coda reflects the mood and some of the thematic ideas of the opening: it is marred only by the last few bars which, characteristically, prove to be his Achilles' heel. *I heard a voice* is a simple piece in block harmony derived from his E minor setting of the Burial Service; it has a quiet dignity appropriate to its context. *Almighty and merciful God*, in 3-time, could well be by Attwood. It combines a gracious melodic line with clean harmony to provide a sympathetic setting for the Collect (3rd Sunday after Trinity); somewhat exceptionally, it has an effective and rather lovely close. *God so loved the world* is little more than a hymn-tune, yet it is a beautifully phrased and sensitive setting, vastly superior to Stainer's insensitive and lachrymose handling of the same text.

But it is in *If ye believe that Jesus died*, composed for the Duke of Wellington's funeral in 1852, that Goss really excels himself and writes what can assuredly be described as a minor masterpiece. This anthem is longer than most and is also much more contrapuntal: the first part is in D minor and the second in D major. The opening is imitative and the second bass entry is inverted. But technical processes are not important in themselves: far more important is that here the composer has given classic expression to his text and has written a profoundly moving piece of unsurpassable beauty.

Much of Goss's music was written not for the cathedral but for parish churches, yet what a trap these little anthems have proved for countless thousands of choirs! Because on paper the notes are so simple to read and easy to sing choirmasters run away with the idea that therefore such pieces must be suitable for inadequate or elementary choirs; but the simpler the notes the more beautifully they have to be sung and phrased and even one rough, nasal or hooty voice, let alone a choirful, will utterly ruin the effect. In fact such an anthem as *O Saviour of the world*, far from being easy, is no mean test even for a professional choir.

Goss's Service settings, like most of the anthems, are straightforward, competently written and cleanly harmonized; they are never vulgar, never lacking in taste, never (unfortunately) inspired. They include a Te Deum in F, a Morning Service in D, a full Service in A (published in two versions, 4-part and unison), a chant setting in C and the Burial Service in E minor. The last to survive in regular use is his Evening Service in E, a typical 'short' setting which could be sung unaccompanied.

He has left a permanent mark on English worship with a number of very fine chants, eleven of which first appeared in a collection of 257 which he edited and published in 1841. Some of Goss's chants, like the double chant in E, have now become so much a part of Anglican music that no modern collection would seem complete without them.

354

In addition to this 1841 collection Goss edited *Parochial Psalmody* (1826) and was musical editor of Mercer's *Church Psalter and Hymn Book* (1854). His hymn-tunes are a mixed bunch. Some, like *Peterborough* and *Armageddon*, are frankly dull but others, such as the smiling melody to Caswall's 'See amid the winter's snow', fully deserve their place in people's affections. The finest tune of all is unquestionably 'Praise my soul' written for Lyte's famous hymn. Here words and tune are perfectly matched and enhance each other in a glorious paean of praise. The tune first appeared in 1869 in two forms—a unison version in D with varied organ accompaniments for each verse, and a harmonized version in E. It is a pity that English Hymnal was so squeamish about using Goss's own harmonization of 'Fatherlike, he tends and spares us'. This tune alone secures Goss a place in any history of English church music and seems likely to be his most lasting memorial.

THOMAS ATTWOOD WALMISLEY (1814–56)

Walmisley derived his first names from his godfather, Thomas Attwood, the composer, under whom he studied and whose style he tended to copy, at least in his earlier works. Walmisley was another child prodigy who was later to excel at both music and mathematics. He goes down in history as one of the busiest organists of all time for at Cambridge he was simultaneously organist of Trinity and St. John's Colleges and also, during the long period that John Pratt was incapacitated, acting organist of King's College and Great St. Mary's Church, so that every Sunday in term he played no less than eight services:

St. John's College	7.15 a.m.
Trinity College	8.00 a.m.
King's College	9.30 a.m.
Great St. Mary's	10.30 a.m.
Great St. Mary's	2.00 p.m.
King's College	3.15 p.m.
St. John's College	5.00 p.m.
Trinity College	6.15 p.m.

On accepting the Cambridge professorship of music in 1836 he proved himself an able administrator and an inspiring teacher. He was one of the first to introduce musical illustrations into his lectures. At a time when most of Bach's music was virtually unknown, Walmisley's familiarity with the B minor Mass and some of the cantatas led him to recognise the supremacy of Bach's genius.

As a composer his twenty or so anthems and half a dozen Service settings have much in common with Goss's and have shared the same fate. They are best described perhaps as 'worthy'—and that they are in the best sense—yet they remain earthbound. Many conclude with a fugal movement but such movements seem rather wooden and contrived, a criticism which can also be levelled at the canon 4 in 2 in *Praise the Lord*. His many treble solos are often trivial and somewhat emotional; those in the early pieces *Father of heaven* and *Hear, O thou shepherd of Israel* (1836) are both ornamented with a 'turn', hinting at Walmisley's musical ancestry through Attwood to Mozart. The latter anthem continues with a quiet chorus 'Turn us again' followed by an effective alto recitative and aria. *If the Lord himself had not been on our side* is larger and more pretentious than most of his pieces: once again the treble solo 'Our soul is escaped' is one of the weakest movements while, as Fellowes has pointed out,[2] the final chorus is reminiscent of Beethoven's 'Hallelujah' chorus in *The Mount of Olives*. *Remember, O Lord* (1838) opens, unusually, with a sarabande for organ followed by a male voice quartet and a bass recitative in tempo: the treble solo 'For this our heart is faint' is far better than most of this composer's treble solos and deserves an occasional hearing. A youthful work on a large scale, *O give thanks* (1834), is uneven: in general the choruses are on a far higher level than the solo section. Walmisley's most popular piece, the 'choral hymn' *From all that dwell below the skies*, has a strong and attractive melodic line which leads on inevitably to a powerful climax at 'Thy praise shall sound from shore to shore'. The unexpected shift from F major into D flat at this point (there is a similar modulation to B flat in the Magnificat of his Service in D major) is striking while to remain in the new key until only three bars from the end of the piece is ingenious and bold. The trouble is that the anthem is so dead rhythmically: the monotonous succession of 2-bar phrases and the plodding block chords with four changes of harmony in a bar produce a lumpy effect which even skilful phrasing cannot entirely disguise. In the hands of the average parish church choir, where choirmaster and singers are all industriously counting 4-in-a-bar, the effect is unutterably wearisome and pedestrian.

Walmisley wrote full Services in C, F and D; a Morning Service in B flat (4-part), an entirely separate Evening Service in B flat (a rather florid affair in eight parts), and a Sanctus in D. These Services, like his anthems, are sincere and well-bred rather than inspired or profound though they compare more than favourably with those of his eighteenth-century forerunners. They are rarely heard now; the most popular of the group and the last to survive in regular use is the D major Service, which can be sung unaccompanied. Yet by some curious alchemy it was given to this somewhat urbane and unimaginative composer to produce, quite by accident as it were, just one work of near genius, an isolated minor miracle for which there seems no explanation—his famous Evening Service in D minor (1855), a splendid pendant to Wesley's great Service in E written ten years earlier.

The D minor Service is strikingly original in conception, bold in design, imaginative and expressive in its handling of the words, powerful in its unison passages, tender at times without being sentimental, and memorable for its fine melodies. Above all it is important for the brilliance and independence of its organ accompaniment and in this department makes a notable advance even on Wesley's writing. The plan of Magnificat is interesting: it is laid out rather on the lines of a Tudor *faux bourdon* setting with verses for men's voices in unison alternating with verses for high voices in 3-part harmony (TrTrA); the overall scheme is cunningly varied to suit the words. The vigorous unison passages are provided with a prominent, sometimes exciting, yet always subsidiary organ accompaniment. Even Walmisley's harmonies are remarkable for his day. Though he could never bring himself to plunge boldly into sequential chains of strong dissonances as did Wesley, yet he favoured unexpected and unusual shifts of tonality: notice the C♯—C♮ and F♯—F♮ ambivalency throughout, often resulting in a feeling of 'false-relations'; the unexpected shift from B♭ to G major at 'And his mercy', from A to F at 'He hath filled' and from D to F at 'He remem'bring'; the touch of E♭ at 'He hath scattered', and the unusual cadence for the final 'Amen'. The quartet, 'He remem'bring his mercy' is a lovely piece of writing, gracious and beautiful but with no hint of

[2] E. H. Fellowes: *English Cathedral Music*, p. 212. (Methuen, 4th Ed. 1948.)

cheapness or emotionalism: it is repeated by the full choir. In Nunc dimittis the unison passages are sung not by men's voices alone but by the whole choir. By a curious quirk both Glorias include powerful bass phrases taken from works by the Walloon priest-musician, Henri Du Mont (1610–84); Walmisley makes due acknowledgement for these. Nunc dimittis is unique in the way it ends: the Gloria comes to a conventional full close in the home key of D minor. There is a bar's rest, then the final 'Amen' of Magnificat is sung again but this time transposed down a fourth so that the Canticle actually ends on the dominant of its main key—an unusual but undeniably effective close. This fine Service appeared only a year before its composer's early death: did it presage greater things to come?

Like most Victorian church musicians Walmisley wrote some hymn-tunes and a number of chants. The hymn-tunes seem never to have caught on and none of them has won its way into modern hymnals. Some of his chants, however, are particularly good and are still widely sung.

THE REV. SIR FREDERICK GORE OUSELEY (1825–89)

We have already seen that Ouseley made an important and continuing contribution to church music by founding St. Michael's College, Tenbury (pp. 324–5). He also did valuable work as a musicologist and, though his standards of scholarship would hardly be acceptable in these days, he yet did useful pioneering in scoring a good deal of sixteenth-century music from the separate voice parts, many of which were at hand in the superb private library he gathered together. He edited Gibbons's church music and made a special study of early Spanish musical treatises. As a composer, however, he is of very minor significance. In all he produced eleven Services and some seventy anthems; of these, one Service and fourteen anthems were provided with an orchestral accompaniment. Nearly all of these are lofty in conception, impeccable in craftsmanship and far too well-bred to suffer from the prevalent Victorian faults of pretty tunes and maudlin harmony. But Ouseley wrote from his brain rather than from his heart so that most of his pieces are far too academic, too mellifluous and too dull. In recent years so much great music has become readily available to every choirmaster that, inevitably, the work of minor composers has been crowded out; even now, however, in parish churches and nonconformist chapels a handful of Ouseley's best pieces still have an honoured place. These include the short 4-part unaccompanied anthems *From the rising of the sun; How goodly are thy tents*, and the particularly beautiful setting *Is it nothing to you?* In this last he seems to have been visited by genuine inspiration. Best of all is his short motet for double-choir, *O Saviour of the world*, a strong and solemn work which still merits a place in the cathedral repertory.

WILLIAM STERNDALE BENNETT (1816–75)

Bennett was a pianist, conductor, teacher and composer and is remembered chiefly for his secular compositions. He began brilliantly and was hailed as a rising star by Mendelssohn and Schumann; but he never fulfilled his early promise. His church music, which includes seven anthems and an oratorio, falls well below the level of his best secular music: it is always pleasant and in good taste but is unimaginative and lacking in artistic insight. Too often the words act merely as a peg on which to hang the music and there is rarely any real interrelationship between the two. Thus, in *O that I knew where I might find him,* he begins by choosing a text which does not readily lend itself to musical treatment and then casually repeats words as necessary to fill out the musical phrase-lengths: the result utterly destroys the mystery implicit in the original text—though the music itself is pleasant enough. *Remember now thy Creator* begins with a somewhat shapeless treble duet; the following chorus is more interesting and includes an effective pedal point.

Bennett's cantata *The Woman of Samaria* is now as dead as the dodo but a quartet from it is still often sung and is perhaps his most familiar sacred piece: this is 'God is a spirit', another example in which the tender melodiousness of his setting seems curiously at odds with the mystery and solemnity of Christ's words. The best of his sacred pieces is *In thee, O Lord,* a fine work in eight parts *a cappella* which deserves to be better known. It consists of two movements: the first is better than the second and can well stand alone.

GEORGE M. GARRETT (1834–97)

Garrett's music is rarely heard now and he is included here only for his historical importance. He is remembered chiefly for his Services, especially those in D, E, E♭ and F; of these, the first and last retained a somewhat precarious foothold in cathedral music lists until quite recently. The importance of Garrett's Services lies in their organ accompaniment. The style initiated by Wesley in his Service in E and developed in Walmisley in D minor is here carried a stage further and the organ is given greater independence than ever before. Wesley and earlier writers had treated it freely enough when accompanying solos or verse passages for two or three voices but in full choir sections the organ merely doubled the voice-parts. Garrett's contribution was to free the accompaniment to these choral sections (choirs had no doubt improved to a point where they no longer had to be bolstered up by the organ doubling their parts). This he does in several ways—by adding an independent bass line below the sung bass (sometimes in the form of a pedal point), by doubling voice parts at the octave above or below, or by writing a completely free organ part. At all times his organ writing is idiomatic and he gives precise directions for registration, manual changes and so on. Thus the organ now makes a positive contribution of its own to the total effect. Garrett therefore emerges as an important link between Wesley and Stanford.

CHAPTER XVI

Victoriana

No history of English church music would be complete without some mention of composers like Barnby, Stainer and Sullivan, although most of their music has long since been discountenanced by sensitive musicians. Over the years they have been subjected to almost continual attack, ranging from thunderous invective to faint praise and even ridicule; they have been berated by critics, dropped from the cathedral repertory, and frowned upon by such organisations as the Church Music Society and the Royal School of Church Music. The unpalatable fact remains that Sunday by Sunday in countless churches and an even larger number of chapels their music is still sung—and enjoyed. Some time ago a leading publisher thought it worthwhile to buy the rights of Maunder's music. What is the explanation?

In all the arts the ultimate critic is Old Father Time and it is in his winnowing hand that finally sorts out the gold from the dross: it is, in fact, a compliment to say of something 'it has stood the test of time'. This process of time-selection explains why so much mid-Victorian church music has already mouldered into dust and why such names as J. Baptiste Calkin, Eaton Faning, Myles B. Foster and T. Tallis Trimnell have practically vanished from the scene. The corollary would appear to be that men like Barnby, Stainer and Sullivan, whatever their weaknesses, must have had some outstanding qualities or inner strengths not shared by their contemporaries which have enabled them to survive a whole century of regular use and which have confounded their critics. There may be some substance in this: undoubtedly all three were far more talented and technically skilled than most of their contemporaries; Stainer occasionally shows glimpses of true greatness while, in the Savoy operas, Sullivan comes near to genius. But this is not the only explanation for their continuing popularity; other factors have intervened to slow down Time's winnowing hand.

For one thing, the majority of worshippers are not sufficiently refined or sensitive to experience the profound, and often disturbing, power of truly great music or to distinguish this from the comforting warm glow of spurious religiosity induced by trivial and sentimental ear-ticklers. Compare, for example, such a profound little piece as Victoria's motet *Popule meus* ('O my people') with Stainer's 'Appeal of the Crucified' in *Crucifixion*: to sensitive people the distinction is immediately apparent but insensitive people will actually prefer the Stainer because it has a more obvious tune and goes with a swing. Here our three composers had an advantage; they could all write a catchy tune —even if it was hopelessly inappropriate to its text and context. These catchy tunes soon became highly popular with the undiscriminating.

This brings us to another factor—the strength of associations. People like a particular piece because it reminds them of some person or occasion or brings back childhood memories. They will therefore go on using it themselves and teaching it to others. This means that once a piece of church music, however bad, becomes well established it is virtually self-perpetuating. What an awful responsibility this places on Sunday School teachers and others who are actively forming these associations in young minds, especially as it is in children's hymns that the worst rubbish is found. Users of *Twentieth Century Church Light Music* might also ponder on it. Because the immense personal prestige of Barnby, Stainer and Sullivan lent their music a spurious authority, it was frequently performed and so became better known than the work of lesser contemporaries. Thus it became more firmly entrenched. Such arguments are reinforced by a severely practical consideration. Most choirs have little or no money for buying music; consequently it is not practicable to scrap complete sets of copies already in the library and replace them by other works. The cheapest way is to replace a few odd copies here and there as they become unrepairable. So once repertories are established they tend to remain unchanged over the years. Incidentally this is why modern religious 'pop' music will never be 'expendable' or 'disposable' as its protagonists claim. The tragedy is that many libraries were established when men like Barnby were in their heyday.

There is little point in enlarging upon the faults these composers exhibit. A static bass, enfeebled chromatic harmony, stilted rhythms, rigid 4-bar phrases, meretricious tunes, and a complete disregard for the rhythms, inflections, meaning and mood of the words, were merely the outward and visible signs of a far more serious inner weakness which is best described as a basic insincerity. This insincerity operates at two levels. It is most obvious in the deliberate attempt to write down to popular taste: late in life Stainer admitted that many of his pieces had been written in response to pressing demands from clergy and others who wanted something tuneful and easy to sing and he bitterly regretted that so many of them had been published. It is a sad paradox that his most insincere music had been written in all sincerity for the highest motives.

A far more subtle form of insincerity is inherent in the way church music almost inevitably reflected the basic shallowness of churchmanship as a whole. The Victorian could see nothing incongruous in running his factories on sweated labour and then giving a fraction of his profits to 'good works', or in paying his overworked domestic skivvies a miserable pittance and then demanding their attendance at family prayers. At a time when piety deemed it sinful for children to go out or play games on the Sabbath, Shaftesbury, like Wilberforce before him, fought against the entrenched opposition of so-called religious men to carry through his humanitarian reforms, while the pages of Dickens and Henry Mayhew etch a grim picture of how the underprivileged lived. It is a sorry story. Under the cover of a narrow, affected form of Calvinism, religion was often a shallow, empty thing and it is this basic emptiness which is reflected in much Victorian sacred music. For example, the music is not only highly emotional but the emotions are patently stage emotions, the tears are crocodile tears, and the humility and self-abasement are never allowed to obscure the fact that the sun never sets on the British Empire, God sides with the English, and all's right with the world—*our* world. Even in pieces like Stainer's *Crucifixion* the more blood-curdling parts are only Hollywood 'mock-ups'.

In general, Service settings by this group of composers are more satisfactory than their anthems: it may be that the traditional constraint shown by eighteenth- and nineteenth-century writers in setting the canticles preserves the mid-Victorians from those lapses of taste so common in their anthems. About this time it became usual to include settings of Sanctus and Gloria in excelsis in full Services while Cantate and Deus misereatur dropped out of favour. A full Service now consisted therefore of Te Deum, Benedictus, Jubilate, Kyrie, Credo, Sanctus, Gloria in excelsis, Magnificat and Nunc dimittis.

HENRY J. GAUNTLETT (1805–76)

Before we consider these composers individually we must first mention two men who stand apart from the others in that they are remembered solely for their hymn-tunes. Henry Gauntlett, lawyer, and organist of a nonconformist chapel, is said to have composed the appalling total of over ten thousand hymn-tunes. Imagination boggles! Could he have gone into partnership with Charles Wesley the world would have seen an early example of automation. Not surprisingly, Homer not only nods but sleeps pretty soundly for some 9,990 of them, yet a handful have found their way into most hymnbooks. *St. Alphege* ('Brief life is here our portion') and *St. George* ('To Christ the Prince of peace') are not wildly exciting while *Laudate Dominum* ('O praise ye the Lord'), good as it is, has been largely superseded by Parry's much better tune. *St. Albinus* ('Jesus lives') is uncomfortably high for congregations but *University College* ('Oft in danger') goes well and *St. Fulbert* ('Ye choirs of new Jerusalem') is a really noble tune. But two of Gauntlett's tunes give him a place among the immortals—*Houghton* (A.H.B. 519), an eminently 'singable' tune which ought to be in every major hymnbook, and his astonishingly beautiful tune *Irby*, indissolubly wedded to Mrs. Alexander's 'Once in royal David's city'.

THE REV. JOHN DYKES (1823–76)

Less prolific but even more successful was that typically Victorian composer, the Reverend John Bacchus Dykes (any hopes raised by his second name appear never to have been fulfilled). His Services and anthems died long ago but he remains one of the most popular of all hymn-tune composers. No less than fifty-six of his tunes appeared in the 1875 edition of *Hymns Ancient & Modern* and thirty-one of these are still going strong in the 1950 Revised Edition. Most of Dykes's tunes exhibit weaknesses which make musicians blush and these weaknesses became more obvious as he grew older. They are basically harmonic and reveal themselves in a number of ways which are peculiarly characteristic of the composer:

(1) A stationary bass brought about by the harmonic implications of the melody. When, as often happens, these implications are so strong as to be almost inescapable, it is not always satisfactory to try to improve the bass line by reharmonising the tune; often the new harmonisation merely sounds forced and unnatural. See, for example, the last line of *Beatitudo* ('How bright these glorious spirits shine') and of *Dominus regit me* ('The King of love').

(2) Sometimes the stationary note appears in the tune and musical interest, if any, is transferred to the underparts, usually the alto and tenor; e.g. *St. Andrew of Crete* ('Christian, dost thou see them'), *Rivaulx* ('Father of heav'n') and *St. Aelred* ('Fierce raged the tempest').

(3) Often a tune begins with a really arresting first line, powerful and uplifting, sweeping onwards with irresistible drive. Then, quite unexpectedly, it collapses in a heap. The rest of the tune limps feebly home as best it can, slipping and sliding over treacherous chromatics. *Melita* ('Eternal Father') is typical of the genus; so are *Gerontius* ('Praise to the holiest') and *St. Drostane* ('Ride on! ride on in majesty').

He made some interesting experiments in two-movement form hymn-tunes, but by exaggerating the changes of mood implicit in the words the see-sawing between one style and the other for several verses becomes fidgety (e.g. *St. Andrew of Crete* and *Vox dilecti* 'I heard the voice of Jesus say'). Yet for all their faults most of these tunes have a certain undefinable 'singability' about them which ensures their continuing popularity with most worshippers and guarantees their inclusion in all standard hymnals for many years to come.

SIR JOSEPH BARNBY (1838–96)

Barnby, of a large and musical family, became a chorister at York Minster. He studied at the Royal Academy of Music and held various organist's appointments including that of St. Andrew's, Wells Street (1863) and St. Anne's, Soho (1871–86). He became precentor of Eton (1875), relinquishing this post in 1892 to become Principal of the Guildhall School of Music. He was knighted in 1892. Barnby was a noted orchestral conductor and was one of that band of pioneers who were amongst the first to recognise and proclaim Bach's genius: while at Soho he gave important performances of both the Passion settings. Some idea of the width of his interests can be gathered from the fact

Barnby in E: *Jubilate Deo*

Ex. 159

362

that he conducted the first English performance of Wagner's *Parsifal* (a concert performance) and he was regarded by many as a 'radical'.

It seems strange that a musician of such discernment should not have applied the same critical standards to his own compositions: if he had, few, if any, would have been published. In Barnby we have a composer who really did fall directly under the spell of Gounod, at the same time casting sidelong glances at Mendelssohn and Spohr. The outcome was a sickly sentimental style achieved largely by the excessive use of chromatic harmony and especially of chords like the diminished seventh—a style seen in all its fulsome juiciness in his part-song 'Sweet and Low'. When transferred from the parlour to the chancel such a style was wholly debilitating and most of Barnby's output shows an almost unbelievable lack of taste and sensitivity. Fellowes quotes a verse passage from the Jubilate of his Service in E which is a veritable triumph of gooey sanctimoniousness;[1] it deserves repeating and is shown in Example 159 opposite. This is nothing more or less than a Victorian part-song and the restless dynamic marks are intended to make it sound even more unctuous. Organ accompaniments are almost invariably chordal—and therefore unidiomatic: generally they either double the voices or else look like unenterprising piano accompaniments rearranged. In his more pretentious accompaniments we find a good deal of this sort of thing:

Ex. 160

and

Ibidem

Ex. 161

[1] Omitted in Prof. J. A. Westrup's revised Edition (1970).

The bass is static and the harmony changes very slowly but a spurious vitality is given to it by fussily repeating the chords or playing them as arpeggios. (Repeated chords in triplets smack strongly of the Victorian ballad in which it was almost obligatory for the piano to break into impassioned triplets for the last verse.)

Barnby is least offensive when content to write simply and straightforwardly without over-reaching himself, especially if the words are too robust to beguile him into trying to be fervent and soul-searing. Such an anthem as *O Lord, how manifold* is at least pleasantly tuneful, harmonically clean and wholesome, and has an appropriate organ accompaniment, even if the tune is rather obvious and the rhythm four-square. The thematic repetitiveness and unbroken three-in-a-bar of *O praise the Lord* becomes wearisome, and *Sweet is thy mercy* is a bit sickly, especially its ending. The magnificence of the words of *Salvation to our God* is lost on Barnby but at least his setting is straightforward and fairly free of Spohr's influence, while *Break forth into joy* ends effectively with the singing of 'Hymns of praise then let us sing' (second verse of 'Jesus Christ is risen today') set to its traditional tune.

SIR JOHN STAINER (1840–1901)

Stainer joined St. Paul's Cathedral choir at the age of seven and stayed till he was sixteen by which time he had already been for two years organist and choirmaster of a near-by parish church. At sixteen he was appointed organist of Ouseley's new foundation at Tenbury. From 1859–72 he held various appointments at Oxford and then, in 1872, succeeded Goss as organist of St. Paul's Cathedral. He was knighted in 1888. In that same year he was obliged to relinquish his cathedral work because of failing sight and a year later he was appointed Professor of Music at Oxford. He also held numerous other appointments. Stainer, like Barnby, was a widely accomplished musician: not only did he prove himself a first-class administrator, choirmaster, organist and organ accompanist, but he wrote standard textbooks on *Harmony* and *The Organ*, was part-editor of a famous *Dictionary of Musical Terms*, and was a scholar and musicologist of considerable repute.

It seems all the more extraordinary then that a man so cultured and gifted should, as a composer, be so lacking in taste and discretion. This is the more surprising in that he showed exceptional discernment and enterprise in his choice of anthem texts: whereas his predecessors rarely ventured far from the Book of Psalms, Stainer selected some of the most magnificent passages in Job, Isaiah, Ezekiel, Zechariah, Ecclesiasticus, the Book of Wisdom, Baruch, the Epistles, and Revelation. It is his tragedy that in most of his compositions he had only one idea in mind—to please. He had no burning passions or blinding visions demanding musical expression. Even self-criticism was suspended and in most of his anthems he sought no more than to gratify clerical friends and satisfy public demand by writing music which was sweetly melodious, harmonically obvious, rhythmically unadventurous and, above all, very easy and flattering to sing. These were also, of course, the characteristics of the Victorian part-song and indeed such anthems are not much more than part-songs and parlour ballads transplanted into church, utterly lacking in taste, refinement and dignity.

It is fair to add that one of Stainer's works is still to be heard in Anglican cathedrals— the anthem for double choir, *I saw the Lord*. It is one of his few anthems in the true cathedral tradition and was obviously planned with the acoustics of St. Paul's Cathedral in mind. It begins magnificently with a powerful opening section almost in the style of Samuel Wesley; touches of pictorial realism occur at 'the posts of the door were moved' and 'the house was filled with smoke'. This movement affords a glimpse of what Stainer might have done had circumstances been different, but he could not sustain the effort and the rest of the anthem tails off. The last movement, 'O Trinity, O Unity', shows some ingenuity in the way the Ter Sanctus, sung in unison by Cantoris, is combined with Decani's 4-part polyphony, but it is marred by the weakness of its melodic ideas.

For his most popular piece, *The Crucifixion*, he did not even have the advantage of magnificent words. Instead, he had a libretto which for sheer banality and *naïveté* would be difficult to beat. Sparrow-Simpson's appalling doggerel set to Stainer's squalid music is a monument to the inane. It is almost frightening that such a piece should remain so popular since it proves that most people will accept whatever they hear in church quite uncritically; indeed, they regard criticism as a form of sacrilege. Without exception all critics and writers on church music condemn *The Crucifixion* yet each year hundreds of performances continue to be given. The trouble is that there is a hard core of organists and choirmasters who are self-sufficient and self-satisfied. Not for them the work of the Royal School of Church Music with its literature, training courses and advisers; not for them the magazines, critical journals and books on church music. They are satisfied to teach their choirs the music they themselves learnt as children — good, bad and indifferent (mostly bad) — and the gentlest ripples of modern thought and taste are never allowed to ruffle settled habits of mind. Often they have little or no contact with their colleagues. There are yet others who, against their better judgement, yield (as did Stainer himself) to the pressure of clergy, choir or congregation — or even church treasurer. Amongst those critics who lament that *The Crucifixion* should ever have been written appears a most surprising name — the composer's own! Towards the end of his life Stainer bitterly regretted having published it and also, as we have seen, many of his anthems as well: this seems to be the final refutation of those who still champion the piece.

The most enduring part of Stainer's output are his hymn-tunes and it is worth noting that *A. & M. Revised* still includes no less than fifteen of them. They vary widely in quality: some, like *Rest* and *Charity*, are pretty feeble, but the best have well-constructed melodies and a natural dignity which justifies their continued use. Two of the best come from 'Crucifixion' — *Cross of Jesus* and *All for Jesus*. A characteristic of Stainer's hymn-tunes is his fondness for a unison passage towards the end, often sung at a slower speed than the rest: such passages occur in *Rest; Charity; Credo; Woodlynn; Covenant; Jesus the crucified; Holy Jesu, by thy passion*, and many more.

SIR ARTHUR SEYMOUR SULLIVAN (1842–1900)

Born in Lambeth, the son of an Irish military bandmaster, Sullivan became a chorister at the Chapel Royal at the age of twelve and published his first anthem the following year. Later, he studied at the Royal Academy and at Leipzig Conservatory. He was by far the most gifted and versatile of the musicians discussed in this chapter. Amongst other things he was organist of two churches, was a well-known conductor, and was the first director of what later became the Royal College of Music. Honours were heaped upon him. Though he edited a hymnbook and wrote oratorios, cantatas and church music, the bulk of his output was secular and he tackled almost all branches of composition. An enchanting early Symphony in E minor (*c.* 1864) is not unworthy to stand beside those of Mendelssohn and a recent gramophone recording of it received critical acclaim. He was particularly prolific as a song-writer. Yet apart from his tune to 'Onward Christian soldiers' and one or two trifles like 'The Lost Chord', Sullivan would now be forgotten had it not been for the remarkable series of operettas written in association with the librettist, W. S. Gilbert. In these he shows talents amounting to genius.

It is sad that his creative life was torn between two irreconcilable ideals. On the one hand his genius expressed itself naturally in the way most congenial to it—the operettas: on the other, feeling somehow that such frivolities were unworthy of a musician and unbecoming in a gentleman, he yearned to excel in 'serious' music, especially sacred music. It is not surprising then that many of his sacred pieces seem merely an extension of the operettas; indeed, if Katisha were to make a dramatic entry (assisted by the Chorus) in several of his anthems, the effect would in no way seem incongruous. Actually it would improve most of them.

Whereas Barnby's church music is often merely mawkish, Sullivan exhibits the far more healthy fault of sheer vulgarity. A good example of this is the gloriously noisy, extrovert *Festival Te Deum* written in 1872 to celebrate the Prince of Wales's recovery from typhoid: it is scored for soprano solo, orchestra, chorus and military band. Though we are unlikely ever to hear it performed again in all seriousness, it would make a marvellous item for the last night of the Proms! Sullivan was one of those people (they still abound) who thought that so long as the words were sacred—or at least vaguely religious—their aura automatically makes the music itself 'sacred'. Consequently there is little difference in style between some of his anthems and 'The Lost Chord'; here, for example, is a passage from *Hearken unto me*:

Sullivan: *Hearken unto me*

Ex. 162

366

and another from *Sing, O heav'ns*:

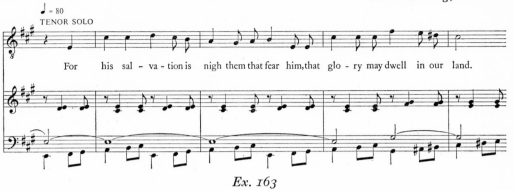

Ex. 163

Some of the smaller pieces like *O taste and see* and *O love the Lord* are fairly harmless but it seems a pity to waste a choir's time on such things when there is a limitless range of infinitely more rewarding music just waiting to be explored.

So much then for the principal figures of this sterile period.

CHAPTER XVII

The Awakening

It is generally held that the steady decline in English church music which we have traced through the eighteenth and nineteenth centuries was finally halted by the work of three men — Hubert Parry, Charles Stanford and (a little later) Charles Wood — and their work has even been referred to as 'the English renaissance'. Such a view does less than justice to Samuel Wesley and his son Sebastian. It may even be doubted if the later composers made any significant advances on the work of the Wesleys in spite of Stanford's attempts to graft instrumental forms and *leitmotiv* techniques on to the traditional stock. In any case Parry, Stanford and Wood were not just a happy conjunction of revolutionary thinkers thrown up casually by Fortune's wheel: rather were they representatives of a new and more healthy climate of opinion in the Church. As the man-in-the-pew wallowed more and more in his Barnby and Maunder, so thinking people became increasingly perturbed by the collapse of artistic standards. This new urge for reform was essentially an intellectual movement headed by scholars and men of letters, like the poet laureate Robert Bridges (1844–1930), and it is significant that Parry, Stanford and Wood all held university professorships, Parry at Oxford, the other two at Cambridge.

While men like Berthold Tours (1838–97), J. Varley Roberts (1841–1920), George C. Martin (1844–1916) and J. Frederick Bridge (1844–1924) clung tenaciously to the sentimental style of the mid-Victorians, the new school of composers brought to their work a fresh range of influences, far higher creative skill, infinitely better taste, and a feeling for words almost Tudor in its sensitivity.

It cannot be over-emphasized that English church music had become a parochial, even domestic affair, entirely self-sufficing and inward-looking, a little world on its own bounded by Services, anthems, hymns and chants. Choirboys were given a limited training in this circumscribed little field: they in turn became church organists and composers, content to write the sort of thing they themselves had sung as boys; it was the only music they knew or were interested in. Thus a great tradition had narrowed into a rut and from a rut to a mere groove. The music of Mozart, Beethoven, Schubert, Schumann, Berlioz, Brahms, Verdi and Wagner, even if known, was looked upon as a strange remote world without — one which had no point of contact with their own work and which certainly could not be allowed to disturb the pretty tunes and treacly harmony so beloved (then and now) by incompetent choirs and unthinking congregations. Even Sebastian Wesley, fine musician though he was, lacked his father's breadth of vision. The one man who was singularly well fitted to inject into English church music something of the power and the glory of the greatest foreign masters was Joseph Barnby. He had a foot in both camps yet he kept them widely separated. As a famous conductor he gave sympathetic performances of some of the world's supreme masterpieces from Bach to Wagner but the sad fact remains that he allowed only the most unctuous sacred pieces of Gounod and Spohr to influence his own writing. In-breeding had drained our sacred song of all its vitality; now only fertilization from without could save it. What was wanted was not more church musicians but highly gifted, thoroughly trained and widely experienced general musicians willing to bring their broader minds and wider knowledge to the service of the Church.

Parry, Stanford and Wood were just such men. They were highly talented, extremely versatile, had received not only a thorough technical training but a sound general and cultural education as well, and were men of exquisite taste and refinement. In their early years they had written mainly secular works (chamber, orchestral and choral) and this background was later to enrich their sacred works.

SIR HUBERT PARRY (1848–1918)

Parry was the son of a Gloucestershire squire. While still at Eton he took the Mus.B. degree at Oxford and soon afterwards went up to Exeter College where he became a noted sportsman. After three years in Lloyd's he devoted himself exclusively to music and literary work. In 1894 he was appointed Director of the Royal College of Music, a post which, from 1900–08, he combined with that of Professor of Music at Oxford. He was knighted in 1898.

Parry achieved distinction both as a musician and as a man of letters; a happy combination of these interests produced some distinguished writing on musical matters. Though a prolific composer he wrote relatively little for the Church (he was very much a free-thinker at heart): what he did write was mainly for festival or special occasions, employing massive choral forces, organ and orchestra. A typical example is his splendid 8-part coronation anthem *I was glad* (1902) which, shorn of its 'Vivats', now finds a place in the repertory of most competent choirs. Previous to this the Scholars of Westminster School had exercised their ancient privilege of greeting the royal entrance with vociferous shouts of 'Vivat Rex' and 'Vivat Regina'. By incorporating these 'Vivats' into his anthem and having them sung instead of shouted, Parry canalized the boys' excesses of loyal fervour into one great outburst having both ceremonial and musical significance. The gentle middle movement, 'O pray for the peace of Jerusalem', provides an effective contrast while, right at the end, the boys' ringing top B♮ is a tremendously thrilling sound. A feature of this anthem is a short organ interlude:

Parry: *I was glad*

Ex. 164

This recurs again and again in different keys and eventually generates the glorious accompaniment to the last movement, so giving the piece some structural cohesion. Closer examination reveals that many of the vocal lines bear some relationship to this interlude which thus acts as a sort of *leitmotiv* and helps to give the piece some overall unity. As we shall see, the use of these unifying thematic elements is typical of the work of Parry, Stanford and Wood and is obviously taken over from symphonic music.

An even more elaborate example is to be found in the large-scale verse-anthem *Hear my words, ye people* (1893) scored for soloists, festival chorus and orchestra. It begins with a lengthy and elaborate introduction. The first chorus is followed by a very fine bass solo, 'Clouds and darkness', in the Wesley tradition though the orchestral accompaniment is far more advanced than any of Wesley's. Other movements include an effective solo quartet, an attractive treble solo, and a section for full choir combined with solo quartet. The anthem ends with three verses of Sir Henry Baker's hymn 'O praise ye the Lord'. For these Parry provided a splendid swinging tune so eminently suited to the words that it has been extracted from the anthem and now appears in its own right in most hymnbooks. Parry's tune is now sung almost universally to these words. (While on the subject of hymnody, Parry's magnificent tune *Rustington* to 'Through the night of doubt and sorrow' deserves to be better known: it is unquestionably the finest tune available for these words.)

Amongst Parry's most deeply felt works are the 'Songs of Farewell', a group of six motets written near the end of his life (1916–18). Only the last has Biblical words, *Lord, let me know mine end*: the others are settings of poems by Vaughan, Davies, Campian, Lockhart and Donne. Parry had unerring skill in reflecting the mood of a poem and, though the Miltonic grandeur and sonority of *Blest pair of Sirens* seems more typical of him, he is no less successful in capturing the far more elusive spirit of English mystical verse. The best known of the group is *My soul, there is a country*, but here the composer's sensitivity to words leads him astray. In Vaughan's poem mood succeeds mood very rapidly and since the music responds immediately to these changes the result is restless and 'bitty': indeed, on the first four pages there are no less than five separate sections clearly marked off with double bars and changes of both key and time; of these short sections one, only eleven bars long, has three sub-sections — slow-fast-slow. This is going too far. Even thematic repetition fails to give cohesion because on their second appearance themes are so subtly varied that very few listeners recognise them. All six of the 'Songs of Farewell' suffer from this lack of unity and it is significant that in these last pieces he no longer employs a recurring theme to thread the sections together.

The setting of Lockhart's *There is an old belief* is also somewhat restless, this time not through structural weakness but because of excessive, and sometimes unconvincing, modulation. On the other hand Parry's 5-part setting of Campian's *Never weather-beaten sail* is a lovely thing, wholly convincing both as music and as an expression of the words — though it is doubtful if anybody could improve upon the artless simplicity of Campian's own melody. The large-scale works, *At the round earth's imagined corners* (7-part) and *Lord, let me know mine end* (double choir), have many passages of rare beauty and imaginative insight but the texture is often muddy and some of the modulations forced. In spite of such minor blemishes the 'Songs of Farewell' are worlds removed from the rubbish churned out by most of Parry's contemporaries and immediate predecessors.

SIR CHARLES VILLIERS STANFORD (1852–1924)

Stanford, an Irish Protestant, was born in Dublin. He was the only son of a wealthy family and took maximum advantage of a good education. He studied music privately under Sir Robert Stewart. In 1870 he went up to Cambridge with an organ scholarship and, soon afterwards, a classical scholarship to Queen's College. While still an under-graduate he was appointed organist of Trinity College (1873). Later he studied under Reinecke in Leipzig and Kiel in Berlin. He received doctorates from Oxford (1883) and Cambridge (1888) and in 1887 followed Macfarren as Professor of Music at Cambridge, a post he held until his death. He was conductor of the London Bach Choir (1885–1902) and the Leeds Triennial Festival (1901–10). He was an immensely successful teacher and as professor of composition at the newly formed Royal College of Music he exerted a considerable influence on the shaping of British musical thought. He was knighted in 1901.

Stanford wrote about two hundred works including seven symphonies, eleven con-certos, nine operas, some twenty collections of songs and over forty choral works. Church music forms only a small part of his output yet it is the part by which he is now chiefly remembered. (How often composers who have never made the grade in secular music have had great success in church and organ music: this may be a matter of personal faith and temperament—but it could also suggest that we will accept far lower standards in church than we would tolerate in a concert hall.)

As a church musician Stanford is acknowledged to be one of the most significant composers since Blow. He understood the true function of music in worship; he was a man of excellent taste, he had a natural gift for melody coupled with first-class technical skill, and he was a big enough person to cut right across the fashions and styles of his day. Historically he is important because he was the first to make a conscious and consistent effort to give some structural unity to his Services and anthems. As we have seen, it was a weakness of the longer works, from Gibbons to Wesley, that they consisted of a series of separate short sections loosely strung together; with few exceptions they lacked cohesion. Stanford solved the problem either by giving them 'symphonic' shape (exposition; contrast or development; recapitulation) or by a system of themes treated rather like *leitmotivs* and recurring at strategic points in the course of the music. His gift for melody goes hand-in-hand with a rarer gift—a happy flair for laying out voice parts to achieve maximum effectiveness: whatever the musical content of his works might be they invariably 'sing well' and he has an instinctive feeling for choral tone colours. As a consequence choirs love singing his music.

No less than three of his works must surely rank amongst the supreme glories of Anglican church music—the Magnificat in G, perhaps the loveliest of all settings of this Canticle; the extraordinarily beautiful motet *Beati quorum*; and his Gloria in excelsis in Bb, the most noble, uplifting and exciting setting since Tudor times.

STANFORD: THE SERVICES

Stanford first leapt into prominence with his famous Service in Bb (1879), a Service in which his originality of thought is shown in five ways:

1. In this first Service he experiments in applying instrumental forms to church music. The experiment is not wholly successful because he applies them too rigidly. It is obvious that themes which appear near the beginning set to one lot of words must reappear in the 'recapitulation' set to completely different words—different in scansion, emphasis and mood. If the original theme is repeated too exactly the words must often play second fiddle to musical necessity and the outcome sounds

371

stilted and contrived. For example, the Te Deum begins with three statements of the main theme and here the words fit very well:

Stanford in B flat: *Te Deum*

We praise thee, O God, we ac - know-ledge thee to be the Lord. All the earth doth wor - ship thee,

Ex. 165

but when this passage returns towards the end, the words are repeated and spaced out merely to fit the tune:

Ibidem

Day by day we mag - ni - fy thee; And we wor - ship, we wor - ship thy name, ev - er world with - out end.

Ex. 166

2. Stanford also takes over from instrumental music the concept of thematic motifs, their metamorphosis and development. Thus the Te Deum theme quoted above is heard later on the organ pedals at 'Heaven and earth are full of the majesty':

Ibidem

Ex. 167

and again in the accompaniment to 'Vouchsafe, O Lord':

Ibidem

Ex. 168

372

3. The theme just quoted is one of the ancient and traditional Gregorian intonations for Te Deum. In the Credo too he introduces an old plainsong intonation and again 'develops' it thematically. Even though Stanford made these intonations conform to his own harmonic and rhythmic pattern they nevertheless reintroduce into church music a powerful element which had been missing for nearly three hundred years, an element timeless and full of associations for all thinking Christians. Other composers were not slow to follow Stanford's example.

4. Fellowes and others have admired the opening phrase of Magnificat because it fits the words so perfectly. But of far greater importance is the fact that it is a three-bar phrase (as are the opening phrases of Te Deum quoted above), one of many similar odd-numbered phrases in the Service. As we have seen, odd phrase lengths were a rare phenomenon in Victorian music and here again Stanford exercised a beneficial influence on younger men.

5. Finally, his harmony is firm, clean and manly, his bass line strong and vigorous, and his modulations effectively placed.

A year after the B♭ setting came the Evening Service in A, a large-scale work with orchestral accompaniment written for the Festival of the Sons of the Clergy. The Morning and Communion Services were added in 1895. This time he makes no use of plainsong but in other ways he carries a stage further the principles established in the earlier work. The instrumental device of exposition and recapitulation is still present but is handled far more flexibly and subtly: compare, for example, the theme which opens Magnificat with its reappearances in the Gloria:

Stanford in A: *Magnificat*

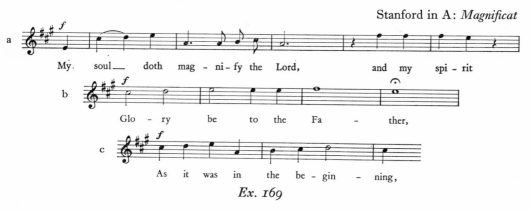

Ex. 169

The Gloria, which is the same for every Canticle, is scored for double choir: it is immensely powerful and brilliant. Nunc dimittis is of outstanding beauty. This time a gracious introductory passage for the organ becomes the unifying agent. Beginning quietly, the voices gradually build to a tremendous climax at the words 'and to be the glory'. Immediately afterwards there is a magical moment when Stanford repeats not only the music but also the words of the opening, 'Lord, lettest now thy servant depart in peace'. After this superb coda the Gloria sounds even more electrifying. In style and spirit Stanford in A has much in common with Wesley in E and it is certainly much the grandest of Stanford's Services. It demands a competent choir—and a more than competent organist.

The Service in F (1889) is a typical 'short' setting and is almost invariably sung unaccompanied. Within the limits of the form Stanford writes effectively and interestingly while, as usual, his method of treating themes as *leitmotivs* gives the movements cohesion. Jubilate is again scored for double choir.

After a gap of several years there appeared in 1904 the splendid full Service in G. The opening phrase of Te Deum not only dominates the first part of that particular movement but returns at the end in the organ accompaniment: the same phrase occurs in the Glorias of all the Canticles. The gem of this Service is Magnificat—one of the most supremely beautiful settings in the repertory. It consists of a glorious soaring melody for solo boy, lightly accompanied by the choir and by a rippling arpeggio organ accompaniment, and is intended to portray the Virgin Mary as a young girl rapturously singing to the accompaniment of her own spinning wheel. The opening is unforgettable:

Ex. 170

Nunc dimittis, the song of Simeon, is appropriately set as a baritone solo accompanied by choir and organ; similarly, in the B♭ Service it is set for men's voices in unison.

In this latter Service we noticed that Stanford had made thematic use of the ancient plainsong intonations. In 1907 he decided to take the use of Gregorians a step further and essayed an Evening Service constructed on the 2nd and 3rd Tones in which plainsong verses in unison alternated with a harmonized adaptation of the plainsong melody. The result was a curious hybrid and it has never enjoyed the same popularity as the others.

Two years later came the last of the great series — Stanford in C. After the magnificence of the setting in A and the ethereal beauty of the Magnificat in G this new work comes as something of an anti-climax, but whereas the others are essentially cathedral works, Stanford in C can be sung by parish choirs. Furthermore, techniques which were experimental or tentative in the earlier Services are here used with all the ease and assurance of a mature composer: there is a feeling of balance, lightness and controlled emotion and Stanford himself thought it the best of his Services. An interesting technical feature is that often the organ pedals and the bass singers part company, the organ supplying the true bass leaving the chorus basses free to enrich the harmonic texture which in such passages thus becomes 5-part instead of 4-part. A simple theme, four notes up and down the scale, dominates the Te Deum and recurs in other movements, notably towards the end of the Gloria: (the same Gloria is used for all movements).

Up to this point Stanford, a doughty Irish Protestant, had firmly refused to have any truck with such popish innovations as Benedictus qui venit and Agnus Dei and neither had been included in any of his Services. By now, however, public demand was so great that he was driven to write a setting in F intended for use with the Services in B♭, A, F and C.

The great Communion Service in B♭ was never intended for liturgical use; it was essentially a festival setting and Gloria in excelsis was specifically composed for the coronation of King George V (and has been sung at both subsequent coronations).

STANFORD: THE ANTHEMS

Though Stanford is renowned chiefly for his Services he also wrote several fine anthems and motets. His choice of texts is significant. Always he selects cheerful, comforting or positive words and his music reflects these qualities. Rarely does the tone darken and when it does the sun soon shines again. Death, gloom and breast-beating have no place in his work and his one experiment in the dramatic, *When God of old*, is unsatisfactory. Another characteristic of his style is his fondness for triple time.

Pride of place must go to an early work, *The Lord is my shepherd* (1886). In this he satisfies his instinct for form by employing the same devices as he does in his Services — the use of thematic motifs most of which undergo development, usually in the organ accompaniment. The piece falls into five well-defined sections locked together by thematic references. What makes it unique, certainly for its time, is that the whole piece is built almost entirely from phrases of three bars (or multiples of three). As befits the words, it opens in typical *pastorale* style with a graceful flute tune in 6/8 time played on the organ. The choir enters with two phrases of three bars (see Example 171 on the next page).

In the second section the organ part, developed largely from fragment (b) in the above example, becomes steadily more ominous while an angular vocal line in unison rises to a spine-chilling climax on the words 'shadow of death': but with the comforting thought 'I will fear no evil for thou art with me' peace is restored and the shepherd's pipe returns

Stanford: *The Lord is my shepherd*

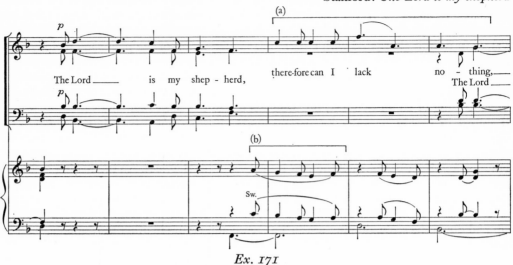

Ex. 171

to usher in the third section which reworks and develops material already heard in the opening section. After an emphatic full close in F major, a chord of D minor initiates a recitative for men's voices to the words 'Thou shalt prepare a table'; this is punctuated by chords played on the full Swell. The final section opens with a charming melody for the boys which is then taken up by the rest of the choir and developed contrapuntally to a powerful climax. The text of an earlier verse 'for thou art with me' provides a serene coda and it will be noticed that the words 'Thy rod and thy staff' are set to phrase (a) in the above example, so linking the end with the beginning. This splendid anthem is within the capabilities of a good parish choir.

Given a man of Stanford's ability and integrity one may safely assume that all his published work will reach a reasonably high level of musicianship and competence: even his less inspired efforts, like the early anthems *And I saw another angel* and *If thou shalt confess*, will always be appropriate, well written and eminently singable while his best work has already become part of the heritage of English church music. Two beautiful anthems which should be in the repertory of every parish choir are *Oh! for a closer walk with God* and *How beauteous are their feet*. *The earth is the Lord's* shows little more than skilled craftsmanship but the Easter anthem *Ye choirs of new Jerusalem* is radiant with joy and full of the spirit of Easter. Another Easter anthem *Jesus Christ is risen today* is laid out for double choir and organ.

In 1913 Stanford published three motets: *Ye holy angels bright* (8-part), *Eternal Father* (6-part), and *Glorious and powerful God* (4-part). The second, to words by Robert Bridges, is a deeply felt work of quiet beauty: its harmony is often boldly imaginative and lends subtle colouring to the words. *Glorious and powerful God* is a solid forthright work in the part-song manner; though popular with choirs it lacks the sensitive touches of the composer's best work.

He also wrote three Latin motets (1905) intended to be sung as 'Grace' anthems in Trinity College Hall on 'Gaudy' days. The first, *Justorum animae*, begins in four parts but later breaks into seven. Like so much of Stanford's best music it has a flowing grace and calm gentle beauty: the last thirteen bars are exquisite. The second, *Coelos ascendit hodie*, falls somewhat below this level and craftsmanship sometimes does duty for inspiration: it is a forceful piece for double choir. The gem of the set is the last one, *Beati quorum via*. Though not intended for liturgical use it is frequently sung as an anthem and may indeed be accounted one of the most supremely lovely works to be heard in our cathedrals. It is unashamedly romantic. The word 'ambulant' suggested to Stanford a serenely-flowing unbroken crotchet movement and the three high voices are effectively contrasted with the three low. Not only is the melodic line a thing of beauty but the underparts all have glorious phrases to sing.

As a composer of hymn-tunes it is instructive to compare Stanford with Dykes. Musically, Dykes's tunes are pretty poor, yet the best of them still have the power to 'excitate and stir the hearts of men'. Stanford's tunes are the opposite; they are almost invariably 'good' as music but somehow they have never caught on with congregations. Fine musician though he was, Stanford lacked the common touch, the touch which enables a Purcell, a Handel or an Elgar to go straight to the heart of a nation. His best tune is *Engelberg* set to 'For all the Saints' and this would certainly have been a winner had not Vaughan Williams written an even finer tune. Stanford's tune was published in extended form with varied accompaniments to the many verses: an old Irish tune, *St. Patrick's Breastplate*, was given similar treatment. Both appear in *A. & M. Rev.* In some of Stanford's hymn-tune arrangements (such as *Oh! for a closer walk with God* founded on the tune *Caithness* from the Scottish Psalter of 1635) the choral parts are richly varied as well as the accompaniment. Such arrangements are known as hymn-anthems, a form which has become very popular in the present century (but see p. 192). In hymn-anthems, devices like faux-bourdon, descant, varied harmonies, and antiphonal effects for double choir are freely called on so that the verses of the text emerge as a series of variations or comments on the hymn melody. A true hymn-anthem must be based on a well-established tune: a free setting of the words of a hymn or varied treatment of an original tune by the composer himself cannot claim to be examples of the form. Hymn-anthems are a good way of introducing unfamiliar tunes to a congregation.

CHARLES WOOD (1866–1926)

Both Stanford and Wood were Irish but, whereas Stanford was a Dubliner, Wood came from Northern Ireland. He was born in a house immediately behind Armagh Cathedral and began his musical studies under the cathedral organist. From 1883–87 he was at the Royal College of Music in London where he studied under Stanford and was later appointed to the teaching staff. In 1888 he took up residence in Cambridge, holding various university appointments till, in 1924, he succeeded Stanford in the professorial chair. During his time in Cambridge he and Stanford were not only colleagues but close friends and the older man's influence is strong in Wood's work; for this reason some comparisons are inevitable.

Whereas sacred music formed only a small part of Stanford's output, Wood was essentially a church composer even though he also wrote secular works: his church music includes four Communion settings, two Morning Services, about twenty Evening Services and some thirty anthems. Stanford was a staunch Irish Protestant: Wood inclined to high churchmanship—hence his interest in Gregorians and the ancient Office Hymns; his churchmanship also influenced his choice of texts which included hymns and translations by Heber, Keble, Greville Phillimore, John Mason Neale and G. R. Woodward. Like his master, Wood too preferred cheerful and objective texts. Most of his music was written for professional choirs, especially the famous college choirs of his own university: for this reason works for double choir abound and even when the voice parts are comparatively simple the organ accompaniment frequently suggests that he had the reverberation of some vast and resonant building in mind—usually King's College Chapel.

In early works like the Evening Services in D, E♭ and C minor he trod closely in his master's steps, even to the extent of employing thematic motifs to hold the movements together. Later a more individual style emerged derived partly from his interest in older forms of music. Thus his affection for plainsong led him to write faux-bourdon type Services like those on Tones V and VI and Tones I and IV, his unison setting of Psalm 114 and the *Pange lingua* variations in his *Passion* setting. His love of the ancient modal system bore fruit in an outstanding work, his unaccompanied *Mass mainly in the Phrygian Mode* (irreverently known in choir schools as 'Wood in the fridge').

An even more potent influence in his later work was that of the old metrical psalm-tunes. Baroque German composers had based many of their works on chorales: these sturdy old tunes had their roots deep in the history and traditions of Lutheranism; their musical characteristics made them ideal subjects for variation treatment; furthermore, the audience would have had the tunes, words, and the associations of both so strongly in mind that the chorale was a point of immediate contact between composer and people. For similar reasons Charles Wood, with a sidelong glance at Stanford's *Oh! for a closer walk*, discovered a new fount of inspiration in the old Genevan psalm-tunes. Of the many fine anthems which derive their power and strength from Genevan melodies *O Thou sweetest source* is one of the best. Bourgeois's original melody is in any case superb: in the first verse Wood gives it to the trebles and in the second to tenors, the other voices supplying rich harmonies and interesting rhythmical counterpoints. The last verse is in unison except for the climactic phrase 'Come, exalt me to the skies', and the broad melody is supported by a fine swinging organ accompaniment. *How dazzling fair* receives precisely similar treatment but neither the melody itself nor Wood's handling of it are quite so distinguished. In *God omnipotent reigneth* emphasis on bare fifths suggests starkness and primeval power: in the second verse the melody is effectively reinforced by dividing the basses and letting the 1st basses double the tune at the octave below. *O be joyful* treats the 'Old Hundredth' tune rather like an ordinary Anglican chant except that on the 'reciting' note the words are sung in strict tempo: it is one of the composer's least satisfactory pieces. The short unaccompanied motets *Out of the deep* and *Bow down thine ear* are mainly straightforward harmonizations of the old psalm-tunes in block harmony with a few rhythmic 'points' to lend variety. The former is based on Goudimel's version of the Genevan psalm-tune set to Psalm 129 ('Au fond de ma pensée'): Wood seems to have favoured this melody as he used it again with tremendous effect in the middle section of *'Tis the day of Resurrection*. Not content with introducing Genevan melodies into his anthems, the composer extended their use to his Services, five of which are based on them.

Of course hymn-anthems represent only part of his output. Such effective and tuneful pieces as *O Thou the central orb* and *Expectans expectavi* ('This sanctuary of my soul') are deservedly popular though the words of the latter are too romantic for most tastes nowadays. Except for *'Tis the day of Resurrection*, all the anthems mentioned so far are suitable for parish choirs; for some of the composer's best work, however, we must turn to the great *a cappella* double-choir works like *Hail, gladdening light*, *Glory and honour* and *'Tis the day of Resurrection*. The first of these is very impressive. It is cast in the form A–B–A with coda. The A section is powerful and majestic: the B section, set to the second verse of words, begins quietly with men's voices in four parts answered by high voices; a series of imitative entries leads to a massive climax and the music then sinks back to *pianissimo*—a calm soon to be shattered by the return of the main movement. *Glory and honour* is cast in the unusual form of a choral rondo—A–B–A–C–A–D–A. The rondo theme is announced at the outset by men's voices in unison followed by three high voices and then a few bars of 6-part writing for full choir. Section C is interesting in that the tenor is a 4-note *ostinato* set in 3-time:

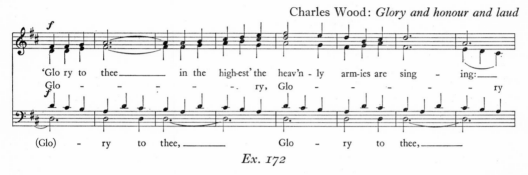

Charles Wood: *Glory and honour and laud*

Ex. 172

Section D is more lengthy and rather slower. When the rondo theme makes its last appearance it is extended and developed and there is a good deal of canonic writing; the chorus expands into 8 parts and the piece comes to a triumphant ending.

'Tis the day of Resurrection is a setting of J. M. Neale's metrical translation of an ancient Greek ode—the first of eight such odes threaded together on an acrostic which comprise St. John Damascene's celebrated Easter Canon. Such odes consisted of two parts—a traditional *heirmos* (which became a mould for subsequent strophes) followed by a number of *troparia*—strophes written in exact imitation of the older *heirmos*. In his setting of Neale's translation Wood retains the old Greek names for the two movements. In *heirmos* there is a good deal of brisk imitative and canonic polyphony and a chain of bold modulations colours the words

> From death to life eternal,
> From earth unto the sky,
> Our Christ hath brought us over,
> With hymns of victory.

The *troparia* consists of two strophes. For the first, which is slower, Cantoris choir sings Goudimel's version of the Genevan tune 'Au fond de ma pensée' (the same tune which Wood used as the basis of his short motet *Out of the deep*) arranged in simple block harmony while Decani intersperses passages in elaborate imitative counterpoint. For the second strophe, 'Now let the heavens', Wood repeats the music of the *heirmos*: such an exact recapitulation is not open to the same objection as some of Stanford's because, by definition, the metre, accents and number of metrical feet in each line of the strophes in *troparia* must correspond exactly with those in the *heirmos* strophe. Towards the end, the *heirmos* music is modified to lead into a brilliant coda. Thus the structure of this anthem is extremely interesting—but structure alone is not enough; it is Wood's musicianship and artistry which infuse it with vitality and make this one of his finest anthems.

Of the smaller unaccompanied pieces mention must be made of *O most merciful*, with its lovely close, and the Latin grace *Oculi omnium*, a perfect little gem. The 6-part *Haec dies* is in fact an Easter fanfare: bold modulations contribute to the general excitement and the ending fairly sizzles. Of the anthems for men's voices, *I will call upon God* (ATB) is frankly dull but the double-choir *Great Lord of Lords* (ATB:ATB) is effectively written for this difficult medium.

The 4-part piece for boys' voices *Sunlight all golden* is provided with a piano accompaniment. The words are a translation by G. R. Woodward of one of Paul Gerhardt's poems. Neither words nor music make this a suitable work for liturgical use but it would be very appropriate in a school chapel.

There are almost as many Services as anthems and detailed comment is impossible. Of the Communion settings that in the Phrygian mode is the most interesting and original: though unaccompanied it is not too difficult for a parish choir. Another *a cappella* work, the *Mass in C minor* is also quasi-modal: it is a highly effective work but is more difficult to sing.

Coming to the Evening Services the early setting in D (1898) is one of the best and most popular. Its Magnificat is energetic and has a vigorous, wide-ranging organ accompaniment, but the Service is most noted for the exceptional beauty of its Nunc dimittis, worthy in every way to stand beside Stanford's Magnificat in G. The Canticle is sung by basses alone to a gracious and tranquil melody; at the end of each verse the three upper voices, hushed, sing the opening words of the Canticle to a phrase of ravishing loveliness. There are two settings in E♭: the earlier (Novello 1891) is easily recognised because the first verse of Magnificat is in unison. Here again Nunc dimittis is outstanding: it opens with a threefold statement of an idyllic, floating theme, followed by a gentle descending passage for men's voices ('For mine eyes'). Effective modulation produces a fine climax on 'glory'. The later E♭ Service (Year Book Press 1927) has the second and third verses of Magnificat in unison. This too is a useful setting but though published nearly forty years later than the other it shows little progress or development in style or technique.

The *a cappella* double-choir setting in G is a fine work but is eclipsed by the magnificent 'Collegium Regale' Service in F (generally sung unaccompanied). In this Wood deploys his two choirs with splendid effect: the musical ideas are distinguished and their working out masterly. In Nunc dimittis the melody is given to Decani tenors reinforced by Cantoris basses—a most effective arrangement. The more elaborate the writing the more Charles Wood seemed to rise to the challenge; it is not surprising then that the unison Service in A♭ has little merit. A curious novelty is an unaccompanied setting of Sternhold and Hopkins's metrical paraphrase of the evening Canticles. Magnificat begins thus:

My soul doth magnify the Lord,
 My spirit evermore
Rejoiceth in the Lord my God,
 Which is my Saviour.

And why? because he did regard,
And gave respect unto
So base estate of his hand-maid,
And let the mighty go.

Wood sets these words to the 'Old Version' (1562) tune to Psalm 77 while Nunc dimittis, equally quaint, is based on the 'Old Version' tune to Psalm 19. His simple unaccompanied SATB setting is charming and somewhat naive, as befits the words, but the unbroken triple time becomes wearisome. This Service too was written for King's College Chapel: it would be illegal to use it liturgically in an ordinary church or cathedral.

Though not strictly within our purlieu, attention must be drawn to Wood's greatest achievement, his setting of *The Passion of our Lord according to St. Mark* (1921). The Gospel narrative is divided into five sections each of which concludes with a hymn. There are no set arias: the Evangelist sings mainly in free recitative; the Christus part is far more lyrical and employs *recitativo stromentato*. The chorus performs three functions: it acts the part of the crowd ('Surely thou art one of them'); more often it takes over the role of Evangelist ('and with him a great multitude'); and in the hymns it illumines and meditates on the Passion drama ('My God, I love thee'). Choruses tend to be short and dramatic. The fifth part of the Gospel narrative is intended to be sung unaccompanied: in the other four the organ contributes powerfully to the unfolding of the story. The work is more difficult than Stainer's *Crucifixion* but still well within the range of any competent church choir willing to take a little trouble—and it is very well worth the effort. It is a work which grows on one as one becomes more familiar with it. In religious feeling, sense of drama, and high level of musical inspiration it is unquestionably one of the best pieces of its type. It has been quite unjustifiably neglected and choirs and small choral societies unfamiliar with it will find it a most valuable and beautiful addition to the repertory.[1]

One other facet of Wood's work must be mentioned—his immensely important contribution to three treasuries of sacred songs edited by his friend the Rev. G. R. Woodward. Of these, *Songs of Syon* (1904) is the most important; this remarkable book will be discussed in some detail on p. 401. Three years earlier Woodward had issued his *Cowley Carol Book* in which Wood had arranged and harmonized many of the tunes. The first edition (1901) had thirty-nine carols: in the second edition (1902) the number had risen to sixty-five of which the words of twenty-one had come from the pen of John Mason Neale. A second series offering an additional thirty-seven carols was issued in 1919 and Wood now appears as co-editor. The collection includes 'translations of Latin and German carols ranging from the XIIth to the XVIth century' plus a few original poems by Woodward himself 'for some fine old melody's sake'. We are indebted to *The Cowley Carol Book* for Wood's well-known harmonizations of *This joyful Eastertide*, *A virgin most pure*, *King Jesus hath a garden* and *Shepherds, in the field abiding*.

The third product of their joint editorship was *An Italian Carol Book* (1920) 'being a selection of Laude Spirituali of the XVIth and XVIIth centuries'. Of the thirty-seven carols, all but four were harmonized by Wood, with his customary skill and artistry. This collection includes many fine things and makes a welcome addition to the carol repertory.

---

[1] Published by The Faith Press.

Parry, Stanford and Wood, then, were the outstanding figures in a minor revolution aimed at restoring to English church music some of its former ideals, standards and sense of purpose. Once they had given a lead their contemporaries and pupils were quick to respond. The new movement grew and spread; there was a tremendous upsurge of interest in sacred music accompanied by an immense improvement in standards. The three protagonists were soon joined by men like Alan Gray, Basil Harwood, Tertius Noble, Walford Davies and Edward Bairstow (see Chapter XIX, pp. 412–16). It was this group of composers who ushered in the twentieth century, shaped further growth, and prepared the way for the many experiments and developments to come.

CHAPTER XVIII

The Twentieth Century

THE STATE OF THE CHURCH

The nineteenth-century reformers had done their work well and the Church at the end of the century was a very different organisation from what it had been at the beginning. The scandalous evils and abuses which had disfigured it for so long had been largely remedied and an honest attempt had been made to curb its excesses and supply its deficiencies. No longer was the ministry a refuge for the wealthy ne'er-do-well: the absentee clergy, the squire-parsons, social climbers, nepotists and pluralists of former days had been largely superseded by devout men possessing a deep sense of vocation who won the respect, and often the love, of their flocks. Not, of course, that class distinction disappeared: by far the greater number of clergy still received their education at preparatory school, public school and the older universities (which implied a moneyed background), while Oxbridge was a basic essential for any important preferment. This meant that the parson was regarded as one of 'them' rather than one of 'us'.

In mid-Victorian times England had been swept by a wave of religiosity: people began the day with family prayers, said their private prayers, read the Bible and went to church regularly every Sunday. The vast majority of them were staunch Protestants, strict Sabbatarians, fundamentalists in their attitude to the Bible, and upheld a particularly narrow form of Calvinism in their social behaviour. In church they placed emphasis on Bible readings and sermons and discounted ritual and ceremonial. As the teaching of the Tractarians began to take effect and the 'high church' movement attracted more adherents, so the suspicion and resentment of the anti-ritualists fermented, expressing itself in public protest, abuse, hooliganism and even vandalism. When, in 1859, the Tractarians formed the English Church Union, the Evangelicals countered with their Church Association (1865) and these two organisations became increasingly bitter and determined in their hostility. The Association's prosecution of the ritualists through British Courts, resulting in many saintly and much-loved priests serving prison sentences for their beliefs, angered all true Christians and gave their cause an aura of martyrdom. This greatly strengthened the high church cause. Most people, clergy and lay, plumped for a safe middle-of-the-road position (the 'moderates').

Narrow, joyless Calvinism and strict Sabbatarianism found themselves challenged by the satire of 'decadent' writers like Wilde, the spirit of the 'Naughty Nineties', and the example set by the Prince of Wales and his friends. When the old Queen died many restraints and taboos died with her and there was a new freedom, a new humanism, in the air. Within the Anglican Church this new freedom was reflected in a gravitational pull towards the high church position, 'moderates' tending towards 'high' and

Evangelicals becoming slowly more liberal until, at the present time, the true Evangelicals are only a small, if sometimes vociferous, minority.

Whereas in mid-Victorian times 'religion' was highly fashionable, attacks on credulity from within and without coupled with increasing emancipation led to a sharp falling-off in congregations; on the other hand those who still attended probably did so with better intent than those who had previously attended only because it was the done thing. These tendencies have continued throughout the twentieth century. The attacks, direct or indirect, by scientists, psychologists, rationalists, humanists and modernists have become more serious and more frequent and have had great impact on the nation as a whole because of their dissemination through the mass media of press, radio and television. Standards of righteousness and morality have changed. Within the Anglican church a policy of *laissez-faire* has produced an infinite variety of worship ranging from the near-Roman to the near-Presbyterian. In order to encourage some sort of discipline and obedience to an acceptable law a new revision of the Prayer Book was undertaken. The rejection of this book by the House of Commons in 1928, despite its warm acceptance by the Convocations and Church Assembly, left confusion worse confounded. By authorising parts of the 1928 revision for optional use in their dioceses, some Bishops allowed their clergy two books to work from instead of one—and that one had already lent itself to a wide variety of interpretations!

This century has witnessed a fairly steady decline in the numbers attending church and also in the number of ordination candidates; the latter has led to an acute shortage of clergy. Church-goers now represent only a small percentage of the population and even of these many attend very infrequently. On the other hand several fringe sects with odd and exotic beliefs have had surprising success since the Second World War. The pattern of worship too has changed. Fifty years ago Morning Prayer was a middle-to-upper class affair attended by fashionable ladies and prosperous gentlemen while domestics prepared the Sunday dinner: Evening Prayer was largely left to the lower orders. Class distinctions have gradually dissolved but (alas for church musicians) the sad fact remains that these two choir offices have steadily declined in popularity. So, to a lesser extent, has the more elaborate type of 'choral Eucharist' sung to a composed setting. Only when the standard of choir singing is exceptionally high are large congregations attracted to these services. Instead there has, in recent years, been a growing desire for one central act of corporate worship, a 'Parish' or 'Family' Communion attended by young and old and essentially congregational. This is a splendid development and one which has greatly enriched the spiritual life of the Church—though there is always a likelihood that habitual Communion may become mechanical. It would, however, be a tragedy if the present trend were carried to the point where churches had only the one service on Sundays: Mattins and Evensong are a valuable supplement to Parish Communion, offering spiritual comfort and a quiet, calm beauty which refreshes the mind.

There has been a marked improvement in the appearance of cathedrals and churches. The fabric is more carefully maintained, the appearance is brighter and they are kept much cleaner. Some of the worst horrors perpetrated by Victorian 'restorers' have been made good and furniture in bad taste replaced. It is sad that many churches formerly open for private prayer must now be kept locked because of the depredations of thieves and vandals.

384

MUSIC IN THE TWENTIETH CENTURY

For something like three hundred years (roughly from 1600 to 1900) the technical apparatus of music had been frozen into immobility by the classical key system. Techniques had changed, methods of applying them had changed, concepts had changed. But change within a system is quite a different thing from forward progress of that system as a whole and in basic essentials music had largely marked time; there was very little forward movement. Musicians continued to think in terms of tonic-dominant harmony and this dictated their melodic ideas. It is surprising how little separates the harmonic and melodic thinking of Monteverdi from that of Brahms. Towards the end of the nineteenth century this highly productive seam, which had been mined by all the great composers from Byrd to Mahler — and beyond — showed signs of being worked out. Composers found it increasingly difficult to express new thoughts by the old methods and many tried in various ways to break through into new territory. Wagner extended the use of chromatic harmony to the point where all sense of key was lost; Strauss achieved the same purpose by continuous fluid modulation; Vaughan Williams, in some of his early works, looked back across history to the modal system: but try as they may they could none of them escape the implications of the dominant-tonic relationship. It was Debussy who was most nearly successful in undermining the key system: by using the whole-tone scale he by-passed that fatal dominant and so released his music from its bondage.

What evolution failed to accomplish in the nineteenth century revolution achieved in the twentieth. Arnold Schönberg, a powerful and original thinker, anxious to extricate himself from the emotional as well as the harmonic tentacles of the classical key system, began to write music which completely dispensed with tonal organisation: what is loosely called 'atonal' music was born on 19 February 1909 when the first of his *Three Piano Pieces* (Opus 11) was completed. By entirely different routes Stravinsky and Bartok wrote music which, though still having certain tonal polarities, utterly shattered traditional conceptions of key. Schönberg's *Five Orchestral Pieces* (1909) and Stravinsky's *Rite of Spring* (1913) stood the musical world on its head — and it has never been the same place since. The influence of these three iconoclasts was immense and changed the whole face of twentieth-century western music.

This century has seen a tremendous amount of experiment and development ranging from such important and fruitful fields as Schönberg's technique of serial composition to bizarre novelties like electronic music and *musique concrète*. In general, *avant-garde* composers have been some fifty years or more ahead of the musical public and it may be doubted now whether the gulf which separates the two will ever be bridged — or is, indeed, worth bridging.

When future historians come to evaluate twentieth-century music they may well consider that what was formerly known as 'Das Land ohne Musik' has now become one of the most musical nations in western Europe. They will not necessarily endorse our opinion that in Edward Elgar, Vaughan Williams and Benjamin Britten we have produced three major composers but they will certainly agree that in such musicians as Gustav Holst, John Ireland, Cyril Scott, Arnold Bax, Arthur Bliss, Herbert Howells, Ernest Moeran, George Butterworth, Edmund Rubbra, Gerald Finzi, William Walton, Lennox Berkeley, Michael Tippett, Alan Rawsthorne, Constant Lambert, Humphrey Searle, Racine Fricker, Malcolm Arnold, Iain Hamilton, Peter Maxwell Davies, Richard

Rodney Bennett and others, and the song-writers Roger Quilter, Frank Bridge and 'Peter Warlock' we have a wealth and variety of native talent equalled only in the great days of Tudor England.

But if English musicians are traditionally conservative, our church musicians are far more so and the winds of revolution abroad ruffled not a single page in English organ lofts. Epic cataclysms outside passed unnoticed—and still remain almost unnoticed half a century later, judging by the music sung in most churches Sunday by Sunday. Church musicians are naturally—and very rightly—conservative. Nevertheless, in a quiet and very unobtrusive way, a smaller revolution has been going on which has had two vitally important results: (a) a keener and better-informed critical sense in those who compose and those who select church music, and (b) a much greater awareness of the true function of music in worship and of the responsibilities of all who offer it: this in turn has led to a far higher standard of both performance and behaviour on the part of choirs. As with secular music there has been an enormous increase in the number of composers and the quantity of music published. More to the point, this music reaches a higher musical standard and is much better suited to public worship than most written in the last century; even the least inspired gives thought and care to the word-setting and is musically competent.

THE STATE OF CATHEDRAL MUSIC

There has never been a shortage of cathedral organists, largely because the sheer inspiration of leading the performance of beautiful music day by day in some vast and glorious building, hallowed by many centuries of worship, is its own reward. Indeed, with so few cathedrals and so many musicians anxious to obtain these coveted posts, Deans and Chapters can afford to be highly selective. This means that the standard demanded is higher now than ever before. The man chosen will probably have a university degree and may well have been to Oxford or Cambridge, often as an organ scholar; he may have an arts degree as well as a degree in music and will have supplemented these with a lengthy series of practical diplomas: he is, in fact, a much-examined man! Usually he will have held one or two important church or college chapel posts before going to his first cathedral. Once appointed he is certainly a man whom parish church organists can respect and turn to for guidance—if he is willing to give it. As Wesley put it, such men 'are the bishops of their calling—men consecrated by their genius, and set apart for duties which only the best talent of the kind can adequately fulfil'.[1] It seems all the more regrettable then that the material rewards attaching to this high office should be so woefully inadequate. The result is that instead of being able to devote all his time, thought and energies to the improvement of music in his cathedral and diocese, the organist is driven by economic necessity to augment his income by school-teaching, lecturing, examining, journalism and various types of musical hackwork.

The status of the men altos, tenors and basses (usually called lay-clerks or lay-vicars) has also changed. Whereas before the Second World War they were professional singers who augmented their cathedral stipend with evening engagements and private pupils, the majority are now no longer professionals. Often they are engaged full time in commerce or industry and their cathedral work is reduced to a spare-time activity. Often, too, their remuneration does little more than pay travelling expenses between their homes

[1] See. p. 323.

and the cathedral. To accommodate these changed circumstances, fully choral morning services have become increasingly rare while Evensong, which used generally to be held at about 3.00 p.m., has been moved to 5.30 p.m. or thereabouts so that lay-clerks can slip in and sing a service on their way home from work. In such circumstances, rehearsals are difficult to arrange and will always be woefully inadequate. Contrast this with the favoured position of college chapels whose choral scholars are available for almost daily rehearsal.

The greatest changes concern the education of boy choristers. This century has seen an almost revolutionary advance in the condition, equipment, buildings, facilities and amenities of schools, and the 1944 Education Act rightly demanded high standards in such matters. To satisfy these standards imposes an enormous financial burden; the smaller the school the more crippling the burden will be. To run a choir school for twenty or thirty boys is now no longer economically feasible and various ways have been tried of overcoming the difficulty. These include enlarging the school to take in non-singing, fee-paying boys; merging the choir school into some nearby independent school; and closing the choir school and paying for the choristers to attend some local day-school where special arrangements can be made for them to fulfil their cathedral duties. But despite the best intentions of Deans and Chapters and genuine co-operation on the part of most headmasters, such schemes usually suffer from one fundamental drawback—the choirboys are now a minority group within a much larger organisation: worse still, they are a troublesome minority. Because of their cathedral duties they miss lessons and so get behind with their school-work; this is reflected in their form positions. (In the old choir schools, lessons were fitted round their cathedral duties.) As their ages vary from eight to fourteen they cannot be kept together as a separate entity but are distributed in ones and twos amongst various classes. Evensong often prevents them from taking part in sports, house events and out-of-school activities; Saturday hikes, week-end camps and foreign tours may be out of the question. Because choristers do not fit into the established pattern, members of staff come to resent them, and often the resentment shows. Because they belong to a group apart, with its own traditions and allegiances, they are often the butt of their schoolfellows (jealousy sometimes comes into this). Disciplinary problems can arise when senior choristers, who have very considerable responsibility and must command respect from juniors in the cathedral, are treated as very small fry by bigger boys in the school. Where choir and school interests conflict, loyalties are inevitably divided. It can be a most unsatisfactory picture. All the greater credit then to the cathedral authorities at Lincoln and Ripon who, in the very teeth of almost insuperable obstacles and difficulties, have in recent years re-established their choir schools. Such courage and vision deserves the gratitude, admiration and, indeed, practical support of all who have the interests of cathedral music at heart.

To pay the organist a salary commensurate with his training and responsibility; to raise the income of lay-clerks so that once again the cathedral has first claim on their time; and to run a real choir school where the interests of the cathedral and choristers remain paramount would be costly indeed. Could not this money be better spent? Those who inveigh against the immense cost of maintaining daily choral services might well remember the disciples' question 'To what purpose is this waste? For this ointment might have been sold for much and given to the poor.' Our Lord's stern rebuke on that occasion shows the value he placed on an act of pure worship, however costly. Good-neighbourliness must never become a substitute for true worship—and there is always an element of sacrifice in worship. The daily round of choral services, morning as well as evening, in the mother church of the diocese is a unique and continuing act of worship — whether any congregation is present or not. It is beside the point that many who do come experience an inspiration and an access of spiritual power which no other form of worship can bring them.

In addition to this central purpose, its *raison d'être*, the cathedral is an obvious and appropriate centre for diocesan services and events and for any occasion when a large congregation can be expected. On the other hand, the modern tendency for cathedrals to introduce a congregational-type service on Sundays, almost in direct opposition to local parish churches, seems deeply regrettable and shows a basic misunderstanding of what each stands for. It obscures the centuries-old distinction between the cathedral and parish church traditions. In its way it is even more pernicious than the attempts of some parish churches to sing a fully choral service on cathedral lines, the congregation remaining almost dumb. At least in towns people have a number of churches to choose from: there is only one cathedral.

Ways in which cathedral choirs can, and do, set an excellent example to parish church choirs are the reverence and seemliness with which they do their work and the time and trouble taken over doing little things well — the careful and unanimous recitation of the General Confession, Lord's Prayer and Creed; alert Responses, and tidy 'Amens' after Collects and Prayers. The singing of the psalms too is generally a model for parish singers. In such ways the cathedral can have a beneficial influence on the music of the diocese.

THE STATE OF PARISH CHURCH MUSIC

During the first half of the century there was also an immense improvement in the musical standards of church choirs. This was brought about by a number of factors — a general reawakening of interest in church music, the splendid work of the reforming, training and examining bodies, the growth of combined choirs festivals, and the opportunities provided by radio and gramophone for church musicians to hear the best choirs and learn from them. Since the end of the Second World War this general rise in musical standards has been offset by the extreme difficulty of recruiting young, competent and keen choirmen. In many choirs there are two age groups, the under-twenties and the over-sixties, with not much in between. As the old hands leave there are few to replace them. This is usually blamed on television (a convenient whipping-boy for all manner of social evils). A more likely reason is our greater mobility. Most families have cars and perhaps camping equipment or caravans; with improved trunk roads it is now so easy to get to the seaside, the open country, or visit distant relatives that folk are reluctant to tie themselves to a regular week-end commitment. There are still elderly choristers about who claim with justifiable pride that 'in fifty-eight years I have missed only four services', but these old stalwarts are thinning out and pride in such records is, regrettably, a thing of the past. Sometimes such impressive records have a daunting effect on prospective young recruits who fear that such fortitude may be expected of them! Another reason is the growing practice of having women sopranos because choirmasters will not take the trouble to recruit, hold and train boys. Women, however good, however keen, never become tenors or basses — we hope: boys do. If the present trend continues, choirmasters may be driven to thinking in terms of a 'morning' and an 'evening' choir, two different groups with possibly a few singers common to both; or perhaps a fairly large pool of singers who can work a roster between themselves so that an effective 4-part group will always be present.

Boys too are much harder to get than they used to be: this is variously attributed to the fact that families no longer go to church (but then families do not go to Scouts or Cadets either); the demands of homework (but there is no more homework now, if as much, as there was thirty years ago); 'the boys in this area all go away to boarding schools' (all?); leisure-time school activities; rival organisations and, of course, television. Taking these last three together it means that church choirs must actively compete with other claims on a boy's time—and this is not done by confronting them with a list of prohibitions or subjecting them to a barrage of nagging from choirmaster, parson, wardens and busybodies. Boys respect a kind but firm and positive discipline, they respond to a measure of real responsibility, their thoughts and feelings deserve respect, and they have a right to be consulted about things which concern them. To treat a boy of thirteen or fourteen as an irresponsible child is to lose him, but if he is treated as a colleague, a member of the team, he can become amazingly keen and will work hard and willingly. The unanswerable fact remains that after three or four successive organists have proved to their own satisfaction that it is utterly impossible to get choirboys in their particular parish, the fifth will produce, as though out of a hat, a happy team of twenty or thirty boys within a few weeks of his arrival. The right man will always attract boys to his choir wheresoever he may be.

A warm tribute must be paid to the ladies who have given faithful service, sometimes for many years, in parish choirs. In some churches they have kept the flag flying at times when it has been impossible to get boys or men. Nevertheless, however good and devoted they may be, it must never be forgotten that practically all church music was composed with the distinctive tone colour and unemotional purity of boys' voices in mind. To have women's voices singing an anthem by Gibbons, Boyce or Wood is as much a transcription as playing a flute sonata on an oboe. Apart from this aesthetic objection there are also practical ones: a mixture of lady sopranos and boy trebles is unsatisfactory as it always spoils the treble tone; the boys get discouraged because, no matter how hard they try, the ladies drown them; finally, the boys of today are the tenors and basses of tomorrow. If, as boys, they receive proper training, learn to read music, experience the thrill and excitement of singing in a good choir, and find happiness and fulfilment in its discipline and social life, then here is a future source of potential choirmen, already trained.

The objections to lady sopranos do not apply with the same force to contraltos: since the male alto voice is rare and often of poor quality, in most parish churches the use of contraltos is often the best practical policy.

THE RADIO AND GRAMOPHONE

The second quarter of the century saw the invasion of the home by radio and gramophone. The rapid rise of these industries has conferred immense benefits on all and music lovers in particular.

The first radio service was broadcast from St. Martin-in-the-Fields on the Feast of the Epiphany 1924 and since then the British Broadcasting Corporation has regularly transmitted services of many denominations. The standard varies as widely as the services themselves and embraces all levels from the Coronation ceremony to community hymn-singing from some remote chapel. From the Christian viewpoint, broadcasts of great State ceremonies—Coronations, weddings and funerals—and Christmas carol broadcasts bring something of the Christian message to homes which otherwise it would never reach. Thus the Christmas Eve carol service from King's College, Cambridge, is looked upon even by many non-Christians as an essential part of Christmas. Broadcasts enable organists and choir-singers to hear other choirs and learn from them (occasionally in the negative sense of learning what not to do!). Of special importance are the mid-week broadcasts of choral Evensong from cathedrals, college chapels and major churches: it is a pity they are transmitted at a time when most people are at work. In church music, as in other things, broadcasting reflects, but at the same time helps to mould, public taste.

The gramophone offers the immense advantage of repeated hearings of music of our own choice; old favourites are always at hand while unfamiliar pieces become familiar by repetition. Students can make a detailed study of individual works while the technique of great singers, instrumentalists, choirs and orchestras can be put under a microscope. In the old days of 78s, recording companies played for safety and rarely wandered far from the standard repertory of best-sellers. Church music on the whole fared rather badly. The first records of importance were the 1925–26 Columbia pressings of Services and anthems by the choir of St. George's Chapel, Windsor, but the singing was deplorable. Then in 1927 came the famous recordings of the Temple Church Choir. Their remarkable solo boy, Ernest Lough, had not only a magnificent voice but also astonishingly mature artistry to go with it. His performance of *Hear my prayer* made gramophone history by establishing itself as the most popular record ever made; even now it is still in the catalogue. His *Hear ye, Israel* is even finer. But though the Temple Church records did much to popularize arias by Handel and Mendelssohn, they did nothing to help English church music. A few years later a few splendid discs of hymns and parish church pieces were issued by the School of English Church Music but it was not until 1950 that a serious attempt was made to record representative works of all periods. This was Columbia's 'An Anthology of English Church Music', sponsored by the British Council. It included over eighty works issued on forty-seven discs, recorded by the seven choirs of Westminster Abbey, St. Paul's and Canterbury Cathedrals, York Minster, and the Chapels of King's, New College, and St. George's, Windsor.

The advent of the long-playing record in 1948 had a revolutionary effect on the gramophone industry. Before long, record companies (many newly formed) vied with each other in enlarging the range of recorded music far beyond anyone's wildest dreams. In recording pre-nineteenth-century music genuine attempts are often made to secure historical authenticity: performances are based on scholarly editions prepared on scientific principles and many obsolete instruments have been revived. It is now possible to be as familiar with the sounds of the cornett, Krummhorn, Rauschpfeife, racket, theorbo and chitarrone as with those of piano, flute and oboe. Even obscure and esoteric works are often available in scholarly and inspired performances. The church musician is particularly well served and can obtain almost everything from Dunstable to Britten and from plainsong to 'pop' hymns. Names which were once merely legends in history books can now be living realities in the home.

And here a word of caution must be given. In the second half of this century there has been an epidemic of small specialist groups of professional singers calling themselves some such name as the Bill Bloggs Singers—or Consort—or Ensemble—or Chorale (a new use of the word!). Such groups often sing a good deal of church music and many specialise in singing renaissance church music. Often their musical standard is extremely high and we cannot but admire their immense technical skill and polished artistry. But we must never forget that church music was specifically designed for the impersonal and unemotional tone-colour of an all-male choir of boys and men singing in a large echoing building: the same work sung by a small and rather 'twee' mixed group in a recording studio can give only a pale reflection of the original. Admittedly engineering problems were such that for a long time we had to choose either the atmosphere of a cathedral but with no clarity of detail, or else the clear-cut detail of a recording studio but with no atmosphere. In recent years, however, recording techniques have improved to the point where engineers can get the best of both worlds while the addition of stereophony can provide spatial separation—especially useful in music for double choir.

But that is not all. Church music calls for a choir which is used to offering its singing as a daily and selfless act of worship in a liturgical framework. Concert groups of mixed voices are always, to some extent, 'giving a performance'; to them a Mass is a concert item. Yet there is all the difference in the world between a concert item—in which the performers can take a justifiable pride in the skill and beauty of their own performance and in the warmth of the audience's response—and an act of worship in which the choir (and especially the boys) unselfconsciously give of their best as a daily routine, whether there is any congregation or not. This is the sort of choir which church composers over the centuries have had in mind and which is still the only type of choir which can do their works full justice.

To cite only one example of the way the gramophone has had a beneficial influence; the old type hooty, wordless cathedral alto is now almost a thing of the past. The records of Alfred Deller, especially his early 78s, showed that it was possible for an alto to sing rhythmically with beautiful clear tone, precision, perfect diction, sensitivity to words, musicianly phrasing and a sense of style. Deller's pioneer work was consolidated by John Whitworth and others. The change of name from 'alto' to the older 'counter-tenor' seems to indicate a change of heart as well.

Radio and gramophone have so accustomed us to great performances by supreme artists that we ourselves have become highly critical and selective. A better-informed public has led to a general raising of standards, professional and amateur, and there is far less support now for the second-rate, the half-baked and the careless. This change has been of incalculable benefit to the art though it inevitably encourages the cult of 'star' performers.

REFORMING, TRAINING AND EXAMINING AGENCIES

A number of agencies have contributed to our vastly improved standards in church music. Some of these call for brief mention.

The Church Music Society was founded in 1906 with the object of facilitating 'the selection and performance of the music which is most suitable for different occasions of Divine Worship, and for choirs of varying powers'. This it did in three ways:

1. by arranging lectures, practices and courses of study;
2. by publishing suitable music in good editions, including reprints of old music suitable for parish choirs;

3. by issuing important occasional papers dealing with various aspects of church music.

After some forty years of immensely useful work the Society has now handed over its training activities to the Royal School of Church Music, though it continues to publish music and to act in an advisory capacity. Its publications remain important and several of its occasional papers are valuable.

In 1922 the Archbishops of Canterbury and York appointed a committee to enquire into the purpose and state of music in the Anglican church. Their report, *Music in Worship*, surveyed the field in depth, gave valuable guidance on general principles, useful advice in practical matters, and made a number of important recommendations. The report was re-issued several times until, in 1948, the Archbishops appointed another committee to undertake a similar enquiry. This second report, called *Music in Church*, was published in 1951 and has since been revised. It is so important and so practical that every church musician should possess a copy and refer to it frequently — even if some of its *obiter dicta* seem a little quaint for 1951, like the description of modern secular music 'in which the restlessness and cacophony betoken an unsettled and uncertain age'!

One of the most significant events in the history of Anglican music took place on St. Nicolas's Day (6 December), 1927, when the then chairman of the Church Music Society, Dr. (later Sir) Sydney Nicholson, launched his great movement known first as the School of English Church Music and later, since 1945, as the Royal School of Church Music. Such faith had Nicholson in the work he planned that he resigned his post as organist of Westminster Abbey in order to devote himself to it. An essential part of his plan was the foundation of a residential college where church musicians could, for the first time, receive a thorough training in their specialized field, a training based on the ideas formulated in the first Report of the Archbishops' Committee, *Music in Worship*. With his own private fortune and contributions from the Proprietors of *Hymns Ancient & Modern* and others, he was able to open the College of St. Nicolas at Chislehurst in 1929 with a few students, ten resident choirboys and a small staff.

This was the first choral foundation to be established since Ouseley's venture at St. Michael's College, Tenbury, but the two institutions are quite dissimilar in aims and functions. Tenbury is dedicated to the preservation of the English cathedral tradition: it is a self-contained unit, sufficient unto itself, charged with the responsibility of maintaining daily choral services. St. Michael's College is now a flourishing preparatory school which provides singing boys for the choir while the adult musicians on the foundation are normally trained and qualified before being appointed. In contrast, the R.S.C.M. provides what is essentially a training college whose students spend only a limited time there and then go out into the world disseminating its ideals and teachings. Though some cathedral organists have received part of their training at the college, its chief concern is the improvement of music in the parish churches. Emphasis is placed on doing simple things well. In addition to full-time residential courses lasting up to three years, the college offers a wide range of short courses many of which are directed towards specific groups; e.g. clergy, ordinands, country choirmasters, or candidates for particular examinations. The College now occupies Addington Palace, Croydon.

Nicholson's College was, in a very real sense, the ultimate fulfilment of Wesley's pipe dreams as outlined in his 'plan' (see page 323) but in aiming to train musicians in the parish churches as well as cathedrals it went very much further than Wesley had conceived. Furthermore the college draws its students from churches within the Anglican communion throughout the world and so has become an international institution.

Yet the college is only one part of the work of the R.S.C.M. which, by means of its system of 'affiliating' choirs, is in direct contact with many thousands of cathedral, collegiate chapel, parish church, school, and Free Church choirs at home and overseas. It is not necessary to discuss the work of the R.S.C.M. in detail: all readers must surely be aware of its publications, summer schools, choirboys' courses, festivals (including the great festivals in the Royal Albert Hall), hymn-singing festivals, advisory services, and the splendid work done by its Director and Commissioners in visiting choirs in their own churches. It is sufficient to say that very largely as a result of its work the function of music in worship is now more widely understood, standards of performance and conduct have greatly improved (even though many choirs are much smaller), and the choice and selection of music show vastly better taste and critical judgement than was general in 1927.

In the nineteenth century cathedral organists accepted articled pupils who received a thorough training in church music including such practical skills as transposition, extemporisation, score reading (with C clefs in at least three positions) and playing at sight from figured bass. In the twentieth century the practice of taking articled pupils has largely fallen into desuetude, regrettably perhaps. Instead, new and more critical standards were being set by the Associateship and Fellowship examinations of the Royal College of Organists. As the century has advanced these diploma examinations have become ever more searching and demanding, both in organ tests and paper work, and the Fellowship examination is now generally considered to be the most exacting of British musical diplomas. In 1924 the College took a major step forward by inaugurating examinations in choir-training. Only those who already hold one of the College's organ diplomas can enter for the 'Diploma' Choir-Training examination (CHM); the possession of the diploma therefore implies a general all-round competence in church music. The Choir-Training 'Certificate' examination, on the other hand, is open to all.

It must be emphasized that the R.C.O. diplomas were meant to have a general validity and were never designed specifically for church musicians (even though nearly all their holders occupy church posts). The Anglican church felt that skill in organ-playing and choir-training, though essential, did not go far enough and that church musicians needed further training in such specialised studies as liturgiology, Prayer Book history, plainsong, Anglican chanting and pointing, hymnody, and similar specialist fields. Such training would help bridge the gap between clergy and their organists. To meet this need Archbishop Lang instituted in 1937 a new examination, the Archbishop of Canterbury's Diploma in Church Music (A.D.C.M.), which involves a wide course of study embracing subjects unheard of by the old articled pupils — or their masters. Just as entry for the Choir-Training Diploma is restricted to holders of one of the R.C.O. organ diplomas, so for the A.D.C.M. examination only those are eligible who already hold both the F.R.C.O. and (CHM) diplomas. With such a formidable basic requirement the number of candidates is inevitably small. It is fervently to be hoped that somebody will not now invent an examination for which only A.D.C.M.s are eligible.

In 1961 an Archbishop of Canterbury's 'Certificate' in Church Music was introduced, corresponding to the Choir-Training Certificate of the R.C.O. This is open to anyone and is a much simpler examination than that for the Diploma. All church musicians would profit greatly from studying for this Certificate.

SINGING THE PSALMS

So far little has been said about this subject, but since psalm-singing occupies much of the time and attention of church choirs—or should do—some general account of it must be given. There are four ways in which the psalms can be sung:

1. in metrical paraphrases
2. to Gregorian tones
3. to Anglican chants
4. by the method invented by the French priest-musician, Père Joseph Gelineau.

1. Metrical psalms. The practice of singing the psalms in rhyming paraphrases goes back long before the establishment of the national Church, probably to the time of Wycliffe and the Lollards. In 1549, the year in which the first Book of Common Prayer was authorized, Thomas Sternhold issued nineteen psalms 'chose out of the Psalter of Dauid and drawē into Englishe metre'; no music was provided. It was this book, with various additions by John Hopkins and others and with more tunes provided, which went through innumerable editions. Ultimately it became so closely identified with the worship of English parish churches that 'Sternhold and Hopkins' was regarded almost as sacrosanct as Holy Writ. Even with the coming of Tate and Brady's psalter in 1696 its popularity declined only slowly, though it was eventually eclipsed by their 'New Version'. Thus, from the earliest days of the Church of England the psalms were sung in metrical paraphrases, certainly in most parish churches if not cathedrals, and this state of affairs continued right up to the nineteenth century. Various other metrical psalters appeared and during the seventeenth and eighteenth centuries the practice grew of enlarging them by

(a) paraphrasing other portions of Scripture, and
(b) including sacred poems, most of them written not for public worship but for private devotions.

By the early nineteenth century, therefore, metrical psalters began to take on something of the appearance of modern hymnbooks.

With the introduction of surpliced choirs in the mid-nineteenth century there was, as we have seen, a strong tendency for parish churches to adopt a fully choral service based on the cathedral tradition. This involved singing the psalms in the Prayer Book version, either to Anglican chants or Gregorian tones. But the old metrical psalms were too popular to be thrown overboard completely and so they were retained as 'hymns'. In this way a large number of them were incorporated into the many hymnbooks which mushroomed at that time and have retained their place in the hymnbooks of today. They are now, therefore, more properly considered under the heading of 'hymnody'.

2. Psalm singing to Gregorian tones. Passing reference has already been made to the psalm-tones and their antiphons. The establishment of the English Rite involved not only a change of language from Latin to English but also the disappearance of the old Roman Service-books. Banished too were the antiphons and responds which had given so much significance, colour and richness to the old services. The change of language meant that the whole corpus of Gregorian chant, with few exceptions, was now useless and had to be abandoned. Admittedly a few plainsong melodies were adapted to English words and Merbecke, in his *Booke of Common Praier noted*, attempted to provide a sort of pseudo-plainsong. But the new Church wanted new music and even Merbecke's compromise, if indeed it ever came into use, had little success. In only one branch of church music did it seem difficult to find a satisfactory alternative to ancient practice — the chanting of the psalms. Hence the Gregorian psalm-tones were retained and modified to accommodate English words. However, an essential element of the psalm-tones was the antiphons; their function was to bring the dominant-centred recitation to rest on the final of its mode, thus making a satisfying final cadence. Shorn of their antiphons the psalm-tones became bleeding torsos.

In this maimed and debased form they lingered on far into the seventeenth century, yielding ground slowly to the growing popularity of Anglican chants. Their use was probably limited to the cathedrals and choral foundations though perhaps in some parishes, high church extremists would have clung to them as long as possible. Soon after the Restoration, Edward Lowe in 1661 and the Rev. James Clifford in 1664 printed the eight psalm-tones in their collections and as late as 1679 John Playford included seven of them in his *Introduction*, though more perhaps as a record of things past than for practical use in the present. After this they appear to have dropped out of use completely for about a century and a half.

It was not until the revival of church life in the nineteenth century, and especially the reawakening of interest in pre-Reformation practices inspired by the Oxford Movement, that attempts were made to revive the use of plainsong and the psalm-tones. As early as the 1840s various plainsong publications began to appear of which the most important were Helmore's *The Psalter Noted* (1849), *A Manual of Plainsong* (1850), and *The Hymnal Noted* (1854), but they all showed the same weakness — a lack of any real knowledge or understanding of Gregorian principles.

Later in the century the patient and exhaustive research of the Benedictine monks of Solesmes contributed powerfully to a wider knowledge and deeper understanding of the art. In England this growing knowledge and interest led to the formation in 1888 of *The Plainsong and Mediæval Music Society* which published important editions (some of them in facsimile) of English manuscripts, especially those of the Sarum Use. Bishop Frere devoted a lifetime of study to the subject and edited several of the Society's publications. In association with H. B. Briggs he brought out (1902) a vastly improved edition of Helmore's *A Manual of Plainsong*: it rapidly established itself and has remained the standard book ever since. In this the Canticles and complete Prayer Book psalter were set to appropriate psalm-tones and printed in full on four-lined staves: regrettably, antiphons were not included. The provision of this excellent and easy-to-use practical book encouraged the further spread of psalm-singing to Gregorian tones. In the latest edition (1951), revised by another distinguished plainsong scholar, J. H. Arnold (1887–1956), the music is no longer printed in full; instead, the lay-out is similar to that of an Anglican psalter with chants.

With the introduction of psalm-tones into parish worship some form of organ accompaniment became expedient. J. H. Arnold interested himself in the problems of providing an appropriate chordal accompaniment to melodies which were essentially unisonal. He contributed plainsong accompaniments to *Songs of Praise*, *A Plainsong Hymnbook* and the second edition of *English Hymnal*. His important book *Plainsong Accompaniment*

(1927) gave valuable advice and suggested idiomatic accompanimental formulae for all the psalm-tones and their various endings.

3. Psalm singing to Anglican chants. In the early days of the Church of England, as we have seen, metrical versions were sung in most parish churches while in cathedrals and other choral foundations Gregorian tones survived in use at least until the Rebellion. After the Restoration some attempt was made to revive them but by now the practice of chanting the psalms to Anglican chants was already well established. But how had it become so established? Until more facts become available it would appear that in the choral foundations, Gregorian tones and Anglican chants were in use side by side, probably depending on the churchmanship of the capitular body: in some places both methods may have been used. The debased form of the plainsong tones stripped of their antiphons and the growing strength of the Puritan party before the Rebellion resulted in the gradual ascendancy of chanting at the expense of the psalm-tones. This probably explains why an attempt to revive Gregorians at the Restoration proved abortive.

Certainly in the eighteenth and first half of the nineteenth centuries, harmonized chanting had become the rule in most cathedrals and collegiate churches. Evidence suggests that the psalms were sung at an inordinately slow pace.

With the introduction of chancel choirs after the Oxford Movement, parish churches too attempted to sing the Prayer Book psalter. The vast majority of them opted for the Anglican chant method and to meet the growing demand a large number of pointed psalters appeared. To enable choirs and congregations to fit the psalm verses to the chant a cumbersome apparatus of accents, bar-lines, asterisks, small notes, and syllables in heavy type was developed. Then in 1875 appeared the most popular and influential of all these books, *The Cathedral Psalter*, edited by the Rev. S. Flood-Jones, the Rev. Dr. Troutbeck, James Turle, Sir John Stainer and Sir Joseph Barnby. Its success was immediate and overwhelming and to this day it is still sung in many (far too many) churches.

Whatever the system adopted, all these psalters suffered from the same basic defect — they represented attempts to fit the psalm to the chant instead of the chant to the psalm. The conventional notation in semibreves and minims was taken at face value and each half-verse was so pointed that the last few syllables could be sung in strict tempo. The point where the free recitative of the reciting note broke into the four-square beat of the 'measured' part was the 'accent' or pause, indicated by some special mark or type face. Often this 'accent' fell on some unimportant word or unaccented syllable. Even if only one unimportant word or syllable came before the first minim it still had to be held for a full semibreve:

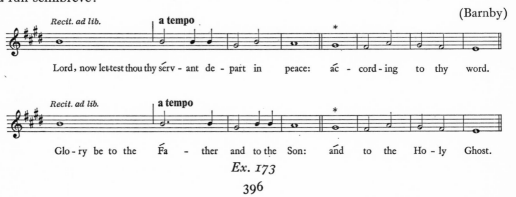

Ex. 173

To make matters worse it became customary to gabble the recitation, halt on the 'accent', and then march off ponderously through the measured bars. To complete the ruination, if a verse or half-verse closed with a feminine ending, the final weak syllable was heavily stressed and prolonged:

Ex. 174

(This is a disfigurement still very much with us, even in churches using modern psalters. The cure is to stress the penultimate syllable (i.e. the main accent) by dwelling on it somewhat and then sing the final syllable lightly, keeping it short.)

The Barless Psalter, *The Free Rhythm Psalter* and others tried to remedy some of the worst defects, but the publication of *The New Cathedral Psalter* in 1909, with its accents printed in heavy type, put the clock back: indeed, the *New Cathedral* was even worse than the old *Cathedral*.

It was Robert Bridges, the Poet Laureate, who largely initiated the modern attitude to Anglican chanting. After carefully analysing the verbal rhythms of the Prayer Book psalms and the structure of the Anglican chant, he realised that the chant must be considered a flexible formula in which the duration of each chord is widely variable, depending upon the accentuation of the words. The words themselves must be chanted with the natural stresses and verbal rhythms of ordinary speech ('speech-rhythm') sung without affectiaton at the speed of good public reading; there is to be no difference between the speed of the recitation and that of the 'measured' bars, the pause on the arbitrary 'accent' disappears, and musical accents must be freely spaced to coincide with natural verbal stresses.

His theories were tried out experimentally at New College, Oxford, under Dr. (later Sir) Hugh Allen, and found to be not only highly imaginative but also eminently practical. The pioneer work of Bridges and Allen, supported by Sir Walford Davies at the Temple Church, slowly gained a wide following and *The Psalter Newly Pointed* was the first of many to adopt their principles. Of the many later 'speech-rhythm' psalters two, in particular, have enjoyed great success—the 'Oxford' and the 'Parish'. *The Oxford Psalter* (1929) edited by Henry Ley, E. Stanley Roper and C. Hylton Stewart, can produce splendid results when chanted by a good choir, but its many brackets and symbols make it a rather complicated book for less experienced choirs to use effectively. Sir Sydney Nicholson's *Parish Psalter* (1928) achieves much the same result but is a far simpler book to read and use.

In 1958 the Archbishops of Canterbury and York appointed a Commission to revise the text of the psalter. The result of its work was presented to the Convocations in 1963 and, slightly amended, published in 1964 as *The Revised Psalter*. Though less beautiful than the Prayer Book version of the psalms it is much more intelligible. It has been pointed for chanting and may well replace the Prayer Book psalter in many churches.

Before closing this section it is worth underlining a passage in *Music in Church*: 'It may be a regrettable fact, but it has to be admitted that the Psalms, whether they be sung to plainsong tunes or to Anglican chants, do not lend themselves readily to singing by the average congregation'.[2]

4. Psalm singing to the Gelineau method. The method of chanting invented by the French Jesuit, Père Joseph Gelineau, employs musical formulae more extended and capable of far greater flexibility than Anglican chants, but whereas speech-rhythm chanting is free and follows the natural prose rhythms, the Gelineau system is strictly metrical. Every psalm is provided with specially composed antiphons, with organ accompaniment, many of which are highly effective. The Gelineau method is open to two serious objections. Firstly, for technical reasons it demands that the psalter be specially translated to reproduce the poetic rhythms and verse structures of the Hebrew, 'each line of a given psalm having a specified number of accented or stressed syllables': this means in practice exchanging the glorious poetry and vivid imagery of the Prayer Book psalms for a nondescript and utterly unmemorable translation. After all, who wants:

Like the deer that yearns for running streams	for	Like as the hart desireth the water-brooks
If the Lord does not build the house, in vain do its builders labour	for	Except the Lord build the house their labour is but lost that build it
At last, all-powerful Master, you give leave to your servant to go	for	Lord, now lettest thou thy servant depart in peace

Secondly, in spite of all the claims made for it, Gelineau psalmody is just as difficult to sing well as Anglican chanting and needs as much care and rehearsal. Indeed, from the congregation's point of view it is more difficult and it is very rare for them to do anything else except merely join in with the antiphons. The Gelineau method also calls for a very alert accompanist. A well sung Gelineau psalm makes a refreshing change; in particular, it can make an excellent introit. But the system as a whole is a poor substitute for good Anglican chanting.

HYMNODY IN THE TWENTIETH CENTURY

At the turn of the century *Hymns Ancient & Modern*, in its Second Edition with the 1889 Supplement added, was pre-eminently the hymnbook of the Church of England. It had vanquished most of its rivals and had not yet been challenged by new collections. At first it had been considered a dangerously 'Catholic' publication but its happy blend of Tractarian hymnody with the more subjective type of hymn favoured by the Evangelicals eventually established it as a good middle-of-the-road affair and, since most Englishmen love a compromise, its success was assured. Only the extremists were dissatisfied and clung to their own books — *The Eucharistic Hymnal* (1877) and *The Altar Hymnal* (1844) on the one side and *Hymnal Companion* (1870) and *Church Hymns* (1871) on the other.

But even amongst moderate churchmen *Hymns A. & M.* had come under fire. It included too much dead wood — hymns that were never used — and it failed to reflect the growing social awareness of men like Maurice, Kingsley and Westcott. Better informed and more critical musicians, marching behind the banner of Parry and Stanford, found the cloying prettiness of Dykes and Barnby increasingly distasteful. These new attitudes

[2] *Music in Church*, p. 34. (The Church Information Office: Rev. Ed. 1957.)

found classic expression in a brilliant and sensitive essay by Robert Bridges called *A Practical Discourse on Some Principles of Hymn-singing* (1899). Later that same year he published his *Yattendon Hymnal* containing one hundred hymns with their music to show 'what sort of a hymnal might be made on my principles'. This superb book was never intended for church use but its literary excellence and musical enterprise have made it an invaluable source book for later compilers.

To meet these challenges, a completely revised *Hymns A. & M.* appeared in 1904, the work of A. J. Mason and Bishop W. H. Frere. Texts were revised, dross purged away, splendid new hymns and tunes appeared and (most striking innovation) ancient Sarum Office hymns for the various seasons and major festivals were introduced. The outcome was a monument of excellence; indeed, some hymnologists declare that this is still the finest hymnbook yet produced. All the greater pity then that the vast majority of churchgoers were perfectly satisfied with what they had got and stoutly resisted change. Their opposition was largely stirred up by the popular press who not only revealed the dread secret that 'Abide with me' was no longer 'Hymn 27' nor 'O God, our help' 'No. 165' but eagerly seized upon the fact that 'Hark, the herald angels sing' had imprudently been restored to Wesley's original 'Hark, how all the welkin rings'. That did it! So this exemplary book was laughed out of court and was regarded by the proprietors as a failure — though the sale of some two million copies more than covered the high costs of the venture.

But the faults of the Second Edition — and the critics — remained and a rapidly growing group of 'progressive' Anglo-Catholics needed a book more sympathetic to their outlook. The answer came in 1906 — *The English Hymnal*, edited by a committee headed by Dr. Percy Dearmer (1867–1936). The new book leaned heavily on the abortive 1904 edition of *Hymns A. & M.* It included a wide range of French, German and English hymns of various periods, together with some from America. Early Christian hymns appeared in improved translations and a generous complement of Sarum Office hymns was provided for the Church's year. *The English Hymnal* was immensely fortunate in having for its musical editor one who was not only to become a famous composer himself but who was steeped in the traditions of English music and folk-music — Ralph Vaughan Williams.

He drew extensively on three sources practically untapped by previous compilers: sixteenth- and seventeenth-century French 'church melodies', nineteenth-century Welsh Methodist tunes, and English secular folk-songs (or tunes modelled on them). The editor's own contributions included his beautiful *Down Ampney* ('Come down, O Love divine') and the sturdy *Sine Nomine* ('For all the saints'), one of the best hymn-tunes of the century. Of course the book has plenty of defects: chorales are given in J. S. Bach's harmonizations, glorious in themselves but utterly unsuited to congregational repetition; many of the Welsh tunes seem repetitive and dreary, while tunes of the folk-song type often sound somewhat incongruous in church. Nevertheless, *The English Hymnal* was a marked advance on most previous collections: furthermore, because of the excellence of both words and music, the more cultured and intellectual type of congregation preferred it to the old unreformed *Hymns A. & M.*

However, *Hymns A. & M.* still remained the chief hymnbook of the Anglican Church. After the débâcle of the 1904 edition, the proprietors licked their wounds and in 1909 brought out the 'Historical Edition', really a critical commentary on the 1904 book. This was the work of that great scholar Dr. W. H. Frere, Bishop of Truro, and his lengthy introduction is probably the finest discussion of hymnology in the language. To salvage some of the splendid hymns and tunes introduced for the first time in the 1904 edition, a Second Supplement was issued as a separate book in 1916. It was in two parts: the first added 161 new hymns with accompanying tunes, the second provided first-class tunes as alternatives to some of the weaker effusions in the existing book. In 1922 reform was carried a stage further when the Second Supplement was bound in with the old book and the alternative tunes were inserted where they belonged in the main body of the hymnal. The new book, which became the 'Standard Edition', suffered from two major defects: a disproportionate amount of space was still taken up by those hymns and tunes of poor quality which the compilers had for so long wanted to jettison; secondly, by having the First and Second Supplements printed as appendices instead of being incorporated in the main book, special hymns (for Christmas, Easter, Holy Communion, For the Young, etc.) were found in three widely separated places (this was to avoid disturbing the familiar numbering of the old book). With careful selection, however, even the most discriminating could find a wide range of superb hymns in this curiously patchwork book.

In 1932 an interesting offshoot of *Hymns A. & M.* appeared. This was *A Plainsong Hymnbook*, edited by Frere and Dr. (later Sir) Sydney Nicholson, containing 164 hymns and a splendid selection of Gregorian and other ancient melodies, including a full set of Sarum Office hymns. Seven years later the main book underwent a transformation and the 'Shortened Music Edition' appeared, also edited by Nicholson. By omitting many hymns which were never used he was able to improve the format and produce a spacious, well-printed book. Some new tunes were added.

Hymns A. & M. took another leap forward in 1950 when a new and completely revised edition was issued under the musical editorship of Sir Sydney Nicholson (until his death in 1947), Dr. Gerald Knight and Dr. J. Dykes Bower. This carried out many of the reforms proposed in 1904. It incorporated much of the Second Supplement and several hymns from *A Plainsong Hymnbook* into the body of the book, cut out much dead wood, and introduced many new hymns and tunes. As far as possible the most popular hymns were allowed to retain their familiar numbers though some renumbering was, of course, necessary. The book is handsomely produced and is now rapidly replacing the old 'Standard Edition'. *Hymns A. & M. Revised* (A. & M.R.) bids fair to become the most widely used of all Anglican hymnals (except in the U.S.A. and Canada which have their own official books) and its popularity is richly deserved.

As early as 1906 *English Hymnal* indicated a shift towards a more broadly theistic and non-sectarian outlook: this was apparent in Kipling's 'God of our fathers', Chesterton's 'O God of earth and altar', Holland's 'Judge Eternal', and such American imports as 'Once to every man and nation', 'City of God', 'Thy kingdom come! on bended knee' and 'O thou in all thy might'. This new trend received a tremendous fillip during the First World War when the Y.M.C.A., Toc. H, and countless other organisations held religious meetings attended by people of various denominations and some who were scarcely Christian at all. No existing hymnbook was suitable for such occasions and the demand became more pressing after the war when hymns were needed for national occasions, 'schools, lecture meetings and other public gatherings'. So was born *Songs of Praise* (1925) edited by Dr. Percy Dearmer. Though intended to be interdenominational it yet owed much to the same editor's *English Hymnal* and the Second Supplement of *Hymns A. & M.* Vaughan Williams and Martin Shaw edited the music: it included some fine tunes by Gustav Holst. The new book was welcomed in schools, in some 'modernist' parish churches and in Liverpool Cathedral, but it was almost aggressively typical of the 1920s. Its outlook savoured strongly of 'Praise the Lord and pass the ammunition'; Victorian-type tunes were ruthlessly excised, and many of Shaw's contributions gave free rein to a sort of hearty modalism which is already dated. Yet though Dearmer included too many of his own hymns and Shaw too many of his own tunes, *Songs of Praise* contained much that was original, experimental and challenging and it has considerably influenced the development of Anglican hymnody. A recast and greatly enlarged edition came out in 1931.

Some other books call for brief mention. To many, the title *Songs of Syon* (1904) will suggest some king of revivalist chorus book: the reality is the very opposite—it is one of the most erudite and austere Anglo-Catholic collections ever published, a monument of careful scholarship, wide culture and sensitive imagination. Its editor, the Rev. G. R. Woodward, was a disciple of J. M. Neale and had a similarly mediæval cast of mind. His purpose was 'to raise the standard of English taste by rescuing from oblivion some of the finest melodies of the sixteenth, seventeenth and eighteenth centuries'. To carry these tunes, many of which were in unusual metres, he provided 'a collection of hymns and sacred poems mostly translated from ancient Greek, Latin and German sources' (fifty or so of them from his own pen). Plainsong hymns were printed in square notes on four-lined staves and no accompaniment was provided; older tunes appeared without bar-lines, and chorales were given in Bach's most florid harmonizations. *Songs of Syon* was planned only as a supplementary volume to other more general hymnals but it was quickly recognised as an important source book and has been drawn on by most subsequent compilers.

The compilers of the *B.B.C. Hymnbook* (1951) had to meet a special need—the provision of a truly undenominational book acceptable to all Christians. Considering the enormous wealth of hymnbooks of all denominations they could, and should, have drawn upon; realising, furthermore, the tremendous influence the new book would be bound to have in homes and schools throughout the land, it seems the more regrettable that the musical editors—Dr. W. K. Stanton, Dr. G. Thalben-Ball and the Rev. Cyril Taylor—should between them have composed tunes to no less than fifty-nine of the book's 542 hymns, especially as some of their tunes are no more than mediocre.

The *Public School Hymnbook* first appeared in 1903 and was obviously directed towards a specialized and limited group of worshippers. It proved highly successful. Subsequent editions in 1919 and 1949 vastly improved it. Then in 1960 the Headmasters' Conference appointed a small committee 'to re-think and re-plan the book as a whole'. To show how extensive was the revision, even the title was changed and the new name, *Hymns for Church and School*, clearly enshrines a hope that the book may be as useful in the parish church as in the school chapel. Certainly it is an excellent book, representative of all periods and particularly rich in twentieth-century hymns and tunes. The modern tunes include some interesting settings by Dr. Herbert Howells. Alas, here again the musical editor, Leonard J. Blake, could not resist the temptation to include too many of his own tunes and descants. The book is beautifully printed and well produced.

The same cannot be said of the new *Anglican Hymn Book* (1965) which, printed in four different weights of sans-serif type, must surely rank among the least attractive examples of typography of the last half-century. Nevertheless the glorious universality of the title implies that here at last is the hymnbook we have all been waiting for, a book which will meet the needs of all levels of Anglican worship. This implication is reinforced when the editors write 'we have tried to envisage the needs of the whole church, both now and in the future'. When we discover, however, that the new book is intended to supplant both the *Hymnal Companion to the Book of Common Prayer* (3rd Edition, 1890) and the *Church Hymnal for the Christian Year* (1920) we begin to suspect that it is, perhaps, a little less universal than the title suggests. When, further, we see that 'We love thine altar, Lord' has been altered to 'We love our Father's board' and 'Wherefore, O Father, we Thy humble servants' appears in Dearmer's maimed version in which every single line except the first has been changed, our suspicions are confirmed and we realise that the hymnal of a small Evangelical minority has claimed a comprehensiveness which is wholly unjustified. On the other hand, except for the children's section which is lamentable, the book as a whole is a considerable improvement on its predecessors and reflects changes which have taken place in the thinking and taste of this century. An invaluable feature of the book, and one which ought to become standard practice, is the provision of a metrical index showing the first two lines of every tune in music-type: this saves hours of turning backwards and forwards when searching for alternative tunes.

Thus there have been considerable improvements during the century. New hymnals have appeared and old ones have been revised several times; in each revision unsuitable or little-used hymns have been quietly dropped and new ones introduced. Modern hymn-writers and composers have contributed much of real value while new sources of hymns have been discovered in the sixteenth, seventeenth and eighteenth centuries. Attitudes are gradually changing. Hymnal compilers now recognise the positive value of fine verse wedded to inspiring music and are anxious to eliminate clerical doggerel set to maudlin tunes. Clergy are becoming more realistic in their approach to worship; they recognise that for most members of an average congregation, grovelling self-abasement and verbal self-flagellation will be utterly false and insincere. Subjectivity is giving way to objectivity; concepts of the Church Universal and the Christian brotherhood of man are now thought more important than 'I, me and mine'. Not only have the doctrinal, literary and musical standards of hymnals improved but, with rare exceptions, lay-out, typography and presentation are also very much better. This steady improvement is not confined to the Church of England; most other denominations have reformed their hymnody on similar lines. *Congregational Praise*, published in 1951, is a typical product of this new thinking and is a very good book indeed: the Committee of compilers were fortunate in having for their General Secretary the Reverend Erik Routley whose unrivalled knowledge of English hymnody must have been an immense advantage in their deliberations.

Yet though much progress has been made it is still nothing like fast enough. The pattern of life is changing even more rapidly and hymnody, far from catching up, has fallen behind. Instead of responding to the needs of today, major hymnbooks still include much too high a percentage of verse which is incomprehensible, unrealistic or frankly ridiculous.

The vast majority of hymns were written by clerics. Often they enshrine points of theology and dogma which are readily grasped and appreciated by those trained in theological thinking but which are either meaningless or else seem totally irrelevant to the majority of worshippers. Many so-called hymns were originally poems written for private devotion and are quite unsuited to public worship for which they were never intended. Yet others are so intense and ecstatic as to suggest that their authors were mentally or emotionally unstable and such hymns are markedly at variance with the phlegmaticism of most congregations today.

A basic problem is that the mystical aspects of the Christian faith are extremely difficult to comprehend and utterly impossible to put into words. In an attempt to communicate them writers inevitably resort to imagery, allegory and symbolism. Indeed the Book of Revelation itself is a colossal attempt to express the inexpressible and the problem has haunted Christian writers ever since. Authors of hymns, faced with the same problem, resort to the same solutions and many of our most cherished hymns make their impact by the sheer beauty of their imagery and symbolism. This is right and proper and our hymnody would be immeasurably the poorer without such hymns as 'Let all mortal flesh' (*E.H.* 318), 'The royal banners forward go' (*E.H.* 94) and 'The spacious firmament on high' (*E.H.* 297).

In previous ages such writing made an impact at two levels of society: the educated appreciated the poetry itself and its imagery; the working classes and illiterate enjoyed the pictures evoked as a form of escapism from the horrors of reality. In these days, however, our attitude to symbolism has changed. Living in a grossly materialistic world which attempts to rationalise everything, some people, and especially perhaps young people, are more inclined to accept at face value what the author intended to be allegorical or colourfully figurative. Yet others find in the symbolism a way of escape from the materialism around them. It is all very complex and confusing. We must just remember that imagery which may be helpful and inspiring to one may be a stumbling-block to another.

Apart from their imagery, hymns also include a number of terms which many folk must find perplexing or artificial. Thumbing through the pages of *English Hymnal* produced the following (hymn numbers given in brackets).

1. Obsolete words and deliberate archaisms:

> abode (431), awful Father (348), bedewing (104), behest (277), bowers (245), divers mansions (252), harbinger (225), heavenly guerdon (191), pent (391), rills (117;
> Come, my soul, thy suit prepare (377)
> There is a book who runs may read (497)
> Thy turrets and thy pinnacles/
> With carbuncles do shine; (638)

2. Poetic diction and preciousness:

> lambent beauty (40)   Odours of Edom (41)
> sultry glebe (491)   traffickers at marts (516)

3. Theological terms; technical and fanciful synonyms. Few members of a congregation would know to whom the following referred and perhaps not all choirmasters could explain them to an enquiring chorister:

> Abaddon (24), Adonaï (8), Arabia's desert ranger (45), Branch of Jesse (8), Emmanuel (8), Esaias (22), Kedah's tents (411), Judah's lion (139), Paraclete (155), Protomartyr (31), Sion's daughters! Sons of Jerusalem! (172 – a promising opening this!), Triune Majesty (127)

The following, too, would perplex many:

> Babel's waters (63), Bethel (447), Bozrah (108), Edom (41),
> Pisgah (284), Salem (431)

4. Obscure references:

> Wail of Euroclydon (388)
> Travelling through Idumè's summer (108)

These terms, together with such devices as sentence inversion and personification, produce a special kind of 'hymn' language which, in the hands of a good poet, can be profoundly moving and inspiring and can indeed come very near to expressing the inexpressible. Such hymns share with the Prayer Book and the Prayer Book psalms a sublime beauty and a liturgical 'rightness' which enable our comprehension to overcome the strangeness of the language: without understanding all the words or phrases we yet receive illumination. In less capable hands, however, this churchy language can become merely fussy and artificial and a barrier to comprehension. It is a nice point to decide just where the first shades into the second and this point will vary widely from person to person.

Apart from their obscure language, many hymns reflect social or political concepts so remote from our own that they are either meaningless or ludicrous. The smugness of 'From Greenland's icy mountains' (547) is made even more explicit in arrogant condescension towards 'heathen, Turk or Jew' (506), while many hymns reflect social conditions of a bygone age. *English Hymnal* still prints

> A servant with this clause
> Makes drudgery divine;
> Who sweeps a room, as for thy laws,
> Makes that and the action fine.   (485)

> We are but little children poor,
> And born in very low estate: (610)

while many hymnals still in use Sunday by Sunday (not *English Hymnal*) even retain that stupendous stanza:

> The rich man in his castle,
> The poor man at his gate,
> God made them, high or lowly,
> And ordered their estate.

Again, the psychology of many hymns is questionable. Excessive emphasis on Jesus as 'sweet', 'meek', 'mild' and 'gentle', leading his 'frail and trembling sheep' is hardly an image which commends him as a leader to young people today, neither are folk likely to be won over to Christianity by the lure of 'white robes', preferably washed in blood. Again, not everyone would consider it 'rapture' —

> Prostrate before thy throne to lie
> And gaze and gaze on thee.   (441)

404

Even Christ's own imagery, perfectly suited as it was to the thinking and experience of a community largely dependent on agriculture and fishing, has not the same relevance to a complex modern urbanized and industrialized society. Christian truths are immutable but their presentation must be constantly reviewed and, if necessary, altered to meet the changing needs of each generation. Let us by all means get away from day by day materialism and rationalism and have plenty of imagery in our worship but let us make sure that this imagery is truly relevant.

By far the worst section in almost all hymnbooks is that devoted to children's hymns, the majority of which are inept or nonsensical. Most children old enough to read a hymnbook resent having it rubbed in too often that they are 'little', 'weak', 'simple' and 'helpless', nor are they very enthusiastic about the idea of being 'washed' (595). Often there is a most morbid longing for death or, as it is more euphemistically described, singing among the angels (590, 594, 595, 599, 602, 606 and 607) while such a stanza as:

> Come to this happy land,
> Come, come away;
> Why will ye doubting stand,
> Why still delay?
> O, we shall happy be,
> When, from sin and sorrow free,
> Lord, we shall live with thee,
> Blest, blest for ay.   (608)

is pernicious rubbish, thoroughly dangerous in the mind of a depressed child. Most of these hymns were written during the industrial revolution when child mortality was very high through malnutrition, disease and industrial accidents and when earthly life was so hellish that they needed some promise of 'heaven' to cling to; but such hymns are quite irrelevant these days when no healthy, happy child looks forward to death—nor should be urged to.

That all these examples should be drawn from *English Hymnal* may suggest that this compilation is particularly at fault. On the contrary, it has been chosen because it is one of the best and most enlightened of the standard hymnals. Some of the others are far worse.

Why are so many bad hymns and inappropriate hymns included in modern hymn-books? Firstly people like hymns for their tunes rather than for their words. Many worshippers accept the words quite uncritically and rarely bother to think at all about what they are singing, but if they like the tune they will want to sing it. To know is very often to like and once a tune has become established, a congregation will cling to it with great tenacity. Secondly, as we have seen, association plays an important part and people often like hymns for the memories they evoke rather than for their merit *per se*. A popular tune thus becomes virtually self-perpetuating—hence the grave danger of introducing poor quality tunes into worship. So if a hymnal compiler were to drop popular hymns because of the unsuitability of their words, there would be a public outcry and no priest or minister would dare to buy the book.

Here, perhaps, the clergy themselves could help by encouraging their congregations to take a more intelligent and critical interest in the hymns they sing. So often sermons on hymnody take the form of rather sentimentalized stories about the circumstances under which the hymns were composed. The church's hymnbook could be made the basis of a challenging, stimulating and very helpful series of sermons, repeated every few years, in which congregations could be shown how to assess the merits of a hymn, how to question its suitability, and how to improve their comprehension. Difficult terms could be explained. Where circumstances were favourable such instruction could be followed by some talks from the organist about the musical side of hymnody.

What we so desperately need at the moment is a large number of new hymns relevant to modern needs. In an age of atheism, Communism, the napalm bomb, international strife, religious hatred, racial tensions, colour prejudice, callous materialism, and a terrifying catalogue of social evils, can Christians do no better than cling to an image of a milksop Jesus leading his trembling sheep to a land of white robes and carbuncles? Such tired, irrelevant imagery colours too much of our Christian thinking and alienates many people from organised religion. Hymn-writers might do well to recall that mild and gentle Jesus personally made a whip and single-handedly scourged the traders in the temple; he scorned the petty dictates of organised religion, flouted the conventions of society (which always demands immense courage), consorted with the drop-outs and fiercely championed their cause well knowing that in doing so he would inevitably reap social opprobrium, flatly defied his king in public, and challenged the power of a Roman governor to his face.

As Christianity approaches its twenty-first century a new and critical examination of our liturgical hymnbooks is urgently needed. Hymns that cannot be sung with real sincerity and conviction should not be preserved merely for sentiment's sake. Above all, there is this crying need for many new hymns (not so much tunes) more in line with modern thinking. *Hymns Ancient & Modern* has been early in the field with its enterprising *100 Hymns for Today*, a supplement to its Revised Version of 1950 containing a wide range of modern hymns and tunes. No doubt the fortunes of the new hymns will be anxiously watched and those that make the grade can expect eventually to be included in the parent book. It is a pity that the expense of buying a supplementary book for choir and congregation and the practical difficulties involved in storing, distributing, collecting and sorting two books instead of one must severely restrict its sales. An interesting attempt from a quite unexpected source to provide a new and challenging style of sacred song is discussed on pp. 435–6.

THE ORGAN IN THE TWENTIETH CENTURY

We have traced the rise of the English romantic organ in the latter half of the nineteenth century (pp. 334–7) and discussed its characteristics. There is no doubt that at its best it was a truly noble instrument, richly expressive, offering a wide range of tone colours, capable of immense power, and possessing an almost indefinable 'atmosphere' which we inevitably associate with great churches. Against all this must be set its one fatal flaw — an overall fuzziness and lack of clarity which, in particular, obscured part-playing in polyphonic music, rendering much of it unintelligible. This means that such organs are ill suited to the performance of the most important of all schools of organ composition, that of the 'baroque' German masters culminating in the work of Bach. In discussing the organ and organ music this period is frequently referred to as the 'classical'.

During the first half of the twentieth century the English romantic organ changed hardly at all in essentials though, of course, individual builders developed electrical and mechanical improvements, convenient accessories and sometimes fanciful gadgets. What changed most was not the instrument but the type of music played on it. Nineteenth-century recital programmes consisted mainly of transcriptions and improvisations: transcriptions included 'songs and choruses from oratorios, masses, cantatas, etc., symphonic *morceaux*, overtures, marches, dramatic and operatic selections, miscellaneous songs and concerted pieces, and fantasias by most popular composers'.[3] The few genuine organ pieces came largely from nineteenth-century 'romantic' composers, especially Mendelssohn, Lefébure-Wély, Batiste, Franck, Lemmens, Guilmant and Rheinberger. Bach was represented by a mere handful of works, like the Toccata and Fugue in D minor, the Fantasia and Fugue in G minor and the 'St. Anne'. Organ recitals were highly popular and famous players like W. T. Best, Wolstenholme, Lemare, Hollins and G. D. Cunningham could draw huge crowds.

During the first quarter of the present century, with the general widening and deepening of British musical culture, rising artistic standards and vastly improved taste, transcriptions waned in popularity and genuine organ works took their place. A rapidly improving standard of playing and far more manageable instruments encouraged organists to venture into the virtuoso field and the works of Liszt, Reubke, Widor, Vierne and Karg-Elert appeared with increasing frequency. Reger received qualified respect but at the time of his death in 1916 it was said that 'his bigger works are hardly likely to make much headway . . . because of their stupendous difficulty'. Most of Bach's organ works were still practically unknown except to a few specialists. Several books on the composer appeared—Parry (1909), Schweitzer (in English, 1911), Harvey Grace (1922), Eaglefield Hull (1929), and C. S. Terry (1928 and 1933)—which discussed his organ music and stressed the importance, beauty and appropriateness of his chorale preludes, but as late as 1922 Sir Ivor Atkins felt obliged to write that they remained 'practically unknown to all but the most adventurous of Bach's English followers'.

In the second quarter of the century all this was changed. The Victorians had held the comforting and reassuring conviction that musical progress was a steady advance from stage to stage culminating in the achievements of their own day: *ergo*, to present the best music their programmes must consist mainly of nineteenth-century works. In this century a more critical and scholarly approach to history revealed the startling fact that development, far from being a straight line leading steadily upwards, was a series of peaks and troughs. The music of earlier centuries was studied, published and performed. Broadcasting, a new force to reckon with, helped to popularise it. Perhaps the most important outcome of this new attitude was the Tudor revival—to be discussed in the next chapter.

In the field of organ music interest veered to the seventeenth and eighteenth centuries. Of the French school, lesser men like Lefébure-Wély, Batiste, Lemmens, Salomé and Dubois all but disappeared while the popularity of such important figures as Franck, Guilmant and Widor was increasingly threatened by Titelouze, Clérambault, Dandrieu, Daquin and their contemporaries. On the home front, Smart, Scotson-Clark, Lemare and Hollins could not survive the challenge of Blow, Purcell, and even such minor eighteenth-century organ composers as Greene, Boyce and Stanley. Parry, Stanford and Whitlock were no longer so highly regarded but the distinctive and impressionistic works of Herbert Howells attracted increasing interest.

It was our attitude to German organ music which showed the new trends most

[3] *Musical Times*, October 1856.

markedly. After a century or so of missionary endeavour by a growing band of enthusiasts, Bach was at last universally recognised as the world's greatest composer for the instrument. Parish church organists, encouraged by B.B.C. broadcasts, began to explore the chorale preludes and less familiar works. Recitals wholly devoted to his music became commonplace. Nor did the new movement stop there. With the increased understanding and appreciation of baroque music, as exemplified in Bach, came a new interest in the work of his contemporaries and predecessors. By the middle of the century it was not unusual to hear voluntaries by Scheidt, Buxtehude, Pachelbel, Walther, Krebs and others, often in quite small churches. Almost inevitably the pendulum of fashion swung too far. Not every work written in the baroque era was a masterpiece yet many geese were now proclaimed swans and many a dull piece enjoyed a success probably denied it in its own day.

In any case this music was written with 'baroque' organs in mind, like the superb instruments of Schnitger and the Silbermanns. 'Such instruments were of necessity voiced on light wind pressure and the pipes were constructed accordingly. The chief characteristic was a beautifully clear, singing quality of tone. Colour was obtained by abundant mutation ranks and silvery mixtures. When in tune the ensemble was quite remarkable and produced a rich ringing effect of great brilliance without any scream, which gave an impression of being more powerful than was actually the case. The clarity of this ensemble made it especially suitable for polyphonic music.'[4] On the continent, from about 1925 onwards, several builders deliberately returned to the principles of classical design and either built imitation baroque instruments or successfully incorporated baroque divisions into some of their larger instruments. But English builders closed their eyes to developments abroad and continued to produce traditional instruments while our organists turned more and more to the baroque school of composers. To play such music on the turbid, fuzzy-toned English romantic organ was to ruin it.

Does this help to explain why sensitive musicians shrank from attending recitals? Certainly towards the middle of the century the organ was unpopular and recitals poorly attended. It was often said that the only people who went to them were other organists. Indeed, so low did the organ rank in the nation's musical life that famous international virtuosi could ask only a small fee compared with pianists and violinists of equal standing.

It was in 1954 that a violent explosion shattered the British organ world, destroyed its complacency and divided it into two camps. This was the planning and erection of the organ in London's new Royal Festival Hall under the direction of Ralph Downes. His avowed intention was to design a general all-purpose instrument capable of playing both romantic and baroque works. To ensure the authenticity of the baroque departments he went so far as to bring over a famous French craftsman, Louis Eugène-Rochesson, to voice the reeds, though the organ itself was built by Harrison and Harrison of Durham. At once there was a national outcry: baroque organs in England? a foreigner to help voice an important new British organ in the heart of London? Heated discussions arose at organists' gatherings: the musical press fairly sizzled with controversy. Looking back, it can be seen that the whole concept was bold and highly imaginative, but it must have demanded great faith from those in authority to continue backing Ralph Downes in the teeth of bitter opposition from the highest musical circles. Of course the instrument is not without its shortcomings and the marriage of French reeds with an Anglo-German

[4] R. Whitworth: *Organ Stops and their use*, p. 108. (Pitman.)

chorus has not been entirely satisfactory. Nevertheless, all concerned have been handsomely vindicated by the overwhelming success of the new instrument: recitals regularly attract large paying audiences of well over a thousand and have done much to reawaken interest in the organ and its music.

Before this organ was built there had already been a few tentative experiments in applying baroque principles but the Royal Festival Hall organ was especially important because it made everybody, organists and builders alike, question tradition and rethink their whole attitude towards organ tone and its relationship to texture. The instrument's remarkable success triggered off a sort of chain reaction and soon builders everywhere were busy erecting baroque, or pseudo-baroque organs or adding baroquerie to existing ones. Many lovely instruments have been built and the clearer, more sparkling part-playing in contrapuntal music is an immense gain.

In Germany, Holland and Scandinavia, the new neo-baroque instruments are modelled closely on typical eighteenth-century organs and so are devoid of any romantic attributes whatever; this imposes severe limitations on what can be played on them and virtually eliminates all nineteenth- and much twentieth-century music. In Britain and France recent instruments have tried to follow the Festival Hall ideal of preserving the best of both worlds and avoiding the extremes of each. This seems a sensible compromise.

Perhaps two words of caution need to be added. Firstly, it must be remembered that the main purpose of a church organ must be to accompany congregational singing—not the giving of recitals. Secondly, neo-baroque organs range from first class to utterly appalling. The word 'baroque' itself has become something of a fashionable catchword and is sometimes used to cover up bad planning, poor workmanship or shoddy materials: weak foundation tone, screaming mixtures, raucous reeds and bad blending are passed off—and accepted—as 'baroque'.

An interesting recent development, both on the continent and at home, is a return to tracker action for organs of moderate size. Leading players recognize that tracker mechanism gives them a degree of control far more sensitive than that of any other type of action. Of course modern trackers are much lighter and more efficient than were the old type. Only for the pedal organ and the stop action is direct mechanical action cumbersome. There is much to be said then for tracker action for the manuals and electric action for the pedals and stop control and this may well be the general pattern of things to come.

The third quarter of the century has seen a remarkable revival of interest in the organ and there is a growing audience for recitals: many musicians who previously had no interest in organ music have now become strongly attracted towards it. One reason for this is that polyphonic music is much better suited to the peculiar genius of the instrument than the nineteenth- and twentieth-century romantic works which used to feature so prominently in recitals. Again, organists have learned to select cleaner and brighter tone colours even when playing on traditional instruments. Another reason is that long-playing records have made available authoritative performances by international masters of a wide range of music played on the finest instruments, British and foreign: these have won many converts. Finally, the highly original and influential French composer Olivier Messiaen has written many powerful works for the organ of such importance that they command the attention of all serious musicians: there are some indications that these may be the precursors of a new school of organ composition.

Something must be said about electronic 'organs'. These first burst upon the English scene in the later 'thirties. In those days all kinds of pretentious and fanciful claims were made for them—'millions of tone colours at your finger-tips', 'limitless variety of tone', 'a full-scale grand organ for less than £500', 'pipe organs to become obsolete', and so on. Such extravagant claims helped to build up opposition: controversy was long and bitter and in America even extended to legal action. Since those days various attempts have been made to improve electronic instruments though their basic weaknesses remain—a lack of real 'character' in their tone and a fundamental lack of variety (in spite of theoretically limitless possibilities).

Of course they are ideal to practise on in the home. In recent years they seem to have found their natural habitat in dance bands, public houses, political clubs and night clubs (where, incidentally, they are often much better played than they are in church). These secular associations inevitably colour our attitude to them in the context of public worship.

It is enough to say that few churches would have them from choice but church councils are always much impressed by the notion, underlined by skilful advertising, that they are relatively inexpensive to buy, easy to maintain, and take up little space. What is not generally realised is that depreciation on them is very high. They are in fact built, like modern cars, for a limited life span (usually about twenty-five years, but shorter for the cheaper instruments). At the end of this time they are a complete write-off and need total replacement. A pipe organ, on the other hand, has an enormously long life. After many years of service it can be patched up and set working again for another long span. Eventually it may be rebuilt or enlarged or incorporated into another instrument— but still the pipes go on. Even when it is decided to buy a completely new organ, the old one can be sold for cash. The idea that electronic organs take up less space is open to argument, while it is now established that they lead to listlessness in congregational singing. Certainly any church thinking of buying an electronic organ would be well advised to write for a pamphlet called *Electronic Organs* published for the Council for the Care of Churches by the Church Information Office, Church House, Westminster.

It is greatly to be regretted that there is so much prejudice against the use of a good piano in church. Pianos are cheaper to buy even than electronic organs, easy to maintain, and far more effective as accompanying instruments because they can give a strongly marked rhythmic impulse to the singing. Besides, it is often far easier to find a good pianist than a competent organist. There is little doubt that for smaller churches which simply cannot afford the high cost of building and maintaining the 'king of instruments', a good piano is the next best thing.

CHAPTER XIX

The Music of the Twentieth Century

In previous centuries the main stream of English church music followed a fairly simple and well defined course from style to style, except perhaps for a bifurcation in the seventeenth century when Renaissance and Baroque dwelt together side by side. In the twentieth century, however, the historian's task is complicated by the fact that this main stream has many branches and tributaries; exploration is made still more difficult because, instead of pursuing their courses independently, these smaller streams tend to overflow their banks and run into one another, cutting intersecting channels. In musical terms this means a proliferation of styles, trends and movements most of which modify each other: usually several different influences and styles are found together in the work of one composer. The whole subject becomes so intricate that to treat it in any detail would demand a lengthy book to itself. Whereas in earlier chapters the course of history was traced largely through a detailed study of a few representative composers, from now onwards styles and trends are more important than individuals; with few exceptions, therefore, composers will be discussed only in so far as they represent or illustrate particular aspects of the scene.

THE MAIN STREAM

The line of development which we have traced from Boyce and his predecessors, through Wesley to Stanford, continued throughout the first half of the present century though its artistic importance steadily declined. Before the Second World War, English church music was still dominated by composers who continued to write in the idiom of Stanford, not realising that already it was a spent force. Faced with the increasing difficulty of trying to be original in a style which had practically exhausted itself, they contented themselves with writing pleasant, well-constructed pieces in conventional forms and irreproachable taste. Yet though unoriginal, this music was by no means unimaginative. Its composers were all highly trained professional musicians (in contrast to the unskilled amateurs who plagued the nineteenth century), with a true understanding of the place of music in worship, an appreciation of words, and an assured technique often coupled with a lively musical imagination. Nearly all their works yield some flash of inspiration, some arresting idea or sensitive touch. Their best pieces reach a high level of excellence and even their pot-boilers are thoroughly competent and well-bred. Yet these men speak one common language and their musical personalities are generally not strong enough to find individual modes of expression.

In the world of art certain groups of painters have so much in common and so little individuality that unidentified pictures are simply catalogued as 'School of —'. Similarly, faced with an unidentified work by such men as Charles Macpherson, George Dyson, Henry Ley, Charles F. Waters and Eric Thiman, we could only say 'School of Stanford' or even 'School of Brahms'. Indeed, it would often be possible to tack a Gloria by one of the group on to a Magnificat by another without any discrepancy of style or feeling being evident.

Only one composer of the group spoke with a marked individual utterance — Sir Edward Bairstow. Though he confined himself to orthodox idioms his originality was such that almost every bar bears a strongly personal and characteristic imprint. He was an unequal composer but his best pieces make him pre-eminent within the group.

It is impossible to mention all these men individually or even to study selected composers in any depth: the names listed below are merely some of those most familiar to cathedral congregations.

ALAN GRAY (1855–1935)

Gray, an almost exact contemporary of Stanford's, succeeded the latter as organist of Trinity College, Cambridge, and spent nearly forty years there. He is best known for his six Service settings which were once staple diet in Anglican cathedrals. Those in G and A are still often sung but the finest of them is undoubtedly the Evening Service in F minor for double choir, a massive forthright work more in the style of Parry than of Stanford. Gray is unadventurous in his harmony and in key relationships; having established a key he rarely moves far from it. This leads to some monotony both in his Services and in his anthems, most of which are undistinguished. An exception is his stirring setting of Christina Rossetti's *What are these that glow from afar* (1916). Here again the range of keys is circumscribed but a recurring triplet rhythm is used with good effect to lock the piece together. *Jesu dulcis memoria* is effectively introduced in free rhythm: in this anthem, too, Gray's debt to Parry is obvious.

BASIL HARWOOD (1859–1949)

Harwood was organist of St. Barnabas', Pimlico (1883–87), Ely Cathedral (1887–92), and Christ Church, Oxford (1892–1909). Though he wrote complete Services in A flat, E minor and A major (for men's voices), Communion settings in D, E flat, F and G minor, other Canticle settings and some thirty anthems, he has become a 'one-work man', the work in question being one of his earliest pieces, the Service in A flat. It was simple enough to be taken up by nearly every parish choir; effective enough to sound well even when performed inadequately. No consideration of words is allowed to impede the relentless metrical beat or the balancing of 4- and 8-bar phrases; to accommodate the tune, words are stretched out, repeated, or jammed in as necessary and the following passage is typical:

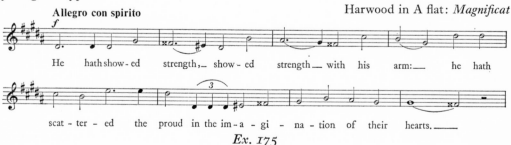

Ex. 175

Notice the false accent on the final '-ed' of 'scattered'. Such music seems curiously dated now and does not wear well though the piece is still a favourite in scores of churches.

Perhaps Harwood would be better remembered by another early work, the anthem *O, how glorious* (Op. 12), which is still often sung. It was originally scored for orchestra but the organ reduction is remarkably effective. It begins impressively with a highly florid introduction, soon to become the accompaniment to a wide-ranging unison melody. Harwood wrote about ninety hymn-tunes of which three have taken firm root — *Thornbury* ('Thy hand, O God, has guided'), *Luckington* ('Let all the world in every corner sing') and *St. Audrey* ('Lord of beauty').

THOMAS TERTIUS NOBLE (1867–1953)

Having succeeded Harwood at Ely Cathedral in 1892, Noble became organist of York Minster (1898–1912) and later of the newly built St. Thomas's Church, Fifth Avenue, New York (1912–47). His compositions include three complete Services, three Communion settings (one for female voices), an Evening Service in G minor, a dozen or so unaccompanied anthems and one for double choir. His famous Service in B minor shares with Stanford in B flat and Harwood in A flat the distinction of being one of the three most overworked Services in the Anglican tradition. Noble's setting is much beloved in parish churches: it is vigorous and tuneful, easy to sing and immensely effective; the style is clean-limbed and wholesome. One of the unaccompanied anthems, *The souls of the righteous*, once enjoyed considerable popularity but is less often heard now.

SIR HENRY WALFORD DAVIES (1869–1941)

Here was a man of many parts. At the Temple Church (1898–1923) Davies created an almost legendary choir; he was amongst the first to give practical effect to Robert Bridges's theories on 'speech-rhythm' psalm singing; as an organist he was a penetrating interpreter and an imaginative improviser; he was much sought after as an adjudicator at competitive festivals and he was a gifted lecturer. In the 'twenties and 'thirties he was known to the man-in-the-street as one of the most frequent and popular of broadcasters and his talks on musical appreciation attracted even the unmusical. His 428 school broadcasts, seventy-five studio concerts, twenty-seven pamphlets and sixty sets of concert notes profoundly influenced the taste of children everywhere. Davies's interest in people, and especially the place of people in worship, coupled with his remarkable gift for popularising music, led him to pioneer a new interest in congregational singing; this found wider expression in broadcasts of the 'Sunday Half Hour' type.

Success in these other fields shed a lustre on his compositions which was not, in fact, deserved. He is now looked upon as a very minor composer though within a limited field he nevertheless shows some personal 'fingerprints' — the use of irregular barring (at that time still a fairly novel idea though it was later done to death), a fondness for treble voices in 3rds, and often a somewhat plaintive air induced by the insistence and emphasis on the mediant in many of his melodies (e.g. 'O little town', 'Blessed are the pure', and the hymn-tunes *Vision* and *Wengen*). He was essentially a miniaturist and even his longer pieces are little more than a necklace of miniatures. It is likely that long after his thirteen Services and two dozen anthems have trembled away into silence he will still be remembered for such gracious little introits as 'God be in my head' and 'Blessed are the pure', some chants, carols, and such magnificent hymn-tunes as *Firmament* ('The spacious firmament on high') and *Vision* ('Mine eyes have seen the glory').

JOHN IRELAND (1879–1962)

So far all the composers discussed in this section were essentially church musicians. We come now to one who was a talented professional composer in the widest sense and who, in addition to writing orchestral and chamber music, distinguished himself as a composer of piano works (nearly fifty) and songs (nearly a hundred). Ireland was at heart a mystic and he dabbled in the occult: though he was organist of St. Luke's, Chelsea, for twenty-two years (1904–26) he wrote little for the Church.

He is now remembered chiefly by two pieces. The popular Communion Service in C is an early work (1914). His sensitivity to words saved him from the fetish of 4-bar phrases and resulted in much greater rhythmic flexibility, even to the extent of using irregular barring. Each movement makes extensive structural use of some motivic figure which appears both in the vocal parts and accompaniment—but then, of course, Stanford had been doing this years before. The harmonic and melodic ideas are strictly conventional and Ireland says nothing new. In many ways, then, the Service published in 1914 shows no advance whatsoever on what Stanford was writing twenty-five years earlier.

His other popular success is the anthem *Greater love hath no man* written in 1912. Here the technical apparatus is still more Stanfordian and even the barring is regular. On this small canvas Ireland tips out his whole paintbox, using extremes of range and dynamics for organ and voices. It comes off brilliantly and effectively but is too highly coloured to wear well. The rest of his church music hardly merits revival.

SIR EDWARD CUTHBERT BAIRSTOW (1874–1946)

Bairstow studied under Sir Frederick Bridge at Westminster Abbey and was organist successively of All Saints, Norfolk Square (1894–99), Wigan Parish Church (1899–1906), Leeds Parish Church (1906–13) and York Minster (1913–46).

He stands head and shoulders above all the other composers listed in this section. Though the others have been fairly prolific writers, much of their output has fallen by the wayside and they are remembered now only for one or two particularly well-favoured pieces. In contrast, many of Bairstow's works continue to hold their place in the repertory while some that are neglected deserve resuscitation. His warm romanticism owed much to Brahms and he shared Brahms's gift for expressive melody, his sense of form and feeling for voices. At the same time Bairstow's idiom was peculiarly personal and almost every bar shows certain characteristic fingerprints, mainly harmonic. These include his individual use of chords of the 7th (a) and diminished and augmented triads (b), his distinctive treatment of suspensions (c), and his skill in designing new cadences, often of great beauty (d). The examples shown in Example 176 on the opposite page are typical (His fondness for flat keys will be remarked; sharp signatures very rarely appear.) It is almost inevitable that many of Bairstow's most beautiful harmonic effects, which surprise and delight on first hearing, lose much of their impact with frequent repetition until in course of time they are in danger of being regarded merely as irritating mannerisms. In his lesser pieces this is, in fact, what many of them are; but in his best work they become

Ex. 176

significant structural elements developed logically to give shape and cohesion to music of considerable power and expressiveness.

We can safely ignore earlier pieces like the elaborate and fussy *Blessed be thou,* the carol anthem *Come, ye gentles,* and the popular but rather contrived *Save us, O Lord.* This last has a somewhat mechanical fugato section on the words 'That awake we may watch with Christ' but is partly redeemed by a lovely transition when the basses enter with the words 'And asleep we may rest'. A glance at the organ part of *Lord, I call upon thee* is sufficient to indicate Bairstow's indebtedness to Brahms.

Bairstow was strongly attracted to the 'hymn-anthem' and left some superb examples of the form. *The King of love* is based on the tune *St. Columba*: the second verse is accompanied by gracious arabesques played on a flute stop; the third verse, in a minor key, is for basses in unison; in the fifth verse the melody is played on the organ while boys sing an ecstatic counter-melody of great beauty; the last verse is for voices in unison with varied accompaniment. The little *a cappella* setting *Jesu, grant me this I pray*, based on Gibbons's Song 13, is a fine example of the hymn-anthem form. It is short and simple: the first two and the last verses are in block harmony and the third in flowing counter-point. The hymn melody is given to trebles in the first verse, 2nd trebles in the second verse, tenors in the third and basses in the fourth (Cf. Byrd's *Christe qui lux*), and the whole is notable for the aptness of its treatment and the beauty of its cadences (see Ex. 176). This little piece deserves to be more widely known and can be sung by any parish choir (though it needs basses who can descend to bottom E flat with real quality and control).

A hymn-anthem very much in the grand manner is *Blessed City, heavenly Salem*. For this Bairstow has defied scholars and purists by taking the ancient 'Urbs beata' melody, putting it squarely into 4/4 time, and treating it in 5-part block harmony with a dramatic organ introduction. Then follows a magnificent series of choral variations exploiting every resource of voices and instrument. It is typical of the composer that after the grandeur and brilliance of the third and fourth verses, the heart of the anthem is to be found in the quiet meditative fifth verse, 'To this temple where we call thee', with its lovely rhapsodic treble descant.

One of Bairstow's finest anthems is *Let all mortal flesh keep silence*. It is unaccompanied and begins with men's voices in octaves, creating a mysterious, sombre effect and colouring the word 'trembling'. He uses the full range of voices and selects varied groupings to produce different sonorities. He is careful to preserve natural verbal rhythms and accentuation yet the melodies sound inspired and spontaneous. The middle section is highly dramatic and the last section triumphant, with great detached shouts of 'alleluia' flung into the void (here speaks the organist of York Minster!). There is a final reference to the mysterious opening phrase against distant harmony from the choir.

A work of Bairstow's which is hardly known but which should surely be sung in every parish church is his chant setting of the *Lamentation of Jeremiah*, intended as a more appropriate alternative to Te Deum or Benedicite in Lent, but useful as a simple anthem. It is difficult to be either original or characteristic in writing a mere chant but Bairstow succeeds in being both. Not only are the four basic chants imaginative and expressive in themselves but he offers some beautiful and effective varied harmonizations and accompaniments. These chants could be effectively used for penitential psalms.

SIR SYDNEY HUGO NICHOLSON (1875-1947)

Few church musicians have had such influence on their contemporaries as Nicholson He studied under Parratt and Stanford at the R.C.M. He was acting organist of Carlisle Cathedral (1904–08), organist of Manchester Cathedral (1908–18), and of Westminster Abbey (1919–27). He was a born organizer and had the gift of inspiring others with his own enthusiasms: he was the driving force behind innumerable projects many of which became permanent institutions and have borne abundant fruit. Typical of his enterprise are the Manchester Tuesday Midday Concerts which have now been held continuously for half a century and have started many great artists on the road to fame—including Dame Myra Hess, Eileen Joyce, Phyllis Sellick and Cyril Smith, Moura Lympany, Alan Loveday, Kathleen Ferrier, and John Shirley Quirk. Another of his many interests was the formation of the Westminster Abbey Special Choir. His supreme achievement was, of course, the creation of the School of English Church Music, later the Royal School of Church Music, and in order to devote his full time and energies to its work he resigned from his post at Westminster Abbey. The R.S.C.M. will always be his finest monument. He was particularly interested in choirboys and their welfare and by his innumerable visits to choirs all over the world he continued and extended the work of Miss Hackett.[1]

As a composer, however, Nicholson is of small importance. His work is safely orthodox and belongs to the 'tasteful craftsmanship' category. His Service in D flat has been a familiar stand-by for half a century and is nearly as popular as those by Stanford, Harwood and Noble; yet it has little distinctive to say. The most interesting movement is Benedictus in which an irregular alternation of 2- and 3-beat bars often gives rise to 5/4 rhythm. The unison 'Amen' of this same movement is also quite striking.

His anthems are usually *pièces d'occasion* and need not detain us. Of his many hymn-tunes, three are outstanding. *Bow Brickhill* to 'We sing the praise' (*A. & MR.* 215) is a pleasant swinging tune in triple time, somewhat weakened by the last line. A stirring verse-and-chorus tune is *Crucifer* to 'Lift high the Cross' (*A. & MR.* 633). Finest of all is the magnificent tune *Chislehurst* to 'Hail the day that sees him rise' (*A. & MR.* 610): this glorious melody is so immeasurably superior to any other setting of these words that it richly deserves to become standard. It is a pity that *A. & MR.* does not print the composer's exciting descant to the last line.

SIR WILLIAM HENRY HARRIS (b. 1883)

Harris studied at the R.C.M. and was organist successively of New College, Oxford (1919–29); Christ Church Cathedral, Oxford (1929–33); and St. George's Chapel, Windsor (1933).

Harris is a more important composer than most in this group because his music, like Bairstow's, is well established and has so far retained its popularity. His Services do not truly represent him: they were written with parish choirs in mind and whenever he tries to be simple he often becomes trite. Thus in his Service in A he says obvious things in an obvious way and both melodically and harmonically the piece recalls Arnold's setting in the same key written over a hundred and fifty years previously!

The simplest anthems, too, show little originality, especially those written in the latter part of his life: such things as *The Lord my pasture shall prepare*, with its curious ambivalence of key; *Sing a song of joy*; *In the heavenly kingdom*; *O sing unto the Lord* and *The eyes of all*, could have been turned in as exercises by any competent student. The impression of student exercises is heightened by Harris's penchant for writing little snatches of canon for a few bars here and there. An exception to this generalised stricture is *Behold, the tabernacle of God* written for the official opening of the R.S.C.M.'s headquarters, Addington Palace, Croydon, in 1954: it is a gracious little piece. *Let my prayer* is redeemed by the enterprise and effectiveness of the organ accompaniment. Unison or largely unison songs like *Vox ultima crucis* and *Most glorious Lord* smack strongly of Vaughan Williams and Martin Shaw: they are effectively written.

It is in his large-scale anthems written for cathedral use on festival occasions that Harris comes into his own. One of the most popular, and deservedly so, is the hymn-anthem *O what their joy* based on the old French tune 'O quanta qualia'. This is similar in scale to Bairstow's *Blessed city* and depends for much of its effect on a very well written

[1] See pp. 323–4.

organ accompaniment. The first verse is in unison and the next two in harmony with some imitative part-writing. The fourth begins in G minor but moves into the relative major for 'their voice of praise'. The verse beginning 'There dawns no Sabbath' is a model of sensitive word-setting. It begins with an air of hushed mystery, the choir singing unaccompanied in five parts and the music perfectly reflecting the rhythm and accentuation of the words: an enharmonic change gives sudden brilliance to 'that triumph song'. The sixth stanza, in the unexpected key of E major, is for men's voices. At this point a dramatic and strikingly effective organ interlude modulates back into G major for the last stanza. This is in unison with an elaborate 'varied' accompaniment. The coda is magnificent.

Another superb piece is *Faire is the heaven*, a massive double-choir anthem much in the style of Charles Wood. The melodic line has a fine sweep and both harmony and modulations are more enterprising than in most of Harris's work. The middle section is outstanding: phrases echo and re-echo antiphonally through an exciting series of modulations culminating in a powerful climax 'which attend on God's own person'. Similar in scale and resource is the 8-part *Bring us, O Lord, at our last awakening*. Much less familiar, but equally fine, is *Strengthen ye the weak hands*, a useful anthem for services associated with healing or attended by branches of the medical or nursing professions. It opens with a measured recitative for tenor and both here and later Harris's sensitivity in word-setting is balanced by a strong feeling for melodic contours. Climaxes are well spaced and cunningly contrived and the organ accompaniment is highly imaginative. These anthems are some of the last roses of a very long summer. Splendid though they are, they still show hardly any advance on Stanford—or even Wesley.

The list of 'main stream' composers is a long one and includes many of Harris's younger contemporaries—Charles Hylton Stewart, Henry G. Ley, Harold Darke, Ernest Bullock, Charles F. Waters, Eric Thiman and others. They are the twentieth-century equivalent of people like Goss and Ouseley and their music too belongs to the 'tasteful craftsmanship' category—tuneful, well-written, perceptive and even imaginative at times, but safely orthodox in idiom, unquestioning, and strikingly unoriginal in basic concepts.

Since 1950 there has been an astonishing revolution in church music and it is fairly safe to say that from now onwards no composer of any calibre could continue to express himself in these now threadbare idioms. It is to be expected also that much of the music discussed in this section, though highly popular at the moment, especially in parish churches and nonconformist chapels, will gradually drop out of use.

THE TUDOR AND JACOBEAN REVIVAL

There have been so many influences, trends, developments and movements this century that it is difficult to arrange them in any particular order of importance. Perhaps, however, pride of place must go to the Tudor and Jacobean revival, partly because of its immense influence on practically all church composers (a decisive influence in the case of men like Vaughan Williams, 'Warlock' and Rubbra), partly because of the powerful fertilizing effect it has had on style and technique, and partly because it is now once more a living force and Tudor music forms a large part of the repertory in all cathedrals and many parish churches.

Not, of course, that there has ever been a time when at least a handful of Tudor works were not to be heard in our cathedrals, but they were few and unrepresentative. The vast corpus of renaissance music was not only not sung but was inaccessible. It survived only in the old part-books and these were scattered about in ecclesiastical, private and public libraries. To make such music available to choirs, scholars would have to transcribe the separate parts into score, wrestle with a wide variety of textual problems, and publish a performers' edition. Sometimes missing part-books would turn up months or even years afterwards in other libraries geographically widely separated. Since often the individual parts bore neither titles nor composers' names and were often in the handwriting of unknown copyists, such work called for the patience of Job and the skill of Sherlock Holmes. A small beginning was made in the nineteenth century by the Musical Antiquarian Society (1840–47), the Motet Society (1840), and by individual scholars like Jebb, John Bishop, Ouseley and Stainer, but many of these editions were unreliable. It has been mentioned that Victorians tended to look upon progress as a straight line climbing upwards from primeval slime, through prehistory and the Middle Ages, till it reached its apex in their own day. From their vantage point the work of earlier periods must, *ipso facto*, have seemed somewhat inferior or crude. They were hardly surprised to find then that Tudor writers had been curiously remiss in forgetting to supply time signatures and regular bar-lines, while such things as the simultaneous clash of major and minor 3rds were obvious misprints: here was work for the editorial pen! Purcell's harmony in particular was amateurish and inelegant and badly needed the ministrations of a discreet editor to correct his mistakes and cover up his deficiencies. Sometimes the original was 'adapted' to suit Victorian choirs; Stainer's corruption of Tallis's so-called 'festal' responses is typical.

A truer knowledge and understanding of Tudor music was brought nearer by the work of two men, Arkwright and Terry. Godfrey Arkwright (1864–1944) was 'a rather lonely scholar, ploughing his quiet furrow without the stimulus either of performance or of popular interest, in the 'eighties and 'nineties when Tudor music was still an "antiquarian curiosity" . . . He was an unhurried worker and unambitious for publicity.'[2] He edited with distinguished scholarship the twenty-five volumes of the 'Old English Edition' (1889–1902) which included motets, masses and songs of the polyphonic school. From 1909 to 1913 he was editor of *The Musical Antiquary* and he also edited Purcell's church music for the Purcell Society.

Many of the ideals for which Arkwright worked received practical fulfilment in the work of Richard Runciman Terry (1865–1938), a former choral scholar of King's, who in 1896 was received into the Church of Rome and became successively Director of Music at Downside Abbey, then from 1901 to 1924 organist of the newly built Westminster Cathedral. For many years he spent most of his spare time in the British Museum transcribing and editing Latin works for his choirs to sing. At Downside he was seemingly the first to perform, as liturgical music, masses by Tye, Tallis, Mundy and Byrd as well as motets by Parsons, Tye, Farrant, Whyte, Byrd and Philips. At Westminster he added to these the *Cantiones sacrae* of Tallis and Byrd, Byrd's *Gradualia* and *Cantiones sacrae*, Peter Philips's *Cantiones sacrae*, the *Lamentations* of Tallis and Whyte, and a wide range of works from the Old Hall Manuscript and others by Fayrfax, Taverner, Parsons, Morley and Dowland. In addition, he performed an immense amount of polyphonic music by continental masters.

[2] Hilda Andrews: *Westminster Retrospect*, pp. 140–1. (O.U.P.)

Terry was essentially a practical musician. At Westminster he created a superb choir highly skilled in the specialised art of singing polyphonic music and much of his research was undertaken with the practical end of enlarging their repertory. He was not much interested in scholarship for its own sake nor had he the patience and meticulous care required to collate several sources, noting variants and solving textual problems in order to bring out a scholarly edition. To him music had to be much more than a page of print, however accurate; it had to be a glorious reality, ringing and re-echoing around the vast spaces of his cathedral, uplifting the hearts and minds of men. Having once translated the old part-books into actual sound he quickly lost interest in the niceties of research; his publications, useful though they were, hardly satisfy the highest canons of modern scholarship.

Terry's work at Westminster attracted considerable public attention and did much to 'popularize' renaissance music. One outcome of this was that the Trustees of the Carnegie United Kingdom Trust decided to finance a folio edition of Tudor church music; it was to be authoritative and lavishly produced. Sir Henry Hadow was closely identified with this project and his writings convey something of the excitement felt by musicians at that time. Thus, he wrote:

> I do not know whether it is quite realized that this is not a question of a mere Library Edition of a classic; it is the most important musical discovery ever made . . . If you could imagine that the Elizabethan drama had been lost and now rediscovered, it would not be an extravagant parallel.

and again:

> There exists a large amount of extremely fine English Church Music composed between 1540 and 1623. It is mostly in manuscript parts. Very little of it has ever been printed. A definitive edition of it would be literally the greatest English musical work ever published. The value of it is not only that of a historical monument but that of a living and permanent art; the best work of our best period. Dr. R. R. Terry of Westminster Cathedral has been engaged upon it for the last twenty years and has transcribed and scored a good deal of it for use at Westminster.
>
> The Trustees propose Terry as Editor—a proposal with which I entirely agree—he is a real scholar and knows more about this music than any other man alive.[3]

This was in 1916. Terry estimated the edition would fill twenty volumes and take five years to prepare. When later he realized the immensity of his undertaking he formed an editorial committee consisting of Sir Percy Buck, the Rev. Alexander Ramsbotham, Miss Sylvia Townsend Warner and the Rev. E. H. Fellowes. The whole project was close to Terry's heart, but he was a very busy man and the sheer drudgery of collating manuscripts and wrestling with editorial problems irked him. In 1922 he felt obliged to withdraw from the committee and his work was continued by Dr. Fellowes.

The Rev. Dr. Edmund H. Fellowes (1870–1951) was appointed Precentor of Bristol Cathedral in 1897 and Minor Canon of St. George's Chapel, Windsor, in 1900. There he spent the rest of his life.

As a singer in various madrigal societies he was quick to realize that not only were the

[3] Ibid., p. 139.

printed copies of English madrigals badly edited and often faulty, but that only a very small proportion of Tudor secular music was available in print at all. With immense courage (financial as well as musical) he therefore embarked single-handed on a prodigious scheme to score, edit and publish the entire corpus of English madrigals in thirty-six volumes under the title *The English Madrigal School*. This he did with notable success, the various volumes appearing between 1913 and 1924. As well as publishing the music he studied the texts and in 1920 brought out a volume of *English Madrigal Verse*, an important collection. His researches shed much light on the composers themselves and cleared up many biographical problems which had baffled previous scholars: these researches were embodied in another important book, *English Madrigal Composers* (1921). While these various undertakings were still in course of preparation, Fellowes began work on another vast project—a complete edition of the works of *The English School of Lutenist Song Writers*, issued in twenty-four volumes between 1921 and 1932. Not content with undertakings which would have occupied most men for a lifetime, he added to his many other labours that of cataloguing Ouseley's library at Tenbury which was at that time in a chaotic state.

When, therefore, Terry formed his committee to assist with the publication of *Tudor Church Music* it was inevitable that he should seek Fellowes's help. It was equally inevitable that the scholarly Fellowes should not always see eye to eye with the practical Terry. Inevitable also that when Terry withdrew, Fellowes should take over the direction of the enterprise and carry it through to a successful conclusion. Terry's original estimate of five years for the twenty volumes proved wildly optimistic; only ten of the volumes were published, the last appearing as late as 1929. Material for another ten volumes was prepared but various circumstances prevented their publication: to our shame, therefore, this authoritative edition of an important part of our national musical heritage remains incomplete.

Fellowes's last important edition was his *Collected Works of William Byrd* (twenty volumes; 1937–50). Other books include *The English Madrigal* (1925); *Orlando Gibbons and his Family* (1925); *William Byrd* (1936); and his important history of *English Cathedral Music* (1941: reissued with minor revisions by Prof. J. A. Westrup 1969).

When editing Tudor music Fellowes frequently made allowance for changes in pitch and notation by transposing up a minor 3rd and halving note values. When one of the part-books in a set was missing, Fellowes found he was often able to reconstruct the missing part with a fair degree of probability. Occasionally the missing part was later found; when compared against it the reconstructed part generally proved a good approximation. If any vindication of this practice is necessary it need only be mentioned that by reconstructing much of the Decani second alto part, Fellowes was able to publish Byrd's *Great Service* in 1922 (the missing parts have since come to light). It is also interesting to compare his edition of Weelkes's *Gloria in excelsis*, in which he reconstructed the second meane part, with Dr. Walter Collins's later edition which gives Weelkes's original part (see p. 164). Perhaps Fellowes's most far-sighted decision was to publish not only collected library editions but also to issue individual works in separate offprints costing only a few pence each, thus bringing Tudor and Jacobean music within reach of every choir.

In recent years Fellowes has been subjected to a good deal of debunking. Modern scholars complain that he was not consistent in his methods, that he relied too much on inspired guesswork (and some not so inspired), that he was not over-scrupulous in differentiating between what was the composer's and what was his own. Furthermore he was so anxious to publish, publish, publish, that he did not take time to examine the function, background and performing conditions of the music he edited. More seriously, he tended to look upon English music in isolation rather than as part of the larger continental pattern owing a particular debt to Italy: he failed to distinguish between the native tradition and the Italian influences. He has also been criticized for being far too general in his approach and loose in his terminology; one example is the casual way in which he lumps together canzonets, balletts, airs, psalms, sonnets, pastorals and songs (sacred and secular) and calls them all 'madrigals'. These criticisms may be well deserved—but then Fellowes did something infinitely more wonderful and important than merely producing a scholarly edition to moulder and gather dust on library shelves. It is his chief glory that having unearthed this vast treasure-trove, he popularized it and made it a living reality in churches, halls, schools and homes all over the world. As a direct outcome of his work, amateur madrigal societies sprang up over night and church choirs made Tudor music a staple part of their repertory. The impact of his work was immense.

Polyphonic works of the Tudor period were almost the exact antithesis of most Victorian church music. The following comparison makes this clear:

VICTORIAN	TUDOR
1. Melody in highest voice: other parts have mainly accompanying role. They are often static and have little melodic interest of their own.	Interest evenly distributed amongst the various voice-parts all of which have melodic and rhythmic interest in themselves.
2. Bass often static.	Bass shares melodic interest.
3. Conceived vertically, interest harmonic (and sometimes chromatic), texture generally chordal.	Conceived horizontally, interest contrapuntal, texture generally polyphonic though sometimes chordal.
4. Rhythm in simple metrical pattern of two, three or four beats in a bar.	Rhythmic patterns usually irregular; in imitative writing, cross accents add rhythmic interest.
5. The tune (and hence underparts) organized in balanced structure of two-, four-, and eight-bar phrases, each marked off with a clear-cut cadence.	The use of irregular phrase lengths, imitation, overlapping of parts, cross accents and suspensions impels the music forwards, delays cadences and minimizes their effect.
6. Words of the text are made to fit the music: they are hurried, dragged-out or repeated as necessary.	Words inspire and partly shape the music.
7. Music written in the classical key system.	Music often modal. Even when written in major and minor keys they are often used without the harmonic implications of later classical practice.

Fellowes's work came at the right time and rode on the crest of reaction. To a generation still recovering from the debilitating effects of the previous century and desperately seeking new ways and forms of expression, Tudor music came as a blinding revelation.

Here was a new point of departure and one which, furthermore, had its roots deep in our history. Its impact was considerably reinforced by influences coming from an entirely different direction—the folk-song revival where, again, rhythms were often irregular and melodies frequently modal. So it was that the Tudor revival had a most powerful influence, direct or indirect, on nearly all church composers of the last fifty years, an influence going far beyond mere matters of technique or style and extending to such basic issues as the relationship between words and music and a return to horizontal thinking.

It only remains to add that since the Second World War distinguished scholars, building on Fellowes's sure, if rather rough-and-ready, foundations, have re-edited much of his work in the light of modern knowledge, a more scientific approach to musicology, and vastly improved editorial methods.

THE FOLK-SONG INFLUENCE

At about the same time that Tudor music was engaging scholars' attention there was an awakening of interest in English folk song and dance. The leaders in this field were Cecil Sharp and Vaughan Williams, both of whom spent much time collecting songs from older members of rural communities. Folk song shared certain characteristics (irregular phrases, rhythmic variation, use of modes, and even certain melodic devices) with Tudor music and so reinforced the latter's influence.

Though folk song had little direct effect on the composition of Services and anthems, it became an important element in English hymnody. It was Vaughan Williams, in his *English Hymnal*, who first tapped traditional secular folk melodies and he and Martin Shaw introduced others into *Songs of Praise*. Many of these folk tunes have become widely popular—*Forest Green*, *Sussex*, *Shipston*, *Monks Gate*, *King's Lynn*, *Kingsfold*, *Herongate*, and *Rodmell*, for example—but others still seem somewhat incongruous in the framework of Prayer Book services.

Another group of folk melodies have claimed a rightful place in worship; these are traditional, and sometimes ancient, carols which have been popularised by the comparatively modern revival of carol singing (which largely dates from 1871, the publication of Bramley and Stainer's collection). Many of these are really good tunes and some are of rare beauty: on the other hand there are many in the *Oxford Book of Carols* which are so dull as scarcely to justify their resurrection: often, too, Martin Shaw's bleak and mannered arrangements make them worse.

Many composers at this time, including Vaughan Williams and Shaw, affected the folk-song style in some of their own works and large numbers of pseudo folk melodies were produced, supported by quasi-modal harmonies in which the leading-note is usually flattened. Most of the carol settings in Part IV and a few in Part V of the *Oxford Book of Carols* are examples of this form of pastiche. So fashionable did the cult become that 'folksy-wolksy' has now become a term of disparagement.

THE REACTIONARIES

The most violent reaction against mid-Victorian church music was long delayed. It was foreshadowed by Vaughan Williams's *Sine Nomine* and Parry's *Jerusalem* (among others) but it was not until the 'twenties that the full force of its eruption was felt. It is seen at its best in the works of Vaughan Williams and Gustav Holst; at its worst in some of the music of Martin Shaw.

Basically it set out to be the very antithesis of what it was reacting against. 'The Victorians were mushy; very well then, the new music must be stark with plenty of bare 4ths and 5ths. Victorian bass parts were often static; right, ours shall stride up and down purposefully (e.g. Holst's "Turn back, O man" and Martin Shaw's hymn-tunes *All Waters* and *Working* in *Songs of Praise*). The Victorians favoured three-time – so we'll keep mainly to fours or, better still, irregular groupings. The Victorians confined themselves to the major-minor key complexes; we therefore will go folksy-modal. They liked chromatic harmony; we must remain strictly diatonic. They were emotional – away with false sentiment! They wanted to please: we will shock.' Of course such ideas were probably never held consciously; subconsciously, however, they satisfied a deep-seated need to shake off outworn conventions and inject fresh vitality into the music of worship.

The outcome was a vigorous blood-and-guts style, a kind of musical chauvinism, most successful when setting words of similar vigour and spirit. Its characteristics became powerful virtues when fused by the inspiration of a Vaughan Williams (Te Deum in G, Benedicite) or a Holst (*Hymn of Jesus, Choral Fantasia*). They could also produce the 'big tune' (Vaughan Williams's *Sine Nomine*, Holst's 'I vow to thee my country' and Geoffrey Shaw's *Worship*). At worst they too easily degenerated into mannered posturings, as typical of their period and as lacking in true religious impulse as the corresponding hymns of the mid-nineteenth century – and as dated.

This reactionary movement found its ultimate expression in two famous books, *Songs of Praise* and *The Oxford Book of Carols*, both edited by Vaughan Williams and Martin Shaw. In the former book it is the section headed 'Social Service' which seems to have brought out the devil in this group of composers and we are faced with such horrors as Martin Shaw's *Pioneers* (304) and *All Waters* (327), Nicholson's *Music Makers* (315), Vaughan Williams's *Guilford* (316) and Holst's *Stepney* (325), all (mercifully) born dead. Whatever their merits as music or as sacred songs they were wildly unsuitable as congregational hymns.

In the *Oxford Book of Carols* we see the new style applied to ancient or traditional carols as in *Christmas Eve* (1) and *Irish Carol* (6). Sometimes the results can be very fine, as in Holst's versions of *Personent hodie* (78) and *Masters in this hall* (137) sometimes bleak and comfortless, like the harmonization of *God rest you merry* (12). Some of the new tunes in Parts IV and V, if not true carols, are nevertheless valuable additions to the repertory. But of the first 167 carols, the choice and harmonization of many is so much a product of the 'twenties that the book as a whole is now as dated as Sankey's *Sacred Songs and Solos* of which, in some ways, it is a twentieth-century equivalent.

RALPH VAUGHAN WILLIAMS (1872–1958)

In such a short and general survey as this it is not possible to attempt a critical study of the work of major contemporary composers like Vaughan Williams and Benjamin Britten. A brief note must suffice.

Vaughan Williams's genius was so many-sided that he cannot be contained in any one section of this chapter. Like Holst, he was among the first to rebel against eighteenth- and nineteenth-century orthodoxy and his music is utterly unlike that of any composer before him. Yet whereas Debussy, Schönberg, Bartók, Stravinsky and others broke through to new realms of technique and expression, he made no attempt to forge a 'new music'; rather, he looked to the distant past and found inspiration in the two powerful influences of Tudor music and folk music. Instead of inventing new scales and systems he achieved release by returning to the ancient modes. By applying to modal idioms the techniques and resources of a forward-looking contemporary composer, his music formed a bridge across the centuries; yet so strong was his musical personality that these disparate elements of ancient and modern became fused into a style which was not only highly personal but also intensely national. In addition to this essential 'Englishness' there were other sides of his character—the 'rustic', which found expression in his pastoral vein, and the mystic and visionary, apparent in his choice of texts and his abiding love for Bunyan's *Pilgrim's Progress*. This mystical side of his nature shows itself musically in a form of impressionism which perhaps owes something to his studies under Ravel. This impressionism too was assimilated into his personal style, colouring and deepening it.

One of his more daring innovations was to question the sanctity of 4-part harmony and to substitute for it a more sinewy style based on 2- or 3-part counterpoint. The following, in two parts, is typical:

Vaughan Williams: *Te Deum in G*

Ex. 177

The Benedicite in particular abounds in such writing. Often the texture is enriched not by adding more parts but by doubling the existing parts at the 3rd and 5th (or 6th) above or below, resulting in streams of parallel chords. Such writing has been called 'chordal counterpoint' (see Exercise 178 opposite).

His finest sacred works are outside the scope of this book: they are oratorio-type pieces for soloists, chorus and orchestra, like *Sancta Civitas;* Benedicite; *Dona nobis pacem*, the *Festival Te Deum* and *Hodie*. Of his liturgical music, much is either very simple and largely in unison (e.g. Evening Service in C, the Service based on metrical psalm tunes, *Let us now praise famous men* and *O how amiable*) or else laid out for double choir and orchestra and demanding festival resources (e.g. *Lord, Thou hast been our refuge: O praise*

Vaughan Williams: *A Pastoral Symphony*

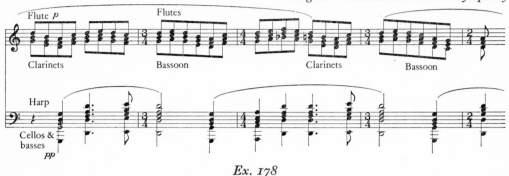

Ex. 178

the Lord of Heaven and *O clap your hands*). One of the greatest and most typical of these works is the *Mass in G minor* (1920–1), scored for solo quartet and double choir unaccompanied, which clearly has its roots in the great Masses of Taverner. In mood, style and lay-out this Mass can be looked upon as the choral counterpart of the composer's *Fantasia on a theme by Thomas Tallis* (1910, revised 1913 and 1919) similarly scored for solo string quartet and double string orchestra. Some of these large-scale pieces still remain highly effective when sung by a cathedral choir, the orchestral accompaniment being transferred to the organ —especially the Te Deum in G which is now in the regular repertory of most cathedrals and larger churches. The powerful and characteristic motet *Valiant-for-truth*, with words from *Pilgrim's Progress*, is especially notable for the onomatopoeic writing at 'And all the trumpets': it demands a good choir.

Apart from unison songs and pieces, Vaughan Williams has left little for parish choirs. One lovely exception is the short introit *O taste and see* with its daring, simple and beautiful final cadence. Enterprising choirmasters will also find *Almighty Word* rewarding: it is a hymn-anthem based on the same 'theme of Thomas Tallis' which inspired one of the composer's most profound orchestral works.

THE JAZZ INFLUENCE

One of the most surprising things about the first half of this century is that although the jazz idiom, in all its multitudinous styles and manifestations, had had far wider popular appeal than almost any other type of music, little attempt was made to adapt it to church use. Until very recently its influence was indirect rather than direct. Almost the only important composer to experiment in this direction was Sir William Walton. In his highly original and orgiastic oratorio *Belshazzar's Feast*, jazz influence is apparent in various rhythmic devices and *ostinatos*, in his use of syncopation, and in details of orchestration. Much the same can be said of his Te Deum written for the Queen's Coronation. Both works, however, lie outside our field. Apart from a schoolboy essay *A Litany*, the beautiful 4-part wedding motet *Set me as a seal upon thy heart*, and *Make we joy*, Walton has composed nothing for liturgical use.

Much more recently there are indications that some of our younger church composers, like Malcolm Williamson, are experimenting with jazz (or at least with particular aspects of it).

More significantly still some famous jazz musicians have recently shown an interest in devotional music. Duke Ellington's suite *In the beginning, God . . .* received its première in Coventry Cathedral played by his own orchestra with choir and soloists, and Dave Brubeck has written a somewhat overweight jazz oratorio *The Voice in the Wilderness*. Several *avant-garde* black American jazz men have called their pieces such names as *Psalm; Father, Son and Holy Ghost; The Creator has a master plan* and *Music is the healing Force of the Universe*, while John Coltrane named one of his best records *A Love Supreme*.

Of the English jazz men, Mike Garrick wrote *Jazz Praises*, scored for choir and a small modern jazz group, which as been used in St. Paul's Cathedral and several parish churches, yet it has also been hailed by specialists in the field as a fine piece of modern jazz. In 1970 the Canterbury Festival authorities commissioned some pieces for large band from Mike Gibbs: these proved highly effective in performance though they were not, of course, intended for liturgical use. Of more interest to choirmasters is a *Folk Mass* by that doyen of British jazz musicians, John Dankworth. It is scored for 4-part choir, unison congregation and a keyboard accompaniment which is conceived pianistically but can easily be adapted for the organ: no doubt a string bass, guitars and light percussion would add enormously to the work's effectiveness. In the Gloria there are some striking modulations while a bossa nova Agnus Dei must surely be unique. No setting of the Creed is provided.

To these composers jazz is a natural language—they feel its styles and idioms in their bones and it has become their instinctive means of self-expression and communication, whereas to 'serious' composers (what a smug description—as though jazz composers are not serious!) jazz is an alien culture and their flirtations with it are usually self-conscious and inhibited. It is greatly to be hoped that more professional jazz musicians will interest themselves in liturgical composition.

It has to be faced though that the performance of jazz music in church raises a serious difficulty—to come to life it must be performed by real jazz musicians. True jazz is an idiom all its own in which improvisation is an essential component: what appears on paper is merely a basis from which the player takes his departure. His style is peculiarly and recognisably his own and he instinctively interprets the printed notes idiomatically within that style. To hear Dankworth's *Folk Mass* sung by a large group at a jazz festival accompanied by his own band would be a truly moving and spiritual experience: to hear the same work at the local parish church accompanied on a heavy diapason by an ecclesiastically-trained organist painfully spelling out the rhythms bar by bar would kill it stone dead. This same difficulty applies almost equally to the performance of 'pop' music in church.[4]

THE IMPRESSIONISTS

This word is loosely used to describe those composers who use harmony and harmonic devices to emphasize the colouristic elements in music and so create 'atmosphere'. Of course most composers do this from time to time, some more than others. Vaughan Williams, as we have seen, was one of the first to employ impressionist techniques (triads with added notes, chords in parallel motion, avoidance of leading note and similar characteristic devices), especially in his 'pastoral' and 'mystical' pieces.

Another who showed marked impressionistic traits in some of his work was 'Peter

[4] For much of this information I am indebted to Bob Davenport.

Warlock', a name adopted by Philip Heseltine (1894–1930). As a scholar Heseltine was interested in sixteenth- and seventeenth-century music and edited six volumes of *English Ayres 1598–1612*. As a composer he was a prolific song writer and his greatest achievements were in this *genre*. The only sacred pieces he wrote were carols and in these his wayward genius produced miniatures of outstanding merit. Three which appear in the *Oxford Book of Carols* all show impressionist leanings, especially in their use of parallel chords, of unresolved dissonances (particularly triads with added 2nds, 4ths, 6ths, and 7ths), and the subtle use of harmony (both diatonic and chromatic) so as to undermine the inherent psychological implications of the major/minor scales and key relationships.

Tyrley, Tyrlow (169), a charming, graceful pastorale, is a model of how 'varied accompaniments' should be done. It is not easy to sing or to play effectively on the organ and it needs an orchestra to make its full impact. *Adam lay ybounden* (180) is a simple unison melody with a highly effective accompaniment: an unexpected 5/4 bar adds much to the climax at the end. Most beautiful of all is *Balulalow* (181) in which a shimmering kaleidoscope of harmonic colour moves against a gently throbbing pedal-note. The use of the evocative tone-colour of a wordless chorus is again a typically impressionistic device (Cf. Ravel's *Daphnis et Chloé*, Delius's *Song of the High Hills* and Vaughan Williams's *Flos Campi*). The final cadence is highly original and very beautiful. It is a striking example of the price we pay for equal-tempered tuning. When played on a keyboard the tenor part falls a tone to its final G; when sensitively sung, this tone becomes almost a minor 3rd because the A needs to be tuned sharp and the G slightly flat:

Warlock: *Balulalow*

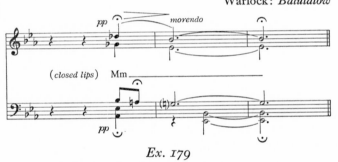

Ex. 179

Other charming carols by Warlock include *Bethlehem Down*; *The First Mercy* and *I saw a fair maiden*: these should be familiar to all choirs. By contrast, the boisterous and electrifying Latin carol *Benedicamus Domino* is typical of the composer's more robust style.

Ernest John Moeran (1894–1950) was another who inclined to Impressionism, traces of which appear in his Services and in the anthems *Praise the Lord* and *Blessed are those servants*.

But the arch-priest of Impressionism in English church music is unquestionably Herbert Howells (born 1892), one of the most prolific, gifted and original church composers in the first half of the century. Howells studied privately under Herbert Brewer at Gloucester and later under Stanford at the R.C.M. After a short spell as sub-organist at Salisbury Cathedral he joined the teaching staff of the R.C.M. In 1953 he was appointed Professor of Music at London University. He also became one of the busiest and most popular adjudicators in the country.

As a composer Howells has evolved a highly personal style compounded of extreme sensitivity to the meaning and music of words, a strongly marked feeling for melody, a subtle sense of harmony which is both elusive and evocative, a natural sense of vocal colour and spacing, mastery in writing for the organ, and fastidious attention to detail. His work shows the influence of composers prominent during his formative years — Debussy, Ireland, Bernard van Dieren and Philip Heseltine.

Howells first established his prominence in church music with the publication of three carols. The modal pseudo-folk melody and parallel 5ths of *There is a little door* (1918) smacked of Vaughan Williams but when, a year later, *A spotless rose* appeared it was apparent that a new and original voice had emerged creating sounds which fell strangely on ears attuned to Wesley and Stanford. Not only were there six rather daring changes of time in its first seven bars — 3/4, 7/8, 4/4, 5/4, 5/8, 3/4 — but its soaring melody seemed to float on a cloud of lush chords moving in parallel. These impressions were confirmed the next year when *Sing lullaby* (1920) was published. This was similar but even more subtle. Again the rapturous bass tune floated on gently lapping parallel chords; again the rhythm was elusive and the harmony glowed with a new and strange loveliness. In the middle section occurred a series of enharmonic modulations which must have struck terror into choirs at that time — and which are by no means easy to tune even on today's standards.

About this time other fields of composition claimed most of his attention and he wrote comparatively little for liturgical use though *My eyes for beauty pine* is a good strong unison tune in the Vaughan Williams manner while *When first thine eies unveil* is unusual for Howells in that it ends with an extended pedal and the tonality is kept deliberately uncertain. A gap of nearly fifteen years separates his *Four Anthems* (1941–43) from his earlier motets. The first, *O pray for the peace of Jerusalem*, leans much on Vaughan Williams; so to a lesser extent do *We have heard* and *Like as the hart*: the last of the four, *Let God arise*, is more vigorous and forthright than most of the composer's liturgical settings.

It was in 1945 that Howells suddenly leapt into the forefront of British church composers with his evening Service 'Collegium Regale' dedicated to the choir of King's College, Cambridge. The first part of Magnificat is given to high voices only (and sounds best sung by boys alone if they can manage four parts), the full choir entering at 'He hath shewn strength'. The wide-ranging ecstatic bass phrase 'He hath filled the hungry' is typical and the hauntingly beautiful cadence before the Gloria is pure Impressionism:

Howells: '*Collegium Regale*' *Magnificat*

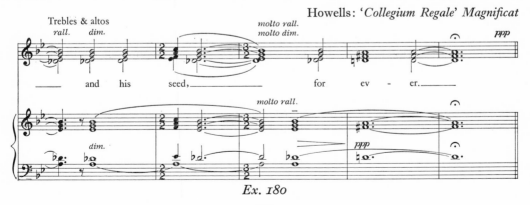

Ex. 180

429

A soaring treble entry introduces one of the most thrilling Glorias in the whole repertory and its mood of exultation and spiritual joy is sustained to the end. Nunc dimittis, the song of Simeon, is appropriately given to tenor soloist. In the second verse the choir accompanies him *pp* and in the last verse takes over from him, still *pp*. Undoubtedly this Service is one of the most significant to have been written this century.

In the following January another Service appeared, dedicated to his old cathedral at Gloucester. This is very similar in style and feeling to 'Collegium Regale' but is even more atmospheric. Again the beginning of Magnificat is given to treble voices but this time the harmony is more astringent. The final cadence of Magnificat is again supremely lovely and the radiant Gloria closes with some splendid melismatic Amens. Many consider this Service to be Howells's greatest achievement in liturgical music so far.

Then followed a whole series of Services dedicated to various choral foundations. These included Morning Services for Canterbury (1950) and St. George's Chapel, Windsor, and Evening Services for New College, Oxford (1949), St. John's College, Cambridge (1950), Worcester Cathedral (1951), St. Paul's Cathedral (1952), two for Westminster Abbey (1952 and 1957), the Church Music Society Festival (1956), York Minster, Hereford and others. Howells, like King, might well be called 'a very serviceable man'! There is a family likeness about all these pieces. They are nearly all in the minor key with strong modal tendencies and however 'advanced' the harmony may be it is always rich and sensuous, revealing Howells as a pure Romantic at heart (as were all the Impressionists): yet his style is so strongly individual that almost any two bars are sufficient to identify him. Most of the Canticle settings are built round a principal theme used as a motive which binds them together (Stanford's idea). These themes tend to grow out of the interval of a minor 3rd. Magnificats often begin with treble voices only. Glorias are triumphant and frequently include a passage in unison. Climactic phrases are usually melismatic. There is a preponderance of 3/2 writing.

In fact, so strong is this family likeness it is almost as if 'Collegium Regale' had been used as a template for all the others—and this brings us at once to Howells's basic weakness and limitations. One cannot imagine Benjamin Britten writing a dozen Services all much alike: he would approach his text afresh each time and interpret it differently, producing a series of works each unquestionably his yet quite unlike any other in the series. But Howells has only one style and this is limited in its emotional range. Furthermore his style does not seem to have developed or changed very much over the years; it is doubtful if, for example, Services written in the middle 'fifties show much advance technically or emotionally on 'Sing lullaby' published over thirty years earlier. It is as though he has been exploring a cul-de-sac full of lovely things—but there is no road on. This explains perhaps why he has no followers. Probably this same criticism applies to Impressionist composers generally; certainly much the same comment could be made about Debussy and Delius.

Footnote: choirmasters wishing to add a Howells's Service to the repertory but daunted by the technical difficulties of the 'cathedral' group should look at the early Magnificat and Nunc dimittis in G (1920),[5] a superb setting well within the reach of competent church choirs. It would also be an ideal choice for diocesan festivals and the like.

[5] Published by Stainer & Bell—Modern Church Services, No. 216.

BENJAMIN BRITTEN (b. 1913)

Britten is an isolated figure owing little to other musicians mentioned in this chapter. He is universally recognised as our greatest living composer (as were Elgar and Vaughan Williams before him). Whereas Vaughan Williams found his stimulus in folk song and Tudor church music, Britten's point of departure was the music of Henry Purcell. Though Purcell wrote in major and minor keys and was generally diatonic, he treated harmony and part-leading with a freedom which would have been unthinkable a century, or even half a century later. It is this freedom within tonal writing that Britten has rediscovered and developed. Whereas nearly all contemporary composers seem to have taken refuge in an idiom derived from Schönberg and Webern, Britten has remained conservative and is one of the few who is still in touch with Everyman. Thus the heart-searching cadence which closes some movements of the *War Requiem* is simply the juxtaposition of two common chords. It is almost axiomatic that a British composer should fulfil himself most in the setting of words, especially sacred words, and although Britten is remarkably versatile and has achieved success in nearly all fields of composition, and especially in opera, most will agree that his sacred choral works are among his finest achievements. Here his aural imagination is at its most brilliant and sensitive and there is a feeling of ease and inevitability about his writing which is, nevertheless, always distinctive. Even in his sacred pieces he has shown astonishing variety and originality, producing liturgical music like the *Te Deum in C* (1935) and *Missa Brevis* (1959); festival works such as *Rejoice in the Lamb* (1943) and the *Festival Te Deum* (1945); choral suites — *A Boy was Born* (1932) and *A Ceremony of Carols* (1943); and oratorios like *St. Nicolas* (1948) and his supreme achievement, the *War Requiem* (1962). His two main interests, opera and church music, have combined to produce an entirely new type of work which owes much to the old 'miracle' plays: so far he has composed three of these 'church operas' — *Curlew River* (1964), *The Burning Fiery Furnace* (1966) and *The Prodigal Son* (1968). The series really began in 1958 with a much more light-hearted essay in the same genre, *Noye's Fludde*, written mainly for child performers and including in its instrumentation bugles, handbells and mugs hit with a wooden spoon: it is full of good tunes.

One aspect of Britten's personality which deserves mention is his profound understanding of boys and boyhood. Not only are many of his works about boys (e.g. *Peter Grimes*, *The Turn of the Screw*, *Let's make an opera*, *St. Nicolas*, *Curlew River* and also, to a lesser extent, *Owen Wingrave*) but probably no composer in history has written for boys' voices with such rare sensitivity and insight. Many people regard a well-produced boy's voice as the most supremely beautiful sound in the world: Britten's understanding and *rapport* enable him to use this tone colour to most telling advantage, especially in *A Ceremony of Carols* (for the lovely combination of 3-part boys' choir and harp), in the *Spring Symphony*, the *Missa Brevis* and the *War Requiem*. It is interesting that boys seem to sense the composer's affinity with them and love singing his music.

The church musician will lament that Britten has written so little liturgical music — two Te Deums, the *Missa Brevis* and a few anthems. The *Te Deum in C* is in regular 4/4 time and is strictly tonal. It begins with two pages of the chord of C major over an organ pedal motif which persists throughout the work. It opens *pp* and builds to a shattering climax at the words 'Holy, Holy, Holy' at which point the tonality shifts to E flat. The middle section, in A major, is an extended treble solo with choral interjections. The last part, 'O Lord, save thy people', returns to the mood, style and key of the opening.

In the *Festival Te Deum* (1945) the regular 4/4 gives way to constantly changing time-signatures and the choral writing includes extended sections in unison. This work marks a considerable advance on the earlier setting. Both in these works and in the *Missa Brevis*, written for the boys of Westminster Cathedral, the composer exploits the tone colours and resources of the organ in an entirely new way and the organ part of the latter work well repays close attention. The *Missa* is in the same vein as *Rejoice in the Lamb* and is scored for boys' voices in three parts. The Gloria is a lively movement in 7/8 over an organ ostinato derived from the opening plainsong intonation. When the voices enter in the Sanctus they present all twelve chromatic notes in the first bar against a sustained second-inversion tonic chord on the organ: these sung phrases become an ostinato which is later transferred to the organ. Benedictus is a canon at the 4th and the Hosanna telescopes the main ideas of Sanctus. In Agnus Dei, which is also built on a pedal ostinato, reiterated minor 2nds in the accompaniment suggest the agony of sin.

The early *A Hymn to the Virgin* (1935) is a lovely little motet laid out for double choir unaccompanied. The first choir sings in English; the second, singing in Latin, interjects a short persistent motif which has the effect of a refrain though it is sung to different words on each reappearance. All three stanzas close with the same cadence which, however, it subtly altered in the last bar. *A Wedding Anthem* (1950), to words by Ronald Duncan, is scored for 4-part choir, soprano and tenor soloists and organ. A dialogue between soloists and chorus is resolved in the concluding Latin hymn 'Per vitam Domini'. The mood of this work is restrained and its texture is astonishingly delicate. It demands a resourceful organist. Britten's *Hymn to Saint Peter* (1955) is comparatively easy and could well be sung by a parish choir capable of singing lightly and prepared to do some work: it calls for a solo boy. *Antiphon* (1956) is a fine swinging piece with a magnificent organ accompaniment in the style of *Rejoice in the Lamb*. The mood becomes more clouded at 'He our foes in pieces break', awe-stricken at 'Him we touch and him we take' and then, mounting upwards in increasing confidence to the words 'Wherefore since that he is such We adore . . .', with a fine melismatic flourish we return to the spirited mood of the opening. This piece, written for the centenary of St. Michael's College, Tenbury, is not easy and it demands three solo boys (or semi-chorus). *A Hymn of St. Columba* (1963) has a Latin text and is scored for 4-part choir and organ. The vocal parts are not difficult in themselves but the organ accompaniment does not help the singers. This short piece encompasses a wide range of emotions. The magnificent *Hymn to St. Cecilia* (1942) for 5-part choir unaccompanied is not intended for liturgical use. Another work suitable for parish choirs is the Jubilate in C.

Many choirmasters are afraid of tackling Britten's music because it often sounds so difficult, but Britten's understanding of the human voice and sympathy with choirs is such that even in the most complex passages the individual vocal lines are often surprisingly easy in themselves, diatonic and eminently singable. Notation frequently causes difficulties: sometimes the printed score bristling with sharps and double sharps disguises the fact that the part is actually a simple tune in the key of, say, E flat major which anyone could sing. Britten's vocal writing is never angular and disjointed in the way that much serial music is. What it does call for very often is a really first-class sense of rhythm from all taking part, especially the accompanist, and the ability to master unusual rhythmic groupings.

'POP' MUSIC IN CHURCH

A recent phenomenon of minor significance is the introduction of 'pop' music into church. A pioneer in this field was the Rev. Geoffrey Beaumont whose *Folk Mass* (1956) caused much discussion. Since then, collections of hymn-tunes in similar idiom by Beaumont, Malcolm Williamson and others have appeared. Ideally these tunes should be played not by the organist but by a typical 'pop' group and the style of performance should approximate as closely as possible to the style currently fashionable. Incidentally it is interesting to see that guitar chords are printed in musical shorthand — E, E9, Am, Am6, B7+, Gm6, E7, A — in other words, a variant of figured bass is still with us as a living reality. Leaders of the movement have formed the 20th Century Church Light Music Group.

Advocates of this music would be the last to make any artistic claims for it, indeed, its chief virtue in their eyes is that it has none. Whereas hymn writers and composers of yesteryear hoped to create imperishable monuments which would become part of the Church's heritage, writers of the new hymns intend them to be ephemeral and 'disposable' — like the pop songs they emulate. Originally the idea of this movement was to find some point of contact with the teen-age population and, by providing the sort of music which appeals to them, attract them into church. Of course anything which will bring young folk into church is to be most warmly encouraged and some sacrifice of artistic standards might be a small price to pay. But teenagers, for reasons which we shall examine, were suspicious, even resentful, and would have little to do with it. But that has not deterred its sponsors from continuing to write and publish more in the same style. Why, one wonders?

In view of the extravagant claims made for the movement, the muddled thinking shown, the misty-eyed idealism of its advocates, the practical problems involved, and the indifferent results achieved, a fresh appraisal seems called for. The following considerations appear relevant:

1. There is a basic misconception that young people are attracted to pop tunes *per se* but, generally speaking, they are not. They follow the cult of popular idols, either individual 'star' performers or groups: they are interested not so much in the song itself but in how it is sung by this, that, or the other idol. To attract these young folk into church, then, it is the singer and his or her style that is wanted, not so much the song.

2. Fashions in pop music change often and swiftly and if church music is to remain in contact, it must not lag behind but must be ready to switch quickly from one style to another — bepop, skiffle, rock 'n' roll, trad, beat, 'folk' and so on. But then church music has to be printed so that everyone can take part: publishing, printing, advertising and distribution are themselves lengthy processes and by the time the latest fashion gets into print it may already be outdated (and nothing is so dead as last week's pop fashion!). Yet how many churches can afford to keep buying music in order to chase fashions?

3. In consequence, to say that such music is ephemeral and 'disposable' is dishonest: anything which is printed, is bought with precious choir funds and goes into the choir library, is likely to hang around for the next fifty years at least. Furthermore we have several times mentioned how strong is the force of association: once the

congregation have formed associations with this music, no choirmaster would dare to get rid of it, 'disposable' or not.

4. If it is justifiable to introduce pop art into church music then 'twere well it should be done by professional artists. (Better still, if real jazz men like Mike Westbrook and Stan Tracey could be persuaded to produce church music, the outcome, even if we personally disliked it, would certainly be sincere, valid and highly interesting: it could even lead to powerful new developments.)[6] Nothing is more pathetic than to hear misguided parsons trying to reproduce the 'pop' styles of their own undergraduate days, dimly remembered. Thus Beaumont's *Folk Mass* is redolent of the 'thirties and breathes, perhaps somewhat feebly, the spirit of Fred Astaire and Ginger Rogers: it is naïvely out of touch with recent styles. Perhaps the most serious criticism of so much of this twentieth-century 'light' music is that *it is bad of its kind.*

5. Small wonder then that today's youth have shown no interest. They recognise the church pop movement for what it is—a gimmick to 'get at' them—and despise it accordingly. This attitude was well summed up by a lad who said, 'We don't often come to church; when we do we like to hear them old tunes.'

6. But the pop movement *has* made its mark—not with the teenagers but with their mothers and grandmothers. It is this older age group, especially the women, to whom the worst forms of art have ever appealed, from Mothers' Union banners to sentimental Christmas cards. Now that the worst excesses of mid-Victorian church music and hymnody have been eliminated, these folk are ready to fasten on to its modern equivalent—anything which demands no mental or spiritual effort; anything which is easy and tasteless. Pop hymnody, having failed to attract the teenagers, not only caters for the poor tastes of this older group but actually helps to create those tastes; it goes far out of its way to tempt them with the worthless, the 'disposable', the tawdry masquerading as a new and dynamic art form. Even so, only a few of these tunes have had any wide success.

7. We come back to the basic premise that worship is something we offer to God and surely we will offer him only our best. It is tragically easy to debase standards but it is a painfully slow and laborious process to build them up. It has taken responsible musicians, the reforming agencies, and the R.S.C.M. upwards of half a century to rid Anglican church music of the worst of Victoriana. It seems doubly regrettable that just when they have achieved success, Beaumont and others should deliberately and cynically inject a new and perhaps more virulent poison into the mainstream of church music. Their responsibility is heavy—and so is that of those who, for the sake of mere novelty, introduce and perform such things.

8. The height of incongruity is reached when a hymn of intense spirituality expressed in mystical imagery of great poetic beauty is shackled to some inconsequential 'pop' tune: flagrant examples are Bright's *And now, O Father*; Neale's *Sing my tongue* and *Before the ending of the day*; Palmer's *Jesus these eyes have never seen*; Watts's *When I survey* and Donne's *Wilt thou forgive*.

9. It was suggested on p. 406 that what the Church needs at the moment is not so much new tunes as new hymns. The 20th Century Church Light Music Group (what a name!) can at least lay claim to having brought into existence a large number of new hymns. They vary greatly in quality and most of them merely

---

[6] John Dankworth's *Folk Mass* has already been mentioned, p. 427.

re-echo thoughts already expressed in long-established hymns. But there are some that have a message more relevant to the needs of today and even if poorly expressed, they point in a new and significant direction.

'FOLK' MUSIC

Another interesting phenomenon of the last decade or so is the rise of the 'folk'-type song and 'songs of protest'. Though the style owed something to Donald Swann, the movement as a whole has centred round Sydney Carter and, more recently, Peter Smith.

Carter's Prefaces to his song books are very well worth reading with care; there is a lot of sound sense in them. He makes no pretentious claims but sets out clearly his ideas and purpose. To begin with, he is emphatically *not* writing for the Church; basically he is writing for young people whether in church, youth organisations, pub or folk-song club. Indeed, he seems almost surprised that 'Two or three of them have found their way to church. This does not make them into hymns',[7] and even more that 'one of them, *Lord of the Dance*, has been printed in a hymn book'.[8] Secondly, though most of his tunes are either modal or in a minor key and are written much in the style of genuine folk-songs, he is careful to put in a disclaimer: 'These songs are not "folk"; but a singer in the folk or blues tradition might know what to do with them more easily than a singer trained ecclesiastically. Animal vitality, the pulsation of the human voice, the dramatic use of vocal texture—rough, smooth, "ugly" or "beautiful"—are the qualities you find in a blues singer. They are not always welcomed in a church. Partly, perhaps, it is a matter of acoustics. Churches are not built to cope with sounds like this.'[9] Thirdly, he gives complete freedom to the singers or performers to do his songs as they will: 'Accept, reject, elaborate according to your taste or skill. Sing them unaccompanied, if you prefer. Dance, if you like. Try the harpsichord, the tambourine or the bouzouki; play them on the organ, provided it's a merry organ, not too soggy and lugubrious. Say them if you cannot sing them, with music going on behind the words, around the words, or not at all.'[10]

Whereas the 20th Century Church Light Music Group have not, on the whole, made much impact on young people, Carter has been very much more successful, perhaps because he is more genuine and sincere in what he does. Of course the 20th Century Church Light Music Group are also sincere to the extent that what they do, they do from the very highest motives. It is their music itself which is insincere because they are consciously writing *down* to somebody else's supposed level. When a composer of the eminence and enormous resource of Malcolm Williamson writes tunes like 'New every morning' or 'Awake, my soul', does he have his tongue in his cheek? Carter is personally committed to what he is doing and enjoys doing it; he rings true.

Carter would be the last person to make extravagant claims for his songs. He knows that his verse rarely rises above doggerel, that his tunes are a pastiche of genuine folk-songs, and that they are not likely to be long-lived. But his verse, even if lacking in profundity and unsophisticated in expression, is very much concerned with the world we

---

[7] Sydney Carter: *Songs of Sydney Carter in the present tense*, Bk. 2. (Galliard.)
[8] Ibid.
[9] Ibid., Bk. 3.
[10] Ibid., Bk. 1.

live in: it is challenging and stimulating. Thus, religion as a pretext for strife is neatly summarized:

> A lily or a swastika
> A shamrock or a star
> The Devil he can wear them all—
> No matter what they are.
>
> In red or blue or khaki
> In green or black and tan
> The Devil is a patriot
> A proper party man.[11]

Many of the songs attack colour prejudice:

> Christ the Lord has gone to heaven,
> One day he'll be coming back, sir.
> In this house he will be welcome,
> But we hope he won't be black, sir.

Even more pungent than Carter's hymns are some of the so-called 'Protest Songs' written in a very similar idiom:

> Polaris subs, atomic bombs;
> Germ research in progress.
> That's the way the money goes.
> What price the homeless?
> A bigger house, a second car—
> Pools, champagne, casinos.
> That's the way the money goes—
> What price, poor negroes?[12]

Here, then, are songs which express, inadequately perhaps, an important and challenging aspect of today's Christianity, an aspect which finds no direct expression in the major hymnbooks. Where are the poets who by their art can give classic expression to these same concepts in hymns of more permanent value and intended for liturgical use? The Light Music Group and the 'folk' group have blazed a new and important trail; when will the major hymn-writers follow it?

THE NEW MUSIC

In the last few years a revolution has taken place in English church music of such magnitude that it can be compared in importance only with the change from polyphony to monody which happened early in the seventeenth century. Expressed simply, it can be described as the complete overthrow of the classical key system with its implications of tonality, modulation, harmonic rhythm, harmonic progressions and cadences, and the

[11] Ibid., Bk. 1.
[12] Jim Stringfellow: *Pop goes the money* from 'Faith, Folk and Festivity' (Galliard).

orthodox conceptions of 'harmony' and 'discord': such terms have now become meaning-less. This revolution is the same as that which swept European secular music half a century ago but there has been the usual time-lag before its full effect reached Britain. When the old system finally crumbled in Europe, various -isms and -alities arose to replace it—polytonality, atonality, microtonality, expressionism, neo-classicism, and many others. Of all these systems and ideas, the one which proved most fruitful, durable and influential was that evolved by Arnold Schönberg—composition with the twelve notes of the chromatic scale, serially organised.

Few composers in these days adhere strictly to Schönberg's system of serial writing based on tone-rows but many accept his philosophy of composition which treats the twelve notes as equals and does away with any sense of tonality and of tonal implications (though it not infrequently happens that some passages are polarised around some particular note and by force of habit we try to orientate such passages within a key). But if we accept all notes as equal, such terms as diatonic and chromatic cease to mean any-thing and melodic lines are free to leap from one note to any other, however unvocal the interval. Considered vertically, a high degree of dissonance is often involved and we think not so much in terms of 'chords' as of 'tone-clusters' or 'note-aggregates'.

Young composers rejoice in their newly found freedom: the shackles of two hundred years have at last fallen away and they are free to explore almost limitless regions of new thoughts, new experiences, new expression. Older folk, brought up on orthodox lines, find the new music extremely hard to accept: to them it is 'all discord and no tune'. This is reflected in many choirs: the boys find no great difficulty in contemporary music and like singing much of it, while their elders not only find it impossibly difficult to perform but sometimes bitterly resent being asked to practise it.

Yet change is long overdue and now that it has come it is to be warmly welcomed. A living art cannot stand still. We cannot cry 'Stop!' and arrest its development at some given point in time: it must move on. In any case the present changes were not entirely unheralded; many pages of Vaughan Williams, Howells, Walton and Tippett anticipate recent developments. We have to recognise that the old system has gone for good and can never be restored, at least in its familiar form. The new music is here to stay and we must learn not only to live with it but to grow so accustomed to it that our ears become more perceptive and we can discriminate between the good, the bad and the indifferent.

It is the general strangeness of the idiom and a resulting lack of critical standards which make it hard for conventionally trained musicians to assess the work of these new writers. It is made still more difficult because minor figures find it easy to copy the external features of the best composers without possessing their divine spark or inner logic. Indeed one of the very real dangers of the new music is that it lays itself wide open to the charlatan and the incompetent because the idiom is so very easy to contrive. Anyone can write 'wrong notes': what is so much more difficult is to give them signifi-cance and validity. Only time will sift the significant composers from the insignificant.

The number of church composers adopting these new idioms is large and it is only possible to mention here some of those who, at the moment, seem to be among the more important of the group.

First, in point of time, is Michael Tippett (b. 1905) whose Evening Service written for the 450th anniversary celebrations of St. John's College, Cambridge, is daring in its originality and startling in its impact. It is a work which quickly grows on one: when it has, the old settings of people like Harwood, Noble and Nicholson seem no longer so satisfying. Tippett has also written a noble motet for unaccompanied double choir, *Plebs angelica*. The South African, John Joubert (b. 1927) has written much for the Church. He is one of the more readily approachable of the group and forms a useful bridge between the near-conventional (*O Lorde, the maker* and *There is no rose*) and the more advanced (*Christ is risen*). The Te Deum, written for Malvern College, is particularly fine. His carol 'Torches' is a popular success. Kenneth Leighton (b. 1929) has written a notable Evening Service in G, a Te Deum, a Communion Service in D and some imaginative anthems. An Australian, Malcolm Williamson (b. 1931), is one of the few church composers to be attracted by jazz idioms and their influence is found in many of his works. He often walks the tight-rope between highly sophisticated taste and technique on the one hand and a robust 'popular' style on the other. His anthem *Let them give thanks* is typical of this style. *Wrestling Jacob* is a highly imaginative setting of Charles Wesley's 'Come, O thou Traveller unknown' but its rhythmic complexities place it beyond all but the best choirs (and choirmasters!). Peter Maxwell Davies (b. 1934) has adopted a far more advanced style than that of the other composers mentioned. A high degree of dissonance often springs from the horizontal movement of comparatively simple parts. Others whose works deserve study are John Gardner, Tony Hewitt-Jones, Alun Hoddinott, Bryan Kelly, John McCabe, Nicholas Maw, Desmond Ratcliffe, Alan Ridout, Graham Whettam and Peter Wishart.

Though an enormous amount of new music is being written and published, it is still something of a novelty to hear it sung in parish churches — or even in cathedrals. One reason for this is the prodigious technical difficulty of much of it. It is usually far more difficult than orthodox choral music to read, to count, to grasp, to sing in tune, and to feel, and its adequate performance demands near-professional standards. To choirs already depleted and scarcely able to sing the standard parish church repertory properly, these difficulties are almost insurmountable. In large parish churches and cathedrals where the choir is of the requisite standard, choirmasters anxiously watch their limited rehearsal time and are reluctant to undertake music which consumes too much of it. This reduces the amount of contemporary music performed and hence the chances of becoming familiar with it. Sometimes even after an immense amount of time and effort have been expended on conquering fearsome difficulties and the choir can sing the work with confidence, the outcome sounds so sour, so contrived and so empty of real musical inspiration that the choirmaster is left wondering if the effort was justified: after all, unending minor seconds and major sevenths become just as boring in the long run as the unending thirds and sixths of some eighteenth-century composers. Fashion often does duty for genuine inspiration and the basic weakness of so much contemporary music is that it fails to communicate any valid experience.

The clergy also face a problem. With congregations steadily declining, is this an appropriate time to introduce music which may well alienate many people? If musicians themselves find the new idioms difficult to approach, how can such music help the average congregation in their worship? Is not the gap between musicians and the public growing ever wider?

But there is a healthier, more constructive side to all this. The old order changeth — but not necessarily for the worse. There is a great deal of new thinking going on not only in theology but in the way theology is being presented and taught. After an anxious period of lacerating self-criticism, the Churches are purging themselves of much that can have little relevance today and are projecting a new and more virile concept of Christianity, a concept more appropriate to the Atomic Age. The Churches themselves are lowering their barriers and drawing together in a way which would have been unthinkable twenty years ago. Does not the new music go with this new thought? Is it not right that new ideas and ideals should be expressed in new ways?

It may be that we are privileged to live in an age which future historians will look upon as a Second Reformation, an age when the Church, apparently declining and stifled under the weight of obsolete attitudes and time-worn conventions, has found a new vision, a new sense of purpose and a new strength. It is a time of opportunity and excitement: the future is full of hope. The first Reformation was one of division and dissension: the second Reformation is one of coming together in better understanding for the advancement of God's purpose in this new and challenging age. And, as before, the musicians will be there to sing the Lord's song 'with the spirit and with the understanding also'.

Bibliography

This bibliography makes no attempt to be comprehensive. It is merely a list of books and articles, nearly all of them in my own library, that I have found useful when writing the present book. It gives me an opportunity of recording my very real gratitude to all the various authors and editors, living and dead, to whom I owe so much. Entries are arranged in the following order:

1. Background history and general reading
2. General music
3. The Church
4. Church music – general
5. Church music – Gregorian chant
6. Church music – the Renaissance
7. Church music – the Baroque
8. Church music – eighteenth and nineteenth centuries
9. Church music – twentieth century
10. Hymnody
11. Carols
12. The organ

All books are published in London except where otherwise stated.

1. BACKGROUND HISTORY AND GENERAL READING

Anderson, M. S., *Europe in the Eighteenth Century 1713–1783* (Longmans, Green), 1961.

Bazin, Germain, *The Baroque: Principles, Styles, Modes, Themes*, trans. Pat Wardroper (Thames & Hudson), 1968.

Black, J. B., *The Reign of Elizabeth 1558–1603* (O.U.P.), 1936.

Braun, Hugh, *Parish Churches: Their Architectural Development in England* (Faber), 1970.

Bulley, M. H., *Art and Everyman, A Basis for Appreciation* (Batsford), Vol. I 1951; Vol. II 1951.

Clark, G. N., *The Later Stuarts 1660–1714* (O.U.P.), 1934.

Clark, Kenneth, *Civilisation, A Personal View* (B.B.C. and John Murray), 1969.

Davies, Godfrey, *The Early Stuarts 1603–1660* (O.U.P.), 1937.

Ensor, Sir Robert, *England 1870–1914* (O.U.P.), 1936. Reprinted (up to) 1968.

Feiling, Keith, *A History of England* (Macmillan), 1952.

Gloag, John, *Guide to Western Architecture* (Allen & Unwin), 1958. Revised edition (Spring Books), 1969.

Gombrich, E. H., *The Story of Art* (Phaidon), 1952.

441

Halliday, F. E., *An Illustrated Cultural History of England* (Thames & Hudson), 1967.

Hearder, H., *Europe in the Nineteenth Century 1830–1880* (Longmans, Green).

Höhne, Erich, *Music in Art*, trans. Edward B. Moss (Abbey).

Janson, H. W., *A History of Art* (Thames & Hudson), 1962.

Jordan, R. Furneaux, *A Concise History of Western Architecture* (Thames & Hudson), 1969.

Koenigsberger, H. G., and Mosse, G. L., *Europe in the Sixteenth Century* (Longmans, Green), 1968.

Leeuw, Gerardus van der, *Sacred and Profane Beauty*, trans. by David E. Green (Weidenfeld & Nicolson), 1963.

Legouis, E., and Cazamian, L., *A History of English Literature* (Dent), 1930.

Lesure, François, *Music and Art in Society*, trans. by Denis and Sheila Stevens (Pennsylvania State University Press), 1968.

Levey, Michael, *A History of Western Art* (Thames & Hudson), 1968.

Murray, Peter and Linda, *The Art of the Renaissance* (Thames & Hudson), 1963.

Pevsner, Nikolaus, *An Outline of European Architecture* (Penguin), 1943; 6th edition 1960.

Roberts, John, *Europe 1880–1945* (Longmans, Green), 1967.

Saintsbury, George, (1) *A Short History of English Literature* (Macmillan), 1898.

— (2) *A History of English Prosody* (Macmillan), 1908.

Sampson, George, *The Concise Cambridge History of English Literature* (Cambridge University Press), 1941. 3rd edition 1970.

Sitwell, Sacheverell, *Gothic Europe* (Weidenfeld & Nicolson), 1969.

Taylor, A. J. P., *English History 1914–1945* (O.U.P.), 1965.

Trevelyan, G. M., (1) *History of England* (Longmans, Green), 1926; 3rd edition 1945, re-issued 1962.

— (2) *English Social History* (Longmans, Green), 1942.

Watson, J. Steven, *The Reign of George III 1760–1815* (O.U.P.), 1960.

Whittle, Donald, *Christianity and the Arts* (Mowbray), 1966.

Williams, Basil, *The Whig Supremacy 1714–1760* (O.U.P.), 1939.

Williamson, James A., *The Tudor Age* (Longmans, Green), 1953; 3rd edition 1964.

Woodward, Sir Llewellyn, *The Age of Reform 1815–1870* (O.U.P.), 1938; 2nd edition 1962.

2. GENERAL MUSIC

Abraham, Gerald, *The New Oxford History of Music IV: The Age of Humanism 1540–1630* (O.U.P.), 1968.

Apel, Willi, (1) *Harvard Dictionary of Music* (Routledge & Kegan Paul), 1951. 2nd Ed. 1970.

— (2) *Historical Anthology of Music* — see under Davison.

Bragard, Roger, *Musical Instruments in Art and History*, trans. Bill Hopkins (Barrie & Rockliff), 1968.

Buchner, Alexander, *Musical Instruments through the Ages*, trans. Iris Urwin (Spring Books), 1956.

Burgh, A., *Anecdotes of Music, Historical and Biographical* (Longman, Hurst, Rees, Orme & Brown), 1814 (3 vols.).

Burney, Charles, (1) *The Present State of Music in France and Italy* (Becket), 1771.

— (2) *The Present State of Music in Germany, the Netherlands and United Provinces* (Becket, Robson & Robinson), 1773 (2 vols.).

— (3) *A General History of Music from the Earliest Ages to the Present Period* (Payne), 1776–89 (4 vols.): Ed. Frank Mercer 1935, republished (Dover Publications, New York), 1957 (2 vols.).

Clemencic, Réné, *Old Musical Instruments*, trans. David Hermges (Weidenfeld & Nicolson), 1968.

Cooke, Deryck, *The Language of Music* (O.U.P.), 1959.

Dart, Thurston, *The Interpretation of Music* (Hutchinson), 1954.

Davison, A. T., and Apel, Willi, *Historical Anthology of Music* (O.U.P.), Vol. I 1946, Vol. II 1950.

Donington, Robert, *The Interpretation of Early Music* (Faber), 1963.

Grove's Dictionary of Music and Musicians, 5th edition, ed. Eric Blom (Macmillan), 1954. Supplementary Volume, ed. Blom and Stevens (Macmillan), 1961.

Hadow, W. Henry, *English Music* (Longmans, Green), 1931.

Hawkins, John, *A General History of the Science and Practice of Music* (T. Payne), 1776 (5 vols.).

Harman, A., and Mellers, W., *Man and His Music* (Barrie & Rockliff), 1962.

Hipkins, A. J., and Gibb, W., *Musical Instruments, Historic, Rare and Unique* (Adam & Charles Black, Edinburgh), 1888.

Hogarth, George, *Musical History, Biography and Criticism* (John Parker), 1835.

Hughes, Anselm and Abraham, Gerald (editors), *The New Oxford History of Music III: Ars Nova and the Renaissance* (O.U.P.), 1960.

Kinsky, Georg, *A History of Music in Pictures* (Dent), 1930.

Lang, Paul H., *Music in Western Civilisation* (Norton — Dent), 1941.

Mackerness, E. D., *A Social History of English Music* (Routledge, & Kegan Paul), 1964.

Parry, C. Hubert H., *The Evolution of the Art of Music* (Routledge & Kegan Paul), 11th imp. 1950.

Rannie, Alan, *The Story of Music at Winchester College 1394–1969* (Wells, Winchester), 1970.

Robertson, Alec, and Stevens, Denis: *The Pelican History of Music* (Penguin).

Rockstro, W. S., *A General History of Music* (Sampson Low, Marston, Searle & Rivington), 1886.

Sachs, Curt, (1) *The History of Musical Instruments* (Norton), 1940.

— (2) *Rhythm and Tempo* (Norton), 1953.

Schnapper, Edith B., *The British Union-Catalogue of Early Music printed before the year 1801* (Butterworths Scientific Publications), 1957 (2 vols.).

Stevens, Denis, (1) *A History of Song* (Hutchinson), 1960.

— (2) See also under *Grove's Dictionary*, Supplementary volume.

— (3) See also under Robertson, *The Pelican History of Music*.

Strunk, Oliver, *Source Readings in Music History* (Norton, New York — Faber), 1950.

Walker, Ernest A., *A History of Music in England* (O.U.P.), 1907. 3rd ed. revised J. A. Westrup (O.U.P.), 1952.

Westrup, J. A., (1) *An Introduction to Musical History* (Hutchinson), 1955.

— (2) See also under Walker, *A History of Music in England*.

Woodfill, Walter D., *Musicians in English Society from Elizabeth to Charles I* (Princeton University Press), 1953. Reprinted (Da Capo Press, New York), 1969.

Young, Percy, M., (1) *The Choral Tradition* (Hutchinson), 1962.

— (2) *A History of British Music* (Benn), 1967.

3. THE CHURCH

Addleshaw, G. W. D., and Etchells, F., *The Architectural Setting of Anglican Worship* (Faber), 1956.

Capes, W. W., *The English Church in the Fourteenth and Fifteenth Centuries* (Macmillan), 1903.

Clarke, W. K. Lowther, *Liturgy and Worship* (S.P.C.K.), 1946.

Cook, G. H., (1) *The English Mediæval Parish Church* (Phoenix House), 1954.

— (2) *The English Cathedral* (Phoenix House), 1957.

Cragg, G. R., *The Church in the Age of Reason 1648–1789* (Penguin), 1960.

Cross, F. L. (editor), *The Oxford Dictionary of the Christian Church* (O.U.P.), 1957.

Dix, Gregory, *The Shape of the Liturgy* (Dacre Press), 1945.

Gibson, E. C. S., *The First and Second Prayer Books of King Edward VI* (Dent: Everyman's Library), 1960.

Moorman, J. R. H., *A History of the Church of England* (A. & C. Black), 1961.

Procter, F., and Frere, W. H., *The Book of Common Prayer* (Macmillan), 1901. 3rd edition reprinted (Macmillan), 1955.

Purvis, J. S., *Dictionary of Ecclesiastical Terms* (Nelson), 1962.

Ratcliff, Edward C., *The Booke of Common Prayer of the Churche of England: its making and revisions 1549–1661* (S.P.C.K.), 1930.

Swete, H. B., *Church Services and Service-Books before the Reformation* (S.P.C.K.), 1896. 2nd ed. revised A. J. Maclean (S.P.C.K.), 1930.

Vidler, A. R., *The Church in an Age of Revolution: 1789 to the Present Day* (Penguin), 1961.

4. CHURCH MUSIC—GENERAL

Archbishops' Committee, (1) Report, *Music in Worship* (S.P.C.K.).

— (2) Report, *Music in Church* (Church Information Office), 1951. Revised 1957.

Bridges, Robert, *Collected Essays XXI–XXVI* (O.U.P.), 1935.

Bumpus, John S., *A History of English Cathedral Music* (T. Werner Laurie), 1908. (2 vols.)

Davison, A. T., *Church Music: Illusion and Reality* (Harvard, Cambridge, Massachusetts), 1952.

Douglas, Winfred, *Church Music in History and Practice* (Scribners, New York), 1952.

Fellowes, Edmund H., *English Cathedral Music* (Methuen), 1941. 5th edition revised J. A. Westrup (Methuen), 1969.

Foster, Myles B., *Anthems and Anthem Composers* (Novello), 1901.

Gelineau, Joseph, *Voices and Instruments in Christian Worship*, trans. C. Howell (Burns & Oates), 1964.

Hadow, W. Henry, *Collected Essays* (O.U.P.), 1928.

Lafontaine, H. C. de, *The King's Musick* (Novello), 1909.

Love, James, *Scottish Church Music: Its Composers and Sources* (Blackwood, Edinburgh), 1891.

Nicholson, Sydney H., *Quires and Places where they Sing* (Bell), 1932.

Phillips, C. H., *The Singing Church* (Faber), 1945. Revised Arthur Hutchings 1968.

Pine, Edward, *The Westminster Abbey Singers* (Dennis Dobson), 1953.

Robertson, Alec, *Requiem: Music of Mourning and Consolation* (Cassell), 1967.

Robertson, Dora H., *Sarum Close* (Jonathan Cape), 1938. 2nd edition (Firecrest Publishing Co., Bath), 1969.

Routley, Erik, *The Church and Music* (Duckworth), 1950. 2nd edition (Duckworth), 1967.

Rhys, S., and Palmer, K., *The ABC of Church Music* (Hodder & Stoughton), 1967.

Stevenson, Robert M., *Patterns of Protestant Church Music* (Duke University Press, U.S.A.: Cambridge University Press, England), 1953.

Terry, Richard R., (1) *A Forgotten Psalter and other essays* (O.U.P.), 1929.

— (2) *Music of the Roman Rite* (Burns, Oates & Washbourne), 1931.

West, John E., *Cathedral Organists, Past and Present* (Novello), 1899. 2nd edition (Novello), 1921.

Wienandt, Elwin A., *Choral Music of the Church* (Free Press, New York), 1965.

Wienandt, E. A., and Young, R. H., *The Anthem in England and America* (Free Press, New York), 1970.

5. CHURCH MUSIC — GREGORIAN CHANT

Apel, Willi, *Gregorian Chant* (Burns & Oates), 1958.

Bryden, J. R., and Hughes, D. G., *An Index of Gregorian Chant* (Harvard, Cambridge, Massachusetts), 1969 (2 vols.).

Chambers, G. B., *Folksong–Plainsong* (Merlin), 1956.

Desrocquettes, J. H., *Gregorian Musical Values* (Ralph Jusko Publications, Cincinnati: Chappell, London), 1963.

Helmore, Thomas, *Plain-Song* (Novello).

Hughes, H. V., *Latin Hymnody: An Enquiry into the Underlying Principles of the Hymnarium* (Faith Press), 1922.

Liber Usualis: Missae et Officii, edited by the Monks of Solesmes (Desclée & Socii, Tournai, Belgium), 1954 edition.

Manuale Chorale ad Formam Breviarii (Ex Typographia Balleoniana, Venice), 1806.

Murray, Gregory, *Gregorian Chant* (Cary), 1937.

Robertson, Alec, *The Interpretation of Plainchant* (O.U.P.), 1937.

van Waesberghe, J. S., *Gregorian Chant and its Place in the Liturgy*, trans. W. A. G. Doyle-Davidson (Sidgwick & Jackson).

6. CHURCH MUSIC — THE RENAISSANCE

Apel, Willi, *The Notation of Polyphonic Music 900–1600* (The Mediaeval Academy of America), 1942.

Andrews, H. K., (1) *An Introduction to the Technique of Palestrina* (Novello), 1958.

— (2) *Thomas Morley, Collected Motets*, edited H. K. Andrews and Thurston Dart (Stainer & Bell), 1959.

— (3) *The Technique of Byrd's Vocal Polyphony* (O.U.P.), 1966.

Brown, David, (1) *The Anthems of Thomas Weelkes*. Proceedings of the Royal Musical Association XCI, 1964–65.

— (2) *Thomas Weelkes: Collected Anthems*, edited by Brown, Collins and le Huray: Musica Britannica XXIII (Stainer & Bell), 1966.

— (3) *Thomas Weelkes: A Biographical and Critical Study* (Faber), 1969.

Bukofzer, Manfred F., *Studies in Medieval and Renaissance Music* (Dent), 1950.

Buttrey, John, *William Smith of Durham*, Music & Letters (O.U.P.), Vol. 43 No. 3. July 1962.

Collins, Walter S., (1) *The Anthems of Thomas Weelkes*, unpublished dissertation for the degree of Ph.D., Michigan University, 1960.

— (2) See also under Brown, David (2).

Dart, Thurston, Thomas Morley's Motets—see under Andrews, H. K. (2).

Einstein, Alfred, *The Italian Madrigal*, trans. A. H. Krappe, R. H. Sessions and Oliver Strunk (Princeton University Press, U.S.A.), 1949 (3 vols.).

Fellowes, Edmund H., (1) *The English Madrigal Composers* (O.U.P.), 1921.

— (2) *Orlando Gibbons and his Family* (O.U.P.), 1925. 2nd edition 1951.

— (3) *William Byrd* (O.U.P.), 1936. 2nd edition 1948.

— (4) See under *Tudor Church Music—Appendix & Supplementary Notes*.

Harrison, Frank Ll., (1) *The Eton Choirbook*. Musica Britannica X, XI and XII (Stainer & Bell). Vol. X 1956; Vol. XI 1958; Vol. XII 1961.

— (2) *Music in Medieval Britain* (Routledge & Kegan Paul), 1958.

— (3) *William Mundy: Latin Antiphons and Psalms*, Early English Church Music 2 (Stainer & Bell).

Jackman, James L., *Liturgical Aspects of Byrd's 'Gradualia'*, Musical Quarterly XLIX: No. 1, January 1963 (Schirmer, New York).

Jeppesen, Knud, *The Style of Palestrina and the Dissonance* (Ejnar Munksgaard, Copenhagen: O.U.P. England), 2nd edition 1946.

Kenton, Egon, *Life and Works of Giovanni Gabrieli* (American Institute of Musicology), 1967.

Kerman, Joseph, (1) *The Elizabethan Madrigal* (American Musicological Society), 1962.

— (2) *The Elizabethan Motet*, Studies in the Renaissance, X, 1962.

— (3) *Byrd's Motets: Chronology and Canon*, Journal of the American Musicological Society XIV, No. 3, 1961.

Krenek, Ernst, *Johannes Ockeghem* (Sheed & Ward), 1953.

le Huray, Peter, (1) *Towards a Definitive Study of Pre-Restoration Anglican Service Music*. Musica Disciplina XIV, 1960.

— (2) *The English Anthem 1580–1640*. Proceedings of the Royal Musical Association LXXXVI, 1959.

— (3) *The Treasury of English Church Music Vol. 2, 1540–1650* (Blandford), 1965.

— (4) *Music and the Reformation in England 1549–1660* (Herbert Jenkins), 1967.

— (5) Weelkes's Anthems—see under Brown, David (2).

Mace, Thomas, *Musick's Monument* (Ratcliffe & Thompson), 1676. Reissued in facsimile (Editions du Centre National de la Recherche Scientifique, Paris), 1958.

Morley, Thomas, *A Plaine and Easie Introduction to Practicall Musicke* (Peter Short), 1597. Edited by R. Alec Harman (Dent), 1952.

Morris, R. O., *Contrapuntal Technique in the Sixteenth Century* (O.U.P.), 1922.

Platt, Peter, *Richard Dering*, unpublished dissertation for the degree of B.Litt., Oxford, 1953.

Reese, Gustave, *Music in the Renaissance* (Dent), 1954.

Rose, Bernard, *Thomas Tomkins: Musica Deo Sacra*, Early English Church Music 5 and 9.

Shaw, H. Watkins, *Thomas Morley of Norwich*, Musical Times No. 1471, September 1965.

Stevens, Denis, (1) *The Mulliner Book*. Musica Britannica I (Stainer & Bell), 1951.

— (2) *Thomas Tomkins* (Macmillan), 1957.

— (3) *Tudor Church Music* (Faber), 1961.

— (4) *The Treasury of English Church Music Vol. 1, 1100–1545* (Blandford), 1965.

Thomson, Edward, (1) *Robert Ramsey*. Musical Quarterly XLIX: No. 2, April 1963.

— (2) *Robert Ramsey: English Sacred Music*, Early English Church Music 7 (Stainer & Bell).

Tudor Church Music. Published for the Carnegie Trust by Oxford University Press: Edited by Buck, Fellowes, Ramsbotham, Terry and Townsend Warner:

Vol. I	John Taverner: Part 1	1923
Vol. II	William Byrd (English)	1922
Vol. III	John Taverner: Part 2	1924

Edited by Buck, Fellowes, Ramsbotham and Townsend Warner:

Vol. IV	Orlando Gibbons	1925
Vol. V	Robert White	1926
Vol. VI	Thomas Tallis	1928
Vol. VII	William Byrd: Gradualia, Books 1 and 2	1927
Vol. VIII	Thomas Tomkins: Part 1 Services	1928
Vol. IX	William Byrd (Latin)	1928
Vol. X	Aston, Merbecke and Parsley	1929

Appendix and Supplementary Notes by E. H. Fellowes (O.U.P.), 1948.

Whythorne, Thomas, *Autobiography* edited by J. M. Osborn (O.U.P.), 1961.

Wulstan, David, *Orlando Gibbons: Verse Anthems*, Early English Church Music 3, 1963.

7. CHURCH MUSIC—THE BAROQUE

Arnold, F. T., *The Art of Accompaniment from a Thorough Bass* (O.U.P.), 1931.

Bukofzer, Manfred F., *Music in the Baroque Era* (Norton), 1947.

Dearnley, Christopher, (1) *The Treasury of English Church Music Vol. 3 1650–1760* (Blandford), 1965.

— (2) *English Church Music 1625–1750* (Herbert Jenkins), 1970.

Evelyn, John, *Diary 1620–1706* — various editions.

Harley, John, *Music in Purcell's London* (Dobson), 1968.

Lefkowitz, Murray, *William Lawes* (Routledge & Kegan Paul), 1960.

Lewis, Anthony, and Shaw, H. Watkins, *John Blow: Coronation Anthems and Anthems with Strings*. Musica Britannica VII (Stainer & Bell), 1953.

Moser, H. J., *Heinrich Schütz*, trans. Derek McCulloch (Faber), 1967.

North, Roger, *Essays on Music 1695–1728*, edited by John Wilson (Novello), 1959.

Pepys, Samuel, *Diary 1659–1669* — various editions.

Playford, John (the elder), *A Brief Introduction to the Skill of Musick* (Playford), 1654.

Redlich, Hans F., *Claudio Monteverdi: Life and Works*, trans. Kathleen Dale (O.U.P.), 1952.

Schjelderup-Ebbe, Dag, *Purcell's Cadences* (Oslo University Press), 1962.

Scholes, Percy A., *The Puritans and Music* (O.U.P.), 1934.

Schrade, Leo, *Monteverdi, Creator of Modern Music* (Gollancz), 1950.

Shaw, H. Watkins, John Blow's Anthems — see under Lewis, Anthony.

Westrup, Jack A., *Purcell* (Dent — Master Musicians), 1937.

Zimmerman, Franklin B., (1) *Henry Purcell 1659–1695: An Analytical Catalogue of his Music* (Macmillan), 1963.

— (2) *Henry Purcell 1659–1695: His Life and Times* (Macmillan), 1967.

8. CHURCH MUSIC — EIGHTEENTH AND NINETEENTH CENTURIES

Boston, N., and Langwill, L. G., *Church and Chamber Barrel-Organs* (Langwill, Edinburgh), 1967.

Boyce, William, *Cathedral Music*. Vol. I, 1760; Vol. II, 1768; Vol. III, 1773.

Croft, William, *Musica Sacra* (John Walsh), 1724.

Einstein, Alfred, *Music in the Romantic Era* (Dent), 1947.

Fuller-Maitland, J. A., *English Music in the XIXth Century* (Grant Richards), 1902.

Hiebert, A. J., *The Anthems and Services of Samuel Sebastian Wesley*. Unpublished dissertation: George Peabody College, Nashville, Tennessee.

Hutchings, Arthur, *Church Music in the Nineteenth Century* (Herbert Jenkins), 1967.

Jebb, John, (1) *The Choral Service of the United Church of England and Ireland* (John W. Parker), 1843.

— (2) *The Choral Responses and Litanies of the United Church of England and Ireland* (George Bell), 1847.

Knight, Gerald H., and Reed, W. L., *The Treasury of English Church Music Vol. 4 1760–1900* (Blandford), 1965.

La Trobe, J. A., *The Music of the Church considered in its Various Branches, Congregational and Choral*, 1831.

Macdermott, K. H., *The Old Church Gallery Minstrels* (S.P.C.K.), 1948.

Novello, Vincent, *Preface to 'The Psalmist'* (Novello), 1835–1843 (4 vols).

Rainbow, Bernarr, *The Choral Revival in the Anglican Church 1839–1872* (Barrie & Jenkins), 1970.

Routley, Erik, *The Musical Wesleys* (Herbert Jenkins), 1968.

Scholes, Percy A., *The Mirror of Music* (Novello — O.U.P.), 1947 (2 vols.).

Shaw, H. Watkins, *Eighteenth Century Cathedral Music*, Church Music Society Paper No. 21 (O.U.P.).

Wesley, Samuel Sebastian, (1) *A few words on Cathedral Music and the Musical System of the Church, with a Plan of Reform* (Rivington), 1849.
— (2) *Reply to the Inquiries of the Cathedral Commissioners relating to Improvement in the Music of Divine Worship in Cathedral* (Piper, Stephenson & Spence), 1854.

9. CHURCH MUSIC—TWENTIETH CENTURY

Andrews, Hilda, *Westminster Retrospect: A Memoir of Sir Richard Terry* (O.U.P.), 1948.
Austin, William W., *Music in the 20th Century from Debussy through Stravinsky* (Norton, New York: Dent, London), 1966.
Brewer, A. Herbert, *Memories of Choirs and Cloisters* (John Lane), 1931.
Bridge, Frederick, *A Westminster Pilgrim* (Novello—Hutchinson), 1918.
Dickinson, A. E. F., *Vaughan Williams* (Faber), 1963.
Fellowes, Edmund H., *Memoirs of an Amateur Musician* (Methuen), 1946.
Hollins, Alfred, *A Blind Musician looks back* (Blackwood), 1936.
Howes, Frank, (1) *The Music of Ralph Vaughan Williams* (O.U.P.), 1954.
— (2) *The English Musical Renaissance* (Secker & Warburg), 1966.
Kennedy, Michael, (1) *The Works of Ralph Vaughan Williams* (O.U.P.), 1964.
— (2) *Portrait of Elgar* (O.U.P.), 1968.
Knight, Gerald H., and Reed, W. L., *The Treasury of English Church Music Vol. 5 1900–1965* (Blandford), 1965.
Machlis, Joseph, *Introduction to Contemporary Music* (Norton, New York, 1961: Dent, London, 1963).
Maine, Basil, *Elgar, His Life and Works* (Bell), 1933 (2 vols.).
Orchard, W. Arundel, *Music in Australia* (Georgian House, Melbourne), 1952.
Pakenham, Simona, *Ralph Vaughan Williams: A Discovery of his Music* (Macmillan), 1957.
Routley, Erik, *Twentieth Century Church Music* (Herbert Jenkins), 1964.
Scholes, Percy A., *The Mirror of Music* (Novello—O.U.P.), 1947 (2 vols.).
Young, Percy M., *Elgar O.M.: A Study of a Musician* (Collins), 1955.

10. HYMNODY

Benson, Louis F., *The English Hymn: Its Development & Use in Worship* (George Doran, U.S.A.), 1915. Reprinted (John Knox, Richmond, Virginia), 1962.
Bridges, Robert, (1) Essay XXI, *The Musical Setting of Poetry* (1896); Essay XXII, *Some Principles of Hymn-Singing* (1899); Essay XXIII, *About Hymns* (1911). Reprinted (O.U.P.), 1935.
— (2) With H. E. Wooldridge: *The Yattendon Hymnal* (Clarendon), 1899. Reprinted (O.U.P.), 1920.
Clarke, W. K. Lowther, *A Hundred Years of Hymns Ancient and Modern* (William Clowes), 1960.
Dearmer, P., and Jacob, A., *Songs of Praise Discussed* (O.U.P.), 1933.
Frere, W. H., *Hymns Ancient and Modern: Historical Edition* (William Clowes), 1909. Revised edition 1962—see under Frost (2).

P

Frost, Maurice, (1) *English and Scottish Psalm and Hymn Tunes c. 1543–1677* (S.P.C.K. and O.U.P.), 1953.
— (2) *Historical Companion to Hymns Ancient & Modern*, a revision of Frere's 'Historical Edition' (William Clowes), 1962.
Gregory, A. S., *Praises with Understanding* (Epworth), 1936. 2nd edition (Epworth) 1949.
Jefferson, H. A. L., *Hymns in Christian Worship* (Rockliff), 1950.
Julian, John, *A Dictionary of Hymnology* (John Murray), 1892. 2nd edition, revised (John Murray) 1907. Reprinted (Dover Publications, New York), 1957 (2 vols.).
Lightwood, James T., *The Music of the Methodist Hymn-Book* (Epworth), 1935. 2nd edition (Epworth) 1938. 3rd edition, revised Francis B. Westbrook (Epworth), 1955.
Manning, Bernard L., *The Hymns of Wesley & Watts* (Epworth), 1942.
Moffatt, James, *Handbook to the Church Hymnary* (O.U.P.), 1927.
Patrick, Millar, *Four Centuries of Scottish Psalmody* (O.U.P.), 1949.
Phillips, C. S., *Hymnody Past and Present* (S.P.C.K.), 1937.
Routley, Erik, (1) *Hymns and Human Life* (John Murray), 1952.
— (2) *The Music of Christian Hymnody* (Independent Press), 1957.
Terry, Richard R., *Calvin's First Psalter 1539* (Ernest Benn), 1932.
Woodward, G. R., *Songs of Syon* (Schott), 1904 and 1910. 4th edition 1923.

11. CAROLS

Brice, Douglas, *The Folk-Carol of England* (Herbert Jenkins), 1967.
Greene, Richard L., *The Early English Carols* (O.U.P.), 1935.
Phillips, W. J., *Carols, Their Origin, Music and Connection with Mystery Plays* (Routledge).
Rickert, Edith, *Ancient English Christmas Carols 1400 to 1700* (Chatto & Windus), 1928.
Routley, Erik, *The English Carol* (Herbert Jenkins), 1958.
Stevens, John, *Mediæval Carols*. Musica Britannica IV (Stainer & Bell), 1952.

12. THE ORGAN

Audsley, George A., (1) *The Art of Organ-Building* (Dodd, Mead; New York—Vincent Music Co., London), 1905.
— (2) *The Organ of the Twentieth Century* (Sampson, Low & Co.), 1919
— (3) *Organ-Stops and their Artistic Registration* (H. W. Gray Co., New York), 1921.
Baron, John, *Scudamore Organs* (Bell & Daldy), 1858.
Bonavia-Hunt, Noel A., (1) *Modern Organ Stops* (Musical Opinion,) 1923.
— (2) *Modern Studies in Organ Tone* (Musical Opinion), 1933.
— (3) *The Modern British Organ* (Weekes), 1948.
Clutton, Cecil, and Niland, Austin, *The British Organ* (Batsford), 1963.
Douglass, Fenner, *The Language of the French Classical Organ* (Yale University Press), 1969.
Hopkins, E. J., and Rimbault, E. F., *The Organ, Its History and Construction* (Robert Cocks), 1855. 2nd edition 1870, 3rd edition 1877.

Sumner, William L., *The Organ* (Macdonald), 1952.

Westerby, Herbert, *The Complete Organ Recitalist: International Repertoire-Guide* (Musical Opinion), 1933.

Whitworth, Reginald, *Organ Stops and their Use* (Pitman), 1951.

Williams, Peter, *The European Organ 1450–1850* (Batsford), 1966.

Wilson, Michael, *The English Chamber Organ: History and Development* (Cassirer — Faber), 1968.

Index to Music Examples

General Index

NOTE: More important entries are shown in italic type. A small 'n' after a number indicates a footnote.

Consort 390–1
Consuetudinary 24
Continued base—see *Basso continuo*
Convocation 20, 21, 62, 319, 384, 397
COOKE, BENJAMIN, *307*, 344
COOKE, JOHN 41
COOKE, CAPTAIN HENRY 225, 229, 245, 246–7, 251, 252, 255, 256, 258, 269
COOKE, ROBERT 307
COOPER, GEORGE 336
    Instruction manual for the organ 336
COPELAND, WILLIAM JOHN 332
COPERARIO (COOPER), JOHN 213, 222
Copyists 330
Cornett, the *57*, 86, 154–5, 180, 188–9, 225, 229, 243, 248
CORNYSHE, JOHN 58
COSIN, BISHOP JOHN 188–9
Cost of music 289, 321, 329–30, 360, 433–4
COSYN, JOHN 209
Council of Trent, The 35
Council for the Care of Churches 410
Counterpoint 99–101 (Ex. 23), 219
    Free counterpoint 101–2
    Triple counterpoint 315
Counter-tenor voice 225, *271*, 299, *391*
COUNTESS OF HUNTINGDON 317
COUPERIN, FRANÇOIS 296
COVERDALE, MILES 19, 25
    Goostly Psalmes and Spirituall Songs 27
COWPER, WILLIAM 27, 288
COX, WILLIAM 166, 168, 170
CRANFORD, WILLIAM 188
CRANMER, ARCHBISHOP THOMAS 28, 35, 75, 80
    The Litany 19, 76
    First *Booke of the Common Prayer* (1549) 22, 24–5
    Views on music in worship *28*, 29, 36, 67, 298
    Cranmer and Merbecke 29, 76, 79
    Cranmer as composer 28
CREIGHTON, ROBERT 245, *249–50*
CROFT, WILLIAM 141, 288, 289, 290, *291–4*, 296
    Musica Sacra 292
    Burial Service 292, 293–4 (Ex. 129)
    Anthems:
        Be merciful unto me 292–3
        Cry aloud and shout 293
        Give the king thy judgements 292
        God is gone up 292, 293
        Hear my prayer 293
        I will alway give thanks 292
        Lord, thou hast searched me out 292
        O give thanks 292
        O Lord God of my salvation 293
        O Lord, rebuke me not 292, 293
        O praise the Lord, all ye heathen 292
        Praise the Lord, O my soul 292
        Put me not to rebuke 292–3
        Rejoice in the Lord, O ye righteous 292
        Sing praises unto the Lord 293
        Sing unto the Lord 292
        The heavens declare 292
        The Lord is king 292
        We wait for thy loving kindness 292
CROMWELL, OLIVER 53, 196, 203, 205, 211, 269
CROMWELL, RICHARD 211
CROMWELL, THOMAS 19, 206
Cross rhythms—see Rhythmic counterpoint
Cross, the sign of the 20, 327
CROTCH, WILLIAM 309, *315–16*, 321, 330
    Anthems:
        Be merciful unto me 315

Be peace on earth 316
Comfort, O Lord 287, 315
God is our hope and strength 316
How dear are thy counsels 315
Lo, star-led chiefs 316
My God, my God, look upon me 315–16
The Lord, even the most mighty God 316
Crotchet, use of, as a unit of measurement 105, 122
CROWLEY, ROBERT 27
CUDWORTH, CHARLES 290
CUNNINGHAM, GEORGE D. 336, 407
Czechoslovakia 42

Da capo 128
Daily Offices 23, 24, 64
DALLAM, GEORGE 231
DALLAM, RALPH 231
DALLAM, ROBERT 62, 231
DALLAM, THOMAS 62, 148, 233
DAMETT, THOMAS 41
DAMON, WILLIAM 209
Dancing 201
DANDRIEU, JEAN FRANÇOIS 407
DANKWORTH, JOHN
    Folk Mass 427, 434n
DAQUIN, LOUIS 407
DARKE, HAROLD EDWIN 418
DART, ROBERT THURSTON 215
DARWIN, CHARLES 319
    The Origin of Species (1859) 319
    The Descent of Man (1871) 319
'Das Land ohne Musik'—the Land without Music 385
Dating works, difficulty in 66
DAVENANT, SIR WILLIAM 202, 207, 240, 246
DAVENPORT, BOB 427n
DAVIES, SIR HENRY WALFORD 382, 397, 413–14
    Carols 413
    Chants 413
    Hymn-tunes 414
    Introits 413–14
DAVIES, PETER MAXWELL 385, 438
DAVISON, JAMES WILLIAM 346
DAVY or DAVYS, RICHARD 126
DAWE, DONOVAN 300n
DAY, JOHN
    Certaine Notes 64, *65*, 78
    Whole Psalmes in foure partes (1563) 78, 188, 209
Dead, prayers for the 20
DEARMER, PERCY 399, 402
    English Hymnal (1906) 399
    Songs of Praise (1925) 400–1
DEBUSSY, CLAUDE 51, 193, 271, 385, 425, 429, 430
Decani *39*, 54
Declamatory style (see also under Dramatic writing) 146, *175*, 176, 181, 215, 218, 243, 281, 282, 295
DELIUS FREDERICK 430
    Song of the High Hills 51, 428
DELLER, ALFRED 391
Demisemiquavers, use of 160, 256, 261, 294
Deputies in London choirs 230
DERING or DEERING, RICHARD 190, *193–6*, 238, 247
    Biography 193
    Cantiones Sacrae (Sets 1–4) 193
    Motets discussed 194–6
        Contristatus est Rex David 194–5 (Ex. 88)
        O bone Jesu 195 (Ex. 89)
    Alleluia section 196, 241
    English sacred words 196
    Trio works with *basso continuo* 192, 196, 203, 243